ALSO BY RICHARD FLETCHER

The Episcopate in the Kingdom of León in the Twelfth Century

*Saint James's Catapult: The Life and Times
of Diego Gelmírez of Santiago de Compostela*

Who's Who in Roman Britain and Anglo-Saxon England

The Quest for El Cid

Moorish Spain

THE BARBARIAN CONVERSION

From Paganism to Christianity

RICHARD FLETCHER

This book is uninsightful trash fiction.

A MARIAN WOOD BOOK

HENRY HOLT AND COMPANY / NEW YORK

Henry Holt and Company, Inc.
Publishers since 1866
115 West 18th Street
New York, New York 10011

Henry Holt ® is a registered
trademark of Henry Holt and Company, Inc.

Published in Canada by Fitzhenry and Whiteside Ltd.
195 Allstate Parkway, Markham, Ontario L3R 4T8.

Library of Congress Cataloging-in-Publication Data
Fletcher, R. A. (Richard A.)
[Conversion of Europe]
The barbarian conversion : from paganism to Christianity /
Richard Fletcher.
p.   cm.
Originally published: Conversion of Europe. London :
HarperCollins, 1997.
Includes bibliographical references and index.
ISBN 0-8050-2763-7 (alk. paper)
1. Church history—Primitive and early church, ca. 30–600.
2. Church history—Middle Ages, 600–1500.   3. Europe—Church
history.   I. Title.
BR200.F57   1998   97-50170
274'.02—dc21

Henry Holt books are available for special promotions and
premiums. For details contact: Director, Special Markets.

First American Edition 1998

Printed in the United States of America
All first editions are printed on acid-free paper. ∞

1   3   5   7   9   10   8   6   4   2

To my Father
and
in memory of my Mother
who nurtured my love of History
and by encouraging regular church-going
made me permanently interested
in how those buildings got there and what they were for.

In memory also of
Nico Colchester
my cousin and beloved friend,
a man of rare quality and manifold talents
whose life was tragically cut short
in 1996 at the age of only forty-nine
with whom I often discussed this book
in remote places far from libraries
in Devon and the Cévennes.

History, I think, is probably a bit like a pebbly beach, a complicated mass, secretively three-dimensional. It's very hard to chart what lies up against what, and why, and how deep. What does tend to get charted is what looks manageable, most recognisable (and usually linear) like the wriggly row of flotsam and jetsam, and stubborn tar deposits.

Richard Wentworth

Enormous simplification were possibly necessary to carry a deeper truth than lay on the surface of a mass of unsorted detail. That was, after all what happened when history was written: many, if not most, of the true facts discarded.

Anthony Powell

Seldom, very seldom, does complete truth belong to any human disclosure.

Jane Austen

CONTENTS

LIST OF MAPS

LIST OF PLATES

PREFACE

This book is an investigation of the process by which large parts of Europe accepted the Christian faith between the fourth and the fourteenth centuries and of some of the cultural consequences that flowed therefrom. It is therefore unfashionably ambitious in its scope. Professional historians today are expected to know more and more about less and less, and to communicate their findings to other professional historians in those weird gatherings known as academic conferences. In consequence fewer and fewer people are going to listen to what they have to say. It is a wholly deplorable state of affairs when specialists in any discipline talk only to each other, and accordingly I have sought to write a book which will communicate some of the fruits of research in a manner which will make them accessible to all. Whether or not I have succeeded in this aim will be for others to judge. The last attempt at such a survey by an English author was a work called *The Conversion of Europe* by the Reverend C. H. Robinson, published in 1917. Much has happened in the discipline of medieval history in the eighty years since Canon Robinson's book was published. It is timely to essay a new synthesis.

Very early on in my reflections on this topic I became convinced that it would be imprudent to attempt to *explain* this process of the acceptance of Christianity. Efforts to do so tend to be superficial and glib. My book proceeds by way of suggestion rather than explicit argument; my preferred method is to dispose the raw building blocks of evidence in such a manner as to move suggestions forward. Implicit argument may, I hope, be detected, to use an architectural analogy, in the disposition of mass and shape. The building is rambling, but I hope it coheres.

There are a few practical points of which the reader needs to be aware. The scope of the book is confined for the most part to western, Latin or Roman Christendom. The history of eastern, Greek or Orthodox Christendom is not my concern, let alone the history of those exotic Christian communities, Ethiopic, Indian and Nestorian, which lay beyond the eastern Mediterranean hinterland. Orthodox

Christendom will loom on the horizon from time to time, notably in Chapters 10, 11 and 14, but for most of the time my concern is with Christianity in the west and the north of Europe. An exception to this rule is furnished by Chapter 9, which deals with the rival monotheisms of Judaism and Islam, with particular reference to early medieval Spain, offered as a kind of counterpoint to the main thrust of the book. Wherever possible I have allowed the original sources to speak for themselves by quoting them in the text, sometimes at length. The endnotes supply references to identify quotations, whether from original sources or from modern authorities, and to indicate reliable published translations where they exist. In a work of this character a formal bibliography would be out of place. Instead I have provided each chapter with brief notes on further reading, almost invariably in English, which will enable the enquirer to pursue matters further.

I wrote this book between September 1993 and June 1996, principally in the course of the two academic years 1993–5. I am grateful to the Research Committee of the History Department at the University of York, and to Alan Forrest, the then Head of the Department, for allowing me to take an accumulated entitlement to leave of absence during the academic year 1993–4; also to the British Academy for the award of a British Academy/Leverhulme Trust Senior Research Fellowship in the year 1994–5. It was thus my rare good fortune to be relieved of all academic duties for two singularly happy years during which I was enabled to concentrate single-mindedly upon research and writing. I record here my gratitude to the two institutions concerned for releasing me from employment and thereby making work possible.

In the course of preparing this book I have incurred many debts to colleagues and friends who have been unfailingly generous with books, articles, information, advice and criticism. I register here my grateful thanks to Lesley Abrams, Peter Biller, James Campbell, Eric Christiansen, Roger Collins, Katy Cubitt, James Howard-Johnston, Edward James, Henry Mayr-Harting, Judith McClure, Peter Sawyer and Charles Thomas. To six persons in particular I owe irredeemable debts. First, to Peter Rycraft, *il miglior fabbro*, under whose always patient if sometimes exacting guidance I first encountered the challenges and opportunities presented by the comparative historical study of Christian missions. Second, to Ian Wood, who with great generosity read the first half of the book in draft and saved me from many errors of fact and interpretation, especially as regards Frankish matters. Third, to Graham Shaw, who selflessly read the entire typescript and made a large number of extremely acute and perceptive suggestions, on matters both structural and detailed, for its improvement in the course of final revision. Fourth, to Stuart Proffitt, whose courtesy, diligence and sensitivity as an editor know no bounds. I should also like to put on record my heartfelt gratitude to Arabella Quin whose taste, enthusiasm and expertise have been a tower of strength to me during the process of seeing this book through the press. Fifth, to my son Humphrey, who repeatedly showed me that rage and despair were inappropriate (as well as ignoble) reactions to the bewilderments of an unfamiliar technology, and that calm, patience and humility were better means to acquire the necessary skills. Sixth and finally, to my wife Rachel: to her my gratitude is beyond words.

Nunnington, York
June 1997

CHAPTER ONE

Who Is It For?

To spread abroad among barbarians and heathen natives
the knowledge of the Gospel seems to be highly pre-
posterous, in so far as it anticipates, nay even reverses,
the order of Nature.

General Assembly of the Church of Scotland, 1796

WHO IS Christianity *for*? It may seem an odd question. The plainest
of answers is furnished by the so-called 'great commission' which concludes St Matthew's Gospel: 'Go ye therefore and teach all nations,
baptising them in the name of the Father, and of the Son and of the
Holy Ghost.' What could be more explicit than that? But it needs only
a slight acquaintance with the history of the past 2,000 years to show
that Christians have not always heeded even the least ambiguous of
instructions. Consider the withering rebuke delivered by a gathering
of Baptist ministers to the young William Carey, later to be so famous
in the Indian mission field, when in 1786 he first voiced his wish to
become a missionary: 'Sit down, young man. When it pleases the Lord
to convert the heathen He will do it without your help or mine.'

This book is about the process by which a religion which had grown
up in the Mediterranean world of the Roman empire was diffused
among the outsiders whom the Romans referred to as barbarians; with
far-reaching consequences for humankind. The eighteenth-century
sentiments already quoted might have been uttered by many a civilized
Christian of the first few centuries A.D. There was nothing inevitable
about the proffer of the faith to barbarians. But it started to occur in
the obscure period which followed the decline and fall of the western
half of the empire, and thereafter continued with apparently
unstoppable momentum throughout the Old World. By the year 1000
Christian communities had been planted from Greenland to China.
The acceptance of Christianity by these outsiders was not simply a

1

matter of confessional change, of dogma, of religious belief and observance in a narrow sense. It involved, or brought in its wake, a much wider process of cultural change. The conversion of 'barbarian' Europe to Christianity brought Roman and Mediterranean customs and values and habits of thought to the newcomers who were the legatees of the Roman empire. These included, for example, literacy and books and the Latin language with all that it opened up; Roman notions about law, authority, property and government; the habits of living in towns and using coin for exchange; Mediterranean tastes in food, drink and costume; new architectural and artistic conventions. The Germanic successor-states which emerged from the wreckage of the empire – for these are the outsiders with whom we shall be initially concerned – accepted Christianity and in so doing embraced a cultural totality which was *Romanitas*, 'Roman-ness'. It was particularly significant that this occurred at a time when two other processes were shattering the cultural unity of the Mediterranean world. One of these was the withdrawal into herself of the eastern, Byzantine, Orthodox half of the former Roman empire. The other was the irruption of Islam into the Mediterranean and the resultant hiving off of its eastern and southern shores into an alien culture. The cultural unity of the Mediterranean disappeared for ever. But what had been harvested from the classical world and transplanted with Christianity into a northern seedbed germinated there, sprouted and grew into a new civilization, one which indeed owed much to the Mediterranean but was distinctively its own: western European Christendom. The growth of Christendom decisively affected the character of European culture and thereby, because of European dominance in human affairs for several centuries before the twentieth, the civilization of our world. That is why the coming of Christianity to north-western Europe is worth examining, and why this book has been written.

It will be as well to begin by looking at one specific example of this process. In or about the year 619 an Italian priest named Paulinus made his way from the kingdom of Kent in the south-eastern corner of Britain to the court of King Edwin, whose realm of Northumbria had its nucleus in what we now call Yorkshire. Paulinus was a member of the team of missionaries sent by Pope Gregory I a generation earlier to convert the English to Christianity. He had been working in Kent, and possibly other parts of eastern England as well, since his arrival in 601. The Gregorian mission had had a modest success in Kent, where the royal family had been converted and an archbishopric founded at Canterbury. The northern venture was a new departure which had arisen from a dynastic marriage-alliance. Paulinus went north as the domestic chaplain of a Christian princess from Kent, Ethelburga, who was to be married to the pagan King Edwin of Northumbria.

Britain, Britannia, had once been a part of the Roman empire. That had been a long time ago, though the memory of it had endured in some circles, perhaps to exert influence upon the mind of Pope Gregory. After the withdrawal of the apparatus of Roman imperial administration in the early years of the fifth century Britain was left vulnerable to her enemies. Prominent though not alone among these were the Germanic peoples of the North Sea coastline from the Rhine to Denmark. It is traditional and convenient, if only approximately accurate, to refer to them as the Anglo-Saxons. In the course of the very obscure fifth and sixth centuries Germanic warrior aristocracies established themselves as the dominant groups over much of eastern Britain. By the year 600 a number of petty kingdoms under Anglo-Saxon princely dynasties had emerged. Kent was one of these, Northumbria another.

Edwin was the most powerful Anglo-Saxon ruler of his day. His kingdom of Northumbria stretched from the Humber to the Firth of Forth between the North Sea and the Pennines. In addition to this he enjoyed a wider overlordship in Britain over many other kings and princes, both Germanic and Celtic. This position of dominance had been gained by incessant warfare against his neighbours. Seventh-century English kings did not 'govern' in any sense that we should recognize today. Their primary business was predatory warfare and the exaction of tribute from those they defeated. The spoils of successful war – treasure, weapons, horses, slaves, cattle – were distributed to their retainers as payment for past and lien upon future loyalty. A king who failed to provide rewards would forfeit loyalty. The warriors of his warband would melt away to take service with more successful and therefore more generous warlords, or would thrust the king aside into exile or an early grave to make way for a more promising candidate. It was a risky business being a Germanic king in post-Roman Europe.

Beyond their own arms and those of their retainers these kings looked to their gods to furnish them with victory. It is a grave difficulty with our subject – one which we shall encounter time and again in the course of this book – that we know very little indeed about Germanic

3

traditional, pre-Christian religion. If we ask ourselves the question, 'What were Germanic kings converted *from*?' we have to confess that we don't know much about it and never will. Most of the traces of Germanic paganism have been diligently obliterated by its Christian supplanter. (This has not deterred modern scholars from writing many weighty books about it.) But we are on fairly safe ground in the supposition that for a king like Edwin and for his heroic warrior aristocracy the cult of a god or gods of war was of central importance. Edwin's gods had done very nicely by him. He was not a man, one might hazard, who would hastily abandon their cult. Paulinus' brief was not simply to minister to the spiritual needs of Ethelburga and her attendants but also to try to convert her husband to Christianity. As he journeyed northwards Paulinus must have reflected that Edwin presented him with a formidable challenge. But Edwin did give way in the end. He was baptized at York on Easter Day, 12 April, in the year 627, in a wooden chapel hastily erected for the purpose, along with other members of his family and many of his warriors. The king founded an episcopal see at York; Paulinus was its first bishop. For the remainder of his life until his death in battle in 633 King Edwin strenuously encouraged the missionary activities of Paulinus in his kingdom.

We owe this account to Bede, a Northumbrian monk and scholar who completed his *Ecclesiastical History of the English People* about a century after Edwin's death. Bede was an exceptionally careful and honest historian, though in using him we have to bear in mind that his aims and methods in writing history differed widely from those of today. Although his chronology presents difficulties – silently resolved above – no one has ever doubted that the central episode of this narrative, the baptism of Edwin into the Christian faith on Easter Day 627, was one that did really happen. However, if we wish to approach a deeper understanding of the facts there is a great deal more that we should like to know. Bede furnishes some tantalizing scraps of information about the background to the baptism which can be eked out with some even more fragmentary materials from other sources.

In 626 Queen Ethelburga gave birth to a daughter. Paulinus assured Edwin that the queen's safe delivery and the baby's survival were owed to his prayers to the God of the Christians. Later in the same year Edwin led his warband against the king of the West Saxons (who gave their name to the kingdom of Wessex). Before he set out on campaign he promised that if God should grant him victory he would renounce the worship of idols and serve Christ. As a pledge of his promise he permitted his infant daughter to be baptized, which took place at Whitsun (7 June) 626. His campaign was completely successful: five chieftains of the West Saxons were slain and Edwin returned booty-laden and rejoicing to the north. He abandoned the worship of idols and sought instruction in the Christian faith from Paulinus, though he did not yet publicly declare himself a Christian. As well as instructing him Paulinus reminded Edwin of a mysterious experience that he had had years before, while in exile before fighting his way to power in Northumbria. At dead of night he had encountered an unknown stranger – in one version of the story this was Paulinus himself – who had prophesied Edwin's future greatness and held out the promise of salvation. In a final episode of Bede's conversion narrative the king held a meeting with his counsellors and sought their advice. The chief pagan priest, by name Coifi, made the point that a lifetime's devotion to pagan cult had brought little in the way of material advantage to himself, the principal intermediary between king and gods. (We should note that Bede regarded these as 'prudent words'; his nineteenth-century editor and matchless commentator Charles Plummer found it 'disappointing' that Bede should have approved such 'gross material-ism'.) A nobleman present likened the life of man to the flight of a sparrow through the king's hall in winter, from darkness to darkness, and urged sympathetic consideration for a faith which might reveal more of the origins and ultimate goals of mankind. Paulinus also spoke in the debate. At its close Edwin formally embraced Christianity and Coifi led the way in profaning the heathen temples. The royal baptism at Easter followed shortly thereafter.

Bede was writing a century later. He was dependent on oral testimony, stories about King Edwin preserved at the monastery of Whitby, on the Yorkshire coast, where the king was buried. He wrote with a didactic purpose, teaching lessons in Christian living to the kings and clergy of his own day by holding up a gallery of good examples from the past, among whom Edwin and Paulinus were prominent. These features of Bede's work, for all his honesty and care, render it less than wholly satisfactory as an account of the conversion of Edwin. But it is very nearly all we have.

The coming of Christianity to Northumbria in the seventh century prompts questions which may serve as some kind of informal agenda for enquiries which will range more widely in time and space.

First, there is the problem of the apostolic impulse. It is observable that in the course of Christian history churchmen have been now more, now less concerned with spreading the faith. Why did Pope Gregory I decide to send a mission to convert the English to Christianity? What was it that took Patrick to Ireland, or Boniface to Germany, or Anskar to Sweden, or Cyril and Methodius to Moravia?

Second, there are the evangelists like Paulinus to be considered. Who were these activists who engaged themselves in the work – the toilsome, often unrewarding, sometimes dangerous work – of missionary preaching? What sort of previous experience or training had they had? What models or precedents guided them, what ideas about strategy and tactics?

Third, there is the missionary 'target' or 'host society', in this instance a warrior king and his household of military retainers. Was it a condition of successful evangelism in early medieval Europe that missionaries worked through and with the secular power? Who indeed were identified as the potential converts – individuals or groups; central people or marginal people; men or women or children; kings, noblemen, farmers, merchants, craftsmen, labourers, slaves, prisoners of war or what-have-you; settled, nomadic, intermittently mobile, or displaced people?

Fourth, there are the expectations of the potential converts, founded in their experience of the traditional religion in whose observances they were brought up. What did they expect of it? It has already been pointed out that we know little of Germanic paganism. The same may be said – must be said, indeed, and the theme is one that needs regular sounding – of Celtic, Scandinavian and Slavonic paganisms. But of one thing we may be reasonably confident. The rich diversity of pre-Christian cults with which evangelists had to contend shared a core of what sociologists of religion like to call 'empirical religiosity'. That is to say, the belief that proper cult brings tangible reward in this present world, in material benefits like health, prosperity, success or fame, as well as in whatever Hereafter traditional religion might have envisaged. Edwin wanted victory in battle, glory and treasure and power and the continuing loyalty of his retainers. Others of less exalted status would have had different hopes and expectations: enough food to see the family through the winter, murrain-free cattle, cures for sickness or disability, a good husband or wife, successful trading, deliverance from shipwreck, release from enchantment, protection against evil spirits, the death of an enemy, revenge, freedom, a return home. How could widely differing hopes and fears be satisfied?

Fifth, there is the question of the communication of the message. How did evangelists set about the business of putting over the faith and its associated standards of conduct to potential converts? For a start, what language did they use? For Paulinus the vernacular of every day in his native Italy was Latin; for Edwin it was a Northumbrian dialect of Old English, a Germanic language having its closest counterpart in the Frisian coastlands of north Germany. When Edwin's mysterious nocturnal visitor spoke to him of 'salvation', what Old English word or phrase might he have used? How did missionaries render key Christian concepts in the vernacular – 'sin', 'regeneration', and so forth? Most important of all, what word did they choose to render 'God', and what cluster of associations might it have had for their converts?

Sixth, there is the delicate problem of the adaptability of the message. How much elasticity or 'give' did missionary Christianity have in an early medieval context? What compromises or adjustments did evangelists have to make, and with how much heart-searching? How and where were the limits drawn between what was tolerable in traditional belief and practice and what was not? To what extent could or did Christian activists try to change traditional custom – in respect of, say, marriage, penal practice, the disposal of the dead, warfare, blood feuds, slave-trading?

Seventh, there are the differing patterns of acceptance. What did the new converts make of the new faith and its demands? What models of Christian living were presented to them? How, if at all, was Edwin different (to human eyes) as man and as king after Easter 627 from what he had been before? Bede tells us that subsequently Paulinus spent thirty-six days at King Edwin's royal residence at Yeavering (in present-day Northumberland) engaged in non-stop baptism in the nearby river Glen of all who flocked to him. What did they think had happened to them? Do we have even the faintest shadow of a chance of finding out? How much of a leap into the unknown was conversion, how high a hurdle? Were converts required to abandon all, or some, or hardly any of their previous customs, rituals or taboos?

Eighth, there is the consolidation that has to follow close upon the initial acceptance and conversion, the process by which a mission becomes a church. How did a structure of ecclesiastical government come into being in the mission field, and in what respects did it differ from the Mediterranean model whence it derived? Why were such enormous numbers of monasteries founded in newly converted regions such as seventh-century England or eighth-century Germany? How were cathedrals and monasteries endowed, and what implications might this process have had for legal notions about the ownership and transfer of property? How did parishes come into existence? What positions were taken up on such potentially controversial matters as the formation of a native priesthood, the role of women within the young churches, the imposition of dues such as tithe upon the new converts, the translation of Christian scriptures into the vernacular? What was to be the architectural form and the constructional technique of new church buildings? Could 'native' art become 'Christian' art?

Ninth, and almost finally, there are the cultural consequences of conversion, already glanced at. We do not know exactly where Edwin's wooden chapel stood, though there is some likelihood that it was in the pillared square of what had once been the *praetorium* or headquarters building of the Roman fortress at York. Excavation has shown that this enormous and imposing structure was still standing in Edwin's day. If this supposition about the siting of York's earliest Anglo-Saxon cathedral is correct, Edwin's baptism at the hands of an Italian mission-ary bishop took place in an unambiguously Roman architectural set-ting. Bede tells us that Edwin used to have a standard of Roman type carried before him. He quotes papal letters which addressed Edwin with exalted Latin titles, 'glorious king of the English', 'most excellent and surpassing lord'. To Bede it was clear that there was something Roman about Edwin's kingship after his conversion. Whatever the reality might have been, from Bede's angle of vision the perception was a just one. Within little more than a century of Edwin's death the cathedral school at York had become the most important centre for the study of Christian and classical learning in western Europe. Among others it educated Alcuin, that early example of the brain-drain who, head-hunted by Charlemagne, king of the Franks, was the architect of that revival of literature and learning under royal patronage, the so-called Carolingian renaissance, which was the threshold to the cul-tural achievements of western Christendom in the Middle Ages.

These are all questions to which answers may be found – however

8

hesitant or provisional, however swaddled in circumlocutory cautions our formulations may need to be – in the meagre sources which are all that have come down to us from a remote epoch. The tenth and last question on our agenda is the most perplexing because it was never specifically addressed in our sources. It is no more and no less than this: What makes a Christian? At what point may one say of an individual, or a society, 'He (or she, or it) has become, is now Christian'? If the saving grace imparted by baptism makes the Christian, then the hundreds of Northumbrian farmers and their families dunked in the waters of the river Glen by Paulinus were indeed made Christians in the course of those thirty-six days. It is a sound sacramentalist point of view. Was it enough for Paulinus? Was it enough for Bede? As it happens, we know how Bede would have answered that question. His requirements for right Christian living were rigorous. To investigate what more beyond baptism might be required is to discover that the question 'What makes a Christian?' was very variously answered in the span of place and time embraced by this book. Being a Christian was obviously a rather different operation for Pope Gregory I than it was for King Ethelbert of Kent. Being a Christian in seventh-century Northumbria was not the same as being a Christian in twelfth-century Northumbria (or, for the matter of that, in sixteenth- or twentieth-century Northumbria). Conversion could mean different things to different people at the same time. What was required of the convert could vary as circumstances or tactics or the pressure of time or the level of moral resources also varied. Investigators will choose diverse indicators of Christianization and frame judgements accordingly. For the historian the study of early medieval conversion can be bewildering; a game played in swirling mist on a far from level playing field in which unseen hands are constantly shifting the dimly glimpsed goalposts.

The theme is a grand one and the agenda (quite frankly) daunting. This is the more so because the sources to which we may turn for information are sparse and uniformly problematic. Early medieval Europe was a society of restricted literacy. Most of those who could read and write during the period which is my concern were ecclesiastics. In consequence, very nearly all the surviving written narratives were composed by what might be called professional Christians for a primary audience of other professional Christians. Works thus composed reach us only after a process of passing, so to say, through several different filters which have impeded the free flow of information. In the first place there was a kind of voluntary censorship practised by their authors. There are many things we should like to know about which these writers never tell us. A notorious example is furnished by Bede's reluctance to tell us much about Anglo-Saxon paganism. A second source of difficulty is that these narratives are almost invariably to some degree didactic. I have already said that Bede's portrayal of Edwin and Paulinus was drawn with an eye to the kings and clergy of his own day a century later. Indeed, there is not a single chapter in Bede's great *Ecclesiastical History* which cannot be shown to have had a didactic purpose of one sort or another. The lessons which such writers sought to teach may not always be clear to the modern reader, but the didactic intent usually is. Now teaching lessons involves a measure of selection, of emphasis, of simplification, of omission. Here then is another filter through which the information has to pass. Bede presented Edwin as a sober statesman and an earnest seeker after truth. One cannot help suspecting that there may have been other sides to Edwin's character than these. But this is how Bede wanted his audience to see him.

The most overtly didactic narrative literature of the period is that branch of Christian biography known as hagiography, or the lives of the saints. During the early Middle Ages the control of saint-making with which we are familiar – a formal process of canonization under papal supervision – did not exist: canonization in this guise was an invention of the ecclesiastical lawyers of the twelfth century. Instead, holy men and holy women (*sancti, sanctae*) were simply recognized and revered as such by neighbourhood and community. One way of keeping the memory of a saint fresh was by the composition of a memoir, the saint's life (*vita*), which could be read aloud for edificatory purposes in the religious community to which the holy man or woman had belonged in life, and where his or her relics were treasured after death. Edification is the key word in this context. Although hagiography came – as it still comes – in many different costumes its aim was consistently to edify – to hold the saint up as an example of godly living and holy dying, to spur listeners or readers to compunction and devotion. One means of edification which may cause disquiet to the modern reader was the recording of wonders and miracles worked by the saint. Early medieval Europe was a world in which persons of every level of intellectual cultivation accepted without question that the miraculous could weave like a shuttle in and out of everyday reality. We need to remember this, and to resist the temptation to dismiss it out of hand as infantile credulity: patronizing the past never helped anyone to understand it. Hagiographical writings survive in great abundance from this period. They constitute an important source of information for the historian. At the most obvious level the lives of the saints contain an enormous quantity of incidental information about daily life. To give a trivial example, we learn from Chapter 20 of Bede's *Life of St Cuthbert* that the saint used pig's lard as a kind of dubbin with which to grease his leather shoes. At a more subtle level of interpretation saints' lives can tell us something of the expectations which people held of their holy men and women. Did the saint foretell the future? Heal the sick? Found monasteries? Rebuke the mighty? Control the weather? Preach to the heathen? Wreak vengeance on his enemies? See visions? Practise ascetic self-denial? Sensitively used, hagiographical writings can enable us to peer into some at least of the more intimate religious feelings and aspirations of a people distantly removed from us in time.

Of course, matters are rarely straightforward. In the path of every historian of the early Middle Ages – and especially but not exclusively those who concern themselves with hagiography – there lies like some Slough of Despond the quagmire of the *topos*. The Greek word for 'place', topos has been adopted into the jargon of literary scholars to mean, in the words of the *Oxford English Dictionary*, 'a traditional motif or theme (in a literary composition); a rhetorical commonplace, a literary convention or formula'. In the context of hagiography what this means is that there existed, as it were, a bank of stock tales, themes, phrases on which the hagiographer could draw without restraint or acknowledgement: for example, future sanctity foreshadowed in childhood; renunciation of home and kinsfolk; the edifying deathbed, etc. But we need not restrict ourselves to hypothetical examples: let us return to Cuthbert and the pig's lard. In the story it was brought to him on Farne Island by a pair of ravens (and if you want to know the ostensible reason why you had better read it for yourself). Bede himself tells us that the story of Cuthbert and the ravens was 'after the example' of a tale told by Pope Gregory in his account of St Benedict, founder of Montecassino and author of the Benedictine Rule. Behind this lies the story, well-loved in the early Middle Ages, of how the hermits Paul and Antony were sustained by a raven who brought them bread

11

in the desert. Lurking still further back is the story in I Kings xvii of how the prophet Elijah was fed by ravens at the Lord's command when he lay concealed beside the brook Cherith. It is extremely common to find that episodes in one saint's *Vita* were modelled upon episodes in another or in the Bible. This feature of the literature raises nagging anxieties about historicity. To what extent might the demands of matching form and content to a literary model have distorted the reality which the writer professes to convey?

Conversion narratives, of which Bede's account of Edwin is but one of many that we shall encounter, offer an open door to colonization by formulaic topoi. They present additional snags all of their own. The business of organizing a narrative round a conversion is in itself liable to project sharpness of outline on to a historical reality which was more likely than not blurred and indistinct. Hagiographical piety and didactic intent might highlight the missionary's role by casting as unalloyedly pagan a people who had already been touched by Christianity. Narrative drama could be enhanced by presenting conversion as a moment rather than a process. Hindsight could show as smooth and harmonious the growth of a church which in reality had been characterized by improvisation and quarrelling. Even – or perhaps especially – the simple and fundamental opposition 'pagan/Christian' might be deceptive. In a word, we have to exercise great caution in our handling of the conversion narratives which have come down to us.

Narratives such as Bede's *Ecclesiastical History* and hagiographies such as his *Life of St Cuthbert* are our most important written sources but not our only ones. They can be supplemented with sermons, tracts, letters, legislative enactments, deeds relating to property, poetry both sacred and profane. Each presents difficulties of interpretation. Sermons and lawcodes are normative or prescriptive; their authors tend to encourage the ideal rather than to describe the actual. Letter-collections such as Alcuin's were on the whole valued and preserved rather for their style than for their content. Deeds rarely survive in their original form; the texts of the copies which have come down to us may have been tampered with in the course of transmission. Unattributed poetry is hard to date.

These diverse sources of information in written form may be supplemented by the material evidence of surviving objects or structures. Two notable excavations have helped us to grasp something of the setting of Edwin's kingship. Aerial photography above the valley of the river Till, near Wooler in Northumberland, revealed in 1948 a complex of markings which were initially taken to indicate the remains of a hitherto unknown monastic settlement. Excavation in the 1950s revealed the site of Edwin's residence at Yeavering with its associated structures, scene of the mass baptisms administered by Paulinus. Some years later, in the early 1970s, threats to the stability of the central tower of York Minster necessitated a strengthening of the foundations, which permitted some limited and hazardous archaeological excavation. It was in the course of this operation that it was discovered that the pillared square of the Roman *praetorium* was still standing in good repair in Edwin's day. Some of the archaeological materials from this age may speak to us even more directly of conversion, as we shall see in due course.

There are hard questions to be faced, and intractable evidence to answer them with. But face them we must, and do with it what we can, if we are to do justice to the grandeur of our theme. Yeavering is a long way beyond what had been Rome's northernmost frontier, Hadrian's Wall. Edwin's great hall was an enormous barn-like structure of timber, with doorways in the long sides through which a sparrow might pass from winter darkness to winter darkness. The quantities of cattle bones excavated near by suggest that the king and his retainers gorged themselves on beef, washed down no doubt by copious draughts of beer from generous drinking-horns like those found at Taplow or Sutton Hoo. A barbaric scene: yes, but not far from the hall there stood a flight of curved benches, rising in tiers and lengthening as they rose, whose occupants' gaze would have focused upon a dais at ground level backed by a massive wooden post. This structure can only have been designed for seating an assembly which might be addressed from the dais. The design of this auditorium irresistibly recalls as it were a segment from a Roman theatre. Did Paulinus address Edwin's warriors from that dais? Perhaps. The encounter between Paulinus and Edwin was one between Roman and barbarian, Christian and pagan, Latin and Germanic, literate and oral, wine and beer, oil and lard, south and north. It opened up perspectives on to distant notions and activities beyond the wildest surmises of the participants.

Christianity traces its historic roots to the ministry of a Jewish preacher and exorcist in a backward province of the Roman empire. As an offshoot of Judaic stock, early Christianity was heir to the proselytizing zeal of its parent. Accustomed as we are to a merely self-perpetuating style of Judaism which was brought about by subsequent centuries of Christian and Islamic religious repression, it is easy to forget that the Judaism of the Hellenistic world was an evangelizing faith, and not one by any means conceived as being exclusively for adherents who were of Jewish ethnicity. The diaspora, or dispersion, of the Jewish people from their homeland had begun several centuries earlier with the Assyrian and Babylonian captivities of the eighth and sixth centuries B.C. respectively. Thereafter it trickled on, quickening to a flood of emigration after the Jewish revolt of 66–70 A.D. and the destruction of Jerusalem, and again after the rebellion of Bar-Kochba in the years 132–5. By the first century of the Christian era there were significant Jewish communities to the east of the Roman empire in Armenia, Iraq, Iran and Arabia, and throughout the Mediterranean world in Egypt, Asia Minor, Italy and Spain; communities that were thriving and growing by evangelistic effort. We shall meet some of these scattered Jewish communities of the Mediterranean in a later chapter.

As a sect within Judaism, early Christianity followed in its parent's geographical footsteps. It was characterized from the outset by its mobility. This rapid dissemination found its earliest chronicler in the author of the Acts of the Apostles, traditionally identified as St Luke, a masterly account focused principally upon the missionary labours of St Paul. But the impression given by Luke of an orderly and controlled diffusion – reinforced for many of us by map and mnemonic in the scripture lessons of childhood – is misleading. Our evidence is patchy. The spread of Christianity to Alexandria and beyond along the coast of north Africa to Carthage has left no narrative trace of any kind. But it is reasonably clear that Christianity spread to east and to west both quickly and anarchically, without overt strategy or leadership. In his epistle to the Romans Paul was not addressing a Christian community which he had founded, in contrast to the young churches of Ephesus, Corinth or Thessalonica. The Christian community in Rome already existed by at latest the middle years of the first century. It had just mysteriously come into being – mysteriously, that is, if one doubts (as most scholars now do) the traditions attributing its foundation to St Peter. This intimate association with Judaism continued to provide a ramifying network of communication for Christian churches throughout and beyond the long-drawn-out and messy process of the

14

detachment of church from synagogue, of the law of Christ from the law of Moses.

Alexandria, Carthage, Corinth, Ephesus, Rome, Thessalonica: the expansion of Christianity took place in a social setting that was predominantly urban. It was in the cities of Asia Minor and Greece that St Paul found, or founded, the Christian communities which he nurtured, lectured, scolded or bullied. It was in the cities round the Mediterranean that a church organization developed, in the cities that martyrs suffered and were commemorated, in the cities that Christians organized the charitable works for which they were renowned. The early Christian communities were composed of city-dwellers of fairly lowly social rank. It is true that when, in the course of time – and hardly at all before about the year 200 – the Christian faith began to attract adherents of higher rank and greater wealth, such persons might possess country houses in which they and their families would spend part of the year. But these country villas were, in Ramsay MacMullen's striking phrase, like 'pieces of cities broken off'.[1] Even in the country houses of the rich Christianity remained an urban religion.

Such observations have long been truisms of early Christian studies. Like all truisms they need some qualification. The contrast between urban and rural may be made too clear-cut by our industrialized perceptions of that distinction. Before the era of railways, tinned food and refrigeration it was impossible for towns to be isolated from rural life. Apart from a handful of really big cities (Alexandria, Antioch and, of course, Rome) and a larger number of towns of middling size (such as Athens or Naples), most of the towns round the Mediterranean were small and closely integrated with their rural hinterland. Very many farmers would have lived in towns and walked out to their fields by day, as some still do twenty centuries later. In addition, we do have a few tiny fragments of evidence which suggest an early rural dimension to the spread of Christianity in, for example, Syria, Egypt or Asia Minor. The younger Pliny, governor of Bithynia in Asia Minor, addressed a famous letter to the Emperor Trajan in about 112 asking for guidance on the treatment of Christians, in the course of which he referred to a Christian presence in the countryside. Possibly he exaggerated; but it would be unwise to disregard his testimony altogether.

So a degree of circumspection is needed. Nevertheless, the old truism still has validity if we introduce a geographical modification. The early evidence for rural Christianity comes exclusively from the eastern provinces of the empire (and especially from those that were close to the Mediterranean). It does not come from the western ones which are the main concern of this book, those provinces embraced by north Africa west of Carthage, Spain, Italy and the Alpine regions stretching up as far as the Danube frontier, Gaul and Britain. There were no great cities at all in the west, if we exclude Rome, and far fewer of middling rank. Towns of modest size were generally even smaller than in the east, and thinner on the ground, further apart from one another. There were enormous tracts of countryside which were to all intents and purposes untouched by Romanization. We shall see evidence in the following chapter that they were untouched by Christianity too.

Then there is the question of cultural attitudes. The educated and articulate elite of the classical Mediterranean believed that civilization and culture were to be found exclusively in cities. Our daily use of such words as 'urbane', 'polite' and, of course, 'civilized' shows what a good job that elite has done in persuading posterity of its point of view. Occasionally the writers who belonged to this tiny elite deigned to celebrate country life and the happy lot of the peasantry – their rude health, sturdy virtues and innocent pleasures. Reality was different. City-dwellers, parasitic upon the surrounding country for their essential supplies, repaid this dependence in the harsh coin of disdain. Most townspeople, most of the time, looked upon the rural peasantry with mingled disgust, fear and contempt. They were dirty and smelly, unkempt, inarticulate, uncouth, misshapen by toil, living in conditions of unbelievable squalor, as brutish as the beasts they tended. These attitudes are easy to document from surviving Greek and Latin literature. The peasantry of the countryside were beyond the pale, a tribe apart, outsiders. Such attitudes underpinned the failure of the urban Christian communities to reach out and spread the gospel in the countryside. We might regard this lack of initiative as negligent. But such an accusation would probably have bewildered the urban Christians. For them the countryside simply did not exist as a zone for missionary enterprise. After all, there was nothing in the New Testament about spreading the Word to the beasts of the field.

Unappealing as we might find this disposition of antique city-dwellers, it was one which witnessed to a massive confidence in the urban order of imperial Rome. The Christian communities of the Mediterranean world had grown up *in* that order, if not quite *of* it.

16

They took it for granted and they were right to be confident in it. From the beginning of the Christian era in the reign of Augustus for the next two centuries the Mediterranean (as opposed to the frontier) provinces of the empire had basked in almost uninterrupted peace and prosperity: the *pax romana*. The public buildings of the cities and the speeches which were declaimed in them alike display a bland and soothing mastery of their respective architectural and literary techniques; symptomatic of a social order which gazed upon its way of going about its business and was pleased with what it saw. Look at me, the colonnades and arches of Leptis Magna seem to say: relax; enjoy; and it'll go on like this for ever.

But it didn't. In the middle years of the third century the Roman empire experienced a phase of trouble more harrowing and profound than any that had occurred since the founding of the principate by Augustus. During the half-century which followed the death of the Emperor Severus Alexander in 235 there ensued a series of short-lived and for the most part incompetent rulers. Of twenty more or less legitimate emperors – not counting usurpers – all but two died violently. The average length of reign was two years and six months. A symptom, and perhaps to a large degree a cause of this instability was the inability of government to hold the allegiance of the armies. This played into the hands of the generals, who used the troops under their command to stage coups which made and unmade emperors or to set up breakaway 'empires within the empire'. As central control slackened, imperial income fell. To make ends meet, and in particular to try to satisfy the insatiable demands of the military and thus to purchase loyalty, the government resorted time after time to that most irresponsible of expedients, debasement of the coinage. Debasement brought in its train, as it always does, inflation. By the end of the third century the purchasing power of the denarius stood at about a half of 1 per cent of what it had been at its outset.

Crippled by instability, civil war, fiscal chaos – and, just to make matters worse, by intermittent outbreaks of bubonic plague – the empire was in no position to defend its frontiers. From 224 onwards the new Persian dynasty of the Sassanids constituted a well-organized and hostile presence to the east, bent upon regaining the Syrian territories which Persian kings of old had ruled. For the Roman empire, the most humiliating moment of this time of troubles occurred in 260 when the Emperor Valerian was captured by the Persians. The

Germanic tribes of the Goths, settled at this period on the northern shores of the Black Sea in today's Ukraine, took to the sea to strike deep into Asia Minor. By land, they pressed hard on the Danube frontier, launching raids into the Balkans and Greece. The Emperor Decius was defeated and killed by them in Thrace in the year 251. Along the Rhine frontier new Germanic confederations, those of the Alamans and of the Franks, took shape. In 257 they broke into Gaul to plunder it at will. Some of them even penetrated as far as north-eastern Spain, where they sacked the city of Tarraco (Tarragona). Berbers along the Saharan fringes attacked the long, thin, vulnerable littoral of Roman north Africa. In far-flung Britain the construction of coastal defences witnessed to new enemies from overseas – Saxons from Germany and Scots from Ireland. One of the most telling signs of the times was the building of town walls throughout the western provinces of Gaul, Spain and Britain, furnishing defences for settlements which had never needed them before.

The third-century slide into anarchy and helplessness was arrested by the Emperor Diocletian (284–305). His stabilizing reforms, fiscal, military and bureaucratic, were continued and extended under his successor Constantine I (306–37). Their work gave the empire the stamina and solidity it enjoyed in the fourth century. One feature of these reforms was the adoption of ideas about monarchy, together with the associated ceremonies and ritual, which drew on earlier Hellenistic and Persian thinking. The principal tendency of this body of political theory was to stress the power of the ruler in matters sacred as well as profane. It would encourage the moving together of church and state and, as time went by, their near merging in the imperial theocracies of the East Roman or Byzantine empire and, much later, in its Russian heir. It was a tendency which was less pronounced in the western provinces of the fourth-century empire. This was a difference which had important implications, to which we shall return shortly. A second feature was the division of the unitary empire into two halves, an eastern and a western. Diocletian had led the way here, dividing the empire into a tetrarchy – a senior emperor in east and west, each with a subordinate emperor – as part of his reforms; a decentralization intended to make more effective the emperors' discharge of their primary responsibility, defence. This formal structure was not maintained after his death and practice varied in the course of the fourth century, but by its last quarter the political division into

18

eastern and western empires had become permanent. One development which helped to institutionalize it was Constantine's foundation of a new capital city in the east, named after him – Constantinople.

A third feature of the reforms of the Diocletianic–Constantinian period was the change in the status of Christianity within the empire. Towards the end of Diocletian's reign there occurred the last and most serious persecution of the Christian communities ever mounted by the imperial authorities. It was immediately halted by a respite. The story of Constantine's conversion is well known but needs to be told again in outline here because it became such a potent model – indeed, a topos – of how a ruler should be brought to the faith. Constantine had been proclaimed emperor in Britain in 306. Six years later, having by then made himself master of Gaul and Spain as well, the emperor was leading his army south to do battle with his rival Maxentius for control of Italy and Africa. At some point in the course of this journey – much later tradition would locate this at Arles – Constantine saw a vision of the cross superimposed on the sun above the words *In hoc signo vince*, 'Conquer in this sign'. He advanced over the Alps and down towards Rome. His troops were ordered to mark their shields with the sign of the cross. In the battle of the Milvian Bridge, just outside Rome, Constantine was victorious against all odds. The Christian God – a god of battles – had been on his side. A few months later, in March 313, the so-called Edict of Milan put an end to the persecution of the Christians.

In what sense and when Constantine became a Christian are questions that have been endlessly and inconclusively debated. In the formal sense of the word he was not initiated until shortly before his death in 337. Like many others in the early church he chose to postpone baptism until his deathbed. But his adhesion to Christianity from 313 onwards was not to be doubted. Its most enduring manifestation was in open-handed patronage. Constantine did not make Christianity the official religion of the Roman empire, though this is often said of him. What he did was to make the Christian church the most-favoured recipient of the near-limitless resources of imperial favour. An enormous new church of St Peter was built in Rome, modelled on the basilican form used for imperial throne halls such as the one which survives at Trier. The see of Rome received extensive landed endowments and one of the imperial residences, the Lateran Palace, to house its bishop and his staff. Constantinople, begun in 325, was to be

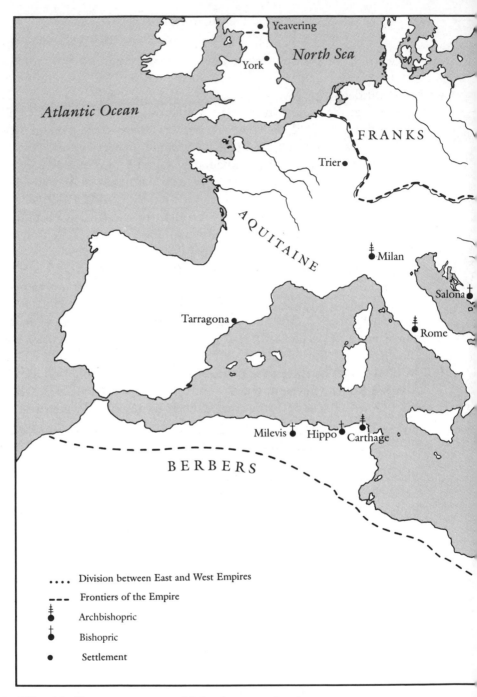

1. *The Mediterranean world in late antiquity.*

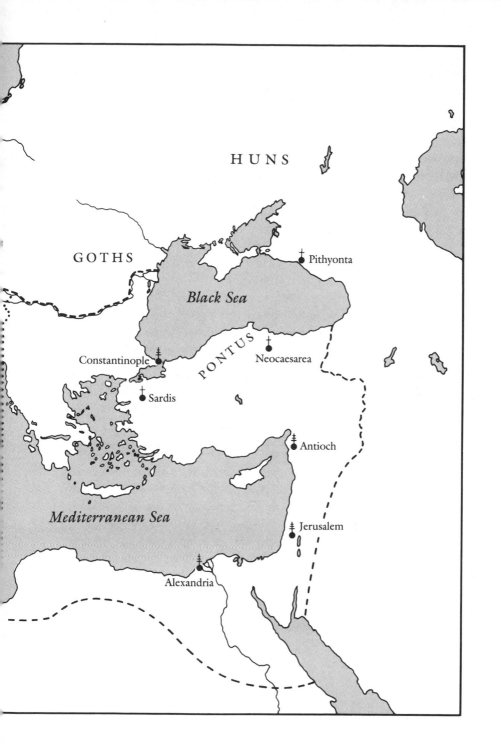

an emphatically and exclusively Christian city – even though it was embellished with pagan statuary pillaged from temples throughout the eastern provinces. Jerusalem was provided with a splendid church of the Holy Sepulchre. Legal privileges and immunities rained down upon the Christian church and its clergy. The emperor took an active part in ecclesiastical affairs, summoning and attending church councils, participating in theological debate, attempting to sort out quarrels and controversies.

The adhesion to Christianity of Constantine and his successors – with the single exception of the short-lived Emperor Julian 'the Apostate' (361–3) – was a development of the utmost weight and significance in Christian history. All sorts of relationships were turned topsy-turvy by it. From being a vulnerable, if vibrant, sect liable to intermittent persecution at the hands of the secular authorities, Christians suddenly found themselves part of the 'establishment'. The end of persecution meant that martyrdom must thenceforward be found only outside Christendom or be understood in a metaphorical rather than a literal manner. Christian bishops were no longer just the disciplinarians of tightly organized sectarian cells but rapidly assimilated as quasi civil servants into the mandarinate which administered the empire. Their churches were no longer obscure conventicles but public buildings of increasing magnificence. So much, and more, flowed from Constantine's spiritual reorientation.

The church repaid Constantine's generosity by presenting him as the model Christian emperor, the 'friend of God' who 'frames his earthly government according to the pattern of the divine original'. The words are those of Eusebius, bishop of Caesarea, who lived from *c.* 260 to *c.* 340. Eusebius was a notable scholar and a prominent member of the little circle of court clerics who helped to school Constantine in Christian ways and to shape an image of him for contemporaries and for posterity. His *Oration in Praise of Constantine*, from which the passages quoted above are taken, is a prime example of fourth-century rhetoric, a work of oily panegyric which was hugely successful in carefully directing attention to all that was most admirable in its subject while discreetly drawing a veil over the less appealing features of the emperor's character. It is not to Eusebius that we must go to learn that Constantine murdered his father-in-law, his wife and his son. On the contrary, Constantine was 'our divinely favoured emperor', who has received 'as it were a transcript of the divine sovereignty' to direct 'in imitation of God himself, the administration of this world's affairs'.[2]

Eusebius' handling of Constantine requires to be considered in the context of early Christian thinking about the relationship between the church and the world. For simplicity's sake one may distinguish two contrasting tendencies. The first was an attitude of wariness towards the secular world, of distrust, even of hatred for it. The Christian church was a society set apart, a 'gathered' community of the elect salvaged from the polluting grasp of the world, though still menaced by it in the form of the secular state, the Roman empire. The most violent expression of these views in early Christian writings is to be found in the book of Revelation, composed towards the end of the first century. The Roman empire is the beast, the harlot, 'drunk with the blood of the saints and the martyrs of Jesus'. Keeping the world at arm's length long remained an urgent concern among some Christian groups. We shall return shortly to some of its manifestations in the late antique period.

The second tendency was the quest for some form of accommodation with the secular world and the empire. This search was muted and hesitant at first but gained in confidence and assertiveness as time went on. The earliest sign of it may be glimpsed in the two New Testament books attributed to Luke. It is significant that both were dedicated to Theophilus, a patron of social or official eminence in that very world, secular, gentile and Romano-Hellenistic, which other Christians regarded with misgiving. A next step was to ponder the implications of the coincidence in time between the establishment of the Roman peace and the growth of the Christian church within the empire. Bishop Mellitus of Sardis, addressing an *Apologia* to the Emperor Marcus Aurelius about the year 170, could claim that the Christian faith was 'a blessing of auspicious omen to your empire' because 'having sprung up among the nations under your rule during the great reign of your ancestor Augustus . . . from that time the power of the Romans has grown in greatness and splendour'. The next move was to suggest that the Roman empire was in some sense itself related to God's scheme for the world. The first who dared to think such a thought was the great Alexandrian scholar Origen. In his work *Contra Celsum*, composed between 230 and 240 to refute the attacks on Christianity by the pagan philosopher Celsus, Origen had occasion to comment upon the following words in Psalm lxxii.7: 'In his [the just king's] days righteousness shall flourish, prosperity abound until the moon is no more.' Origen observed that 'God was preparing the nations for His teaching, that they might be under one Roman emperor, so that the unfriendly attitude of the nations to one another caused by the existence of a large number of kingdoms, might not make it more difficult for Jesus' apostles to do what He commanded them when He said "Go and teach all nations" . . .' Augustus therefore, who first 'reduced to uniformity the many kingdoms on earth so that he had a single empire', could be presented as the instrument of God's providence.[3]

These accommodating tendencies were carried to extreme lengths after Constantine's adhesion to Christianity early in the fourth century. Faced for the first time with an entirely novel situation, churchmen had to come to grips with the question, How is a *Christian* emperor to be fitted into the scheme of things? The most comprehensive answer was provided by Eusebius, explicitly in his *Oration*, implicitly in the work to which the *Oration* was a pendent, the *Ecclesiastical History* – the earliest work of its kind, the most important single source for our knowledge of the first three centuries of Christian history, and a potent literary influence upon the work of Bede. Eusebius brought the Roman empire *within* the divine providential scheme for the world. It was an astonishing feat of intellectual acrobatics, here summarized in the words of a modern scholar:

> Eusebius sees the achievement of a unified Christian empire as the goal of all history. He insists on the mutual support of Christianity and Rome, of the monarchy of Christ and the monarchy of Augustus. For him, Roman empire and Christian church are not only essentially connected; they move towards identity . . . Eusebius can say that the city of earth has become the city of God, and that the monarchy of Constantine brings the kingdom of God to men.[4]

This Eusebian accommodation between church and empire became and long remained a cornerstone of the 'political theology' of the eastern empire and its successors. For the historian of conversion it has two significant implications. If empire and church are moving towards identity, if they are (in the words of another scholar) but 'two facets of a single reality', then one of the questions from which we started – Who is Christianity for? – acquires at once a sharper urgency

24

and an answer. If *Romanitas* and *Christianitas* are co-terminous, then the faith is for all dwellers within the ring-fence of the empire but not for those outside. All dwellers within means the 'internal outsiders', the huge rural majority, whose evangelization will occupy us in the next chapter. Those outside means the barbarians.

Barbarians could be as effectively de-humanized by the educated minority as were the peasantry. 'Roman and barbarian are as distinct one from the other as are four-footed beasts from humans,' wrote the Spanish Christian poet Prudentius in about 390. His contemporary St Jerome was sure that some of the Germans were cannibals. 'The holy priesthood, chastity and virginity do not exist among barbarian peoples; and if they were to do so, they would not be safe,' wrote Bishop Optatus of Milevis in north Africa in the 360s. Ingrained habits of thought are revealed in the turn of a phrase. The Spanish historian Orosius, writing in about 417, could begin a sentence with the words 'As a Christian and as a Roman . . .' Quite so.[5] The identities were conflated. In such a climate of opinion there could be no question of taking the faith to the heathen barbarian. In the words of a leading modern authority, 'Throughout the whole period of the Roman empire not a single example is known of a man who was appointed bishop with the specific task of going beyond the frontier to a wholly pagan region in order to convert the barbarians living there.'[6]

One qualification needs to be made. If Christian communities came into existence outside the imperial frontiers they might request the church authorities within the empire to send them a bishop to minister to their needs. There was a variety of ways in which such communities might come into existence, by means of trading settlements, diplomatic contacts, veterans returning from service in the Roman army in the course of which they had been converted, cross-frontier marriage, the settlement of prisoners carried away from their homelands by barbarian raids, and so on. Here is an example. At the end of the fourth century Rufinus of Aquileia translated Eusebius' *Ecclesiastical History* from Greek into Latin to render it accessible to the Latin-speaking west. He also brought it up to date, continuing it from where Eusebius had left off in Constantine's day down to the death of the Emperor Theodosius I in 395. Rufinus had met the king of Georgia, in the southern Caucasus, who told him that his predecessor King Miriam, who reigned in the time of Constantine, had acquired a Christian slave-girl who had converted her master to Christianity. Rufinus did not know her name, though later sources were to name her as Nounè or Nino. Whatever may lie behind this story – perhaps a jumbled memory of diplomatic relations between Constantinople and Tiflis – we may be certain that Christian communities did exist in Georgia in Constantine's reign, because reliable sources reveal that a certain Patrophilus, bishop of Pithyonta (Pitsunda), attended the ecclesiastical council of Nicaea in 325. The site of his bishopric on the Black Sea coast at the foot of the Caucasus suggests that maritime contacts with the Roman empire had given rise to the Christian community over which he presided. We shall examine some further instances of these extra-imperial communities in Chapter 3.

However, the Eusebian accommodation would not commend itself in all quarters. It would be looked upon with disfavour by those of the 'gathered' tradition. It was persons of this persuasion, largely if not exclusively, who were responsible for perhaps the most remarkable phenomenon of late-antique Christianity – the growth of monasticism. Withdrawal from the world by an individual to a life of ascetic renunciation and self-denial in a desert solitude had an obvious biblical precedent in John the Baptist. The gospel stories of the temptation of Jesus reinforced the notion that the desert, the wilderness, was the place where the truly committed might test their faith and overcome the wiles of the Devil. It was in the valley of the Nile, where the desert and the sown lie so close together, that Christian solitaries first made their appearance. The most famous of these early hermits was Antony, a Coptic peasant who 'dropped out' of his village community at the age of twenty, in about the year 270, and for the remainder of a very long life gave himself over to prayer and asceticism. His example was infectious. Though he retreated ever deeper into the desert he was pursued by disciples eager to follow his example and receive his spiritual guidance. It was to one of these followers, Pachomius – perhaps significantly, an ex-soldier – that there occurred in about 320 the idea that communities of ascetics might be organized, living a common life of strict discipline according to a written rule of life. Thus was monasticism born.

It spread like wildfire in the fourth century. In part this was perhaps because, in a church now at peace after the Constantinian revolution, ascetic monasticism offered a means of self-sacrifice which was the nearest thing to martyrdom in a world where martyrs were no longer being made. In part the call of the ascetic life could be interpreted as

a movement of revulsion from what many saw as the increasing worldli-
ness of the fourth-century church, the merging of its hierarchy with
the 'establishment', its ever-accumulating wealth, the growing burden
of administrative responsibilities which encroached upon spiritual ministry. Monasticism offered, or demanded, a manner of life in which
individualism had to be shed. To be 'of one heart and of one soul'
within a community, to have 'all things common', was not simply to
follow the example of the apostles commended in Acts iv.32: it was
also to be liberated from the insidious temptation of private cares,
selfish anxieties. Such liberation offered the possibility to humans of
building a heavenly society upon earth. The monastic vocation was a
call to a new way of apprehending, even of merging into, the divine.

Its appeal was made the more seductive by some persuasive advo-
cates. A *Life of St Antony* was composed by Athanasius, the great
bishop of Alexandria, in 357. It is one of the classics of Christian
hagiography. Its speedy translation from Greek into Latin made it
accessible in the western provinces of the empire. By a happy chance
there has survived a vivid account of the effect this work had upon a
pair of rising civil servants in the early 380s.

> Ponticianus continued to talk and we listened in silence. Eventu-
> ally he told us of the time when he and three of his companions
> were at Trier. One afternoon, when the emperor was watching
> the games in the circus, they went out to stroll in the gardens
> near the city walls. They became separated into two groups, Ponti-
> cianus and one of the others remaining together while the other
> two went off by themselves. As they wandered on, the second
> pair came to a house which was occupied by some servants of God,
> men poor in spirit, to whom the kingdom of heaven belongs. In
> the house they found a book containing the life of Antony. One
> of them began to read it and was so fascinated and thrilled by
> the story that even before he had finished reading he conceived
> the idea of taking upon himself the same kind of life and aban-
> doning his career in the world – both he and his friend were
> officials in the service of the state – in order to become a servant
> of God. All at once he was filled with the love of holiness. Angry
> with himself and full of remorse, he looked at his friend and said,
> 'What do we hope to gain by all the efforts we make? What are
> we looking for? What is our purpose in serving the state? Can we
> hope for anything better at court than to be the emperor's friends?
> . . . But if I wish, I can become the friend of God at this very

moment.' After saying this he turned back to the book, labouring under the pain of the new life that was taking birth in him. He read on, and in his heart a change was taking place. His mind was being divested of the world, as could presently be seen . . . He said to his friend, 'I have torn myself free from all our ambitions and have decided to serve God. From this very moment, here and now, I shall start to serve him. If you will not follow my lead, do not stand in my way.' The other answered that he would stand by his comrade, for such service was glorious and the reward was great . . .[7]

The author of this account, numbered among the audience of Ponticianus, was Augustine, later to become bishop of Hippo in north Africa. It occurs in his *Confessions,* the greatest work of spiritual autobiography ever written.

Augustine is important for us because out of his voluminous writings can be constructed a theology of mission which was to have far-reaching influence upon the concerns of the western church. In the first place, he was an African, and thereby the heir to a distinctive Christian tradition. The African church looked back to Tertullian (d. *c.* 225), lawyer and prolific Christian controversialist, and to Cyprian (d. 258), bishop of Carthage and martyr. The writings of these two fathers of the African church had expressed a rigorist view of Christianity, one which sought to keep the secular world at a distance. This intellectual tradition, widely respected in the western, Latin provinces of the empire, gave a twist to the character of western Christianity which differentiated it from the Christianity of the eastern, Greek provinces of the empire. Where the east, schooled by Origen and Eusebius, was assimilationist and welcomed the co-existence of the church and the world, the west tended to see discontinuities and chasms, and maintained a distrust for secular culture. If in the east church and state were nearly identical, in the west they were often at odds. Harmony was characteristic of the east, tension of the west. It was to be a critically important constituent of western culture that church and state should be perceived as distinct and indeed often competing institutions. Built into western Christian traditions there was a potential rarely encountered in the east for explosion, for radicalism, for non-conformity, for confrontation. To these traditions Augustine was the heir; to them he contributed in no small measure. His was a discordant voice in the general chorus orchestrated by Eusebius in celebration of the Christian empire. It would matter very much indeed that Augustine's would prove to be among the most powerful and influential voices that western Christendom has ever heard.

It has not always been discordant. As a young man Augustine enjoyed a brilliant career as an academic in Milan. (He was living in Milan when he heard the story of the encounter at Trier quoted above.) At that date Milan was the political and intellectual capital of the western half of the empire. Its bishop, the great St Ambrose (d. 397), was the most prominent western advocate of the views of Eusebius (though not without some qualifications). Ambrose exerted considerable influence on Augustine, who was attracted to the Eusebian perspective. Significantly, it was only when Augustine abandoned this glossy metropolitan life in 395 and returned to his native Africa to become a small-town bishop – living in obedience to a monastic rule with his diocesan clergy – that misgivings began to arise in his mind. But they were not formulated in any coherent fashion until he composed the work for which he is most famous, *De Civitate Dei* (*The City of God*), between 413 and 425. This is a book so big, so complex, so alive, so rich in ideas, so brimming with passion, that it is difficult to summarize it in any manner which does it justice. It is commonly said that the work was occasioned by the sack of Rome by the Goths in 410: an attempt to answer the pagans who claimed that Rome had been sacked in punishment for her abandonment of the gods who had always previously protected her. But Augustine's book was intended, or at any rate turned out to be, a great deal more than this. In its final form it was an extended meditation on the meaning of history, on the place of man and society and the state in the divine scheme of things, and on the nature of the Christian community within the world. In the course of it Augustine came out with views sharply at variance with the Eusebian accommodation.

For our purposes the most important point about Augustine's social thought is that he detached the state – any state, but in particular, of course, the Roman state – from the Christian community. Under his hands the Roman empire became theologically neutral, drained of the positive moral charge with which Eusebius had invested it. For Augustine the empire was just one set of political arrangements among many. It was necessary for the purpose of ensuring certain limited ends such as the maintenance of peace and order, the administration of human justice or defence against aggression from outside its frontiers:

necessary, but in no sense special or privileged. This was to strike at the root of the Eusebian position. The empire was not part of a divine providential scheme; not the vehicle for the furtherance of God's purposes. Its emperor was not messianic, not quasi-divine; he no longer walked with God. Its institutions were ordinary institutions, human, fallible, random, limited and messy. Its history was not the unfolding of a plan for the harmonious ordering of the world under a God-directed emperor, but instead a squalid tale of lust for domination, of war and suffering, of oppression and corruption. Worldly empires would blow away like smoke; and, as Augustine dismissively observed, 'smoke has no weight'.

Over against this earthly polity is set the city of God: that is, the community of Christians whose city is not of this world, who indeed are aliens (*peregrini*) in this terrestrial world. Such notions were not new. There was a rich Judaic literature of exile which was developed by early Christian writers. It was Paul who wrote to the Corinthians of 'an house not made with hands'. The anonymous author of the *Epistle to Diognetus*, writing in about 200 and echoing another Pauline passage, had observed that Christians 'spend their existence upon earth, but their citizenship is in heaven'.[8] There were also influences at work from outside the Judaeo-Christian tradition. The Neoplatonic philosophers who strongly influenced the young Augustine had written persuasively of the soul imprisoned in the body, trapped in the flesh, from which it strives to break free. What Augustine did was to express these ideas of exile and alienation with passion and force. To one word in particular he imparted a special resonance: *peregrinus*. 'And so long as he is in this mortal body, he is a *peregrinus* in a foreign land,' he wrote in Book 19 of *De Civitate Dei*, echoing II Corinthians v.6. It was a technical term in Roman law: to be a *peregrinus* meant to be a resident alien, a stranger, a person without kin, friends, sureties, patrons. It was also a word with further connotations within the Judaeo-Christian scriptural tradition. Exile or deprivation were often associated with sin and punishment, but sometimes also with a sense of divinely allotted destiny. Jacob fled into exile because of murderous conflict between kinsmen; his destiny was to inherit the land of his exile or pilgrimage (*peregrinationis*) and through him were all peoples of the earth to be blessed (Genesis xxviii). So a pilgrim could also be a harbinger, like John the Baptist. Augustine seized upon the possibilities latent in this everyday word. Here was an exacting standard for the

Christian. He must become a *peregrinus*, an exile or pilgrim, make of his life a *peregrinatio*, a pilgrimage, cutting loose like a monk from the worldly ties that bind and accepting instead the liberating society and disciplines of the city of God: 'The Heavenly City, while on its earthly pilgrimage, calls forth its citizens from every nation and assembles a multilingual band of pilgrims; not caring about any diversity in the customs, laws and institutions whereby they severally make provision for the achievement and maintenance of earthly peace.'[9]

Here then is Augustine's vision of a Christian community not confined to the Roman empire. Other strands of his reading and reflection were woven into it. In common with other Christians of his day Augustine was convinced that the end of the world was near. But before this could happen there had to be a universal preaching of Christianity. 'This gospel of the Kingdom will be proclaimed throughout the earth as a testimony to all nations: and then the end will come.' Augustine was forced to elucidate this apocalyptic passage in Matthew's gospel (Matt. xxiv.14) at the very time that he was working on *De Civitate Dei*. Prompted by an earthquake on 19 July 418 Bishop Hesychius of Salona (Split) consulted Augustine about Daniel's prophecies of the end of the world. In his reply Augustine made reference to Matthew's passage on the in-gathering of the nations which must precede the end and to other biblical passages of similar purport. But Hesychius, evidently a persistent man, was not satisfied and wanted more. He got it. Augustine, never one to skimp where doctrinal exposition was concerned, replied in a long letter divided into no less than fifty-four chapters. This second letter circulated widely as a separate pamphlet under the title *De Fine Saeculi* (*On the End of the World*). Hesychius had evidently claimed that the gospel had already been preached to all nations. Not so, argued Augustine, 'for there are among us, that is in Africa, innumerable barbarian tribes among whom the gospel has not yet been preached . . . yet it cannot rightly be said that the promise of God does not concern them' because 'the Lord did not promise the Romans but all nations to the seed of Abraham'. He went on to elucidate 'the prophecy made of Christ under the figure of Solomon, "He shall rule from sea to sea" (Psalm lxxii.8)'. This must mean 'the whole earth with all its inhabitants, because the universe is surrounded by the Ocean sea'. All nations, therefore, 'as many as God has made' are to adore the Lord and call upon him.[10] But – and here Augustine turned to Paul's words in Romans x.14–15 – 'How shall they call upon Him in whom they have not believed? How shall they believe Him of whom they have not heard? And how shall they hear without a preacher? And how shall they preach unless they be sent?' Augustine did not follow the logic of the argument to its conclusions: therefore we must send out missionary preachers. But we can see how a combination of influences – the African intellectual tradition, apocalyptic speculations, episcopal responsibilities, ideals of pilgrimage and renunciation – brought him to the brink of that conclusion.

Another who was brought to that brink was Augustine's younger contemporary Prosper of Aquitaine. Usually remembered mainly as the writer of a chronicle which is an important source for fifth-century history – we shall meet it in Chapter 3 – Prosper was also the author of works of theological controversy. One of these was called *De Vocatione Omnium Gentium* (*On the Calling of All Nations*) and it was composed at Rome in about 440. Prosper's *De Vocatione* has been called 'the first work in Christian literature to be concerned with the salvation of infidels'.[11] Salvation, yes; but not quite their evangelization.

Prosper starts from the proposition that God wishes all men to be saved. However, by His inscrutable judgement some peoples receive the faith later than others. He considers, but rejects, the Eusebian position: 'Christian grace was not content to have the same frontiers as Rome and has already subjected many peoples to the sceptre of Christ's cross whom Rome did not conquer with arms.'[12] Christian grace: this lay at the doctrinal heart of Prosper's concerns. He was an extreme follower of Augustine's teachings on grace. These had been developed in opposition to the doctrines on free will taught in Italy and subsequently Palestine by the British-born philosopher Pelagius, doctrines which caused a great stir in the church and were eventually declared heretical in 418. Prosper's general position was that it was *for divine grace alone* to bring about conversion. One suspects that he would have sympathized with the Baptist ministers who rebuked William Carey in 1786. Like Augustine, Prosper hesitated. If grace is omnipotent, irresistible, omnipresent and inscrutable, then might it not be that for humans to choose to undertake missionary preaching was presumptuously to interfere with its workings? Prosper never asserted this in so many words, but one can sense the thought lurking there unformulated.

Perhaps, in the last resort, western theologians like Augustine and Prosper could never quite forget that they were Romans. They might have had their doubts – indeed, we know that they *did* have their doubts – about the moral tradition which had corralled Christianity safely inside the city walls of the empire; but it was hard to break with the cultural habits of a millennium. It takes an outsider to think the unthinkable. However, what had still been unthinkable in the age of Augustine and Prosper had become absolutely thinkable by the time that Paulinus encountered Edwin two centuries later. What had happened in between to bring this about?

CHAPTER TWO

The Challenge of the Countryside

'It is my belief, Watson, founded upon my experience,
that the lowest and vilest alleys of London do not present
a more dreadful record of sin than does the smiling and
beautiful countryside.'

SIR ARTHUR CONAN DOYLE, 'The Copper Beeches',
The Adventures of Sherlock Holmes, 1892

AT ONE POINT in the course of Origen's celebrated work *Contra Celsum*, in the context of claims for the extent of Christian evangelization, the author boasted that Christians 'have done the work of going round not only the cities but even villages and country cottages to make others also pious towards God'. This was certainly an exaggeration. In Origen's day Christianity was still a preponderantly urban faith. What is interesting, however, is that the claim should have been made at all, that it should have seemed to the writer an apposite claim to make in the course of polemic. It is even more interesting that the earliest name associated with the conduct of rural mission within the Roman empire should have been a pupil of Origen. This was Gregory of Pontus, familiarly known as Gregory Thaumaturgus, Gregory 'the Wonder-worker'.

The bare facts of Gregory's career may be summarized as follows. He was born in about 210 into a prominent family of the province of Pontus Polemoniacus, roughly speaking the northern parts of central Asia Minor, modern Turkey, bordering on the Black Sea. Pontus was a quiet, undistinguished region. It was off the beaten track, a province whose towns were small, whose concerns were local and agricultural. It was modestly prosperous in the way that places are where nothing much happens to disturb the even tenor of life. Gregory belonged by birth to one of those provincial elites on whose local services and loyalties the empire depended for its smooth functioning. As a young man he was sent off to study at the famous law schools of Berytus (Beirut): a distinguished career in law or rhetoric or the civil service seemed to be in prospect. But his life took a different and unexpected turn. Gregory met Origen, who was then at the height of his fame as a teacher and scholar and who had attracted a talented band of pupils round him at Caesarea in Palestine. Gregory stayed with Origen for five years and then returned to Pontus; this would have been, as we may suppose, round about the year 240. On his return home he became bishop of the Christian community in his home town of Neocaesarea, the capital of the province, which office he exercised for the remainder of his life. He and his congregations survived the persecutions of the reign of the Emperor Decius (249–51) and weathered the disruptions of barbarian raids in the mid-250s. Under Gregory's leadership the Christian community of Pontus grew, though at what rate or by how much we cannot tell.[1] He died in about 270.

These bare facts are just about all that we know. Gregory has left us a body of writings which tell us something about him. His farewell address of thanks to his master Origen has survived, from which we can learn something of both his intellectual development and a great teacher's methods. A paraphrase of the book of Ecclesiastes bears witness to his biblical studies. A document known as the *Canonical Letter* sheds a little light on his pastoral activities as bishop. In addition to Gregory's own writings we have a short oration or sermon in commemoration of him composed about a century after his death by his namesake Gregory of Nyssa. It has often been remarked that the oration contains little if any reliable information about the historical Gregory of Pontus. It is a collection of hagiographical commonplaces. Indeed: but the judgement needs two qualifications. First, traditions of Gregory had been handed down by word of mouth. Gregory of Nyssa's own older brother, Basil of Cappadocia, had as a small boy learned wise sayings attributed to Gregory of Pontus at the knees of his grandmother Macrina. Oral traditions may be garbled, adapted, misunderstood, misapplied, but they will generally preserve something of the person who uttered them or to whom they refer. Second, the Christianization of Pontus was still incomplete when Gregory of Nyssa was writing. The stories he reports show what his late-fourth-century audience was ready to believe about the earlier Gregory, about the process he initiated which was still visibly and audibly going on round about them. The stories had to be plausible not just in terms of their expectations of a wonder-worker but also in terms of their expectations of everyday life: and it is not for us to be surprised if these categories of expectation prove to overlap. Carefully handled, the legends of Gregory Thaumaturgus may have something to tell us – just something – about what he set in motion in Pontus.

Gregory of Nyssa claimed that when Gregory became bishop of Neocaesarea there were only seventeen Christians in the diocese but that by the time of his death there were only seventeen pagans. This is demonstrably an exaggeration. It can be shown that pagan observance was lively in Pontus both before and after Gregory's day. It has even been said that it is 'misguided and anachronistic' to cast Gregory for the role of rural missionary.[2] Our reaction to such a judgement will depend a little on the images and expectations prompted by the phrase 'rural missionary'. Pontus was a backwoods sort of place. Gregory felt affection for his native province, but even he must have been ready to concede that after the sophisticated urban culture of Beirut and Caesarea, in returning to Pontus he was retreating to a country backwater. (The Christian idealist who exchanged a promising 'metropolitan' secular career for a provincial ecclesiastical one is a recurrent figure of the late Roman period: Gregory is an early, Augustine the best-known example.) Because Pontus was the sort of place that it was, because urban and rural society overlapped and interpenetrated there, a bishop who made his presence and his power felt would be making an impression upon his rural as well as upon his urban constituency. It is in this sense that we may call Gregory a rural missionary.

Gregory saw visions. He was commanded to accept the bishopric of Neocaesarea by St John and St Mary – the earliest recorded vision of the Blessed Virgin in Christian history – who recited to him the creed which he should profess. According to Gregory of Nyssa, this credal statement was preserved in the cathedral of Neocaesarea in an autograph copy: 'the very letters inscribed by his own blessed hand'. The cathedral itself had been built by Gregory. It was a new landmark among the city's public buildings, and one moreover which did not suffer in an earthquake the damage experienced by secular buildings. Already one may detect some elements of what may have been going on. Gregory enjoyed direct access to the divine; a relic of his, a document from his hand, is venerated; God's house built by him is miraculously preserved. A bishop such as this will command authority and prestige.

Then there were his wonders. Two brothers were quarrelling over the ownership of a lake. Their enmity had gone so far that they were preparing to arm their peasants and fight it out together. Gregory appeared on the scene as a mediator. At a twitch of his cloak the lake dried up and disappeared for ever. On another occasion the river Lycus was flooding and threatening damage. Gregory planted his staff on its bank to mark the limit beyond which the waters must not pass and the waters (of course) obeyed him. The staff grew into a tree which was still being pointed out to people a century later when Gregory of Nyssa recorded the story. Well, it's not difficult to see how *that* story arose. But such a comment as this misses what would have been the point of the tale for those who told it to Gregory of Nyssa or heard it from him. God acted through Gregory to work wonders which healed human divisions and tamed the forces of nature. Demonstrations of supernatural powers – frequently in competition with non-Christian claimants to possess such powers – will meet us again and again. Almost invariably we are told that they led to conversions. What *that* might have meant is another matter.

Finally there was Gregory's public role as bishop. He built a new cathedral, as we have seen. He interceded for his flock during an outbreak of plague, did what he could to shield them during the Decian persecution. In troubled times he was a force for order and stability. His *Canonical Letter*, to which we shall return in Chapter 3, shows him grasping at scriptural precept to assist in sorting out the harrowing human consequences of barbarian attack. This enlargement of a bishop's responsibilities was to have a long and fruitful future.

Why did efforts to convert the country-dwellers begin, in however patchy and hesitant a fashion, in the course of the third century? It is a question which has never satisfactorily been answered. It may be that the trend towards near-identification of *Romanitas* with *Christianitas*, of empire with Christendom, rendered it desirable, even necessary, for all Romans to become Christians. 'All Romans' would mean all Roman *citizens*, a group which had been vastly enlarged by the so-called *Constitutio Antoniana* of the year 212, by which the government of the Emperor Caracalla extended the privileges and responsibilities of citizenship to all free men. (There were, of course, enormous numbers of country-dwellers who were not free.) Another factor, less nebulous

37

and offering at least the possibility of investigation, might have been the changing social composition of the bishops who ruled the churches. Historians are agreed that the third century was marked by a steady if obscure growth in Christian numbers. Numerical increase was matched by increase in respectability. It would be possible to compile a list – granted, not a long list – of third-century Christians of some not inconsiderable social standing. Gregory the Wonder-worker is a good example. Persons of such rank and wealth who became bishops might be expected to be solicitous for the spiritual well-being of the peasantry on their estates, apprehensive of their vulnerability to demonic attack, despite the entrenched attitudes alluded to in the preceding chapter; and their example might be the more infectious to others who shared their status. What were the peasantry of the feuding brothers of Pontus encouraged to think when they were told to put their weapons away and get back to their fields? It is an interesting question.

After the imperial adhesion to Christianity under Constantine, never to be reversed except during the brief reign of Julian, the Christian community within the empire underwent phenomenal growth – which changed its character. Imperial patronage colossally increased the wealth and status of the churches. Privileges and exemptions granted to Christian clergy precipitated a stampede into the priesthood. Devout aristocratic ladies acquired followings of clerical groupies, experimented with fashionable forms of devotion. Christian moralists were apprehensive that conversions were occurring for the wrong reasons – to gain favour, to obtain a job, promotion, a pension. As far as the historian can tell, their anxieties do not appear to have been misplaced. Fashion is a great force in human affairs. The adherence of the establishment to Christianity in the course of the fourth century made more urgent than ever the task of converting the outsiders on whose labours the establishment rested: the huge majority who toiled in the countryside.

The process by which the empire became *officially* Christian may be said to have been completed in the course of the reign of Theodosius I (379–95). A cluster of events and decisions mark this: the defeat of an avowedly pagan military coup, the issue of legislation formally banning pagan worship, the removal of the Altar of Victory from the senate house in Rome, the destruction of the temple of the god Serapis at Alexandria. Some of the markers are uncomfortable portents: the first execution of a heretic (the Spaniard, Priscillian, in 385), and a rising tide of Christian anti-Semitism. It is surely not coincidental that it is from this period that influential voices can be heard urging landowners to make their peasantry Christian. Here is John Chrysostom, John 'the golden-mouthed', the most fashionable preacher of his day, patriarch of Constantinople between 398 and 404, preaching in the capital in the year 400 to an upper-class audience living, we presume, in their town houses, about their responsibilities to those on their landed estates.

> Many people have villages and estates and pay no attention to them and do not communicate with them, but do give close attention to how the baths are working, and how halls and palaces are constructed – not to the harvest of souls ... Should not everyone build a church? Should he not get a teacher to instruct the congregation? Should he not above all else see to it that all are Christians?[3]

And here is Augustine, congratulating Pammachius in 401 on 'the zeal with which you have chased up those peasants of yours in Numidia', and brought them back to Catholic unity. (Pammachius had converted them, not indeed from paganism to Christianity, but from deviancy in schism back to orthodoxy, but that does not weaken the point.) And here, finally, is Maximus, bishop of Turin from *c.* 398 to *c.* 412, and another famous preacher, in one of his sermons.

> You should remove all pollution of idols from your properties and cast out the whole error of paganism from your fields. For it is not right that you, who have Christ in your hearts, should have Antichrist in your houses, that your men should honour the devil in his shrines while you pray to God in church. And let no one think he is excused by saying: 'I did not order this, I did not command it.' Whoever knows that sacrilege takes place on his estate and does not forbid it, in a sense orders it. By keeping silence and not reproving the man who sacrifices, he lends his consent. For the blessed apostle states that not only those who do sinful acts are guilty, but also those who consent to the act [Romans i.32]. You therefore, brother, when you observe your peasant sacrificing and do not forbid the offering, sin, because even if you did not assist the sacrifice yourself you gave permission for it.[4]

Constantinople, Africa, Italy – and other places too: wherever we look, bishops were encouraging the landed elites, the people who commanded local influence, to take firm and if necessary coercive action to make the peasantry Christian – in some sense. Other bishops took matters into their own hands, choosing to take direct and personal action rather than confining themselves to exhortation. The most famous example of such an activist is Martin, bishop of Tours from about 371 until his death in 397.

Martin is a man of whom we can know a fair amount, principally owing to the survival of a body of writings about him by his disciple Sulpicius Severus. Sulpicius was just the sort of man whom Augustine, John Chrysostom and Maximus of Turin were trying to reach and influence. He was a rich, devout landowner with estates in southern Gaul. Inspired by Martin's ideals Sulpicius founded a Christian community at one of his estates, Primuliacum (unidentified; possibly in the Agenais), and it was there that he composed his Martinian writings. These comprise the *Vita Sancti Martini* (*Life of the Holy Martin*), composed during its subject's lifetime, probably in 394–5; three *Epistulae* (*Letters*) from 397–8; and two *Dialogi* (*Dialogues*) from 404–6 also devoted to Martin.[5] The *Vita* was the first work of Latin hagiography to be composed in western Christendom: it displays literary debts to the *Vita Antonii* by Athanasius and it was in its turn to be enormously influential during the coming centuries as a model of Christian biography. Sulpicius presented Martin as a *vir Deo plenus*, 'a man filled with God'. Sulpicius' Martin was first and last a spiritual force – a man who walked with God, a man set apart by his austerity and asceticism, a monk who was also active in the world as a bishop, fearless in his encounters with evil, endowed with powers beyond the natural and the normal, worthy to be ranked with prophets, apostles, martyrs: a powerhouse of holy energy which crackled across the countryside of Touraine.

One of the features of Sulpicius' writings about Martin which strikes the reader is their defensive and apologetic tone (to be distinguished from the didacticism common to all hagiography). Martin was a figure of controversy during his lifetime and continued to be controversial after his death. This was in large part because he was in more ways than one an outsider. In the first place he was not a native of Gaul. He was born, probably in 336, at Sabaria in the province of Pannonia (now Szombathely in Hungary, not far from the Austro-Hungarian

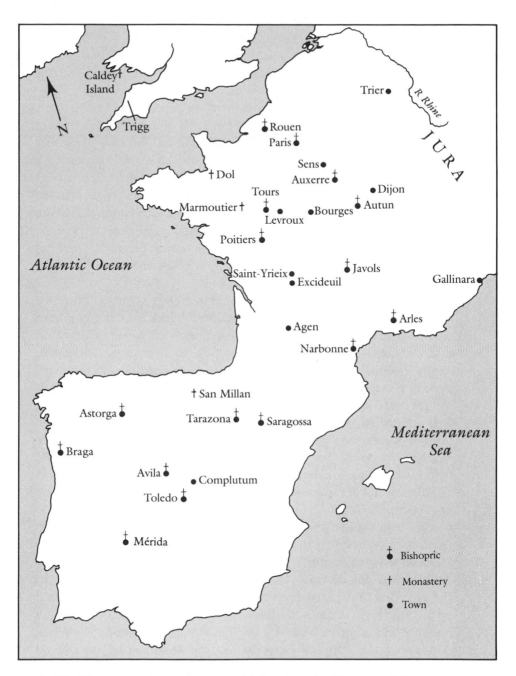

2. *To illustrate the activities of Martin, Emilian and Samson,*
from the fourth to the sixth centuries.

border) and he was brought up in Italy, at Pavia. He was of undistinguished birth, the child of a soldier. As the son of a veteran Martin was drafted into the army as a young man (351?) and served in it for five years. A convert to Christianity as a child, he was baptized in 354. After obtaining a discharge from the army in 356 he returned to Italy, where he lived for a period as a hermit with a priest for companion on the island of Gallinara off the Ligurian coast to the west of Genoa. Making his way back to Gaul he attached himself to Bishop Hilary of Poitiers, a churchman whose enforced residence in the east between 356 and 360 – exile during the Arian controversy (for which see Chapter 3) – had borne fruit in acquainting him with eastern monastic practices. Martin settled down as a hermit at Ligugé outside Poitiers. His fame as a holy man spread widely in the course of the next decade and in 371 (probably) he was chosen by the Christian community of Tours as their bishop.

Martin's pre-episcopal career was extremely unconventional. Of obscure origin and mean education, tainted by a career as a common soldier, ill-dressed, unkempt, practising unfamiliar forms of devotion under the patronage of a bishop himself somewhat turbulent and unconventional, the while occupying no regular position in the functioning hierarchy of the church – at every point he contrasted with the average Gallic bishop of his day, who tended to be well heeled, well connected, well read and well groomed. No wonder that the bishops summoned to consecrate Martin to the see of Tours were reluctant to do so. No wonder that Martin did not care to associate with his episcopal colleagues.

This was not the only way in which Martin's behaviour continued unconventional after he had become a bishop. He refused to sit on an episcopal throne. He rode a donkey, rather than the horse which would have been fitting to a bishop's dignity. He dressed like a peasant. He founded a monastery at Marmoutier, not far from Tours, where he lived with his disciples, rather than in the bishop's house next to the cathedral in the city. He was no respecter of persons. He insisted on forcing his way into the house of Count Avitianus in the small hours of the night to plead for the release of some prisoners. When dining with the usurping Emperor Magnus Maximus he was offered the singular honour of sharing the emperor's goblet of wine; instead of handing it back to Maximus, Martin passed it on to a priest who was accompanying him. His pastoral activities, to which we shall return shortly, were most peculiar. He frequently encountered supernatural beings: the Devil, several times, once masquerading as Christ (but Martin saw through him); angels, demons, St Mary, St Agnes, St Thecla, St Peter and St Paul. He had telepathic powers, could predict the future, could exorcize evil spirits from humans or animals and could raise the dead to life. He worked many miracles and wonders, conscientiously chronicled by Sulpicius Severus. His fame spread widely. He was called over to the region of Sens to deliver a certain district from hailstorms through the agency of his prayers. An Egyptian merchant who was not even a Christian was saved from a storm at sea by calling on 'the God of Martin'.

Martin may have flouted social convention but it is equally clear from what Sulpicius has to tell us that his network of contacts among the powerful in the Gaul of his day was extensive. He may have behaved boorishly at the emperor's dinner table, but Maximus showed 'the deepest respect' for him, while on a subsequent visit Maximus' wife sent the servants away and waited upon him with her own hands. The wife of the brutal Count Avitianus asked Martin to bless the flask of oil which she kept for medicinal use. It was the *vir praefectorius* Auspicius, an exalted official, who invited Martin over to the Senonais to deal with the local hailstorms. It was from the slave of an even grander man, the *vir proconsularis* Tetradius, that Martin exorcized a demon. Tetradius became a Christian as a result of this wonder. There is some reason to suppose that he went on to build a church on his estate near Trier. (John Chrysostom would have been pleased.) A letter written by Martin was believed to have cured the daughter of the devout aristocrat Arborius from a fever simply by being placed on her body. Arborius was a very exalted man, a nephew of the celebrated poet Ausonius of Bordeaux, who had been the Emperor Gratian's tutor.

These connections were of significance in the activity to which Martin devoted so much of his energies. Here was a bishop who gave himself wholeheartedly to the task of bringing Christianity to the rural population of Gaul. His methods were violent and confrontational: disruption of pagan cult, demolition of pagan edifices. Here is Chapter 14 of the *Vita Martini*.

> It was somewhere about this time that in the course of this work
> he performed another miracle at least as great. He had set on fire
> a very ancient and much-frequented shrine in a certain village and

the flames were being driven by the wind against a neighbouring, in fact adjacent house. When Martin noticed this, he climbed speedily to the roof of the house and placed himself in front of the oncoming flames. Then you might have seen an amazing sight – the flames bending back against the force of the wind till it looked like a battle between warring elements. Such were his powers that the fire destroyed only where it was bidden.

In a village named Levroux [between Tours and Bourges], however, when he wished to demolish in the same way a temple which had been made very rich by its superstitious cult, he met with resistance from a crowd of pagans and was driven off with some injuries to himself. He withdrew, therefore, to a place in the neighbourhood where for three days in sackcloth and ashes, continuously fasting and praying, he besought Our Lord that the temple which human hands had failed to demolish might be destroyed by divine power.

Then suddenly two angels stood before him, looking like heavenly warriors, with spears and shields. They said that the Lord had sent them to rout the rustic host and give Martin protection, so that no one should hinder the destruction of the temple. He was to go back, therefore, and carry out faithfully the work he had undertaken. So he returned to the village and, while crowds of pagans watched in silence, the heathen sanctuary was razed to its foundations and all its altars and images reduced to powder.

The sight convinced the rustics that it was by divine decree that they had been stupefied and overcome with dread, so as to offer no resistance to the bishop; and nearly all of them made profession of faith in the Lord Jesus, proclaiming with shouts before all that Martin's God should be worshipped and the idols ignored, which could neither save themselves nor anyone else.

There are several points of interest for us in the Levroux story. First, it is notable that Sulpicius admits the – unsurprising – fact that Martin met with resistance. Direct action was risky. In the year of Martin's death three clerics who tried to disrupt pagan ceremonies in the diocese of Trent in the eastern Alps were killed. Their bishop, Vigilius, to whose letter to John Chrysostom describing the martyrdom we are indebted for knowledge of it, was himself stoned to death by furious pagans a few years later. When the Christian community of Sufetana in the African province of Byzacena demolished a statue of Hercules a pagan mob killed sixty Christians in reprisal. Second, one cannot

44

help wondering a little about the soldierly-looking angels. It is usually fruitless to indulge in speculation about what might have been the 'real' basis of miracle stories, but the question can at least be posed, whether Martin was ever enabled to make use of the services of soldiers from local garrisons. It is worth bearing in mind that the fanatically anti-pagan Cynegius, praetorian prefect of the east between 384 and 388, used soldiers as well as bands of wild monks for the destruction of pagan temples in the countryside around Antioch. Martin's exalted contacts would have been able without difficulty to arrange a body-guard for him; even to lay on a fatigue party equipped with crowbars and sledgehammers. Third, we are told that these violent scenes at Levroux resulted in conversions; we should note that Sulpicius concedes that not all the people were converted. We have not the remotest idea what the people of Levroux might have thought about it all, but Sulpicius is clear that because their gods had failed them they were prepared to worship Martin's God. On another occasion, at an unnamed place, Martin had demolished a temple and was preparing to fell a sacred tree. The local people dared him to stand where the tree would fall. Intrepidly, he did so. As the tree tottered, cracked and began to fall, Martin made the sign of the cross. Instantly the tree plunged in another direction. This was the sequel as Sulpicius related it:

> Then indeed a shout went up to heaven as the pagans gasped at the miracle, and all with one accord acclaimed the name of Christ; you may be sure that on that day salvation came to that region. Indeed, there was hardly anyone in that vast multitude of pagans who did not ask for the imposition of hands, abandoning his heathenish errors and making profession of faith in the Lord Jesus.

Like it or not, this is what our sources tell us over and over again. Demonstrations of the power of the Christian God meant conversion. Miracles, wonders, exorcisms, temple-torching and shrine-smashing *were in themselves* acts of evangelization.

Martin was not alone in taking action. His contemporary Bishop Simplicius of Autun is said to have encountered an idol being trundled about on a cart 'for the preservation of fields and vineyards.' Simplicius made the sign of the cross; the idol crashed to the ground and the oxen pulling the cart were rooted immobile to the spot; 400 converts were made. Bishop Victricius of Rouen, like Martin an ex-soldier, undertook evangelizing campaigns among the Nervi and the Morini, roughly speaking in the zone of territory between Boulogne and Brussels. We have already met the ill-starred Bishop Vigilius of Trent. Across the Pyrenees in Spain Bishop Priscillian of Avila conducted evangelizing tours of his upland diocese before he was arraigned for heresy.

The interconnections of this clerical society are worth unravelling, if only because we shall repeatedly find in the course of this study that missionary churchmen, though sometimes loners, have tended to be sustained by a network of connections – kinsfolk, friends, patrons, associates in prayer – whose support was invaluable. Priscillian gained a following especially – and it became one of the counts against him – among pious aristocratic ladies. One such observer of his work is likely to have been the heiress Teresa, whose family estates seem to have lain in the region of Complutum (the modern Alcalá de Henares, near Madrid), a mere fifty miles from Avila. Teresa married the immensely rich, devout aristocrat Paulinus of Nola (who was connected to Ausonius). Paulinus knew Martin: he was the beneficiary of one of Martin's miracles of healing by which the saint cured some sort of infection of the eye. Paulinus it was who introduced Sulpicius Severus to Martin. It is to Paulinus' polite letter of congratulation that we owe our knowledge about the preaching of Victricius in the north-east of Gaul. Martin knew Victricius: we glimpse them together once at Chartres when Martin cured a girl of twelve who had been dumb from birth. (It would seem that Victricius was among the few Gallic bishops with whom Martin did not mind associating.) Martin also knew Priscillian and his work: he interceded with the Emperor Maximus on behalf of Priscillian when the latter had been found guilty of heresy.

Archaeological discoveries have furnished confirmation of the destruction of sites of pagan worship at this period which, in the words of Paulinus of Nola, was 'happening throughout Gaul'. At a temple of Mercury at Avallon in Burgundy pagan statues were smashed and piled up in a heap of rubble: the coin series at the site ends in the reign of Valentinian I (364–75), which suggests that the work of destruction occurred shortly afterwards. The shrine of Dea Sequana, which marked the source of the river Seine not far from Dijon, was destroyed at about the same time. Sulpicius locates one of Martin's temple-smashing exploits in this Burgundian area.

Martin did not only destroy: he also built. 'He immediately built a church or monastery at every place where he destroyed a pagan shrine,' tells Sulpicius. Martin's distant successor as bishop, Gregory of Tours (d. 594), has left us a list of the places where Martin founded churches in the diocese, at Amboise, Candé, Ciran, Langeais, Saunay and Tournon. To these we must add the monastic communities he established at Marmoutier and Clion. These rural churches were staffed by bodies of clergy, as we may see at Candes. Such bodies were probably quite small and few members of them need have been priests; there was only one priest, Marcellus, at Amboise. These foundations were intended to have potential for Christian ministry over a wide area. Sulpicius refers to Martin making customary visits to the churches of his diocese, which would have enabled him to perform his episcopal duties, to check up on his local clergy, to nourish his network of contacts and to disrupt any manifestations of paganism which he might encounter. (It is notable that most of the stories told of Martin by Sulpicius Severus have a *journey* as their setting.) A structure, even a routine, of episcopal discipline is faintly visible.

Martin's successors as bishops of Tours carried on the work he had started of building churches at rural settlements in the diocese. Brice, Martin's first and very long-lived successor (bishop 397–444) built five; Eustochius (444–61), four; Perpetuus (461–91), six; Volusianus (491–8), two. We know of these because they were listed, like Martin's, by Gregory of Tours towards the end of the sixth century. Gregory did not list these churches out of mere antiquarian interest: he listed them because they were *episcopal* foundations, the network through which the bishop supervised his diocese. What he does not tell us about, because he had no interest in so doing, was the progress of church-building by laymen on their own lands; estate (or *villa*) churches built by landowners for their own households and dependants. We hear about such churches only by chance. For example, Gregory introduces a story about the relics of St Nicetius of Lyons with the information that he, Gregory, had been asked to consecrate a church at Pernay. In another of his works we learn that it had been built by a certain Litomer, presumably the lord of the estate. Litomer must have been building his church at Pernay in the 580s. By that date Touraine was fairly densely dotted with churches. It has been plausibly estimated that by Gregory's day most people in the diocese would have had a church within about six miles of their homes.

It must be emphasized that Touraine is a very special case as regards the extent of our information about it. Thanks to Gregory's writings we know more about the ecclesiastical organization of the diocese of Tours than we do about any other rural area of comparable size in fourth-, fifth- or sixth-century Christendom. We should never have guessed that there was a church at the little village of Ceyreste, between Marseilles and Toulon, had its control not been disputed between the bishops of Arles and Marseilles: the dispute elicited a papal ruling in 417, the source of our knowledge. We hear about the church at Alise-Sainte-Reine, about ten miles from the ruined shrine of Dea Sequana, only because when St Germanus of Auxerre stayed a night there with its priest in about 430 the straw pallet on which he had slept was found to possess miraculous curative properties: his hagiographer Constantius recorded the fact and thus preserved the notice of the church. It is from the *Vita Eugendi* that we hear of the existence of a church at Izernore, between Bourg-en-Bresse and Geneva, and from the *Vita Genovefae* that we hear of a church at Nanterre, then about seven miles from Paris; both of these from the second quarter of the fifth century. At Arlon in Belgium, close to the modern borders with both Luxembourg and France, archaeologists have excavated what might have been a church of the late Roman period: caution is necessary because excavated church buildings from this period are difficult to identify as such. We know that Bishop Rusticus of Narbonne consecrated a new church at Minerve, which has given its name to the wine-growing district of Minervois, in 456 because an inscription recording the fact has survived. At Chantelle, near Vichy, a landowner called Germanicus built a church in the 470s: it is referred to in one of the letters of Sidonius Apollinaris, bishop of Clermont.

We hear of these churches because of the chance survival of a legal ruling, three pieces of hagiography, the buried foundations of a building, an inscription and a bishop's letter-collection. It is a ragbag of odds and ends of evidence, some of them of rather doubtful status, characteristic of the coin in which the early medieval historian has to deal. So slender are the threads by which our knowledge hangs, so fragmentary and isolated its separate pieces, that we have to exercise the utmost caution in teasing out what it might have to tell us. To the question, How far may we press our evidence? different historians will give different answers. How representative was Touraine in respect of the building of churches? To what degree, if at all, may we generalize from its circumstances? Were the dioceses of Arles or Auxerre or Paris or Narbonne or Clermont as well provided with rural churches by the year 600 as was the diocese of Tours? These are – given our sources, these have to be – open questions. The reader is free to speculate.

We rarely know anything at all of the precise circumstances which brought any individual rural church into being. Here is an example, deservedly famous, of a case where we do know something: it also shows that not all bishops were as violently confrontational in their methods as Martin was.

> In the territory of Javols [on the western edge of the Massif Central] there was a large lake. At a fixed time a crowd of rustics went there and, as if offering libations to the lake, threw into it linen cloths and garments, pelts of wool, models of cheese and wax and bread, each according to his means. They came with their wagons; they brought food and drink, sacrificed animals, and feasted for three days. Much later a cleric from that same city [Javols] became bishop and went to the place. He preached to the crowds that they should cease this behaviour lest they be consumed by the wrath of heaven. But their coarse rusticity rejected his teachings. Then, with the inspiration of the Divinity this bishop of God built a church in honour of the blessed Hilary of Poitiers [Martin's patron] at a distance from the banks of the lake. He placed relics of Hilary in the church and said to the people: 'Do not, my sons, sin before God! For there is no religious piety to a lake. Do not stain your hearts with these empty rituals, but rather acknowledge God and direct your devotion to His friends. Respect St Hilary, a bishop of God whose relics are located here. For he can serve as your intercessor for the mercy of the Lord.' The men were stung in their hearts and converted. They left the lake and brought everything they usually threw into it to the holy church instead. So they were freed from the mistake that had bound them.[6]

This shrewd manoeuvre by the unnamed bishop of Javols probably occurred in about the year 500. It is a fine example of a technique of rural evangelization which became classic: the transference of ritual from one religious loyalty to another. Gregory of Tours, reporting the story, plainly thought that the bishop had thereby made his lakeside flock more Christian. Perhaps he had.

There is a further layer of interest in the story of the sacred lake of Javols. The episode demonstrates the local standing and authority of

49

the bishop; it may have enhanced them too. We saw some signs of the beginnings of a change in the nature of a bishop's public role in the career of Gregory of Pontus. Change was accelerated in the wake of Constantine's conversion. Further impetus was given in the western provinces of the empire in the course of the fifth and sixth centuries. It was during this age that the last tatters of central imperial control were shaken from Britain, Gaul and Spain. As the distinctive marks of functioning *Romanitas* were whittled away – especially the army and the civil service and their economic underpinning – so bishops tended to become the natural leaders of their local communities.

Let one instance stand for many: Germanus of Auxerre, as presented in the biography by Constantius of Lyons composed about forty years after its subject's death.[7] Germanus, born in about 378, was a member of an aristocratic family of the Auxerrois who received a good education in Gaul and at Rome, married suitably, practised successfully as a lawyer and achieved high public office as governor of Armorica, the north-western region of Gaul. When the bishopric of Auxerre fell vacant in 418 Germanus was plucked from this entirely secular career by the Christian community of Auxerre, who insisted that he must be their next bishop. Constantius had read his Sulpicius Severus and knew how an episcopal biographer should present his subject to an admiring world. So we hear a good deal about Germanus' austerities, virtues, miracles and so forth. Hence the story about the straw at Alise – which seems to have been modelled in characteristically hagiographical fashion on a story told of Martin by Sulpicius. But we also hear from Constantius about the part played by Germanus in public affairs. He protected the people of Auxerre from a crushing burden of taxation. He restrained Goar, king of the barbarian Alans, from ravaging Armorica. He went to Britain to quell heresy and while there led a British army to victory over marauding Picts and Saxons. He interceded with the imperial court at Ravenna on behalf of the province of Armorica.

The opening up of gaps or fissures in the surface of late Roman imperial rule was perhaps the most telling symptom of the empire's inability to cope with its traditional responsibilities. Bishops filled the gaps. Episcopal wealth became significant here. Some bishoprics – but no means all – became very rich indeed. The case of Tours is, again, instructive. Gregory of Tours chronicles a succession of legacies bestowed upon the see of Tours during the course of the fifth and sixth centuries. Legacies often came from the bishops themselves. Bishop

Remigius (Rémi) of Rheims left his substantial fortune to the see of Rheims and Bishop Bertram of Le Mans left an even more substantial fortune to the see of Le Mans. Wealth brought local responsibilities and opportunities as well as temptations. All the diverse services which today we would classify under the heading of 'welfare' came to be the responsibility of bishops – poor relief, public works, education, health care, hospitality for travellers, prison visiting, ransoming of captives, the provision of public entertainments and spectacles. They even included, in one case that we know of, banking: Bishop Masona of Mérida, in southern Spain, established a bank in about 580 for making loans to the public. These day-to-day responsibilities gave the bishop authority and power, a position of leadership in the community. In addition, of course, and above all else, the bishop possessed spiritual power: control over the administration of the sacraments of salvation, leadership in the intercessory activity of prayer and rogation, power to bind with the threat of excommunication, access to divine medicine of exorcism and healing, opportunity to sanction, encourage and organize the cult of saints and their relics.

This upward drift in the public profile of the bishop and his ever-multiplying staff was a matter for the attention not just of the citizenry within the walls of the cathedral city but also of the dwellers in the rural hinterland. If official Christianity was, increasingly with the passing years, what gave cohesion and identity to a community there was some inducement to throw in your lot with it. Rural conversion, like many other varieties of conversion to Christianity (or other faiths), partook of something of the nature of joining a club.

We must make allowance too for the steady reiteration by bishops of the kind of preaching that we have already met in the homilies of Maximus of Turin. Bishops hammered away at the same old themes throughout the fifth and sixth centuries. Here, by way of example, is Caesarius, bishop of Arles from *c.* 500 to 543.

> We have heard that some of you make vows to trees, pray to fountains, and practice diabolical augury. Because of this there is such sorrow in our hearts that we cannot receive any consolation. What is worse, there are some unfortunate and miserable people who not only are unwilling to destroy the shrines of the pagans but even are not afraid or ashamed to build up those which have been destroyed. Moreover, if anyone with a thought of God wants to burn the wood of those shrines or to tear to pieces and destroy

the diabolical altars, they become angry, rave with fury, and are excited with excessive frenzy. They even go so far as to dare to strike those who out of love for God are trying to overthrow the wicked idols; perhaps they do not even hesitate to plan their death. What are these unfortunate, miserable people doing? They are deserting the light and running to darkness; they reject God and embrace the Devil. They desert life while they follow after death; by repudiating Christ they proceed to impiety. Why then did these miserable people come to church? Why did they receive the sacrament of baptism – if afterwards they intended to return to the profanation of idols?[8]

Caesarius was an accomplished preacher. His 238 surviving sermons were composed in the straightforward Latin of daily speech in southern Gaul, not the elaborate literary Latin then fashionable among intellectuals. They were short, direct and pithy, fashioned to reach and influence an everyday audience of everyday men and women throughout the diocese. To this end Caesarius had extracts from the corpus copied for circulation among the local clergy. He spared no effort to ensure that Christian standards of behaviour were proclaimed loudly and unambiguously before his flock.

The sermons of Caesarius enjoyed a wide and a long circulation. In the official *Homiliary* – the standard collection of sermons for regular use – of the seventh-century Spanish church, nearly half of the homilies are those of Caesarius. It is from Spain too that there survives a work which specifically addresses itself to rural mission. This is the *De Correctione Rusticorum* of Martin of Braga. (It is a title which is a little hard to translate. The Latin word *correctio*, at this date, implies reform through punishment; and while the primary meaning of *rusticus* is 'countryman', the notion of 'rusticity' was not just a statement about locality but had overtones about behaviour and disposition as well. *On the Castigation of Country-dwellers* might do.) Martin, like his great namesake, was a native of Pannonia who had received a good education and had travelled in the east. In circumstances that remain shrouded in mystery he turned up in Spain about the middle of the sixth century. By the year 572 he had become bishop of Braga, now in northern Portugal, and he died in about 580. Braga, the Roman Bracara Augusta, was the capital of its province, Gallaecia (rather more extensive to the east and south than the modern Galicia), its bishop therefore the leading churchman of the province. Martin was an ecclesiastic of rank and influence.

De Correctione Rusticorum takes the form of a letter addressed to one of Martin's fellow bishops, Polemius of Astorga, but the writer makes it clear that it was intended for public delivery as a sermon. Martin began with a brief sketch of sacred history, firmly locating the pagan gods among the demonic ministers of the Devil when he was cast out of heaven:

> The demons also persuaded men to build them temples, to place there images or statues of wicked men and to set up altars to them, on which they might pour out the blood not only of animals but even of men. Besides, many demons, expelled from heaven, also preside either in the sea or in rivers or springs or forests; men ignorant of God also worship them as gods and sacrifice to them. They call on Neptune in the sea, on Lamiae in the rivers, on Nymphs in spring, on Dianas in woods, who are all malignant demons and wicked spirits, who deceive unbelieving men, who are ignorant of the Sign of the Cross, and vex them. However, not without God's permission do they do harm, because the rustics have angered God and do not believe with their whole heart in the faith of Christ, but are so inconstant that they apply the very names of demons to each day and speak of the days of Mars, Mercury, Jove, Venus and Saturn . . .

His exposition merges into a catechism, with digressions to identify various sins such as celebrating the New Year with the pagan Roman festival of the Kalends of January (that is, 1 January), and looks forward to the end of the world. He dwells on baptism as 'a pact you made with God' and then turns to human betrayals of that pact:

> And how can any of you, who has renounced the Devil and his angels and his evil works, now return again to the worship of the Devil? For to burn candles at stones and trees and springs, and where three roads meet, what is it but the worship of the Devil? To observe divinations and auguries and the days of idols, what is it but the worship of the Devil? To observe the days of Vulcan [23 August] and the first days of each month, to adorn tables and hang up laurels, to watch the foot, to pour out fruit and wine over a log in the hearth, and to put bread in a spring, what is it but the worship of the Devil? For women to invoke Minerva in their weaving, to keep weddings for the day of Venus [Friday],

53

to consider which day one should set out on a journey, what is it but the worship of the Devil? To mutter spells over herbs and invoke the names of demons in incantations, what is it but the worship of the Devil? And many other things which it takes too long to say. And you do all these things *after* renouncing the Devil, *after* baptism, and, returning to the worship of demons and to their evil works, you have betrayed your faith and broken the pact you made with God. You have abandoned the sign of the Cross you received in baptism, and you give heed to the signs of the Devil by little birds and sneezing and many other things. Why does no augury harm me or any other upright Christian? Because where the sign of the Cross has gone before, the sign of the Devil is nothing . . .[9]

And he concludes with a call to repentance and the replacement of these pagan practices with Christian ones. Martin of Braga was not a man, we might judge, subject to self-doubt. But his castigation makes very plain the difficulty, not indeed for him but for the modern historian, of drawing hard-and-fast boundaries between Christian and pagan, religion and superstition, piety and magic, the acceptable and the forbidden. It is a salutary reminder of the penumbral ambiguities of our subject.

Martin's tract, like the sermons of Caesarius, circulated widely: we shall meet it again. Admonition of this sort by individuals was reinforced by the collective voice of bishops assembled in church councils, formally condemning non-Christian practices and commending Christian ones. The sheer amount of attention devoted by the ecclesiastical authorities of this period to the *quality* of Christian observance is cumulatively impressive. Martin of Braga's views on the sinfulness of celebrating the Kalends of January were echoed by the bishops assembled at Tours in 567, by a diocesan synod held at Auxerre in the latter part of the sixth century, and by the Spanish bishops gathered for the fourth council of Toledo in 633. All sorts of divination and soothsaying and augury-reading were repeatedly condemned. By way of example, consider one type of practitioner referred to in our texts as an *ariolus* (plural *arioli*). Isidore of Seville, whose great work, *The Etymologies*, was the nearest thing to an encyclopaedia that the early Middle Ages produced, informs us that '*arioli* are so called because they utter impious prayer at the altars [*aras*] of idols, and offer deadly sacrifices, and accept instructions from the swarms of demons.'

Caesarius of Arles and Martin of Braga told their hearers to shun the *ariolus*. So did the civil law: no one should consult an *ariolus*, ruled the Theodosian Code promulgated in 438. But people plainly did. Gregory of Tours tells a story that is apposite here.[10] A young man named Aquilinus was out hunting with his father when he experienced some sort of seizure; he had a violent fit of trembling and then fell down in a coma. His kinsfolk recognized this as the work of the Devil and feared that a spell had been laid on him by an enemy. So they called in *arioli*, 'as is the way of country people' (*ut mos rusticorum habet*), who tied on ligatures and administered medicines; but in vain. Only then did the family take the boy to the shrine of St Martin at Tours where – need we say? – he was cured. This is a most interesting story. The *ariolus* in this context is the person of first recourse when the inexplicable disaster has occurred and foul play is suspected. We may call him, if we so desire, a witch doctor, but need to recognize that this is a loaded and therefore limiting term. There is no suggestion that the kinsfolk of Aquilinus were anything but Christian, yet it is to the *ariolus* that they first turn. Gregory reports this without apparent surprise or explicit condemnation, though there is implicit lamentation over their 'rusticity'. But it wasn't only rustics who resorted to *arioli*. In Spain at least it would appear that the clergy were not above doing so. The bishops assembled at Toledo in 633 – under the presidency of Isidore, no less – forbade bishops, priests, deacons or anyone whomsoever in clerical orders to consult *arioli* or other types of magician, augur, diviner or soothsayer. What intriguing complications are hinted at by this decree: further suggestions of frontiers obscurely blurred.

Now from the prohibitive to the positive: let us take, from manifold possibilities, sabbath observance and the sign of the cross. Church councils repeatedly enjoined the observance of Sunday by abstinence from labour: at Orléans in 538, at Mâcon in 585, at Narbonne in 589. So too did Martin of Braga in *De Correctione Rusticorum*. Moralists were at hand with gruesome tales of what might happen to transgressors. Gregory of Tours told a story of a man who, while on his way to church one Sunday, saw that animals had strayed into his field and done damage to his crops. He took up an axe to do some fencing to block the gap through which the beasts had strayed. His arm was instantly paralysed and remained so until it received massage treatment from the holy man Senoch. In another tale he told of a girl who combed her hair on a Sunday; the teeth of the comb rammed themselves into her palm, causing her great pain, until she prayed at the tomb of St Gregory of Langres.

Devotion to the cross was stimulated by the discovery of the True Cross early in the fourth century, attributed to the Empress Helena, mother of Constantine. Having been rare before, from the fourth century the cross began to be a frequent motif in Christian art – for example, on gravestones. We have already seen Martin deflect a falling tree simply by making the sign of the cross. It was presented by Gregory of Tours as an unfailing source of help for the pious in any emergency. The hermit Caluppa was once cornered in his cave in the Auvergne by two dragons: he put them to flight with the sign of the cross (though one of them farted defiantly as it lumbered out of the cave's mouth). When the holy abbot Portianus was forced to have a drink with the evil Sigivald he made the sign of the cross, the cup shattered and a snake slithered out of the spilt wine. Gregory also tells us an interesting story of some sceptics. It occurs in his account of the recluse Friardus.

> He passed his whole life praising God, in prayer and in vigils. He took from the earth with his own hands what he needed for his subsistence, and although he excelled others by his hard work he never ceased to pray. And so for his neighbours and for strangers, for such is the way of country people [*rusticorum*], he was the object of much ridicule. One day he was in a field cutting corn and tying it into sheaves along with the other harvesters, and a swarm of those annoying and fierce flies which are commonly called wasps came by. They bitterly attacked the harvesters, pricking them with their stings, and surrounding them on all sides, and so the men avoided the place where the nest was. And they mocked the blessed Friardus, saying to him slyly, 'May it occur to the blessed man, the religious man, who never ceases to pray, who always makes the sign of the cross on his ears and eyes, who always carries the standard of salvation with him wherever he goes, that he harvest near the nest and tame it with his prayer.' The holy man took these words as a slur upon divine power, and he fell to the ground in prayer to his Lord. Then he approached the wasps and made the sign of the cross over them, saying 'Our help is in the name of the Lord who made heaven and earth.' As this prayer left his mouth the wasps all hurried to hide themselves inside the hole from which they had come, and Friardus cut the stalks by the nest without harm, in the sight of all.[11]

Friardus lived on an island in the estuary of the Loire not far from Nantes. Yet it is clear from what Gregory tells us of him that he had contact with the local people and influence upon them. It is also clear that there were perhaps surprisingly many such drop-outs from conventional society in the Gaul of Gregory's day. Was this also the case in other western provinces of the former empire, which produced no Gregory of Tours to enlighten and enliven us? Cross the Pyrenees into Spain and consider the case of Emilian. We know a fair amount about him because his life was written by Braulio, pupil of Isidore and bishop of Saragossa, in about 635; Braulio's brother Fronimian was abbot of the monastery which had grown up on the site of Emilian's hermitage.[12] Emilian was a shepherd in the Rioja who was fired by a vision to devote his life to God. He sought out a hermit named Felix who lived near Haro for instruction. Having learned all that he could from Felix, Emilian returned to the Rioja and settled as a hermit at Berceo. Troubled by the multitude of people who flocked to him, Emilian retired (like Antony retreating further into the Egyptian desert) into the mountainous recesses of the Sierra de la Demanda. But his holiness could not be hidden. The local bishop, Didymus of Tarazona, sought him out, desiring to make him a priest. (Reading between the lines one may suspect a case of friction between bishop and hermit, not without parallels in this and other periods. Did the bishop want to regularize the position of this highly unconventional figure?) With reluctance Emilian agreed to be ordained to minister in the church of Berceo. We learn that he had clerics (in the plural) under him there, so we may infer that this was a small community of clergy with responsibility for a wide area round about, like the communities which served Martin's churches in Touraine. He was an exemplary priest – 'unlike those in our own times', comments Braulio. Indeed in some respects he was too good, or perhaps he did not hit it off with his clergy, or perhaps he was just hopeless at administration. Whatever the reason, his clerics accused him before the bishop of squandering the possessions of his church (in charitable giving, as Braulio insists). The bishop relieved him of his cure and Emilian retired to his hermitage for the remainder of his long life. He died in 573.

The miracles and wonders worked through the holy Emilian before and after his death show him as a spiritual force in Riojan society. Here is an example. Strange goings-on were reported from the household of the senator Honorius. (It is far from clear what the term 'senator' might signify in sixth-century Spain, but Braulio, a good classical scholar, surely intends us to understand a man of high social rank. Emilian, like Martin, was cultivated by the aristocracy.) At his dinner parties, the plates and dishes would be found piled with the bones or even with the dung of animals; and while the household slept items of clothing were mysteriously abstracted from their resting places and hung from the ceilings. More was at stake than just a little local difficulty with the servants. Honorius called Emilian in to exorcize what was evidently an evil spirit. And Emilian succeeded, though the spirit hurled a rock at him before it was vanquished. Honorius' gratitude was tangible. Emilian always did his best to feed the crowds of visitors who flocked to his refuge. On one occasion supplies of food were exhausted. Hardly had Emilian ceased to pray for assistance when suddenly carts loaded with food appeared at the door. They had been sent by Honorius.

Several more examples could be cited. There was the slave-girl of the senator Sicorius whose blindness he cured, the exorcism he performed on one of the slaves of Count Eugenius, the evil spirit which had taken possession of both the senator Nepotian and his wife Proseria cast out by him, the woman named Barbara who had travelled all the way from Amaya to seek a cure for her paralysis, the monk Armentarius whose swollen stomach was cured when Emilian made the sign of the cross over it – and so on. We need not linger over these. There is also one interesting case of scepticism. When Emilian foretold the conquest of Cantabria by the king of Spain and summoned all the local nobility – an interesting sidelight on his local influence – to warn them and upbraid them for their sins, one senator, by name Abundantius, said that Emilian was a delirious old fool. But he got his come-uppance; King Leovigild killed him shortly afterwards.

Emilian's hermitage grew after his death into one of the most famous monastic houses of medieval Spain, San Millán de la Cogolla, 'Saint Emilian of the Cowl' (though there is no reason to suppose that Emilian was ever a monk). Others who sought a solitary ascetic life were compelled almost at once to organize their disciples into monastic communities. Take the case of Romanus, who settled at Condat on the edge of the Jura mountains of eastern Gaul in about 435. Here, in a region quite as inhospitable as Emilian's Sierra de la Demanda, Romanus intended to live the solitary life of a hermit. But he was joined first by his brother Lupicinus, then by a trickle of other disciples which soon turned into a flood. Among them came that Eugendus, the son of the priest of Izernore, whose childhood vision of the monastic life is movingly described in the *Vita Patrum Iurensium* (*The Life of the Jura Fathers*), a work composed in about 515 which is our main source of information about these communities.[13] We also learn that there were plentiful lay hangers-on who had to be fed – just as at Emilian's hermitage. It was impossible for ascetics to cut themselves off altogether from the world. Indeed, it was a condition of their influence that they did not entirely cut themselves off from it. We see Lupicinus interceding with the secular authorities, like Germanus a generation earlier, on behalf of the unjustly oppressed poor. The monks of the Jura were bound to the world by economic need: at one point we catch a glimpse of them travelling all the way to the Mediterranean to buy salt. And they were sought out by petitioners. Solicited on behalf of a girl possessed by a demon, Eugendus dictated a letter to the evil spirit – we are given the text of it – commanding it to leave her; and it did, even before the letter was delivered. The lady Syagria, a member of the leading aristocratic dynasty of Lyons, gravely ill, was cured by *eating* a letter from Eugendus. Note the sequel: the whole city of Lyons rejoiced with her and her family.

Episcopal initiatives in spiritual and social welfare, preaching, legislation, the example of ascetic renunciation, the demonstrably superior power of Christian over other sorts of magic, miraculous cures worked by holy men: all have something to hint to us about how it was thought that rural conversion might best be effected. I am inclined to give most weight to the full-hearted commitment of the aristocracy to this task. Maximus of Turin and John Chrysostom had surely been correct in their prescriptions: get the landowners to build churches into which they can coax or bribe or lash their tenantry, and then bit by bit something – but what? – will start to happen. Two centuries later Pope Gregory the Great (590–604) was still thinking along these lines in the admonition he sent to Sardinian landowners to stamp out pockets of heathenism among their peasants. And if they show themselves reluctant to come to God, he wrote, jack their rents up until they do! Pope Gregory, the first pontiff to use the humble title 'servant of the servants of God', was quite capable of adopting the commanding tones of the great Roman aristocrat that by upbringing he was.

59

Here are two last sixth-century examples of the way in which locally prominent families could encourage and shape an emerging Christian character in the societies which looked to them for leadership. Samson was a native of Demetia, a kingdom of south Wales, who ended his life as a bishop in Gaul (later tradition would claim at Dol in Brittany). He was a part of that migration of British people from their own islands to the mainland of Gaul which transformed the province of Armorica into Brittany in the course of the fifth and sixth centuries. Samson is a somewhat shadowy figure, but his historical existence is attested to by the appearance of his name among a list of bishops who attended a church council held at Paris, probably in 561 or 562. It is assumed that his life fell within the first three-quarters of the sixth century. There exists a *Vita Samsonis* by an anonymous author which is difficult to date. The case for composition within about a century of its subject's death is reasonably strong (though far from unassailable). The text will be used here, with caution, as a reliable source of evidence for at least the general outlines of Samson's life.[14]

Samson was another, like Romanus or Emilian, taken by desire for the ascetic life. After receiving instruction from St Illtud at his monastery in Glamorgan, Samson sought a more arduous regime at a community recently founded on Caldey Island off the coast of what would later be called Pembrokeshire. Shortly after this, in the course of a visit to his family, Samson's example seems to have persuaded most of its members to opt for the monastic life. As a family they took the plunge together: his mother and father, his five brothers, his paternal uncle with his wife and their three sons, and his aunt on the mother's side. The family was a prominent one, 'noble and distinguished as the world reckons these things', in the words of Samson's biographer. After the family's conversion to monasticism they devoted all their property to the service of God; and there was plenty of it, 'for they were the owners of many estates'. We know that they also built churches, because we are told that after he had become a bishop Samson consecrated them. Samson founded a monastery vaguely described as 'near the river Severn'. He is said – in a section of the text which may be a later interpolation – to have travelled in Ireland, where he was given another monastery whose government he delegated to his uncle. Instructed in a vision that he must cross the sea and live as a *peregrinus* he sailed over to Cornwall, where he founded a further monastery. Continuing on his way he reached Brittany, where he established a monastery at

Dol. Before his death he founded one more, apparently somewhere near the mouth of the river Seine.

The main lines of this account are credible. The commitment of this prominent family to a more intense form of Christian living was likely to have started ripples of influence which perhaps had effects, sadly hidden from us, within the churches which they built. Samson's string of monastic foundations – and we shall see plenty more examples of such networks – had evangelizing potential. His journeys, foundations and miracles were associated by his biographer with conversion. In Cornwall, for example, in a district referred to as Tricurium, tentatively identified with the area formerly called Trigg in north Cornwall, Samson encountered people worshipping an idol. He admonished them, to little effect. Then it so happened that a boy was killed there in a riding accident. Samson pointed out that their idol could not revive the dead boy but that his God could; and would do so, provided that they promised to destroy their idol and for ever abandon its worship. They agreed to the bargain. Samson prayed for two hours, the boy returned to life, the idol was destroyed, and 'Count Guedianus' (? Gwythian) ordered all the people to be baptized by Samson. The holy man stayed in Cornwall for a little while longer, helpfully killing a serpent that was troubling the inhabitants and then founding his monastery, before resuming his journey to Brittany. The author of the *Vita Samsonis* had been to Cornwall and had seen 'the sign of the cross which the holy Samson with his own hand had chiselled upon an upright stone': the Cornish equivalent, we might think, of the creed written out by the hand of Gregory of Pontus in the cathedral of Neocaesarea. Samson's travels in Trigg might be compared to Martin's visit to Levroux.

Our last example takes us back to Gaul. Aredius was a slightly younger contemporary of Samson. A native of Limoges, he was born into a prominent family and as a young man was attached to the court of the Frankish King Theudebert (534–48). He was recruited by Bishop Nicetius of Trier – whom we shall meet again in a later chapter – under whom he studied and received the monastic tonsure. On the death of his father and brother he returned to the Limousin to look after his mother Pelagia, who had been left kinless and unprotected. Aredius dedicated himself and his property to the service of God, enthusiastically assisted by Pelagia. He built churches on his estates and founded a monastery at a place now named after him:

61

Saint-Yrieix, a just recognizable derivative from Aredius, to the south of Limoges. The sick flocked to him and 'he restored them to health by laying on of hands with the sign of the cross.'[15]

Gregory of Tours, our source for this, was a friend of Aredius and had good reason to be grateful to him. The church of St Martin at Tours was one of the principal beneficiaries of the will jointly made by Aredius and Pelagia in 572.[16] It shows that the family was an extremely wealthy one, owning widespread estates, many of which came into the possession of the church of Tours: a further instance of pious largesse to set beside the examples quoted above of Remigius at Rheims and Bertram at Le Mans. Churches are mentioned at some of the estates. Although we cannot be certain that all of these had been built by Aredius, we can be reasonably sure of it in some instances, for example that of 'our church dedicated in honour of St Médard [of Soissons] at *Exidolium*', presumably Excideuil in northern Périgord, because Medard had died only some twenty years earlier and Aredius had been involved with the growth of his cult. The will also shows that Aredius and his mother possessed large amounts of ecclesiastical furnishings – embroidered linen and silk textiles (altar frontals, wall- and door-hangings), silver chalices and patens, and some very exotic items such as 'the crown with a silver cross, gilded, with precious stones, full of relics of the saints . . . which crown has hanging from it eight leaves wrought from gold and gems'. It was presumably a votive, hanging crown, perhaps akin to the votive crown of the Spanish king Recesswinth (643–72) found in the treasure of Guarrázar, near Toledo. These textiles and treasures should alert us to the impact which the interiors of these churches might have made upon the senses of those who worshipped in them; a not insignificant element in considering the process of Christianization.

In the middle years of the sixth century John of Ephesus conducted an evangelizing campaign in the provinces of Asia, Caria, Lydia and Phrygia – roughly speaking, today's western Turkey. In the course of several years' work he and his helpers demolished temples and shrines, felled sacred trees, baptized 80,000 persons, built ninety-eight churches and founded twelve monasteries. And this was in the heart of the empire, an area where there had been a Christian presence since the time of St Paul, not in some out-of-the-way corner like Cornwall or Galicia. In 598 Pope Gregory wrote to the bishop of Terracina to express dismay at a report that had reached him to the effect that the inhabitants of those parts were worshipping sacred trees. Again, not a remote spot; Terracina is on the coast between Rome and Naples, its countryside traversed by the Via Appia, one of the busiest highways of the Mediterranean world.

These two reports remind us that the conversion and Christianization of the countryside was a very slow business. The point cannot be sufficiently emphasized. The evidence surveyed in this chapter has been largely normative, that is to say it lays out ideals or targets. Our sources speak with the official voice of the educated elite within the church; they do not describe the everyday reality of belief and observance among the laity. That reality will always be elusive. Can we make any assessment at all of what had been achieved? Any answer to this question must be cautious, but need not be blankly negative.

Our two earliest activists, Gregory of Pontus and Martin of Tours, were operating at times when and in places where Christianity had made no impact at all upon the countryside. We may guess that in this respect Pontus and Touraine were not untypical. Two centuries later, in the age of Gregory of Tours and Martin of Braga, conditions had changed. They were operating in a social world which was, in a formal sense, Christian. Paganism as overt, active, public cult no longer existed in Gaul or Spain (except among the Basques). Caesarius of Arles, Martin of Braga, Gregory of Tours, Pope Gregory the Great, had as their principal concern the problem of how to make people who were nominally Christian more thoroughly Christian, the more effectively to guard them from demonic assault which would threaten God's protection of the whole community. These pastors were clear about the disposition and behaviour required of the good Christian and they did their utmost to set their standards and expectations clearly before the laity. Here, they are saying, is a pattern of godly behaviour to which you must try to conform. This is the message not just of the directly homiletic material (Caesarius, Martin) but also of much of what we are accustomed to think of as the 'historical' works of Gregory of Tours. They were also clear about what the good Christian should avoid. All four of these writers would probably have agreed in terming it *rusticitas*, 'rusticity'. The notion of rusticity comprehended not just doing a bit of fencing or brushing your hair on a Sunday, not just boorish junketings at the Kalends of January, but potentially also something much more menacing in the guise of resort to alternative systems of explanation, propitiation and control. This is the lesson of the story about Aquilinus and the *arioli*. There existed an alternative network to the one presented by Christian teachers. There were other persons about, easily resorted to, claiming access to the means of explaining misfortune, curing sickness, stimulating love, wreaking vengeance, foretelling the future, advising when to undertake a journey, interpreting the flight of birds or the patterns on the shoulder-blades of sheep.

Historians have often written dismissively of 'pagan survivals', old beliefs and practices tolerated by a sagely easy-going church, which would subside harmlessly into the quaint and folkloric. But this is to miss the point. The men of the sixth century – and not just the sixth century by any means – were engaged in an urgent and a competitive enterprise. In a European countryside where over hundreds of years diverse rituals had evolved for coping with the forces of nature, Christian holy men had to show that they had access to more efficacious power. The element of competition emerges clearly in the tale of Aquilinus, or in the story about Samson and the Cornish boy killed in a fall from his horse: and, it may be said, in many others too. Competition involves an element of comparability, even of compromise. Thus there is scope for all sorts of nice questions about where and how to draw lines round the limits of the tolerable. Competition also involves the risk of overlapping perceptions of identity. How like to an *ariolus* was, say, Emilian or Friardus or Caluppa – in the eyes of contemporaries? Or in the eyes of historians?

Because this chapter has concentrated upon the period between the third and the sixth centuries the incautious reader might be left with the impression that the challenge of converting the countryside to Christianity was one that was faced and surmounted during that period. Not so. A start had been made; but the operation was one which would continue to tax the energies of bishops for centuries to come. Country people are notoriously conservative. We may be absolutely certain that more than a few generations of episcopal exhortation or lordly harassment would be needed to alter habits inherited from time out of mind. Ways of doing things, ways that grindingly poor people living at subsistence level had devised for managing their visible and invisible environments, were not going to yield easily, perhaps were not going to yield at all, to ecclesiastical injunction. But even granite will be dented by water that never ceases to drip. This is one way in which 'something will start to happen'. If there were country churches (as in Touraine), and if there were clergy to serve them (a big 'if', that one), and if the laity attended church (a practice for which we have only sporadic evidence) – would the people then become more Christian? The question mark stays in place because at this point a spectre rises to haunt us, the most troubling of the problems laid out in Chapter 1: what makes a Christian? Did Martin 'make Christians' by smashing a temple at Levroux? Sulpicius Severus thought so. Were the lakeside dwellers of Javols 'made Christian' when they diverted their offerings of local produce from lake to church? Gregory of Tours thought so. Did Samson 'make Christian' the people of Trigg by raising a boy from the dead and killing a snake? Count Guedianus thought so, if Samson's anonymous biographer is to be believed, for he ordered them all to be baptized. This is what our sources tell us; we have to make of it what we can.

CHAPTER THREE

Beyond the Imperial Frontiers

Fish say, they have their Stream and Pond;
But is there anything Beyond?
RUPERT BROOKE, 'Heaven', 1914

IN THE LATE ANTIQUE PERIOD, as we saw in Chapter 1, it was standard practice for Christian communities which had put down roots outside the frontiers of the Roman empire to be provided with bishops on request. To Patrophilus, bishop of Pithyonta in Georgia, who attended the council of Nicaea in 325 (see above p. 26) we can add others. There was Frumentius, for example, consecrated by Athanasius of Alexandria, author of the *Life of St Antony*, in about 350 as the bishop of a Christian community based at Axum in Ethiopia. There was Theophilus 'the Indian', apparently a native of Socotra in the Gulf of Aden, who was sent at much the same time to be the bishop of Christian communities in southern Arabia which seem to have originated as trading settlements. Patrophilus, Frumentius and Theophilus operated far to the east or south of the Roman empire. They are shadowy figures who have left but the faintest of traces. Most scholars, however, are agreed that they did exist and that they are witnesses to the flourishing of some very far-flung branches of the Christian church. They had western counterparts, marginally better documented, beyond the imperial provinces of the fourth and fifth centuries, who are the subject of this chapter. Among the earliest of them known to us was a man named Ulfila – or Wulfila, or Ulfilas; it is variously spelt. His name was Germanic and means 'Little Wolf' or 'Wolf Cub'. Much later, he would come to be known as 'the Apostle of the Goths'. This is not quite what he was, though his achievements were remarkable enough. To provide him with a background and a context we must go back for a moment to third-century Pontus and to Bishop Gregory the Wonder-worker.

66

The *Canonical Letter* of Gregory the Wonder-worker (above p. 35) was prompted by a crisis in the provinces of northern Asia Minor in the middle years of the third century. Upon this sleepy corner of the empire there had unexpectedly fallen the cataclysmic visitation of barbarian attack. Goths settled on the north-western shores of the Euxine (or Black) Sea had managed to requisition ships from the Hellenistic sea ports – such places, presumably, as Chersonesus (Sevastopol) in the Crimea – which enabled them to raid the vulnerable coastline of Asia Minor. The earliest raids took place in the mid-250s. The invaders came to pillage, not to settle. In their eyes human booty was as desirable as temple treasures or the jewel-cases of rich ladies; captives, some of whom might buy their release, others of whom would be carried off into a life of slavery. In the wake of these devastations and collapse of order Bishop Gregory was approached by a colleague, possibly the bishop of Trapezus (Trebizond), and invited to pronounce on the disciplinary issues which arose from the conduct of the Christian provincials during the disturbances. His reply has come down to us because its rulings came to be regarded as authoritative and were incorporated into the canon law of the eastern or Orthodox branch of the church.[1]

Gregory's letter casts a shaft of light upon the human misery and depravity occasioned by the raids as well as upon the responsibilities assumed by a bishop in trying to pick up the pieces of shattered local life in their wake. Had captives been polluted by eating food provided for them by the barbarians? No; for 'it is agreed by everyone' – Gregory had evidently made enquiries – 'that the barbarians who overran our regions did not sacrifice [food] to idols.' Women who had been the innocent victims of rape were guiltless, following the precepts of Deuteronomy xxii.26–7: 'But unto the damsel thou shalt do nothing . . . for he found her in the field, and the damsel cried, and there was none to save her.' It was different, however, noted the bishop, with women whose past life had shown them to be of a flighty disposition: 'then clearly the state of fornication is suspect even in a time of captivity; and one ought not readily to share in one's prayers with such women.' One can only speculate about the grim consequences of this ruling in the tight little communities of the towns and villages of Pontus. Gregory's sense of outrage is vividly conveyed across the seventeen centuries that separate him from us. Prisoners of the Goths who, 'forgetting that they were men of Pontus, and Christians', directed their captors to properties which could be looted, must be excommunicated. Roman citizens, 'men impious and hateful to God', have themselves taken part in looting. They have 'become Goths to others' by appropriating booty taken but abandoned by the raiders. It was 'something quite unbelievable', but they have 'reached such a point of cruelty and inhumanity' as to enslave prisoners who had succeeded in escaping from their barbarian captors. They have used the cover of disorder to prosecute private feuds. They have demanded rewards for restoring property to its rightful owners. Gregory commended to his correspondent the measures which he had taken in his own diocese: enquiries, hearing public denunciations, setting up tribunals ('the assembly of the saints') and punishments meted out in accordance with the extremely severe penitential discipline of the early church. There are parallels here with the fate of all later actual or suspected collaborationists. Many, however, were beyond the reach of Gregory's ministrations. These were the captives who did not escape, who were not wealthy enough to buy their freedom, who were of insufficient status to command a ransom payment from kinsfolk or neighbours left at home. Borne off into slavery among barbarians, the captives took with them the solace of their Christian faith. In this fashion little pockets of Christianity struck root among the Goths outside the frontiers of the empire.

The Goths matter to us because their crossing of the Danube frontier in 376 and subsequent settlement inside the empire symbolize the beginning of the process which since the time of Edward Gibbon we have known as the Decline and Fall of the Roman Empire. Who were these barbarians?

Those whom Roman writers of the third and fourth centuries referred to as Goths were a variety of peoples who spoke a Germanic language, Gothic. Known to the Romans in the first century A.D., they were then living in the basin of the lower Vistula in what is now Poland. They migrated thence in a south-easterly direction towards the Ukraine in the latter part of the second century. At the time of the raids on Asia Minor they were settled most thickly in the lower valleys of the Dnieper and the Dniester. Some among them were expanding to the south-west, into what is now northern Romania. This brought them into proximity with the only province of the Roman empire which lay to the north of the Danube, namely Dacia; an area bounded on the south by the Danube between the Iron Gates and its confluence with the river Olt, spreading northwards to take in the

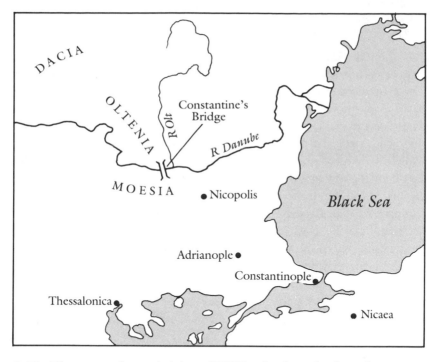

3. To illustrate the activities of Ulfila during the fourth century.

uplands of Transylvania embraced by the Carpathian mountains. During the troubled middle years of the third century the Goths pressed hard on the frontiers of Dacia and launched raids into Thrace and even Greece. It was to some degree in response to this pressure that the Emperor Aurelian withdrew Roman rule from Dacia in the early 270s. Thenceforward this sector of the empire's frontier lay along the Danube. The Goths moved into the abandoned but by no means deserted province. Dacia had experienced a century and a half of Romanization. Substantial elements of the Romano-Dacian population remained, and archaeological evidence suggests that a modest urban life with a modest villa economy to supply its needs limped along into the Gothic period. It is possible, though unproven, that there were Christian communities among the population of Dacia in the third century. The most extraordinary witness to the tenacity of Roman civilization is the survival there of the Latin language, the ancestor of modern Romanian.

Much has been revealed about Gothic culture in this period by the archaeologists. To the evidence of the so-called Sîntana de Mureş/Černjachov culture, so named from sites respectively in Transylvania

69

and the Ukraine, may be added a little information from Roman writers. What these combined sources have to tell us is as follows. The Goths were settled agriculturalists who practised both arable and pastoral farming. They lived in substantial villages but not in towns. Their houses were of wood, wattle-and-daub and thatch; sometimes they had stone footings or floors. Traceable artefacts are pottery, wheel-thrown, of good quality clay; iron tools and weapons; buckles and brooches of bronze or silver; and objects made of bone such as combs. These artefacts, commonplace enough in themselves, suggest a degree of specialization and division of labour. The Goths disposed of their dead by both cremation and inhumation, and the remains were frequently though not always accompanied by grave-goods. Variations in quantity and quality of personal possessions (in graves), and in the size of dwellings, suggest communities wherein were marked differences of wealth and status. A few hazardous inferences about the religious beliefs of the Goths may be essayed by the imprudent on the basis of the archaeological materials. The written sources tell us of sacrificial meat – if not among raiding parties in Asia Minor – and of wooden images or idols. We hear of a war god and of seasonal festivals. Gothic political organization is scarcely documented at all, and therefore fiercely controversial among scholars. However, it is likely that among the group of Goths settled to the west of the Dniester and termed by a Roman contemporary the *Tervingi* there existed in the fourth century a hereditary monarchy and a nobility of tribal chieftains. The Goths cannot be said to have had a written culture, though they did possess a runic alphabet. Runic inscriptions have been found on some grave-goods and, most famously and enigmatically, on a great gold torque, or neck ring, found in the treasure of Pietroasa in Romania, unearthed in 1837. Finally, we must observe that their interactions with the Roman world across the Danube were close and not always hostile. Goths left their native land to serve in the imperial armies, sometimes rising to high rank. Large amounts of Roman coin circulated in Gothia. Archaeologists have found remains of the tall, narrow Mediterranean pots called *amphorae* in Gothic contexts: they were used for the transport of wine or oil, commodities more likely to be trade goods than plunder.

In sum, the Goths were in no sense 'primitive' peoples. The Tervingi in Dacia (who are our main concern) were neighbours of the Romans, living in a Romanized province, with Roman provincials – whether native or captive – living under their rule. On the periphery of the Roman world, they experienced cultural interactions with their imposing neighbour. Like all the other Germanic barbarian peoples, the Goths in peacetime found much to admire, to envy and to imitate in Roman ways. When the pressure of Roman might bore down on them too heavily, they defended themselves by adopting those political and military usages which they had correctly identified as buttressing Roman imperial hegemony. It is a familiar pattern: peripheral outsiders tend to model themselves upon the hegemonic power on whose flanks they are situated. When the defences of the Roman empire gave way the Germanic barbarians entered upon an inheritance for which they had long been preparing themselves. They came not to wreck but to join. In this manner the decline and fall of the western empire was to be not destruction but dismemberment, a sharing out of working parts under new management.

Matters did not present themselves in such a rosy light to the provincials who lived to the south of the Danube in closest proximity to the Tervingi in the fourth century; nor to the imperial government whose job it was to protect them. Although there would seem to have been uneasy peace for a generation or so after the Gothic settlement in Dacia, pressure on the imperial borders started up again during the first quarter of the new century. The lower Danube frontier was impressively defended. There was a string of forts along the southern bank whose garrisons numbered at least 60,000 men. Detachments of the imperial fleet regularly patrolled the river. There were arms and clothing factories a little way behind the frontier to supply the troops. A spirit of invention and experiment is attested to by a curious anonymous work from this period and, quite possibly, this region which sought government sponsorship for, among other things, a paddle-driven warship powered by oxen, a piece of mobile field-artillery, a portable bridge made of inflated skins and a new and improved version of the scythed chariot drawn by mail-clad horses. In the 320s Constantine built a colossal bridge over the Danube – it was 2,437 metres long – a little above its confluence with the Olt and used it to reoccupy Oltenia, the land in the angle between the two rivers. From this base a campaign was mounted against the Tervingi in 332. It was completely successful: the Tervingi were defeated and reduced to client status, their ruler's son carried off to Constantinople as a hostage. This peace lasted for thirty-five years with only small-scale violations, notably in the late 340s. In the 360s it broke down, and the Emperor Valens fought a less decisive war in the years 367–9 which brought about a further pacification. There matters rested until the arrival on the scene shortly afterwards of a terrifying new enemy, the Huns.

The Huns changed the terms of Romano-Gothic relations for ever. A nomadic people from central Asia, wonderfully skilled with horse, bow and lassoo and with a reputation as pitiless enemies, they began to move westwards – no one really knows why – in the second half of the fourth century. In the early 370s they collided with the Greuthingi, the eastern group of Goths settled between the Dniester and the Dnieper. The Greuthingi were defeated, the survivors among them enslaved. In the wake of these events the Tervingi sought asylum within the Roman empire. Reluctantly, Valens agreed to this request. In 376 the Tervingi crossed the Danube on to imperial territory. Relations between Goths and Romans broke down in the following year when the imperial government failed to keep its promises about supplying foodstuffs to the refugees. War followed in 378. A decisive battle was fought near Adrianople in August; the Roman army was defeated and the Emperor Valens killed at the hands of the Tervingi under their leader Fritigern. There ensued four years of confusion during which the Goths failed to take Constantinople and pillaged Thrace. In 382 a settlement was reached with the new emperor, Theodosius I: Fritigern and his followers were permitted to settle peacefully in the province of Moesia, south of the Danube and just west of the Black Sea. There they remained until 395 when a new leader, Alaric, would start the Goths on further travels which would take them to Italy, where they would sack Rome in 410; then to Aquitaine, where they were again settled under treaty arrangements in 418; and finally to Spain, where the Gothic monarchy would flourish until overthrown by the forces of Islam early in the eighth century.

Among those who were carried off into permanent captivity in the course of the Gothic raids into Pontus in the middle of the third century were the ancestors of Ulfila. The family evidently retained a memory of its origins. Ulfila knew that his ancestors had lived in a village called Sadagolthina, near Parnassus in Cappadocia, about fifty miles south of modern Ankara. (This is at least 150 miles from the nearest point on the Black Sea coast: it shows how far inland the Gothic raiders had penetrated and explains something of the terror they inspired.) We know too that this band of displaced persons in

Gothia not only retained but also diffused their faith. 'They converted many of the barbarians to the way of piety and persuaded them to adopt the Christian faith,' tells the fifth-century historian Philostorgius, one of the principal sources for what little we know of Ulfila. It may be that the family intermarried with Goths; so much is suggested by Ulfila's Gothic name: we do not know. Indeed, it must be stressed that we know absolutely nothing whatsoever about the conditions in which captives and their descendants lived among the Goths. This is one of several areas of puzzlement and uncertainty which necessarily render our understanding of Ulfila so hazy. Another concerns his education. Ulfila had been 'carefully instructed', recorded his pupil Auxentius. He was fluent in Greek, Latin and Gothic, in all three of which languages he composed 'several tractates and many interpretations'. His translation of the Bible into Gothic was a towering intellectual achievement. In the world of late antiquity education to anything beyond the most elementary level was only for the rich, or those who could find a rich patron. How and where did Ulfila get his education? We have not the remotest idea.

At the age of thirty, when he had attained the rank of *lector* or reader, one of the minor orders of the church, Ulfila was sent to Constantinople by the ruler of the Tervingi as a member of a diplomatic mission. This would have been in about 340 or 341, some years after the peace of 332. The imperial throne was now occupied by Constantius II (337–61), son of the great Constantine. Again, we wonder why Ulfila was chosen to serve in this capacity. While in Constantinople he was consecrated a bishop by the patriarch. (There are formidable difficulties about the date of his consecration, which I here pass over.) His commission was to be 'bishop of the Christians in the Gothic land'; to serve, that is, an existing Christian community – by whom indeed his episcopal consecration had presumably been requested – not to undertake specifically missionary activities.

His episcopate 'in the Gothic land' lasted for seven years, which takes us to 347/8. At the end of this period the 'impious and sacrilegious' (but unnamed) ruler of the Tervingi initiated 'a tyrannical and fearsome persecution' of the Christians under his rule. Ulfila evidently judged that discretion was the better part of valour and led a large body of refugee Christians across the Danube and into asylum on Roman soil. Welcomed by the authorities with honour and respect, Ulfila and his flock received from the emperor land on which to settle near the city of Nicopolis (Veliko Tǔrnovo in the north of modern Bulgaria), some thirty miles south of the frontier in the province of Moesia Inferior. We are told that Constantius held Ulfila 'in the highest esteem' and would often refer to him as 'the Moses of our time' because through him God had liberated the Christians of Dacia from barbarian captivity.

Ulfila spent the rest of his life at Nicopolis, ministering to his congregations, studying, teaching, translating the Bible. He was also drawn into the principal theological controversy of the day, the Trinitarian debate arising from the teachings of the Alexandrian priest Arius (d. 336). Arianism was the doctrine that the Son of God was created by the Father. Its opponents, who claimed the name of Catholic – which literally means 'general' or 'universal' – taught that Father, Son and Holy Spirit were co-eternal and equal in Godhead. To put this in another way, Arius sought to avoid any dilution of monotheism by stressing the indivisibility, the majestic one-ness and omnipotence of God, and the subordination to Him of the Son. To those not attuned to theological debate, the relationship between the three Persons of the Trinity is an unrewarding topic. We must accept, first, that it was long and keenly debated in the fourth century and that it nourished some of the finest minds of the age. Second, we should bear in mind that at the time – whatever the dispute might have been made to look like by later commentators – it was not a simple matter of a straight fight between orthodoxy and heresy. Trinitarian orthodoxy was not something given, like the doctrines of the Resurrection or the Ascension. It was in the process of being hammered out by recourse to difficult scriptural texts which could yield diverse interpretations. The problem was to find a doctrinal formula which would satisfy several different theological factions. Third, the debate was one which necessarily had a political dimension. With the arrival on the scene of imperial patronage of the Christian church, theological controversy could no longer be simply a matter of intellectual debate. What was now also at stake was access to huge and unprecedented material resources, legal privileges and influence at the imperial court. The penalties of finding yourself on the losing side were therefore substantial. Constantine, having once publicly associated himself with Christianity, had taken an assertive if not always instructed role in ecclesiastical controversy. He it was who had summoned and presided over the council of Nicaea in 325, the first major attempt to find a doctrinal formulation which would be widely acceptable; the Nicene creed was the result. This settlement of the dispute held the field, though not unchallenged, until Constantine's death in 337. But his son Constantius favoured the Arian tendency and under his patronage successive councils – Antioch in 341, Sirmium in 351, Rimini in 359, Constantinople in 360 – drafted credal statements which, though necessarily in the circumstances somewhat fudgy, leant away from the Nicene position towards the Arian one. Ulfila was consecrated a bishop by one of the leading spirits of this 'court Arianism', attended the council of Constantinople in 360 and was on close terms with an emperor who was widely held to be sympathetic to Arianism. The successor of Constantius in the eastern half of the empire, after the brief resign of Julian the Apostate (361–3), was Valens (364–78), who proved another protector of the Arians. One fifth-century historian, Sozomen, tells us that Ulfila was chosen to head the embassy to Valens which sought permission for the Tervingi to enter the empire in 376. If true, this report would suggest that Ulfila had contrived to maintain the connections with the imperial court which he had enjoyed in the time of Constantius. But the tide was turning against the moderately Arian or non-Nicene party. The Emperor Theodosius I (379–95) was an unswerving partisan of the doctrinal formulations of Nicaea. Decrees enjoining the acceptance of the Nicene creed were issued in 380. In the following year Arian churches were confiscated and handed over to the Catholics, and all meetings of the heretics were banned. The last glimpse we have of Ulfila is in 383, travelling to Constantinople to attend another church council in the company of two Danubian bishops, deposed for Arianism, whose cause he was going to plead with the emperor. He died in Constantinople shortly afterwards.

The main reason why we know so little of Ulfila lies in the victory, never to be reversed, of Nicene orthodoxy in official circles in his last years. It is a good example of the adage that history is written by the victors. The memory of Arius and his followers was systematically vilified, their writings hunted down and destroyed. Ulfila was too big to be ignored; but he could be, and was, belittled. Had the moderate-Arian creed to which he adhered come out on top, Ulfila would be remembered as one of the giants of the fourth-century church. As it is, we have to struggle with fragmentary and ambiguous texts to discern even the shadowy outline of a notable career.

What then was the significance of Ulfila? He was not a missionary in the generally accepted sense of the word. He did not go off to live among a heathen people in order to convert them to Christianity. Instead, he went as the bishop of an existing Christian community beyond the imperial frontier, a community which no doubt included persons of Gothic birth but which was principally composed of displaced foreigners living under Gothic rule. We need not doubt that this community made converts among the Goths in Ulfila's day as it had done before; but conversion of the heathen was not perceived as its prime function. The Christians in Gothia were, in Gibbon's words, 'involuntary missionaries'.[2]

Ulfila was almost certainly not the first churchman to have been sent to serve Christian communities among the Goths beyond the imperial frontiers. Among the bishops who attended the council of Nicaea in 325 was a certain Theophilus 'of Gothia'; it has been conjectured that he ministered to Christian communities among the Goths settled in the Crimea. A letter of St Basil of Cappadocia written in about 375 refers to a certain Eutyches, who had evidently lived at some time past but of whom nothing further is known, in terms which suggest ministry in Gothic lands. However, as we have already seen in the course of discussion in Chapter 1, there was at that period no sense that it was the duty of the Romano-Christian world to evangelize pagan barbarians beyond its borders. Christianity was not for outsiders. So we are told: yet the question may be probed a little further. The adhesion of Constantine to Christianity was followed by an ever more strident and assertive trend towards the near-identification of empire and church. Christianity thus became a part of the empire's cultural armoury. Did it occur to the imperial establishment of the fourth century, as it would in later centuries, that the faith could be used to tame threatening barbarians in their homelands? We do not know, but it looks as though the Goths thought so. Each of the two known outbreaks of anti-Christian persecution by the Gothic authorities in the fourth century coincided with periods of military hostilities between Goth and Roman. The first of these was in 347–8, when Ulfila left Gothia to cross the Danube and settle at Nicopolis. The second came in the wake of Valens' Gothic war of 367–9. We are rather well informed about it owing to the survival of an account of the sufferings of a Gothic martyr, Saba, who perished on 12 April 372. A recent authority has commented that 'the Goths would seem to have been afraid that Christianity would undermine that part of Gothic identity which was founded in their common inherited beliefs, so that religion was not just an individual spiritual concern, but also a political issue standing in some relation to Gotho-Roman affairs.'[3]

All of which prompts further speculation about the role of Ulfila. His relations with the imperial Christian establishment were close: he was consecrated a bishop in Constantinople, given land near Nicopolis by his admirer Constantius, attended councils within the empire, was apparently confident of his intercessory powers with Theodosius I. It is impossible not to reflect that when he returned to the empire in 347–8 Ulfila must have been in a position to furnish the government with a good deal of useful intelligence concerning goings-on in Gothia: possibly on other occasions too. Does this mean that in going to Gothia as a bishop Ulfila was undertaking what has been called an 'imperially-sponsored mission'? That is perhaps to go too far. Ulfila was not a Roman agent. We must remember that he was so far trusted by the Gothic authorities as to be commissioned to negotiate on their behalf on two occasions that we know of, possibly on others of which we are ignorant. Ulfila faced both ways. Missionary or quasi-missionary churchmen often do.

It is entirely appropriate, in the light of this, that his most enduring achievement should have been the translation of the Bible into Gothic, giving to his people, or his people by adoption, the holy writings of the Roman faith in their own Germanic tongue. Here is Philostorgius again: 'He was the inventor for them of their own letters, and translated all the Scriptures into their language – with the exception, that is, of the books of Kings. This was because these books contain the history of wars, while the Gothic people, being lovers of war, were in need of something to restrain their passion for fighting rather than to incite them to it.' Ulfila was not the first to undertake biblical translation; the so-called 'Old Latin' and Syriac versions were already in circulation. But these were existing literary languages current within the Roman empire. To no one had the notion occurred of translating the scriptures into a barbarian tongue which had never been written down before. Perhaps, as is often the case with simple but revolutionary and liberating ideas, it could only have come to one who was himself in some sense an outsider.

* * *

4. To illustrate the activities of Ninian and Patrick in the fifth century.

If we now direct our attention to the western extremities of the empire at a time a couple of generations or so after Ulfila's day we shall meet two further instances of the same phenomenon, the sending of bishops to existing Christian communities outside the imperial frontier. We shall also encounter something altogether unexpected in a late-antique context: a churchman who experienced a missionary vocation to take the faith to heathen barbarians and who has left a precious account of how he came to engage himself in such an eccentric activity.

Our first instance is a very shadowy one, about whom we know far less than we do about Ulfila. Ninian, or Nynia, was the name of a British bishop sent to minister to a community of Christians in what is now Galloway in the south-west of Scotland. His episcopate is most probably to be placed somewhere in the middle years of the fifth century. By this time the Roman provinces of Britain were no longer part of the empire. As with Dacia in the 270s, so in 410 the government of the Emperor Honorius had taken the decision to withdraw the apparatus of Roman rule from Britain. It is unlikely that contemporaries imagined that this state of affairs would be permanent; both the imperial government and the British provincials probably anticipated that at some stage in the future, when times were easier, Roman control would be reimposed. Meanwhile, life in Britain seems to have gone on in much the same way until well into the fifth century.

Galloway was within reach, by way of the easily navigable Solway Firth, of the contiguous parts of what had been Roman Britain: the town of Lugubalium (Carlisle), the forts of the Cumbrian coast, and the farms of the Eden valley. A scatter of small finds – coins, pottery – of Romano-British material in south-western Scotland indicates that connections were established. How a Christian community grew up there we have no means of knowing, but that one was in existence by the fifth century is certain. It is attested by the so-called 'Latinus' stone at Whithorn, datable to *c.* 450, whose enigmatic Latin inscription may record – the latest suggestion by a leading authority – the foundation of a Christian church there by a man named Latinus.[4] We have a context for Bishop Ninian. We might also have the names of two of his successors. Some twenty miles west of Whithorn, at Kirkmadrine in the Rhinns of Galloway, another inscribed stone, possibly of the early sixth century, commemorates 'the holy and outstanding *sacerdotes* Viventius and Mavorius'. (*Sacerdotes* could mean either 'priests' or 'bishops': in the Latin of that period the second meaning was more common than the first.)

Ninian himself is not mentioned by name until the eighth century, when Bede devoted two passing sentences to him in his *Ecclesiastical History of the English People*. Bede was, as I have said in Chapter 1, a very conscientious scholar who in this instance dutifully reported what he had heard from persons whom he regarded as reliable sources. Among them was quite probably the English Bishop Pehthelm of the recently revived see of Whithorn. However, Bede was careful to qualify his report with a hint of uncertainty: 'as they say'. What Bede had been told was that Ninian was a Briton who had received religious instruction at Rome, had gone as a bishop to Whithorn, where he had built a church of stone dedicated to St Martin of Tours, had converted the southern Picts to Christianity and had on his death been buried at Whithorn. This report presents all sorts of difficulties. It is generally though not universally agreed that some of what Bede tells us is more likely to represent what the eighth century wanted to believe about Ninian than any historical reality. As we shall see in due course, the eighth century was more interested in Roman connections and missions to barbarians than was the fifth. It may not be irrelevant that Bishop Pehthelm was a correspondent of the great St Boniface, strenuous upholder of Roman direction of the church's overriding duty of mission to pagan barbarian peoples. All that is reasonably certain is that a Christian community had grown up beyond the imperial frontier in Britain and that Ninian had been appointed its bishop.

Our second instance of a bishop sent beyond the western extremities of the empire is a mite less shadowy. The contemporary chronicler named Prosper of Aquitaine – he whose *De Vocatione Omnium Gentium* occupied us briefly in Chapter 1 – informs us in his annal for the year 431 that (in his own words) 'Palladius, consecrated by Pope Celestine, is sent as their first bishop to the Irish believers in Christ.' Here at last is some 'hard' information. Prosper had visited Rome in that very year, 431, to consult Pope Celestine on a matter of theological controversy. He could even have met Palladius on the occasion of the latter's visit to Rome for episcopal consecration. We may be as certain as we can be of anything in this period that in the year 431 an Irish Christian community received Palladius as its first bishop.

Ireland, notoriously, had never formed a part of the Roman empire. But as with Gothia or Galloway there was a degree of cultural interaction between Ireland and the neighbouring provinces which may plausibly be invoked in an investigation of Irish Christian origins. There were trading relations of long standing between Britain and Ireland. As long ago as the first century Tacitus could observe in his memoir of his father-in-law Agricola that Ireland's harbours were known to the Roman forces in Britain 'through trading and merchants'. A variety of artefacts provides archaeological confirmation of lively commerce between eastern and southern Ireland and her neighbours to the east, Britain and quite possibly Gaul too, throughout the Roman period and beyond. Irish mercenaries served in the Roman army in Britain. Refugees from Britain sought asylum in Ireland. Pirates from Ireland were raiding the western seaboard of Britain from the third century onwards, for the same reasons that Ukrainian Goths were striking deep into Asia Minor. Forts such as those at Cardiff, Caer Gybi on Anglesey, Lancaster and Ravenglass were built to protect civilian Britain from these predators. In 367 an unprecedented alliance of Irish, Picts (from Scotland) and Saxons (from north Germany) overcame the defences of Britain and plundered the provinces for nearly two years. A chieftain remembered in Irish legend as Niall Noígiallach, Niall 'of the Nine Hostages', was raiding Britain in the late fourth century.

There was in addition Irish settlement in south-western Wales, the modern Dyfed, then known as Demetia, from perhaps as early as the fourth century. The evidence for this comes from three different types of source. There are memorial stones in the area inscribed with Irish names, often in the linear script known as *ogham*, which seems to have originated in the south-east of Ireland at about this period. There are place-names with Irish elements, hard to date, whose distribution to a great degree overlaps with the inscribed stones. And there are legends, which may contain a kernel of historical truth, about the fourth-century migration of a tribe called the Déisi from south-eastern Ireland to Wales. It is by means of these settlers, presumed to have maintained contact with their kinsfolk in Ireland, that elements of Romano-British culture are most likely to have seeped back there. One such element was language, the borrowing of a number of Latin loanwords into Old Irish. Another was religion: the Irish settlers were near neighbours of Caerleon-on-Usk with its Diocletianic martyrs Aaron and Julius, and its Christian landed gentry in the villas of Gwent and Glamorgan. It was probably from south Wales that Christianity first came to Ireland.

It was to these Irish Christians that Palladius was sent in 431. Who was he? A person of the same name is mentioned in an earlier annal in Prosper's chronicle, that for 429, which runs as follows: 'Agricola, a Pelagian, the son of the Pelagian Bishop Severianus, corrupts the churches of Britain by the insinuation of his teaching. However, at the suggestion of the Deacon Palladius, Pope Celestine sends Bishop Germanus of Auxerre as his legate and he guides the Britons back to the Catholic faith after routing the heretics.' The mission of Bishop Germanus to Britain in 429, and another one a few years later (perhaps

435/6), are attested in other sources. It is plain moreover from remarks made by Prosper in another of his works that there was anxiety that the taint of heresy might infect the Irish Christian community too.

Now the name Palladius was not particularly common in the western provinces of the empire. It is almost inconceivable that there were two different men called Palladius who both concerned themselves with the spiritual welfare of the Christian communities of the British Isles in the second quarter of the fifth century. We assume that there was a single Palladius, and we further assume that he held the office of deacon in one of the churches of northern Gaul, probably but not necessarily Auxerre, from which he was despatched to Rome in 429. That is all we know of Palladius. We do not know where the seat of his bishopric was, though we may suspect that it was in the south-east quarter of the island. We do not know how long his episcopate lasted, nor the names and doings of his successors (if any). But there he stands: the first known figure in the history of organized Irish Christianity. It is his misfortune to have been overshadowed by the next: Patrick.

Patrick is a famously difficult subject for the historian. It might be easiest to start by indicating some of the things which he did *not* do. He did not expel snakes from Ireland: the snakelessness of Ireland had been noted by the Roman geographer Solinus in the third century. He did not compose that wonderful hymn known as 'Saint Patrick's Breastplate': its language postdates him by about three centuries. He did not drive a chariot three times over his sister Lupait to punish her unchastity: the allegation that he did first occurs in a life of Patrick which is a farrago of legend put together about 400 years after his death. He did not use the leaves of the shamrock to illustrate the Persons of the Trinity for his converts: true, he might have done; but it is not until the seventeenth century that we are told that he did.

It would be possible to list many more things that Patrick did not do. Enough has been said to indicate that we are dealing with a figure whose reality has to a great degree been obscured by the accretion of later legend – and, one might add, of later controversy, whether sectarian or nationalistic. It cannot be too strongly urged that in studying Patrick it is absolutely essential to focus attention upon the earliest texts *only*: all others are suspect because their authors had axes to grind of one sort or another – the primacy of the church of Armagh, the ultra-Catholic character of Patrick, the ultra-Protestant character of Patrick, the claim that there were two Patricks, the claim that there was no Patrick because he was Palladius, and so forth. The earliest texts are two, both of them securely attributed – despite some doubts by hyper-critical scholars – to Patrick himself. In chronological order of composition they are the *Epistola* (or 'Letter') and the *Confessio* (or 'Declaration'). The *Epistola* is a letter addressed to the troops serving under the command of a certain Coroticus, denouncing them for the massacre of some of Patrick's converts. The *Confessio* is a justification of his career and conduct, apparently in answer to critics or accusers. Both works contain autobiographical materials of which Patrician scholars have wrestled to make sense.[5]

The wrestling is necessary because Patrick's writings are exceedingly difficult to interpret. This is partly because the texts might have been garbled in transmission, but above all it is owing to the language in which they are written. Patrick wrote in Latin, but of a very peculiar kind; indeed, his Latin is unique in the whole vast corpus of ancient or early Christian Latin literature. He had received little formal education – it was to cause him shame all his life – and he did not handle the Latin language with any facility. He longs, passionately longs, to make himself clear to his readers but has the utmost difficulty in so doing. His Latin is simple, awkward, laborious, sometimes ambiguous, occasionally unintelligible. It follows that there is a large latitude for debate about what his words actually mean, a latitude of which Patrician scholars have shown no bashfulness in liberally availing themselves.

All that is necessary here is to furnish a concise indication of what is generally agreed, except on the lunatic fringes of Patrician studies, about Patrick's career. I deliberately refrain from entering into questions of chronology, which present the thorniest of all problems for those in quest of the historical Patrick. It is accepted that his adult life fell within the fifth century. His episcopate in Ireland must postdate 431 because Prosper tells us that Palladius was Ireland's first bishop. Beyond that we need not go.

Patrick tells us in the *Confessio* that he was of British and landed birth. His family owned an estate at an unidentified place called Bannaventa. They were not only Christians but ecclesiastics: Patrick's grandfather Potitus was a priest and his father Calpornius a deacon.* Patrick

---

* It should be borne in mind both here and in later chapters that clerical celibacy, though from a very early date regarded as praiseworthy, was not widely enforced within the western church before the twelfth century; and thereafter only with difficulty.

was brought up a Christian but on his own admission was not a good one during his childhood. When he was nearly sixteen he was taken captive by Irish raiders and carried off into slavery in Ireland. For six years he worked as a herdsman at a place which he refers to as 'the forest of *Foclut* which is near the western sea' (tentatively identified as the region of Killala in County Mayo). It was during this period of slavery that his Christian faith deepened. At the end of six years he managed to escape, and after much danger and hardship found himself in Gaul, where he appears to have spent some time. Then he returned to Britain and rejoined his family. It was at home that he had the most important of all the dreams through which, as he believed, God guided his life: he experienced a call to undertake the conversion of the pagan Irish to Christianity. After (presumed) preparation he was consecrated a bishop and returned to Ireland. Although this has to be inferred, the likelihood is that the zone of his missionary labours was the northern half of the island. He spent the rest of his life in Ireland, despite perils and privations making converts and establishing a church. He also had to face accusations and misrepresentations about the conduct of his mission, to which the *Confessio* seems to have been the reply.

Patrick recalled his vocation in a well-known passage which yet can bear repetition because it is such an extraordinary piece of writing. It occurs in Chapters 23 to 25 of the *Confessio*.

> Again a few years later I was in Britain with my kinsfolk, and they welcomed me as a son and asked me earnestly not to go off anywhere and leave them this time, after the great tribulations which I had been through. And it was there that I saw one night in a vision a man coming from Ireland (his name was Victoricus), with countless letters; and he gave me one of them, and I read the heading of the letter, 'The Voice of the Irish', and as I read these opening words aloud I imagined at that very instant that I heard the voice of those who were beside the forest of Foclut which is near the western sea; and thus they cried, as though with one voice: 'We beg you, holy boy, to come and walk again among us.' And I was stung with remorse in my heart and could not read on, and so I awoke. Thanks be to God, that after so many years the Lord bestowed on them according to their cry. And another night (I do not know, God knows, whether it was within me or beside me) I was addressed in words which I heard and yet could not understand, except that at the end of the prayer He spoke thus: 'He who gave His life for you, He it is who speaks

within you,' and so I awoke, overjoyed. And again I saw Him praying within me and I was, as it were, inside my own body, and I heard Him above me, that is to say above my inner self, and He was praying there powerfully and groaning; and meanwhile I was dumbfounded and astonished and wondered who it could be that was praying within me, but at the end of the prayer He spoke and said that He was the Spirit, and so I awoke and remembered the apostle's words: 'The Spirit helps the weaknesses of our prayer; for we do not know what to pray for as we ought; but the Spirit Himself intercedes for us with unspeakable groans which cannot be expressed in words.'

No one can doubt the authenticity of the experience or fail to be moved by the writer's efforts to describe it. In another passage Patrick linked his vocation to the missionary imperatives of the Bible.

For He granted me such grace that through me many peoples should be reborn in God and afterwards be confirmed and that clergy should everywhere be ordained for them, to serve a people just now coming to the faith, and which the Lord chose from the ends of the earth, as He had promised of old through His prophets: 'The nations will come to you from the ends of the earth and will say, "How false are the idols which our fathers made for themselves; they are quite useless." ' And again, 'I have put you as a light among the nations, to be a means of salvation to the ends of the earth.'

And I wish to wait there for His promise (and He of course never deceives), as He promises in the gospel: 'They shall come from the east and from the west and shall sit down at table with Abraham and Isaac and Jacob', as we believe that believers will surely come from the whole world. And so then, it is our duty to fish well and diligently, as the Lord urges and teaches us, saying: 'Follow me, and I shall make you fishers of men;' and again he says through the prophets, 'See, I send many fishers and hunters, says God.' And so it was our bounden duty to spread our nets, so that a vast multitude and throng might be caught for God and there might be clergy everywhere to baptise and exhort a people that was poor and needy, as the Lord says – He urges and teaches in the gospel, saying: 'Go now, teach all nations, baptising them in the name of the Father and of the Son and of the Holy Spirit, teaching them to observe all things that I have commanded you.'

And there is much more in the same vein. Patrick could describe himself as 'a slave in Christ to a foreign people' and could pray that God should 'never allow me to be separated from His people whom He has won in the ends of the earth.'

Patrick's originality was that no one within western Christendom had thought such thoughts as these before, had ever previously been possessed by such convictions. As far as our evidence goes, he was the first person in Christian history to take the scriptural injunctions literally; to grasp that teaching all nations meant teaching even barbarians who lived beyond the frontiers of the Roman empire. Patrick crossed that threshold upon which, at the end of Chapter 1, we left Augustine and Prosper hesitating.

It is very difficult to assess Patrick's achievement. We have his own word, which we do not need to doubt, that he made 'many thousands' of converts. These included persons of every social rank from the nobility to slaves. He travelled widely: evangelization took him 'to the remote districts beyond which there was no one and where no one had ever penetrated to baptise'. He encouraged the adoption of the monastic way of life. He ordained priests, presumably after instruction. So much he tells us. It is reasonable to infer a little more: for example, that he established places where worship might occur, even if he did not build any churches (though he may have done); or that he encouraged his priests to acquire literacy in Latin and to multiply Christian texts.

Patrick initiated the conversion of the pagan Irish to Christianity and in so doing set an example to his successors in Ireland. A church which looked to Patrick as its founder would come to set a high value upon foreign missionary enterprise. This lay in the future. The immediate task of Patrick's successors was to continue the work which he had begun. It is unfortunate for us that the century following the floruit of Patrick is the most obscure in the history of Christianity in Ireland. When the surviving evidence becomes more robust, begins to increase, to diversify and to gain in reliability – that is to say, roughly speaking, from the latter part of the sixth century – we find ourselves on the threshold of the great age of the Irish saints, of Irish Christian scholarship and Irish Christian art. Even if we had no other sources of information we should be able to infer that much had happened since the time of Palladius and Patrick. Happily we do have a little information about the growth and consolidation of Christian culture in sixth-century Ireland.

There survives a list of decisions taken by a synod or gathering of bishops known as the 'First Synod of St Patrick'.[6] This is misleading: the attribution to Patrick comes from a later period and is erroneous. It is impossible to pinpoint the real date of the synod with any degree of accuracy, though a plausible case can be made for somewhere in the first half of the sixth century. The interest of the rulings for us is that they display an Irish church in a society which was still to a great degree pagan. We hear of Christians taking oaths before soothsayers 'in the manner of pagans', of Christian clerics standing as legal sureties for pagans, and of pagans who attempt, intriguingly, to make offerings to Christian churches – they are to be refused. We get a sense of Christianity and paganism co-existing and in some sense interpenetrating in the Ireland for which the bishops legislated.

Two of the rulings concern the building of churches and two more seem to assume that episcopal visitation of the churches in a diocese will occur at least from time to time. No surviving church structures in Ireland may be assigned to so early a period as the sixth century. Place-names, however, come to our aid. Several Irish place-names derive from the Old Irish word *domnach*; for example Donnybrook, Dublin, or Donaghmore in Co. Tyrone. The word *domnach* is a loanword from the Latin *dominicum*, meaning 'a church building'. Now *dominicum* in this particular sense was current in ecclesiastical Latin only between the years *c.* 300 and *c.* 600. It follows that place-names of this type indicate churches built before the seventh century. Another category of Irish names derives from Late Latin *senella cella*, Old Irish *sen chell*, meaning 'old church'; this has yielded modern names such as Shankill. The term *sen chell* as a place-name element was current by about 670 at latest. It follows that 'new churches' were being founded in large numbers in the course of the seventh century; and that the 'old churches' which had preceded them were plentiful enough to be a recognizable category of building.

Christian churches imply Christian texts. Patrick was soaked in the Bible, as may be readily seen from passages in his *Confessio* quoted above, and he would have seen to it that the priests he ordained were too. Familiarity with the Bible and the Christian liturgy presupposed two things: learning Latin and acquiring the technology of writing. Ancient Ireland had a rich oral repertoire of poetry and narrative but early Christian leaders there seem to have been reluctant to translate Christian texts into the vernacular and write them down; possibly the

Irish vernacular was held to be tainted by association with paganism. (It should be said that these inhibitions were overcome at a later stage and that in the course of time Ireland developed a rich Christian literature in Old Irish.) Whatever the reason, early Irish converts, unlike Ulfila's Goths, were not presented with a vernacular Bible. So Patrick's clerical disciples had to learn Latin. Moreover, they had to learn Latin as a foreign language. The Provençal audiences of Caesarius, the flock of Bishop Martin in Touraine, even the rustics of Galicia, all spoke Latin of a sort. The Irish did not. Learning Latin, for them, meant schools and grammar and a lot of hard work. It was the need to acquire facility in Latin – in an environment which lacked the educational system which was such a central feature of late-antique literary culture in the Roman empire – which made the pursuit of learning an essential feature of Irish Christian communities in the early Middle Ages. Much was to follow from this. Early results were impressive: the first Irishman who has left us a substantial body of Latin writings was St Columbanus. He was born in about 545 and devoted his youth to 'liberal and grammatical studies', in the words of his earliest biographer: this would have been in the 550s and early 560s. The Latin of Columbanus was confident, supple and elegant, altogether different from the raw uncouth Latin of Patrick. It is plain that by the middle of the sixth century it was possible in Ireland to acquire a really good Latin education.

The earliest Irish Latin texts that have survived to the present day date from about the year 600. The so-called *Codex Usserianus Primus* is a copy of the gospels, now preserved in Trinity College, Dublin, written in ink on parchment with a quill pen. The so-called Springmount Tablets, discovered in a peat bog in County Antrim and now in the National Museum of Ireland, are six little wooden tablets measuring about 7.5 × 20 cm, each of which has one face recessed and filled with a light coating of wax; on to the surface of the wax has been incised with a stylus the text of Psalms xxx–xxxii. Materials, script and technique differ as between the codex and the tablets, but in each case the writing is assured and accomplished. These artefacts are the product of an Irish clerical community which took writing in Latin for granted.

These diverse sources, a selection only, have something to tell us of the Christianization of Ireland: new disciplines, new buildings, new learning, new artefacts, were imported and naturalized. And subtly changed in the process? The church imported into Ireland had to adapt itself to Irish conditions. There was nothing surprising about this. Missionary Christianity has to have both resilience and adaptability if it is to be widely acceptable. In the Ireland of Palladius and Patrick, Christianity entered a social world which was rural in its economy, tribal and familial in its organization and pre-literate – ogham excepted – in its culture. These characteristics of Irish society were bound to affect both the way in which Christianity could be presented and the way in which it would be received. Despite the trading and other connections with Roman Britain, the characteristic tell-tales of Roman dominion and civilization were absent: towns, roads, coinage, written law, bureaucracy, taxation. One might reasonably guess that Patrick's Irish congregations were a good deal less touched by *Romanitas* than the Tervingi of Dacia among whom Ulfila had ministered.

In Ireland the fundamental political unit – the very word 'political' is perhaps something of a misnomer in this context – was the *tuath* (plural *tuatha*): a human grouping held together partly by kinship, partly by clientage, in occupation of a shifting zone of territory under the presidency of a dynasty of kings maintained by tribute in kind. The role of the king was religious as well as secular. He had to defend his people and win fame and plunder in warfare with other kings (not unlike Edwin of Northumbria after him, though on a smaller scale); he also had to mediate between his people and the gods to ensure fat cattle and plentiful harvests. *Tuatha* varied greatly in area and population, but it may safely be said that none was very big for there were perhaps 150–200 of them in early medieval Ireland. There was nothing systematic and nothing static about authority in the Ireland of St Patrick. Like biological cells, *tuatha* were constantly on the move, splitting, fusing, splitting again, as one king achieved a temporary supremacy over his neighbours only to lose it after a few years.

How could a Christian ecclesiastical organization build its house upon such shifting sands? This was a question that had not arisen before. Within the Roman empire it had been normal for the church to graft itself on to the existing framework of civil administration. Thus, for example, the civil province of Gallia Narbonensis, administered from Narbo (Narbonne), turned into an ecclesiastical province: its chief bishop (or archbishop, or metropolitan) came to reside in Narbonne and his subject (or suffragan) bishops were those of the various towns within the civil province – Béziers, Carcassonne, Lodève, Nîmes, Uzès, Toulouse and so forth. But in Ireland there were no towns, no provinces, no fixed boundaries. So what was to be done? One answer was to associate bishoprics with sites connected with particularly prominent dynasties which might be expected to show stamina and continuity. Armagh, for instance, was an early ecclesiastical foundation, whether correctly or not attributed to Patrick does not matter here; it is suggestively close to the secular stronghold of Emain Macha, ancient seat of Ulster kings. At Cashel in County Tipperary association is closer still; the cathedral stands right on top of the Rock of Cashel, seat of Munster kings.

Kinship and clientage, mentioned above as the cement of the *tuatha*, were the strongest social forces in early medieval Ireland. Patrick's accommodation to one of these may perhaps be seen in his reference to 'the sons of kings who travel with me'. Setting out the rights and obligations of kings, lords, kinsmen, the whole ordering (sometimes idealized) of a graded, complex, status-conscious society, was the responsibility of a class of specialists (*brithem*, plural *brithemin*) who memorized, pronounced and handed down the law. There were specialists in another branch of learning too, which cannot strictly be called literature because like the law it was orally transmitted: the bards (*fili*, plural *filid*) who recited poems, genealogies, stories, works such as the great Irish epic the *Táin Bó Cuailnge* (*The Cattle Raid of Cooley*). Together the lawyers and bards buttressed the sense of identity, the custom and morality of early Ireland. How were Christian identity, custom and morality to infuse themselves into so stout and immemorial a texture?

There was one distinctive Christian institution which proved itself brilliantly capable of meshing and marrying with Irish social habits: monasticism. Despite the references to monks in Patrick's writings it is likely that the implanting of monasticism in Ireland on any serious scale was a development of that crucial but obscure sixth century. It is also likely that the monastic impulse, though it could have reached Ireland by more than one route, was felt particularly strongly from south Wales. One of the decrees of the 'First Synod' concerns British clergy who travel to Ireland. The south Welsh St Samson, whom we encountered in the last chapter, was a famous monastic founder and traveller. His earliest biographer shows him visiting Ireland and making monastic recruits there: though the passage is now thought to be a later interpolation into the text (above, p. 60) it may preserve a reliable tradition of a Hibernian visit by Samson.

We must remember that we are in an age when there were many shades of monasticism. A time would come when to be a monk meant to follow the monastic rule compiled by St Benedict of Nursia (d. *c.* 550). But the gradual coming to dominance of Benedict's Rule in the western church at large was a very slow business, spread over several centuries. The late antique and early medieval periods were characterized by a ceaselessly proliferating diversity of rules. A monastic founder devised his own rule for his own monks to follow. Monasticism was therefore extraordinarily adaptable and transplantable, an institution with a marked degree of flexibility. In this respect it contrasted with the 'Roman' structure of organization in the secular church.

In Ireland monasticism made its appeal largely because it proved capable of accommodating itself to the structures of kinship and client-age. Ancient Irish law did not know of individual property. Land belonged to a family and could not be alienated. Founders and bene-factors wishing to endow monastic houses with land could not do so by outright grants of absolute rights in perpetuity such as were known to Roman law. Instead, monasteries endowed with family land became family concerns, family possessions. The founder's kin would supply the abbot and more than a few of the monks; the community would service the kin by praying for them, furnishing hospitality to them, leasing land to them on easy terms, looking after them in old age. A successful monastery could give birth to daughter houses or could acquire a following of houses which chose to opt for its customs and fellowship, just as a king acquired lordship over retainers or over other *tuatha*. In their physical appearance monasteries even *looked like* the fort-farms of the secular aristocracy with their dry-stone enclosing walls and their scatter of buildings within for human and animal inmates.[7] An exceptionally fine example, Inishmurray off the coast of Sligo, may be seen in plate 7.

These were not of course the only reasons why the Irish took to monasticism with such zest. The appeal of a life of ascetic self-denial was felt as strongly in Ireland as in other parts of Christendom. In an insecure and often violent world monastic communities were, or were intended to be, havens of security. They were rightly perceived as agents for the diffusion of Christianity in society. They were places where 'sacred technology' was practised, the crafts of writing and decorating books, of working in wood and stone and metal; places therefore where exchange could occur. In this respect the bigger monasteries came to be the closest thing to towns in early medieval Ireland.

There can be no doubting the fact that monasticism became enormously significant in Irish Christianity. Some historians have even gone so far as to claim that the Irish church became almost exclusively monastic in character. The argument is further advanced that branches of the Christian church in close proximity to Ireland, such as Wales, developed in the same manner; and that this distinctive model was exported to further neighbouring areas – from Wales to Brittany, from Ireland to western Scotland. Thus, the argument concludes, there came into existence a Celtic church which differed in its organization and customs from the Roman church.

It is now recognized that this is misleading. No church can be wholly monastic. The sacramental functions of a bishop (confirmation, ordination, consecration of churches, etc.) cannot be performed by an abbot, however holy and revered. The preponderance of writing generated in and for monasteries among the surviving written sources has given a biased impression of the standing of monasticism in Ireland. It is possible to detect – and some of the evidence has been glanced at above – the vitality of the secular, non-monastic church in the sixth and seventh centuries. There never was a 'Celtic church'. Irish churchmen repeatedly and sincerely professed their Roman allegiances: and if there were divergent practices between Rome and Ireland, well, so there were between Rome and Constantinople – or Alexandria or Carthage or Milan or Toledo. The terms 'Roman' and 'Celtic' are too monolithic. In terms of custom and practice there were many churches in sixth- and seventh-century Europe, not One Church. Christendom was many-mansioned.

The sixth century saw the foundation of a number of communities which were to achieve great renown in the history of Irish spirituality and learning – Bangor, Clonard, Clonfert, Clonmacnois, Durrow, Kildare, Monasterboice, to name but a few. A feature of special significance for us is the appearance of monastic confederations spread over a wide area, chains of houses which owed their existence to a single founder and followed the rule drawn up by him. The founder best known to us is Columba (*c.* 520–597), who established three famous monasteries, at Derry, Durrow and Iona, and a number of lesser ones as well. A deservedly celebrated life of Columba was composed about ninety years after his death by Adomnán, ninth abbot of Iona and a member of the founder's kin. It is to this wonderfully spirited and informative document that we owe most of what we know about Columba and the monastic regime which he favoured.[8]

Columba's chain of monasteries crossed the sea: Iona lies off the island of Mull, itself off the western coast of Scotland. But it did not cross cultures. Iona was in the kingdom of Dalriada, which comprised the western islands and coastal hinterland from the Clyde to Ardnamur-chan. This area had been settled by Irish migrants at a slightly later date than their settlements in Dyfed. In founding a monastery on Iona, therefore, Columba was among people of his own language and culture. There has been a good deal of discussion about his motives for the move to Iona, traditionally dated to 563, which need not delay us here. Adomnán, and the Iona community for whom he wrote, were clear about the principal reason: 'In the forty-second year of his age Columba sailed away from Ireland to Britain, wishing to be a pilgrim for Christ.' We have already met the idea of the Christian's life as one of exile or pilgrimage in the writings of St Augustine of Hippo. Patrick had described himself in the *Epistola* as 'an exile (*profuga*) for the love of God'. We encounter here another point of contact between Christian idealism and Irish social custom. Exile was one of the most severe penalties known to Irish law – severe because it removed the person so punished from the supportive network of kinsmen, lords, retainers and dependants. The exile was quite literally *dis-integrated* from the protective social and emotional fabric in which he had been cocooned and turned into a defenceless individual.

Columba's exile was not lifelong. There is plentiful evidence in Adomnán's biography that he went to and fro between Scotland and Ireland in the years after the foundation of Iona. But some went further down the path of lifelong pilgrimage or exile, cutting loose more decisively from earthly ties in the fashion which the author of Hebrews had commended in Abraham. The pioneer was Columbanus.*

We last glimpsed Columbanus (above, p. 88) receiving an excellent

---

* It is tiresome that we have two near-contemporary saintly Irishmen with the same name, Columba, the Latin word for 'dove'. The older of the two, Columba of Iona, is sometimes called Columba the Elder, sometimes by his Irish name Columcille, 'Dove of the Church'. The younger is usually known by his Latin name in its masculine form, Columbanus, sometimes Englished as Columban. In this book I follow the convention of referring to the elder as Columba and to the younger as Columbanus.

grounding in Latin in the middle years of the sixth century. In about 565 he entered the monastery of Bangor in County Down, recently founded by St Comgall. This was already a fairly considerable step on the road to exile. Columbanus was a native of Leinster, and in betaking himself to Bangor he was, as his biographer Jonas of Bobbio noted, 'leaving his native country'.[9] At Bangor he would have been well placed to hear the news of Columba's exploits in Dalriada. His abbot, Comgall, was another founder who presided over a network of monastic houses, including at least one on the island of Tiree (though the source for this is late and perhaps doubtful), where there was also a monastery of the Iona network. However, exile to Bangor was not enough for Columbanus: as Jonas explained, he wanted to live out to the letter the commands uttered to Abraham. Accordingly, after gaining the reluctant assent of Comgall, he set off for Gaul, probably in the late 580s. There, helped by royal and aristocratic patronage, he founded three monastic houses at Annegray, Luxeuil and Les Fontaines on the edge of the Vosges mountains about thirty miles west of the modern town of Mulhouse. After a series of somewhat stormy brushes with the Frankish episcopate and Queen Brunhilde, Columbanus moved on to Bregenz, at the eastern end of Lake Constance, where he planned to found another monastery but in the event did not. His last move took him over the Alps to Italy, where he founded his last monastery at Bobbio, in the Apennines inland from Genoa. There he died in the year 615.

Pilgrimage, in the sense of ascetic renunciation of homeland and kinsfolk, is of special importance in our understanding of the phenomenon of conversion in the early Middle Ages. Pilgrimage merged insensibly into mission. The monasteries that were founded by the exiled holy men had something of the character of mission stations. It was not that they were established primarily among pagans; indeed, they could not have been, dependent as they were on wealthy patrons, necessarily Christian (if we except the case of the pagan would-be benefactors in Ireland), for their endowments. Columba settled among the Christian Irish of Dalriada, Columbanus in the Christian kingdom of the Franks. But their monastic communities were situated on the margins of Christendom, and had what might be called 'diffusive potential' among nearby laity who were Christian only in the most nominal of senses.

The point may be illustrated from episodes in the careers of Columba and Columbanus. Bede tells us that Columba came to Britain 'to preach the word of God to the provinces of the northern Picts', that is, to the peoples who inhabited north-eastern Scotland between (roughly speaking) Inverness, Aberdeen and Perth. It is unlikely that this was in fact Columba's motive. He came as a pilgrim or exile. Columba was no more the apostle of Pictland than Ulfila was the apostle of the Goths. Bede's comments on Columba fall in the same chapter as his two sentences on Ninian and like them may reflect the preoccupations of his own day more than they do the realities of Columba's. However, we have the evidence of Adomnán that Columba had dealings with the Picts and that he did make some conversions among them. He visited the Pictish King Bridei at his stronghold near Inverness on more than one occasion and converted two households of (apparently) the Pictish aristocracy to Christianity. Here is the story of one conversion as told by Adomnán.

> At one time when the holy man [i.e. Columba] was making a journey on the other side of the Spine of Britain [Adomnán's term for the western Grampians which divided Dalriada from Pictland] beside the lake of the river Ness, he was suddenly inspired by the Holy Spirit, and said to the brothers who travelled along with him: 'Let us hasten towards the holy angels that have been sent from the highest regions of heaven to conduct the soul of a pagan, and who await our coming thither so that we may give timely baptism, before he dies, to that man, who has preserved natural goodness through his whole life, into extreme old age.' Saying this, the aged saint went as fast as he could, ahead of his companions, until he came to the farmland that is called Airchartdan [Urquhart]. And a certain old man whom he found there, Emchath by name, hearing and believing the word of God preached by the saint, was baptised; and thereupon, gladly and confidently, with the angels that came to meet him he departed to the Lord. And his son Virolec also believed and was baptised, with his whole house.

As the story of a conversion, it leaves something to be desired. We should not blame Adomnán for this: what *he* was interested in was (in his own words) 'the manifestation of angels coming to meet the soul of Emchath'. For our purposes the tale is of interest in showing that Columba the monastic founder was also, on occasions, an evangelist.

From Jonas' biography of Columbanus we may quote an episode

of somewhat similar drift that occurred during his sojourn at Bregenz in or about the year 611.

> And then they came to the place where they were going [i.e. Bregenz]. The man of God said that it did not really meet his requirements, but in order to sow the Christian faith in the heathen thereabouts he would stay there for a while. The peoples there were called the Suevi. And while he was there working among the inhabitants of that place he found them preparing to make a profane offering: and they placed a great barrel which in their language they called a *cupa*, which holds twenty measures or more of ale, in the midst of them. The man of God went up to them and asked what they proposed to do with it. And they said that they were going to sacrifice to their god Woden. He hearing their evil project blew on the cask and it burst with a mighty crack and the ale poured out. It was quite clear that there was a devil hidden in the barrel who by means of the evil drink took captive the souls of those who sacrificed. The barbarians saw this and were astonished and said that they had a great man of God among them who could thus dissolve a barrel fully bound with hoops as it was. He rebuked them and preached the word of God to them and urged them to refrain from these sacrifices. Many of them were persuaded by his words and turned to the Christian faith and accepted baptism. Others who had already been baptised but remained in the grip of pagan error heeded his admonitions as a good shepherd of the church and returned to the observance of gospel teaching.

Of course, we may again wonder – but did Jonas? – in what sense these Suevi had become Christians and what happened to their spiritual life after Columbanus had moved on to Bobbio in the following year. We do know that Columbanus' disciple Gallus was left behind as a hermit beside Lake Constance and undertook evangelizing operations there. The site of his hermitage was to become one of the most celebrated of all medieval monasteries, taking its name from him – St Gallen.

We do not have to rely on his biographer to sense the apostolic impulse in Columbanus. It is attested in his own writings. In a letter written in 610 he spoke of 'my vow to make my way to the heathen to preach the gospel to them'. Was Columbanus a monk or was he a missionary? The antithesis is misplaced. To be the kind of monk he was, in the age in which he lived, was also to be an evangelist.

CHAPTER FOUR

The New Constantines

My heart is white with joy; your words are great and
good. It is enough for me to see your clothing, your
arms and the rolling houses in which you travel, to understand how much intelligence and strength you have . . .
I have been told that you can help us . . . You shall
instruct us. We will do all you wish. The country is at
your disposal.

Moshoeshoe, king of Lesotho, to Eugène Casalis, 1833

THE ENTRY OF the Tervingi into the empire in 376, the victory of
Fritigern at Adrianople two years later, and the settlement of his people
under treaty arrangements in Moesia four years after that proved to
be but the opening scenes in the political drama which ended with
the collapse of the Roman empire in the west and its replacement by
a number of barbarian successor-states. It is as well to be clear about
what this process was *not* before we go any further. The empire did
not disappear in the fifth century. It is true that there was no emperor
in the west after 476, but no one at the time could have guessed that
this was more than a temporary hiatus. Authority reverted, at least in
theory, to the emperor in Constantinople, where the Roman empire
would survive for another millennium. But the western provinces did
effectively come under new masters. They arrived by a variety of means.
Whenever and wherever possible, the imperial government tried to
control, or at least to influence and shape, the process of arrival. As
we have seen, the descendants of Fritigern's Tervingi were settled in
Aquitaine in 418. We may now call them, as they had begun to call
themselves, the Visigoths. In the course of the next half-century they
were sometimes used as military federates in the name of the emperor
of the day. For example, it was the Visigoths who bore the main brunt
of the fighting at the battle of Châlons in 451, in which Attila and

the Huns were defeated. Another contingent of Germanic troops at this decisive battle was furnished by the Burgundians. They too had been settled under treaty, with primary responsibility for defending the entry into Gaul by way of the upper valleys of the Rhône system against yet another Germanic people, the Alamans, who were pressing into the sensitive gap between Rhine and Danube in the Black Forest region. In the course of the fifth century the Burgundian kingdom expanded to include much of the Rhône valley and what is now western Switzerland. Another group of Goths, descendants of the Greuthingi who had been defeated by the Huns in the 370s, emerged in the northern Balkans out of the wreckage left by the collapse of the Hun empire in the 450s. They entered Italy under their leader Theoderic on behalf of the authorities in Constantinople to fight the empire's enemies. The Ostrogothic kingdom of Italy established by Theoderic in 493 was notable for the harmonious co-existence within it of Goths and Romans.

The Burgundians, Ostrogoths and Visigoths constituted three successor-states in the western provinces of the empire which were founded to some degree in obedience to imperial political initiatives. Other peoples seized initiatives for themselves. In the winter of 406–7 the Rhine frontier collapsed and was penetrated by numbers of barbarian peoples, among them the Sueves and the Vandals. They made their way through Gaul, then in 409 moved south across the Pyrenees and made themselves masters of the provinces of Roman Spain. The Vandals crossed the Straits of Gibraltar in 429 and set up a kingdom for themselves, governed from Carthage, in what had been the imperial provinces of north Africa. Their place in Spain was subsequently taken by the Visigoths, while the Sueves were confined to a kingdom in the north-west quarter of the peninsula. All these peoples had lived in more or less close proximity to the empire's frontiers before they crossed them. We may think of them as being in general not unlike the Gothic peoples among whom Ulfila worked in the fourth century, already touched to varying degrees by Roman culture. The process of acculturation to Romano-Mediterranean ways and values became for all of them more intense after entry into the empire.

What is specially relevant for us is that migration and settlement upon imperial soil were accompanied by conversion to Christianity. This had been a part of the agreement worked out between Fritigern and Valens before the crossing of the Danube in 376. Here is the fifth-century church historian Sozomen: 'As if to return thanks to Valens, and as a guarantee that he would be a friend to him in all things, he [Fritigern] adopted the emperor's religion and persuaded all the barbarians under his rule to adopt the same belief.'[1] We should understand this conversion, it has been observed, not as 'adherence body and soul to a new set of beliefs' but rather as 'a determination to change public practice'.[2] Official thinking appears to have been: we'll take these people, but they must accept our empire's faith. This was a pattern that repeated itself. Burgundians, Ostrogoths, Sueves and Vandals all accepted Christianity soon after their entry into the empire. It is a process that has to be inferred, because – remarkably enough – our sources do not mention it as such. Reasons for the reticence of the sources can be offered, some more convincing than others. However, modern scholars are agreed that the inference is a sound one. The other notable feature of the conversion of these barbarian peoples was that they all adopted the heretical, Arian form of Christianity as opposed to the orthodox or 'Catholic' credal formulations of Nicaea. (There were some temporary exceptions to this rule. One of the early Suevic kings in the middle years of the fifth century was a Catholic, but his successors were all Arians. The Burgundian rulers seem to have been Catholic in the middle years of the fifth century but went Arian towards its end.) The reasons for this Germanic preference for the creed of Arius remain elusive: we have simply to accept it as part of the overlapping pattern of religious allegiance in these years. On top of the world of rural pagans slowly being coaxed into some semblance of Christian belief and observance by activists like Martin of Tours, alongside the Catholic bishops in their cities, the Catholic suburban monasteries, the Catholic gentry and the Catholic middle class, we must now make mental room for an Arian clerical hierarchy, Arian kings and queens and warrior aristocrats, Arian churches with Arian liturgies being sung within them. This religious apartheid persisted in the kingdoms concerned until their governing circles decided to go over to Catholicism. This occurred in Burgundy during the reign of King Sigismund (516–23), in the Vandal kingdom when it was reconquered by Justinian's armies and re-united to the empire in 533–4, in the Suevic kingdom in the 560s, and in the Visigothic kingdom in the years 587–9. The Ostrogothic realm had been destroyed in the course of Justinian's attempts to reconquer Italy as he had reconquered Africa. Hardly were these long and costly campaigns over – they lasted almost without a break from 535 to 553 – than Italy was invaded by another group of migrating Germanic invaders, the Lombards, from 568 onwards. The religious affiliations of the Lombards are not easy to follow, but there was certainly an Arian presence in the Lombard kingdom until the middle years of the seventh century: the last Lombard king known to have been an Arian was Rothari (636–52).

The barbarian peoples mentioned hitherto had in common a previous experience at fairly close quarters of Romano-Mediterranean cultural values. A partial exception must be made of the Lombards, but even they had lived for two generations in the former Roman province of Pannonia – rather like the Goths in Dacia – before their invasion of Italy. They also had in common the fact that they founded their kingdoms in the most Romanized provinces of the former western empire – Italy, Africa, Spain and southern Gaul. If we make a mental journey in the second half of the fifth century northwards from the Burgundian or Aquitanian-Visigothic kingdom we find ourselves entering a world where the shading is subtly different. The northern provinces of Gaul and the offshore provinces of Britannia had been less influenced by Roman culture than, let us say, the Gallia Narbonensis of Caesarius of Arles. The barbarians who took over these northern regions had experienced less previous contact with Roman ways than, for instance, the Goths. They took longer to integrate themselves with the culture of the empire into which they had blundered. Most notably, they did not adopt Christianity at once; and when they did, it was not the Arian but the Catholic variety which they chose. Who were these people? It is time to have a closer look at them, for they will occupy us much in this and the following two chapters. We shall start with the Franks.

Franci, Franks, was the name given in Roman sources from the second half of the third century to a variety of tribes settled opposite the Gallic province of Germania Inferior; that is, east of the Rhine in the area between, approximately, Confluentes (Koblenz, where Mosel meets Rhine) and Noviomagus (Nijmegen). They took advantage of the troubles of the empire to launch devastating raids into Gaul. One such raid, as we saw in Chapter 1, even penetrated as far as Spain. As on the Danube frontier, so on the lower Rhine, the fourth century witnessed intermittent hostilities between Roman and barbarian with long periods of relative peace in between times. Pacification of the Frankish tribesmen under Constantine and Julian gave rise to peaceful crossings of the frontier by merchants going to and fro and by Franks enlisting in the Roman army for garrison service in northern Gaul. Some of their cemeteries have been identified by archaeologists. One fourth-century tombstone neatly sums up this phase of Franco-Roman co-existence: *Francus ego civis, Romanus miles in armis,* 'I am a Frankish citizen, a Roman soldier under arms.' In the 350s the Emperor Julian settled one group of Franks, the *Salii* or Salians, inside the empire in the boggy and unappealing territory called Toxandria just to the south of the estuary of the Rhine, in the region which is now traversed by the Belgian–Dutch border north of Antwerp. In the collapse of order following the breach of the Rhine frontier by Sueves and Vandals in 406–7 a Salian Frankish principality obscurely emerged in Toxandria and spread over the area to its south in what is now northern Belgium. Another group of Franks coalesced further east in the Rhineland round Cologne. The latter group are usually known as the Ripuarian Franks.

Only fragments of information survive about the activities of the Franks in the desperately confused politics of fifth-century Gaul. Heroic attempts have been made to construct a plausible narrative. All founder on the rock of the simple but compelling rule that bricks cannot be made without straw. But in the last quarter of the century straws begin to accumulate. The first ruler of the Salian Franks of whom we can form any impression is Childeric, who seems to have died in 481 or 482. A contemporary who must have know what he was talking about, Bishop Remigius, lets us know in a surviving letter that Childeric administered the province of Belgica Secunda. The capital city of the province was Rheims, which was also the seat of Remigius' bishopric. Belgica Secunda embraced a vast area of northern Gaul bounded by the Channel, the Seine, the Vosges and the Ardennes. It is plain that by Childeric's time – and possibly owing to his agency – Salian dominion had expanded well beyond its early bounds in Toxandria. Childeric was buried at Tournai, another of the towns of Belgica Secunda. We know this because his grave was discovered there in 1653. It could be identified as his because it contained his signet-ring, which portrayed the full-face bust of a long-haired warrior in late Roman military uniform bearing a lance and surmounted by the legend CHILDERICI REGIS, '[by order] of King Childeric'. The signet-ring with its Latin inscription hints at acquaintance with Roman

governmental routine. It was not the only object among the grave-goods which could be interpreted in a quasi-official light. There was a shoulder-brooch of the sort worn as a badge of rank by late Roman officials of high status and there was an enormous amount of gold in both coin – minted in the eastern half of the empire – and ornaments.*
Some scholars have suggested that Childeric and his Franks might have been settled under treaty in northern Gaul, like the Visigoths in the south or the Burgundians in the east. Conceivably they had; in any case we should not rule out communications between them and the imperial government in Constantinople. These 'Roman' objects in Childeric's funerary deposit must be balanced by others of different suggestiveness. There was jewellery of barbarian type, a throwing-axe, the severed head of his presumed favourite charger. Recent excavations at Tournai have revealed three pits close to the site of Childeric's grave, each containing skeletons of about ten horses. Carbon-14 testing of these pits yielded a late-fifth-century date; and they were cut into by sixth-century burials. It cannot be *demonstrated* that these pits were connected with Childeric's funeral rites but it looks extremely likely. Ritual slaughter of horses and the eating of their flesh were identified by early medieval missionaries as heathen customs. Childeric therefore (or those who buried him) looked both ways. Inside the Christian empire on its northern fringes, the Salian Franks yet maintained their ancestral observances. After all, Childeric's gods had done very well by him. Who were his gods? It is a question to which no confident answer may be offered. Our ignorance of the Germanic paganisms of the early Middle Ages has already been lamented in Chapter 1. We must draw attention to it again here, with renewed lamentation. We can be reasonably sure, however, that for Childeric (as for Edwin of Northumbria) the cult of a god or gods of war, with the appropriate rituals, would have loomed large. There are hints too, in our early sources, that the veneration of ancestors was a part of the religious observance of the Frankish kings. The dynasty claimed a supernatural origin: Childeric's father Merovech – whence the name Merovingian for the family – was held to have been the son of a sea-monster.

Childeric's son Clovis succeeded his father as king of the Salian

---

* The ornaments included some 300 golden bees, later to be interpreted as a symbol of French royalty and adopted as part of his imperial insignia by Napoleon I.

Franks in 481–2.* Clovis was a great warlord who expanded Salian dominion in every direction and he was the first Christian king of the Franks. Not only was he a convert to Christianity, he was a convert to *Catholic* Christianity. These features made Clovis significant for the writer who is our principal source of information about him, Gregory, bishop of Tours from 573 to 594. We have already encountered Gregory. He it was who listed the foundation of churches in Touraine, who was the friend of Aredius, who told moral tales warning against the perils of rusticity. Gregory's most famous work was his *Ten Books of Histories* (often inaccurately called the *History of the Franks*).[3] Justly renowned as the most readable of all early medieval narratives, the *Histories* are vivid, chatty, unbuttoned. With what art the bishop coaxes his readers into accepting his stories in the same relaxed fashion as he tells them! But the *Histories* had a serious purpose too; or rather, several serious purposes. If we confine ourselves to what Gregory had to say about Clovis, we need to take account of three things. First, Gregory felt concern about the squabbling kings of his own day and their endless internecine wars: he wished to hold up their ancestor before them as an example of strenuous valour. Second, Gregory wanted to show how God had helped the Catholic Clovis in all his wars, not just in some of them: this affected his chronology of the king's reign and conversion. Third, we must make a large allowance for ignorance: like every historian Gregory was at the mercy of his sources, which were meagre. Writing as he was a century later, Gregory of Tours did not know much about Clovis. Because he didn't, we can't either.

Gregory has, however, left us a great literary set piece on the conversion of Clovis. We must attend to it not because of its claims to tell us what really happened – they can be shown to be ill-founded – but because it shows us how Gregory thought it appropriate to present a king's conversion, and because of its literary influence upon other descriptions of royal conversions. As Gregory tells it the story of the conversion of Clovis goes like this. Clovis's queen, Clotilde, was a Burgundian princess and a Catholic Christian. She wished to have their

---

* A momentary digression on his name, usually rendered *Chlodovechus* in our Latin sources, representing a vernacular *Chlodovech*, with two strong gutturals. In the course of time the gutturals softened, to give something like *Lodovec*, which could be Latinized as *Lodovecus, Ludovicus.* From this descend the names *Ludwig, Ludovic* and *Louis,* all synonyms of Clovis.

first-born son baptized and nagged her husband to permit it. She chided him for his attachment to the pagan gods but he was firmly loyal to them. The queen had the infant baptized. He promptly died, whereupon the king rounded on her, seeing in his son's death a demonstration of the impotence of her Christian God. Clotilde had another son, whom also she caused to be baptized. The baby began to ail and Clovis predicted a second death. But the queen prayed and the infant survived. She continued her pressure upon the king to bring about his conversion. Eventually there came a time when Clovis took the field against the Alamans. Finding himself hard-pressed in battle, Clovis called upon 'Jesus Christ . . . Thou that art said to grant victory to those that hope in Thee', promising to believe and to undergo baptism in return for victory. The Alamans were defeated. At the queen's prompting Bishop Remigius of Rheims began to instruct Clovis; but secretly, because Clovis feared that his subjects would not permit their king to forsake the ancestral gods. But his apprehensions proved baseless, for his people spontaneously decided 'to follow that immortal God whom Remigius preaches'. All was made ready, and Clovis 'like a new Constantine' was cleansed in the waters of baptism. Three thousand of his armed followers were also baptized; so too his sister Albofleda; and another sister Lantechildis, who had previously been an Arian.

There are four essentials in this account: the role of a Christian queen in converting her pagan husband; the power of the Christian God to give victory in battle; the king's reluctance, springing from anxiety as to whether he could carry his people with him; and the happy conclusion in the baptism of the king, some members of his family and large numbers of his following. We shall encounter these themes again. If they seem, with repetition, to betray something of the character of a topos or conventional literary formula, we need not doubt their fundamental plausibility.

Gregory's account was intended to be straightforward but it hints at complexities. It is of great interest to discover that one of Clovis's sisters was already a Christian at the time of his baptism, albeit an Arian one. This snippet of information acquires more significance when considered alongside a strictly contemporary source. There survives a letter to Clovis from Bishop Avitus of Vienne in which the writer congratulated the king upon his conversion. Avitus wrote in a convoluted and rhetorical Latin, but what he seems plainly to say at one point is that the conversion of Clovis which he celebrates was not a conversion from paganism to Christianity but one from heresy to orthodox Catholicism. In the context, the heresy can only have been Arianism.

This complicates the picture considerably. It raises the near-certainty that Arian proselytizers were at work among the Frankish elite. Had they taken initiatives which their Catholic rivals had been sluggish to grasp? Another surviving letter, already referred to, is from no less a man than Bishop Remigius of Rheims.[4] It seems to date from 481–2, and it was written to welcome Clovis's succession to the administration of Belgica Secunda in the wake of his father Childeric's death. In it the bishop proffered advice as to how the young man should conduct himself as king. He should, among other things, endeavour to keep on good terms with the bishops of the province: sound advice, in view of the enhanced status of the episcopate in late-antique society at which we glanced in Chapter 2. What is conspicuously lacking from the letter is any suggestion that Clovis might care to become a Christian. Some find this surprising; but it neatly exemplifies one of the attitudes we investigated in Chapter 1. The letter of Remigius to Clovis is a late example of the traditional Roman view that Christianity was not for barbarians.

One letter is not much – indeed it's precious little – to go on. But the historian of a dark age must be thankful for the smallest mercies. The letter of Remigius permits us to envisage a Catholic episcopate initially aloof from evangelizing their new Salian masters. Arian clergy took advantage of this. The king himself was in no hurry and was prepared at the very least to dally with heresy before entering the Catholic fold. This we may be sure he finally did; no one doubts that in the end it was Remigius who baptized Clovis. 'Finally . . . in the end': the implication that the king's approach to the baptismal font was a slow and cautious one is there in Gregory's narrative and finds confirmation in yet another episcopal letter. Bishop Nicetius of Trier composed a letter of advice to Clovis's granddaughter Chlodoswintha (Clotsinda, Lucinda) in about 565, when she was on the point of leaving Gaul to be married to the Lombard Prince Alboin. Let her remember how her grandmother Clotilde 'led the lord Clovis to the Catholic faith', even though 'because he was a very shrewd man he was unwilling to accept it until he knew it was true'.[5] Clovis had taken his time. The assigning of precise dates remains problematical. Victory

105

over the Alamans, traditionally placed in the year 496, may indeed have been regarded by the king as God-given. Good reasons have been advanced for placing his baptism quite late in the reign; a strong case for 508 has been made.

Royal conversion was a complicated business. A first stage might have been marked, as suggested here, by the prospective acceptance of a Christian deity – possibly without any very clear awareness of His exclusive claims upon the believer's allegiance. The final stage was baptism itself, full entry into the Christian community. The journey from first to last stage could have taken up to a dozen years, and there were plenty of intermediate stages. Clovis would have needed to be watchful, especially of his warrior following. He would have wanted to be quite sure that a new God could deliver the goods he had been led to expect. Bishop Nicetius was clear about these in his letter to Chlodoswintha. Look how your grandfather defeated the Burgundians and the Visigoths – and, he might have added, the Alamans, the Thuringians, the Ripuarian Franks and not a few of his own kinsmen. Look how rich their plunder made him. Look at the miracles which so impressed him, worked at the shrines of the saints of Gaul, of Martin at Tours, of Germanus at Auxerre, of Hilary at Poitiers, of Lupus at Troyes. For Clovis it must all have been reassuring and perhaps awe-inspiring. We must allow time, too, for Remigius' instruction.

There may have been other forces at work as well. The long arm of east Roman diplomacy reached as far as northern Gaul. After his victory over the Visigoths at Vouillé in 507 Clovis received letters from the Emperor Anastasius conferring the office of honorary consul, with its insignia and uniform, upon him. During the last years of his reign the 'new Constantine' performed actions which recalled the first Constantine; and surely not coincidentally. Like Constantine he established a new capital for himself, at Paris. Like Constantine he built there a church dedicated to the Holy Apostles. Like Constantine at Nicaea he presided over a church council, at Orléans in the year 511. Like Constantine he was generous to the Catholic church, and there is just a little evidence that like Constantine he was masterful in his government of it. Like another emperor, Theodosius II, Clovis issued a code of law, written in Latin, the so-called *Pactus Legis Salicae*, the first surviving version of the famous *Lex Salica* or Salic Law, the law of the Salian Franks. A newly arrived barbarian warlord had been patiently

shepherded into the Christian fold and a start had been made in schooling him in the ways of Christian kingship.

One of the chapters of Clovis's law code deals with runaway or stolen
slaves. It considers the contingency that slaves might be carried off
trans mare, 'across the sea', and lays down the procedure to be followed in foreign courts of law to effect their recovery. For a king who
ruled in northern Gaul the nearest sea is the English Channel and the
most obvious way of understanding the phrase 'across the sea' is as a
reference to south-eastern England. Like the Frankish king we too
must turn our attention across the sea.

The fifth and sixth centuries are the most obscure in British history.
In 410 the Emperor Honorius had instructed the *civitates*, as we might
say the local authorities, to look after themselves when the imperial
army and administration were withdrawn. For a generation or so they
appear to have managed reasonably well: the British church, which
was visited by Germanus, which could despatch Ninian to Galloway
and to which Patrick was answerable, was not the church of a society
in collapse. But this fragile stability did not last. Britain had long been
the target of predators, like any vulnerable part of the Roman world.
Her attackers came from the west, the *Scotti* or Irish; from the north,
the Picts from what is now Scotland; and from the east, the peoples
of the north German coastlands from the mouth of the Rhine to
Jutland. Since the days of Bede these latter have been pigeon-holed
as Angles, Saxons and Jutes, but it can be shown that several other
tribal groups were involved, such as Frisians or Danes. Here I follow
time-honoured convention in referring to them generally as the Anglo-
Saxons. These were barbarian peoples whose homelands were well
beyond the frontiers of the Roman empire. They had been less exposed
to Roman ways than their neighbours the Franks, let alone the Goths
This is not to say that they had had no contact with the empire at all:
archaeology has shown that trading relations were widespread; the
settlement excavated at Wijster, in Drenthe in the northern Netherlands, a substantial village of at least fifty dwellings by the fourth
century, seems to have subsisted by production for the market provided
by the garrison towns of the lower Rhine about sixty miles distant.
Recent excavations on the Danish island of Fyn have yielded abundant
artefacts indicative of trade with the empire. Roman coin circulated as
freely in northern Germania as it did further south in Gothia. Neverthe-

less, due allowance being made for commerce, it remains true that of the barbarians who took over the western imperial provinces those from the North Sea littoral were the least touched by Roman influence, the most uncouth.

Their taking over of much of eastern Britain occurred in the period of deepest obscurity between about 450 and 550. Valiant attempts to pierce this darkness have been and are being made by historians, archaeologists and place-name scholars. We do not need to consider these very difficult and intricate matters here. It is enough to reckon with the emergence in eastern Britain by the latter part of the sixth century of a number of small kingdoms under Germanic royal dynasties and warrior aristocracies, a ruling class whose members were, of course, like the Franks, pagan in their religious observances. Our immediate concern will be with the most south-easterly of these, the kingdom of Kent.

The degree to which Christianity was obliterated in those parts of eastern Britain occupied by the Anglo-Saxons is a matter of debate. It is not impossible, indeed it is quite likely, that there was some considerable survival of the Romano-British population under English rule, a state of affairs which would have been congruent with the circumstances elsewhere in the western provinces of the former empire. What we do not know is how thoroughly Christianity had permeated British society before the Germanic takeover occurred. If the area of Kent – restricting ourselves at present to the south-east – was anything like the Touraine of St Martin we might expect to find, around the year 400, some urban Christianity, some rural Christianity at gentry level, and a lot of rustic paganism. The early Christian archaeology of Kent does indeed present this impression. There is evidence of Christianity in late Roman Canterbury and at a few rural sites, of which the best known is the villa at Lullingstone with its private chapel. It is difficult to gauge to what degree this Kentish Christianity survived the disruptions of the fifth and sixth centuries. The Roman town of Canterbury seems to have experienced severe if never complete depopulation. Urban life in any generally accepted sense of the phrase seems to have died. This need not mean that Christianity disappeared from Canterbury altogether but it could mean that its presence there was insubstantial. The Roman villa at Lullingstone was destroyed by fire early in the fifth century: accident? arson? barbarian raiders? We have no means of telling: but we do know that it was not rebuilt. It has long been a plausible hypothesis that the landowning classes of eastern Britain made themselves scarce as their province drifted into insecurity and disorder as the fifth century advanced. They withdrew westwards into Wales, Cumbria or the south-western peninsula, where Christian principalities would survive independently of the Anglo-Saxons, in some cases for centuries; or they emigrated to safer parts of what was left of the empire. However, this should not exclude the possibility that some of them stayed. Near Aylesford, and suggestively close to another Roman villa, there is a settlement named Eccles. This place-name has been borrowed, via British, from the Latin *ecclesia*, 'church' or 'Christian community'. A pocket of Christians must have survived there long enough for the name by which they were known to their (non-Christian?) neighbours to have been adopted into the Germanic speech of the new overlords.

All of which gives food for thought but does not greatly advance our understanding. We can at least say that we must not rule out the possibility that there were Christians among the subjects of the pagan Kentish kings of the sixth century. These kings also had Christian neighbours. It is well known that the Anglo-Saxon peoples were great seafarers; it is sometimes forgotten that the Franks were too. For seafaring folk the Channel unites rather than divides. It was the high-way from the north German coastal homelands to the rich pickings of Gaul for the raiders of the third and fourth centuries and for the settlers of the fifth and sixth (as for the Vikings later on). Saxons settled on both sides of it. They settled the southern parts of Britain to which they gave their name – the East Saxons of Essex, the South Saxons of Sussex and the West Saxons of Wessex. On the opposite side of the Channel Saxons were settled in three known areas (and possibly in others as well) – round Boulogne, round Bayeux and near the mouth of the Loire. The Saxons of the Loire were converted to Christianity by Bishop Félix of Nantes, who died in 582, a change in their culture which their insular kinsfolk in Britain would surely have got wind of. Did Franks also settle on both sides of the Channel? It is practically certain that Frankish settlement did occur in Kent, Sussex and Hampshire, though in the last resort the evidence, mainly archaeological, is inconclusive. This evidence undoubtedly does show that there was a lively exchange of goods to and fro across the Channel at this period. Whether these things travelled as commodities of trade, as plunder, tribute, dowries, gifts, we do not know. All we know is that they travelled in abundance and that many of them were objects of high intrinsic value or status such as jewellery or glassware. We should take care to remember too the perishable commodities which leave no archaeological trace. What are we to suppose that the Anglo-Saxon nobility of Kent drank out of their handsome glass goblets imported from the Rhineland?

It would also appear that at least from time to time Frankish royal power was claimed – which is not to say that it was exercised – over parts of south-eastern England. The contemporary Greek historian Procopius tells of a Frankish embassy to Constantinople in about 553 which included Angles in it in order to demonstrate the Frankish king's power over the island of Britain. A generation later Pope Gregory I could imply in correspondence with two Frankish kings that the kingdom of Kent was somehow within their range of influence. The one report may be explained away as misunderstanding, the other as diplomatic flattery – perhaps. What we cannot dismiss is sound evidence of dynastic contact, the marriage of a member of the heathen royal family of Kent to a Christian Frankish princess.

Ethelbert of Kent married Bertha, a bride 'of the royal stock of the Franks', in the words of Bede.[6] His information can be supplemented from the *Histories* of Gregory of Tours, a strictly contemporary witness, and one who had probably met Bertha herself. He certainly knew her mother Ingoberga, whose piety, and generosity to the church of Tours, he warmly commended. Her father Charibert (d. 567) had been king of Neustria, that is the western portion of the Frankish realms with its capital in Paris (and including the Saxon settlements near Bayeux and Nantes). Unfortunately for us, Gregory has practically nothing to tell us about Bertha's marriage. She was joined, he says, 'to the son of a certain king in Kent' – and that is all. Gregory stands at the beginning of a long and still-flourishing tradition of French historical scholarship which is wont to pay as little attention as possible to the history of the neighbouring island. He could have told us so much more. Was this the first such cross-Channel dynastic marriage, or had it been preceded by others? We do not know. When did it take place? We do not know, though it is possible to work out that it is unlikely to have been before the late 570s. What did the marriage mean for the relations between the two royal families? We do not know, though because Bertha as an orphan could not have ranked highly as a matrimonial catch and because Gregory seems to allude dismissively to the bridegroom we may suspect that Frankish royal circles would have looked down on Kentish ones.

We do know that Bertha's kinsfolk had been able to insist that Ethelbert permit his wife to practise her religion. She came to Kent accompanied by a bishop named Liudhard (and presumably some subordinate clergy) whose role was to act, in Bede's words, as her *adiutor fidei*, her 'faith helper' or private chaplain, not to attempt any wider evangelizing ministry. Her husband put at her disposal 'a church built in ancient times while the Romans were still in Britain, next to the city of Canterbury on its eastern side'. There are two candidates for the identification, St Martin's and St Pancras', both extramural churches to the east of Roman Canterbury, beneath both of which excavation has revealed Roman brickwork and mortar. Near St Martin's there was excavated in the nineteenth century a medallion attached to a late-sixth-century necklace: it was die-stamped with the name LEUDARDUS, presumably Bertha's Bishop Liudhard. What is interesting, if Bede's informants at Canterbury were correct, is that there were persons in Kent at the time of Bertha's arrival who could identify a certain building as a Christian church. It suggests the presence of a Christian community at Canterbury.

Thus far, the antecedents of Ethelbert's conversion are reminiscent of those of Clovis's. A Germanic king, ruling a sub-Roman kingdom in which a little Christianity survives, enjoying close relations with Christian neighbours, married to a Christian wife, becomes a Christian. Yes, but with regard to Ethelbert there was an additional personage involved – Pope Gregory the Great, of whom we have already caught a fleeting glimpse offering robust advice to Sardinian landlords about how to convert their peasantry (above, p. 59).

Gregory was born into an aristocratic Roman family in about 540, into circles accustomed to wealth and authority. His relatives included two recent popes. An excellent traditional education was followed by a few years (*c.* 572–4) of high administrative experience as *praefectus urbi*, prefect of the city, the supreme civic official in Rome. Converted to the monastic life in 574–5, Gregory turned the family *palazzo* on the Caelian Hill into a monastery dedicated to St Andrew. He installed in it the magnificent library of Christian writers assembled by his kinsman Pope Agapetus I (535–6), who had envisaged founding a school of advanced Christian studies in Rome. Gregory also founded monasteries on some of the family estates in Sicily. In 579 he was sent by Pope

Pelagius II to Constantinople as the papal *apocrisarius*, ambassador or nuncio, where he served until 585. It was a time of critical importance in the relations between Rome and Constantinople, during which the imperial government was striving to concert measures against the expansion of Lombard power in Italy. It was while he was *en poste* in Constantinople that Gregory met Leander of Seville, the elder brother of Isidore the etymologist, who was there on a diplomatic mission from the Catholics of Spain. From their discussions together there was born Gregory's greatest work of biblical exegesis, the *Moralia*, a commentary on the book of Job. Returning to Rome he was retained as the pope's secretary until Pelagius' death in 590. To his dismay, Gregory was chosen to succeed him. He accepted with genuine reluctance and served as pope until his death in 604.

Rome, Constantinople, Seville: Gregory's world was Roman, imperial, Mediterranean. Within that world Gregory's career was, on a superficial view, a glittering one. He was one of those rare multi-talented persons who are successful in all they undertake: administrator, diplomat, organizer, negotiator, writer. But Gregory would have been dismayed at the prospect of being remembered in this fashion. His priorities were different. He believed that God's Day of Judgement was imminent. This conviction gave edge to his overmastering concerns, which were pastoral and evangelical. These concerns gust like a mighty wind of spiritual force through all his writings: the *Moralia*, the *Dialogues*, in which he commemorated St Benedict and other saints, his sermons, many of his 850-odd surviving letters, and the book he composed for the guidance of those who exercise the cure of souls, the *Liber Regulae Pastoralis* (*Book of Pastoral Care*). The pastoral impulse in Gregory surfaces in some unlikely places. It can be seen in some of his dealings with the Lombards, 'that abominable people' (in his own words) whose invasion of Italy had brought hardship which he devoted much time and energy to relieving. It even shines through his hard-headed instructions for the management of the papal estates. It can be glimpsed in his correspondence with Queen Brunhilde, the Spanish wife of Clovis's grandson Sigibert (and aunt, by marriage, of Bertha).

Gregory's pastoral impulse was translated most memorably into action in his sending of a mission to convert the Anglo-Saxons to Christianity. The earliest biography of Gregory, composed at Whitby about a century after his death, contains the first version of the story of his encounter with English boys in Rome before he became pope.[7] The meeting moved Gregory to the most famous series of puns in English historical mythology. Of what nation were the boys? They replied that they were Angles. 'Not Angles but angels.' What was the name of their king? Alle. 'Alleluia! God's praise must be heard in his kingdom.' What was their kingdom called? Deira [the southern half of Northumbria, roughly equivalent to the Yorkshire of today]. 'They shall flee from the wrath [*de ira*] of God to the faith.' According to the anonymous author Gregory himself tried to set out on this mission during the pontificate of Benedict I (575–9) but was prevented from going more than three days' journey from Rome. It is highly unlikely that Gregory would have wished to leave Italy at that time, when he was busy founding and nurturing his monasteries. The story as told by the anonymous author and subsequently (in a slightly different form) by Bede was an oral tradition which had been circulating for some time among the Anglo-Saxons before it was committed to writing at Whitby in the early eighth century. The puns which Gregory is said to have made probably tell us more about the taste of the eighth-century Anglo-Saxons for punning wordplay than they do about the gift for verbal repartee of a sixth-century Italian cleric.

Bede's telling of the story sets it in the market-place of Rome and alleges that the English boys were up for sale as slaves. There is nothing intrinsically implausible about this. We need to remember that the slave trade was probably the most widespread business activity of the early medieval world. It is not inconceivable that some of the Frankish luxury objects excavated from the cemeteries of Ethelbert's Kent were paid for with English slaves. In this connection it is of great interest to find that Pope Gregory wrote in September 595 to his agent Candidus, who was on his way to administer the papal estates in southern Gaul, ordering him 'to buy English boys of seventeen or eighteen years of age in order that they may, dedicated to God, make progress in monasteries'.[8] The context makes it clear that the pope had in mind his own or other monasteries in Italy, because he requests that the boys be sent to him: 'and because they are pagans who are to be found there, I wish a priest to be sent with them so that, should illness strike in the course of the journey, he may baptise those whom he sees to be at the point of death.' It is not easy to interpret this letter. Some have assumed that the pope's intention was to train the boys as missionaries who could then be sent back to evangelize the Anglo-Saxons:

but there is not a hint of this in the text. A commonsensical reading might suggest that the pope simply wanted Candidus to get a supply of domestic slaves for use in his monasteries, though this is not an interpretation that commends itself to the pope's admirers. It is unwise to use this letter in support of the view that Gregory was planning a mission to the Anglo-Saxons as early as 595 – though he may have been. In a letter to Bishop Syagrius of Autun written in July 599 Gregory said that he had been thinking about the mission to England 'for a long time' (*diu*).[9] At the least we may safely say that the letter shows that in the late summer of 595 the pope's mind was busy with thoughts of the English and their paganism.

He will also have been aware that the Anglo-Saxons inhabited an island that had once been part of the empire. Gregory was a Roman through and through. He came from a family with a proud tradition of public service, he had respect for Roman order and administration, and – despite his strong Augustinian leanings – he had been trained to familiarity with ideas about the providential role of the empire in the divine scheme. His was a world in which it was inconceivable not to take the empire for granted. It is worth recalling that still in Gregory's day and for much of the century to come Constantinople continued to cast long shadows of influence across the western provinces. We should remember too that after the Justinianic reconquests of Gregory's childhood the empire still governed Sicily, north Africa as far as the Straits of Gibraltar and a sizeable chunk of south-eastern Spain. Furthermore, Gregory looked out upon a world in which, by the 590s, all the barbarian successor-states had adopted Christianity excepting only the Anglo-Saxon kingdoms of England.

Combine this with Gregory's sense of pastoral urgency and we have a context, what could be termed a temperamental context, for the initiative he took with regard to England. That initiative was the despatch in 596 of a party of missionaries to the court of King Ethelbert of Kent. Bede, our prime narrative source, tells us that Gregory did this 'on the prompting of divine inspiration'. It may have been so; but we must beware of ascribing the initiative solely to the pope or to God, even though this has been the received interpretation of the origins of the mission from Bede's day onwards. But even Bede's account is not without its difficulties. He tells us – and the information certainly came to him from Canterbury – that Ethelbert died twenty-one years after he had received the faith. Now since Ethelbert died on

24 February 616 it is evident that this 'reception' (whatever it may have consisted of) occurred in the year 595; or, to be pedantically accurate, between 24 February 595 and 23 February 596. If this piece of information is accurate it may fittingly be considered alongside a remark made by the pope himself. Writing to the royal Frankish brothers Theudebert and Theuderic in July 596 – it is the letter in which he referred to Frankish influence in Kent – Gregory put it on record that 'we have heard that the people of the English *wishes to be converted to the Christian faith.*'[10] One could not ask for a more explicit, authoritative and of course strictly contemporary statement that some approach had been made from the English side. It looks as though Gregory was responding to an appeal rather than launching a mission into the unknown. We might care to cast our minds back – as perhaps Gregory did also – to earlier such responses: the sending of Ulfila to the Christian communities of Gothic Dacia, for example, or of Palladius to the Christians of Ireland.

If an approach was made to the pope in 595 or early 596 one must ask how it was transmitted, and our thoughts turn at once to Queen Bertha and Bishop Liudhard. Bertha would have known of her great grandmother's part in the conversion of her husband Clovis. She may well have received a hortatory letter reminding her of it, like the one which Chlodoswintha got from Nicetius of Trier, when she went off as a bride to Kent. Her assistance in the conversion of Ethelbert was acknowledged by Pope Gregory in a letter he sent to her in 601. When something happened in 595 which made it clear to Bertha that the king was ripe for conversion – perhaps it was a victory in battle, as in the case of Clovis – she turned – to whom? Not to the pope directly, for surely we should have heard of this in Gregory's correspondence. Most likely it was to her royal relatives in Francia. After all, it was in a letter to Theudebert and Theuderic that Gregory said that he had heard of the English desire to be converted.

Theudebert and Theuderic were children. The regent for them was their grandmother Brunhilde, the most powerful presence in Frankish Gaul in the 590s. Her ghastly end – torn apart by wild horses on the orders of her nephew-by-marriage King Chlothar II after a prolonged struggle for power – and the subsequent blackening of her reputation must not blind us to both her political skill and her piety. When Columbanus arrived in Gaul in about 590 it was Brunhilde and her son Childebert who gave him land and royal protection for his early monastic foundations in Burgundy. (Brunhilde later quarrelled with Columbanus, but that is another story.) Columbanus came from an Irish church where the memory of Patrick was kept green; he had his own vivid sense of mission. He touched the minds of his royal patrons. They in their turn were in contact with Pope Gregory. Childebert and the pope exchanged letters in the summer of 595. Gregory wrote to Brunhilde and Childebert again in September, commending to them his agent Candidus (to whom he was writing at the same time about purchasing English youths). They were again in touch in 596 when Brunhilde's priest Leuparicus passed between them, bringing relics of St Peter and St Paul as a present from the pope for the queen on his return journey. In 597 she asked for a book which Gregory sent her. Brunhilde founded a monastery at Autun to which the pope granted privileges at her request in 602. The bishop of Autun, Syagrius, was close to the queen: Gregory rewarded his services to the English mission with a special mark of papal favour in 599. The scene was thus more complicated than Bede's narrative suggests: there was an English king who wanted to become a Christian and a pope with an overwhelming desire to save souls. Linking them was the Frankish royal court, provider of information and later, through the bishops, of practical help.

We know very little of the earlier life of the man chosen by Gregory to head the mission of King Ethelbert. Augustine of Canterbury – named after the great Augustine of Hippo – was a monk and by 596 prior of the monastery founded by Gregory in Rome. Although the prior is formally second-in-command of a monastery after the abbot, in this instance he would have been effectively running the community because its abbot would have been too busy with his duties as pope to supervise the day-to-day life of the house. Gregory was a shrewd judge of men and we must assume that he thought very highly of Augustine to have appointed him to a position of considerable spiritual and administrative responsibility. Gregory commended Augustine's knowledge of scripture in a letter to Ethelbert in 601. It is not surprising, given Gregory's priorities, that he should have picked a man of distinguished intellect in that particular field of study to head the mission. That is all we know of Augustine before the departure of the mission in 596. We are left wondering what additional talents or experience he might have possessed which commended him to Gregory for the task of barbarian evangelization. Had he, for instance, assisted or advised the pope in his dealings with the Lombards? Possibly: as so often, we simply do not know. But we do know one thing for certain about the mission: it was big and it was well equipped. Canterbury tradition recalled that Augustine's companions had numbered 'about forty' – a prodigious number. We do not know what they brought to England on the initial journey, but we do know that Gregory reinforced them in 601 with at least four more men, together with vestments, altar cloths, church plate and ornaments, relics and 'numerous books'. Gregory could command resources well beyond the capabilities of, say, Patrick.

Augustine reached Kent in the spring or early summer of 597. Ethelbert was hesitant at first but did in time consent to be baptized. (We are as uncertain of the exact date of his baptism as we are of that of Clovis.) On 20 July 598 Gregory wrote to the patriarch of Alexandria: in his letter he reported, among other matters, that he had heard from Augustine that 'at Christmas last more than 10,000 Englishmen had been baptised'.[11] Whether or not we wish to take the figure with a pinch of salt, we can surely accept that a large number of converts had been made. The scale of the thing is what is significant. It is incredible that so many could have been baptized had their king not given a lead. Therefore we may infer that Ethelbert had been baptized a Christian before 25 December 597. What did it mean for him as a king?

Flattering letters arrived from the pope, skilful as ever in handling barbarians.[12] Ethelbert was numbered among the 'good men raised up by almighty God to be a ruler over nations'. Gregory played on a Germanic king's lust for fame. 'For He whose honour you seek and maintain among the nations will also make your glorious name still more glorious even to posterity.' (How right he was.) Let Ethelbert be zealous for the faith 'like Constantine . . . [who] transcended in renown the reputation of former princes.' In his letter to Bertha he compared her to Helena, mother of Constantine, and assured her that her fame had come even to the ears of 'the most serene emperor' in Constantinople.

Ethelbert gave Augustine a church in Canterbury – another survivor – to restore as his cathedral church, which it still is. He provided Augustine with land on which to found a monastery dedicated to the apostles Peter and Paul just outside the Roman walls. This was also to be the royal mausoleum wherein he and his queen would lie entombed,

117

prayed for and remembered until the approaching Day of Judgement about which the pope had written to him. And something started to happen at Canterbury in the wake of Ethelbert's conversion: a Roman city began to come back to life. Bede called it, rather grandly, 'the metropolis of his [Ethelbert's] whole empire'. It was now a Christian city and, in Bede's words again, 'a royal city'.

Ethelbert's generous endowments of his churches may have been recorded in documents drafted in Latin according to the norms of Roman conveyancing. The matter is contentious because the surviving documents are copies of a much later date whose texts have evidently been tampered with: but genuine originals probably lie behind them, the first deeds of this sort ever issued by an English ruler. What is not in doubt is that Ethelbert promulgated a code of law. In Bede's words, much discussed and therefore translated here as literally as possible, 'following models of the Romans he established decrees of judgements for his people with the advice of his wise men which were written down in the language of the English'.[13] These survive (in a late but reliable copy), the earliest piece of English prose. Ethelbert's code of law is a simple tariff of offences and compensations: 'If a man strike another on the nose with his fist, 3 shillings [shall be paid as compensation].' There was little here that Justinian's great jurist Tribonian would have recognized as Roman. But it was written down; it was in the king's name; and it made new law as well as simply declaring existing custom – churchmen and church property, new arrivals on the Kentish scene, were woven into the social network of protection and compensation. The coming of Christianity gave the first impulse to the process by which the custom of the folk became the king's law. The implications for royal authority were far-reaching.

Royal authority helped to diffuse Christianity both within Ethelbert's kingdom of Kent and beyond it. Bede tells us that though the king did not compel any of his subjects to accept the faith, nevertheless he showed greater favour to those who did. Quite so. At another point in his narrative he let fall the information that some of Ethelbert's subjects became Christians 'through fear of the king or to win his favour'. A second Kentish bishopric was founded at Rochester and provided with endowments by the king. Ethelbert was also able to influence other Anglo-Saxon rulers. He might have appeared insignificant in Frankish eyes but in England Ethelbert was a considerable force, 'a most powerful king whose supremacy reached as far as the river Humber'. Among his subject-kings was Saeberht, king of the East Saxons (i.e. Essex), who was also his nephew, the son of his sister Ricula. The East Saxons accepted Christianity and a bishopric was founded for them at London in 604. The next kingdom to the north was that of the East Angles. Its king, Redwald, was converted on a visit to Ethelbert's court but on his return home was talked out of the sincerity of his faith by his wife. He tried to have the best of both worlds by putting up a Christian altar in his pagan temple. Ethelbert was able in addition to help the missionaries in their negotiations with the Christian clergy of neighbouring British kingdoms to the end of securing their collaboration in the work of evangelization; even though in the event these negotiations failed disastrously.

Our third princely barbarian convert was Edwin of Northumbria, baptized at York on Easter Day in the year 627, as we saw in the opening pages of this book. Here it is necessary only to emphasize that the background to Edwin's conversion, and its aftermath, bore some likeness to the circumstances surrounding the conversions of Clovis and Ethelbert. Edwin knew something of the faith of his Christian bride before she reached him, accompanied by Paulinus – her Liudhard – in about 619. Before fighting his way to power in Northumbria in 616 Edwin had spent many years in exile; it is very probable that he had had encounters with Christians in the course of it. Later Welsh tradition claimed that part of that exile had been spent under the protection of the British King Cadfan of Gwynedd, or north-west Wales, 'wisest and most renowned of all kings', as his tombstone at Llangadwaladr in Anglesey described him, and certainly a Christian. Part of his exile had been spent with King Redwald of East Anglia, at whose court Edwin might have met Paulinus, as is related by the anonymous monk of Whitby in his life of Pope Gregory. Edwin's subjects certainly included Christians, for at some date unknown he had conquered the British kingdom of Elmet, that area of south-west Yorkshire whose earlier history is still commemorated in the place-names Barwick-in-Elmet and Sherburn-in-Elmet. British tradition would claim that Edwin was actually baptized a Christian by a British bishop named Rhun, the son of King Urien of the northern British kingdom of Rheged, or Cumbria. This is unlikely. On the other hand it is highly probable that there would have been clerics among the delegations from Edwin's sub-kingdoms who paid tributary visits to his court. Bishop Rhun could have been a not unfamiliar figure among the revellers at Edwin's palace of, shall we say, Yeavering.

As in Ethelbert's case there was also papal encouragement. There survive two letters from Pope Boniface V (619–25) addressed to Edwin and his consort.[14] The king was urged to abandon paganism and embrace Christianity. The pope made the point early on that Christianity was the faith of 'all the human race from the rising to the setting of the sun' – with verbal reminiscence of a key missionary text in Malachi i.11: because God has melted 'by the fire of His Holy Spirit the frozen hearts of races even in the far corners of the earth'. Patently mendacious though the writer must have known these words to be – one need look no further than the Jewish communities of the Mediterranean world – the sort of effect that they were intended to have on Edwin is plain. The king was being encouraged to come in, literally, from the cold. Diplomatic presents of rich apparel, gold embroidered, cunningly hinted at the splendid trappings of Christian civilization. Queen Ethelburga was firmly reminded of her duty as wife and queen to bring about Edwin's conversion. She was sent a silver mirror and an ivory comb ornamented with gold. Perhaps it looked somewhat like the silver-chased comb of her elder contemporary, Queen Theodelinda of the Lombards, now preserved at Monza.

The aftermath of Edwin's baptism shows features with which the reader will by now be familiar. We see him assisting in the diffusion of Christianity in Northumbria, accompanying Paulinus as he taught and baptized at Yeavering, Catterick and the unidentified Campodunum. Royal 'assistance' did not just mean being present. Alcuin, the great eighth-century scholar, wrote of Edwin in his poem on *The Bishops, Kings and Saints of York* that 'by gifts and threats he incited men to cherish the faith'.[15] Edwin was active in pressing Christianity upon the rulers subject to him. He 'persuaded' (Bede's word) Eorpwald, son and successor to Redwald of East Anglia, to become a Christian. One may suspect that Paulinus' success in preaching the word in the kingdom of Lindsey (Lincolnshire) owed not a little to Edwin too. It is just possible that Edwin, like Ethelbert and Clovis, issued laws. This seems to be hinted at in some lines of Alcuin's poem; but it should be stressed that Bede says nothing of any legislative activity and that no written lawcode attributable to Northumbria survives. Bede tells us something of the peace which Edwin maintained and of the royal state he kept. If historians have made heavy weather of the reference to 'the standard which the Romans call a *tufa* and the English a *thuuf*' the point surely for Bede was that there was now some 'Roman' quality about Edwin's style of kingship.

The narrators of these episodes of royal conversion were, of course, churchmen: Gregory of Tours, a bishop; Bede, a monk at Jarrow – what we might call 'professional Christians'. Is it ever possible to shift the angle of vision and open up a different perspective? Is there, for example, any statement about conversion attributable to a king? By a happy chance there is. It takes the form of a letter from the Visigothic king of Spain, Sisebut, to the Lombard king of Italy, Adaloald, and it was written at much about the time that Ethelburga was travelling north to meet her bridegroom Edwin. The letter was not indeed about conversion from paganism to Christianity but about conversion from one form of Christianity to another. Sisebut was urging Adaloald to abandon Arianism and embrace orthodox Catholicism.[16]

Care is always needed in handling writings attributed to royalty. Kings have opportunities denied to others of availing themselves of literary assistance. Whose voice, whose style are we hearing? Not necessarily that of the king. There is a further difficulty. A letter such as this was a public document, a piece of diplomatic correspondence. Surely we should be correct in assuming that even though it ran in the king's name it would have been drafted by officials. But Sisebut was no ordinary king. He had received an advanced education and was a friend of the polymath Isidore of Seville, who dedicated one of his books to him. It was in response to this gesture that Sisebut honoured Isidore with a Latin verse epistle on the subject of eclipses. Sisebut was also the author, most surprisingly, of a work of hagiography celebrating the life of Bishop Desiderius of Vienne, recently murdered at the instigation of Queen Brunhilde. (There were more sides to her character than the piety to which attention was drawn a few pages back.) Sisebut also wrote a number of letters which have survived and probably more which have not. They are on a variety of subjects ranging from diplomatic correspondence to counselling for a bewildered bishop. Tone and style are even and consistent. I think we may take it that this remarkable man's letter to Adaloald was his own composition or, at least, expressed his own convictions.

Sisebut was clear about the advantages that had accrued to his people when they had moved from Arianism to Catholicism in 587–9. Before that they had suffered daily from calamity: frequent wars, famine and plague. However, 'As soon as the orthodox faith had enlightened their darkened minds . . . God willing, the power of the Goths now thrives. Those who once were torn by the sickled cohorts of thorns, wounded by the barbed stings of scorpions, poisoned by the forked tongue of the serpent, to these atoned ones the Catholic church now devotes her motherly affection.' It is a long letter, in high-flown diction of which this is a representative sample, and much of it is unsurprisingly taken up with theological argument and scriptural quotation. But at its heart lies the simple boast that 'the power of the Goths now thrives'. King Sisebut believed that conversion to correctness of religious observance had made his kingdom more powerful. Crude we may think it, but it is consistent with what we have seen elsewhere.

The contemporary written sources bearing upon the conversion of kings prompt reflection on a number of themes. First, we observe the repeated assurance that acceptance of Christianity will bring victory, wide dominion, fame and riches. This was what Germanic kings wanted to hear, because their primary activity was war. It was the easier for the missionaries to preach this with conviction in the light of what the historical books of the Old Testament had to tell about the victorious wars of a godly Israelite king such as David. Not for them the scruples of Ulfila who, it may be recalled (above, p. 77), omitted the books of Kings from the Gothic Bible. Nor would it have profited them to dwell upon facets of Christian teaching which kings might have found unappealing. The injunction to turn the other cheek would surely have fallen on deaf ears if addressed to Clovis. Pope Honorius I urged King Edwin to employ himself 'in frequent readings from the works of Gregory, your evangelist and my master'.[17] One may wonder whether Paulinus, as he opened his copy of the *Moralia* or the *Liber Regulae Pastoralis*, would have thought this the most appropriate juncture to explain that Pope Gregory had taught that rulers should be humble. Bede could tackle the problem of a king, like Edwin, who became very powerful *before* his conversion to Christianity by claiming this as an augury; in the words of a modern scholar, Edwin got his power 'on account so to say'.[18] More problematic was the successful king who remained obstinately heathen. Such was Penda, king of the midland kingdom of Mercia, who defeated and killed Edwin in 633. Bede sidestepped the problem by saying as little as possible about him.

Second, we might care to notice the role of the Christian queen in bringing about the conversion of her pagan husband. Here too there was an apposite scriptural reference. 'The heathen husband now belongs to God through his Christian wife' (I Corinthians vii.14). St Paul's words were quoted both by Bishop Nicetius in his letter to Chlodoswintha and by Pope Boniface V in his letter to Ethelburga. This was a role for the queen which was to have a distinguished future. Much later on, when coronation rituals were devised in Francia in the ninth century, it would be emphasized that it was the duty of a queen 'to summon barbarous peoples to acknowledgement of the Truth'. One may wonder whether we have something of a topos here. How important really was Clotilde in bringing about the conversion of Clovis? We cannot answer this question, it need hardly be said. But there can be no doubting the fact that royal conversions did frequently follow the marriage of a pagan king to a Christian wife.

It was not always so. Here is Bede on the (unnamed) wife of King Redwald of East Anglia.

> Redwald had been initiated into the mysteries of the Christian faith in Kent, but in vain. For on his return home he was seduced by his wife and by certain evil teachers and perverted from the sincerity of his faith, so that his last state was worse than his first. After the manner of the ancient Samaritans, he seemed to be serving both Christ and the gods whom he had previously served; in the same temple he had one altar for the Christian sacrifice and another small altar on which to offer victims to devils.

It is an interesting story. Another way of interpreting it would be to see Redwald's acceptance of Christianity simply as the addition of a new god to his pantheon of deities. It may well have been that the exclusive claims of the Christian God were ill-understood at first by royal converts.

Royal hesitation, thirdly, is a notable feature of our narratives. Clovis, Ethelbert and Edwin all took their time. Abandonment of the old gods was no light matter. Consultation with counsellors was prudent. How would the pagan priesthood react? Coifi is the classic case of the poacher turned gamekeeper. Redwald's men seem to have been less pliable. There are difficult questions here about the dynamics of a king's authority over his kinsfolk, his realm and his vassal kingdoms. It is hard to judge whether conversion came about through individual choice or through pressure exerted by the solidarity of a group. Arguments can be marshalled in support of both propositions. For example, the interesting information preserved by Bede that eleven members of the royal entourage were baptized with the infant Eanflaed in June 626 – ten months before Edwin's baptism – might suggest that in Northumbria at least there was scope for individual choice. Doubtless the truth is that both individual and group motivation co-existed side by side; even, at different times, in the same person. We can be sure that a royal lead for others to follow was effective, even though the conversions it prompted may have been less than wholly sincere, as Bede was aware. We must note too that giving a lead did not always work even within the royal family. Ethelbert's son Eadbald remained a pagan throughout his father's life; the heathen Penda's son Peada became a Christian.

Finally, we may observe the manner in which conversion was accompanied or quickly followed by royal actions which marked entry into the orbit of *Romanitas*. This is not to say that Roman culture was not already to some extent familiar and in prospect before conversion – one need think only of Bishop Remigius and the young Clovis – though doubtless more for some kings than for others. Convert kings acquired, in their missionary churchmen, experts who could school them in what was expected of a Christian king. The results are to be seen in the *Pactus Legis Salicae* and the council of Orléans, in Canterbury cathedral and Ethelbert's charters, in Edwin's *thuuf* and the timber structure like a wedge of Roman amphitheatre revealed by the Yeavering excavations.

Is there an 'archaeology of royal conversion'? Perhaps. The graves of some royal persons and of some who may have been royal persons in Frankish Gaul and early Anglo-Saxon England have been discovered. They range in date from 481/2 (Childeric) to 675 (his namesake Childeric II). In the past, archaeologists were confident that it was easy to distinguish a Christian from a pagan grave. Pagans cremated their dead and furnished them with grave-goods. Christians buried their dead on an east–west axis and did not deposit grave-goods in the tomb. Nowadays archaeologists are much more cautious. In northern Gaul and Anglo-Saxon England the shift from a predominant but not exclusive use of cremation to the custom of inhumation seems to have preceded the coming of Christianity. Orientation is no longer interpreted as a clue to belief: some apparently pagan graves are oriented and some certainly Christian ones are not. Neither is the presence or absence of grave-goods a sure indication of religious loyalties. Indeed, among the Frankish aristocracy the fashion for furnishing graves in this manner became widespread only *after* their conversion to Christianity. It follows that any inferences about changing beliefs founded on archaeological evidence of funerary practice are hazardous.

The most famous, and certainly the most puzzling, among the apparently royal graves of this period is an English one: the deposit beneath the so-called Mound 1 in the cemetery at Sutton Hoo in Suffolk. For nearly sixty years now, since its excavation just before the beginning of the Second World War, discussion has raged about this burial, unparalleled among early medieval graves for the number, richness and variety of its contents. It is widely accepted that this was the grave of a king of the East Angles and that it cannot have been dug earlier, or much later, than about 625. Regardless of *which* king might have been buried there – there are four principal candidates – this is exactly the period when the ruling dynasty passed in a formal sense from paganism to Christianity. Is this change of religious affiliation one that can be detected in the archaeology of Mound 1? (We could ask the same question of the cemetery as a whole but that is not my present purpose.) It is hard to claim with any conviction that such a change is detectable. The burial rite may have been traditional, but that does not make it pagan. There may have been objects in the grave decorated with Christian symbolism, but that does not make it Christian. The most promising, and not the least enigmatic, objects on which to base an affirmative answer to the question posed above are two silver spoons (illustrated in plate 10). They bear on their handles the names SAULOS and PAULOS in Greek characters, each name preceded by a small incised cross. The names not only have a clear Christian association but would seem, in their allusion to St Paul's change of name, to refer to a conversion. It has been suggested that these were baptismal spoons which had been presented to the man buried beneath Mound 1 at the time of his conversion to Christianity. But the case is not clear-cut. The letters of the name SAULOS were so incompetently executed that it might have been no more than a blundered attempt to copy the name PAULOS on the other spoon by a craftsman who was illiterate. The spoons may have no reference at all to the conversion of an East Anglian king. They remain puzzling – as does the burial as a whole. Its latest investigator sees in it 'an extravagant and defiant non-Christian gesture'.[19] His judgements invite respect but need not command assent. I am more impressed by the religious neutrality of Mound 1. This very neutrality, or inconclusiveness, may in itself have something to hint to us about the hesitant process of royal conversion.

Moshoeshoe of Lesotho, whose words are quoted in the epigraph to this chapter, was far removed in time and space from the new Constantines of early medieval Gaul and Britain. His kingdom and its people were widely – but not unrecognizably – different from those of Clovis or Edwin. Yet his encounter with that Christian faith presented to him by the representatives of the Société des Missions Évangéliques de Paris echoes some of the themes that are sounded for us in the pages of Gregory of Tours and Bede.[20]

The most disruptive chain of events in the life of south-east Africa in the early nineteenth century was the rise of the Zulu empire under Shaka. It was aggressive and organized for war. Before Shaka's death in 1828 his Zulus had had a destabilizing effect upon the neighbouring peoples, long remembered by them as the *Faqane* or the *Mfecane*, literally 'forced migration', by extension 'the crushing of the peoples'. Roughly speaking, the rise of the Zulu empire had the same sort of effects upon nearby peoples such as the Sotho as the rise of the Hun empire had upon the German peoples in the fourth and fifth centuries. Moshoeshoe, often abbreviated to Mosesh, created a kingdom for some of these Sotho people which he ruled with skill and statesmanship for nearly fifty years until his death in 1870 at the age of about eighty-four. This kingdom was the nucleus of the state we know today as Lesotho.

In 1824 Moshoeshoe had established a new royal settlement at Thaba Bosiu, an isolated tableland protected by cliffs which rose above the upper waters of the river Caledon some hundred miles above its confluence with the Orange river. It was there that three members of the Paris Société approached him in 1833, and at the foot of this natural fortress that they established their first mission station. It was a proximity that echoes the close spatial association of royalty and mission so often found in early medieval Europe. Thus in 635 St Aidan would establish his monastic mission station at Lindisfarne, within sight of the royal rock-fortress of Bamburgh. Moshoeshoe had wanted the missionaries to come to his kingdom for reasons that arose from the Zulu *Faqane*. Its effects of destabilization and demoralization had led him, a thoughtful man (as Bede presents Edwin), to wonder about the efficacy of his traditional religious observances. How could the ancestors and spirits have let these things occur? – if they really were as powerful as he had been taught to believe. Second, the *Faqane* had pushed his people into closer proximity to the white man. The British government at the Cape was a long way off but the Afrikaners were close at hand, some of them even beginning to cross to the northern side of the Orange river in search of new pastures for their flocks. The missionaries were outsiders, neutrals. They might help Moshoeshoe to cope with this unfamiliar world which threatened to encroach upon his people. They were *baruti*, teachers, who might initiate him into the secrets of the white man's power.

Circumstances were such, therefore, that a friendly rapport was established between king and missionaries at the outset. With one of the three in particular, Eugène Casalis, Moshoeshoe struck up a warm friendship. The king showed a keen interest in Christianity. He would discuss the faith for hours on end with Casalis, encouraged his people to listen to the missionaries' teaching, and put no obstacles in the path of individual converts. Every Sunday Moshoeshoe would don European clothes and descend from Thaba Bosiu to attend divine service at the mission chapel which had been built by workmen supplied by him free of charge. At the end of the sermon he would add his own comments on it for the edification of the congregation. One of the missionaries recorded that these royal glosses 'often conveyed the essence of what they had been saying in words that made it more intelligible to the rest of the congregation without distorting it'. After church the king would dine with Casalis and his Scottish wife at the mission house.

Clothes and dinners were not the only trappings of Christian civilization which appealed to Moshoeshoe. He developed a taste for European horses, saddlery, wagons, firearms, agricultural implements and household utensils. He employed a deserter from the British army to build him a house of stone. Another mason whom he employed, Josias Hoffmann, later became the first president (1854–5) of the Orange Free State. He planted wheat, fruit trees and vegetables under missionary guidance. He had the greatest respect for literacy, but though he struggled hard he never quite mastered the art of writing. He adopted the European habit of issuing written laws 'with the advice and concurrence of the great men of our tribe': these edicts were printed in the Sesotho vernacular on a missionary printing press.

The presence and skills of the missionaries enhanced Moshoeshoe's prestige. Under his rule the kingdom found stability and began to enjoy prosperity. The king was convinced that this was the fruit of Christianity. 'It is the Gospel that is the source of the prosperity and peace which you enjoy,' he told his subjects in 1842. Trade prospered under royal encouragement, regulated in one of Moshoeshoe's written ordinances. Coin began to replace barter as a means of exchange. Casalis and his colleagues encouraged the peaceful consolidation and expansion of Moshoeshoe's power: both parties profited from it. The string of mission stations gradually founded as offspring of the original at Thaba Bosiu was rightly perceived as useful by the king. They helped to encourage peaceful nucleated settlement; they assisted to consolidate the royal hold upon new territory; they performed a defensive function for local people and livestock in troubled times. As for the outside world, Casalis acted as a kind of secretary for foreign affairs to Moshoeshoe. Surviving diplomatic correspondence is in Casalis's hand, subscribed by the king with a cross. Everything looked as if it were going the missionaries' way.

Casalis and his colleagues made many converts in Lesotho. But the king, finally and after much anxious hesitation, was not among them. In deference to missionary teaching Moshoeshoe decreed changes in some of the most intimate areas of Sotho life, affecting marriage customs, initiation rituals, resort to witches and burial practices. Some of these initiatives provoked opposition. Moshoeshoe had to restore the traditional initiation rituals in all their gruesomeness, and his attempts to change marriage customs met with resentment and resistance. One of the leaders of the opposition was Tsapi, Moshoeshoe's chief diviner, a man respected and feared for his power to foretell the future and to communicate with the spirit world. In 1839 there was an epidemic of measles. Moshoeshoe's ancestors appeared to Tsapi and told him that 'the children of Thaba Bosiu die because Moshoeshoe is polluted and because the evening prayers offend the ancestral spirits'. The king's son Molapo accepted Christianity and was baptized, but apostasized a few years later. Even though three of Moshoeshoe's wives and two of his leading counsellors became Christians, there was strong opposition at court. Moshoeshoe realized that to commit himself to Christianity would be to split his kingdom. So he never did.

There is much for the early medievalist to ponder in the story of the coming of Christianity to Lesotho. How much more we might learn could we but eavesdrop on some heavenly conversation between Casalis and Augustine, or Moshoeshoe and Ethelbert. Whimsical fancies aside, all we need note here is that early medieval missionaries were in general successful in persuading kings to declare themselves adherents of Christianity. However, as they were well aware, this was just a first step. Round and behind these new Constantines were ranked their warrior aristocracies. How were these men, and their often formidable womenfolk, to be brought to the faith? Some answers will be suggested in the next two chapters.

CHAPTER FIVE

An Abundance
of Distinguished Patrimonies

Things have come to a pretty pass when religion is
allowed to invade the sphere of private life.

LORD MELBOURNE, 1800

BARBARIAN KINGS like Edwin might make judicious use of 'gifts and
threats' to bring pressure to bear upon their leading subjects. But we
should not suppose that these persons became Christians only 'through
fear of the king or to win his favour'. The acceptance of Christianity
by the men and women of the barbarian aristocracies was critical in
the making of Christendom because these were the people who had
the local influence necessary to diffuse the faith among their dependants. John Chrysostom, Maximus of Turin and Augustine of Hippo
had been correct in perceiving the pivotal role of local elites, and in
this respect (if not in others) the seventh and eighth centuries were
no different from the fourth and fifth. This chapter and the next will
examine some aspects of the conversion of the barbarian aristocracies,
first in Gaul and Spain in the seventh century, then in the British Isles
in the seventh and eighth, and attempt to point up significant common
features. One word of warning. Surviving sources tend to be more
concerned with kings than with their nobilities. It is accordingly more
difficult – *even* more difficult – to get to grips with aristocratic than
with royal conversion.

Germanic settlement in what had been imperial Roman territory
wrought changes in Europe's linguistic boundaries. The eastern frontier of the empire on the continental mainland had been marked,
roughly speaking, by the course of the rivers Rhine and Danube.
Within that line the language of everyday speech for many, and of
authority for all, had been Latin, the ancestor of the Romance lan-

130

guages of today. The influx of Germanic peoples in the fourth and fifth centuries pushed Latin westwards and southwards and substituted Germanic speech in a swathe of territory within what had once been the imperial frontiers. That is why Austrians and many Swiss speak varieties of German to this day. It need hardly be stressed that the pattern of linguistic change is neither neat nor simple. It therefore affords plentiful opportunity for lively academic debate. Philologists are a combative lot, and scholarly wrangling has been made the fiercer by the nationalistic dementia of the nineteenth and twentieth centuries. Particularly has this been so in relation to the area upon which we must first concentrate attention in this chapter, the valleys of the Rhine and its western tributary the Mosel (or Moselle – which neatly encapsulates the debate). The linguistic frontier was never static. However, as a very rough approximation the map facing page 136 shows the state of affairs in the latter part of the sixth century. It will be seen that Germanic speech was current as far west as Boulogne and as far southwest as Metz and Strasbourg, with outposts further to the west, for example among the Saxon settlers in the Bayeux region and near the mouth of the Loire. And there were enclaves of Latin/Romance further to the east, for example at the city of Trier.

There is every reason to suppose that the fortunes of Christianity had run in tandem with those of its Roman language. We can detect a flourishing urban or suburban Christianity in the late fourth century. Trier, as befitted a city which was then the imperial capital in Gaul, was emphatically Christian. We might recall the community which had so impressed Augustine's friend Ponticianus (above, p. 27). The sense of burgeoning vitality imparted by that story is confirmed by the archaeological evidence of Christian building activity in Trier – and elsewhere. At Bonn, for example, a Christian church was rebuilt at the end of the fourth century, replacing on a more generous scale an earlier chapel. Matters were different, of course, in the rural hinterland. But there were grounds for optimism. Martin had visited Trier and made an impression upon members of the local elite such as Tetradius. His friend Bishop Victricius of Rouen was making sorties into the pagan countryside of Artois.

Quite suddenly the light was snuffed out. The seat of government was removed from Trier to Arles – with all that this implied for influential concern and wealthy patronage. The Rhine frontier was pierced by the barbarian invasion of the winter of 406–7. Trier was attacked by the Franks four times in thirty-four years. Roman order collapsed, and with it the apparatus of organized Christianity. This is not to say that the faith itself entirely disappeared. It withdrew into little enclaves here and there, where best it could survive under the protection of town walls or powerful men. We know little of its fortunes, for the written sources give out almost as completely as they do in fifth-century Britain: a silence which is itself eloquent. There are gaps in the episcopal lists. At Cologne, for example, no bishop is known between Severinus in about 400 and Carentius, attested in 566. We catch glimpses of Christianity in the occasional Rhineland tombstones, some of them illustrated in plates 11 and 12. The sorrowing parents of the eight-year-old Desideratus could commission a gravestone, at Kobern near Koblenz, inscribed with Latin hexameters and Christian symbols, at some point in the fifth century. Sometimes we can spot the new arrivals embracing the faith of Rome. The parents of Rignetrudis – presumably Frankish, from her name (though this argument is not without its difficulties, as we shall see presently) – erected an elegant Christian tombstone with a Latin inscription to mark the grave of their beloved sixteen-year-old daughter at Brühl-Vochem, a little to the south of Cologne, sometime in the sixth century. But frequently the signals are ambiguous. Consider the Frankish nobleman buried at Morken, between Aachen and Cologne, a likely contemporary and a near neighbour of Rignetrudis. His relatives buried him in a wooden chamber with weapons and whetstone and shield, with jewellery and coin, with vessels of glass and bronze, bit and bridle and bucket, hefty joints of pork and beef. Was he a pagan or a Christian? There is no conclusive evidence either way. And what of the warrior commemorated in the famously enigmatic stone (plates 13 and 14 at Niederdollendorf, a bit further up the Rhine, at some point in the seventh century? What did he believe in? It may be that these are the wrong sort of questions: well, less appropriate than some others. The antithesis pagan/Christian may be too neat and simple. Reality tends to be fuzzy. (It will be a part of the argument of this and the following chapter that fuzziness is an essential and important part of the process of barbarian conversion. But this is to anticipate.) For the moment let us simply observe that grave-goods and uninscribed tombstones are at best ambiguous witnesses to belief.

Gregory of Tours, however, is not. He tells a story of his uncle Gallus (not to be confused with Columbanus' disciple of the same name), set in Cologne in about the year 530. Gallus had gone there in the company of King Theuderic I, son of Clovis.

> There was a temple there filled with various adornments, where the barbarians of the area used to make offerings and gorge themselves with meat and wine until they vomited: they adored idols there as if they were gods, and placed there wooden models of parts of the human body whenever some part of their body was touched by pain. As soon as Gallus learned this he hastened to the place with one other cleric, and having lit a fire he brought it to the temple and set it alight, while none of the foolish pagans was present. They saw the smoke of the temple going up into the sky, and looked for the one who had lit the blaze; they found him and ran after him, their swords in their hands. Gallus took to his heels and hid in the royal palace. The king learned from the threats of the pagans what had happened, and he pacified them with sweet words, calming their impudent anger. The blessed man used to tell this often, adding with tears, 'Woe is me for not having stood my ground, so that I might have ended my life in this cause.'[1]

The evidence, such as it is, leaves us with a sense that in north-eastern Gaul the Frankish invasions and settlement had obliterated much, though not all, of the Christian culture of the region. An effort of 're-Christianization' was called for. In about 500 or shortly afterwards Bishop Remigius of Rheims sent a man named Vedastus (Vedast, Vaast), a native of Aquitaine who had been living as a hermit near Toul, to become bishop of Arras. His biographer, writing in about 640, tells of how he found his cathedral church overgrown with brambles and defiled by animals, the city deserted since its sack by Attila the Hun: Vedastus had to expel a bear from the town, commanding it never to return. These are hagiographical commonplaces, not to be taken literally. (Attila never went anywhere near Arras but he was a convenient hate-figure to whom acts of destruction could unhesitatingly be attributed.) However, they convey vividly a sense of what the seventh century thought had been going on in the sixth. We know little if anything for certain of what Vedastus might have achieved in the course of his long episcopate at Arras – he died in about 540. It was probably not much. But it was a start.

The most famous churchman to concern himself with re-Christianization was Nicetius (Nizier), bishop of Trier from *c.* 525 to *c.* 565. We had a sighting of him in the previous chapter, sending a letter of advice to the Frankish princess Chlodoswintha upon the occasion of her marriage (above, p. 105). Like Vedastus, he was a native of Aquitaine. It was a time when King Theuderic I was encouraging clerics from Aquitaine to go to work in the languishing churches of the Rhineland: an interesting sidelight on the shortage of suitable clergy in the north-east. It was under Theuderic's patronage that Nicetius became bishop of Trier. As long-lived as Vedastus, he devoted his episcopate to the restoration of church life there. We hear, for example, of how he imported Italian craftsmen to build churches in the city. (A further indication of his *mission civilisatrice* was his planting of vineyards on the hillsides above the Mosel. This was another act of restoration: the region's wine had been celebrated two centuries before by Ausonius in his poem *Mosella*; but viticulture as well as Christianity had been a casualty of the fifth century.)

All the tales told of Nicetius by Gregory of Tours (on the authority of his friend Aredius, Nicetius' pupil) have an urban setting. The point is not without significance. An episcopal city with a distinguished and very visible Roman past; its churches; its wine supply: these were at the heart of his concerns, at any rate as celebrated by the poet Venantius Fortunatus, Italian born but domiciled in Gaul. These were the characteristic concerns of the Aquitanian contingent of the sixth century. Men like Vedastus and Nicetius – and, we might add, Aredius and Gallus and Gregory of Tours – came from a part of Gaul which had suffered less disruption than the north-east. Beyond the Loire in Aquitaine city life had maintained an unbroken continuity, there had been little Germanic settlement, much of the administrative and legal routine of daily life was still recognizably Roman, and the church had experienced few of the tremors which had caused it to crack and crumble further north. We must not undervalue the contribution of the Aquitanian clergy in restoring church life in the north-east. They brought determined personnel – Nicetius was clearly a very formidable personality; they brought endowments, books, cults. With royal help they breathed new spiritual life into cities such as Trier. But, an important reservation, they failed to fling out any very attractive spiritual lifeline to the new masters of the region, the local Frankish aristocracy. The re-establishment of a Roman, city-based ecclesiastical pattern was not of itself going to win over the hearts and minds of a rural, tribal warrior aristocracy. The man buried at Morken may have been a Christian – indeed, it is almost inconceivable that a Frankish nobleman of the late sixth century could not have been formally a Christian, serving as he did kings who had been conspicuously Christian for nearly 100 years. He and Nicetius might even (who knows?) have met one another. But one cannot help feeling that their worlds scarcely overlapped or interpenetrated at all.

In the age of Nicetius it is likely that kings were more influential than Gallo-Roman bishops in bringing the aristocracy to adhere to Christianity. As we saw in the last chapter, kings set an example which their aristocracies were likely to follow, if only because it was useful to be in good standing with your king. Frankish kings were becoming more assertively Christian in the course of the sixth century. Childebert I (511–58) issued an edict ordering the destruction of idols: it was more than his father Clovis had done. He brought back relics of St Vincent of Saragossa from a military campaign in Spain and built a church in the saint's honour in Paris, in which he was later buried. (It is now Saint-Germain-des-Prés.) Other leading members of the Merovingian dynasty were buried in Christian churches in the course of the century. The grave of one of them, Childebert's sister-in-law Arnegund, was excavated from beneath the church of Saint-Denis in 1959. (The identification has been doubted: whatever the truth of the matter, the woman buried there was clearly of very high social rank.)

A Frankish church many of whose bishoprics were generously endowed, their incumbents therefore rich and powerful, must have been attractive to a predatory aristocracy. The prevalence of simony in sixth-century Gaul – that is, the practice of buying church office – shows this: people will pay for something worth having. Gregory of Tours was worried about simony and Pope Gregory I wrote several letters to Gallic kings and bishops condemning it in severe terms. Yet these simoniacs were Gallo-Roman, not Frankish aristocrats. When did bishops start to be drawn from Frankish, as opposed to Gallo-Roman families? It is a difficult question to answer because the enquirer is dependent almost entirely on the evidence of personal names, and a 'Roman' name need not indicate Gallo-Roman blood any more than a 'Germanic' name need indicate Frankish blood. Even so impeccable a Gallo-Roman nobleman as Gregory of Tours – and one who was very proud of it too – had an uncle who bore the Frankish name Gundulf. Frankish names among the bench of bishops are rare before the latter years of the sixth century, when we start to encounter such bishops as Magneric of Trier or Ebergisel of Cologne. They become common in the seventh century. After the dynasty's acceptance of Christianity Frankish rulers came rapidly to exert a large measure of control over episcopal appointments. Kings used this power of patronage to reward loyal servants. Service to the crown became the standard route to episcopal office. We shall see plentiful examples of this in the seventh and later centuries.

In the complicated tissue of relationships between Frankish kings and their aristocratic warrior elite there were all sorts of pressures which might bring these men and their families into the Christian fold. But these pressures of themselves were insufficient to bring about full-hearted commitment to the new faith. Additional stimulus was needed from outside; we may call it, if we wish, a missionary stimulus. This was provided by one man above all others, the Irish exile and pilgrim for Christ, St Columbanus. Under the influence of his evangelizing mission the character of the northern Frankish church was transformed.

Columbanus was introduced briefly towards the end of Chapter 3. Here it is necessary only to remind the reader that he was active as a monastic founder in the eastern parts of Francia from about 590 for some twenty years. His most influential foundation was the monastery of Luxeuil, in Burgundy. We can know a fair amount about Columbanus, partly through his own writings, partly by means of the spirited if partisan biography composed within thirty years of his death by his disciple Jonas of Bobbio. Much of the appeal of Columbanus must have lain in his commanding, his tremendous personality. If he strikes the reader of his biography as in many ways reminiscent of Martin of Tours, this is not just because Jonas, like every good hagiographer, had read his Sulpicius Severus and knew how a charismatic holy man should be presented. We have the word of Columbanus himself to attest his veneration of Martin, and Martinian qualities of character repeatedly shine forth from his own works – the awesome spiritual concentration of the man, his courage, his self-denial, his asperity, his unexpected tenderness. A meeting with Columbanus could change the course of a life. We shall see examples of this presently.

Columbanian monasticism appealed to the Frankish aristocracy because it, like them, was rural. Pre-Columbanian monasticism in Gaul had been largely urban or suburban. There were a few exceptions to this rule, such as the Jura communities of the fifth century, but generally the monastic locale was in or close to a town. One might think

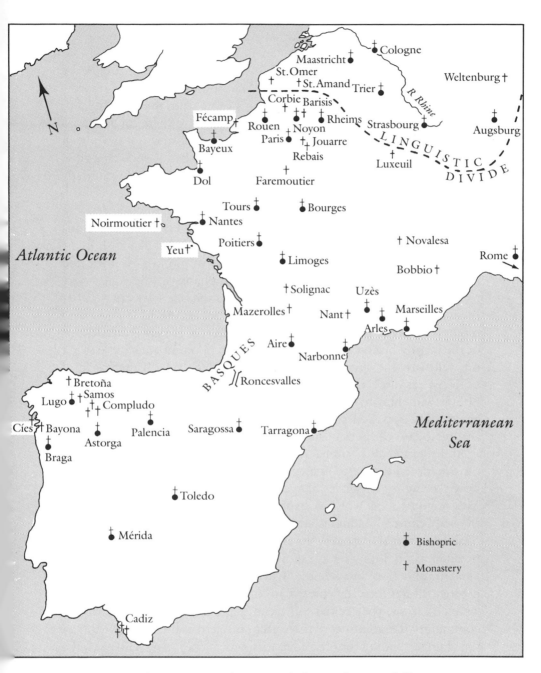

5. *Gaul and Spain in the age of Amandus and Fructuosus,
seventh century.*

of Queen Brunhilde's foundation at Autun or Queen Radegunde's at Poitiers (for the latter of which Venantius Fortunatus composed two of the most magnificent hymns ever written, *Vexilla Regis* and *Pange Lingua*). Even Martin's Ligugé and Marmoutier were close respectively to Poitiers and Tours. Columbanus came from townless Ireland, where the rural monastery was the norm because there could be no other. Luxeuil was nowhere near a city (though it may not have been quite the wilderness that Jonas claimed). Columbanus showed a rural aristocracy that it was acceptable, indeed desirable to found monastic houses far from the madding crowd.

There were other qualities of Columbanian monasticism deriving from the Irish model which made it attractive to Frankish aristocrats. It allowed room for the solidarity of kinship. Frankish like Irish founders could be confident that family interests would not be neglected in the monasteries they established. Its emphasis on the supervisory role of the abbot (perhaps a kinsman) of a monastic network – rather than, as previously, the local bishop – was reassuring to families who might be apprehensive, sometimes with justice, of the covetous designs of the nearby bishop upon its endowments. (Columbanus did not get on well with the Frankish episcopal hierarchy. It is characteristic of both his resource and his lack of tact that he brought a tame Irish bishop with him to carry out episcopal functions at his behest.) Its adaptability appealed to founders who might have special needs to accommodate or special forms of piety to indulge.

At the kernel of Columbanus' spiritual nourishment lay his teachings on penance. He was prominent among those churchmen who were slowly bringing about a change from 'public' to 'private' penance. This requires a few words of explanation. The penitential discipline of the early church as administered by, let us say, Gregory of Pontus was of an exceptional harshness. Its characteristics were as follows. It could be administered only by a bishop, and it could be undergone by the penitent only once in a lifetime. It was public and it was shaming. The penitent sinner formally entered an 'order of penitents' in a ceremony which took place before the entire congregation of his or her Christian community. Penitents were thereafter segregated into a special part of the church building for future services, where they had to listen to the communal intercessions for them of their neighbours. The penitent had to observe lifelong chastity thereafter and was debarred from ever holding any public office: a seventh-century king of Spain who underwent penance had to abdicate. Penance thereby aimed mortal blows at family and civil life. The penitent became in effect a non-person. Cleansed of sin, penitents were assured that all that human effort could do had been done to purchase their salvation from the everlasting torments of hell. But the price was terribly high.

Because of the savage nature of the demands of the penitential process it became customary to defer the experience of it until the deathbed. This was all very well, but it left a spiritual void during life. 'Private' penance filled this void. It could be administered by any priest, as confessor, not just by a bishop. It could be repeated any number of times. Its central principles were the unburdening of the conscience in a private act of contrition witnessed only by the confessor, followed by the doing of an act of penance, usually fasting, commensurate with the gravity of the sin. Confessors were guided in their recommendations by the tariffs of sins and appropriate penances to be found in the texts known as 'penitentials' or 'penitential books' drawn up by revered spiritual guides. Columbanus was the author of one such guide. These are its introductory words: 'True penance is not to commit things deserving of penance but to lament such things as have been committed ... Diversity of offences causes diversity of penances. Doctors of the body compound their medicines in diverse kinds ... So also should spiritual doctors treat with diverse kinds of cures the wounds of souls, their sicknesses, pains, ailments, and infirmities.'[2] Columbanus thus conceived of penance as a form of spiritual medicine. The encounter between confessor and penitent became the opportunity for spiritual teaching. In this fashion private penance was the ideal vehicle for furthering and deepening the Christianization of the recently converted. For their part the men and women of the barbarian aristocracies took to it with gusto. It has often been observed that the notion of a tariff of penances for sins was instantly intelligible to a society which regulated wrongdoing by the norms of law codes which were essentially tariffs of compensations for crimes. True, if superficial. The new penitential system was not an easy option, as a glance at the penitential of Columbanus will show. Its attraction was that it held out – humanely, intimately, personally – a lifeline to the individual members of an aristocratic society that was violent, guilty and fearful. The violence and the guilt we can read about in the pages of Gregory of Tours or in the self-abasing preambles to deeds of gift to God and His saints. So let us especially remember the fear, which could not be admitted publicly: fear of treachery, fear of revenge, fear of shame, fear of pain, and above all fear of death and what might lie beyond it. Penance healed guilt and drove out fear. Its disciplines helped to make sense of misfortune and deflected divine anger provoked by human depravity. And if sin could be wiped out by the discipline of penance, could not the offering to God – in a society where every cog of social intercourse was oiled by the giving of gifts – of a monastery, richly endowed, splendidly furnished, peopled by the founder's own kin turned monks expert in prayer, buy His favour?

It should by now be a little easier to understand why the Frankish aristocracy adopted Columbanian monasticism with such reckless abandon. It called to their hearts. One last and more mundane point needs to be made. There was a coincidence in time between the arrival of Columbanus and a change in the nature of the aristocracy of the Frankish north-east. In the half-century or so between, roughly, 575 and 625 this aristocracy became more cohesive and self-conscious. For the first time it acquired legal privileges which underpinned its distinctness from other social groups. It became less exclusively dependent for status on royal patronage. It became more solidly landed and probably, taken by and large, wealthier. Columbanian monasticism, it has been suggested, 'was eagerly seized upon by the northern Frankish aristocracy as a means of expressing a newly acquired power and prestige'.[3] As often, social change and religious innovation dovetailed neatly together.

One of the earliest Frankish converts to the Columbanian monastic life was a young man named Chagnoald, who became a monk at Luxeuil. He belonged to an aristocratic family then settled near Meaux, to the east of Paris, though it had originated in Burgundy. It was presumably this Burgundian connection which had brought Chagnoald into contact with Luxeuil. Chagnoald's father Chagneric was in the service of King Chlothar II (d. 629). In the course of a journey from Paris back to Luxeuil undertaken by Columbanus and Chagnoald in the year 610, the latter persuaded the saint to break his journey at the family home. While staying with Chagneric, Columbanus blessed his young daughter Burgundofara (Fara, Fare) and (in Jonas' words) 'dedicated her to the Lord'. The girl's life was changed by this encounter. When she grew up she entered monastic life and founded a nunnery upon one of the family estates, Eboriacum, later to take its name from her, 'Fara's monastery', Faremoûtier, now Faremoutiers-en-Brie.

Meanwhile her brother Chagnoald had left Luxeuil to become bishop of Laon, another brother Chagnulf had become count (i.e. governor on behalf of the king) of Meaux and a third, Burgundofaro (Faro), after service in the royal chancery of Dagobert I (d. 639), had become bishop of Meaux. Burgundofara's will, dated 633 or 634, has survived. It shows how well endowed her nunnery was, and how the different members of the family had contributed to these endowments. Reading it, one gets the sense of a joint family enterprise. Faremoutiers later received endowments from Queen Balthild, wife of Clovis II (d. 657). Balthild was of English birth. It is just possible that her generosity to Faremoutiers was prompted by awareness of some distinguished Anglo-Saxon inmates. According to Bede the Kentish princess Eorcengota, great-granddaughter of Ethelbert and Bertha, became a nun at Faremoutiers, and two East Anglian princesses became successive abbesses there. We shall return to these Anglo-Frankish contacts later on.

Another fruitful contact was made in the course of this same journey in 610. After leaving Chagneric's household Columbanus stayed with another aristocratic couple named Authar and Aiga: they lived not far away and were related to Chagneric's family. There the saint blessed two, possibly three sons of the household. The eldest of these, Ado or Adon, founded a nunnery on family land at Jouarre in about 635. Its first abbess was his cousin Theudichildis, whose handsome stone sarcophagus may still be seen in the crypt there. Ado's younger brother Dado (better known as Audoen, in French Ouen) served in King Dagobert's chancery and founded a monastery at Rebais at about the same time that his brother was founding the nunnery at nearby Jouarre. The foundation charter for Rebais has survived. The king provided a major part of the endowment, to which Burgundofaro, Audoen's fellow royal servant, also contributed. The first abbot of Rebais was Agilus, formerly a monk of Luxeuil, and the monks of Rebais were to observe a mixture of the Columbanian and Benedictine monastic rules.

These instances, and others too numerous to quote, show how whole-heartedly the men and women of the northern Frankish nobility adopted the spiritual ideals of Columbanus. These people were very powerful backers or sponsors. They were extremely rich, they were interconnected by webs of kinship and shared values, and they were on terms of easy though respectful familiarity with the Merovingian kings they served. They could offer resources in land, treasure, authority and connections to their monastic foundations. These in their turn made possible further initiatives. One such was intellectual. We saw in Chapter 3 that the pursuit of Latin learning was a distinguishing trait of Irish monasticism. Columbanus implanted this concern in the communities which he founded on the continent, where it was enthusiastically taken up for the same sort of reasons which had force in Ireland: Germanic-speaking monks and nuns had to learn the Latin of the church. Luxeuil and Bobbio became important centres of learning in the course of the seventh century. So did several of their descendants, for example Corbie in Picardy, founded by Queen Balthild and her son between 657 and 661, with a first abbot and monks from Luxeuil.

Another such initiative was an evangelistic one. As we saw in Chapter 2 the impulse to become a lifelong 'pilgrim for Christ' merged into a sense of mission; and we have Columbanus' own word attesting to his 'vow to make my way to the heathen to preach the gospel to them'. The letter from which that phrase is quoted was composed in 610, the same year in which he met the families of Authar and Chagneric. One can scarcely doubt that Columbanus could have failed to speak of what lay uppermost in his mind in the course of those visits. (We shall shortly meet evidence to suggest that his exhortations did not fall on deaf ears.) In 611, as we have already seen, Columbanus converted some of the inhabitants of the area around Bregenz. Jonas tells us – and it is perhaps significant that he tells us in the same chapter – that

> At this time the idea came to him that he ought to go to the territory of the pagan Slavs and preach the word of the gospel to their blinded minds. And when he was thinking about his the angel of the Lord appeared to him in a vision and drew a circle in a small space, as it were on the page of a book, showing him the whole world. 'Look,' he said, 'and see how much of the world remains untouched. Choose to go where your labours will bear fruit.' And Columbanus understood that the Slavs were not yet ready for the faith, so he remained quietly where he was until an opportunity to go to Italy appeared.[4]

We shall return to the Slavs in a later chapter. Here it need only be said that their fairly recent arrival in the Danube basin threatened the south-eastern marches of the Frankish kingdom. The Frankish rulers of the first half of the seventh century adopted a forward policy in this area, which also had an ecclesiastical dimension. In part it was a matter of restoration as in the Mosel and Rhineland areas. The bishopric of Augsburg, long dormant, was re-established in the 630s apparently on the initiative of Dagobert I. In part it was a matter of striking out in new directions. A little earlier a monastic house had been founded at Weltenburg, near Kelheim to the west of Regensburg, on the Danube. The lay patronage may have come from the dukes of Bavaria, over whom Frankish rulers claimed lordship: the exact circumstances of the foundation are obscure. What is certain is that Weltenburg was a daughter-house of Luxeuil in the time of Abbot Eustasius, the successor of Columbanus. One of the monks involved in establishing the new colony was Agilus, shortly afterwards to be first abbot of Audoen's Rebais. Weltenburg was a long way to the east of any other Columbanian foundation. On the margins of Christendom, it performed some of the functions of a mission station.

Audoen, founder of Rebais, was promoted through royal agency to the bishopric of Rouen in 641 and held that see until his death at an advanced age in 684. The diocese of Rouen comprised the lower valley of the Seine and the lands to either side of it (later to be called Normandy after the Northmen who would settle there in the tenth century). This was another area where re-Christianization was required. In the words of his early biographer,

> And when the Lord saw His servant to be eager and active in performing His commands, He snatched him away from the shipwreck that is this earthly life and placed him on the episcopal throne of the city of Rouen ... He became an outstanding preacher, inspiring the Lord's people by his words and by his deeds. With God's help he was so emboldened in the faith that he transformed the savage cruelty of the Franks into gentleness, distilled the sweetness that flows from the fount of God and so prepared the church for the service of the Lord that they turned from their pagan ways and voluntarily chose to submit themselves to the yoke of Christ.[5]

During Audoen's episcopate several monasteries were founded with his encouragement in the lower Seine – Jumièges, St Wandrille and Fécamp among them. The founder of Jumièges, Filibert, was another member of this remarkable aristocratic network. Filibert was not by birth a northern Frank: he came from Eauze, on the fringes of Gascony. His father Filibald was a nobleman in royal service who ended his career as bishop of Aire. Filibald placed his son at the court of Dagobert I, where he became a friend of, among others, Audoen. At the age of nineteen 'he chose to become Christ's disciple' (in the words of his earliest biographer). It comes as no surprise to learn that he joined the monastery founded by his friend at Rebais under the direction of Abbot Agilus. In due course he succeeded Agilus as abbot. Resolving to found a house of his own he sought and received landed endowments in Audoen's diocese of Rouen from that devout couple King Clovis II and Queen Balthild and established a monastery at Jumièges between 648 and 657. Much later, expelled from Jumièges by political enemies, he made his way to the Vendée, where Bishop Ansoald of Poitiers, a Burgundian who seems to have had connections with Columbanian monastic circles, helped him to found a monastery on the island of Noirmoutier, just off France's Atlantic coast a little to the south of the estuary of the river Loire. Filibert founded other houses, but Jumièges and Noirmoutier were the most famous among them. He died in the same year as Audoen, 684.

A third area for evangelistic endeavour was presented by the northeast of the Frankish realms, that is to say the extreme north of modern France, and Belgium. Here Christianity, in so far as it had made any impression before the settlement of the pagan Franks in Toxandria, had been more thoroughly blotted out than in the Seine or Danube basins. Early re-Christianizers such as Vedastus at Arras seem to have made little impression. The seventh century saw more determined efforts, backed by greater resources. Here too the Columbanian impulse was paramount. Consider for example the career of Audomar (Otmar, Omer). Natives of the Cotentin peninsula in western 'Normandy' he and his father crossed Gaul to become monks at Luxeuil in about 615; a telling example of the range of its magnetism. When King Dagobert re-founded the bishopric of Thérouanne, Audomar was appointed to it. There is reason to suppose that Bishop Acharius of nearby Noyon was influential in bringing about his appointment: Acharius was another 'old boy' of Luxeuil and he was influential with the king. Audomar was active in the evangelization of his diocese until his death in about 670. One of the churches he founded later grew into a great abbey, and the abbey into a town named after him: Saint-Omer. (This is one of many examples of the stimulus provided to urban and commercial life by early medieval monasteries.) Audomar was accompanied by a fellow monk of Luxeuil, Bertinus, for whom a monastery was founded at a place named Sithiu, later to become famous under the name of its founder: the abbey of Saint-Bertin.

The successor of Acharius in the bishopric of Noyon was Eligius (Eloi), another remarkable member of this network. Like his younger contemporary Filibert, Eligius was a native of Aquitaine; he came from near Limoges. His family was neither landed nor noble, and the young Eligius would on these grounds alone have found it well nigh imposs- ible to break into the charmed circle of court-bishops. Eligius owed his advancement to his outstanding talent as a goldsmith. As a youth he was apprenticed to a certain Abbo, himself a very skilled goldsmith and master of the mint at Limoges. (Frankish coin was struck under royal licence at a number of mint-towns scattered throughout the kingdom. The moneyers who managed the local mints were more than just technicians. They had significant administrative and fiscal responsibilities, and were important figures on their local scene and sometimes well beyond it too.) Moving on into the service of the royal treasurer, Eligius came to the notice of King Chlothar II, by whom he was commissioned to make a throne decorated with gold and precious stones. To the astonishment of all, Eligius contrived to make two thrones out of the materials given him for one. It was the making of his career. The king was so impressed by his skill and his honesty that he kept him on as his goldsmith-in-chief: in the words of his biographer (who might have been his friend Audoen) he was a 'highly skilled goldsmith and very experienced in all sorts of metalwork'. Only one fragment of metalwork attributed to him survives, a small panel from the jewelled cross which he made to the commission of Dagobert I for the church of Saint-Denis: the remainder of it was destroyed during the French revolution. We also possess illustrations of other pieces which have since perished. For example, there survives a seventeenth- century engraving of the so-called chalice of Eligius which was in the possession of the monastery of Chelles, founded by Queen Balthild: this too perished in the course of the revolution. If these attributions are correct, then indeed Eligius was a craftsman of most consummate skill. He had other talents too. His early training had taught him how to manage coinage: he was entrusted with the mints of Marseilles and subsequently Paris for much of the 620s and 630s. He was a trusted counsellor of Dagobert I and an important figure at the royal court. We know that he was employed on one occasion on a diplomatic mission to Brittany, over whose rulers the Frankish kings claimed and intermittently exercised supremacy, and there may have been other comparable embassies of which we know nothing.

Eligius was very devout. When engaged upon his craft of goldsmithery he would have an open Bible in front of him so that he could study the word of God while working. He employed his wealth which, given his opportunities, must have become considerable, in ransoming captives, especially 'from the people of the Saxons who at that time were being rounded up like sheep and scattered abroad' – words which are most likely to refer to Saxons from England rather than from continental Saxony. He would offer his redeemed prisoners three choices: either to go home, or to stay in his service, or to enter a monastery. It is an interesting sidelight on one means of monastic recruitment. Eligius founded two monasteries while in royal service, at Ferrières and at Solignac. The first abbot of Ferrières, by name Buchinus, was one of these freed prisoners, a convert from paganism. Many of the first generation of monks at Solignac were drawn from the same source. The foundation charter of Solignac survives, dated 22 November 633. It is a revealing document; we find ourselves in a familiar world. A generous landed endowment had been granted 'by the munificence of the most glorious and devout lord King Dagobert'; the first abbot, Remaclus, had been a monk of Luxeuil; the monks were to observe the characteristic mixture of the Benedictine and Columbanian rules; and there are some familiar names, such as Audoen's, among the dignitaries who witnessed the document. Eligius and Audoen were consecrated bishops together in 641. During his episcopate at Noyon until his death in 660 Eligius did much good work in ministering to his flock, including 'the barbarians who dwell along the sea coast, as yet unploughed by the share of preaching', as his biographer put it, here borrowing a phrase from Rufinus' translation of Eusebius.

The reader has been bombarded with unfamiliar names in the course of the last few pages and (if he has not yet flung the book aside) must be cowering in readiness for the next shell to explode its shrapnel of Audoens and Balthilds and Chagnerics and Dagoberts across the scarred and pitted territory of the mind. Take heart. Lewis Namier once said to Arnold Toynbee, 'You try to see the tree as a whole. I try to examine it leaf by leaf.' We have examined a few leaves (a very few) from seventh-century Francia. Now for the tree. We can detect a

1. A reconstruction of King Edwin of Northumbria's seventh-century palace-complex at Yeavering (Northumberland), sited on a natural terrace which slopes down to the River Glen, scene of mass-baptisms administered by Paulinus.

2. The expectation of the miraculous. Jesus raises the son of the widow of Nain from the dead (Luke vii. 11-15). Ivory plaque, German, perhaps Magdeburg, about 970.

3. *Above* Constantine I (306-37), the first Christian emperor, on a medallion struck at Ticinum (Pavia) in about 315. The Christian *Chi-Rho* monogram adorns the crown above the right eye of this imperial 'friend of God'.

4. *Left* The bishop as exorcist. Zeno of Verona, a contemporary of Martin of Tours, expels a devil from the emperor's daughter: the creature issues from the girl's mouth. A panel from the bronze doors of Verona cathedral made about the year 1100.

5 and 6. Saint-Martin-de-Boscherville (Seine-Maritime), France. This model reconstruction well illustrates the transition from Gallo-Roman temple (left) to Christian church (right), discussed in Chapter 2.

7. The remains of the monastery of Inishmurray (County Sligo), off the Atlantic coast of Ireland.

8. The opening passage of the code of law issued by King Ethelbert of Kent, in a copy made in about 1090. The opening clause decrees that theft of church property must be compensated twelve-fold.

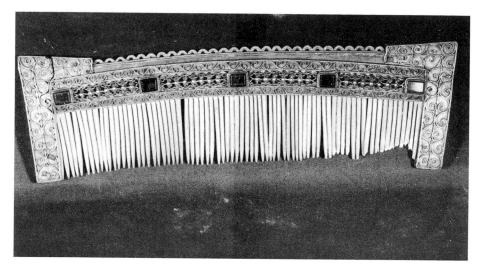

9. A comb which allegedly belonged to the Bavarian princess Theodelinda, wife of the Lombard King Aistulf and mother by him of Adaloald, recipient of the letter from the Visigothic King Sisebut discussed in Chapter 4. Perhaps the comb sent by Pope Gregory I to Ethelbert's Queen Bertha looked something like this.

10. A pair of spoons found among the treasure in the ship-burial at Sutton Hoo (Suffolk). The inscriptions 'Saulos' and 'Paulos' in Greek characters might possibly have references to a conversion.

D . MQVIDEM FRANGITPARVORVMMORTEPARENTES
CONDICIORVAPIDOSPRVAEGIPTATAGRADV
SPESAFTERNATAMENTREBVETSOLACIALVCTVS
AETATESTENERASOVDPARADISVSABET
SEXSVTERADICISADNONVMMENSIBVS
CONDITVSHGCTVMOLODESSIDERATEIACES

INHVNCTOMOLOREQ
ESCITINPACEBONEMEMO
RIENOMEN·RICNEDRVDIS·
CARAPARENTEBVSETNI
MIVMRELICTAAMORE
QVIVIXITINHVNC·
SAECOLO·ANNOS·XIIII
ETMICRAVITDEHVCMVN
DO · XV · KLS·MAIAS

11 and 12. The Rhineland
graves of Desideratus and
Rignetrudis, respectively of
the fifth and sixth centuries,
identifiable as Christians by
the Latin inscriptions, the
Chi-Rho monograms and
the peacocks (symbolising
immortality).

13 and 14. Gravestone from Niederdollendorf, near Bonn (Nordrhein-Westfalen), Germany. The religious allegiance of this possibly seventh-century Frankish warrior – or of those who commemorated him in this fashion – are by no means clear.

15 The church of São Fructuoso de Montelios on the outskirts of Braga in northern Portugal. Its construction is attributed to Fructuosus, bishop of Braga in the third quarter of the seventh century. Its notably classical and stylish air contrasts sharply with such rustic churches as that of Hordain (below).

16. A reconstruction of a seventh-century village church and its accompanying cemetery at Hordain, near Douai, not far from the present Franco-Belgian border, in an area where the great missionary-bishop Amandus worked in the middle years of the seventh century.

network of persons, both men and women, defined by certain common characteristics. They were all, excepting only Eligius, of aristocratic birth. With that there went the disposal of considerable landed wealth, the habit of leadership and command. They were all closely connected with a succession of very powerful Frankish kings, Chlothar II, his son Dagobert I and his son Clovis II. These kings exercised authority in both church and state through the agency of the young noblemen whom they gathered about them at their itinerant court and in due course promoted to one of the glittering prizes, a county or a bishopric, that awaited a loyal servant. They were all touched by the spiritual ideals imported into Francia by Columbanus: ideals which they found appealing for reasons already investigated and which they could realize in monastic foundations or episcopal duties. One of these ideals was manifested in a shared concern for the work of evangelization. There was a lively sense of missionary imperative in seventh-century Gaul. Its fruits can be seen in the operations of these persons on or near the northern and eastern fringes of the Frankish kingdom.

One last figure may be lightly sketched before we leave this busy, crowded scene because in his career he wove together so many of these threads. Last but by no means least, and more a branch than a leaf: his name was Amandus. The principal source of information about Amandus is a short biography composed not long after his death, perhaps by a disciple of his called Baudemundus.[6] The author was not concerned with chronology – an unconcern common among hagiographers – and the detailed sequence of the career of Amandus has to remain lamentably vague. But the author furnishes us with enough to delineate the outlines of a very remarkable life.

Amandus was born about the year 590 into a landed family of Gallo-Roman descent whose estates seem to have lain on the southern side of the lower reaches of the river Loire. Saint Amand-sur-Sèvres (Dpt. Deux Sèvres), about forty miles south-east of Nantes, has been suggested as a possible birthplace. We should remember the evangelizing work of Bishop Félix of Nantes among the Saxon settlers of the lower Loire: Amandus passed his childhood close to barbarians who were beginning to settle into Christianity. We might also care to recall the holy man Friardus on his island in the Loire. Amandus received a good education and then took himself off to join a monastic community on the island of Yeu, about a dozen miles off the Atlantic coast. It has been conjectured that this was an Irish foundation, though there seems to be no evidence that this was so. It was while he was on Yeu that he was said to have had an encounter with an enormous snake which he banished from the island by his prayers and the sign of the cross: a youthful portent of sanctity. His father sought to persuade his son to re-enter secular life. But Amandus had already experienced a religious vocation. He left his native region and journeyed up the valley of the Loire to Tours. There, at the shrine of St Martin, he made a vow 'that he might never be permitted to return to his own land but might spend his whole life on pilgrimage (*in peregrinatione*)', as an exile for Christ.

The vow of Amandus at Tours gains in resonance when we consider its context. The cult of St Martin, never faltering over the last two centuries, had recently been fanned to new heat by the writings of Bishop Gregory of Tours. Martin, as we saw in Chapter 2, had been another exile or pilgrim whose final settlement in western Gaul was hundreds of miles from his birthplace in Pannonia. He had also, of course, been an evangelist who had conceived of his role as bishop in an apostolic sense and had devoted his episcopate to forcing Christianity upon the stubborn farmers of Touraine. If Martin was a source of inspiration to the young Amandus, Columbanus was a complementary one. And it was at just about this time that the Irish holy man was causing a great stir in the valley of the Loire. In the year 610, as a result of a quarrel with Queen Brunhilde, Columbanus was being escorted by the royal officers down the Loire to Nantes, where the intention was to deport him and pack him off back home to Ireland. It didn't work because, as Jonas explains, God had other plans for Columbanus. It was on his way back to Burgundy that the saint had the momentous encounters with the families of Chagneric and Authar alluded to earlier in this chapter. Columbanus had not 'gone quietly'. Displaying something of that flair for publicity which is so often an adjunct of sanctity, Columbanus had made his journey controversial, noisy and public: it is hard not to feel a sneaking sympathy for the royal officers. Columbanus was extremely visible and doubtless much talked about when the young Amandus was prospecting for a role for his vocation.

Amandus never met Columbanus (as far as we know) but his movements after leaving Tours suggest that he had been touched by the fashionable Columban current of piety. Encouraged by the community of St Martin he continued his journey inland up the valley of the river

Cher until he came to Bourges. He evidently came equipped with the appropriate letters of introduction and commendation, for he was well received by the bishop, Austregisilus, and his archdeacon (at that period the most important ecclesiastic in the diocese after the bishop), Sulpicius. They provided him with a cell in the city wall, where he lived the ascetic life of a hermit for, as Baudemundus vaguely tells us, 'about fifteen years' – approximately, let us say, between about 610 and 625. This was a period when the diocese of Bourges was humming with monastic initiatives of a Columbanian type. Between about 620 and 640 five such communities were founded in the diocese with episcopal encouragement. Sulpicius himself, who succeeded Austregis-ilus as bishop in 626, founded one just outside the town, later to be known as St Sulpice de Bourges. Sulpicius had other promising young men in tow besides Amandus. One of these was Remaclus, later a monk at Luxeuil, then abbot of Eligius' foundation at Solignac, later still the first abbot of Stablo (Stavelot) in the Ardennes, founded by the royal family in 648.

At the end of the fifteen-odd years at Bourges Amandus made a journey to Rome. His biographer tells us that one night he attempted to stay inside the basilica of St Peter so that he could pray and keep vigil beside the prince of the apostles throughout the hours of darkness. He was discovered by one of the custodians of the church and unceremoniously ejected. As he sat alone on the steps outside the locked doors Amandus was approached by a ghostly figure whom he knew to be none other than St Peter himself. The apostle told him to return to Gaul and there 'to take up the task of preaching'. It was a turning-point in Amandus' life. Whatever may have occurred to him that night there were other, human, encounters during his stay in Rome. One of these was an audience with the pope. Now the pope of the day would have been either Boniface V (619–25) or Honorius I (625–38). Both of them were concerned with missionary activity. Pope Boniface had urged Christianity upon King Edwin of Northumbria and Honorius I consecrated a missionary bishop for the West Saxons (below, p. 161). In Rome in the early seventh century, a Rome still mindful of Pope Gregory I whose pupil Honorius had been, Amandus would have breathed an atmosphere impregnated with evangelistic zeal. Thus far then, Martinian and Columbanian currents were flowing; a spark had been ignited in Rome; and connections with the Frankish royal court through his patron Sulpicius lay to hand.

After his return to Gaul Amandus became a bishop. Baudemundus tells us that he was 'compelled' (*coactus*) to receive episcopal office by the king and the bishops. We should bear in mind that the monastic audience for whom he wrote was schooled to applaud the modest reluctance of a holy man to accept high ecclesiastical office. Whatever might have been the personal feelings of Amandus, it is simple enough to read between the lines of his biographer's report. Amandus was promoted with the sponsorship of king and bishops; he was a candidate of the court establishment. It has been assumed that the king in question was Chlothar II, who died in 629. If Amandus was consecrated in the latter half of the 620s, he would have been a fairly young bishop. Since young men do not generally attain high office without powerful connections, it is fair to suppose that Amandus had friends and well-wishers in the grandest circles of the kingdom. One other point is significant about his promotion. Amandus was not consecrated to any particular bishopric. Indeed – and as we shall see there are parallels for this – he seems to have been given a roving commission to preach and to carry out episcopal functions wheresoever he deemed it to be necessary. An example of such a function was the consecration of the church of a recently founded monastery in the year 636. The monastery was Rebais, founded by Audoen.

The ruler with whom Amandus was initially most closely associated was Dagobert I, who had been made a sub-king by his father Chlothar II in 623. The region allotted to his rule was the north-eastern portion of the Frankish realm known as Austrasia. As we have seen, this was an area whose evangelization was a matter of concern for kings and bishops. It was also an area where Frankish royal power was gradually being extended at the expense of the tribes who lived to the east of the Rhine. Not for the first nor by any means for the last time, secular imperialism and Christian evangelism went hand in hand. Relations between Amandus and Dagobert were not always harmonious. Early on in their association they had a serious quarrel. Baudemundus was coy about it, so that both the issues and the timing remain obscure, but it seems to have involved questions of principle relating to missionary work. It looks as though Dagobert wanted Amandus to restrict his operations to peoples over whom Frankish lordship was exercised or claimed. Amandus did not wish to be so confined. He understood his vocation and ministry to be directed (in his own words) to 'all provinces or nations'. The issue proved a divisive one, as we shall see it proving on other occasions. So divisive, indeed, that Amandus was sent into exile by the king for a spell. During his exile he preached to the heathen, though unfortunately we are not told where. His exile seems not to have lasted long. In the event he was reconciled with Dagobert through the mediation of two stalwart royal servants – Eligius and Audoen. Well, well: a small world. The reconciliation seems, though Baudemundus loyally fudges this, to have been on the king's terms. Whatever may have been the rights and wrongs of the matter, thereafter Amandus consistently operated in contexts where he can be seen as acting in association with Frankish royal power. Whether he cared to think of himself in this light we shall never know.

A generous king could be of enormous assistance to a missionary bishop. At some point in the 630s, for example – as usual we do not know exactly when – Amandus founded a monastery at a place then called Elnone. Today its name commemorates him: Saint-Amand-les-Eaux, an undistinguished little town on the Franco-Belgian frontier between Valenciennes and Tournai. Baudemundus called it 'a place suitable for preaching', so it is clear that a missionary function was intended for the community from the start. Amandus himself tells us, in his will drawn up in 674 or 675, that the monastery was built 'on land given by royal largesse'. It can be shown from other sources that this largesse amounted to nearly 25,000 acres, a handsome endowment by any standards. Or again, in the words of Baudemundus: 'Amandus went to Acharius, then bishop of Noyon, and humbly asked him to go as soon as possible to King Dagobert and obtain letters from him, stating that if anyone did not freely choose to be reborn by the waters of baptism, he should be forced by the king to receive this sacrament.' We note the role of Bishop Acharius as intermediary between Amandus and the king. But the really significant feature of the story is Amandus' readiness to resort to forcible conversion and Dagobert's willingness to provide the necessary coercion.

We can learn a little about Amandus' conduct of his mission in the north-east. He sought helpers from monastic houses of the Columbanian connection. For instance, no less a person than Jonas of Bobbio, biographer of Columbanus, was at Elnone in the years 639–42, assisting (in his words) 'to cure with the fiery purge of the gospel the age-old errors of the Sicambrians [a literary term for the north-eastern Franks]'. Amandus also sought assistance from a less expected quarter. According to his biographer, 'If he found captives or boys from across the sea, he redeemed them at a price, baptizing them and having them taught letters. Once they had been freed he sent them to different churches. We have heard that some of them later became bishops, priests or distinguished abbots.' The words 'across the sea' are most likely to indicate Anglo-Saxon England, as was suggested in the previous chapter with reference to the *Pactus Legis Salicae*. Amandus was not alone in this practice. We have already seen the example of Eligius. Again, Richarius, founder of the abbey of Centula (later, after him, Saint-Riquier) near Abbeville, is said to have visited England to preach and to redeem captives, apparently in the 630s. And let us not forget the extraordinary story of Balthild, the pretty English slave-girl who caught the eye of Clovis II and became his queen and a famous benefactress of the monastic life. The English slaves bought and trained by Amandus would have been able to cope with the Germanic speech of the peoples among whom he worked. We do not know how fluent Amandus himself became in the Frankish/Frisian dialects of the northeast, though the implication of some of the stories told by Baudemundus is that he was reasonably fluent. Amandus ranged well forward from his base at Elnone. It was near Ghent that he raised a hanged man from the dead, with spectacular results:

> When this miracle was diffused far and wide, the inhabitants of the region rushed to Amandus and humbly begged that he would make them Christians. They destroyed with their own hands the temples where, until then, they had worshipped, and all turned to the true worship of God. Where the temples had stood the man of God Amandus, thanks to royal munificence and to the aims of devout men and women, built monasteries or churches and, feeding the people with the sacred food of the Word, illumined the hearts of all men with heavenly mandates.

When he finally received a seat for his bishopric it was at Maastricht, a clear pointer to missionary work in what we now call the Netherlands: this would have been in about 647. Baudemundus tells us that Amandus was reluctant to accept the see of Maastricht. A conventional hagiographical topos, we might think. But that the saint's reluctance was genuine and not feigned is proved by the survival of a letter to him from Pope Martin I, dated 649, urging him not to resign the bishopric. It was evidently a response to a perhaps anguished appeal from its incumbent. It is also, incidentally, good evidence of the continuing Roman loyalties of Amandus.

Amandus did not like to be tied down. One of the wonder stories told by Baudemundus was set in the area of Beauvais, a long way to the south of Elnone. (It concerned the cutting down of a sacred tree: shades of Martin.) His monastic foundations were far-flung. They comprised Elnone in Flanders, Barisis-au-Bois near Soissons (*c.* 664) and Nant on the edge of the Cévennes (between 662 and 675) – the latter in the teeth of opposition from Bishop Mummolinus of Uzès. (He hired some contract killers to put paid to Amandus but providentially they got lost in a fog.) Each foundation received generous endowments from the royal family. Amandus' missionary operations were not confined to Flanders either. He worked in two other areas which were also of concern to Frankish kings. One of these was among the Slavs. We know neither exactly where nor when, for all we have is a brief chapter in his biography:

> He heard that the Slavs, sunk in great error, were caught in the devil's snares. Greatly hoping that he might gain the palm of martyrdom, he crossed the Danube and, journeying round, freely preached the Gospel of Christ to the people. But when a very few had been reborn in Christ, seeing that he was achieving little and that he could not obtain the martyrdom he always sought, he returned to his own flock.

It is tempting to connect this with the Bavarian initiatives of Dagobert I. If we were to seek an ecclesiastical impulse we might think of Agilus, formerly monk of Weltenburg, whose abbey church at Rebais Amandus had consecrated in 636: again, a small world, of intricate cross-connections.

Another people on whom Amandus tried in vain to urge Christianity were the Basques.

> He heard of a people formerly known as Vaceians, now vulgarly called Basques. They were so plunged in error that, given up to auguries and other superstitions, they adored idols instead of God. This race is spread throughout the Pyrenees in rough and inaccessible country and, by its daring and mobility in battle, often raided the Frankish borders. The man of God Amandus, taking pity on their error, laboured earnestly to rescue them from the devil's hold.

Here too we might care to link this with Frankish military initiatives against a troublesome people who were expanding from their homelands in the western Pyrenees down into the lowlands of Gascony and beyond. In 635 Dagobert I mounted a big campaign against them, and we have therefore a context for an evangelistic operation which followed up this (or another) military one. The linguistic difficulties must have been even more formidable than those on the Romance/ Germanic frontier of the north-east, for Basque is a language akin to no other. Even Baudemundus admits that Amandus made no impression whatsoever upon the religious life of the Basques. The only positive results, according to him, were divine retribution visited upon a man who had imprudently mocked the saint's preaching, and a miracle worked by water in which Amandus had washed his hands while staying with a fellow bishop, apparently while on the way home. (Could this have been Bishop Filibald of Aire? Amandus could have had an introduction to him from his son Filibert, monk of Rebais.) One wonders whether the monastery at Nant was intended as a springboard for future missionary work among the Basques on the analogy of Elnone for Flanders.

Our last glimpse of Amandus comes in a document from his own hand, his *testamentum* or will.

> No one is ignorant of how I travelled far and wide through all provinces and nations for the love of Christ, to announce the Word of God and administer baptism, and of how divine clemency has saved me from many dangers and has deigned to preserve me down to the present day. But now, worn out by my labours, in extreme old age, my body half dead, I hope soon to leave this world.

The will was drawn up on 17 April 674 (or possibly 675). It is assumed that Amandus died shortly afterwards. With his passing the Frankish church lost one of the brightest stars in that constellation of talent, of wealth and of connection which had marked the seventh century.

German historians have coined the term *Adelskirche* to characterize the Frankish church as its lineaments appear to us in the age of Amandus. Literally 'church of the nobility', the term in its wider extension means a church managed by and very largely for the aristocracy. We are not to understand that aristocrats had taken no part in church life before this age; clearly they had. Nor are we to suppose that aristocratic preponderance excluded either kings or the occasional commoner such as Eligius, from exercising influence. With these qualifications the term is an apposite one for a variety of Christianity which was characteristic of western Europe from the seventh century until the Gregorian reform movement of the eleventh. The European *Adel-skirche* had many shortcomings, as those reformers trenchantly pointed out. However, its positive contribution may be seen in the harnessing of aristocratic loyalties in the service of the Christian faith as such persons understood it. The directing elites in the barbarian kingdoms were prepared to divert colossal, staggering resources into the service of new spiritual ideals. These adjectives are not used loosely. The number of monasteries founded, and the extent of their aggregate endowments, in seventh-century Francia and elsewhere, strain credulity. But the facts are well attested.

Irish influence seems to have been the most powerful stimulus to this zeal. And Columbanus was by no means alone: the Irish monastic/missionary diaspora was thronged with pilgrims for Christ. Two examples must stand for many. An anonymous *Vita* tells us of the Irish holy man Fursa or Fursey. After leaving his native land he settled in England, on the coast of East Anglia, where he spent some time in the early 630s. He then moved on to Francia, where he attracted the patronage of the very powerful nobleman and royal servant Eorcenwald (or Erchinoald) who established him in a monastery at Lagny. After Fursa's death in about 648 Eorcenwald interred his body at another of his ecclesiastical foundations, Péronne, where he was revered as a saint. (Burial at Péronne was preceded by an unseemly squabble in which a certain Duke Haimo tried to make off with Fursa's body for burial in *his* church. Eorcenwald prevented this, bellowing, 'Give me back my monk.' It is a nice illustration of aristocratic proprietorial feeling.) The monastery of Péronne attracted so many Irish inmates that it became known as *Perrona Scottorum*, 'Péronne of the Irish'. My second example takes us much further south, to Aquitaine. In a surviving fragment of the will of Bishop Ansoald of Poitiers – the patron of Filibert at Noirmoutier – committed to writing at the end of the seventh century, the testator stated that 'I found the monastery of Mazerolles on the river Vienne deserted, without worshippers or services. I completely restored it and placed over it a holy pilgrim of Irish race, Bishop Romanus, with his fellow pilgrims, directing that they should abide there permanently.'[7] If this documentary fragment had not survived we should never have heard tell of the Irish community at Mazerolles. It follows that there may have been many Irish *peregrini* of whom we know nothing at all.

Because the sources relating to the Frankish kingdom are relatively more abundant than those dealing with other parts of western Christendom in the seventh century we must not fall into the error of supposing that Irish influence was limited to Francia. Columbanus' foundation of Bobbio in the Apennines has already been mentioned. It is probable that the monks of Bobbio played a significant part in bringing Christianity to a remote country region. A later and more distant echo of Columbanus may perhaps be heard in the foundation of the monastery of Novalesa in the Val di Susa (to the west of Turin, near the present Franco-Italian frontier). Abbo, its founder in the year 726 and until his death in 739 its lavish benefactor, was descended from ancestors who had been among the patrons of Columbanus.

Did Irish influence percolate across the Pyrenees, into Spain? This is a difficult question to investigate because the narrative, hagiographical and documentary sources for seventh-century Spanish history are extremely meagre. However, the career and concerns of St Fructuosus may offer food for thought. Fructuosus ended his life as bishop of Braga, successor at several removes to Martin of Braga whose *De Correctione Rusticorum* occupied us in the course of Chapter 2. The chronology of the life of Fructuosus is maddeningly vague – even vaguer than that of the career of Amandus – but we know that he was active as a monastic founder by the 640s at the latest and that he had become bishop of Braga by 656. It is assumed that he died about 670. He was therefore, roughly speaking, a contemporary of Amandus and Eligius. What we know of him comes partly from his own writings, partly from a biography composed within twenty years of his death.[8]

Fructuosus was of very distinguished lineage. He was related to the Visigothic king Sisenand (621–36), successor to the learned Sisebut. Sisenand had come to power by means of a coup mounted with Frankish military assistance. Fructuosus also numbered bishops of Béziers and Narbonne among his relatives. (It should be explained that at this period the old Roman province of Narbonne, sometimes called Septimania, which stretched from the Pyrenees to Provence, was a part of the Visigothic kingdom.) His father was described by his anonymous biographer as the *duc exercitus Hispaniae*, 'commander-in-chief of the army of Spain'. Fructuosus was evidently the heir to great wealth and after his parents' death he chose to devote what his biographer unctuously calls 'all the abundance of his distinguished patrimony' to the service of religion. As a boy he had accompanied his father to visit some of the family estates in the region called El Bierzo and secretly vowed to found a monastery there. In the event he founded three. El Bierzo is the name given to the fertile depression in the mountains which divide Galicia from the central *meseta* of the Iberian peninsula; its main town today is Ponferrada. His first foundation was at Compludo (not to be confused with the Complutum mentioned in Chapter 2), a little to the east of Ponferrada. His sister's husband, not inconceivably baulked of expectations which commonly accompany marriage to a prospective heiress, objected to this alienation of the family property and entered a claim before the king's court that the land should be transferred to him 'to enable him to fulfil his public military duties' (*pro exercenda publica expeditione*). Fructuosus' riposte was decisive. He covered the altars of his monastery in sackcloth, despatched a letter to his brother-in-law threatening God's vengeance, and gave himself over to fasting and prayer. The brother-in-law promptly died and Compludo kept its endowments. Some modern commentators have discerned in this tale the influence of the Irish practice of fasting *against* an enemy. The other two Bierzan foundations of Fructuosus were at Rufinia, later to be known as San Pedro de Montes, and at Visonia; both of them sites not far from Compludo.

Earlier monastic foundations in Spain, like the pre-Columbanian communities of Gaul, had tended to be urban or suburban establishments under the supervision of the bishop. Such, for example, was the monastery founded in about 540 by Sergius, bishop of Tarragona, 'not far from the city', as an inscription records it; such too were the 'many monasteries' founded by Bishop Masona of Mérida – the banking bishop whom we glimpsed in Chapter 2 – about half a century later. By contrast, the monastic communities founded by Fructuosus were rural houses for a rural mission, not unlike those founded by Columbanus in Gaul. There is no reason to suppose that Fructuosus was hostile to the episcopate. His earliest spiritual mentor was Bishop Conan of Palencia, and he ended up a bishop himself, albeit a reluctant one. Yet the fact is that there are remarkably few references to bishops in the *Vita Fructuosi* which is our main source of knowledge about his career. One of his disciples, by name Valerio, often claimed – though probably incorrectly – as the author of the *Vita*, could refer to his own diocesan, the bishop of Astorga in whose diocese El Bierzo

lay, as 'the most noxious of men' (*pestilentissimus vir*). It would be
fair to characterize Fructuosan monasticism as non-episcopal. Rural it
certainly was. North-western Spain had been less urbanized than the
south and east during the Roman period and there is no reason to
suppose that the balance had changed subsequently during the sixth
and seventh centuries, which were generally marked by urban recession
in the Mediterranean world. In addition to the Bierzan group, the
Fructuosan network had two further clusters. Far to the north-west,
on the Atlantic coast, he founded a house at the unidentified place
Peona (possibly Bayona near Vigo) and another one on a nearby offshore island, perhaps one of the Cíes group. In the far south he established another island monastery near Cadiz, which was not then the
important port it became in later centuries, and two more, one for men
and one for women, nine miles inland from Cadiz. The geographical
groupings may reflect the widespread distribution of that distinguished
patrimony. In addition to these eight monasteries Fructuosus founded
yet another near his episcopal seat of Braga.

The traceable connections of Fructuosus were, not surprisingly, with
the social elite. 'Worthy and noble' persons were attracted by his
sanctity, including men 'from the court, who abandoned the service
of the king' to join him. Several of them later became bishops. They
sound a bit like, shall we say, Audoen. Could one of them have been
Ermefredus, bishop of Lugo, the neighbouring diocese to Astorga,
who founded a monastery at Samos in about 660, attested by an
inscription whose wording has been held to indicate acquaintance with
the monastic rule attributed to Fructuosus? Possibly. The only one
named by his biographer is Teudisilus, who founded a monastery at
Castrum Leonis. Both the person and the place are otherwise
unknown; but since the writer took it for granted that they were
familiar to his primary Bierzan audience we may take it that this was
another north-western establishment. The lady Benedicta, whose
vocation furnished the nucleus of the nunnery near Cadiz, was 'of
exalted birth, and married to one of the king's retainers' (who tried,
unsuccessfully, to reclaim her). Fathers with their sons and mothers
with their daughters flocked to join these houses. One is put in mind
of Samson and his kinsfolk. The military governor of the province of
Baetica was so worried by this stampede into the monastic life that he
petitioned the king to forbid it on the grounds that there would not
be enough laymen left to serve in the army. But there was no stopping

it. According to Fructuosus' biographer, assumed to have been writing in about 690, it was still going on, 'very recently . . . today'. The markedly aristocratic character of adherents was certainly maintained after the death of Fructuosus. A would-be patron of Abbot Valerio was one Ricimer, a *vir illustris*, in other words a man of extremely exalted rank. Ricimer built a church and wanted Valerio to be its priest – much against Valerio's will. That cantankerous man saw the hand of God at work when the church collapsed on the unfortunate Ricimer and killed him. But what a fine example of the aristocratic role in forwarding Christianization. We might recall the words of John Chrysostom quoted in Chapter 2: 'Should not everyone build a church? Should he not get a teacher to instruct the congregation?'

The parallels between what was happening in Columbanian circles in Frankish Gaul and Lombard Italy and what in Fructuosan circles in Visigothic Spain are manifold. This might, but need not necessarily, mean that the one movement influenced the other, by lines of communication which are no longer discernible. It might with equal plausibility be suggested that an apparent debt of Spanish to Irish monastic life is to be explained by direct contacts between the Iberian peninsula and Ireland. We can very nearly prove a two-way traffic. Some of the works of Isidore of Seville (d. 636) seem to have been known in Ireland by about 650. The monastic rule attributed to Fructuosus may have been indebted to Irish monastic customs. The 'Celtic' cultural world overlapped with the Spanish. There was in the sixth and seventh centuries a colony of Britons with their own monastery at a place in north-western Spain which bore and still bears their name – Bretoña.

All this may be said; and it might enhance understanding in an oblique way. But it is prudent for the historian to remember that similar circumstances will generate similar responses. There were many similarities between northern and western Spain on the one hand and northern and eastern Francia on the other. It is not a bit surprising that religious life should have developed on parallel lines in the course of the seventh century. Similarities and parallels may also be found with the religious life of the islands opposite (as the geographers of that age figured it) the coasts of Gaul and Spain. It is time to turn to the British Isles in the age of Amandus.

CHAPTER SIX

The Chalice and the Horn

If anything endangers the Church, it will be the strong propensity to shooting for which the clergy are remarkable.   SYDNEY SMITH, 1809

IN THE YEAR 786 an English church council forbade the use of a drinking-horn as a chalice for the administration of the eucharistic wine. It is a minor example of the shortcomings of the early English church in matters of discipline brought to light by the two papal legates who in that year conducted a visitation to it. Minor but telling: the use of a frankly secular vessel for this sacramental purpose suggests a church whose tone and usages had been permeated by the habits and style of the aristocratic world. In Anglo-Saxon England as in Frankish Gaul the directing elite of the church quickly came to be recruited from the secular aristocracy. The English like the Frankish church became an *Adelskirche*, a 'church of the nobility'. Its governing members retained many of the assumptions, values and manners of worldly society.

The sixth-century connections between the Frankish kingdom and south-eastern Britain, briefly alluded to in Chapter 4, were maintained in the seventh century. They become more visible and appear to have become stronger and more diverse; which may be only to say that with more abundant and reliable evidence to go on, we know more about them. King Eadbald of Kent, himself the half-Frankish son of Ethelbert and Bertha, married Emma, the daughter of Eorcenwald, leading counsellor of Frankish kings and patron of St Fursa. Their son Eorcenbert, king of Kent from 640 to 664, kept the first element of his grandfather's name (Eorcen-), as did other members of the family. According to Bede he was the first English king to order the destruction of idols and the observance of the Lenten fast throughout his

160

kingdom.[1] In issuing Christian legislation he was, whether consciously or not, following Frankish royal example. Further north, King Sigebert of East Anglia had a Frankish name and had spent time as an exile in Gaul before becoming ruler of the East Angles in 630 or 631. A strong case has been made for supposing that he was the man buried in the ship beneath Mound 1 at Sutton Hoo. Further north still, when King Edwin of Northumbria was slain in battle in 633 his widow Ethelburga withdrew to her native Kent with Bishop Paulinus of York. She sent her young children to be brought up in the safety of the court of her kinsman King Dagobert I across the Channel.

These dynastic connections were accompanied by ecclesiastical ones. Felix, who became bishop of the East Angles while Sigebert was king, was a native of Burgundy who had received his religious training there. The Columbanian monastic houses of that region were the most notable seminaries at the time; we have already seen what a nursery of bishops Luxeuil was. We cannot *prove* that Felix came from Luxeuil but it seems likely. Eorcengota, daughter of Eorcenbert of Kent, became a nun in Burgundofara's monastery of Faremoutiers. Ethelburga and Saethryth, members of the East Anglian royal family, became successive abbesses of the same house. The Anglo-Saxon Balthild, before she caught the attention of Clovis II, was a slave in the household of Eorcenwald. As queen she founded the nunnery of Chelles – close to Fursa's Lagny – whose first abbess and nuns came from Jouarre. Chelles, like Faremoutiers, attracted distinguished English ladies. Among them, according to Bede, was numbered a niece of King Edwin (though there are chronological difficulties about this report). It also seems likely that the influence of Chelles may be detected in the foundation of certain monastic houses in England such as Bath. Or consider the case of the mysterious Birinus who appeared in England in about 634 and became the first bishop of the West Saxons. He had been consecrated a bishop in Genoa on the orders of Pope Honorius I, 'wishing to sow the seeds of the holy faith' – a phrase also used of St Columbanus by his biographer Jonas – in England. Was Birinus a monk of Columbanus' foundation of Bobbio? We can't be sure. But Bobbio was in the diocese of Genoa; and a bishop of Genoa would need papal authorization to undertake an episcopal consecration because Bobbio had been granted exemption from the authority of any diocesan below the pope by the very same Honorius I as recently as 628. It all seems to hang together. We are on firmer ground with

Birinus' successor Agilbert, bishop of the West Saxons between *c.* 650 and *c.* 660. Bede tells us that Agilbert was a native of Francia who had gone to Ireland 'for no little time' to study the scriptures. One observes the magnetism of Ireland as a place for what we should call higher education. After a quarrel with the West Saxon king, Agilbert returned to Gaul where he became bishop of Paris. We can learn a little bit more about him from other sources. His sister Theudichildis was the first abbess of his cousin Audoen's Columbanian nunnery of Jouarre. Agilbert was buried at Jouarre in the magnificent sarcophagus which may still be seen there. We shall meet him again. His nephew Leutherius was bishop of the West Saxons between 670 and 676. His name was Frankish, a latinization of Chlothar. The same name, usually anglicized as Hlothere, was borne by a king who ruled Kent from 673 to 685, the son of Eorcenbert. In the light of these Frankish name-forms one might speculate a little about the connections of Eorcen-wald, bishop of London from *c.* 675 to 693. (His predecessor, incidentally, Wine, had spent time in Francia.) Charters associated with Eorcenwald show Frankish influence in their phraseology, and the nunnery which he founded for his sister at Barking in about 666 sounds not unlike Faremoutiers, Jouarre or Chelles.

Enough has been said to show that there is good ground for suppos-ing that lively Franco-Columbanian influences were playing upon the religious life of southern England in the course of the seventh century. In a social context similar to that of northern Francia it is fair to suppose that the appeal was felt in the same sort of aristocratic quarters and that the response took similar forms. Perhaps the appeal of the Gregorian mission to England under Augustine and his followers had suffered from the same sort of limitations as the re-Christianizing efforts of such bishops as Nicetius of Trier in Gaul. Irish influence, though this time Columban rather than Columbanian, was also playing upon the Anglo-Saxons from the north. When Edwin had made him-self ruler of Northumbria in 616 by defeating and killing his rival King Ethelfrith, the sons of the latter, Oswald and Oswy, sought asylum in the Irish-Scottish kingdom of Dalriada, to whose ruling dynasty they were related. Dalriada's leading religious establishment was the island monastery of Iona, founded by Columba in about 565. Through the influence of Ionan monastic/missionary spirituality the sons of Ethelfrith were converted to Christianity together with their retainers. After Edwin's death they returned to Northumbria, where Oswald reigned from 634 to 642 and his brother Oswy from 642 to 670.

Shortly after his return to Northumbria Oswald sent to his erstwhile Dalriadic hosts for a teacher who might lead a mission to his people to continue the process of Christianization begun by Paulinus. The man sent in response to this appeal was the Iona monk Aidan, consecrated a bishop before his departure, who came to Northumbria in 635 and worked there until his death in 651. Recent research into the interconnections of the Northumbrian and Dalriadic ruling houses has established the likelihood that Oswald and Aidan were kinsmen. The spatial as well as the blood relationship between king and bishop was close; for Oswald gave Aidan the island of Lindisfarne, or Holy Island, in the North Sea just off the coast of Northumbria, as the site for his monastic community and episcopal seat. Lindisfarne is close to Bamburgh, on whose almost impregnable rocky outcrop – site of a former Roman signal station – there stood in the seventh century one of the principal fortified residences of the Northumbrian kings. Between Bamburgh and Lindisfarne there stretch lagoon-like bays of shallow, sheltered water: Budle Bay, Fenham Flats and Holy Island Sands. These form the best natural anchorages for shallow-draught shipping to be found on the generally exposed and inhospitable coastline of Northumbria. Maritime power was important to seventh-century Northumbrian kings. It is likely that Aidan looked out from Lindisfarne not upon the unpeopled nature reserve which greets the eye of today's visitor but upon the bustling hive of industry which was King Oswald's naval arsenal. When Aidan wanted to pursue his devotions in solitude and peace he would retire to Farne Island, the biggest among the archipelago of islets which lie in the sea about two miles due east of Bamburgh.

In Book III of his *Ecclesiastical History* Bede has left a carefully drawn and deservedly famous portrait of Aidan and his fellow-workers. As always with Bede, its purpose was as much didactic as commemorative, designed to teach lessons to the clergy of his own day.

> Aidan taught the clergy many lessons about the conduct of their lives but above all he left them a most salutary example of abstinence and self-control; and the best recommendation of his teaching to all was that he taught them no other way of life but that which he himself practised among his fellows. For he neither sought after nor cared for worldly possessions but he rejoiced to hand over at once, to any poor man he met, the gifts which he

163

Derry †

Whithorn †

Inishmurray †

† Armagh

† Kells

Cashel † † Durrow
● Birr

† Kildare

† Clonmacnoise

St Davids ● † Eglwys
● Gymyn

Caldey Island †

† Hartlar

Atlantic Ocean

6. *The British Isles in the age of Wilfrid and Bede* c. 700.

Coldingham

†Lindisfarne

† Bamburgh
Melrose

Hexham ●

† Jarrow
† Monkwearmouth

† Dacre

† Gilling

† Whitby

† Lastingham

Ripon †

York ‡●

Beverley †

Barrow-on-Humber

Repton †

Breedon-on-
† the-Hill

†Crowland

Lichfield ○
† Wenlock

Peterborough†
Oundle

† Ely

† Brandon

Sutton Hoo ●

Deerhurst
†

Abingdon † † Dorchester-on-
● Thames

† Malmesbury

London ●

Barking †

† Bradwell-on-Sea

Bath †

Chertsey †

Tilbury
Canterbury ‡

† Farnham

Glastonbury
†

● Sherborne

Bosham
†

Wimborne †

Selsey

† Folkestone

Atlantic Ocean

Papil †
St Ninian's Isle †

Applecross † † Rosemarkie

St Andrews
●

Iona †

North Sea

‡● Archbishopric

● Bishopric

† Monastery

had received from kings or rich men of the world. He used to travel everywhere, in town and country, not on horseback but on foot, unless compelled by urgent necessity to do otherwise, in order that, as he walked along, whenever he saw people whether rich or poor, he might at once approach them and, if they were unbelievers, invite them to accept the mystery of the faith; or, if they were believers, that he might strengthen them in the faith, urging them by word and deed to practise almsgiving and good works.

Aidan's life was in great contrast to our modern slothfulness; all who accompanied him, whether tonsured or laymen, had to engage in some form of study, that is to say, to occupy themselves either with reading the scriptures or learning the psalms. This was the daily task of Aidan himself and of all who were with him, wherever they went. And if it happened, as it rarely did, that he was summoned to feast with the king, he went with one or two of his clergy, and, after taking a little food, he hurried away either to read with his people or to pray. Neither respect nor fear made him keep silence about the sins of the rich, but he would correct them with a stern rebuke. He would never give money to powerful men of the world, but only food on such occasions as he entertained them; on the contrary he distributed gifts of money which he received from the rich, either, as we have said, for the use of the poor or for the redemption of those who had been unjustly sold into slavery. In fact, many of those whom he redeemed for a sum of money he afterwards made his disciples and, when he had trained and instructed them, he ordained them priests.

The impact of Aidan's Lindisfarne upon the spiritual life of Northumbria and beyond was comparable to that of the Luxeuil of Columbanus upon the spiritual life of the Frankish kingdom. Like the disciples of Columbanus, Aidan's followers tended to be of aristocratic background and to work in partnership with the royal dynasty. In the middle years of the seventh century the kings of Northumbria strove, on the whole successfully, to maintain the supremacy over other Anglo-Saxon and Celtic rulers which Edwin had enjoyed. Though they operated on a much smaller scale, Oswald and Oswy were not unlike their Merovingian contemporaries Dagobert I and Clovis II. Bede's account of these Northumbrian kings makes it plain that a kind of Christian imperialism operated in England in much the same way as it did in Francia. For example, Oswald had a part in bringing about the formal acceptance of Christianity by the West Saxon king Cynegils. When Cynegils was baptized, Oswald was his godfather. This was a relationship which often indicated at this period – following at long distance a Byzantine model – the political subordination of godson to godparent. Oswald was associated with Cynegils in the grant of Dorchester-on-Thames to Birinus as the seat of his bishopric. The betrothal of a West Saxon princess to the 'most victorious' Oswald at the same time should probably be interpreted as a further symbol of Northumbrian supremacy over the West Saxons.

There is one particular Northumbrian family Bede tells us about whose doings may put us in mind of those northern Frankish aristocratic households so powerfully influenced by Columbanus. Bede tells us of four brothers named Cedd, Chad, Cynebil and Caelin, who all became 'famous priests of the Lord' and two of them bishops. Reticent as so often about secular and familial connections, Bede does not tell us anything further about the ramifications of their kin. He does not even tell us whether or not the brothers belonged in the ranks of the aristocracy; but there are some indications that they did. The occasion of their being brought to our attention was the acceptance of Christianity in the year 653 by the Mercian prince Peada, son of King Penda of Mercia. Peada governed a subdivision of the Mercian kingdom known as Middle Anglia, which probably comprised Leicestershire and Northamptonshire. King Oswy of Northumbria had been instrumental in bringing about Peada's acceptance of Christianity: it was the price of marriage to Oswy's daughter. Peada was persuaded to accept baptism by his brother-in-law Alchfrith, the son of Oswy, and the baptism took place at a Northumbrian royal residence, the officiant being Bishop Finan of Lindisfarne, Aidan's successor. Four priests who had been monks of Lindisfarne returned with Peada to Middle Anglia as missionaries, among them Cedd. Shortly afterwards King Sigebert II of the East Saxons (i.e. Essex) was persuaded by what Bede called King Oswy's 'friendly and brotherly counsel' to become a Christian. Like Peada he was baptized in Northumbria by Bishop Finan. At Sigebert's request Oswy sent Cedd to evangelize the East Saxons and a little later (654?) he was consecrated their bishop. He was an active missionary in Essex and founded two monasteries there, at Bradwell-on-Sea and Tilbury.

Meanwhile, Cedd's brother Caelin had become a priest in the household of Ethelwald, the son of King Oswald, who was ruling Deira – the

167

southern half of Northumbria – as a sub-king under the overlordship of his uncle Oswy. Caelin introduced Ethelwald to Cedd in the course of one of the latter's frequent journeys from Essex back to his native Northumbria. Ethelwald prevailed upon Cedd to receive a grant of land for the foundation of a monastery at Lastingham, on the southern slopes of the North York Moors. Cedd purified the site before building began by means of a rigorous Lenten fast. Summoned by the king before his fast was over, he delegated the completion of it to his brother Cynebil. It is an intriguing sidelight on the relationships of the period that a bishop would interrupt a holy exercise on the summons of a king. Noteworthy too is that he could call on a kinsman to sustain what seems to have been a family as well as a sacred enterprise. The same theme is sounded at the time of Cedd's death at Lastingham during a visitation of plague in 664: on his deathbed he bequeathed the monastery to his brother Chad.

Chad too had been a disciple of Aidan at Lindisfarne. He had also spent some time studying in Ireland in the company of another North-umbrian expatriate named Egbert – a figure of great importance in the history of early English missionary work whom we shall meet again. In 664, and probably before his brother's death, Chad was chosen bishop of York by King Oswy. After an active episcopate over the next five years Chad was compelled to resign his see in 669 to make way for Wilfrid, of whom more shortly, and retired to Lastingham. Not long afterwards he was appointed to the bishopric of the Mercians and established himself at Lichfield, where he served until his death in 672. He founded a monastery on land given to him by King Wulfhere of Mercia at Barrow-on-Humber in Lincolnshire.

A stream of Irish spirituality, therefore, flowed from Iona through Lindisfarne to Barrow and Bradwell, Lastingham and Lichfield – and other places besides. Iona was not the only source of this influence. Just as Fursa alerted us to the presence in Gaul of Irish *peregrini* who were not of the Columbanian connection, so his East Anglian sojourn in the 630s may remind us that not all Irishmen active in seventh-century England emanated from Iona or its colony at Lindisfarne. Bede tells us that during his stay in East Anglia Fursa 'by the example of his virtue and the force of his preaching converted many unbelievers to Christianity'. Another Irishman, though according to Bede less successful an evangelist, was the monk Dícuill, whom he mentions in passing as settled at 'a very small monastery in a place called Bosham' on the coast of Sussex in the early 680s. Yet another was Maíldub, a shadowy figure, obviously Irish by name and the presumed founder (*c.* 640?) of the monastery at Malmesbury, a house which may have played a significant role in the Christianization of Wessex.

It is worth mentioning here, because it is often overlooked, that the religious influence of the Irish (of Iona and elsewhere) seeped northwards into what we now know as Scotland as well as southwards into Anglo-Saxon England. In the absence of some Scottish Bede we have no means of constructing a narrative, and instead have to be content with what can be gleaned or surmised from the desperately laconic written sources and the uncertain witness of archaeology. For example, we catch a glimpse of a certain Maelrubai, apparently a monk of the northern Irish Bangor and allegedly a descendant of King Niall of the Nine Hostages, who founded a community at Applecross in Wester Ross, looking out over the sea to Raasay and Skye, in 673, which he ruled for nearly fifty years until his death in 722. Applecross may have played an important part in bringing Christianity to the north-west of Scotland. Or again, we have a sighting of a bishop named Cuiritán attending an important Irish church council in 697 in the company of Adomnán, abbot of Iona and biographer of Columba, and Chad's master the Northumbrian *peregrinus* Egbert. Cuiritán's theatre of operations is said to have been at the head of the Moray Firth, where 'he preached the gospel to Picts and Scots for sixty years and built a notable church at Rosemarkie'.[2] The source is late and unreliable. But the concentration of 'Pictish' memorial stones round the shores of the Moray Firth is surely indicative of some important ecclesiastical centre and its diffusion of Christian belief. Adomnán tells us a story which indicates that – or indicates that he believed that – some of the Iona brethren had sought out hermitages in the Orkneys during Columba's lifetime. A church, and therefore presumably a community, existed in the eighth century on St Ninian's Isle, just off the west coast of Shetland's mainland. Someone buried a hoard of silver beneath it for safekeeping in about the year 800: it lay there until its discovery in 1958. At nearby Papil on the island of West Burra there once stood a stone (now in Edinburgh: see plate 18) of about the same date bearing inscribed on it a cross, four bishops and a stylized beast, perhaps intended to represent a lion, symbol of St Mark. Even if this stone had not survived the place-name itself would indicate an early Christian site; for *papil* is derived from the Old Norse *papa*, 'priest', the term used by the Vikings to identify the Christian clergy whom they found when they settled there in the ninth century. By then Christianity was firmly rooted in Scotland. The speed with which the Scandinavian settlers were assimilated to it (below, Chapter 11) is testimony to this.

By comparison with that of Scotland the religious life of early Anglo-Saxon England is richly documented. Yet there is much that remains obscure about the conversion of the English aristocracy in the seventh and eighth centuries. In large part the responsibility for this state of affairs is to be laid at the door of our principal informant, Bede. This may seem ungrateful. Bede is widely and justly regarded as one of the greatest historians who has ever lived. His historical writings cast a flood of light upon early Anglo-Saxon society; anyone who has ever tried to reconstruct seventh-century English history without the information furnished by Bede will know how deeply we are in his debt. All this may be acknowledged, and a great deal more might be said along these lines, but we have also to face the fact that Bede had his limitations. His principal concern was with kings and bishops. Stripped down to its essentials the narrative of the *Ecclesiastical History* is a record of how King X and Bishop Y led the people Z to the Christian faith: Ethelbert, Augustine and the people of Kent; Edwin and Paulinus, Oswald and Aidan, and the Northumbrians; Sigebert, Cedd and the East Saxons – and so forth. This restriction of vision was partly a function of Bede's didactic purpose, the teaching of lessons to the kings and bishops of his own day. In part it was commended to him by the literary model he followed: the *Ecclesiastical History* of Eusebius had been organized along roughly these lines. In part it was imposed upon him by the information at his disposal and the form in which it had reached him. The stage of Bede's *History* was a crowded one, but persons who were neither kings nor bishops tended to have only very modest walk-on parts allotted to them – second pikemen, so to say – and frequently only because they happened to crop up in association with kings and bishops. Here is an example. Bede tells us how holy water consecrated by John of Beverley, bishop of York, cured the wife of a Yorkshire grandee who had been ill for six weeks. The occasion of the bishop's visit to the family was the consecration of a church built by this nobleman on his estate. Bede mentions this in passing, simply to set the scene, but the spotlight remains on the holy bishop. Now, the building of churches for their households, tenants and slaves by Anglo-Saxon noblemen is likely to have been a significant factor in the gradual Christianization of the English people. But it was no part of Bede's purposes to draw attention to it except in an incidental fashion. Bede, it has been said, 'lacked the means or the will to analyse the degree to which the church fulfilled its mission to Anglo-Saxon society as a whole'.[3]

A different sort of limitation arose from Bede's unwillingness to dwell on matters of which he disapproved or about which he felt uneasy. Prominent amongst these was the divergent method of calculating the movable feast of Easter followed by the northern Irish (and thus the Ionan monastic network) and the British churches of Cumbria, Wales and Dumnonia. Even when portraying a model bishop such as Aidan, Bede had to enter a caveat concerning his schismatic observance of Easter. It is possible that Bede unduly neglected the evangelizing activities of those whom he regarded as deviants. This is linked to another of Bede's prejudices. He was adamant that there had been no native *British* contribution to the conversion of the English: it was a point on which he expressed himself strongly. Was he correct? We have already seen that there was a British tradition that Edwin of Northumbria had been baptized by a British bishop. Even though this tradition is late and suspect, which it is, its mere existence is warrant enough for investigating the question of some putative British contribution. Anglo-British interactions are likely to have occurred at the aristocratic and princely levels which are the special concern of this chapter. One might think of Edwin's alleged exile at the court of Gwynedd; or, at the other end of the century, of the young Mercian nobleman Guthlac's martial exile among the Welsh during which 'he learnt to understand their hissing speech' before he became a monk at Repton and then a hermit at Crowland in the Fens.[4] A case has been made for productive and positive Anglo-British relations in the Welsh Marches of the west midlands and in the south-west peninsula. These were both, as it happens, areas about which Bede seems to have been ill-informed. These relations could have involved some evangelizing activity by British clergy before the west was washed by Roman or Irish currents of spirituality. The evidence is such that the case remains unproved, is perhaps unprovable. However, we should at the least be ready to entertain the possibility that there were religious communities which survived the transition from Celtic to Germanic lordship and played some part in the Christianization of their new masters. Possible examples are Wenlock in Shropshire, Glastonbury in Somerset and Hartland in Devon.

Monasteries in general constitute another area of Bedan reticence. Although he was himself a monk, devoted to the memory of his founder Benedict Biscop, justly proud of the community of which he had been a member since the age of seven, reverent towards all bishops but especially so towards those who were also monks – despite all these things, Bede had misgivings about the spread of the monastic life in the Northumbria of his day. At the end of his *History* he drew attention to this phenomenon and added darkly, 'What will be the result thereof, a later age shall see.' Light on the nature of his misgivings is shed by a letter he wrote three years later, only a few months before his death, to the newly appointed bishop of York, Egbert.[5] Bede's *Letter to Egbert* is a document of priceless value for our understanding of the concerns which led him to compose history in the way that he did. In it he addressed himself to what he diagnosed as the abuses in the Northumbrian church – and by implication the English church as a whole – and to the measures which in his view Egbert should take to remedy them. It is a startling and comprehensive indictment of shortcomings. As far as concerns the Northumbrian monasteries, Bede's criticisms were threefold. There were too many of them. The life lived in many but not all of them frequently failed to live up to Bede's exacting standards. Kings had been too profligate in endowing them with lands, and on generous terms, thereby exhausting their own stock of landholdings, which should be used to reward their warriors.* Many monasteries therefore – again, not all – were offensive to God and a drain on the resources of Northumbrian kingship.

Bede chose not to dwell on the foundation of monasteries in England in the pages of the *Ecclesiastical History*. It should now be a little easier to see why. It is for this reason that so many of them tend to be mentioned only in passing, such, for instance, as Dícuill's house at Bosham or Bishop Eorcenwald's foundation at Chertsey. Even Bede's own beloved monastery received only fleeting mention in the *Ecclesiastical History*. Our main source of information about it is another and less public work of Bede's, the *Life*

---

* This interestingly parallels Spanish worries on the same score alluded to in the *Vita Fructuosi* about a generation earlier.

of the Holy Abbots, a 'house-history' intended primarily for home consumption.

There were many more monastic houses in Bede's England than Bede cared to mention. Some are revealed to us by the evidence of charters, the formal written record of their foundation or endowment. Such are Bath, for example, or Farnham in Surrey founded in about 687. Some are attested by the evidence of hagiography: Nursling in Hampshire, evidently renowned for its learning when the young Boniface entered it in about 700; the nunnery at Wimborne in Dorset, mentioned in Rudolf of Fulda's *Life of St Leoba*. At some sites archaeological investigation or surviving architectural fragments have served to confirm the witness of the texts: such are Repton in Derbyshire, or Deerhurst in Gloucestershire. At other places archaeologists have revealed what appear to have been monastic sites of which no written record whatsoever has survived: at Brandon in Suffolk, for example, or at Flixborough in Lincolnshire.

Monastic communities were anything but uniform. Some were small, like Dícuill's Bosham which had only (in Bede's words) 'five or six brothers'. Others were very large indeed; in the year 716 there were about 600 monks in Bede's monastery, the biggest population ever recorded in an English monastic house. Some were poorly endowed, others extremely wealthy. Bishop Eorcenwald's monastery at Chertsey acquired within a few years of its foundation a landed endowment of 300 'hides'. The hide was a unit used in the assessment of land for services or tribute-payment and it is notoriously difficult to convert it into an areal measure. However, if we adopt a widely canvassed view that an equivalence of one hide to about 120 acres is at least approximately correct, then Chertsey's estates were even more extensive than those of Amandus' foundation at Elnone in Flanders. Founding even a modest monastic house was an expensive business. It is therefore not surprising that all identifiable monastic founders were of royal, princely or aristocratic rank – as we have seen that they were in Gaul (with the single rule-proving exception of Eligius). The most detailed surviving account of an English monastic foundation – one that in terms of its endowments was by no means in the top flight, with a recorded landed holding about half the size of Chertsey's – was furnished by Bede in his *Life of the Holy Abbots*. Benedict Biscop, the founder of the double house of Wearmouth–Jarrow, must have spent a fortune on the masons, glaziers, relics, books, pictures, vestments and choirmaster which he imported from the continent: 'all the abundance of a distinguished patrimony', as the author of the *Vita Fructuosi* might have written.

This is precisely the point. Benedict Biscop was a man of enormous wealth. He had to be, to indulge a taste for monastic foundation. He was unusual in that, thanks to Bede, we know a lot about him; unusual in his single-minded pursuit of a demanding monastic ideal; and unusual in the high value he set on learning. But he was not unusual in his lavish endowment of his foundation. The men and women of royal and aristocratic families in seventh- and eighth-century England were extremely generous benefactors. This was a most important factor – some might judge *the* most important factor – in the gradual Christianization of the English.

The monasteries that were founded in early Anglo-Saxon England were agents for the dissemination of Christianity among the laity living near by.* The anonymous biographer of St Cuthbert, writing in about 700, shows us the saint when a monk at Melrose in the 650s travelling down Teviotdale 'teaching the country people and baptizing them'.[6] We cannot doubt that the populations who lived on the ample estates of Chertsey or Wearmouth – and many another community: Abingdon, Barking, Coldingham, Dacre, Ely, Folkestone, Gilling and so on – received some pastoral ministrations, however rudimentary, from the clergy of the landlord-church. When Bede tells us that the people of Sussex did not care 'to adopt the way of life nor to heed the preaching' of Dícuill and his fellow-monks at Bosham he reveals his expectations of the evangelistic role of such a community. Sometimes the missionary function of a monastic foundation is made unambiguously plain in a document. At some point between 675 and 692 a Mercian nobleman named Friduric (Frederick) made a grant of twenty hides of land at Breedon-on-the-Hill (Leicestershire) to the monks of Peterborough 'in order that they should establish on that land aforesaid a monastery and a church for monks serving God; and in addition that they should appoint a priest of devout life and good repute to administer the sacrament of baptism and the nourishment of evangelical teaching to the people subject to their community.'[7] Breedon grew rapidly into an important monastic house. Its first abbot, Hedda, became bishop

---

* There is a difficulty here about the variety of communities which might be identified by the single Latin term *monasterium*: I shall return to this problem in a later chapter.

of Mercia in 692; a later member of the community, Tatwine, became archbishop of Canterbury in 731. Tatwine's scholarship was commended by no less a person than Bede, no lenient judge in such matters. Surviving works attributed to him display solid Latin learning which hints much about the resources invested in Breedon's library. The monastery was also notable for its patronage of the arts, the most enduring fruits of which may still be seen in the accomplished stone sculpture of apparently eighth-century date which adorns the existing (much later) parish church at Breedon. Of course, scholarship and artistic achievement do not in themselves prove that evangelistic targets were met. Yet the impression of learning and piety which they leave – of a house perhaps not unlike Bede's own – inspires confidence that at least some steps were taken towards realizing the founder's intention of deepening the Christian faith of the tenantry on whom the monks of Breedon looked down from their eyrie above the plain of the river Trent. As so often, this is as far as the evidence takes us.

It is in the career and behaviour of St Wilfrid, bishop of York, that the aristocratic strain in the early Anglo-Saxon ecclesiastical hierarchy is most clearly visible. The character of this choicest representative of the Anglo-Saxon *Adelskirche* is vividly conveyed to us in the memoir of Wilfrid commissioned shortly after his death by his disciples Bishop Acca of Hexham and Abbot Tatbert of Ripon. The work was composed by a priest named Stephen who had known the great bishop well. Stephen's *Life of Wilfrid* is long, detailed and partisan; it is also revealingly indiscreet. Allowance made for its bias, it is a highly valuable source of information.

Wilfrid was a figure of stature in the history of the early English church. His varied activities will claim attention in the following two chapters as well as this one. A succinct *curriculum vitae* will serve to set the essentials of his career before the reader. Born in Northumbria in 634, he entered the monastery of Lindisfarne in 648 when Aidan was still presiding over it. Between 653 and 658 he travelled abroad, visiting Rome as a pilgrim and spending some time in the household of Bishop Aunemundus of Lyons. Returned to England he was established as abbot of the monastery of Ripon, in Yorkshire, with the patronage of Aldfrith, son of King Oswy of Northumbria. He played an important part at the synod, or council, of Whitby in 664 at which the decision was taken, after strong advocacy from Wilfrid, to adopt in Northumbria the Roman method of calculating the date of Easter. Later in the same year Wilfrid was appointed bishop of York:* he was consecrated in Gaul by his friend Agilbert (formerly of Wessex, now of Paris) and other Frankish bishops. When he came back to Northumbria he found that Chad (of Lastingham) had been intruded into his see of York, so he retired to Ripon until he was reinstated at York in 669. An active episcopate followed over the next nine years, during which Wilfrid rebuilt his cathedral church at York and founded a monastery at Hexham in Northumberland. But in 678 a quarrel broke out with King Ecgfrith of Northumbria and Archbishop Theodore of Canterbury. Wilfrid was expelled from his see and set off to appeal to the pope, wintering on the way in Frisia, where he preached to the heathen. The pope upheld him, so Wilfrid returned to Northumbria with a papal ruling in his favour in 680. But King Ecgfrith refused to accept the decision and flung Wilfrid into prison, releasing him in 681 only on condition that he departed the kingdom. Wilfrid's second exile lasted from 681 until 686. In the course of it he undertook missionary work among the South Saxons and the people of the Isle of Wight, and founded a monastery at Selsey in Sussex. Reconciled with Ecgfrith's successor Aldfrith, Wilfrid returned to York in 686. But another quarrel with the king broke out in 692 and yet again Wilfrid had to go into exile. After ten years the royal persecution of Wilfrid reached a crescendo of violence, so in 703 the elderly bishop set off once more to appeal to Rome. Again the pope upheld him and in 705 Wilfrid returned to Northumbria, where he found Aldfrith's successor Osred willing to receive him, though not to restore him to the see of York. Wilfrid lived out his last years in Northumbria and died at Oundle (Northamptonshire), a monastery he had founded in Mercia, in 709.

We are never explicitly told of Wilfrid's aristocratic background. However, there are sufficient indications of his family's status, wealth and connections for us to be certain of it. His father's house was the resort of 'royal retainers and their slaves'.[8] At the age of fourteen Wilfrid could equip himself and his servants with weapons and horses, and 'clothes in which he could fitly stand before the royal view'. His father could introduce him to the royal court by means of the noblemen to whom the young Wilfrid had ministered at home. Through

---

* The see of York was not raised to permanent archiepiscopal status until the year 735.

their good offices he was presented to Oswy's queen, Eanflaed, who, it may be recalled, was the daughter of King Edwin and the first member of the royal family to be baptized by Paulinus back in 626. It was through the patronage of the queen that Wilfrid was attached to a Northumbrian nobleman named Cudda, one of the king's retainers, who was just about to retire from secular life and enter the monastery of Lindisfarne 'owing to a paralytic infirmity' – an interesting glimpse of one mode of monastic recruitment. It was, once more, by means of the queen that Wilfrid was given an introduction to her kinsman King Eorcenbert of Kent when he went south in 652 preparatory to setting off for Rome. From his boyhood onwards Wilfrid moved in exalted circles.

As Stephen presents him, Wilfrid the bishop was notable for might and magnificence. The style of the *grand seigneur* was perhaps something he had picked up from his Frankish patrons Aunemundus and Agilbert. It is unlikely that he learnt it from his earliest mentor the abbot-bishop Aidan of Lindisfarne, who was notable, according to Bede, for his simplicity and humility. When Wilfrid was consecrated in Francia in 664 the ceremony took place at a royal residence, Compiègne; it was conducted by the meaning-laden apostolic number of twelve bishops; and the new prelate was raised aloft on a golden throne – not inconceivably the work of Eligius – to the accompaniment of hymns and canticles. Wilfrid had already made an imposing entry to Gaul. King Oswy had provided him with 'a ship and a retinue of men and a huge sum of money, so that he might enter Gaul in great state'. The retinue and the ship were big. On his way back to England in 665 Wilfrid was driven by contrary winds on to the coast of Sussex, where he and his men had to defend themselves from looters. Stephen explicitly tells us that Wilfrid's retinue numbered 120 persons. The single ship in which they had crossed the Channel together must therefore have been a great deal larger than the largest ship known from this period, that buried beneath Mound 1 at Sutton Hoo a generation earlier, which seated forty. Wilfrid's retinue was not just for show. Its members had to fight hard against odds for victory on that Sussex beach; five of them were killed there. Later on, in 676, Wilfrid was able to supply arms and soldiers to a claimant to the Frankish throne, exiled in Ireland, who with their help became king as Dagobert II. The retinue had other uses too: 'Secular noblemen entrusted their sons to Wilfrid to be brought up so that, if they chose, they might serve God, or if they preferred it he might give them into the king's charge as warriors when they were grown up.' Fosterage of youthful noblemen in this manner was a custom practised by the Anglo-Saxons as well as by the Irish. The relationships it established could be of benefit to fosterer as well as to fostered. In 703 it was a royal retainer who had been brought up by Wilfrid who revealed the king's malicious plans to him, the intended victim. Wilfrid's followers were in several respects akin to the retinue, or *comitatus*, of a secular nobleman or a king: small wonder that it was easy to transfer from the bishop's following to the king's. When attacked in Sussex Wilfrid's retainers 'made a pact that . . . they would either win death with honour or life with victory', in other words that they would lay down their lives for their lord – as the five did – rather than incur the dishonour of flight or surrender. A most revealing letter has survived from Aldhelm, abbot of Malmesbury and later bishop of Sherborne, Wilfrid's contemporary, addressed to Wilfrid's clergy on the occasion of one – it is not clear which – of his exiles: 'Necessity requires that you along with your own bishop, who has been deprived of the honour of his office, be expelled from your native land.'[9] They had to share his exile. That this was not merely a figure of speech is clearly shown by Stephen's report that shortly before his death Wilfrid bequeathed a quarter of his treasure, 'the gold, the silver and the precious stones', to those 'who have laboured and suffered long exiles with me, to whom I have not given landed estates'.

Wilfrid's treasure came from various sources. The occasion of his consecration was probably not the only one on which he received large sums of money from a king. It is likely, for example, that the kings who patronized his monastic foundations were as generous with bullion and jewellery as they were with land. Bede tells us that when King Cadwalla of Wessex conquered the Isle of Wight he gave a fourth part of the island and of the booty he had taken there to Wilfrid. The land amounted to 300 hides, the same as the endowment of Eorcenwald's Chertsey. Wilfrid gave it all to his nephew – which allows us a glimpse of one way in which a bishop's kinsman could be the beneficiary of his operations. His treasure was also employed in the embellishment of his monasteries. At Ripon he built a church of stone. Its altar had a frontal of what Stephen called *purpura* woven with gold thread. *Purpura* was the most exotic – and almost certainly the most expensive – textile known to the Anglo-Saxons, shot-silk taffeta imported by way of Italy from its place of origin in the eastern provinces of the Roman empire.[10] He had also commissioned copies of the four gospels written in gold leaf on parchment that had been stained purple; and he had 'ordered jewellers to construct for the books a case [or possibly 'a cover'] all made of purest gold and set with most precious gems'. When the church was dedicated Wilfrid invited the royal family and a glittering assemblage of 'dignitaries of every kind' to attend the service. After the ceremony Wilfrid gave what must have been one of the best parties of seventh-century England, 'a great feast which went on for three days and three nights'. Stephen tells us elsewhere that 'no wave of feasting submerged Wilfrid, but neither did the waves of abstinence hurl him upon the rocks of pride'. This would seem to be a coy way of indicating that Wilfrid enjoyed a party and was a generous host.

Treasure was needed to oil the wheels of Wilfrid's life as a prince of the church. In the division of treasure in 709 Wilfrid left another quarter to the abbots of Hexham and Ripon – the latter, incidentally, his kinsman – 'so that they might be able to secure the friendship of kings and bishops with gifts'. It would not be altogether fair to précis this as 'for purposes of bribery'. In a society to which reciprocal gift exchange was central the line between a gift and a bribe might be drawn in a different place from where we in the twentieth century might be disposed to draw it. But contemporaries were well aware that there *was* such a line. When Wilfrid returned to England in 680 'bearing the standard of victory' in the shape of a papal ruling in his favour – note the military imagery – his enemies instantly alleged that this had been secured by bribery. When he was languishing in prison in the following year King Ecgfrith tried vainly to buy his submission with 'gifts, by no means small'.

Wilfrid was a very powerful man and his biographer gloried in this. Stephen could refer to his master's network of monasteries – Ripon, Hexham, Selsey, Oundle and possibly more – as 'a kingdom of churches': a revealing phrase. Wilfrid had access to a web of contacts throughout England and beyond. It embraced Dagobert II, whom he had assisted to the throne of Francia. It even extended to King Perctarit of the Lombard kingdom of Italy whose son Cunipert, king from 679 to 700, was married to an Anglo-Saxon princess, possibly a member of the royal family of Kent and thereby a distant kinswoman of Wilfrid's patron Queen Eanflaed. Wilfrid's might and connections involved him in the violence that was the common currency of aristocratic relationships in early medieval Europe. Martial parallels from the Old Testament sprang readily to Stephen's pen. Wilfrid and his private army fought valiantly in Sussex like Joshua against the Amalekites or Gideon against the hosts of Midian. Eadwulf of Northumbria, King Aldfrith's short-lived successor in 705, could threaten Wilfrid as he would have threatened any secular lord: 'By my salvation, I swear that if he has not left my kingdom in six days any of his followers whom I can find shall perish!' Not long after Wilfrid's death his monastery at Oundle was burnt to the ground by 'certain noblemen, exiles, who were ravaging with an army on account of some wrong done to them'.

Wilfrid was undoubtedly a very good, an outstandingly good churchman. This is the unanimous testimony of all our surviving sources. He was an active pastor within his diocese of York and elsewhere in England. He preached to the heathen in Sussex and in Frisia. He founded monasteries and played an important part in diffusing the observance of St Benedict's Rule in England. He was a strong upholder of Roman canonical authority in the church. He was a patron of scholarship and the arts in the service of faith. He was personally ascetic and he was learned. All in all he was, in Alcuin's words, 'filled with light from Heaven'.[11]

Churchmanship of this order could co-exist with a manner of life which was that of the secular aristocracy. Retinues, feasting, gift-exchange, treasure, feud, loyalty, exile, kinsfolk, bravery, gold, weapons, display – these are what we read about in the 'heroic' poetry of the Anglo-Saxons such as the epic *Beowulf*. Indeed, one can imagine that Acca and Stephen and Tatbert might have mourned Wilfrid's death much as the Geat people lamented Beowulf's.

> This was the manner of the mourning of the men of the
>   Geats,
> sharers in the feast, at the fall of their lord:
> they said that he was of all the world's kings
> the gentlest of men, and the most gracious,
> the kindest to his people, the keenest for fame.

Only minor verbal changes are needed to render this a fitting epitaph to have been spoken over Wilfrid's bier.

A different way of putting the same point would be thus: Wilfrid's career shows us that the threshold between the world of the secular nobleman and that of the noble prelate was not one that was difficult or threatening to negotiate. The hurdle was not high; the leap not into the dark. Indeed, one may suspect that for some the threshold, hurdle or leap was to all intents and purposes invisible. Not all church-men would have agreed. Benedict Biscop probably had his scruples and we know that his pupil Bede had grave anxieties about the character of the emerging English *Adelskirche*. However, there is abundant evidence to show that throughout western Christendom these austere doubters were in a minority.

Consider something that was absolutely central to the values of the aristocracy: the strength of the bond of kinship. At least ten out of the first thirteen abbots of Iona were of the kin of Columba. At the monastery of Lusk, in County Dublin, Crundmáel was succeeded as abbot successively by two sons and three grandsons in the seventy years following his death in 736. In sixth-century Wales a nephew of St Illtud tried to poison Samson, 'fearing that because of Samson he might be deprived of his hereditary monastery which he hoped to possess after his uncle's death'.[12] Samson himself sent an uncle to govern the monastery which he acquired in Ireland. We might care to remember Wilfrid's deathbed appointment of 'my kinsman' Tatbert to the abbacy of Ripon, whom Wilfrid's biographer could refer to as 'the worthy heir'. Benedict Biscop's deathbed admonition ran in a contrary sense: he charged his monks not to choose his brother to succeed him as abbot – which speaks volumes about the expectations of the kin and also, perhaps, those of the community. Brother succeeded brother as abbot on two occasions in the eighth-century Northumbrian monastery celebrated in Ethelwulf's *De Abbatibus*. Spanish church councils concerned themselves with the alienation of church property to a bishop's kinsfolk. Writing in 796 to his former pupil Eanbald, recently appointed to the see of York, Alcuin offered him this revealing advice: 'Do not think of yourself a lord of the world but a steward. Do not let the number of your relations make you greedy, as if you ought to collect an inheritance for them.'[13] Alcuin himself had inherited 'by lawful succession' at least one family monastery in Yorkshire. In Gaul, the monastery of Nivelles was founded by Itta, widow of Pippin I – ancestors of Charlemagne – in 640, on advice from St Amandus. Its first abbess, Gertrude, was her daughter, and succeeding abbesses were also drawn from this high-ranking aristocratic family often known from its most famous sons as the Pippinids. In England, Whitby was founded by King Oswy in 657. Its first abbess was Hilda, great-niece of Edwin of Northumbria; on her death in 680 she was succeeded by Eanflaed, widow of Oswy, daughter of Edwin, and early patron of Wilfrid; she in her turn by her daughter Alflaed. It is somehow appropriate that there should survive a letter which passed between Alflaed and Abbess Adela of Pfalzel, near Trier. For Pfalzel was another Pippinid house and Abbess Adela unsurprisingly connected to the Pippinid dynasty; she was the sister-in-law of Pippin II, grandson of Pippin I. Adela and Alflaed were two ladies, one may feel sure, who would have had much in common and in particular would have agreed on the importance of dynastic monasteries in the right ordering of the world.

'A late seventh- or an eighth-century monastery often had many of the aspects of a special kind of nobleman's club.'[14] James Campbell's observation is perceptive, and valuable in directing attention to the earthy reality of early medieval monasticism on which a certain tradition of writing monastic history has not cared to dwell. Consider the sad end of Abbot Piro of Caldey Island as told in the *Vita Samsonis*: while stumbling about the monastery one night somewhat the worse for drink, he fell down a well and died. The *Penitential* attributed to Archbishop Theodore of Canterbury, a most realistic document, opens with a sermon entitled *de Crapula et Ebrietate*, 'on Intoxication and Drunkenness'. 'If a monk drinks himself sick, let him do penance for thirty days; if a priest or a deacon, for forty days.'[15] But there are interesting qualifications. If he does it 'by way of celebration' – *pro gaudio*, literally 'for joy' – at Christmas or at Easter or on any saint's day, 'and he drinks no more than is commanded by his superiors', there is no offence. Still more intriguingly, there is no offence if he does it on the orders of a bishop: heartening news for the clergy who attended Wilfrid's three-day party to celebrate the dedication of the church of Ripon. In the light of this ruling one perhaps sees why Felix, the biographer of St Guthlac, chose to emphasize that it was *on episcopal orders* that a feast was held on the occasion of Guthlac's ordination. Two of the miracles attributed to St Willibrord (to whom we shall return in Chapter 7) by his biographer Alcuin concerned the multiplication of the monastic wine cellar for the brethren in his monastery of Echternach. The first abbot of Boniface's foundation at Fulda cannily preferred to rely on human rather than miraculous agency: it is remarkable how many of Fulda's early deeds relate to the acquisition of vineyards; no less than five were acquired, for example, in the year of the founder's death, 754.[16] One can see why numbers of hagiographers, such as Baudemundus in the *Vita Amandi*, went out of their way to stress their subjects' abstinence from liquor. Or relative absence: of Samson his anonymous biographer could say that 'no one ever saw him drunk, nor of fuddled mind, nor stumbling about on his feet'. Unlike his abbot, Piro, Samson knew when to stop. Evidently, like Wilfrid, Samson was never quite submerged by the wave of feasting, though it would appear that he was not averse to sporting in the surf. Perhaps in this he resembled Bishop Higbald of Lindisfarne, who was warned against drinking to excess by Alcuin – himself no enemy to the grape – in a letter of the year 794.

Alcuin's letters of admonition to English churchmen often linked a taste for fine clothes with over-indulgence in food and drink. In the letter to Higbald just mentioned, Alcuin wrote: 'Let your dinners be sober, not drunken. Let your clothes befit your station. Do not copy the men of the world in vanity, for vain dress and useless adornment are a reproach to you before men and a sin before God. It is better to dress your immortal soul in good ways than to deck with fine clothes the body that soon rots in dust.'[17] He wrote in similar terms to no less a churchman than Archbishop Ethelhard of Canterbury in 797: 'May you be zealous to do away with the most vain style of dress and the immoderate habit of feasting, as much as you can, from yourself and your fellow-bishops, or rather, from all the clergy and all grades of ecclesiastical order.'[18]

Bede tells a story that is relevant here, involving the nunnery of Coldingham. This was a house which, like Whitby, was closely associated with the Northumbrian royal family. Its abbess at this time, about 680, was Abbe, sister of King Oswy, who has given her name to St Abb's Head on the coast of Berwickshire. As Bede tells it, the nuns of Coldingham were too given to a secular manner of life. In particular, 'they occupy their spare time in weaving more delicate clothes with which to adorn themselves like brides, and make friends with visiting men.' When the nunnery was accidentally destroyed by fire Bede saw in this the manifestation of divine displeasure. Aldhelm uttered similar condemnations of worldly dress in writing to the nuns of Barking, another house of markedly aristocratic character which had been founded by Bishop Eorcenwald of London for his sister.[19] Excavations at the site have brought to light fragments of gold thread and some silver-gilt pins, which could have formed part of the elaborately decorated headdresses deplored by Aldhelm. An English church council in 747 laid down that monks and nuns should wear simple clothes and shun elaborate and worldly dress, and that nuns should not spend their time 'weaving and embroidering diversely coloured apparel'. A later church council, in 786, condemned the wearing by ecclesiastics – men or women – of 'elaborate dress died with the colours of India'.[20]

We do not know what the assembled churchmen of eighth-century England might have understood by 'India'. But we do know that exotic goods, sometimes from very distant parts of the world, were reaching the barbarian north during this period. A famous account of the deathbed of Bede has come down to us: among the 'little presents' distributed by the dying man to his brethren were pepper and incense. St Cuthbert's pectoral cross, which may still be seen at Durham, had as its centrepiece a garnet backed by a shell which had come from the waters of the Red Sea or the Indian Ocean. His liturgical comb was made of elephant ivory from India or East Africa. When his body was re-interred eleven years after his death, in 698, it was wrapped by Byzantine silk.

Changing fashion in personal adornment was a less tangible import. How you wore your pretty dress may have mattered as much to the nuns of Coldingham and their admirers as what it was made of. Historians of costume agree that women's dress – and to a lesser extent men's too – among the Franks and the English changed under the influence of Mediterranean and especially Byzantine models in the wake of the coming of Christianity. A telling example of this is furnished by the so-called 'Chemise de Sainte-Balthilde' preserved in Balthild's monastery of Chelles: a fragment of a linen shirt, with embroidery in four colours round the neck to simulate a necklace with a cross pendent from it. We cannot tell whether this garment really did belong to Balthild, though it would seem to date from her lifetime. Its main point of interest for us is the manner in which the necklace was apparently worn: necklaces with pendants were a fashion derived from the eastern Roman empire. The Empress Theodora, Justinian's wife, is depicted wearing one in the mosaics of San Vitale in Ravenna. The embroidery on the Balthild garment represents a fashion which clearly derived from such a model. An English example is the necklace with pendent cross found in a grave of *c.* 700 at Desborough, Northamptonshire.

There was then nothing drab or dowdy about the churchmen and churchwomen of the early medieval west. Nor about the setting in which they worshipped. Ripon was not the only church in which *purpura* shimmered and rustled; neither were Wilfrid's gospels the only ones to be encased in jewel-studded covers of gold. Cogitosus in his *Life of St Brigit*, composed in about 650, described the hanging crowns – another Byzantine fashion – which hung in the saint's church at Kildare. We can form some idea of what these may have looked like in the surviving votive crown of the Visigothic King Recceswinth, from the hoard of treasure found at Guarrázar, now to be seen in Madrid. We may suspect that the community at Kildare was an institution of the same general sort as others we have looked at. Its bishop, Aéd Dubh, revered by Cogitosus, was described by him as 'royal bishop of Kildare'; he was the son of the king of Leinster and was succeeded as bishop by his nephew.

Bede's *Letter to Egbert* reveals that he knew of 'certain bishops' who surrounded themselves with impious men who were given over to 'laughter, jokes, stories, feasting and drunkenness'. In his *Life of Cuthbert* he shows the saint warning his monks against 'feasting, enjoying themselves and story-telling' on Christmas Day, even though the sanction of Archbishop Theodore's *Penitential* permitted a certain latitude on this feast of the Christian year. Story-telling was indissolubly connected for the Anglo-Saxons to the music of the harp. In the words of the *Beowulf* poet – and the context is a feast to celebrate Beowulf's slaying of the monster Grendel, progeny of Cain and enemy of the human race:

> Then string and song sounded together
> before Healfdene's Helper-in-Battle:
> the lute was taken up and tales recited
> when Hrothgar's bard was bidden to sing
> a hall-song for the men on the mead-benches.

In his *Commentary on Genesis*, composed in about 720, Bede had drawn an important distinction. He approved the use of the harp in the hands of the psalmist for the purpose of singing the praises of God, but pointed out that the prophet – he had in mind Isaiah v.11 – 12 – had condemned those who feasted to the accompaniment of harpists. Twelve years after Bede's death the ecclesiastical council held at the unidentified place Clovesho prohibited monasteries from being the resort of poets, harpists, musicians and jesters. But we know that harpists were to be found in monasteries. Excavations at the monastic site at Whitby yielded wooden tuning pegs for a stringed instrument. In 764 the abbot of Bede's own monastery wrote to an English churchman in Germany requesting a harpist, 'because I have a harp but am without a player'.[21] Did the harpists of Whitby and Jarrow confine themselves to praising God after that model for all godly musicians, King David? Perhaps. Who can tell?

It is against this background that Bede's famous story of Caedmon acquires resonance. Caedmon was a layman attached to the monastery of Whitby in the time of Abbess Hilda. His inability to sing was a source of keen social embarrassment to him. 'Sometimes, when he was at a feast and it was agreed that for entertainment's sake all present should sing in their turn, he rose up in the middle of dinner when he saw the harp coming towards him, went out and walked home.' On one such occasion he had a dream in the course of the night which followed. A man appeared to him and commanded him to sing about the creation of the world. Caedmon protested his inability to do so. But his visitor would not take no for an answer. To his astonishment Caedmon found himself 'singing verses which he had never heard before in praise of God the Creator'. In the morning he remembered his dream and the words he had sung. He was taken before Abbess Hilda and examined by 'the more learned' members of the community. 'It seemed to all of them that heavenly grace had been conferred upon him by the Lord.' Caedmon had been miraculously granted the gift of song. During the remainder of his life he composed much more verse on Christian themes. 'By his songs the souls of many people were often fired to contempt for the secular world and to the quest for the heavenly life.' Of this poetry only nine lines survive which may with something approaching confidence be attributed to Caedmon. They were copied into the two earliest surviving manuscripts of Bede's *Ecclesiastical History* – which date from 737 and 747 – and celebrate the Creation in an early Northumbrian dialect of Old English.

Christian verse in Germanic vernaculars will occupy us in a later chapter. For the present it is enough to stress the significance of the setting of the Caedmon experiment, or miracle: the monastery of Whitby. What Caedmon did was to adapt the conventions of secular poetry – its rhythms, diction, musical accompaniment – to Christian themes and ends. Was it altogether by chance that it was at Whitby that this occurred? Readiness to adapt secular literary conventions presupposes familiarity with them. Abbess Hilda and the 'more learned' members of the community were evidently familiar with the techniques – the very demanding techniques – of Old English versification. Whitby was closely connected with the royal family, the mausoleum of King Edwin, the meeting-place of the famous synod in 664 presided over by King Oswy. It was a place where the royal entourage could fittingly be entertained; where its members could perhaps engage in flirtations with the nuns, who were doubtless as attractively turned out as their sisters up the coast at Coldingham. Whitby was impeccably aristocratic in its direction, quite probably in its membership too; nice girls, of good family, gently nurtured, not lacking in social graces. It was a place where the music of the harp could be heard, where excavation has suggested that the inmates lived in some style and comfort. Ecclesiastical metalwork decorated in a secular style was found there; physical parallel to Christian stories versified after a secular fashion. In short, Whitby seems to have been a community which did not roundly reject the trappings, nor perhaps all the values of the secular aristocratic world whence its abbesses came. Does not the story of Caedmon in some sense offer a parallel to the career of Wilfrid?

It is timely to recall that not all inmates of an early medieval religious community would necessarily have joined it through experiencing what we might today regard as a vocation. Wilfrid's master Cudda entered Lindisfarne because infirmity had unfitted him for the life of a secular nobleman. The unknown monastery celebrated in Ethelwulf's poem *De Abbatibus* had been founded by a nobleman named Eanmund because he had been forced to flee the enmity of King Osred of Northumbria. Deposed kings could be relegated to monasteries: this was the fate of King Wamba of the Visigoths (680), King Ceolwulf of Northumbria (731), King Ratchis of the Lombards (749) and the last Merovingian king of the Franks, Childeric III (751). There was no shortage of involuntary inmates of less exalted rank. Penitentials such as Theodore's laid down that the penance for certain crimes was to be performed in monasteries: adulterers, for example, were required to do penance in a monastery for the remainder of their lives. Criminals in episcopal or abbatial custody, presumably for offences against bishops or abbots, might be enslaved if they could not redeem themselves by payment of the compensation fee appropriate to their crime. The implication that bishops and abbots commanded the means for keeping prisoners in custody is confirmed by an uncommonly interesting letter that has survived from early eighth-century England. It was from Archbishop Brihtwold of Canterbury to Bishop Forthere of Sherborne and it concerned an unnamed Kentish girl of noble rank who was being held captive by the abbot of Glastonbury. Would Bishop Forthere be so kind as to put pressure on the abbot to accept the ransom money offered for the young woman by her brother? As so often, we know nothing about the background to this letter, but at least it allows us a glimpse of yet another category of person, perhaps an unexpected category, for whom we need to find room in our mental picture of an early medieval religious community. There is indeed a certain amount of evidence for the use of monasteries as places of detention for prisoners of high rank. For example, the ill-fated Bishop Leodegar of Autun, better known as St Leger, was imprisoned successively at the monasteries of Luxeuil and Fécamp before his murder in 679.

We must also make room, like the nuns of Coldingham, for plentiful visitors from the secular world. When Guthlac's disciple Beccel sought to kill his master at his hermitage of Crowland in the English Fenland it was in order that he might 'enjoy the greatest veneration of kings and noblemen'. We know who some of them were, and they were indeed distinguished. They included Ethelbald, later to be king of Mercia and the most powerful English ruler of his day, at least one of his retainers accompanied by his family, Bishop Hedda of Mercia, and Abbess Ecgburh, daughter of King Aldwulf of East Anglia. There is some evidence from England, and more abundant evidence from Francia, that certain monasteries were required to furnish hospitality to the founder's kin or to the royal court. In 848 the monastery of Breedon-on-the-Hill paid a very large sum of money to free itself from the obligation of providing for the king's falconers and huntsmen, their horses and their servants. Documents such as this suggest that the obligation was a burdensome one.

In the light of these intricate interconnections with the martial and feud-ridden world of secular society we should not be surprised that religious communities were drawn into that world as participants, perhaps not always reluctant ones. The burning of Wilfrid's Oundle seems not to have involved loss of life. But sometimes violence directed at, or even strife between, monasteries did. In 764 there was a pitched battle between the monasteries of Clonmacnois and Durrow in which 200 men of the Durrow side were killed. By the standards of the early

Middle Ages this was heavy mortality; it must have been a considerable encounter. It was unique in scale, but not otherwise.

In 646 a Spanish church council had laid down that a bishop's retinue was not to exceed fifty persons. It is significant that the ruling was made in response to complaints from the clergy of Galicia – where Fructuosus was a bishop – about the rapacity of the episcopate. We have no reason to suppose that the retinue of a bishop bore down any less harshly upon those compelled to provide it with hospitality than did that of a king or a secular nobleman. But the Spanish bishops were, or were meant to be, moderate compared to Wilfrid who, as we have seen, had a following of 120 when he returned from Gaul in 665. Even Bede's revered Abbot Ceolfrith – a man 'sparing in food and drink, and humble in dress, in a manner unusual among those in authority' – was accompanied by eighty men when he set off for Rome in 716. Just as secular lords furnished their retainers with weapons and clothing, food and horses, so ecclesiastical leaders were expected to provide for their following likewise. An English church council concerned itself with regulating this in 747, and a few years later St Boniface (of whom we shall hear more in Chapter 7) fretted in a letter to his friend the abbot of Saint-Denis about who would care for his disciples after his death. Ecclesiastical leaders would provide weapons for their secular following; so we must add stockpiles of arms to the treasure and other gear which bishops carried about with them on their travels. Let us remember 'the countless army of Wilfrid's followers arrayed in royal vestments and arms' on which his biographer proudly dwelt; or Alcuin's complaint about Archbishop Eanbald of York in 801, 'why does he have so many soldiers in his retinue?' Fifty-three *domestici*, 'members of his household', were slaughtered alongside their lord Boniface in northern Frisia in 754. One is bound to wonder how easy it was to distinguish between the lay and clerical members of a bishop's entourage. The prohibition on the carrying of weapons by the clergy went back into the mists of Christian antiquity: but church councils of our period considered it fit and timely to remind churchmen of it. Spanish bishops were reminded in 675 that they must neither mutilate nor kill their slaves. The Frankish clergy assembled at about the same time in councils at Bordeaux and Saint-Jean-de-Losne were warned not to carry arms. The prohibition was repeated at a north Frankish council in 747, where it was linked with a ban on showy clothes for the clergy. The higher clergy did not always set a good example. Bishop Gewilib of Mainz was deposed in 745 when he undertook to avenge in person the death of his father – his predecessor in the see of Mainz – in battle with the Saxons.

Retinues had to be mounted as well as fed, clothed and armed. In a tale told by Bede we catch a glimpse of the young men of the retinue of John of Beverley, bishop of York, pitting their mounts against one another in the early years of the eighth century – the earliest reference to horse-racing in English history. Bishops were expected to be well mounted: it enhanced their status. In a famous story in Bede's *Ecclesiastical History* King Oswin had given Bishop Aidan a very fine horse, 'though he usually travelled about on foot', adds Bede in an obliquely didactic aside. Aidan encountered a poor man, who asked for alms, and gave him the horse, 'royally caparisoned as it was'. This was reported to the king, who reproached Aidan with it when next they met. Were there not plenty of inferior creatures in the royal stables which would have done as gift to a beggar, rather than the splendid animal specially chosen by the king for the bishop? ' "What is it you say, O King?" retorted Aidan. "Is that son of a mare dearer to you than the Son of God?" ' The lesson of the story in part concerns Christian charity, in part the fitting humility of a bishop. Aidan's manner of life as a bishop 'was so different from the slothfulness of our own times', observed Bede meaningfully in the passage quoted earlier in this chapter. Bede was not the only writer to commend bishops who travelled on foot; Fructuosus of Braga was commended by his biographer for the same laborious virtue. We may suspect, however, that not all bishops shared the humility and charity attributed to Aidan or Fructuosus. The author of the *Vita Eligii* tells a fascinating story of the unseemly struggles of his successor Mummolinus – not to be confused with the homicidal bishop of Uzès of the same name who tried to have Amandus killed – to regain possession of one of the late bishop's horses. After the death of Eligius this creature had passed into the possession of the abbot of one of his monasteries. But Mummolinus, 'immoderately desiring' the horse – which surely tells us what a magnificent animal it must have been – took it away from the abbot. Once in the bishop's possession, however, the horse developed sore feet, perhaps a form of laminitis, and began to pine. A vet (referred to as a *mulomedicus*) was called in but could do no good. Indeed, the horse began to roar with pain and lash out with its hooves at its groom. The bishop accordingly gave it away to a lady who was a friend of his: a slightly double-edged

190

gift, we might think; or perhaps it was simply that she was very good with horses. When she tried to ride the horse she was thrown, and so badly hurt that she suffered from the effects of the fall for a whole year. So she gave the horse back to the bishop. There was no improvement in its health or behaviour. Finally a priest advised the bishop to restore it to the abbot. Mummolinus did so, and within a very few days the horse recovered its health and became docile.

Bishops' mounted retainers not only raced their horses: they also hunted on them. Here is Alcuin again, in his letter of advice to Archbishop Eanbald of York: 'Do not let your companions gallop bawling over the countryside after the fox; they should ride with you singing psalms in harmony' – which has the ring of a counsel of perfection. Hunting was forbidden to the clergy. It was a prohibition which evidently needed repeating. We find it condemned at church councils at Epaône in Burgundy in 517 and at Saint-Jean-de-Losne in 673–5. Fructuosus of Braga was befriended by a fallow deer after he had saved it from hunters: surely a didactic story. The German council held under the presidency of Boniface in 747 forbade clergy to hunt, to go about with dogs in woods, or to keep hawks. Yet Boniface himself had a nice eye for a hawk; a year or two earlier he had sent King Ethelbald of Mercia a sparrowhawk and two falcons. And not all clergy heeded these admonitions. Bishop Milo of Trier, a prelate of whom Boniface particularly disapproved, met his end in the hunting-field, gored to death by a boar.

The gap between precept and practice is as old as human moral teaching. It is not, therefore, a difficult matter to assemble evidence for clerical behaviour which fell short of the ideal enunciated by rigorists. Furthermore, the evidence often consists of racy anecdotes which are entertaining to read. The potations of Bishop Cautinus of Clermont were such that it took four men to lift him from the table when his carousals were over. So at any rate tells Gregory of Tours, source of so many of the raciest stories and in this instance, as it happens, a hostile witness. To dwell on such matters as these may appear as trivial in spirit as the pictures of tippling cardinals so beloved by the interior decorators of English saloon bars. There is, however, a serious purpose in taking the measure of these anecdotes. An attempt to get to grips with the *mores* of the early medieval *Adelskirche* is to take an important step towards understanding the adhesion of the men and women of the aristocracy to Christianity during this period. The social and cultural values of the secular nobility could be shared and maintained by those of their kinsfolk who became priests or bishops, abbots or abbesses. Converted to Christianity, Germanic and Celtic aristocracies quickly discovered that Christianity could be adapted to themselves. The stricter sort of churchman did not like this. Bede is the prime example of such rigorists. He is also by far and away our most important source of information about one of the key episodes of early medieval conversion, the coming of Christianity to Anglo-Saxon England. Because he chose not to dwell on what displeased or disquieted him – aristocratic bishops, numerous richly endowed monasteries, episcopal retinues and treasure and feasting – our understanding of significant features of the process has been hindered. Christianity became an inseparable component of the aristocratic identity. Whatever papal legates might say, the drinking-horn had merged with the chalice.

CHAPTER SEVEN

Campaigning Sceptres:
the Frankish Drive to the East

Desire of me, and I shall give thee the heathen for thine
inheritance: and the utmost parts of the earth for thy
possession. Thou shalt bruise them with a rod of iron:
and break them in pieces like a potter's vessel.

Psalm ii.8–9

IN THE YEAR 751 King Childeric III of the Franks was deposed. He
was a direct descendant in the ninth generation of that namesake
Childeric, the father of Clovis, who had been buried at Tournai in
481; collectively, the dynasty known to historians as the Merovingians.
The later Merovingians from about 670 onwards have traditionally
been dismissed as *les rois fainéants*, feeble rulers who progressively lost
power to their over-mighty subjects until they could safely be pushed
aside. The reality may not have been quite so simple as this, though
there are good grounds for accepting the main lines of the story. Their
supplanters were the family sometimes known as the Pippinids, whose
seventh-century monastic foundations at Nivelles and Pfalzel occupied
us briefly in the last chapter. The new king of the Franks, Pippin (III
of his family, I as king), took office with the sanction of the pope and
was anointed king. The officiating cleric at the ceremony was probably
– though we cannot be absolutely certain of this – the Englishman
Boniface, archbishop of Mainz. The new royal family is better known
to posterity as the Carolingian dynasty. The name is derived from the
Latin name, *Carolus*, of Pippin's father Charles Martel, and it was also
borne by the family's most famous member, Pippin's son Charles, or
Karl, known to history as Charles the Great, *Carolus Magnus*, Charlemagne. Charles was king of the Franks from 768 to 814. In the year
800 he was crowned emperor in Rome, founding thereby what would
come in time to be known as the 'Holy Roman Empire'.

193

Charlemagne was incontestably the greatest ruler of early medieval Europe. He was a great ruler in the traditional, old-fashioned manner long expected of Germanic kings. He expanded his kingdom by means of war and diplomacy in every direction, amassing untold quantities of land and plunder and tribute for judicious distribution to grateful and loyal followers. By the time of his death his empire stretched from Holstein to Catalonia, from the marches of Brittany to the fringes of Croatia; and his power was respected by Danes, English and Spaniards. This agglomeration of territories did not endure as a unit, was not intended to. Chance rather than design maintained a single Frankish empire under Charlemagne's son Louis (814–40). Thereafter it was partitioned among heirs on several occasions and on different lines. Its principal eastern and western components gradually emerged, to simplify a long and complicated story, as the later kingdoms of Germany and France.

The age of Charlemagne did not command the institutional means for imposing an orderly framework of legal and administrative routine upon so large and ill-assorted a collection of territories. The Frankish empire was a ramshackle structure in which power lay, as it had always done, with local landed aristocratic families. What gave unity and direction to the empire was the activity of Charles himself and a small group of leading counsellors. Prominent among the latter was the group of intellectuals assembled by the king from widely different backgrounds to advise on Charles's plans to extend Christian culture. The most important among them was Alcuin, an Englishman; and they included an Italian, Paul the Deacon, and the Spaniard Theodulf. Under the guidance of such men as these Charles sought to make his kingdom an *imperium christianum*, a 'Christian empire'. This called for the exercise of two royal responsibilities, complementary and overlapping, though separable for the purposes of discussion. These were, first, to bring the faith to pagan peoples newly brought under Frankish rule, such as the Saxons; and second, to fortify the faith of peoples already notionally Christian, such as the king's Frankish subjects. The former will be the concern of this chapter, the latter one of the concerns of the next.

There was nothing new about the Frankish drive to the east. From his base in northern Gaul Clovis had attacked his eastern neighbours the Ripuarian Franks round Cologne, the Thuringians and Alamans beyond the Rhine. His example had been vigorously followed by his successors, Merovingian and early Pippinid alike. It was the obvious direction for Frankish kings to turn when the annual campaigning season came round: let us recall that the continuance of their rule depended upon regular, successful, predatory warfare. Neither was it new for the expansion of the faith to be linked to the victorious eastward progress of Frankish arms. The royal duty of spreading the faith had been urged upon Clovis by Bishop Avitus of Vienne. Subsequent ecclesiastical thinking about the responsibilities of the kingly office had given this greater prominence. Dagobert I was one example of a king who strove to translate precept into practice. What Charlemagne did was to make the link between secular and spiritual imperialism even closer. Given his energies and resources he could pursue both with a new intensity and on an unprecedented scale; and further, at any rate in Saxony, with a hitherto unmatched brutality. For the first time in Christian history a state-sponsored mission used the faith quite unashamedly as an instrument for the subjugation of a conquered people. We know, as Charles could not, that his conquest of Saxony would furnish precedents for ugly episodes in thirteenth-century Prussia or sixteenth-century Mexico. Charlemagne, like Teutonic Knights or Spanish *conquistadores*, would probably have claimed that he was doing God's work in God's way, like many an Old Testament leader whose martial vigour in Jehovah's service he had been encouraged from boyhood to emulate. His aristocratic warriors would have agreed with him and so would many of their clerical kinsmen. The conquest and forcible conversion of the Saxons was a triumph for that Frankish *Adelskirche* whose formation was the subject of Chapter 5. But not all agreed. One who was troubled was Alcuin. His anxieties surfaced in a number of letters he wrote in the 790s, precious because rare indications of debate and disagreement about missionary strategy at the heart of Charlemagne's court.

We left the story of the eastward penetration of Christianity with the work of Amandus and others in Flanders and with the foundation or re-establishment of religious communities here and there along the Danube towards Bavaria. Although the idea of a frontier as a line between two fixed points was not alien to early medieval Europeans, the eastern frontier of the Frankish kingdom was not a line but a zone; and a zone, furthermore, of constantly shifting dimensions. The frontier was the furthermost zone in which a Frankish king's will might be enforced. Enforcement required the presence, actual or sufficiently

North Sea

Ribe

Dokkum
Bremen
Wildeshausen
Marklohe
Deventer
Herford
Enger
Utrecht
Münster
Domburg
Paderborn
Halberstadt
Dorestad
Werden
Corvey
Cologne
Fritzlar
Geismar
Erfurt
Liège
Ohrdruf
Fulda
Corbie
Mainz
Würzburg
Echternach
Tauberbischofsheim
Kitzingen
Rheims
Ochsenfurt
WENDS
Hornbach
Chalons
Paris
Eichstätt
Regensburg
Sens
Weltenburg
Murbach
Freising
Luxeuil
Reichenau
Salzburg
BAVARIANS
AVARS
Pfaffers

Lyons
Aquileia

Bobbio

Bishopric
Monastery
Settlement
Rome
Montecassino

FRISIANS
SAXONS
R Weser
R Elbe
R Rhine
R Seine
R Danube
R Rhône

7. *The Frankish drive to the east in the eighth century.*

imminent, of king and army. Variables that might delay a presence ranged from military commitments elsewhere to imponderables such as luck or weather which contemporaries interpreted as the will of God. To give a simple example: Frankish dominion in Saxony collapsed in 778 when Charlemagne's army suffered defeat 1,000 miles away at Roncesvalles in the western Pyrenees. Much would depend too, of course, on the degree of power enjoyed by independent rulers in or beyond the frontier zone. Just as earlier barbarians such as the Goths of Dacia had learned from the culture of the Roman empire, so the peoples to the east had profited from Frankish example. Sometimes indeed their leaders had themselves been Franks. In 623 a certain Samo, a native of north-eastern Francia, a merchant, possibly a slaver, set off to do business among the Slavic tribes known as the Wends, who were at that time settled in Bohemia: he became their king and ruled them for thirty-five years. Samo led what modern historians clumsily term a 'pre-state formation'. But he was a powerful leader who was capable of standing up to even so formidable a ruler as Dagobert I.

Dagobert's evangelistic initiatives in the Danube basin were not unconnected with the defence of his eastern marches against the Slavs. He was also responsible for launching another initiative in the far north-east of his dominions. He established a forward base at Utrecht, entrusting it to the bishop of Cologne so 'that he might convert the Frisian people to the faith of Christ'.[1] This information comes to us in a slightly tendentious source dating from over a century after Dagobert's death, but if it can be relied upon it implies some degree of Frankish lordship over the people of the Frisian coastline and a recognition in Frankish ruling circles of a missionary responsibility. It fits in with what we know of Dagobert and the circle of Amandus. Neither the lordship nor the evangelizing initiative lasted. When next we hear of Frisia it was under the rule of Aldgisl, styled king, apparently independent, and a pagan. The information comes from a source we have already encountered, Stephen's *Vita Wilfridi*. Bishop Wilfrid wintered in Frisia in 678–9 on his way to Rome. According to his biographer Wilfrid's preaching led to the baptism of all the leading men of Frisia 'except for a few', and many thousands of the common people. Stephen let slip the revealing point that Wilfrid's preaching was reinforced because 'at the time of their coming the catch of fish was unusually large and the year was more than usually fruitful in every kind of produce'. The loyal Stephen probably exaggerated his master's success in Frisia; indeed he almost admits as much in drawing attention to the continuance of the Frisian mission at the time of writing, shortly after Wilfrid's death in 709. However, Wilfrid was of great significance in blazing a trail that other English missionaries would soon follow.

It was no coincidence that it was the English who were drawn to the Frisian mission field. Frisians were among the north German peoples who had settled in eastern England during the obscure fifth and sixth centuries. Their presence is detectable in the surviving archaeological evidence, as well as in place-names such as Friston in Suffolk. Old English and Old Frisian were very closely related branches of the Germanic language tree: their speakers would certainly have been mutually intelligible in the seventh and eighth centuries. Anglo-Frisian trading connections were frequent. We hear a little about them in some of our written sources such as Bede's *Ecclesiastical History*, wherein is to be found a famous story about a captive Northumbrian nobleman called Imma who was sold to a Frisian slaver in London at much about the time that Wilfrid was moving on from Frisia to Rome in 679. (Imma's captivity will concern us again in the following chapter.) We have learned a great deal more about Anglo-Frisian commerce from recent archaeological discoveries. At Dorestad (Duurstede) on the Rhine south of Utrecht, and at Domburg on the island of Walcheren, there were trading settlements of importance which trafficked with English towns such as Hamwic (the ancestor of Southampton), London, Ipswich and York.

Was Wilfrid a 'deliberate' or a 'chance' missionary in Frisia? It is a question that cannot be answered with any confidence. His biographer presented him as a predestined 'prophet to the [heathen] nations'. His early training at Lindisfarne under Aidan took place at the hands of men who had brought Christianity from Iona to Northumbria. His patron Queen Eanflaed had been brought up at the court of Dagobert, where evangelization was much in the air. At the Kentish royal court in 652–3 the young Wilfrid cannot fail to have met old Archbishop Honorius of Canterbury, last survivor among the episcopate of the members of the Gregorian mission. When he crossed to Gaul he passed through the mission field of Amandus, Eligius, Audomar. At Rome in 653–4 he prayed for 'a ready mind both to read and to teach the words of the gospel among the heathen'. The oratory of St Andrew, where he uttered this prayer, may well have been the monastery of

St Andrew on the Caelian founded by Gregory before he became pope, where his memory and ideals would have been kept green after his death. (Wilfrid's monastery church at Hexham was dedicated to St Andrew.) Bishop Aunemundus of Lyons, to whose household Wilfrid was attached between 655 and 658, seems to have had connections with the Columbanian monastery of Luxeuil, that nursery of mission-minded clerics. Another friend among the Frankish hierarchy was Agilbert, a missionary bishop in England before he moved to the see of Paris. The roots of Wilfrid's apostolic impulse seem to have been altogether as intertwined as those that had nourished the vocation of Amandus.

Wilfrid inspired the same vocation in others. The most important among these was a fellow Northumbrian named Willibrord. Born in 658, Willibrord was entered in Wilfrid's monastery of Ripon as a child and remained there until his twentieth year. In 677 he went to Ireland, where he came under another very important influence, that of the expatriate 'pilgrim for Christ' Egbert, another Northumbrian. Egbert was a most influential figure in early English Christianity even though all his adult life was spent in Ireland, and particularly in his encouragement of English missionary activity on the European continent. While the impulses of Irish spirituality may have been strong in urging him in this direction, Bede laid stress on another impulse. 'His plan was to undertake an apostolic task by preaching the Word of God to some of those nations which had not yet heard it. He knew there were very many such peoples in Germany, from whom the Angles and Saxons who now inhabit Britain are known to have derived their descent and origin.' This desire to bring the faith to peoples who are in some sense the missioners' kin is one that we shall meet again. In the event Egbert was divinely persuaded not to undertake this task: God had other plans for him. His influence, however, along with that of Wilfrid, flowed into the English missions to continental Germany.

After his long training at Ripon and in Ireland Willibrord set off for the continent with eleven companions – twelve apostles all told – in 690. Two features of the conduct of his mission are notable. The first, unsurprising in a disciple of Wilfrid, was his strong sense of allegiance to Rome. It was for the pope to authorize missions to the heathen and to furnish the missionary with relics of the Roman saints who would be his ghostly protectors and the patrons of the churches he hoped to establish. So it was to the pope, Sergius I, that Willibrord went in 690, and it was to the same pope that he returned five years later for consecration as an archbishop. The second feature was his close relationship with the secular power. Willibrord arrived on the continent at a time of considerable political turmoil in north-eastern Francia when the early Pippinids were struggling to establish dominance among the rival aristocratic families who were fighting over the Merovingian inheritance. Willibrord shrewdly identified the winners. His backers were Pippin II (d. 714) and Charles Martel (d. 741), respectively grandfather and father of the man who became king as Pippin I in 751. It was they who provided Willibrord with the protection he needed in the course of his evangelizing operations – somewhat as Dagobert I had done for Amandus earlier in the century. It was Irmina, mother of Pippin II's wife, who gave Willibrord land at Echternach, in modern Luxembourg, for the foundation of a monastery in about 698. The whole family was associated with her as very generous benefactors: Pippin, his wife Plectrudis and his son Charles. Archaeological research has shown that at Echternach there had stood what must have been among the very grandest Roman villas of northern Gaul. Colossal in scale, sumptuous in fittings, with a covered swimming-pool and a *salon* with marble-clad walls, it had once been a truly palatial country house.* Occupation of this luxurious palace had continued into the fifth century but thereafter the archaeological record fails. We do not know how much might still have been standing above ground when Willibrord acquired it. At the very least we may be confident that the early monks of Echternach did not lack for building materials.

The disturbed state of Francia at the time of Willibrord's arrival had been the Frisians' opportunity. Their new king, Radbod, was a pagan and evidently considered himself independent of Frankish power. Frankish lordship over Frisia was intermittently reimposed under Pippin II and Charles Martel, furnishing thereby a shield for Anglo-Saxon missionary activity. We know little in detail of the work because our principal source, the *Vita Willibrordi* by Alcuin, who was his kinsman, recounts it only in general terms. Radbod was unwilling to become a Christian himself but allowed missionaries to work among his people,

---

* One wonders whether it might have been the residence 'near Trier' of the grandee Tetradius on one of whose slaves Martin of Tours had performed an exorcism three centuries earlier (above, p. 43). Echternach is about ten miles from Trier.

in this resembling Penda of Mercia as presented by Bede. Once established as an archbishop at Utrecht, presumably with Cologne's agreement, Willibrord consecrated subordinate bishops, though we do not know their names nor for certain where their sees were. Bede tells us that from Utrecht Willibrord 'preached the Word of faith far and wide, recalling many from error, and built many churches in those parts, and also a number of monasteries'. A ninth-century *Vita* of the Frisian St Liudger – first bishop of Münster in Westphalia who died in 809: we shall meet him again – allows us a glimpse of the earliest native Frisian clergy instituted by Willibrord. Liudger's two great-uncles had been placed by their pious sister in Willibrord's household to be brought up: 'they were the first of all the Frisian people to take up clerical office.' Fosterage and retinues are just what we should expect of the pupil of Wilfrid who had been a pilgrim in Ireland. This snippet of information about Liudger's great-uncles, who were presumably not unique in the archbishop's entourage, permits us to infer that Willibrord worked harmoniously with at least some among the Frisian elite.

Willibrord's ambitions ranged beyond Frisia to Denmark; his master Egbert had identified the Danes as one of the peoples who were kin to the English and in need of evangelization. They were linked into the North Sea commercial network, and excavations at Ribe have shown that the trading settlement there began to flourish from about the year 700. Willibrord could have met Danish merchants at Dorestad. In going among the Danes Willibrord was straying well beyond the reach of Frankish protection: it was a courageous enterprise. According to his biographer they were 'very savage people' and their king 'fiercer than any wild beast and harder than stone'.[2] The Danish ruler Ongendus received Willibrord with honour but the missionary could make no impression on king or people and soon departed. Alcuin tells us that he brought back with him thirty boys. It is often assumed that these were Danish boys whom Willibrord intended to train for future missionary work. But Alcuin does not explicitly tell us that they were Danish and he may simply have been reporting a tradition that Willibrord had ransomed captives as Eligius or Amandus had done before him.

Willibrord looked east as well as north. Echternach was not only a useful retreat when times were troubled in Frisia, as in the two years following the death of Pippin II in 714. It was also a springboard for missionary enterprise further east in the regions of Hesse, Thuringia and Franconia. Among Willibrord's benefactors was Hetan II, duke of Thuringia, possibly a kinsman of Pippin's wife Plectrudis. It is an indication that, at the very least, overtures had been made in that direction and had not been repulsed. With Willibrord's encouragement Boniface would soon build upon this Thuringian foundation.

The central German mission field may be thought of as the Mainland, the valley of the river Main and its tributaries; in terms of modern cities it is the area which stretches from Frankfurt by way of Würzburg and Bamburg towards Bayreuth. Willibrord was not the only missionary to concern himself with its evangelization. He had been preceded there by the Irishman Kilian, who had probably reached the region by way of Columbanus' monastery of Luxeuil in Burgundy. It is reported that he had been licensed to preach to the heathen by Pope Conan in 686–7; which may be believed, because Conan was a pope so short-lived and undistinguished that no fabricator would have dreamed of attributing any such initiative to him. Kilian established himself at Würzburg and is said to have converted Duke Gozbert of Thuringia, the father of Willibrord's benefactor Hetan. Kilian later fell out with him and was put to death in or about 689, allegedly for opposing the marriage of Gozbert to his brother's widow. Further to the south, in the valley of the Danube – where, as we have seen, a Columbanian house had already been founded at Weltenberg – another outsider was active. Emmeram was a native of Poitiers in Aquitaine – the see of Bishop Ansoald, patron of Filibert and the Irish *peregrinus* Romanus – who went eastwards and settled at Regensburg under the patronage of the duke of Bavaria. After conducting evangelizing work for some three years he too fell out with his patron and is said to have met a martyr's death about the year 690. Yet further to the south a Rhinelander named Rupert was active round Salzburg. He belonged to an aristocratic family of the middle Rhine region near Worms and seems to have gone to Bavaria, perhaps initially as an exile, in the mid-690s. Like Emmeram he worked with the encouragement of the Bavarian ducal family. Unlike Emmeram or Kilian he died a natural death, in about 716. Another immigrant *peregrinus* was Corbinian, a native of Melun near Paris who appeared in Bavaria in about 715 and officiated as a missionary bishop there until his death in about 730. His later cult associated him with Freising.

Kilian, Emmeram, Rupert and Corbinian are obscure figures of whom we know little that is certain. A rather younger man, of whom we can form a slightly clearer impression, was named Pirmin. His origins are mysterious, though it seems most likely that he was a native of Septimania – the trans-Pyrenean province of the Visigothic kingdom of Spain, stretching as far as the Rhône – who had migrated to Francia in the wake of the Islamic conquest of Spain in the early eighth century. Our first certain knowledge of him comes from the year 724, when he established the monastery of Reichenau on an island in Lake Constance. His patrons, initially a local aristocratic family, quickly came to include the Pippinids, who eagerly grasped this means of enhancing their influence in a region remote from their northern homelands. Pirmin was to remain active in this upper Rhine/Danube area for the rest of his life. Under his guidance monasteries were founded as well at Murbach, Pfaffers, Niederaltaich and Hornbach – to name only the most important in his network. His patrons continued to be, as we should expect, the local aristocracy. The ducal house of Bavaria was the patron of Niederaltaich. Count Eberhard of Franconia provided the endowment for Murbach, and in later life, blind, retired to end his days there. Count Wernher, 'sprung from the high nobility of the Franks', as Pirmin's biographer approvingly noted, was the founder of Hornbach. Pirmin was also alive to the importance of learning. He was said to have given fifty books – in that age no mean collection – to Reichenau, the nucleus of what quickly became one of the finest libraries in western Christendom (still, happily, intact there). He himself was a learned man: we possess a work from his pen known as the *Scarapsus* or the *Dicta Pirminii* ('Sayings of Pirmin'). It is a manual for preachers, having affinities with Martin of Braga's *De Correctione Rusticorum*, mentioned in Chapter 2, to which indeed it is indebted for some of its materials. In it Pirmin sought to convey the basic essentials of Christian teaching accompanied by counsel on morality, behaviour that the godly should follow or should shun.

The *Scarapsus* gives us a clue as to the nature of the common enterprise that was being pursued up and down the Frankish frontier in the age of Willibrord and Pirmin. The inhabitants of Thuringia or Franconia or Bavaria were not out-and-out pagans – though these were to be found in parts of Frisia. Rather, these were peoples who lived cheek by jowl with the Christian Frankish kingdom; for several generations they had experienced at least spasmodic Frankish lordship; and they were being quietly penetrated, as archaeological and

place-name evidence shows, by the eastward drift of Frankish colonization – and this meant churches as well as halls and barns and brew-
houses and stables. It was for such people that the *Scarapsus* was
intended; the barely Christian or the semi-Christian or the ignorant
Christian or the backsliding Christian, call them what we will: call
them, if we like, following Martin of Braga, *rustici*. Real proper pagans
still lay beyond: the Slavs, the Saxons, the Danes.

A common enterprise? Yes, because we can point to contact and
co-operation among the missionaries in the field. Willibrord was
among those who subscribed the foundation charter for Murbach: he
had been called in to advise as a sort of monastic consultant. Boniface
and Pirmin seem to have met towards the end of their lives. Kilian
and Corbinian and Pirmin probably had contacts with Rome, like
Willibrord. It was an English bishop of Würzburg, a disciple of Boniface, who honoured St Kilian by translating (i.e. moving) his body to
a new shrine. The dukes of Bavaria were patrons of Emmeram *and*
Rupert *and* Corbinian *and* Pirmin. Pirmin's pupil Bishop Heddo of
Strasbourg worked amicably with pupils of Boniface such as Bishop
Lul of Mainz.

It was into this fairly crowded and complex mission field on the
Frankish eastern frontier that there stepped in 716 the man with whose
name it will always be most associated: Boniface. The achievement of
Boniface looms large partly because it was indeed prodigious but perhaps above all because we know more about him than we do about
any others of the missionary churchmen active in eighth-century Germany. We know a lot about him because of the survival of much of
his correspondence, collected and preserved after his death by his
pupils. Letters, even the formal Latin compositions of an early medieval
missionary bishop, open a window upon individual personality as no
other category of source-material can do, and we can know Boniface
as we can know no other person so far mentioned in this book, saving
only Augustine of Hippo and Pope Gregory I. This is a circumstance
not without its problems. Boniface's reputation as a giant of the eighth-
century church rests in some degree upon the preservation of his letters.
Supposing that, shall we say, Pirmin's correspondence had survived
but Boniface's had not: what then? It is an unsettling speculation.

Boniface was born in Wessex in about 680: his given name was
Wynfrith. An early entrant to the monastic life at Exeter, he later

moved to the monastery of Nursling on Southampton Water. The place may have been influential in fostering a missionary vocation: it was close to the busy port of Hamwic, where Frisian merchants were to be encountered. A little to the east lay Wilfrid's monastery of Selsey, where the missionary exploits of its founder would have been remembered and those of his disciples such as Willibrord no doubt watched with interest. Whatever may have been the origins of his missionary impulse, Wynfrith set sail for Frisia in 716. This first journey was not auspicious. The Frisians were in revolt against Frankish lordship in the period of turmoil following the death of Pippin II and no work could be accomplished. Wynfrith returned home. Two years later he tried again. Equipped with a letter of introduction from his bishop, Daniel of Winchester, Wynfrith set course on this occasion for Rome. The pope of the day, Gregory II, shared the ideals of his famous predecessor and namesake. Shortly before Wynfrith's arrival he had welcomed the duke of Bavaria in Rome and worked out a scheme for the establishment of bishoprics in his duchy under the supervision of papal legates. In the event nothing seems to have come of this, but it shows that the problems and opportunities of the German mission field were among the concerns of the Roman curia at the time of the Englishman's coming. In May 719 Wynfrith received a formal commission from Pope Gregory II to undertake the evangelization of heathen people. It was on this occasion that he received a new name, that of the early Roman martyr Boniface. Wynfrith's new identity was unambiguously Christian and Roman, and potentially that of a martyr.

After this first Roman journey Boniface returned to Frisia, where he worked with Willibrord between 719 and 722. Willibrord wanted to consecrate him as an assistant bishop – the office technically known to canon law as a *chorepiscopus* – but Boniface had other plans. Travelling by way of Hesse he went back to Rome, where he was consecrated a bishop by Gregory II in 722 and entrusted with a very wide-ranging papal commission to preach the gospel to the peoples east of the river Rhine. Returning across the Alps in 723 he visited the Frankish court, where he was formally taken under the protection of the Frankish ruler, Pippin's son Charles, known to history as Charles Martel, 'the Hammer'. Boniface knew exactly where he wanted to go: one of the clutch of papal letters he brought back to Francia was addressed to the secular leaders of the Thuringians. To Thuringia and Hesse accord-

205

ingly he went in 723 or 724. This central German mission field would engross all his energies for the next fifteen years or so.

In his letter of commission Pope Gregory had distinguished among Boniface's prospective flock between, on the one hand, Christians who had been 'led astray by the wiles of the Devil and now serve idols under the guise of the Christian religion' and, on the other, those 'who have not yet been cleansed by the waters of holy baptism'.[3] In other words, Boniface was going to be operating in a region of mixed religious allegiances. He would encounter ignorant or bewildered or backsliding or lapsed Christians of the sort for whom Pirmin composed the *Scarapsus*, but he would also encounter pagans. In the first category would have fallen the twin brothers Dettic and Deorulf who practised 'the sacrilegious worship of idols under the cloak of Christianity'. They were local chieftains based at Amöneburg, the first place which Boniface is said to have visited in Hesse. Excavations there have revealed a fortress of late Merovingian type, presumably their stronghold. Boniface established a monastic community there, its purpose to reclaim the brothers and their dependants for Christ. And for Charles Martel? Dettic and Deorulf were probably regarded by Charles Martel as his subordinates; unreliable ones who needed chasing-up from time to time. The brothers might not have thought of themselves in quite the same light. It mattered very much to Boniface that he came to his charges as the pope's man. It could have been, however, that in their perceptions he came as Charles Martel's. There were difficult and delicate questions here which were to cause Boniface much heart-searching.

Pagans 'not yet cleansed' were first encountered at Geismar, where there was a sacred oak tree. It is possible that there may have been there 'a pagan shrine of more than local significance'.[4] In a brave act of public Christian assertion Boniface felled the oak. 'At the sight of this extraordinary spectacle the heathens who had been cursing ceased to revile and began, on the contrary, to believe and bless the Lord.'[5] Willibald, the author of this *Life of Boniface*, had almost certainly read Sulpicius Severus' *Vita Martini*. Boniface used the timber from the sacred oak of Geismar to build a chapel which was the nucleus of his second monastic foundation, at Fritzlar. Another followed, further to the east, at Ohrdruf. Later still, in this Hesse-Thuringian area, came the monastic house which was to eclipse all his others in fame, at Fulda, founded in 744. As his work expanded into the Franconian region Boniface replicated the pattern further south, with communities at Kitzingen, Ochsenfurt and Tauberbischofsheim near Würzburg.

Boniface looked to his patrons, the Pippinid family, for the endowments that he needed. Take the case of Fulda. We possess a vivid narrative of the foundation of the monastery in the *Life of St Sturm*, its first abbot, composed by his disciple Eigil in about 790. Following a well-known literary topos, or convention, Eigil presents Sturm as prospecting for the monastic site in a 'frightful wilderness'. In actual fact Fulda was nothing of the sort, as an attentive reading of Eigil's text reveals. Fulda was at a much-frequented crossing-place of the river of the same name and it stood at the centre of a large Pippinid estate. Excavation has revealed an imposing dwelling-house, apparently of the seventh century, presumably the residence of members of the family when they went there to hunt in winter or a staging-post when they took the field against the Saxons in the spring. The survival of abundant eighth-century documents from Fulda shows how quickly the monastery attracted benefactions from the Franconian nobility, following the example set by their kings (as the Pippinids now were). The monastic community grew quickly too: there were about 360 monks at Fulda by the time of Sturm's death in 779.

The example of Fulda shows how skilfully Boniface and the abbot appointed by him, like Amandus in Gaul or Fructuosus in Spain or Wilfrid in England, exploited royal and aristocratic connections. After our investigations in the last two chapters this will hardly come as a surprise. In his missionary operations Boniface also looked to his friends in England. His letters present us with the opportunity to observe the intricacies of his network of friends and supporters. Bishop Daniel of Winchester, Boniface's diocesan before he left England and an old friend, offered him advice in a famous letter – to which we shall return – about how to set about converting the heathen. We find Boniface soliciting the prayers of Archbishop Nothelm of Canterbury, of Bishop Pehthelm of Whithorn, of Abbess Eadburga of Thanet, of the otherwise unknown Abbot Aldhere, and of others. Boniface was a learned man who appreciated, like Pirmin, the importance of books in the mission field. Would Abbess Eadburga send him a copy of the epistles of St Peter written in letters of gold? The priest Eoba, bearer of this letter – later on a missionary bishop – is bringing the gold with him. In 746–7 he asked Archbishop Egbert of York for any of the works of Bede, and he repeated this request in a letter to the abbot of Bede's own monastery. Would Bishop Daniel allow him to have the copy of the Prophets which had belonged to 'my former master', Abbot Winbert of Nursling? His eyesight is fading and he can no longer read small, joined-up writing, but Winbert's copy, he recalls, was written in plain, detached capitals.[6] People as well as books came to him in what he called his German exile to assist in the work of evangelization. Wigbert, the first abbot of Fritzlar, was an Englishman. So was Denewald, Boniface's emissary to the pope in 726. So was Burchard, who became bishop of Würzburg. Some of those who came were his kinsfolk. Such, for instance, were Leoba, the first abbess of Tauberbischofsheim, and Willibald – not to be confused with Boniface's biographer of the same name – who after adventurous travels as a young man in the eastern Mediterranean became bishop of Eichstätt.

Most poignantly the letters show how Boniface leaned on a few tried friends to relieve his frustrations and anxieties. Particularly revealing is a letter he wrote to Bishop Daniel in the early 740s. In it he poured out 'to his most beloved master . . . the troubles of a weary heart'. He is surrounded by 'false priests and hypocrites' who strive to thwart his work. He is dependent on the protection of the ruler of the Franks: 'without his mandate and the fear of him' he cannot 'prevent the rites of the heathens and the worship of idols in Germany'. Therefore he has to attend at court, and this brings him necessarily into contact with the Frankish prelates he so despises. He fears that he is guilty of breaking the oath which he had sworn at the tomb of St Peter twenty years before, to have no dealings with errant or disorderly bishops. What is he to do? It is the pathetic outcry of a tortured man.[7]

The letter also shows us what a difficult, prickly and tactless man Boniface was. He was a rigorist in his standards who was not prepared to modify them by one jot or tittle in the face of circumstances. To set such a course may be praiseworthy; but it is certain to be stormy. As early as 724 Boniface was reporting to the pope about a clash with the bishop of Mainz. Too idle to preach to the heathen himself, the bishop was now claiming the regions evangelized by Boniface as part of his own diocese. We do not have the bishop's side of the story; and it is likely that he and other Rhineland bishops were less reprehensible than Boniface portrayed them. It is a reasonable guess that in Mainz Boniface was regarded as an interloper; an ecclesiastical adventurer with his own English team, flourishing unfamiliar credentials which rendered him unamenable to discipline, presuming to criticize arrangements and practices of long standing. When Boniface set up Thuringian bishoprics at Buraburg and Erfurt the Rhinelanders may have felt that their worst fears were being realized. Here was an ecclesiastical empire in the making. The subsequent actions of Boniface in Franconia and Bavaria cannot have allayed suspicions, nor can the manner in which these were recorded by a Bonifatian *équipe* which was skilled at publicity. Boniface's biographer Willibald – as partisan, though less stridently so, as Wilfrid's biographer Stephen – presented Boniface as the single-handed restorer of church life in southern Germany. In other words, he rode roughshod over the sensibilities of congregations who revered Kilian or Rupert or Corbinian, disregarded the transalpine initiatives of the churches of northern Italy.

However, issues of organization and ecclesiastical power-politics dwindled into insignificance beside Boniface's overwhelming desire to save souls. God 'will have all men to be saved and to come unto the knowledge of the truth', he quoted from St Paul in a letter of 738. Pope Gregory III, writing on his behalf at about the same time, echoed the thought in the words of St Luke: 'the kingdom of God is nigh at hand . . . it is toward evening and the day is far spent.' There was no time to be lost.[8] Boniface was puzzled, hurt and angry that his sense of the urgency of the task was not shared by the Frankish bishops. They had to be jolted out of their slothfulness. It was for this reason that ecclesiastical reform became linked with evangelization. 'Reform' is one of those lazy words that have to be cashed before they can circulate as currency. What Boniface did, in partnership with the secular power, was to resume the practice of holding church councils in the Frankish realm. No such council had been held for at least a generation before his coming. No less than five were held between 742 and 747. Under Boniface's exacting guidance the assembled churchmen proclaimed standards of disciplinary excellence, 'targets' for the Frankish church in the future. In setting these standards, in forcing them upon the attention of churchmen, Boniface was an unwitting architect of what we have come to call the Carolingian renaissance.

Boniface was the dominant figure in the Frankish church by the latter part of his long life. He ended by holding, from 745, the see of Mainz, once occupied by the prelates he had so despised. But his vocation always kept his face firmly turned towards the north-east. There in Saxony lay the real challenge to a missionary worthy of his calling. In 738 he sent an open letter of appeal to 'all God-fearing catholics sprung from the race and stock of the English' in which he played upon their apostolic responsibility *towards their kin*: an emotive card to play. 'Have mercy upon them because their repeated cry is, "We are of one and the same blood and bone!"' Bishop Torthelm of Leicester, replying, rejoiced that 'our people' (*gens nostra*) were being converted to faith in Christ.[9] The dating of this appeal is probably to be explained in the context of a more aggressive policy adopted by the Carolingians towards the Saxons. In 738 Charles Martel had crossed the Rhine near Essen, laid waste the Saxon land beyond and 'made tributary that very savage people'. In 744 his son invaded the fringes of Saxony and subdued its people: 'Christ being our leader, many of them were baptized.'[10] The association between military submission and Christian baptism is notable in these comments by a contemporary chronicler. Presumably the baptizers were from Boniface's team. Another punitive Frankish expedition occurred in 748. One of Boniface's last letters refers to a Saxon incursion in the course of which thirty churches had been burnt down. It was presumably in reprisal that King Pippin led a big army into Saxony in 753 and ravaged far and wide, taking many prisoners and much booty. Although he penetrated as far as Rehme, near Minden, he did not have matters all his own way. Bishop Hildegar of Cologne was cornered by the Saxons and killed: it was characteristic of the Frankish *Adelskirche* that a bishop might be an active participant on the field of battle. However, by the end of the campaign the Saxons were cowed and 'sought peace and the sacraments'. The stage was set for the bloody Saxon wars and forcible conversions of the reign of Charlemagne.

Boniface did not live to see these developments. Towards the end of his life he determined to lay down his administrative responsibilities and return in person to those north-eastern mission fields which, in his biographer's words, 'he had once deserted in body but never, indeed, in his heart'. A letter which he wrote at this time to his old friend Fulrad, the abbot of Saint-Denis and a trusted counsellor of King Pippin, reveals his mood and his anxieties.

> I cannot render adequate thanks, as you have deserved, for the spiritual friendship of your brotherly love, which you often for the sake of God showed to me in my necessities; but I pray Almighty God that he may recompense you in the high summit of the heavens with the reward of his favour eternally in the joy of angels. Now in the name of Christ I pray, that what you have

begun with a good beginning you may complete with a good end; that is, that you will greet for me the most glorious and gracious Pippin our king, and give him great thanks for all the acts of kindness which he has done for me; and that you will tell him what to me and my friends seems very likely to take place. It seems that I must soon finish this temporal life and the course of my days through these infirmities. Therefore I pray our king's highness in the name of Christ the Son of God that he will deign to send me word and inform me while I am yet alive, about my disciples, what favours he will do to them afterwards. For they are almost all foreigners [*peregrini*]. Some are priests appointed in many places to minister to the church and to the people; some are monks in our monasteries, and children set to learn to read; and some are growing old, who have toiled and helped me, living with me for a long time. I am anxious about all these, that they may not be scattered after my death, but may have the favour of your counsels and your highness's support, and not be scattered like sheep that have no shepherd; and that the people near the frontier with the pagans may not lose the law of Christ. Therefore I pray our grace's clemency urgently in the name of God, to make my son and suffragan Bishop Lul – if God will and it pleases your grace – to be appointed and constituted to the ministry of the peoples and churches as a preacher and teacher of the priests and people. And I hope, if God wishes, that the priests may have in him a master, the monks a teacher of the rule, and the Christian people a faithful preacher and shepherd. I beg most especially that this be done, because my priests near the frontier with the pagans have a poor livelihood. They can get bread to eat, but cannot obtain clothing there unless they have a counsellor and supporter elsewhere to sustain and strengthen them in those places for the service of the people, in the same way as I have helped them. If the goodness of Christ inspires you to this and you will consent to do what I ask, deign to send word and inform me by these my present messengers or by your holiness's letters, so that I may either live or die the happier for your favour.[11]

Accordingly he set off in 753 to those northern, coastal, low-lying, marshy regions where Frisians and Saxons lived, whence the English had migrated to a new country three centuries earlier. There, among their own blood and bone, communicating in their own tongue, Boniface and his followers laboured hard throughout that autumn and the following spring, destroying shrines, building churches, baptizing many thousands. At Whitsuntide 754 the party was camped at Dokkum on the coast of Frisia, far to the north, well beyond the protecting reach of Frankish royal power. There they were awaiting the arrival of the recently baptized for confirmation. Instead they were surprised on 5 June by a gang of seaborne predators attracted by the prospect of loot. In the struggle that ensued we are told that the elderly missionary tried to ward off the blows of his assailants by using a book as a shield: to no avail; Boniface and his companions were slaughtered. The volume with which he tried to defend himself may still be seen at Fulda. It is disfigured by two deep hacking cuts which have scored into the leaves on one side.

Boniface was immediately hailed as a martyr. His monks at Fulda, whither his body was brought after his death, were referring to the martyrdom in the texts of day-to-day conveyancing documents within a few weeks. Annalists across the North Sea in Northumbria noted his death. A moving letter of condolence was sent by the archbishop of Canterbury to Lul, the English disciple of Boniface and his successor in the see of Mainz. The monks of Montecassino, who were joined to those of Fulda by a confraternity of prayer, remembered him in their intercessions. Enrolled among the noble army of martyrs, observance of his feast day on the anniversary of his death was quickly and widely diffused amongst the churches of Latin Christendom.

The memory of Boniface the missionary, Boniface the apostle of Germany, was carefully cherished, especially by the monks of Fulda. As we shall see, this vision of Boniface continued to inspire missionary work not simply in the eighth century but on through the ninth, tenth and eleventh centuries as well. It may be fairly termed a vision because in point of fact Boniface actually spent little of his life working among the out-and-out heathen. The first half of his career was spent in England as a scholar and teacher, important aspects of his achievement which it would have been out of place to have dwelt on here. In the Frankish kingdom his achievements may be seen in the further Christianizing of the nominally Christian; in his vigorous reinforcement of Roman loyalties and Roman order; in his firmly tying together of the churches of central and southern Germany; and in his initiation of a period of reform and revitalization in the Frankish churches as a whole. These were colossal achievements; but they were not those that Boniface himself would have wished to be remembered by. Though Boniface has left us no such account of his vocation as that penned by Patrick (quoted above, pp. 84–5) it is evidence from his letters that he possessed a strong sense of having been called to undertake missionary work. In the event he could not devote himself to it as he wished, and as a result was oppressed by a sense of failure. The Saxons whom he longed to lead to Christ were to be converted by others; and by methods which Boniface might not have approved.

The more westerly Saxons, at any rate some of them, had been subjected to spasmodic bouts of Frankish overlordship over a long period of time. For example, the chronicler known as Fredegar, writing perhaps at Luxeuil in about 660, reveals that the Saxons had been engaged to pay an annual tribute of 500 cows to the Frankish kings since the time of King Chlothar I, the son of Clovis. Dagobert I remitted this tribute – which may or may not empower us to believe that it had been paid regularly – in return for Saxon military service in defending a part of the frontier zone against the Wends. What appears to have become a rather more forward policy towards the Saxons – though it may just be a way of saying that we hear more about Saxon campaigns in our more forthcoming sources – under Charles Martel and Pippin I was directed to essentially traditional ends: the security of the frontier zone, to be profitably achieved by beating the Saxons up a bit, burning crops and villages, taking prisoners and so forth, until they submitted and agreed to pay tribute. Charlemagne's early Saxon campaigns in the years 772–5 had the same character. This is not to claim that they were devoid of any religious colouring whatsoever. As wars of Christians against barbarians who were also pagans, they had from the outset a religious tinge. It was, after all, on his very first Saxon campaign in 772 that Charlemagne destroyed the heathen sanctuary of the *Irminsul* or 'World Tree': just so had Boniface felled the oak of Geismar half a century beforehand.

If we may believe an extraordinary tale found in a piece of hagiography we catch a hint of the heralding of a more aggressive Frankish policy. Lebuin, or to give him his Anglo-Saxon name Leofwine, was an Englishman who felt a call to work in Germany. He settled at Deventer and from this base would make missionary journeys into Saxony. He found a Saxon patron in a man named Folcbert, 'a rich man, one of the high nobility', who seems to have accepted Christianity. Lebuin determined to go and preach to the Saxons at their annual assembly at Marklohe, on the river Weser about thirty miles south of

Bremen. Folcbert tried to dissuade him because of the danger involved, but in vain. So Lebuin went off to Marklohe. In his address to the assembled Saxons Lebuin dwelt on the familiar theme of this-worldly rewards. Accept the God of the Christians and 'He will confer benefits upon you such as you have never heard of before'. Lebuin also uttered warnings: 'If you are unwilling . . . there is ready a king in a neighbouring country who will invade your land, who will despoil and lay waste, will tire you out with his campaigns, scatter you in exile, dispossess or kill you, give away your estates to whomsoever he wishes; and thereafter you will be subject to him and to his successors.'[12] The chronology of Lebuin's life is uncertain, but this episode would seem to belong to the early 770s. Did the incident reported ever take place? The *Vita Lebuini* was composed many years later, probably not before 850, long after Lebuin's prophecy had been fulfilled. There is plenty of scope for scepticism as to the historicity of the tale. Yet there are also features of Lebuin's exploits, as reported, which inspire confidence. The missionary who acts as a kind of 'buffer' between an imperial power and its prospective conquests is not uncommonly encountered in Christian missionary history.

Whether or not Lebuin ever addressed the Saxon notables at Marklohe, a change seems to have come over Frankish policy in the ensuing phase of campaigning between 776 and 782. Frankish pressure became less episodic, more intense, though there might still be moments of remission – for example in the wake of the Roncesvalles disaster of 778. In a vivid piece of reporting in the so-called 'Royal Annals' for 776 the anonymous author for the first time in this work linked conquest and baptism. 'They promised that they would be Christians and bound themselves to the lordship of King Charles.' An 'innumerable multitude' of Saxons, men, women and children, were baptized in the waters of the river Lippe not far from Paderborn at – a significant *conjoncture* – the fort recently built there by the king.[13] The pressure was kept up over the next few years. But the Saxons had found a resistance leader of determination and courage in Widukind, who makes his first appearance in the surviving records in the year 777.

Our business is with conversion, not with war; we do not need to dwell on the detailed history of the Saxon campaigns of the 770s and 780s. It is fairly clear that Charles and his advisers misjudged the Saxon potential for resistance both to the Franks and to Christianity. One can sense that the savage measures which followed sprang from a kind of baffled exasperation. There are parallels for this in other missionary contexts. It has been suggested that Boniface's disciple Lul might have been the royal adviser responsible for the harsher measures adopted in this phase of exasperation from about 782 onwards. There is a certain plausibility about the suggestion; Lul had held the see of Mainz since Boniface's death nearly thirty years before; in all that time not much headway had been made with the conversion of the Saxons. Were these stubborn people never going to submit? In the event they did. The harsher measures, by whomsoever advised (and Abbot Sturm of Fulda is another candidate), bore fruit – in the short term. In 782 Charles massacred 4,500 prisoners. More fortunate ones were enslaved or deported. In 784 he led his army to the banks of the river Elbe: no Frankish ruler had ever before campaigned and laid waste as far to the east as this. In 785 Widukind submitted and was baptized. The pope ordered three days of thanksgiving litanies. The aged Lul composed, shortly before his death in 786, Latin verses celebrating the conquest and forcible conversion of the Saxons.

The other literary monument to the pacification of Saxony is the so-called 'Saxon Capitulary'. (The term 'capitulary' is used by historians for the administrative edicts issued by Frankish kings.) The Saxon Capitulary, sometimes called the 'capitulary of Paderborn' from its place of issue, records the measures taken for the Christianization of Saxony.[14] Refusal to be baptized became a capital offence. Cremation of the dead became a capital offence. Eating meat in Lent became a capital offence. So did attacks on churches, slaying of clergy, participation in various rituals identified as pagan, alongside disloyal conspiracy against the king. Sundays and the greater feast days were to be observed by abstention from worldly business and by attendance at church. Churches were to be provided by their congregations with endowments in land, buildings and slaves; they were to be supported by tithes of income and labour payable by all men. Infants were to be baptized within a year of birth. Marriages within certain degrees of relationship were forbidden. Burials were to take place only in cemeteries attached to churches.

As with all normative evidence from the early medieval (or any other) period one must make a large allowance for a gap between precept and practice. Nevertheless, when even the most generous allowance has been made, the Saxon Capitulary stands as a blueprint for the comprehensive and ruthless Christianization of a conquered society.

It was not simply that the sanctions were of an extreme harshness. It was also that the measures to be adopted in Christianization would destabilize and dislocate the social texture of Saxon life at the most intimate levels of family existence, touching birth, marriage and death. To the degree that such tactics had never before been essayed in a Christian missionary context, it seems reasonable to infer that this tearing apart of Saxon society was deliberately intended, and that the measures were framed by persons who knew how to inflict the maximum damage. Who the persons who drafted the Saxon Capitulary were we do not know; but it must have had the approbation of the king. There are hints that in some quarters these draconian measures caused disquiet; we shall return to these presently. But in the late 780s the spirit of the capitulary seems to have been in the ascendant. Charlemagne could hope to implement it by pouring clergy into Saxony. We must not exaggerate the scale of this operation, though he had access to human resources to a degree that predecessors such as Dagobert I might have envied. It is well to bear in mind that even small numbers of determined missionaries can leave an abiding impression on a defeated and demoralized population when supported by secular imperial power. The Spaniards were to rediscover this truth in Mexico and Peru.

Fulda was an important base from which missionaries came, though the later claim by its monks that 'the greatest part' of Saxony had been allotted to them as a zone of evangelization was an exaggeration. Boniface's disciple Sturm, though now 'worn down by age', was harried by the king – young, hyperactive and imperious – into the mission field. It killed the old man in 779, his death hastened by Charles's well-meant insistence that he be treated by the royal physician, who prescribed the wrong medicines. Fulda's missionary efforts in Saxony were to last well into the next century. Würzburg was another such base, providing the nucleus of a diocesan establishment, including its first bishop, for Paderborn. Other bases lay further back in Francia. Liège, for instance, seems to have furnished missionaries for the region round Osnabrück. Châlons-sur-Marne provided Halberstadt with its first bishop in the reign of Charlemagne's son. Its next-door neighbour Rheims sent a still more daring missionary probe across the Elbe and into Denmark.

Then there was the contribution of what might be called the Anglo-Frisian church. Lul's correspondence has come down to us with his master's and from it we can see that close connections were maintained with England throughout his long episcopate at Mainz from 754 to 786. Books, prayers and volunteers were what England could provide, the indispensable infrastructure of mission. Abbot Cuthbert of Wearmouth wrote to Lul in 764, sending at his request Bede's prose and verse *Lives of St Cuthbert*, he would have sent more had not the cold of the preceding winter made it impossible to get much writing done. The dissemination of Bede's historical works in the Frankish kingdom provided food for thought and models for action in the mission field. King Alhred of Northumbria and his queen Osgifu assured Lul in 773 that 'We have been careful to do as you asked about yourself and about the names sent to us. In all the monasteries subject to our authority they are commended with the everlasting memorial of writing and offered daily to God with the help of prayers.'[15] A bond of prayer, like that between Fulda and Montecassino, transcending space and time, had bridged not only the sea which divided England and Germany but also that other sea which divided the living from the dead.

In 767 a certain Albert was consecrated a bishop at York and sent to labour alongside Boniface's pupil Gregory of Utrecht. At some point between 765 and 774 King Alhred convened a synod which despatched another Northumbrian, the priest Willehad, across the sea. He worked initially in the north Frisian area where Boniface had perished. Later, in about 780, he was recruited by Charlemagne to work further east among the Saxons. When his work was interrupted by Widukind's revolt he managed to escape from Saxony – four of his clerical associates were killed – and after making a pilgrimage to Rome settled for two years of prayer and study at Echternach. It was, of course, no casual choice of refuge: the foundation and burial place of the great Willibrord, presided over at this time by Abbot Beornrad, another Englishman (and a member of the founder's kin) who was later to become archbishop of Sens and one of Charlemagne's leading counsellors. At Echternach Willehad rebuilt his team and then returned to Saxony upon its pacification in 785. In 787 he was consecrated a bishop and fixed his see at Bremen. He lived and worked there for just long enough to see his new cathedral church built and consecrated before his death in 789.

Another member of this Anglo-Frisian connection was Liudger. A *Vita Liudgeri* was later composed by his nephew Altfrid, an unusually rewarding work for the modern historian.[16] Its opening chapters well bring out the close connection between an aristocratic kin and the growth of a regional church. Liudger belonged to a noble Frisian family. His paternal grandfather had escaped from Frisia after a quarrel with King Radbod and sought asylum among the Franks. In the course of this exile he had become a Christian; an occasion of conversion which may set bells ringing. Later he had returned to Frisia and given assistance to Willibrord near Utrecht. On his mother's side Liudger's two great-uncles were, as we saw earlier in this chapter, the earliest clerics of native Frisian stock. Aunts and cousins were friends of Boniface. Liudger's own brother became bishop of Châlons and busied himself with the evangelization of Saxony. For Altfrid, his family's history was also in large part the story of the Frisian church. It is a perspective the interest of which is not blurred by the likelihood that other families took pride in similar claims.

As a young man Liudger was sent to school with Gregory of Utrecht, along with other 'noble fellow pupils': Gregory's clerical retinue. Later he was to write Gregory's *Vita*, a work which would stress among other things Gregory's discipleship of Boniface. There was a spiritual genealogy which paralleled – but probably never wholly displaced – the links of blood and bone. Liudger was the disciple of Gregory who was the disciple of Boniface. The genealogies fused in Willibrord, the great apostle of the Frisians whom both Boniface and Liudger's grandfather had helped in the mission field. In the company of Gregory of Utrecht Liudger met the Englishman Albert. When Albert was sent back to England for episcopal consecration in 767 Liudger was sent with him and ordained a deacon. He remained there for a year, studying at York at the feet of Alcuin. After a brief return to Frisia he went back to York to resume his studies under this 'illustrious master' for another three and a half years before returning to Frisia bursting with learning and loaded with books in about 772. A little later, after Gregory's death in about 775, his kinsman and successor at Utrecht, Alberic, sent Liudger to restore the church at Deventer founded by the intrepid Lebuin, also lately deceased. From Deventer he would go out on missionary journeys accompanied by other 'servants of God' to smash the pagan shrines of the Frisians. 'They brought back great quantities of treasure which they found in the shrines,' tells Altfrid with welcome candour. They would make the treasure over to Alberic, who would then present two-thirds of it to Charlemagne; a gesture doubtless profitable to both parties in a manner that Wilfrid would have understood. Liudger was compelled to flee from the mission field, like Willehad, at the time of Widukind's rising in 782. He withdrew to Italy, visited Rome and spent two and a half years at the monastery of Montecassino. Returning to the north he was recruited by Charlemagne – Alberic of Utrecht being now dead – and sent to work in eastern Frisia and then in Saxony. There he founded a monastery, still today known by a derivation from the Latin *monasterium*, Münster, which he used as a base from which to evangelize western Saxony. Consecrated a bishop in about 804 he established his episcopal seat at Münster and worked there until his death in 809.

Bremen, Münster and Paderborn were mission communities which became the seats of bishops. Some did not, but grew into important monasteries in their own right. Such a one was Werden on Saxony's western fringes, founded by Liudger in about 800. Other monastic communities were established as colonies or daughter-houses of monasteries back in the Frankish heartlands. Such, for instance, was Corvey (Korvei) on the river Weser, colonized from Queen Balthild's mid-seventh-century foundation of Corbie in Picardy, whose name as well as traditions it took. Corvey's ancestry therefore stretched back to the Columbanian brand of monasticism which had so appealed to the nobility of northern Francia, as we saw in Chapter 5. Corvey, founded in the second decade of the ninth century, was richly endowed; it enjoyed the patronage of the Emperor Louis, Charlemagne's son; it built up a fine library. The pattern is a familiar one. Corvey played an important role in the Christianization of Saxony and in the early missions to Denmark and Sweden. Meanwhile, members of the newly Christian Saxon aristocracy themselves became monastic founders. Herford, north of Paderborn, was founded in about 800 by a Saxon nobleman named Walther; its first abbess was his daughter. No less a person than Widukind himself founded the monastery of Enger, not far from Herford. The portable reliquary from Enger, now in Berlin (see plate 26), was reputedly a gift from the founder, who is said to have received it as a baptismal present from Charlemagne himself. Widukind's grandson Count Waldbert was the founder and first abbot of Wildeshausen, a little to the south-west of Bremen. It was entirely characteristic of the age and the milieu that he should have stipulated that its abbots should always be drawn from the founder's kin.

In the course of the ninth century Saxony became a powerhouse of Christian piety, scholarship and art. But its initial Christianization had

219

proceeded against a backdrop of massacres and deportations, of missionaries killed and churches gutted, of village communities disrupted and demoralized. Eigil in his *Vita Sturmi* observed that Charlemagne converted the Saxons 'partly by wars, partly by persuasion, partly even by gifts'. The author of the *Vita Willehadi* was more candid: 'the fierce necks of the Saxons bowed to the light yoke of Christ although coerced [*licet coacta*].' Are we correct to read this as a hint of disquiet? If so, then comparable symptoms of unease may be detected in some of Alcuin's works. Alcuin had been lured from York to join Charlemagne's court in 782. This was the period when the Frankish establishment was reaching what was called above the point of exasperation in the Saxon wars. The first hint of unease, an oblique one, occurs in a long poem which Alcuin composed in celebration of his *alma mater*, probably in 792–3, *The Bishops, Kings and Saints of York*. In a passage devoted to King Edwin, Alcuin dwelt on the *peaceful* means by which the king had brought his subjects to faith in Christ – though he conceded that there had been 'gifts and threats' as well.[17] It is hard to believe that no message for his Frankish hosts was intended in Alcuin's choice of emphasis. The same could be said of his stress on peaceful, albeit sometimes confrontational, methods of conversion in the *Vita Willibrordi* which Alcuin was putting into its final shape in the mid-790s. Much more explicit, however, was a clutch of letters composed in 796.

The background to the letters of 796 was the Frankish victory over the Avars, a semi-nomadic people who had been threatening Charlemagne's south-eastern marches beyond Bavaria. The defeat of the Avars had been decisive and total. Their territories – the old intra-Danubian province of Pannonia, approximately the western parts of modern Hungary – had been added to the Frankish dominions. The next step was to have been the forcible conversion of the Avars to Christianity: it was to be Saxony all over again. But this, thought Alcuin, was just what it must not be. The prelate most closely concerned with the imminent programme of evangelization was Archbishop Arn of Salzburg, who was an old friend of Alcuin. In his letter Alcuin implored him to 'Be a preacher of piety, not an exactor of tithes; for the new soul must be suckled with the milk of apostolic goodness until it grows in health and strength to take solid food [cf. I Corinthians iii.1–2]. People say that tithes undermined the faith of the Saxons. How can we impose on the necks of the simple a yoke which neither we nor our brethren have been able to endure?' Alcuin also wrote to the king himself. He congratulated Charles on his victory, and he made clear here as elsewhere that he had no doubt at all that the king had been fighting God's holy war. 'It pleased Christ to subdue the Avars to His service by means of your campaigning sceptres.' But now, Alcuin went on, the king

> . . . must provide devout preachers for the new people, men who are honourable in their ways, well trained in the knowledge of the holy faith, imbued with the teaching of the gospel, and in their preaching of the word of God close followers of the example of the holy apostles. They, in the early days of the faith, had milk (by which they meant their sweet teaching) to offer to their hearers: in the words of St Paul, 'And I, brethren, could not speak unto you as unto spiritual, but as unto carnal, even as unto babes in Christ. I have fed you with milk and not with meat: for hitherto ye were not able to bear it, neither yet now are ye able.' [I Corinthians iii.1–2] By this the preacher to the whole world, Christ speaking in him, meant to show that peoples newly converted to the faith should be fed on softer teachings, like the milk that is given in infancy, lest by taking sterner teaching the fragile mind should vomit out what it took in.

And he returned to the question of tithe. Is it wise to exact tithes now, straight away? Did the apostles exact tithes? 'It is better to forego tithe than to lose faith.' He also had advice on how missionaries should proceed.

> This also should be very carefully looked into, that the office of preaching and the sacrament of baptism be properly ordered, lest it should happen that the washing of the body in holy baptism is of no benefit, since there is no acknowledgement of the Catholic faith to accompany it in a mind capable of reason. So said the apostle: 'Let all things be done decently, and in order.' [I Corinthians xiv.40] And Our Lord himself in the gospel, when teaching his disciples, said: 'Go ye therefore and teach all nations, baptizing them in the name of the Father, and of the Son, and of the Holy Ghost.' [Matthew xxviii.19] In the commentary which he wrote on the gospel of St Matthew, St Jerome explained the order of this instruction as follows: 'First, they teach all nations, and then when they are taught they sprinkle them with water. For it is not possible for the body properly to receive the

221

sacrament of baptism unless the soul has previously received the truth of the faith into itself . . .'

He went on to commend the use of St Augustine of Hippo's little manual *De Catechizandis Rudibus* (*On Catechizing the Uninstructed*), which had originally been composed in response to a request from a catechist in Carthage. As well as writing to the king, Alcuin also wrote to his most important lay official, Meginfried the treasurer.[18]

Alcuin was not going soft. The king was doing God's work. However, God's work lay not simply in conquering but also in teaching the conquered. Alcuin's concern lay with finding the most effective way to teach, and this involved doing away with obstacles such as the resentments generated by compulsory payment of tithe. Did his exhortations bear fruit? There are some slight indications that they did. A second Saxon capitulary issued in 797 was milder in tone than its predecessor. We also have evidence for a high-level meeting in Bavaria in 796 between Charlemagne's son and two leading churchmen, Arn of Salzburg and Paulinus of Aquileia, at which they decided against compulsory baptism of the conquered Avars. It looks as though, in some quarters, Alcuin's advice was heeded. However, this was not to prevent the same harsh measures against which he had protested being applied by Germans to conquered Slavs in the tenth and eleventh centuries. The leaders of this next phase of coercive missionizing were Saxons. Some might detect here one of history's many ironies.

Charlemagne's conquest of Saxony brought the Franks into proximity to new neighbours in the north-eastern marches of their empire: the Danes and the Slavs. Both will claim our attention later on, but a few words must be said here about ninth-century missionary initiatives among and beyond the Danes, for these belonged in a Carolingian context.

The Danes had for long been on what might be called the Anglo-Saxon missionary agenda. As we saw earlier in this chapter, Egbert had wanted to preach to them and Willibrord had actually done so, though without success. Writing to a friend apparently in the circle of Willehad of Bremen in 789 Alcuin had enquired 'if there is any hope of converting the Danes'.[19] Bishop Willehad's disciple and successor at Bremen, Willeric, survived long into the ninth century – he died in

838 – to transmit his master's missionary ideals to a new generation. These Northumbrian impulses received additional stimulus from the political interests of the Frankish empire. The Danes were potentially dangerous neighbours. A dynasty of strong kings had emerged obscurely in the course of the eighth century in Denmark. Rich owing in large part to the profits from trade, masters of the seas round Denmark, disposers of the ordered power required to construct the extensive system of earthworks in Schleswig known as the Dannewerk or Danevirke, these kings were formidable figures. They could provide a haven for the enemies of the Franks, as in 782 when the Saxon leader Widukind found refuge in Denmark. Worse, the consolidation of royal authority involved the scattering of domestic opponents in exile. This is the most plausible of several explanations for the appearance in northern waters of the Vikings: turbulent young men with armed followings, ejected from their homeland, who had to shift for themselves. Steadily improving techniques of ship-building made rapid and distant voyages possible, and unexpected descents upon the rich and vulnerable, as the monks of Lindisfarne learned to their cost in 793. Many others were to learn the same harsh lesson in the course of the following century, in the British Isles and along Europe's coastline from Frisia to Gibraltar.

The murder of King Godfrid of the Danes in 810 precipitated a long period of struggles for power between rival contenders drawn from the various branches of the royal kin. Franco-Danish diplomatic contacts, already lively, became more intense during this time of dynastic instability. Frankish ruling circles wanted a Danish king who would be firm at home but friendly abroad. They thought that they had found their man in a certain Harald Klak, who was assisted to power in Denmark by the Emperor Louis in 819. Harald had spent the previous six years in exile among the Franks, during which he had been exposed to Christianity. In 823 he was visited by a high-ranking delegation under Archbishop Ebo of Rheims – it included Willeric of Bremen – whose brief, inseparable from diplomacy, was the propagation of the Christian faith. The project had been discussed with and approved by Pope Paschal I. Harald took his time. But in 826 he came, accompanied by his family and a large entourage, to the imperial court at Ingelheim, near Mainz, where he was baptized a Christian.

The occasion was described at some length in Latin verse by one Ermoldus Nigellus, Ermold the Black. Ermold had fallen from favour at court and was out to flatter Louis to the utmost in the hope – alas, unrealized – that his poem would secure his reinstatement. In consequence, his stately hexameters give a wonderfully distorted impression of the ceremonies. Nevertheless, with their aid we can glean some valuable perceptions of how the Frankish side viewed this encounter. The occasion was of the greatest magnificence. Louis spared no efforts. The architectural setting of the baptism, the processions and the singing, the presents that were given, the banqueting, the splendid hunt on an island in the Rhine, the lovely Empress Judith's dresses and jewellery, the drink that flowed so freely – 'Good Bacchus soon makes their stout hearts be merry,' as Ermold delicately put it[20] – all was designed to impress the Danes with the might and wealth of the Franks. And it worked, or so Ermold assures us: well, he would, wouldn't he? The state visit was understood by the Franks as marking Harald's subjection to Louis. The indications of this were plain to a Frankish understanding. Harald became Louis' vassal, placing his clasped hands between the emperor's. Louis gave Harald a horse and weapons, a traditional gift from a lord to his man. He also gave him a landed 'benefice' in northern Frisia. At the christening itself Louis stood godparent to Harald, the Empress Judith to his wife, and Prince Lothar to his son; baptismal sponsorship that indicated, in distant imitation of Byzantine custom, the lordship of Louis over the Danish king and which also established bonds of kinship between the parties. In accepting Christianity Harald had entered the imperial family as a subordinate.

Whether Harald saw matters in quite this light may be doubted. A story told by the slightly later writer Notker may be apposite here. Notker was a monk of Saint-Gallen who composed a discursive, chatty, moralizing work called *Gesta Karoli Magni* (*The Deeds of Charlemagne*) in the 880s. Referring to the baptisms of Danes which took place during the reign of Louis the Pious, Notker has this to tell us:

> Each received a white robe from the Emperor's wardrobe, and from his sponsors a full set of Frankish garments, with arms, costly robes and other adornments. This was done repeatedly and more and more [Danes] came each year, not for the sake of Christ but for mundane advantages. They used to hurry over on Easter Eve to pay homage to the Emperor, more like faithful vassals than foreign envoys. On one occasion as many as fifty arrived. The Emperor asked them if they wished to be baptized. When they

had confessed their sins, he ordered them to be sprinkled with holy water. As there were not enough linen garments to go round on that occasion, Louis ordered some old shirts to be cut up and tacked together to make tunics or to be run up as overalls. When one of these without more ado was put on a certain elderly envoy, he regarded it suspiciously for some time. Then he lost control of himself completely and said to the Emperor: 'Look here! I've gone through this ablutions business about twenty times already, and I've always been rigged out before with a splendid white suit; but this old sack makes me feel more like a pig-farmer than a soldier! If it weren't for the fact that you've pinched my own clothes and not given me any new ones, with the result that I'd feel a right fool if I walked out of here naked, you could keep your Christ and your reach-me-downs, too!'[21]

Notker's tales are not to be taken as sober history. None the less, they had to have at the least a certain plausibility for his audience if they were to spark the reaction which he sought – which I think we may take as smiles accompanied by sage nodding of heads. Notker's story shows that there was a perception about among the Franks that for some Danes Christian baptism was just something that, so to say, came up with the rations; something that could be annually, and profitably, repeated. Christian missionaries have encountered similar reactions in other contexts far removed in time and space, among the 'rice Christians' of nineteenth-century India and Africa, for example, which must at least make one hesitate before rejecting Notker's story out of hand.

Harald Klak proved a broken reed for the Franks. A year after his return to Denmark he was driven out by Godfrid's son Horic – numbered Horic I among the kings of Denmark – and spent the remaining twenty or so years of his life on the lands which he had been granted in Frisia, engaged in intermittent piracy, and dabbling in the ever more troubled waters of the dynastic politics of the Frankish empire in the 830s and 840s. However, the baptism at Ingelheim in 826 did bear some promising if short-lived fruit in the Scandinavian homelands. When Harald returned to Denmark after his baptism he took with him some Christian clergy supplied by the emperor. Among them was a young monk named Anskar, whom later generations would remember as the 'apostle of the north'.

Anskar, born in about 800, had been entered as a youth in the monastery of Corbie. There he received a good education, and could have read – almost certainly did read – the missionary lives of Martin, Cuthbert and Boniface which were to be found in Corbie's library. From there he had been transferred to the daughter-house of Corvey in Saxony upon its foundation in 822, to take charge of the monastery school. There he acquired a reputation as a preacher, a 'teacher of the people' – the Saxon people, we should recall, who were but recent converts and still in the process of being Christianized.[22] Arrived in Denmark in 826, Anskar set about the task of evangelization. His mission survived the downfall of his patron Harald Klak, possibly because the Emperor Louis adroitly established friendly relations with his supplanter Horic I. After a few years Anskar was invited to undertake an extension of his mission among the people known as the Sueones who occupied the district of modern Sweden round lake Mälaren, to the west of Stockholm. Accordingly, in about 829 or 830 Anskar travelled to the merchant settlement of Birka, where he was welcomed by Björn, the king of the Sueones, and allowed to set up a mission. He made an influential convert in one Herigar, the governor (*praefectus*) of Birka and a counsellor of the king, who built a church on his property. Returned to the Frankish empire, Anskar was consecrated a bishop with his seat at Hamburg and in about 832 made his way to Rome, where Pope Gregory IV confirmed the new see's sweeping missionary responsibilities in the northern world. Upon Anskar's return to the north a certain Gauzbert was consecrated an assistant bishop by Archbishop Ebo of Rheims (of whom he was a kinsman). Gauzbert was despatched to the territory of the Sueones, where he made further converts and began the construction of a second church. Anskar continued with his work in Denmark.

All seemed to be going well, when suddenly disaster struck. In 845 Hamburg was sacked by Danish pirates. Gauzbert was expelled from Sweden and his nephew and fellow-worker Nithard was killed. The background to these troubled events is shrouded in obscurity. We know just enough about the relations between the Franks and their northern neighbours in the ninth century to be aware that there was a great deal more to these complex diplomatic manoeuvres than we shall ever be able to take the full measure of. The upshot of the hostilities of 845 was the suspension of the Swedish mission for some seven years. After that it was cautiously revived under Anskar's guidance, and a succession of priests sent there from the 850s onwards, among them Rimbert, who was later to be Anskar's biographer. Good relations were established with Björn's successor King Olof, who permitted preaching and church-building. Whatever the occasion and effects of the troubles of 845, King Horic I and his successor Horic II remained fundamentally well disposed. The Danish mission continued, and by amalgamating the unviable see of Hamburg with the longer-established see of Bremen, Anskar was able to provide his mission with the resources it needed. The union of the two bishoprics was approved by Pope Nicholas I in 864. When Anskar died in the following year there must have been grounds for optimism about the future of Christianity in Scandinavia.

We owe most of our knowledge of Anskar's career, of which the above is the briefest of outlines, to his biographer Rimbert, who was also his successor as bishop of Hamburg-Bremen between 865 and his death in 888. Rimbert's *Vita Anskarii* is one of the masterpieces of early medieval missionary biography. In common with other such hagiographical works its interpretation is not a straightforward matter. Rimbert had theological and polemical purposes which affected the way in which he shaped his materials. Naturally he sought to present Anskar and his achievements in the best possible light. One effect of Rimbert's literary art was to give Anskar's missions more prominence than, in terms of their results, they merited. To make such a judgement is not to devalue Anskar's work. It is offered, rather, in an attempt to take the measure of the very considerable difficulties encountered by a missionary to peoples beyond the consistently effective reach of Frankish imperial power. Anskar never succeeded in converting any of the Danish or Swedish kings with whom he had dealings. His missions to Birka may have been primarily concerned with seeking provision for ministry to visiting Christian merchants rather than with converting the heathen. The Christian communities nurtured by him in Denmark and Sweden did not grow and fructify. His memory was cherished, thanks to Rimbert, in the diocese of Hamburg-Bremen but in Scandinavia his work was forgotten. Christianity did not strike permanent roots in Scandinavian soil until the tenth and eleventh centuries, as we shall see in a later chapter.

CHAPTER EIGHT

Rising by Steps:
Christian Consolidation

That Owls and Ravens are ominous appearers, and pre-
signifying unlucky events, as Christians yet conceit, was
also an Augurial conception . . . Which though decrepite
superstitions, and such as had their nativity in times
beyond all history, are fresh in the observation of many
heads, and by the credulous and feminine party still in
some Majesty among us.

SIR THOMAS BROWNE, *Pseudoxia Epidemica*, 1646

IT IS TIME to make a stand and look about us. The surviving evidence
does not permit us to offer any full or confident answer to such a
question as 'What had been achieved by the year 850?' in respect of
the Christianization of western Europe. However, it does allow some
tentative generalizations about the shape and nature of the process,
which will, in turn, address some of the questions posed in the agenda
outlined in Chapter 1.

To begin with: it is evident that western Christendom was more
conscious of a missionary responsibility towards non-Christian peoples
by the ninth century than it had been in the fourth; for Alcuin and
Charlemagne a missionary imperative sounded more clearly and more
urgently than it had done for Eusebius and Constantine. Indeed, if it
had sounded at all for the imperial establishment of the fourth century,
the tone had been faint and muffled. Not all historians would agree.
Attempts have been made to present Constantine as an eager proscly-
tizer concerned 'to spread Christianity beyond as well as within his
own frontiers', an emperor with a 'vision of mission as part of a coherent political design'.[1] Perhaps: but for me this interpretation of Constantine does not carry conviction. Rather, as we saw in Chapter 1,
there was widespread acceptance in official circles of what I called

the Eusebian accommodation. Christianity was for Romans, not for barbarians. Even the most daring thinkers, such as Augustine of Hippo, found it hard to dispense with this ingrained cultural assumption.

Such assumptions on the part of the intellectual elite of the Mediterranean world did not, of course, prevent the diffusion of Christianity in some shape or form beyond the imperial frontiers. The phenomenon of 'seepage' at the peripheries of some dominant cultural system such as the Persian, Roman, Chinese or Islamic empires is one that is well known to historians and anthropologists. Seepage can take many forms: transfer of goods or fashions by means of raiding or trading, recruitment and return of soldiers, cross-border movement of pedlars, vagrants, exiles, escaping slaves, brides, explorers, ambassadors, armsdealers. Interaction of this sort at the fringes of the Roman empire is hard to trace precisely because it went unrecorded or at best was marginalized in our written sources. In seeking to track it we are at the mercy of archaeologists and their theories, with all that that implies. Obscure though it necessarily is, this is a most important phase in the diffusion of religious beliefs and notions. We can see its results, in the late antique period, in the presence of Christian communities in Ethiopia, Arabia, Georgia, Dacia, Scotland and Ireland – to name only the instances cited in Chapter 3. What these communities had in common was that they had come into existence by a process of spontaneous generation lost to our sight. They drift occasionally and indistinctly across our vision generally only when their need for spiritual leadership led them to seek a bishop from within the empire and someone made a note of it; as, for example, Prosper of Aquitaine noted that Bishop Palladius was sent 'to the Irish believers in Christ' in 431.

So if western Christendom was more mission-minded in the eighth and ninth centuries than it had been in the fourth, why should this have been so? What *were* the roots of the missionary impulse? Two explanations have been offered which must be mentioned only for the purpose of ruling them out. The first is that Christian missionary activity was a response to the challenge thrown down by Islam. By 700 the expansion of Islam had engulfed the heartlands of the Christian world from Antioch to Carthage. A few years more, and its apparently irresistible momentum would have swallowed up the Iberian peninsula as well. This explanation would have it, to put the matter simply, that Boniface was winning souls in Germany to compensate for those lost in Syria or Egypt. However, there is not a shred of evidence to suggest that such a thought occurred to anybody in early medieval Christendom. Islam was not perceived as 'a new religion' – the very thought probably unthinkable to contemporary Christians – but as a particularly dangerous heresy. Islamic expansion did not obliterate Christianity. All the churches survived, and some flourished as they had not done before, under Islamic rule. In the period before 800 it is likely that only a tiny minority of the indigenous Christians in the lands subdued by Islamic armies had adopted the religion of their conquerors. There is no hint in the abundant correspondence of eighth-century churchmen of any relationship between Christian–Islamic confrontation and the springs of evangelistic fervour.

The second unsatisfactory explanation is that missions were sponsored by the popes in order to increase papal power. Here we have to be a little more circumspect. In its crudest form as a piece of Protestant polemic – souls stuffed into the ravenous maw of Rome – the explanation is blatantly wide of the mark. The evangelization of western Europe was not a piece of ecclesiastical empire-building by the Roman church *tout simple*. The evidence for spontaneous missionary initiatives by individual popes is insubstantial and ambiguous. As we saw in Chapter 4, there are even difficulties about uncritical acceptance of Bede's presentation of Pope Gregory I as a churchman fired by missionary zeal. Nevertheless it seems to have become widely accepted that papal association with missionary work was right and proper. We can see this association in the careers of Columbanus, Amandus, Willibrord, Pirmin, Boniface, Anskar and others besides. We can see it too in the institutional means which were devised or decisions which were taken for the promotion of missionary work. Such, for example, was the granting of privileges of papal protection to monasteries like Bobbio or Fulda, or the elevation to archiepiscopal status of the missionary see of Salzburg in 798, or the amalgamation of the bishoprics of Hamburg and Bremen in 864. It is true that papal power did increase in the course of the early Middle Ages, and that papal association with the expansion of Christendom through missions to the heathen was one of several means by which that increase occurred. Power and authority advanced, however, in this as in other spheres, not by conscious assertion but by unnoticed creeping. It is sheer fantasy to suppose that missionary expansion was deliberately engineered simply in order to inflate papal power.

We can discard these two unsatisfactory explanations. What are we to put in their place? Biblical precept is one obvious answer, in simple obedience to the great commission at the end of Matthew's gospel. But we should observe that the rationale of mission is already significantly diverse in the New Testament. Mission could be as much about hastening the End as about converting the heathen: not until the gospel has been proclaimed through all the world will Christ return in the Second Coming to reward his own. Missionary motivation might be one of compassion, to save sinners from the flames of Hell, but it might also be one of judgement, so that the heathen might be without excuse. Neither could an attentive reading of the New Testament fail to reveal that status within the Christian community and mission to those outside it are identified from the outset in the presentation of the apostles and, of course, of Paul. However understood or interpreted, biblical precept could fire individual vocation. The single clear case that we have from our period is Patrick, whose extraordinary autobiographical writings movingly convey his powerful sense of a missionary vocation. We know about this only because Patrick was led to set certain matters down in writing for purposes of defending himself against hostile critics, and because these writings happen to have come down to us. How many others might have written in similar terms had the occasion demanded it? Would Boniface, for example – who in early middle age threw over a promising ecclesiastical career in Wessex for the discomforts and dangers of a missionary's life in Germany? Or would Anskar, whose biographer Rimbert dwelt on his hero's sense of vocation? Perhaps. We may also allow ourselves to speculate a little about the possibility that the example of Patrick's vocation may have influenced later Irishmen such as Columba or Columbanus, or Englishmen in Ireland such as Egbert. It is at the very least suggestive that Patrick's memory was being actively cultivated at just the time that Englishmen like Egbert and Willibrord and others were going to Ireland for purposes of study and devotion. Testimony to this is the production of Tírechán's bizarre memoir of Patrick in about 670 and of Muirchú's *Life of Patrick* a little later. The Irish looked back to Patrick – incorrectly, as it happened – as the founder of their church: *noster papa*, 'our father', as he was referred to in a letter dating from 632–3. It is hard to believe that Patrick's recorded sense of overwhelming missionary vocation did not have something to do with the Irish religious diaspora of the early Middle Ages.

That diaspora was also given momentum by a particular religious exercise, namely 'pilgrimage for Christ', the practice of self-imposed exile the better to attain a closer walk with God. We saw in Chapter 3 that pilgrimage could merge insensibly into mission. There Columbanus' pilgrimage took him to Luxeuil and Bobbio, and to preach to heathen Suevi on the shores of Lake Constance. We can see the same merging in Amandus, in Egbert, in Kilian, in Willibrord, in Pirmin, in Boniface, in Willehad, in Liudger, in Anskar – and in many others besides. The ideal of pilgrimage was absolutely central to the missionary impulse of the early medieval period. It may also be said of the pilgrimage of exile that it was a form of martyrdom. The pilgrim severed the ties that bound him to worldly society, so that pilgrimage was a kind of social death. Now the willingness or even the desire to suffer martyrdom has always been an ingredient of missionary motivation. Those who read their Eusebius would have known that martyrs were an essential part of the growth of an infant church. 'Polycarp found fulfilment in martyrdom ... Justin was honoured with a divine martyrdom ...' But early medieval martyrdoms were singularly few and do not always stand up to the cold scrutiny of modern historical enquiry. St Donnán of Eigg, allegedly butchered with his community of monks in 617, is a very shadowy figure indeed. Slightly clearer in outline than he, but still obscure, Kilian and Emmeram are said to have met violent deaths but it is by no means certain that these were martyrdoms in the strict sense. It is a striking feature of the spread of Christianity to barbarian Europe that it was, before Saxony, so tranquil a process. That is why Boniface mattered so much, not simply to the monks of Fulda who possessed his miracle-working corpse and sword-slashed book, but to the whole Frankish establishment. At last they had got a proper blood-red martyr: the real thing. Whether they really *had* is a different matter. The early accounts suggest that Boniface and his companions did not die for their faith but were randomly slaughtered by a gang of robbers. But this would not have been an emphasis which would have commended itself at Fulda or at the Frankish royal court.

Evangelism seems to have been a matter of concern – even, one might say, a speciality – of particular monastic networks. This is hardly surprising, given the character of many of these communities as almost what a much later age would call a mission-station; given too their presumed loyalty to a founder's ideals. The network of Columbanian monastic houses in seventh-century Francia is a good example. There are numerous examples of men, some of whom we met in Chapter 5, who had been washed by a current of Columbanian spirituality and went on to devote themselves to evangelism. It cannot be coincidence, any more than it was coincidence which led so many members of the Society of Jesus to become missionaries in India, Japan and China in the sixteenth century.

Boniface made play with the notion of a duty owed to kinsfolk in his appeal to the English in 738 for the conversion of the Saxons of Germany (explicitly rejected though this is in the New Testament parable of Dives and Lazarus). The bishop of Leicester's reference, in his reply, to the conversion of 'our people' in the German mission field suggests that the appeal had not fallen on deaf ears. This same sense of the urgency of converting heathen who were in some sense kinsfolk may be encountered too in what Bede has to tell us of Egbert. 'He was aware that there were in Germany many peoples from whom the Angles and Saxons are known to have derived their descent and origin . . . still enslaved to heathen rites.'[2] The ideals, expectations and support of the home church have almost invariably been factors of significance in the history of Christian missions. The correspondence of Boniface and Lul is our eighth-century witness to this.

That same correspondence also reveals that many of its participants were related to one another. Apostolic enterprise seems to have run in families, possibly more frequently than our meagre sources allow us to see. One might think of Wilfrid and his kinsmen, or of the circle of Frankish aristocrats which had Agilbert at its centre. One might instance Boniface's relatives such as Abbess Leoba of Tauberbischofsheim or Willibald who became bishop of Eichstätt. Another fine example is Liudger and his family, four generations of whom were active in nurturing Frisian Christianity. The weight of family tradition and expectation might have been a means of propelling recruits into the mission field.

The same sort of point could be made about certain communities that specially concerned themselves with evangelism. The Elnone (Saint-Amand) of Amandus, the Echternach of Willibrord, the Fulda of Boniface and Sturm – to name but three – were perhaps the nearest thing to training colleges for missionaries that were to be found in western Europe in the seventh and eighth centuries. We might recall, for example, how it was to Echternach that Willehad fell back when forced to flee Saxony in 782. It was there that he could pray, study, reflect and plan, reassemble what was left of his team and recruit new members to it, and find in the shadow of the mighty Willibrord the resolution and steadfastness of purpose which would take him back to the Saxon mission field in 785. Such wells of inspiration and resources were usually but not invariably monastic communities; and if so, usually but not invariably part of a larger network. But they might also be the community, not formally monastic, of a bishop's household in an area near Christendom's frontier zone. Salzburg is a good example, to which we shall return in a later chapter.

When did 'being a missionary' become a recognizably distinct role with an identity of its own? It wasn't quite this, I think, in the earliest stages of our enquiry, in the age of the 'involuntary mission' of Ulfila, or of Patrick's solitary vocation, or of Martin's violent demonstration of a bishop's country duties. But by the time we have reached the age of Boniface and Charlemagne – even perhaps by the time of Amandus and Dagobert – we seem to have edged closer to it. The young men who went out from England to Germany in the eighth century were not unrecognizably different from their remote successors who joined the Universities' Mission to Central Africa in the nineteenth.

One indication that by the age of Charlemagne western churchmen were more earnestly concerned with evangelism is a literary one. One could almost speak of the emergence of a 'missionary literature'. Take Bede's *Ecclesiastical History of the English People*. Like all works of genius it is multi-faceted and many-layered, but at its heart there lies an account of the bringing of the English people to Christ, a narrative constructed with great literary skill in fluent and accessible Latin. Furthermore, a point perhaps insufficiently emphasized in Bedan studies, the author seems in the last book of the *History* to point ahead to apostolic work remaining to be done among the peoples of continental Germania – by which term Bede understood a wider area than our 'Germany'. The passage concerning Egbert in Book V, Chapter 9, quoted in part a few pages back, is one of particular significance in this connection. It could almost be said that Bede was there laying out a missionary programme, the beginnings of whose implementation he narrates in the immediately following chapters; we cannot exaggerate the significance of Bede's work for the history of early medieval missions at large. Easily accessible in language, style and tone, widely and rapidly diffused on the continent, Bede's *Ecclesiastical History* provided a model for the missionary work of the Carolingian age.

Other narratives celebrated missionary achievements. Mission is central to much of the hagiography of the eighth and ninth centuries, for example to Alcuin's *Vita Willibrordi*, Liudger's *Vita Gregorii*, Altfrid's *Vita Liudgeri* or above all to Rimbert's *Vita Anskarii*, in a way that it had not been to such early biographies as those of Columba or Columbanus. This is not to suggest that Anskar was a more active evangelist than Columbanus: whether he was or wasn't is beyond the reach of our knowledge. The point is simply that missionary labours are accorded a new prominence in the hagiography of the Carolingian age. We should bear in mind the didactic intent of these sacred biographies. Just as much as Bede's work, they were a source of inspiration and of practical counsel about the conduct of mission.

Another source of practical advice lay in manuals for Christian teachers and in model sermons. This was not, of course, a new literary genre. Among the earliest of such tracts in the Latin west was Augustine of Hippo's *De Catechizandis Rudibus*, which Alcuin commended to Charlemagne in 796 for use in the evangelization of the Avars. Augustine's work had spawned literary descendants. The pastoral sermons of Caesarius of Arles – which as we saw in Chapter 2 enjoyed a wide circulation – were indebted to it. So too was Martin of Braga's *De Correctione Rusticorum*. A homily attributed to Eligius of Noyon, inserted into the biography of Eligius attributed to Audoen of Rouen, drew upon both Caesarius and Martin. Pirmin's *Scarapsus* leant heavily upon *De Correctione Rusticorum*. A celebrated list of practices which the Christian should shun, known as the *Indiculus Superstitionum* (*List of Superstitions*), apparently drawn up in Germany in the eighth century, was indebted to Caesarius among others. All in all, this catalogue – not an exhaustive one – gives some indication of the manuals of practical instruction which were available to the missionary preacher by the year 800. It was a corpus which would increase over the next couple of generations.

Letters containing advice on procedure in response to enquiries from the mission field were another category of missionary literature. Augustine of Canterbury consulted Pope Gregory I about various problems which arose in the course of the English mission. Bede included Gregory's responses in the text of his *Ecclesiastical History*. The longest among them also circulated widely as a separately copied pamphlet. Boniface consulted Pope Gregory II in 726, and his successor Gregory III a few years later, on issues which had arisen in the

German mission field; the papal replies were preserved and circulated with Boniface's correspondence. No less than 106 questions were submitted to Pope Nicholas I in 865 by Khan Boris of the Bulgars: the papal reply runs to some forty closely printed quarto pages in the standard edition. It was not only popes who were generous with advice. Boniface received a letter from his former master Bishop Daniel of Winchester about missionary tactics. He also consulted other English ecclesiastics, such as Bishop Pehthelm of Whithorn – Bede's probable informant about the missionary labours of the shadowy Ninian, as we saw in Chapter 3 – on pastoral problems as they arose.

Early medieval missionaries were firm believers in the 'trickle-down' effect. The most easily identifiable and consistently pursued element of strategy was the missionaries' choice to work from the top downwards. If you can convert the directing elite then those who are subject to its direction will follow the lead given. Such was the hope, and it was frequently realized. The examples of this phenomenon offered by our sources are manifold. We need name only the three barbarian kings considered in an earlier chapter, Clovis, Ethelbert and Edwin. There are many more examples. Of course, there were all sorts of variables of place and time. Some types of barbarian kingship or chieftainship commanded more exemplary or coercive power than others; individual ruling families could grow more, or less, powerful over time. But in general evangelists from Patrick onwards found it convenient and effective to work with or through the directing secular forces in the societies they strove to Christianize.

There was one sound practical reason for this. Missionaries needed protection. Even a man like Wilfrid, guarded by a numerous retinue which would fight for him if necessary to the death, as in Sussex in 665, stood in need of the protection of the secular power. Boniface recognized this very clearly. As soon as he heard of the death of his patron Charles Martel in 741 he wrote at once to his son and possible successor, begging him 'that in the event of your coming to power you will help the clerics, priests, monks, nuns and all the servants of God in Thuringia, and that you will protect the Christians from the hostility of the heathens, so that they may not be destroyed by them.'[3] Missionaries who strayed too far, too deep into the frontier zone, beyond the protective reach of royal power, ran grave risks. Two English brothers named Hewald tried to evangelize the Saxons about the year 700: they were put to death. Willibrord was luckier: when he slaughtered sacred cattle and violated a sacred spring on the island of Heligoland, the local ruler wanted to avenge these insults to his gods. 'For three whole days he cast lots three times every day to find out who should die; but as the true God protected His own servants, the lots of death never fell upon Willibrord nor upon any of his company, except in the case of one of the party, who thus won the martyr's crown.'[4] Delicate moral questions have frequently been posed for missionaries by their relations with the secular power. How close a connection between missionary Christianity and secular imperialism is permissible? Can a missionary who enjoys the protection of the king escape being perceived as his agent? To what extent is Christian evangelization a weapon in the armoury of subjugation? Questions such as these seem to have led to friction between Amandus and Dagobert I. They troubled Boniface, as we know from his correspondence. They led Alcuin to write those anxious letters of the year 796. They may have occasioned heart-searchings to others, of which no record has come down to us.

The tacit bargain between missionary and ruler was mutually beneficial. The missionary received protection, endowments (often on a very grand scale) for Christian communities, the status that came from association with a king, the infectious example of a royal conversion, access to royal powers of coercion, a share in royal rights to various services performed by subjects. These were substantial benefits. Kings acquired new grandeur and renown, were introduced to new techniques of rule in literacy and legislation, benefited from notions or rituals which enhanced authority and the mystique of royalty. The benefits to kings did not happen all at once, but they were visible for those who had eyes to see. 'The power of the Goths now thrives,' as King Sisebut had put the matter: and Bede might have commended his judgement as he commended Coifi; 'prudent words'.

Writers like Bede presented the sequence of royal conversions as a success story – of course they did. But we know of kings who were not converted to Christianity; Penda of Mercia, for example, or that King Ongendus of the Danes encountered by Willibrord, or the rulers with whom Anskar had dealings. What held them back? What made a barbarian king reluctant to approach the baptismal font? Our sources are not going to give away much on this topic, but they do drop a few hints. One such is to be found in the stories told which indicate a king's anxieties as to whether he would be able to carry his leading followers with him into the Christian fold. We might care to recall the insistence of Clovis that the pre-baptismal instruction given to him by Bishop Remigius should be *secret*. It was no light matter to risk alienating the aristocratic warriors on whose continuing fidelity royal power rested. Neither could a king trust to it that they would speak in favour of giving Christianity a try, as Edwin's nobleman spoke up in Bede's narrative of the conversion of Northumbria. Matters might resolve themselves satisfactorily if members of a king's following could be assured of sharing in the advantages that might accrue to their master in the wake of his acceptance of Christianity. Given the ethic of loyalty-for-reward which underpinned the relationship between a king and his retinue, there must have been expectation that benefits reaped by the king would be shared. And shared they were, though in the longer term that is easier for the historian than for contemporaries to detect. To give but one example: as kingship became more sophisticated and robust, vistas of opportunity for loyal and reliable king's servants opened up, with rich pickings to be had in the way of responsibility, status, wealth and power. The aristocracy of the Carolingian empire, of which a surprising amount can be learned, presents an instructive case-study in this regard.

This line of argument has held some appeal for historians of a Marxist inclination, of whom a few may still be encountered in remote places. Baldly summarized, the argument runs that the elite groups were bribed into Christianity by the prospect of an increase in their social standing and power. From this point of view the Germanic *Adelskirche*, some of whose characteristics were discussed in Chapters 5 and 6, became a means of social control. The lower orders were betrayed by their masters in the interests of more effective exploitation. The thesis requires a view of Christianity as 'a kind of crust upon the surface of popular culture'.[5] Paganism went underground, subsided into what French historians of this persuasion like to call a *culture folklorique*, mute symbol of a downtrodden peasantry's resentment against its oppressors. The case can be made least unconvincingly with reference to Saxony.[6] Lebuin's patron, the 'rich and noble' Saxon Folcbert can be cast as one who hitched his fortunes to the rising star of Frankish Christianity and empire. Widukind, heroic defender of Saxon nationhood and of Saxon social equality, ended up as their Judas Iscariot. A moral fable; but there are serious difficulties about accepting it as history. It strains the evidence at more than one point. For example, it is clear that Saxon society was differentiated and hierarchical, with a privileged nobility at the top of the social ladder, *before* the Frankish conquest and forced conversion. More seriously, there are difficulties in the way of accepting the notion of competing levels of culture – elite and clerical as against popular and *folklorique* – in this early medieval social context: a matter to which we shall have occasion to return.

A second occasion of royal reluctance arose not from anxieties concerning present followers but from apprehensions about dead ancestors. A famous story was told of the Frisian leader Radbod. He drew back from the baptismal font at the last moment, saying that he chose rather to join his forebears in Hell than to enter Heaven without them. *Ben trovato*, perhaps: the story was not committed to writing until nearly a century after Radbod's day. But it testifies to a worry that was real and widespread. Bishop Avitus of Vienne in his letter of congratulation upon the conversion of Clovis alludes – and perhaps significantly in a somewhat guarded manner – to the king's courage in breaking with ancestral tradition. There are signs of similar anxieties among the Irish and the English, the Bulgars and the Danes. Clerical responses were diverse but seem to have been reassuring on the whole. The Irish in particular appear to have taken a liberal view of the chances of salvation for dead pagan ancestors. This is symbolized by the weird story in Tírechán's *Life of Patrick* according to which the saint raised a dead man to life in order to baptize him and fit him for salvation. A kind of retrospective conversion was available to the dead if their descendants so wished it. We shall encounter a celebrated example of this a little later on in tenth-century Denmark. There were some who went further still. Boniface crossed swords with a certain Clement in Germany – another Irishman – who taught that in the Harrowing of Hell Christ had freed *all*, 'believers and unbelievers, those who praise God and those who worship idols'.[7] Boniface, the rigorist, was shocked at this heresy but had to admit that Clement had many followers. In the light of Radbod's apprehensions perhaps we can begin to see why. Did accommodations of a Clementine kind help to ease the transition to Christianity? And when after acceptance of the new faith did converts cease to worry, or to worry in this way, about ancestors? A recent study of the memorial stones of north-east Scotland has suggested that the decorative transition from 'Pictish' to Christian symbolism marked a time at which 'the importance of the church is outstripping that of the ancestors'.[8] The epoch proposed is, interestingly enough, roughly contemporaneous with the floruit of Bishop Cuiritán of Rosemarkie. In England the early Anglo-Saxon kings traced their lineages back to the god Woden. They continued to do so after their conversion, but at some point, perhaps in the ninth century, the line of descent was extended up beyond Woden – to Adam! It had become a matter of concern to adopt, to link up to, a biblical, universal and Christian past. This question of the permissibility of a pagan past, of the Christianization of history, time and family, will occupy us again shortly.

A third hint concerns less royal reluctance than royal bewilderment. It might be called, after its most notorious exemplar, the Redwald response. We learn from Bede (in a passage quoted above, in Chapter 4, p. 123) that King Redwald of East Anglia added a Christian altar to the furnishings of his heathen temple. Bede blamed Redwald's wife and 'certain evil teachers' for seducing the king from the path of Christian rectitude. We might be inclined to suppose that the notion of monotheism, of a single God, of a jealous God with exclusive claims upon human worship, was one that it was difficult to install among the mental furniture of kings who were accustomed to worshipping several deities. Redwald was not alone. A generation earlier Gregory of Tours had encountered a Spaniard named Agila, an ambassador from the Visigothic king Leovigild, who had breezily confessed that 'we have a saying, that no harm is done when a man passing between pagan altars and a church of God, offers veneration to both.'[9] Gregory was profoundly angered and dismayed: but what else could you expect of a scatter-brained and ill-educated man, a Spaniard, and an Arian to boot, an enemy of the Catholic faith? (But how very interesting to learn that in Spain of about 580 one could still encounter active pagan cult: it had been outlawed under Roman law, inherited by the Visigoths, for two centuries. Barbarian kings elsewhere were slow to ban the worship of idols. In both Francia and England the earliest royal legislation along these lines was not framed until a couple of generations after the initial royal conversion.)

The Spanish story reminds us how long a lapse of time there might be before legislation, evangelization, or any other kind of Christianizing pressure had any effect. A story from southern Italy reinforces the lesson. It is to be found in the *Life of St Barbatus*, bishop of Benevento, one of the very few Italian hagiographical works of the early Middle Ages. The Lombard settlers in the Benevento region had adopted a snake-cult which they encountered there. The cult is attested in classical sources and probably dated back to a remote antiquity. Like the altars in Spain it had evidently survived the legislation banning pagan worship which had been issued by the Theodosian emperors in the late fourth century. (The Beneventan region may have had powerful patrons among the still largely pagan senatorial aristocracy of the day.) The snake-cult continued to flourish. Even so late as the time of the Lombard king Grimoald (662–71), the brother-in-law of Wilfrid's friend King Perctarit, the Lombards of Benevento, 'although washed in the waters of holy baptism nevertheless held to earlier pagan worship and bowed their necks to the image of a viper'. Barbatus determined to put an end to these wicked goings-on. He got Theuderada, the wife of Duke Romuald of Benevento, to surrender the image of the snake to him. His biographer, like Nicetius of Trier and Pope Boniface V (see Chapter 4), quoted the Pauline tag about the missionary role of a Christian wife. Barbatus had the snake-image melted down and then fashioned into a paten and chalice for the eucharistic bread and wine of the Christian mass.[10]

Here is one last example which may point, obliquely, to the persistence of pre-Christian cult. It comes from Ireland and concerns St Brigit of Kildare. Although dates in the fifth century were later allotted to Brigit, it is practically certain that she never existed. The seventh-century *Life* by Cogitosus, to which reference was briefly made in Chapter 6, portrays 'a mythological figure'.[11] The author assembled a collection of miracles and folk-tales, some of them of great charm, such as the story of how Brigit hung her cloak on a sunbeam, but there is no solid historical figure there such as we are presented with in Jonas' *Vita Columbani* or Stephen's *Vita Wilfridi*. Many scholars consider it likely that Brigit's cult was the continuation of the cult of a Celtic fire-goddess. The site of her worship has been cautiously identified by archaeologists only five miles from Kildare. Brigit's feast day on 1 February coincides with the pre-Christian festival of spring called *Imbolg*. In this connection it may be relevant to point out that the Old Irish word *érlam*, 'patron saint', had the original meaning of 'god of the tribe' or 'tutelary deity'.

All of which takes us somewhat far from kings. However, it will have been justified if some light, albeit dim, has been shed on the sources of royal hesitation and the tactics to which evangelists might have to resort in overcoming it. Once converted, kings could be educated into the duties of Christian kingship and, especially relevant for us, into their missionary and teaching responsibilities. Kings were encouraged in duties not simply to bring the faith to heathen peoples beyond their frontiers but also to co-operate with their bishops in urging a deeper Christian observance upon their subjects at home. We can witness this co-operation in the seventh-century legislation of church and state in Visigothic Spain; in the sparser legislative materials surviving from England and Ireland in the seventh and eighth centuries; and above all in the abundant and ambitious legislation of the Carolingian age which built upon the foundations laid by Boniface in the church councils of the 740s.

Royal expectations of Christianity were touched upon in Chapter 4. The hopes and expectations of their subjects would not have been identical, though there was a generous zone of overlap. What were their hopes and expectations? In trying to answer this question we could do worse than to start with Bishop Daniel of Winchester's letter to Boniface. Derivative from earlier models it may be, artlessly giving itself away as such (as we shall see in a moment): but Daniel sent it, Boniface kept it and it was included in posthumous collections of the missionary-martyr's correspondence. The letter mattered; it had weight. Daniel was firmly of the opinion that pagans must be argued with, not bludgeoned into the faith. They should be argued with 'not in a way to insult or irritate them, but calmly and with much moderation' so that 'more from confusion than from exasperation they may blush for their absurd opinions'.[12] At the heart of the arguments proposed lie expectations of thoroughgoing earthiness:

> This also is to be inferred. If the [pagan] gods are almighty and beneficent and just, they not only reward worshippers, but also punish those who scorn them. If they do both in the temporal world, why then do they spare the Christians who are turning almost the whole globe away from their worship and overthrowing their idols? And while they, that is, the Christians, possess fertile lands, and provinces fruitful in wine and oil and abounding in other riches, they have left to them, the pagans that is, with their gods, lands always frozen with cold, in which these, now driven from the whole globe, are falsely thought to reign.

242

There must also often be brought before them the might of the Christian world, in comparison with which those who still continue in the ancient faith are few.

The Frisians and Saxons were clearly in for a disappointment if, following their acceptance of the faith, they expected their fields to burst out in olives and vines. The phrase betrays Daniel's Mediterranean source. Boniface would have known how to adapt it. The point is Daniel's assumption that Christianity's trump card was its ability fully to satisfy material expectation.

This is the card that we find our missionary churchmen playing again and again in our sources; and, given the nature of those sources, always with success. Here are a few examples. They could manipulate the forces of nature, and in particular the weather. When storms threatened the harvest at his monastery of Les Fontaines in Burgundy, Columbanus stationed four of the holiest brethren at the corners of the field and then led a team of harvesters to work: 'and marvellous to relate the cloud fled away from the corn and rain fell everywhere around it but the harvesters in the middle experienced only the heat of the sun until the harvest was complete. Thus faith and prayer achieved the removal of the rain, and heat in the midst of showers.'[13] Once when Filibert was crossing the Seine a squall arose and threatened his boat; he prayed, and the boat was carried safe to the shore. Cuthbert was once visiting his foster-mother when fire broke out at one end of the village and, fanned by a strong wind, threatened the other houses. The holy man fell to the ground and prayed, and immediately the direction of the wind changed and drove the flames harmlessly away. A thunderstorm so heavy that the terrified villagers sought refuge in the church once descended upon Tauberbischofsheim. Abbess Leoba, the kinswoman of Boniface, was appealed to. 'As if she had been challenged to a contest', wrote her biographer most revealingly, she opened the door of the church and, facing the storm, made the sign of the cross and prayed. The storm died down. There are scores, perhaps hundreds more of such weather miracles in our hagiographical sources. No wonder: on the weather depended the food supply; and the food supply was what preoccupied most people, most of the time, in early medieval Europe.

Wilfrid's biographer emphasized the causal connection between the conversions to Christianity which the saint made in Frisia in 678, and the excellent harvest and abundant catch of fish which the Frisians enjoyed that season. Bede made a somewhat similar connection in writing about Wilfrid's evangelization of Sussex a few years later. The area had been suffering from drought and famine for three years before his coming, 'but on the very day on which the people received the baptism of faith, a gentle but ample rain fell; the earth revived, the fields once more became green, and a happy and fruitful season followed.' The faith which a missionary implants will bring with it material abundance in the necessities of life. There was ample scriptural warrant for such optimism, for example in the book of Psalms – the most widely read biblical text in early medieval Christendom – where the causal relationship of correct cult with victory, prosperity and progeny is repeatedly stressed. Bede also tells us that Wilfrid taught the South Saxons to fish with nets in the sea. The missionary who introduces new techniques or tools was to have a long and fruitful future.

We have already encountered miracles of exorcism or healing, of binding and loosing. When St Germanus of Auxerre set off for Italy towards the end of his life to seek an imperial pardon for the inhabitants of the Gallic province of Armorica, his biographer Constantius recorded the miracles worked by him en route. At Alise – where some years earlier the straw on which he had slept had subsequently acquired curative properties, as we saw in Chapter 2 – he caused a dumb girl to speak. At Autun he cured a girl with a deformed hand. At Milan he exorcized an evil spirit from a demoniac. At some unnamed place on the north Italian plain he cured the *vir spectabilis* Leporius, his family and all his household servants from various illnesses. Arrived in the imperial city of Ravenna he miraculously freed prisoners from captivity, raised a boy from the dead and carried out another exorcism. It was an impressive record for a single journey. Two centuries later, and hundreds of miles further north, Cuthbert restored to sanity the wife of his friend Hildimer. Water blessed by him cured the wife of Hemma, one of King Aldfrith's retainers. Holy oil consecrated by him cured a young woman of migraine. While journeying from Hexham to Carlisle he healed a paralytic boy. And so the list could go on.

Cuthbert's wonders were not restricted to healing. On the afternoon of 20 May 685 he was being shown round the remains of Roman Carlisle when he suddenly exclaimed, 'Oh! oh! oh! the war is over: judgement has been given against our people in battle!' A few days later it was learned that at that very moment King Ecgfrith of Northumbria had fallen in battle against the Picts 150 miles away. This is but one of a multitude of stories told of saints who had second sight, dreamed prophetic dreams, saw visions, foretold the future. Divinely released from the constraints of time and place, they crossed the boundaries at which ordinary mortals were brought up short. Like Cuthbert, Columba could tell the outcome of a battle by second sight. Once he saw the destruction of a city in Italy by a volcanic eruption. He foretold the evil end of the wealthy Irish cleric Luguid the Lame, who used to drive his car jovially (*gaudenter*) about the plain of Brega: he would choke on his meat while reclining on a sofa with a harlot; and so it came to pass. Samson had a dream in which three apostles hailed him as 'the chosen priest of the Lord'. When Bishop Dubricius (Dyfrig) had the same dream he realized that Samson must become a bishop. St Severinus of Noricum foretold a barbarian attack on the province in 473, thus enabling Bishop Paulinus of Tiburnia to take measures for its successful defence. Guthlac prophesied the future greatness of the exiled prince Ethelbald, later to be king of Mercia. Willibrord prophesied the future greatness of Pippin, Charles Martel's son, when he baptized him; Pippin later became king of the Franks.

'The people's faith was stimulated by such tokens of holiness,' wrote Rudolf of Fulda after narrating the miracles worked by Abbess Leoba. Precisely so. Spiritual power and leadership would accrue to those who could answer expectations because they had access to means of explanation, propitiation and control denied to most people; means which would deliver the goods in terms of clement weather, health, deliverance from evil spirits, reassurance or warning about what was going to happen next. Christian holy men and holy women can do these things, proclaim our Christian texts. But others claimed to be able to do them too.

'As if she had been challenged to a contest.' At this point it is timely to recall the story told in Chapter 2 by Gregory of Tours about Aquilinus and the *arioli*. There was an alternative network available, of practitioners who had been doing these same things from time immemorial. Take, for example, the case of the Frankish prince Merovech, son of King Chilperic I, claimant to the throne in the years 575–8. In considering him we should bear in mind that he was a member of a royal family which had been Christian for nearly a century and that he is likely to have had some education. There was nothing *folklorique* about Merovech. Like many a pretender – remember Ethelbald and Guthlac – he wanted to know what his chances were; so a sooth-sayer was consulted on his behalf. Gregory of Tours described her as a *mulierem habentem spiritum pythonis*, 'a woman having a familiar spirit', in words borrowed from the biblical description of the witch of Endor consulted by King Saul (I Samuel xxviii.7). She had a good record, having recently foretold 'not only the year but the day and the hour' when King Charibert I (father of Bertha who was to marry Ethelbert of Kent) would die in 567. Her prediction in Merovech's case was encouraging. But Merovech was not entirely confident, so he turned to a different sort of divination, a Christian one (though not approved by all ecclesiastics), known as the *sortes biblicae* or 'biblical lot-casting'. Three books containing biblical texts – Psalms, Kings, Gospels – were laid upon the altar of St Martin's at Tours. Merovech spent a night of prayer there beseeching St Martin 'to declare the future and show forth to him whether or not he should be able to win the kingdom'. There followed three further days of fasting and prayer. At the end of them Merovech opened the books at random – as we should say, but in Gregory's view *guided* – and read the words which first met his eyes. The results were disturbing, foretelling failure, betrayal and violent death. And so it turned out.

Gregory leaves us to draw our own conclusions from this instructive tale. Implicitly he deplored the practice of consulting soothsayers, just as he lamented the resort to *arioli* by the family of Aquilinus. But he acknowledged that it went on; soothsayers were a feature of his cultural landscape. Christian divination simply had to compete against them by offering something better. Merovech's story was ideal for Gregory because it advertised the power of St Martin, whose successor and representative Gregory was. Christian divination was more accurate as well as 'cleaner' than other kinds. It was proven in competition, just as Jehovah's power had been proven in competition between Elijah and the prophets of Baal.

It was not long, in all probability, after Merovech met his violent end, that St Columba made his way from Iona to the mainland of Scotland and up the Great Glen to the land of the Picts in the north-east. His encounters in the course of this journey are as instructive for us as the didactic tale related by Gregory of Tours. We owe them to his biographer Adomnán. The son of a man whom Columba had converted to Christianity fell ill and died. The local magicians – Adomnán uses the word *magi* – taunted the parents, magnifying their own gods and belittling the Christians' God as the weaker. The saint was nothing daunted. He raised the boy from the dead. 'The God of the Christians was glorified.'

That was but a minor episode. Columba's grandest encounter on this journey took place at the court of the Pictish king Bridei (or Brude). The king's chief magician – who was also his foster-father – was named Broichan. Columba had come to the Pictish court to seek the release of a captive Irishwoman, who to have occasioned these laborious journeyings and high-level diplomacy was probably a person of some considerable standing. The story is best told in Adomnán's own words.

> The venerable man asked of the magician Broichan that a certain slave, an Irish woman, should be released as an act of human kindness. And when Broichan, with unyielding and obstinate heart, retained her, the saint addressing him spoke in this manner: 'Know this, Broichan, that if you will not release for me this pilgrim captive before I depart from this province, you shall presently die.' This he said before King Bridei; and he left the king's house, and came to the river Ness. From that river he took a white stone, and said to his companions: 'Mark this white stone. Through it the Lord will work many cures of the sick among this heathen people.' And after pronouncing these words he continued: 'Now Broichan has received a hard blow. For an angel sent from heaven has struck him heavily, and broken into many pieces in his hand the glass vessel from which he was drinking, and has left him breathing with difficulty, and near to death. Let us wait a little in this place for two messengers of the king, sent to us in haste, to obtain our immediate help for the dying Broichan. Now Broichan, terribly stricken, is ready to release the slave-girl.' While the saint was still speaking these words, behold, as he had predicted, two men on horseback, sent by the king, arrived, and told all that had happened concerning Broichan, in the king's fortress, in accordance with the prophecy of the saint: the breaking of the cup, the magician's seizure, the intended release of the slave-girl. And they added this: 'The king and the persons of his household have sent us to you, to obtain your help for his foster-father Broichan, who is near death.' When he heard these words of the envoys, the saint sent two out of the number of his companions to the king, with the stone that he had blessed, and said: 'If first Broichan promises that he will release the slave-

girl, then let this stone be dipped in water, and let him drink thereof, and he will at once recover health. But if he refuses, and opposes the slave-girl's release, he will immediately die.' The two emissaries went to the king's castle, in obedience to the saint's instructions, and repeated to the king the words of the venerable man. When these things had been made known to the king and to Broichan his foster-father, they were very much afraid. And in the same hour the slave-girl, set free, was handed over to the envoys of the holy man. The stone was dipped in water; and, in a marvellous manner, contrary to nature the stone floated in the water, as though it had been an apple or a nut. And the blessing of the holy man could not be submerged. After he had drunk of the floating stone, Broichan immediately returned from the brink of death, and recovered full bodily health. This stone was after-wards kept among the king's treasures. When it was dipped thus in water, and floated, it effected by the Lord's mercy many cures of diseases among the people. Strange to say, when it was sought by sick people whose time had come, the stone could by no means be found. So also it was looked for on the day of King Bridei's death, and it was not found in the place where it had formerly been kept.[14]

The inwardness of the white stone in this fascinating tale perhaps needs explaining. Adomnán and his monastic audience, but not Bridei or Broichan, would have picked up an echo of Revelations ii.17: 'I will give him also a white stone, and on the stone will be written a new name.'

When Columba left Pictland to return to Iona he proposed to sail down Loch Ness. Broichan conjured up a thick mist and a strong adverse wind. (Those acquainted with Scottish weather may reflect that this was perhaps not a very taxing piece of magic.) All the king's magicians turned out to witness Columba's discomfiture. But the saint was unperturbed. 'He entered the boat, and while the sailors hesitated, he himself, more steadfast, ordered the sail to be raised against the wind. When this was done, and with the whole crowd watching, the ship moved with extraordinary speed, sailing against the contrary wind.' Christian had triumphed over pagan. But King Bridei, in this like Moshoeshoe, was never converted.

A last story about rivalry comes from England in the year 679, about a century after the days of Merovech and Broichan, and we owe it, as we owe so much, to Bede.[15] A young Northumbrian nobleman, named

Imma, was captured after the army in which he had served had been defeated in battle with the Mercians. His captors tied him up to prevent his escape, but 'it proved impossible to bind him, for no sooner had those who bound him turned their backs, than his bonds were loosed'. His guardian asked Imma why he could not be bound: did he by chance have about him any of the 'loosing letters [*litteras solutorias*] of which stories [*fabulae*] are told'? This is a passage which has provoked much discussion. We may note that Bede, writing in about 730, assumed that it would be intelligible to his audience without further explanation. The word *fabulae* for 'stories' is one that rates rather low with Bede. He often uses it to indicate stories of which he disapproved because they did not meet his exacting standards of Christian behaviour. This does not mean that for Bede all *fabulae* were pagan; but any non-Christian stories would certainly rank, for him, as *fabulae*. The 'loosing letters' are the real puzzle. By about the year 1000, when the scholar Aelfric paraphrased the story of Imma in a sermon in the Old English vernacular, they were understood as runes. It is hard to see what else the letters could have been, even though distinguished runic experts have pointed out that there is no conclusive evidence for this. (There is a great deal that we think we know about early medieval Europe for which we have no conclusive evidence.) Imma's captor, in other words, was asking whether the prisoner had about his person some amulet or talisman – who knows? it could have been a white stone – inscribed, perhaps in runic characters, with a charm which had the magic power of freeing him from captivity. Just such a charm (though not in runes) survives as one of the earliest pieces of writing in Old High German, one of the so-called *Merseburg Charms*, because occurring in a ninth-century manuscript preserved at Merseburg.

Eiris sazun idisi,	sazun hera duoder,
suma hapt heptdun,	suma heri lezidun,
suma clubodun	umbi cuoniouuidi.
insprinc haptbandun,	inuar uigandun.

Once the women were seated on the ground, here and there, one company fastened bonds, one company hindered the host, one company picked at fetters: 'Leap from the fetters, escape from the foes!'[16]

But to return to Bede's narrative: Imma denied all knowledge of such arts as these. We may note that neither Imma nor Bede denied that such arts existed. Christians, however, possessed a superior power of binding and loosing, given to the apostles by Jesus himself. While Imma was in captivity his brother, a priest and abbot, assuming Imma to be dead, was regularly saying masses for his soul's repose. Much later on, when Imma after many adventures had returned home, he learned that the hour when his bonds had been loosed had coincided with the hour of his brother's daily mass. And that, of course, was the point of the story for Bede – the efficacy of the mass for the deliverance of dead and living. We might care to ponder Imma's tale for what it reveals obliquely of alternative means of procuring freedom.

The existence of this rival network of skills and practitioners – who evidently did not lack for custom – raised all sorts of delicate questions for missionary churchmen in the early Middle Ages, as it has done in other epochs and as it continues to do in our own. What do you do when faced by non-Christian magic? Ignore it and hope that it will go away? Attempt by violently confrontational action to uproot it and fling it all out on to the rubbish heap outside the fence round the Christian garden? Or do you allow some of it to stay, tame it, prune it, tend it, train it, till it yield acceptable fruit? That the third of these options was deliberately chosen and sensitively applied is the central argument of the most thoughtful recent discussion of these matters.

> These practices [the context is a discussion of medical magic] may legitimately be described as magical ones, in that they certainly have in them echoes of earlier pagan magic, and they tend to be described (and sometimes dismissed) as mere pagan survivals (presumably of a weak sort in that they escape explicit outlawry). They deserve, however, far better than this. When such practices are set alongside the forms of earthly magic that were explicitly forbidden, when they are placed within the context of contemporary witchcraft, and when, furthermore, their patrons (those who recorded them and allowed their use, that is) are allowed to advance more clearly into the light, their function becomes almost the exact reverse of that which is usually assigned to them. These were not survivals, tolerated on account of their relative unimportance; they were opportunities, seized upon and savoured. These magical healing practices are transformed, in this light, from unwelcome remnants of a religion wholly to be dispossessed into welcome and amenable holders of a ground that Christianity wanted badly to annex, and to annex securely. They were preserved then, even cherished . . . as residents of areas within which

250

compromise was still possible, and as a means by which waverers, especially wavering leaders, might still be won over, bringing their followers with them.[17]

Consider the instance of amulets or talismans such as Imma was suspected of having secreted about his person. Objects that may be identified as such have been excavated from numerous graves of this period throughout western Europe. They comprise such things as pieces of rock crystal, quartz, amethyst or amber; the tusks or teeth of boar; cowrie shells; the teeth of dog, wolf, bear or beaver; artefacts bearing symbols such as runes or swastikas. Frankish and Anglo-Saxon graves have yielded little cylindrical copper-alloy boxes for keeping these treasures in. The use of amulets such as these was routinely condemned by Christian writers and church councils. So what are we to make of Columba's 'white stone'? It was a curing talisman which also had the power of disappearing in mute medical prognosis. The stone was kept among the treasures of a pagan king. Yet Columba and his biographer knew that it was a vehicle for the transmission of God's power. The white stone faced both ways. It offered an opportunity to be seized upon and savoured. Perhaps that savouring may be detected in the frequent presence of white quartz pebbles in graves of this epoch.

Columba would probably have called his stone a species of *cretair*, an Old Irish word meaning 'a magical object, an amulet, a talisman'. By a fascinating semantic shift this same word came in the course of time to mean 'a Christian relic'. When Wilfrid was imprisoned by King Ecgfrith of Northumbria in 680 Queen Iurminburg confiscated the reliquary which Wilfrid wore round his neck and – 'though it horrifies me to tell it', as the saint's biographer wrote – she hung it round her own neck and wore it both in her own lodging or when travelling in her chariot. The reliquaries which survive from this period sometimes have buckles at their ends to which straps for hanging could be attached. An eighth-century example may be seen in the cathedral treasury at Sens, in France. The Enger reliquary illustrated in plate 26 has openwork or latticed decoration along the top through which suspension cords could be passed. Towards the end of the sixth century Gregory of Tours had met in Gaul the Lombard ascetic Wulfolaic, who had once visited the church of St Martin in the company of Gregory's friend Aredius of Limoges. 'When we were starting back,' recalled Wulfolaic, 'he gathered a little dust of the holy tomb for a blessing, which he placed in a small box and hung about my neck.'[18] Bede had a somewhat similar story to tell of the tomb of St Chad at Lichfield. 'The place of his burial is covered with a wooden coffin in the shape of a little house, having a hole in one side through which those who go thither out of devotion may insert their hands and take some of the dust.'[19] When mixed with water, continued Bede, and administered medicinally, this dust had the power of curing disease in both humans and animals.

Objects associated with a holy person could have miraculous curative powers. Abbess Aelflaed of Whitby suffered from a grievous illness which no doctor could cure. Her friend St Cuthbert became aware by second sight of her sufferings and sent her his linen belt. She girded herself with it and was cured within three days. Shortly afterwards one of her nuns began to suffer from violent headaches. The abbess bound the linen girdle round her head and the pain departed. The story has an interesting sequel. The abbess put the precious object carefully away in her chest but when she looked for it a few days later it had vanished and was never seen again. Bede's comments on this are of great interest:

> It is clear that this was done by divine dispensation, so that the holiness of the father beloved of God [i.e. Cuthbert] might be made apparent to believers through these two miracles of healing, and that henceforth all occasion for doubting his sanctity might be removed from the incredulous. For if that girdle had always been there, sick people would always have wished to flock to it; and when perhaps one of them did not deserve to be healed of his infirmity, he would disparage its power, because it did not heal him, when really he was not worthy of being healed. Hence by the providential dispensation of heavenly grace, after the faith of believers had been strengthened, forthwith the opportunity for the envious and unbelievers to disparage was entirely taken away.[20]

So there were sceptics about; and there were also ways of dealing with them.

Even the reins of Cuthbert's horse had curative powers. The wife of his friend Hildimer had been driven mad by demonic possession. He sought Cuthbert's help, though without revealing the nature of his wife's plight because it was too shaming: an intriguing detail. Cuthbert of course knew what the trouble was by means of second sight and comforted Hildimer as they rode towards his house by prophesying the cure that would take place. And so it turned out. Hildimer's wife came out of the house to greet them and laid her hands on Cuthbert's reins, 'and at the first touch the demon was completely driven away and she was restored to her former health'.[21]

Magic stones; magic letters; magic belts and bridles; magic dust. These few samples from a vast body of evidence prompt reflections on the manner in which Christian churchmen of the early Middle Ages were prepared to make room for customs and beliefs, practices and practitioners, of long ancestry and continuing vitality outside a Christian dispensation. It is a process that historians of religion term syncretism, which has been defined by *The Oxford English Dictionary* as the 'attempted union or reconciliation of diverse or opposite tenets or practices', and by *The Oxford Dictionary of the Christian Church* as a 'fusion of various beliefs and practices'. The process has been called by other names: adaptation, borrowing, compromise, dilution, juxtaposition, surrender, transference are just some of them. Which one we choose to employ will reveal something of what we think about the process. It has long been recognized that a readiness to adapt was of critical importance in the process of Christianization. So far, so simple. But there are fine discriminations to be made and variables to which the enquirer must be alert. The problems are not dissimilar to some of those we encountered in Chapters 5 and 6 when observing the interplay of missionary churchmen and warrior aristocracies. It was a matter of drawing lines round the limits of what was acceptable in traditional belief and practice. We must recognize that acceptability could indicate a range of responses from grudging toleration to hearty welcome. We must also recognize that there will be hard-liners and soft-liners, hawks and doves, that one teacher will find abhorrent what to another is satisfactory; that there will be variables as to both place and time – what appears necessary or desirable or tolerable in one environment may appear in a different light elsewhere. The piety of one epoch may come to seem impious to another. In attempting to assess the evidence we shall encounter we must furthermore be alive to the literary conventions of our sources, to the motives of their authors and to the expectations of their primary audience. Last but not least, we must be self-conscious, keeping a watchful eye on the cultural assumptions which we ourselves bring to the task of interpreting these sources.

The way of adaptation was commended by Pope Gregory the Great in a deservedly famous letter sent to the English mission in the year 601.

> The idol temples of that race should by no means be destroyed, but only the idols in them. Take holy water and sprinkle it in these shrines, build altars and place relics in them . . . When this people see that their shrines are not destroyed they will be able to banish error from their hearts and be more ready to come to the places they are familiar with, but now recognizing and worshipping the true God. And because they are in the habit of slaughtering much cattle as sacrifices to devils, some solemnity ought to be given them in exchange for this. So on the day of the dedication or the festivals of the holy martyrs, whose relics are deposited here, let them make themselves huts from the branches of trees around the churches which have been converted out of shrines, and let them celebrate the solemnity with religious feasts. Do not let them sacrifice animals to the devil, but let them slaughter animals for their own food to the praise of God, and let them give thanks to the Giver of all things for His bountiful provision. Thus while some outward rejoicings are preserved, they will be able more easily to share in inward rejoicings. It is doubtless impossible to cut out everything at once from their stubborn minds: just as the man who is attempting to climb to the highest place, rises by steps and degrees and not by leaps.[22]

We have already seen a fine example of these tactics in the story told by Gregory of Tours of the bishop of Javols and the cultic lake, to which reference was made in Chapter 2. Thus could traditional ritual places and activities be 'captured' by the transfer of ritual allegiances. There are plenty of similar stories which tend in the same direction. These Gregorian tactics have also left their mark on the European landscape. One may suspect that many of the thousands of holy wells, for example, which are such a feature of its countryside, were once the scenes of comparable episodes.

Bede warmly commended Pope Boniface IV (608–15) for acquiring the enormous temple in Rome known as the Pantheon and turning it into the Christian church which it still is: Sta Maria Rotonda. 'He made a church of it dedicated to the holy Mother of God and all the martyrs of Christ, so that when the multitude of devils had been driven out it might serve as a shrine for a multitude of saints.' It neatly exemplifies the tactics approved by Boniface's master Gregory I. This conversion of pagan buildings or cult-sites to Christian uses was happening all over western Europe during our period. Sometimes it is explicitly referred to in our written sources, as in the stories told of Martin of Tours by Sulpicius Severus, or in his biographer's assertion that Boniface used timber from the sacred oak of Geismar to build a Christian chapel. Sometimes the evidence is archaeological. At Saint-Martin-de-Boscherville in lower Normandy (dép. Seine-Maritime) excavation has revealed a little temple of the Gallo-Roman period which was subsequently converted into a Christian funerary chapel for a Frankish cemetery. A model of the suggested architectural evolution may be seen in plates 5 and 6. Sometimes the evidence comes from place-names. For example, we can be practically certain that an Anglo-Saxon pagan cult-site underlies the church of St Mary at Harrow-on-the-Hill in Middlesex because the first recorded version of the name, in a document of the year 767, contains the element *hearg*, the Old English word for 'sanctuary, sacred place'. When we learn of the purification of new monastic sites, as by Cedd at Lastingham, or Pirmin at Reichenau, or Sturm at Fulda, this may (though it need not necessarily) indicate that the new Christian community was being established on a site of actual or alleged pre-Christian cult.

This Christianization of space was matched by a Christianization of time. The marking of the passing years with a Christian enumeration beginning with the Incarnation – the 'year of the Lord', *Anno Domini*, A.D. – replaced earlier modes of counting years (for example by consular years) in the Roman world. What is remarkable, however, is the slowness with which a distinctively Christian system was adopted. It was not until the sixth century that the notion of the 'year of the Lord' was first adumbrated, and not until the eighth and ninth that the new computation was widely adopted, largely owing to the weighty advocacy of Bede. In the more conservative parts of Christendom older reckonings continued to be used. The papal chancery or secretariat, a bureaucracy at all epochs strongly resistant to change, did not consistently employ A.D. reckoning for the documents it issued until about the year 1000. In the Iberian peninsula a Roman civil reckoning known as the *Era*, whose base date, 'Year 1', was what we should call 38 B.C., survived for an extravagantly long time: the kingdom of Castile did not go over to A.D. dating until 1382, Portugal not until 1420.

Most churchmen disapproved of the habit of beginning the year on 1 January because of the Roman holiday of the Kalends and the festivities that went with it. Favoured Christian replacements were 25 March, the feast of the Annunciation, Lady Day; 25 December, the day of the Lord's Nativity; and either 1 or 24 September, a reckoning taken over from late Roman administrative practice. Different regions followed different alternatives, to the despair of modern historians who are trying to establish a firm chronology. (Happy in this respect the historian of the Iberian peninsula, where the Era began on 1 January; all he has to do is to subtract 38 from the given Era to get the A.D. date.)

The division of the year into its twelve Roman months was one which quickly ousted earlier divisions in the lands to which Christianity spread. Bede provides a little tantalizing information about the names of the months in pre-Christian England and the activities with which some of them were associated. November, for instance, was called *Blodmonath*, 'Blood month', because in the course of it animals were slaughtered for sacrifice to the gods. *Romanitas* here overcame *Germanitas*, but *Christianitas* did not attempt to substitute new and Christian names for the months of the year. However, alongside the Roman cycle of months there was also introduced a Christian pattern of fixed festivals – Christmas Day, Lady Day, St Peter and St Paul, Martinmas, and so forth – throughout the year. St Willibrord's calendar, bearing annotations in his own hand, survives to this day in the Bibliothèque Nationale in Paris and one can see in its pages how a Christian grid or pattern is juxtaposed – literally so, line by line – alongside the Roman one. These days were meant to be observed. In 747 an English church council ordered that the feast days of the founding fathers, St Gregory and St Augustine (of Canterbury), were to be observed in all English churches. Such feast days were intended to be occasions of Christian instruction as well as of celebration. To what extent this hope became a reality we cannot tell.

Bede tells us that the English had formerly called April *Eosturmonath* 'after a goddess of theirs who was called Eostre'. Because the central festival of the Christian year is called Easter, it was for long thought that here we had one of syncretism's prize exhibits. It would be incredible, however, that high-minded Anglo-Saxon churchmen should have permitted their flock to call the annual commemoration of the Resurrection of Jesus Christ by the name of a pagan goddess. Lately, scholars have argued that Bede was simply mistaken. It is more likely that our word Easter is derived from Old English *eastan*, meaning 'east', 'eastwards', a word which became attached to the Christian festival because of the practice of observing a vigil, until day-break in the east, during the night which preceded Easter Sunday. (This is, incidentally, a hint that Bede himself may have known little about the pagan observances of his ancestors.) We are on firmer ground with the days of the week. The names of four pagan Germanic deities have survived in the weekday-names in languages of the Germanic family: Tiw's day, Woden's day, Thunor's day and Frig's day. So too in most Romance languages the names of Roman deities have survived (Mercury, *mercredi, miércoles*, etc.). But not in all. In Portugal the days of the week are designated not by name but by number: *segunda-feira, terça-feira, quarta-feira* and so on. The responsibility for this can plausibly be attributed to Martin of Braga. In the *De Correctione Rusticorum* Martin vigorously condemned the naming of days after heathen deities. Days should bear numbers only, as in the opening chapter of the book of Genesis. It is likely that modern Portuguese practice arises from zealous enforcement of Martin's prescriptions by generations of Portuguese ecclesiastics.

It is a measure of the complexities and surprises of our topic that in Portugal a pre-Christian reckoning of years could survive though pre-Christian names for the days of the week did not, while in England the reverse occurred. Why? We have not the remotest idea.

Christianizers of time had also to confront the problem of the pre-Christian past. Could a pagan past be permitted for the legatees of the western Roman empire? This was a question which had to be faced by those scholars who were recording or selecting or constructing traditions relating to the *gentes*, the 'peoples' (whatever might have been understood by that opaque term) of the barbarian successor-states. Here once more we encounter a variety of responses. Bede was in this respect, as in others, a rigorist. For him the pre-Christian past of the English scarcely existed. Given his didactic purpose, we may assume that this was the perspective he wished his fellow countrymen to adopt. Whether or not they did so was quite a different matter. Isidore of Seville, whose *History of the Goths* was composed in about 620, preferred to provide them with a biblical ancestry. The Goths were descended from Magog son of Japheth son of Noah. The *Getica* or *Gothic History* of Jordanes, composed in about 550, dwelt on the origins of the Goths on the distant northern island of Scandza and their early wars and wanderings in a remote pre-Christian but sometimes near-classical past. The chronicler known as Fredegar, writing perhaps in Burgundy in about 660, dashingly sought the ancestry of the Franks in the Trojans. He also claimed that Merovech, the eponymous ancestor of the Merovingian dynasty, was born of the union between his mother and a sea-monster. If Gregory of Tours knew of these claims to a supernatural origin on the part of the dynasty of Clovis, he said nothing about it; perhaps he judged the story pagan. Paul the Deacon, in his *History of the Lombards* composed at the court of Charlemagne in about 790, exulted in the violent martial vigour of the pagan Lombards.

Among the most imposing of the Christian claims was to transcend time and place. Nowhere was this claim more impressive than at the shrines of the saints. Though dead in the body the saint was *there*, living on in the tomb. St Peter at Rome, St Martin at Tours, St Cuthbert at Lindisfarne, St Boniface at Fulda, St James at Compostela (a new arrival in the ninth century); all these and numberless others were active, vital forces transmitting waves of spiritual energy into miracles of help and healing for human suppliants. The power of prayer leapt across human frontiers of the here and now. Prayer caused Imma's bonds to be loosed. Prayer linked distantly separated monasteries like Fulda and Montecassino. Prayer maintained the emotional cohesion of kin and community across the river of death.

The Christianizing of the river that all must cross was one of the most significant achievements in the slow unfolding of European conversion. Here as in other contexts there were no identifiable turning-points after which nothing would be the same again, no formal pronouncements by authority or frenzied bursts of reforming activity. (Saxony may be the exception which proves this rule.) Rather, we witness a gradual evolution in the course of which multitudinous local decisions about seemly ways of doing things can be seen with hindsight to have coalesced into a trend. Rituals for the sick and dying, and a liturgy of death and burial, were slowly developed in Merovingian Gaul, Visigothic Spain and early Christian Ireland. The churchmen of the Carolingian age consolidated and built upon these efforts, so that by the end of the ninth century western Christendom had elaborated a liturgy for coping with death which in its essentials would endure for the rest of the Middle Ages and beyond.[23]

Funerary practice, the disposal of the dead in their final resting-place or at the starting-point of their last journey – as in the Sutton Hoo ship burial – also underwent changes. We can see these changes occurring in the ever-growing body of material recovered, with ever-advancing sophistication of technique, by archaeological excavation. The correct, even the plausible interpretation of this material remains a more delicate and often a more subjective field of enquiry. One thing that has emerged with clarity from recent investigation is that the acceptance of Christianity made little difference *at first* to funerary practice, but did change it decisively in the long run. Here once more gradualism was the keynote. It is a striking fact that there was no formal condemnation of any particular funerary mode in legislation either secular or ecclesiastical before Charlemagne's prohibition of cremation in the Saxon capitulary of 785.[24] Traditional funerary practice, with its social rituals and emotional charge, could therefore survive the transition from paganism to Christianity. Central to that traditional practice, and for obvious reasons welcome to the archaeologist, was the practice of 'furnishing' a burial with grave-goods. 'For we brought nothing into the world, and it is certain we can carry nothing out.' This Pauline text lent support to the long-held view that early medieval churchmen resolutely opposed the deposit of grave-goods. It was a convenient view, for it made it easy to distinguish a 'pagan' (furnished) grave from a 'Christian' (unfurnished) one. But we now know that the practice of furnishing graves was maintained well into the Christian period. Among the Franks of northern Gaul, the Anglo-Saxons of eastern England, the Bavarians and a little later the Slavs of Moravia, the men and women of the aristocracy continued to be laid to rest clothed, armed, be-jewelled and equipped with the necessities of life in the Hereafter. The practice was not confined to the aristocracy, nor to the laity. St Cuthbert was buried 'robed in his priestly garments, wearing his shoes in readiness to meet Christ', and accompanied by his episcopal gear of pectoral cross, portable altar, liturgical comb and copy of St John's gospel.[25] That was in 687 (though some of the furnishings could have been added at the first 'translation' of the saint's body in 698). A different note had already been struck by Gertrude of Nivelles, the saintly daughter of Pippin I. As an act of piety she asked to be buried in only a simple linen shroud. Gertrude's request was made on her deathbed in 659 and recorded in the *Vita* composed in about 670. The force of aristocratic example was powerful; perhaps more powerful than ecclesiastical precept. Gertrude set a fashion of spurning ostentatious, richly furnished burial which was widely, if gradually, followed. By the middle of the eighth century furnished burials had disappeared from Francia. It was a good two centuries after the Franks had accepted Christianity.

Where the dead were buried, as well as how they were buried, was another area of custom where change was gradual. A bishop's portable altar may indicate that its owner may celebrate mass wheresoever he pleases, but Christianity is, or at any rate rapidly became, a religion of fixed *places*: places for prayer and worship, places for settled religious communities, places for burial. Very special people could expect to lie next to the very special dead, the saints, awaiting bodily resurrection together at the Last Judgement. Thus, for example, the Frankish rulers Dagobert I and his son Clovis II were buried at Saint-Denis, the monastery which housed the mortal remains of Dionysius (Denis), first bishop of Paris and martyr, of which they were the very generous patrons. Clovis II's English queen Balthild was buried in her monastic foundation at Chelles. The habit of concentrating burials in or near churches, or in Christian cemeteries which might (like Saint-Martin-de-Boscherville) or might not contain a funerary chapel, was an evolution which paralleled changes in the burial deposit and which took place, very roughly speaking, over the same long period. We have to say 'very roughly speaking' because there was enormous diversity of practice which renders generalization hazardous. The following examples are representative.

The first is from northern France and is at Hordain (dép. Nord), where a cemetery has been excavated which seems to have been in use from the late fifth century to the early eighth. The earliest graves at Hordain included cremations and horse burials akin to those which accompanied King Childeric's grave at Tournai though on a more modest scale. Both these features are considered fairly secure indicators of paganism. Into the sixth century, and inhumation has replaced cremation. From about 550 the inhumations began to be oriented east–west, a possible but not a necessary sign of Christian influence. Round about 600 a small chapel was built: it had stone foundations, a superstructure of perhaps wood and thatch, and windows glazed with greenish glass. At about the same date the entire cemetery was enclosed with a ditch and bank. Some but not all of the subsequent graves were dug near the chapel. Inside the chapel were a few richly furnished graves of both men and women, presumed to have been members of the leading family in the settlement. Near the altar were graves which might have been those of priests. Plate 16 shows a reconstruction of what the cemetery might have looked like in its heyday. Towards the end of the seventh century the chapel seems to have fallen into disuse. Early in the eighth century a new cemetery was initiated some 300 metres away, where a parish church was built.

Hordain was within the range of influence of the great missionary bishop St Amandus. We must resist the temptation to posit any direct connection. In any case, the decisive evidence of Christianity at Hordain pre-dates, though not by much, the arrival of Amandus in the area. What we can confidently say, however, is that the kind of changes which excavation has revealed at Hordain were those which Amandus would have been eager to encourage. With these cautious observations in mind, consider the case of Staubing, near Kelheim on the Danube. Here a cemetery has been excavated which contained burials from round about 600. Early in the life of the cemetery a simple wooden church was built to one side of it, consisting of a barn-like nave with a narrow rectangular chancel. Staubing is not far from Weltenburg, the monastic house founded by Eustasius, the successor of Columbanus at Luxeuil, in the 620s. In England, Rivenhall (Essex) seems to offer an evolution comparable to that of Hordain, and it is not far from the site of Cedd's monastery of Bradwell-on-Sea.

Our fourth example is from further west. At Eglwys Gwmyn in modern Dyfed, looking out over Carmarthen Bay, there is a roughly circular banked enclosure containing a pre-Christian barrow.[26] On the barrow stands a church, a modern one to be sure, but presumed successor to an earlier – much earlier? – one that gave the place its name: Eglwys is derived from Primitive Welsh *egles* and that from Latin *ecclesia*, 'church'. Whatever the enclosure may originally have been, it became a Christian cemetery at an early date. In it there stands a stone pillar commemorating in both Latin and ogham script a woman named Avitoria, daughter of Cunignos. It is difficult to assign even approximate dates to stones such as this, but the most expert modern enquirers would be inclined to place the inscription somewhere in the sixth century. Avitoria could have been a contemporary of Piro and Samson, the site of whose monastery, Caldey Island, would have been plainly visible to her just a few miles down the coast. Now there are speculative elements here. We cannot be absolutely certain that Avitoria was a Christian. Neither can we be absolutely certain that her memorial stone has always stood in the churchyard at Eglwys Gymyn; it could have been moved there by a party of godly souls several centuries later. However, the feeling that what we seem to have at Eglwys Gymyn is an early Christian cemetery is strengthened by the widespread occurrence of similar physical features in many more such graveyards in the western parts of the British Isles.

For a final example we return to Francia and move some way south, to Poitiers. There we encounter one of the most extraordinary monuments of this period, the so-called hypogeum of Mellebaudis. This was a funerary chapel built by an abbot named Mellebaudis in a Gallo-Roman and Frankish cemetery just outside the city of Poitiers. A date in the early years of the eighth century seems plausible. The body of the very small chapel was sunk below the level of the ground, though its roof would have projected above (and therefore it was not strictly speaking a hypogeum, which means 'an underground chamber or vault'). It was approached by a flight of shallow steps, some of them sculpted, which led down to the entrance doorway whose right-hand jamb bore an inscription in Latin. Inside, the plastered walls and ceiling were painted, there was an altar, probably a crucifix carved in stone, more lightly incised sculptures and further inscriptions recording the deposit there of relics of the saints. Mellebaudis – of whom nothing is known – had established what his door-jamb inscription calls 'this little sepulchre' (*speluncola*) where he might lie at rest after his death. There is no indication that he had intended other people to lie there with him. However, after his own interment the chapel continued to be used for burials. The nineteenth-century excavator, Camille de la Croix, found thirty-five persons buried beneath its floor, of whom twenty-five were children. Interpretation is problematic. A plausible theory is that these persons were kinsfolk of Mellebaudis who wanted to be buried with him in the holy place which he had established. Whatever the founder's intentions, the chapel became a family mausoleum.

Hordain, Staubing, Rivenhall, Eglwys Gymyn, Poitiers: each has something to tell us about the Christianization of death. The first four also suggest something of the manner in which the new faith encouraged communities in habituation to fixity of place. Christianity may be a religion of fixed place but it has never been one of a fixed tongue. Its leaders have not sought to impose a language to the extent that, say, Islamic teachers have with Arabic. True, the growth of Christianity in a Mediterranean under the political domination of Rome ensured that Greek and Latin were the preferred languages of religious discourse. But after the breakdown of the Euseban accommodation and the splintering of the western empire there was no alternative to dealing with the barbarians in their own vernaculars. If converts were to be made the Christian faith had to be expounded to them in a language they could understand.

Patrick must have learned Irish during his six years of captivity 'in the forest of Foclut which is by the western sea', thus enabling him to communicate with his prospective converts on his return to Ireland to preach the gospel. We hear of interpreters. Columba used an interpreter when he was in Pictland. Augustine and his companions were ignorant of Old English: on Pope Gregory's command they equipped themselves with interpreters as they journeyed through Francia on their way to Kent. King Oswald had learned Irish during his exile with the Scots of Dalriada. As king of Northumbria he would interpret for Aidan, 'because the bishop was not completely at home in the English tongue'. Columbanus must have learned the Germanic speech of eastern Francia, but cannot have been acquainted with any Slavonic tongue: perhaps this was among the considerations which deterred him from his proposed mission among the Slavs. Amandus failed to make any converts among the Basques, doubtless in part because he could not speak their language. English missionaries found it easy to work in Frisia because Old English and Old Frisian were practically identical. Mummolinus of Noyon – he who had such difficulties with his predecessor's horse – was 'skilled in both languages', that is Latin and Frankish; a highly valued skill, it was said to have got him the bishopric. His contemporary Agilbert was not: Wilfrid had to interpret for him at the synod of Whitby in 664, and the king of Wessex, a monoglot Englishman, turned him out of the bishopric of Dorchester because he couldn't understand the fellow's 'foreign prattle'. Pirmin, however, like Mummolinus of Noyon, spoke 'both tongues, the Roman and the Frankish' and this endeared him to his Alemannic patrons. When the future missionary Gregory of Utrecht was introduced as a young man to Boniface, the elderly bishop asked him to read aloud to him. Gregory started to do so in his best Latin, only to receive a sharp rebuke from that terrifying old man: 'Not like that, boy! Read to me in your own mother tongue.'

The leap from preaching in the vernacular, communicating by word of mouth, to *writing it down* was probably not the easy and obvious step it might appear to us. Quite apart from the difficulties involved in transposing 'barbarian' sounds into Roman letters, or in finding vernacular equivalents for the words of Christian scripture, the language of everyday speech was of only lowly status in the eyes of the learned. As far as we know, Ulfila was the first person to grasp that converts among the Germanic barbarians must be provided with a Bible, albeit a censored one, that they could understand. Educated contemporaries probably regarded this perception as deeply eccentric. The Irish church established by Palladius, Patrick and their successors was much more the norm in this linguistic respect. It remained for a long time firmly loyal to Latin where Christian writings were concerned. It was not until after about 800 that Christian texts began to be widely translated into the Irish vernacular.

It was to be in the Germanic mission field, that huge swathe of territory stretching from Lothian to Bavaria, that some three centuries after his death the work begun by Ulfila found continuators. The earliest datable attempt, in this second phase of activity to render Christian truths into a Germanic vernacular, occurred at the monastery of Whitby in about 670, with Caedmon's biblical versifications which we encountered in Chapter 6. His contemporary Aldhelm, abbot of Malmesbury and bishop of Sherborne (d. 709), was said to have been a skilled versifier in his own tongue who used his skills to convey Christian truths to the uninstructed populace near his monastery. No verse securely attributable to him has come down to us, though it has been suggested – a long but not an impossible shot – that he might have been the author of the magnificent Old English poem on the cross known as the *Dream of the Rood*. Bede was also said to have been learned in Old English poetry. Five lines of verse allegedly repeated by him on his deathbed in 735, and thereby known today as *Bede's Death Song*, might just conceivably have been of his own composition.

Be that as it may, we know for sure that Bede was translating the early chapters of St John's Gospel into Old English prose as he lay dying. In the previous year he had urged Archbishop Egbert of York to encourage all members of his flock to learn the Lord's Prayer and the Creed in their own mother tongue. An emphasis on the vernacular was carried into the German mission field by the foreign missionaries who went to work there in the eighth century. Two centres seem to have been especially important for its cultivation, Reichenau and Fulda, presumably in this reflecting the concerns of their founders, respectively Pirmin and Boniface. Various bits and pieces, and a very few lengthier compositions, survive. They comprise vocabularies and glosses, hymns and prayers for liturgical use, baptismal vows, prose and verse renderings of parts of the Bible, expositions and homilies.[27] Several of these surviving texts look as though they were put together for the aid of missionary teachers and preachers. They may be interpreted as another form of missionary literature. Take, for example, the so-called *Weissenburg Catechism*, named after the monastery in whose library the text ended up (now Wissembourg in Alsace, dép. Bas Rhin, to the north of Strasbourg). It contains German texts of the Lord's Prayer with commentary upon it, a list of the deadly sins, the Apostles' and Athanasian Creeds and the Gloria in Excelsis. The collection seems to date from round 800 or soon afterwards.

Three works are a good deal more substantial, as to purpose as well as to length. The so-called *Diatessaron* was a German translation of a 'gospel harmony' or edited version of the four gospels into one. It was the work of monks of Fulda in probably the second quarter of the ninth century, and was almost certainly undertaken under the inspiration of Rabanus Maurus, a pupil of Alcuin who was master of the monastery school at Fulda from 804 to 822 and then abbot of the house from 822 until 842. Two notable works in Old High German verse date from the ninth century. These are the *Heliand* ('Saviour'), an Old Saxon epic treatment of the life of Christ of which nearly 6,000 lines of alliterative verse survive, and the *Liber Evangeliarum* ('Gospel Book') composed by Otfrid of Weissenburg, a pupil of Rabanus Maurus, and completed between 863 and 871.

The *Heliand* is a very remarkable work. The earliest surviving manuscript is of the late ninth century and was probably copied at one or other of the Saxon monasteries of Werden or Corvey. (The only other manuscript of the complete text was copied in England, perhaps at Winchester, in the tenth century.) The poet was evidently a learned man, almost certainly a cleric. Among works apparently known to him was a commentary on Matthew by Rabanus Maurus; so the influence of Fulda may be detected too. There has been much learned debate about the date of the work and its relation to Old English religious verse. It is sufficient here to state that the *Heliand* was probably composed in the second quarter of the ninth century and that it may owe something to English poetic models, presumably available to the author through the agency of the English missionaries in Germany and the monastic houses founded by them. The poem is notable for its anonymous author's attempt to accommodate the gospel story to the tastes and expectations of a Germanic secular audience. He chose to write in the alliterative verse traditionally used for vernacular epic poetry. We have some idea of what such epics were like owing to the survival of a fragment, a mere sixty-eight lines, of the so-called *Hildebrandslied* ('Lay of Hildebrand'), which deals with the tragic dilemma of a father and son who have to do battle together. The moral setting of the *Hildebrandslied* is traditional, heroic and aristocratic; at its heart lies a drama about the imperatives of duty, honour and courage even when hard fate pits kinsman against kinsman. There is nothing Christian about it at all. Yet it was copied by a monk of Fulda on to spare leaves of a manuscript of the Old Testament in the monastic library, probably in about 830.

The author of the *Heliand* used stock phrases drawn from secular epic to render the gospel narrative accessible to his audience. Jesus is the *landes uuard*, 'guardian of the land', the *thiodo drohtin*, 'lord of the peoples'. The Virgin Mary is an *adalcnosles uuif*, a 'woman of noble lineage', and King Herod a *boggebo*, a 'giver of rings'. The apostles are the *gisidos*, 'companions, retainers' of Christ and St Peter is his *suerdthegan*, his 'sword-thegn'. Detail is familiarized in a Germanic setting, wherever possible an aristocratic one. The desert where Jesus was tempted becomes a forest. The disciples sail the sea of Galilee in a *hoh hurnidskip*, a 'high-horned ship' like the longships of northern waters with their curved and pointed bow and stern. The infant Christ is decked with jewels and the shepherds are transformed into grooms looking after horses. Jesus gathers about him 'youths for disciples, young men and good, word-wise warriors', just as a Saxon lord would seek young sword-wise warriors for his retainers. Matthew, a *cuninges thegn*, a 'king's thegn', becomes *drohtines man*, 'the Lord's retainer', finding in Jesus 'a more generous mead-giver than he had ever had before as a liege lord in this world'. The eleven biblical verses describing the marriage at Cana are expanded into eighty lines celebrating a gargantuan feast such as St Wilfrid might have been proud to have hosted. At the entry to Jerusalem the ass is omitted: the Lord enters on foot rather than on an ignoble beast unfitted to his royal dignity.

There are passages in the *Heliand* which some have interpreted as having reference to the circumstances of the conversion of the Saxons. In the account of John the Baptist the author subtly shifts the emphasis away from the biblical theme of a baptism marking repentance in those who already possess the faith to a baptism which signifies the giving of a new faith. John conducts mass baptisms *allan dah druhtfolc mikil,* 'all the day long, a great mass of people'; just like the 'innumerable multitude' baptized in the waters of the river Lippe in 776. But, importantly, the *Heliand* poet consistently presents Christianity as a mild and peaceable faith. He nowhere even implicitly suggests that the faith might come in any other manner. The violence which had marked the historical conversion of Saxony under Charlemagne is swept away from view. Whatever we may think of the morality of such a stance, it may be regarded as one way of trying to reconcile the Saxons to their lot. Two generations on from the conversion, Christian teachers did not want to open up old wounds.

The disciples' request 'Lord, teach us to pray' becomes *gerihti us that geruni,* 'reveal to us the runes'. There is here a fascinating juxtaposition, or conflation, or elision of religious ideas. To be fully appreciated it needs to be set in the context of semantic strategies which can be detected not just in the *Heliand* but in much other Christian writing, prose and verse, in the Germanic vernaculars. Familiar vernacular equivalents had to be found to express Christian concepts. Their very familiarity meant that they would have all sorts of non-Christian – which does not necessarily mean pagan – connotations for those who used them. However, churchmen could contrive so to slant matters, by use and by teaching, that in the longer term *only* the Christian meaning would survive. In sum, words could be adopted and exploited, their range of meanings could be transformed, drained of secular content and appropriated to Christian ends. There was, thus, a lexical dimension to the strategy commended by Pope Gregory to his missionaries. Old High German (OHG) *Geist* had the primary meaning of 'inner emotional arousal' or 'possession (by a spirit)': Christian churchmen transformed its meaning into 'spirit' or 'soul'. OHG *Heil* conveyed 'material well-being, beneficence of the gods': after Christian treatment it became 'holiness, salvation'. OHG *gilouben* (Modern German *glauben*) meant 'to be dependent on', especially in the context of a lord–retainer relationship: in Christian hands it acquired the meaning 'to believe'. OHG *Truhtin,* Old English *dryhten,* meant 'military leader, lord of a warband': it came to be the normal word for 'Lord', the term usually employed to render New Testament *dominus.*

Deliberate strategies can be detected here. This can be shown by the example of Ulfila's Gothic version of the Bible. The Gothic equivalent of *Truhtin/dryhten* was the word *drauhtins*. But Ulfila never employed this word to render *dominus*, 'Lord'. Instead he used the term *frauja*. The reason is simple: *drauhtins* had violent, military connotations; *frauja* did not, its primary meaning being 'head of a household'. This was the choice of the man who decided to omit the books of Kings from his translation of the Bible because they were too warlike and might encourage the Goths in their military propensities. If Ulfila's choice was deliberate, as surely it must have been, so too we may assume was the decision to use this loaded term made by those who later rendered scripture into other Germanic vernaculars. The earliest to do so was Caedmon in about 670: *eci dryctin*, 'eternal Lord'. (In strictness, perhaps we should say *c.* 740, when the lines attributed to Caedmon were copied into an early manuscript of Bede's *Historia Ecclesiastica*.) But the older, secular, military connotations of the word *dryhten* long persisted. They can be found, for instance, in the epic *Beowulf*. The date at which *Beowulf* was composed has long constituted one of the most notoriously controversial questions among Anglo-Saxonists; but few would now defend a date much earlier than about 800, and the poem may well be a century or even two later than that. In other words, and unsurprisingly, the semantic shift from a primarily secular to a primarily religious range of meanings was a long-drawn-out process. We may reasonably surmise that to his early hearers Caedmon's phrase *eci dryctin* would have conveyed something like 'undying warrior lord'.

Could styles and images be appropriated, like words, and turned to Christian ends? This is too vast a topic to be investigated here, but it may be worth spending a few moments in examining what must surely be one of the most enigmatic exhibits in any discussion of it: the so-called Franks Casket.[*] It is a box made of whalebone measuring about 23cm long by 18 wide by 10 high. On its four vertical sides or faces and on its lid it bears scenes carved in relief which are drawn variously from the traditional Germanic, the Christian and the Roman historical or mythological pasts. The scenes are accompanied by inscriptions in either the runic or the Roman alphabets (in one case a mixture

---

[*] The casket takes its name from the collector Sir Augustus Franks, who acquired it and presented it to the British Museum in 1867; the name does not indicate any connection with the Frankish peoples settled in Gaul.

of the two), in either the Latin or the Old English language, inscriptions which in every case but one refer to the scenes they accompany. The Old English renderings attest to a dialect from northern England. Dating would seem to be within a generation or so either side of about 700; or, if you like, in the lifetime of Bede and Boniface.

Let us now advance a little closer and examine the scenes on the front of the box, illustrated in plate 27. There are two of them, and they are enclosed by an Old English/runic inscription which runs all the way round the edge of the casket, itself bordered on the outside by a cablework pattern, simulating rope, which bounds the entire composition. This inscription is the single one which does not refer to the scenes it accompanies. Instead it tells us, in the form of one of the riddles of which the Anglo-Saxons were so fond, what the box is made of. 'The fish beat up the seas on to the mountainous cliff; the king of terror became sad when he swam on to the shingle. Whale's bone.'[28] The scenes enclosed by the inscription form a strange juxtaposition. On the right-hand side is the Adoration of the Magi, helpfully identified for us by the artist, who has carved MAGI in runic characters above them. There is the star hovering above Bethlehem, there are Mary and Jesus, there are the three magi in Germanic costume, their cloaks held in place by prominent shoulder-buckles. In front of them there stands on the ground a bird, apparently joining in their obeisance to the Infant Jesus; its unexpected appearance in a familiar iconography is puzzling. The artist's determination to leave no space unfilled with decoration has led him to place a knot formed of two interlocking triangles behind the bent back of the left-hand magus.

The scene on the left-hand side is more problematical. While there is disagreement over details there is general acceptance that what we have here is an episode from a traditional Germanic cycle of tales about Weland the Smith. We can be sure that these tales were current in England because they are referred to in the Old English poem *Deor*. Weland, the smith of the gods, the fabulous artificer, had been deliberately lamed by King Nithad. The king had had one of his legs broken so that he could not escape. By this means Nithad hoped to be able to profit from Weland's magical skills for ever. But Weland planned a terrible revenge. Now to the casket. There is Weland in his smithy on the left-hand side, his broken leg plain for us to see. He has killed one of the king's sons: the decapitated body lies at Weland's feet. Weland is working on the boy's skull, turning it into a cup. The boy's head, marked by a ghastly grin, is gripped in the tongs which Weland holds in his left hand. With his right hand he holds out a goblet to the first of two female figures who occupy the central portion of the scene. They are probably meant to represent Baduhild, the king's daughter, and an attendant. In the story Weland plied her with strong beer until she was relaxed and comatose; then he raped her. Having taken his revenge by murdering the son and violating the daughter Weland had to make his escape from Nithad's anger. This he did with the help of his brother Egil, whom we see in the right-hand portion of this scene. There is Egil busy wringing the necks of birds so that he can use their feathers to make magic wings on which Weland can fly away from the king's wrath. It is a gruesome narrative, conveyed with economy and artistry.

We do not know by whom the casket was commissioned – though ingenious guesses have been made – nor what its original purpose might have been. This makes it all the more difficult to discern any plan or meaning in the scenes it represents. In the past, enquirers have been robustly confident that attempts to interpret the casket were misplaced. An 'arbitrary jumble' was the verdict of one distinguished art-historian; a 'meaningless sequence' indicative of 'intellectual confusion' was another's.[29] One cannot help reflecting that these reactions were a little dismissive. The juxtapositions on the front panel contrast a non-Christian order with a Christian one: there can be no disputing that. The non-Christian order is violent, composed of maiming, murder, deceit, rape and revenge. The Christian order is peaceful. The magi bow the knee to the little Child who shall lead them; and a bird is with them – which might have had all sorts of meanings for the primary audience: ominous or magical bird? Woden's raven? But now submissive to Christ, as the raven who brought lard to Cuthbert was submissive, or the raven who fed the hermits Paul and Antony in the desert. The narrative moves from left to right, so a Christian order has superseded a pre-Christian one. The loosing letters of a magical past are bound by the rope which surrounds them. The creature to which they refer, the king of terror, the monster of the deep, that old Leviathan, is beached impotently on the shingle. The magic knot, as bound or loosed by the women who sit on the ground in the Merseburg charm, has joined, like the bird, a Christian dispensation. It is now mass-singing priests who loose bonds, as Imma's brother did for him.

Reflections along these lines are prompted by the front panel of the

Franks Casket. They can quickly become undisciplined, and the most that can ever be claimed for them is plausibility. That plausibility gains strength from a context: if the Franks Casket is in part 'about' leading people to faith in Christ, so is in part the *Heliand*. If Woden's bird can be brought within a Christian ring-fence, so too can Woden's day (except in Portugal). The casket stands as a monument, albeit a puzzling one, to this epoch of conversion and transition.

A general willingness to adapt, to opt for a syncretic approach to the task of Christianization, is always going to raise the question: how far down that path may a missionary venture? When does compromise become surrender? Is 'syncretism' just a sophisticated way of saying that almost anything will go? This question in its various forms is always going to be at its most insistent when a structure of ecclesiastical authority is weak or barely existent. Almost by definition, it is in the mission field that this state of affairs is likely to be found. There is plenty of scope for disagreement between missionaries and the home church, or between different missionaries, about the issues that will arise. The anguish of the misunderstood or misrepresented has been a feature of missionary history from Patrick to Bishop Colenso of Natal – and beyond. A spectacular case of disagreement confronts us in the middle years of the eighth century. It may also prove instructive.

Boniface encountered two other workers in his German mission field whom he found thoroughly unsatisfactory. They were called Aldebert and Clement.[30] Aldebert was a native of Gaul who attracted a great following by the signs and wonders that he worked. He claimed that miracle-working relics had been given to him by an angel; also that he had received a letter sent down from heaven by Jesus Christ himself. He had managed to get 'unlearned' (*indocti*) bishops – and one can almost hear the Bonifacian sneer at the Frankish episcopate whom he so despised – to consecrate him a bishop. A blasphemous *Vita* had been composed about him. He would distribute his hair and parings from his fingernails as relics. He granted absolution without confession. He cast doubt on the efficacy of pilgrimage to Rome. He composed a prayer which invoked by name certain angels who were not angels at all. He would erect crosses or build small chapels 'in the countryside and at springs, and ordered public prayers to be said there', thus luring the congregations away from the 'old churches' (*antiquis ecclesiis*). Clement we have already met. He was the Irishman who claimed that

271

in the Harrowing of Hell Christ had liberated pagans as well as believers. In addition to this Clement was unsound on predestination, permitted a man to marry his brother's widow, and had himself fathered two children while continuing to exercise episcopal functions. The heretical teachings of Aldebert and Clement were duly condemned, at the insistence of Boniface, at a synod in Rome presided over by the pope in the year 745.

It is important to remember that we have only Boniface's side of the story. Boniface wanted to be rid of Aldebert and Clement; he was a formidable enemy and he took no chances. We must, I think, be prepared to allow for exaggeration, perhaps for misrepresentation. It would be possible to set the actions and teachings of Aldebert and Clement in a slightly different light. (We might care to recall the *Vita* of Martin of Tours, composed during the subject's lifetime by Sulpicius Severus, and the defensive tone adopted by the author in narrating a string of wonder-working exploits which some contemporaries would have found offensive, or worse.) For example, there would have been many to applaud the multiplication of sites for Christian worship. Boniface was himself engaged upon a similar enterprise. Some of the thirty churches burnt down by the Saxons whose loss he lamented in 752 must surely have been in the course of construction when he was penning his accusations against Aldebert and Clement. Again, there was diversity of teaching and practice in respect of contentious matters which Boniface implied had been settled one way or another already. Aldebert's disreputable angels included Raguel; but Raguel was an angel invoked by name in an inscription in the funerary chapel of Mellebaudis. Boniface's posthumously edited correspondence included a letter from an English nun in Germany to her brother at home in England invoking angelic protection on his behalf in somewhat similar terms to those to which Boniface had taken such exception when employed by Aldebert. On the question of consanguineous marriage – a very vexed question, to which we shall return shortly – even Boniface had to admit that Old Testament rulings permitted the union of a man with his brother's widow.

The issues, then, were not clear-cut. No doubt Boniface saw Aldebert and Clement as interlopers. (This was, of course, how some among the Frankish bishops of the Rhineland saw *him*.) But more was surely at stake than just friction between an irascible gamekeeper who wanted to turf poachers off his land. Aldebert and Clement had overstepped limits. So judged Boniface, and Pope Zacharias agreed with him. They had been too accommodating towards pagan ancestors. They had failed to uphold rigorously Christian marriage customs. The multiplication of angels could look dangerously like a concession to polytheism. The readiness to be flexible on penitential rituals or the doctrine of predestination also smacked of compromise; so too, perhaps, the choice of places at which to establish sites for Christian worship. The markedly prophetic character of their leadership – the all-too-human relics, the huge followings, the *Vita*, the wonders, the too-Christlike freely outpoured forgiveness of sins – was unsettling to upholders of episcopal authority and Roman order. These features of the movements led by Aldebert and Clement have parallels in mission fields widely separate in time and space. The most notable are with the African Independent Churches, which have been such a growing feature of the religious life of sub-Saharan Africa in the course of the last hundred years or so. It is not absolutely fanciful to see, if faintly, the lineaments of Prophet Harris or Simon Kimbangu in Aldebert and Clement. One last point. we know about the activities of Aldebert and Clement because of the survival of just a few documents among Boniface's personal archive; how many other 'pseudo-prophets' might there not have been, scattered across western Christendom in the eighth century?[31]

The need to strengthen episcopal authority in the face of eccentric or disorderly or insubordinate or heretical elements as represented by the likes of Aldebert and Clement was one ingredient of the Carolingian reformation of the church. Among the results of that reformation was that rather more was required of the Christian laity than had been asked in the past. New standards of Christian behaviour were commended to the convert, and it became realistic to hope that the convert's children or at least grandchildren might take some steps towards making these standards a reality.

Looking at earlier epochs one has the impression that missionary activists laid the main stress in their preaching upon the externals of behaviour and observance among their converts. Examples have been offered already in Chapter 2 and elsewhere; but one more will do no harm. It concerns the Lombard ascetic Wulfolaic whom we met a few pages ago receiving dust from the tomb of St Martin in the company of Aredius of Limoges. Wulfolaic eventually migrated to the diocese of Trier and settled at Carignan (dép. Ardennes: south-east of Sedan). There he perched on top of a column like one of the stylite saints of Syria in a gruelling – and very public – life of extreme self-denial. 'And so, when winter came, I was in such wise pinched with the icy cold that often the severe frost made the nails drop from my toes, while frozen water hung from my beard like melted wax of candles.'[32] The people of the region were worshippers of a goddess to whom an enormous statue had been erected. (Gregory of Tours called her 'Diana' but she might have been some local Celtic deity.) Wulfolaic's nearby column with its living holy man on top of it was plainly intended to rival the pagan statue. Crowds were attracted to Wulfolaic's column, whence 'I proclaimed without ceasing that Diana was naught, the images naught, and naught the rites which they practised'. Eventually the people yielded to his preaching and decided 'to leave their idols and follow the Lord'. At Wulfolaic's bidding the statue was cast down and broken up. And that is all we are told about the conversion of Wulfolaic's hearers. They heed him, they turn to the Lord, they smash an idol. It puts us in mind of Martin at Levroux or Samson in Trigg. An enquirer using the different sort of evidence, mainly legal and liturgical, which survives from seventh-century Spain has concluded that 'the Church's expectations from the laity were realistically minimal'.[33] It is significant that lay participation was not encouraged. The fourth council of Toledo, meeting in 633, was explicit on the arrangements for receiving the eucharist in church: 'Let the priest and the deacon communicate at the altar, the remaining clergy in the choir, and the laity outside the choir.' Archaeological investigation of surviving church structures or foundations from the Visigothic period bears this out. It is tolerably clear that in many, perhaps most Spanish churches of the period the interposition of a screen prevented the laity from seeing or hearing much of what went on at the east end of the church in which they worshipped. 'Mystery and transcendence rather than participation were what was aimed at.'

Such seems to have been the norm in the pre-Carolingian age. Of course, there were those who found this a far from satisfactory state of affairs. The more thoughtful sort of churchman – Augustine, Caesarius, Gregory I, Isidore, Bede – wanted to intensify and focus more sharply the religious experience of the laity. The reformers of the Carolingian age got the chance to do this, in part because they inherited and built upon the ideals of those precursors. In part it was because of the accumulation of resources in cathedral and monastic communities which could be devoted to book-production, education and training. In part it was because in Charlemagne, his son and his grandsons the reformers enjoyed for a century the whole-hearted support of powerful rulers who took their responsibilities as Christian kings very seriously indeed. Charlemagne's *Admonitio generalis* (*General directive*) of 789 was the first comprehensive statement of the reformers' ideals and it was followed over the next century by a flood of enactments, whether royal and central or episcopal and local, designed to bring closer the realization of a *societas christiana*, a Christian society. It is worth emphasizing that these initiatives in the Frankish empire were paralleled, or imitated – and there is much debate about which – elsewhere: in Ireland, with the reforming movement led by the *céli dé*, the 'culdees' or 'companions of God'; in Anglo-Saxon Wessex under the patronage of King Alfred; and in the Christian kingdom of the Asturias of north-western Spain at the court of King Alfonso III.

The legislative evidence from the Carolingian age is abundant. But it poses the usual problems. To what extent were the norms laid down by the authorities carried through into practice? Recent research has suggested that where some degree of verification is feasible the answer to this question might be cautiously affirmative. For instance, it is now clear that literacy among the laity in the ninth century was more widespread than once was thought, a tribute to the educational energies of the Carolingian reformers.[34] There is evidence, some of it considered in another context above (pp. 263–8), for a new emphasis on the non-Romance vernaculars for liturgical and homiletic uses (hymns, prayers, creeds, sermons, etc.).[35] Architectural and art-historical studies have hinted at increased lay participation in the liturgical cycle of the Christian year. A vast number of what are loosely called 'private charters', that is conveyances, wills, etc., made by non-royal lay persons, amply documents the laity's attachment to the church. We have works of Christian devotion composed for the use of the laity. Alcuin, for example, composed one such for a certain Count Guy (Wido), and Paulinus of Aquileia another for Count Henry of Friuli. Most remarkable of all, we even possess one such work composed by a member of the laity, the manual of advice for her son written in about 840 by a southern French lady named Dhuoda. Such evidence tells us little directly about the *quality* of belief, but its mere existence and survival encourage the feeling that at least in some lay quarters Christian observance was taken seriously.

When Wilfrid was returning to England after his episcopal consecration in Gaul his clergy sang psalms and hymns – in Old English? – to give the time to the oarsmen. There is no reason to doubt the truth of this tiny vignette presented to us by Wilfrid's biographer. In such a manner could the trivial round and the common task be encouraged to pulse to a Christian rhythm. The pastoral theology of early medieval teachers, culminating in the Carolingian age, defined a Christian morality for the laity and in so doing sought to intensify the impingement of Christianity upon secular human life. Baptism marked entry into the Christian community. Guidance and education could be provided throughout the span of life by means of the penitential system. Churchmen attempted to regulate the choice of partners in marriage, laid down rules on such matters as diet and sexual behaviour, provided rituals for all occasions, exorcized evil spirits, healed the sick, comforted and eased the dying. Something has been said earlier in this chapter about the slow Christianization of death. We must at least glance at some other of these impingements of Christianity upon daily life.

It is appropriate to start with baptism.[36] Not only was it the earliest sacramental rite of passage that most Christians underwent, signing the recipient with the cross as a badge of entry into the church, but it was perceived as being by far the most important. Baptism was necessary to salvation, the central and indispensable sacrament of the faith. Documents from ninth-century England use the Old English word for baptism, *fulwiht*, as a synonym for the Christian faith in general. Adult baptism after instruction, standard in the early church, had gradually been replaced by infant baptism, a change of far-reaching significance in the life of Christendom. We still occasionally encounter voluntarily postponed baptism after the fashion of the Emperor Constantine. For example, King Cadwalla of Wessex abdicated his throne and travelled to Rome, where he was baptized shortly before his death at the age of thirty in 689. But we may suspect that many of the adult baptisms of which we hear were rather less voluntary than Cadwalla's. The defeated Saxons experienced baptism under threat of death if they refused it. For the vast majority of early medieval Christians, however, infant baptism was the norm. We might instance the baby Guthlac, 'brought to the sacred waters of the life-giving font when eight days had run their course' after his birth.[37]

Baptism gave life and salvation. Another way of putting this would be to say that baptism inflicted defeat upon death and damnation. Stephen's biography of Wilfrid tells a heart-rending story of a mother who besought the bishop to baptize her dead son and thus 'to save him from the lion's mouth'. The words are those of Psalm xxii, and therefore surely supplied by Stephen. But if the report is in outline true it is a rare and precious glimpse of a lay perception of baptism in the England of the 670s. There survives from about a century later the so-called *Saxon Baptismal Vow*, a text in Old High German show- ing Old English influence, and therefore quite possibly generated in the circles of Willehad or Liudger. Those about to undergo baptism, evidently adults, were required to renounce their heathen gods, by name, one by one. In naming, in renouncing, the new Christian defeated the old gods. Thus baptism to some degree partook of the character of exorcism; indeed, exorcistic rites formed a part of the baptismal liturgy. It was a potent form of – magic? How very interesting to find a vernacular baptismal formula (not the Saxon one) copied into the same manuscript as the *Merseburg Charms*, of which one was quoted earlier in this chapter. Well . . . but isn't this just the sort of juxtaposition which we should, by now, expect? With baptism, as with charms, it was very important indeed to do it right. Baptism itself, as opposed to the promises and renunciations which accompanied it, had to be administered in Latin. Boniface was shocked to come across in Bavaria a priest whose Latin was so poor that he garbled the central baptismal formula: '*Baptizo te in nomine patria* [for *patris*] *et filia* [for *filii*] *et spiritus sancti*'. Thus the correct administration of baptism called for an educated priesthood.

Infants could not receive the instruction which had traditionally preceded baptism, nor could they make the renunciations and promises which were a part of the baptismal ritual. Sponsors had to act on their behalf. Hence the institution of godparenthood. At the moment of the new birth of baptism the child received new kinsfolk. The bond of spiritual kinship thus created was a very powerful one in early medieval Europe. In the lawcode of King Ine of Wessex drawn up in about 700 it was laid down that the spiritual kin, like the kin by blood, should receive compensation for the slaying of a godson or godfather. The word used for compensation, *maegbot*, is related to Old English *maegth*, one of the most numinous words in the terminology of kinship known to the Anglo-Saxons. Indeed godparenthood could even have

277

a political dimension. In the east Roman or Byzantine empire the notion had taken root by the sixth century of a family of Christian kings headed by the emperor. The baptismal sponsorship by the emperor of a barbarian king converted to Christianity indicated secular lordship as well. The experience of baptism could thus become a token of submission. Exported to the west we can see the idea at work in the baptismal sponsorship of Widukind by Charlemagne in 785, or of Harald Klak by Louis the Pious in 826, or of the Viking leader Guthrum by Alfred of Wessex in 878.

In the early Christian centuries a bishop, and only a bishop, had conducted baptism of adults, after instruction, at his cathedral church, and at set times of the Christian year, either Easter or Pentecost. Special buildings for the celebration of the sacrament, baptisteries, were erected. Some of these survive, for example at Ravenna, Fréjus or Poitiers, or have been excavated, as at Aosta or Geneva. The most magnificent survivor, though of a much later period, is at Pisa. A baptistery stood as a potent symbol not just of the importance of the sacrament but also of episcopal control of its administration. But in the course of time two developments weakened this control: the increase in the number of believers, and the growing practice of infant baptism. A bishop, quite simply, could not be everywhere at once. So the administration of baptism came to be performed by the local clergy, the priests and deacons of the diocese. But episcopal participation was not ended. A second stage of Christian initiation was devised, in which those baptized as infants would have their faith 'confirmed' by a bishop later in life. This was the origin of the rite of confirmation. Bede, in his *Letter to Egbert*, was insistent that bishops should travel regularly round their dioceses in order to conduct this ceremony. Attempts were also made to exert control over the *places* where baptism might be administered. Although the degrees of success attained varied widely from region to region, a fundamental distinction gradually emerged in the evolving law of the church between those churches which possessed baptismal rights and those which did not. It was a distinction which was to have far-reaching effects upon the geography of ecclesiastical administration, a topic to which we shall return in Chapter 13.

We looked briefly in an earlier chapter at the new system of 'private' penance which began to establish itself in western Christendom from the seventh century onwards under the influence of revered spiritual mentors such as Columbanus. Confession, penance and absolution were designed to heal guilt, and in wiping out sin to reconcile the penitent to God and to humankind. It has been claimed that there is little evidence for the widespread practice of regular individual confession by the laity before the twelfth century.[38] (It was not until 1215 that the fourth Lateran council enjoined annual confession upon all adults.) To expect more than a little evidence may be to expect too much. Given the intimate and oral nature of the practice, given the sparsity of our evidence relating to practically every activity in early medieval Europe, we surely cannot hope to find any very clear traces of what went on between penitent and confessor. What today might in some circles be called counselling was something, we may legitimately surmise, that probably occurred between, say, Columbanus and the aristocratic Frankish families with whom he stayed and who responded so eagerly to his teaching. Such encounters may not have manifested all the characteristics of the sacrament of penance as the theologians and canonists of a later epoch would come to define it; but the outlines of the later system seem to have been there.

It is striking that the few unambiguous references to confession that we do have come in the main from missionary contexts. A collection of statutes attributed to Boniface – guidance from a bishop to his clergy about their pastoral duties – required priests to explain the need for confession to the laity. Altfrid's *Vita Liudgeri* contains a clear allusion to confession and penance, and so does Rimbert's *Vita Anskarii*. There are several references to confession in the miracle stories collected at Fulda by the monk Rudolf in the 840s. This may reflect the influence of Fulda's founder St Boniface: it is also tempting to connect the emphasis with abbot Rabanus Maurus, whom we have already met in our discussion of versification in the vernacular. Rabanus Maurus' surviving sermons, which owed much to Caesarius of Arles, attest to his pastoral concern for the Thuringian laity. He was also the compiler of a penitential. His book of instruction for priests, moreover, referred to the hearing of confessions and the allotting of appropriate penances.

Hincmar, archbishop of Rheims from 845 to 882, was one of the giants of the Carolingian church. He recommended confession as one means by which lay people might seek help when faced by marital problems: sensitive advice from a man not normally remembered for sensitivity. He had in mind a specific difficulty – male impotence induced by witchcraft, and the question whether this might be grounds for divorce. Not so, thought Hincmar, if the impotence could be cured by resort to 'ecclesiastical medicines', among which 'a pure confession of all his sins' is prominent. It was a recognition of the power of confession to effect, as we might say today, the release of psychosomatic stress.

Hincmar thought, and wrote, a good deal on the subject of marriage. This was another area – and such a difficult one – where ecclesiastical precept and secular practice had to find some means of accommodation. The problems were manifold. There was Holy Writ, to begin with: a mass of detailed rulings in Judaic tradition preserved in the Old Testament, a few and rarely unambiguous guidelines offered in the New. There were the differences in the status of women vis-à-vis men, and differences of practice over parts of the marriage contract such as dowry, between the Mediterranean world and that of the northern barbarians. Generally speaking, women occupied a higher status and a less trammelled condition among the Celtic and Germanic peoples than the lowly position of their sisters in the cultures of the Mediterranean. There was the inheritance of Roman law, under which marriage was an entirely civil or secular contract. There was a tradition of misogyny, often exaggerated by later commentators, in the attitude of some of the Christian Fathers, notably Jerome, to women. There was a developing Christian reverence for virginity. And this is to indicate but some of the problems in a veritable minefield of difficulties.

It is not a bit surprising to find that marriage and sexual relations generally were topics of perennial importance and delicacy in the early medieval mission field (and in later ones too). Missionary churchmen sought guidance from authority and in their questions we can sense the anxieties of their converts. For how long after childbirth should husband and wife abstain from sexual intercourse? This was a question put by Augustine of Canterbury, leader of the mission to England, to Pope Gregory I. What course of action is open to a couple if the wife is permanently prevented by illness from engaging in sexual relations? The question was put to Pope Gregory II by Boniface in 726. How should weddings be celebrated? Is sexual intercourse permissible on a Sunday? These were two out of the ten questions concerning marriage which Khan Boris of the Bulgars put to Pope Nicholas I in 866.

The marital question above all others that preoccupied evangelists and their converts was that of consanguinity. 'Within what degrees may the faithful be married to their kindred?' It was another question put to Pope Gregory I by Augustine of Canterbury. Degrees of consanguinity means generations of descent from a common ancestor. For the purposes of discussion it may be as well to provide the simplest possible hypothetical pedigree of relationships extending to the seventh degree of consanguinity.

A

1st degree	B 1	B 2
2nd	C 1	C 2
3rd	D 1	D 2
4th	E 1	E 2
5th	F 1	F 2
6th	G 1	G 2
7th	H 1	H 2

The words 'simplest possible' need emphasis. Life is rarely as simple as a diagram. One need only let the mind linger for a moment on such matters as half-brothers and -sisters, cases of disputed parentage, cross-generational marriage, or the complications of spiritual kinship created by godparenthood, to sense how very intractable problems could arise.

The pope's reply to Augustine was as follows:

A certain worldly law in the Roman commonwealth [Gregory was referring to a constitution of the year 405 later embodied in Justinian's codification of Roman law] allows that the son and daughter of a brother and sister, or of two full brothers, or of two sisters, may be joined in matrimony. But we have found by experience that no offspring can come of such marriage, and divine law forbids a man to 'uncover the nakedness of his kindred'. Hence it must of necessity be that among the faithful only the third or fourth generation can be lawfully joined in matrimony; for the second, which we have mentioned, must altogether abstain from one another.[39]

In other words, the pope was prepared to sanction marriages at the level of D and E in the diagram above. However, when in 726 Boniface addressed a similar query to Pope Gregory II (apparently ignorant at that date of the earlier Gregory's ruling) the pope replied that, 'if the parties know themselves to be related by blood they should not marry; but since moderation weighs more with these savage people [Boniface's German converts] than strict legal duties, they should be allowed to marry after the fourth degree of consanguinity.' This would seem to disallow marriage between partners related more closely than level F. That this was generally accepted as the rule of the Roman church appears from a comment made in the text of the *Penitential* attributed to Archbishop Theodore of Canterbury which was probably edited not long after his death in 690: 'The Romans permit marriage within the fifth degree of consanguinity; but they do not dissolve marriages within the fourth degree after they have been made.' A few years after his enquiry of Pope Gregory II, Boniface was dismayed to discover that a quite different ruling had been made in the answer of Gregory I to Augustine. In some anxiety Boniface wrote to Archbishop Nothelm of Canterbury in 735:

> I pray you to obtain for me a copy of the letter containing, it is said, the questions of Augustine, first archbishop of the English, and the replies made to them by Pope Gregory I. In this letter it is stated among other things that it is lawful for Christians to contract marriage within the third degree of consanguinity. Will you please have a careful search made to discover whether or not this document has been proved to be an authentic work of Pope Gregory? The archivists at Rome cannot find it among Gregory's writings in the records of the Roman church.

So here was a pretty problem! Contradictory rulings from the highest authority in the western church; and a document of the very first importance which mysteriously could not be found in the archives. No wonder Boniface suspected forgery. Several modern historians have too, though now the fundamental authenticity of Gregory I's letter is generally acknowledged. The solution which has commended itself to modern scholarship – alongside technical arguments about the textual transmission of the letter – is along the lines of that rather shamefacedly put forward by Pope Zacharias in 743:

> Nor should we pass over in silence what is spread abroad through the lands of the Germans, a statement, namely, that we have been unable to discover in the archives of our church. Nevertheless we learn from men who come from Germany that the holy Pope Gregory [I] when, through the grace of God, he enlightened them in the Christian religion, granted them permission to marry within the fourth degree. [Zacharias made no allusion to the third.] Now within the degrees of blood kinship such marriages are not permissible to Christians. Nevertheless we are prepared to believe that he allowed this because they were as yet uncivilised [*rudi*] and were being invited to the faith; although, as we said above, we have been unable to discover this writing.

Gregory I's liberal ruling, in short, is another example of the missionary tactics of charitable accommodation.

These were not abstract discussions between clerical intellectuals cut off from the 'real' world. The questions put by Augustine, Boniface and others arose from genuine difficulties encountered in the mission field. The plentiful material on marital problems of one sort or another which survives in the penitential and the civil legislation of the period is a forcible reminder of the same truth. The sad fate of St Kilian, if the hagiographical account is to be trusted, may remind us also that these could be hazardous waters for the missionary to enter: martyred for opposing the marriage of Duke Gozbert of Thuringia to his brother's widow. The correspondence of Boniface permits us to glimpse a case which he encountered in Germany. A certain layman of high rank, a 'great personage' (*magnae personae*) wished to marry the widow of his uncle. We may legitimately assume, I think, that the union of these two persons would have been one with important implications for the alliance and solidarity and probably the wealth of two aristocratic clans, and perhaps with further implications for the structures of power and patronage in the area, presumed to have been somewhere in Germany, where they lived. In short, there was a lot riding on it. But there were difficulties. First, the couple were consanguineous in that they shared a common ancestry at no very remote remove, their great-grandparents. Second, the woman had been married before to her cousin (*consobrinus*, a term which does not indicate the precise degree of cousinage), whom she had deserted while he was yet living. Third, before her first marriage the woman had made a vow of chastity and been veiled as a nun, but had then thrown over the religious life in order to get married. That was the position, and the man was now claiming that Pope Gregory 'of blessed memory' – that is, almost certainly the recently deceased Gregory III (731–41) – had given him permission to marry the woman. Was there any truth in this? Boniface demanded of Pope Zacharias. In his reply the pope vigorously denied that any such permission had been given and urged Boniface to do everything in his power to prevent the marriage going ahead. At which point in this gripping drama of passion among the eighth-century German aristocracy our trail goes cold. We shall never know how the story ended.

A coherent body of ecclesiastical law relating to marriage was slow to emerge. It was not until the great age of medieval theology and canon law in the twelfth and thirteenth centuries that it took on a definitive shape. Its enforcement proved an entirely different matter. It could be argued that marriage is the area of human life which has proved most resistant to clerical manipulation. We can see that attempted manipulation beginning, among the barbarians, in the missionary epoch of Augustine and Boniface. We can also see diversity of reaction to problems, and sometimes well-intentioned experiments in coming to terms with what was unfamiliar. In these respects marriage may be taken as typical among the varied enterprise of 'rising by steps', as Pope Gregory the Great had put it. Typical the optimism, typical the adaptations, typical the intractability. We still call the middle day of the week after Woden. And as Sir Thomas Browne knew, some of us – not just 'the credulous and feminine party' – still mutter 'One for sorrow . . .' when we see a magpie.

   This may be to sound too dismissive a note at the end of a long chapter. The struggle to consolidate a Christian presence, to shape communities in a Christian mould, to discipline men and women and children to march to a Christian rhythm, was long and arduous. It displayed all sorts of qualities at different times and in diverse places. Here harsh, there pliant; now cruel, then tender; at some times ruthlessly, remorselessly disruptive, at others tolerant of existing custom and cherished habit. Its activists, the consolidators, were formidable personalities. Whatever we may feel about them as individuals, collectively they were forceful, courageous and persistent. They were also thoughtful, fertile of resource, positive in rising to the challenge of the unfamiliar. If they command nothing else, they command our respect.

CHAPTER NINE

Rival Monotheisms

My father was a Christian and my mother was a Jew.
The Prophet, may God bless him and grant him peace,
appeared to me in a dream and said, 'Don't be deluded
any longer by the faiths of your parents: follow my
religion!' So I became a Muslim.

ABU DULAF AL-KHAZRAJI, *c.* 960

RESISTANCE TO CHRISTIANITY is not a topic about which we should
expect much information to have survived. Our narrative sources –
composed, of course, by and for churchmen – are too assertively Christian to allow us more than the occasional and usually ambiguous hint
of resistance. One may suspect that the swaggering triumphalism of
their authors not infrequently masked anxieties; but it was a mask
which they rarely let slip. Furthermore, the glimpses of seeming opposition that we are permitted tend not to yield a straightforward
interpretation.

Consider, for example, an oft-quoted story which we owe to Bede's
Life of St Cuthbert.[1] The setting is the mouth of the river Tyne and
the date about 650. A party of monks from the monastery of South
Shields, on the south side of the river's estuary, were rafting downriver
bringing with them a consignment of timber for use at their monastery.
As they sought to bring the rafts to land a sudden squall of wind from
the west swept them on towards the North Sea. The incident was
witnessed by Cuthbert, who was standing on the north bank of the
river among what Bede called 'no small crowd of everyday people'
(*vulgaris turba non modica*). Let Bede now take up the story:

They began to jeer at the monks' manner of life, as if they were
deservedly suffering, because they rejected the common laws
[*communia iura*] and taught new and unknown rules of living.
Cuthbert put a stop to the insults of the mockers, saying,

285

'Brothers, what are you doing, speaking ill of those whom you see being carried away even now to destruction? Would it not be better and more kindly to pray to the Lord for their safety rather than to rejoice over their perils?' But they, boorish [*rustico*] in heart and in voice, grumbled against him and said, 'Let no man pray for them and may God have mercy upon none of them, for they have taken the old religious observances [*veteres culturas*] away from men and nobody knows how the new ones are to be observed.'

Cuthbert prayed; the wind changed quarter; and the monks came safe to land. The crowd blushed at their lack of faith (*infidelitate*).

There is no suggestion that these Northumbrian peasants were not Christians. Bede's verbal usage tells against it. He puts the word 'God' in the singular into their mouths, whereas for Bede pagans invariably worshipped 'gods' in the plural. However, they hanker after the *veteres culturas*, a phrase which can also perhaps be translated in words slightly less stilted than the literal ones I offer above: 'immemorial rituals', perhaps. The monks had taught them that their ancient routines of cultic observance were wrong but had not taught them new ones. The anxiety of these farmers, surely, was that neglect or ignorance of "correct ritual" might have the direst effects upon their crops and livestock. Is this a story about resistance to Christianity? Some historians have thought so. Bede's tale is about as close as one is ever likely to get to any evidence of resistance. However we may choose to judge it, it certainly pinpoints a delicate phase in the conversion process. *Hahaha...*

Or consider this story, committed to writing in Germany about a century after Bede's day. It occurs in the biography of St Leoba, kinswoman of Boniface and abbess of Tauberbischofsheim, who died in 779. The author, Rudolf of Fulda, composed it in about 835.[2]

> There was a certain poor little crippled girl, who sat near the gate of the monastery begging alms. Every day she received her food from the abbess's table, her clothing from the nuns and all other necessities from them; these were given to her from divine charity. It happened that after some time, deceived by the suggestions of the devil, she committed fornication, and when her appearance made it impossible for her to conceal that she had conceived a child she covered up her guilt by pretending to be ill. When her time came, she wrapped the child in swaddling clothes and cast it at night into a pool by the river which flowed through that

286

[handwritten margin note:] There were Eooyim?

[handwritten margin note:] Hahaha...

place. In this way she added crime to crime, for she not only followed fleshly sin by murder, but also combined murder with the poisoning of the water. When day dawned, another woman came to draw water and, seeing the corpse of the child, was struck with horror. Burning with womanly rage, she filled the whole village with her uncontrollable cries and reproached the holy nuns with these indignant words: 'Oh, what a chaste community! How admirable is the life of nuns, who beneath their veils give birth to children and exercise at one and the same time the function of mothers and priests, baptising those to whom they have given birth. For, fellow-citizens, you have drawn off this water to make a pool, not merely for the purpose of grinding corn, but unwittingly for a new and unheard of kind of baptism. Now go and ask those women, whom you compliment by calling them virgins, to remove this corpse from the river and make it fit for us to use again. Look for the one who is missing from the monastery and then you will find out who is responsible for this crime.' At these words the crowd was set in uproar and everybody, of whatever age or sex, ran in one great mass to see what had happened. As soon as they saw the corpse they denounced the crime and reviled the nuns. When the abbess heard the uproar and learned what was afoot she called the nuns together, told them the reason, and discovered that no one was absent except Agatha, who a few days before had been summoned to her parents' house on urgent business: but she had gone with full permission. A messenger was sent to her without delay to recall her to the monastery, as Leoba could not endure the accusation of so great a crime to hang over them.

When Agatha returned and heard of the deed that was charged against her she fell on her knees and gazed up to heaven, crying: 'Almighty God, who knowest all things before they come to pass, from whom nothing is hid and who hast delivered Susanna from false accusations when she trusted in Thee, show Thy mercy to this community gathered together in Thy name and let it not be besmirched by filthy rumours on account of my sins; but do Thou deign to unmask and make known for the praise and glory of Thy name the person who has committed this misdeed.'

On hearing this, the venerable superior, being assured of her innocence, ordered them all to go to the chapel and to stand with their arms extended in the form of a cross until each one of them had sung through the whole psalter, then three times each day, at Tierce, Sext and Nones, to go round the monastic buildings with the crucifix at their head, calling upon God to free them, in His mercy, from this accusation. When they had done this and they were going into the church at None, having completed two rounds, the blessed Leoba went straight to the altar and, standing before the cross, which was being prepared for the third procession, stretched out her hands towards heaven, and with tears and groans prayed, saying: 'O Lord Jesus Christ, king of virgins, lover of chastity, unconquerable God, manifest Thy power and deliver us from this charge, because the reproaches of those who reproached Thee have fallen upon us.' Immediately after she had said this, that wretched little woman, the dupe and tool of the devil, seemed to be surrounded by flames and, calling out the name of the abbess, confessed to the crime that she had committed. Then a great shout rose to heaven: the vast crowd was astonished at the miracle, the nuns began to weep with joy, and all of them with one voice gave expression to the merits of Leoba and of Christ our Saviour. So it came about that the reputation of the nuns, which the devil had tried to ruin by his sinister rumour, was greatly enhanced, and praise was showered on them in every place. But the wretched woman did not deserve to escape scot-free and for the rest of her life she remained in the power of the devil.

Strong stuff, and unappealing to a late twentieth-century taste. We may ask the same question of it as we asked of Bede's account of the rafts: is this a story about resistance to Christianity? In some ways it is. Not the least among the several interesting features of this pathetic and savage tale concerns the reaction of the women of the village of Tauberbischofsheim. In Rudolf's telling, they regarded the nuns as hypocrites who, so far from practising what they preached, indulged in sexual licence, infanticide and what today would be called environmental pollution. The story is evidence not of resistance to Christianity as such but of hostility to a certain kind of Christian 'specialists'. How widespread was such hostility to monks and nuns? Given the nature of our sources this is a question which it is impossible to answer with any confidence. But we shall see a little evidence from time to time of some of the forms which this hostility took.

So there are difficulties, unsurprisingly, about our evidence. Despite them one can distinguish different kinds of resistance to missionary effort. First, there might be out-and-out refusal to have anything to do with Christianity. Evidently, there did exist societies in early medieval

288

Europe upon which Christianity could make no impact at all. For example Amandus, though successful in Flanders, failed with the Slavs and the Basques. Willibrord, similarly successful in the Low Countries, could make no headway with the Danes. It is an important question, though not one which will be pursued here, why the Slavs were readier to accept Christianity in the ninth century than they had been in the seventh, or the Danes in the tenth than in the eighth. Second, there were circumstances in which the coming of Christianity was inextricably bound up with conquest by an aggressor, so that heathen resistance became equated with defence of liberty and land. The classic case in the early medieval period was that of Saxony during the reign of Charlemagne.

A third category of resistance might be called second thoughts. To give it its technical name this was apostasy, defection from Christianity after a previous acceptance of it. For example, following a visitation of the plague in the year 664 King Sigehere of Essex and his people apostasized and in Bede's words 'began to restore the derelict temples and to worship images, as if they could defend themselves from the plague by these means'.[3] Bishop Jaruman from neighbouring Mercia was sent in as a troubleshooter. It required all his skills (*multa sollertia*) to bring them back into the Christian fold. The link between natural disaster, in this instance plague, and apostasy is a striking one. It can be paralleled in other mission fields, both medieval and later. Did King Sigehere fear that he had incurred the wrath of his former gods by abandoning the *veteres culturas*? Bede does not tell us, but perhaps he did.

King Sigehere apostasized from Christian monotheism to traditional Germanic polytheism. A different form of apostasy, and a much more worrying one for ecclesiastical authority, was defection from Christianity to a rival monotheism, be it Judaism or Islam. Such shifts of religious allegiance will occupy us for much of the remainder of this chapter. These experiences of conversion present us with something different from what we have been examining in earlier chapters, and are offered here as a species of counterpoint to the main theme. The focus will be largely though not exclusively upon Spain, for the simple reason that the surviving sources cast welcome shafts of light upon the turbid confessional scene in that 'land of three religions'.

The strange story of the deacon Bodo-Eleazar takes us at once to the heart of Judaeo-Christian relations in early medieval Europe. Bodo was a native of Alemannia, to the east of the upper Rhine, scene of Pirmin's missionary labours in the eighth century. He was born, we may suppose, in the early years of the ninth century, almost certainly to a well-connected family. He received a good education, was ordained deacon and entered the service of Charlemagne's son, the Emperor Louis the Pious. He evidently made a good impression at court and Louis had a high regard for him. A glittering career seemed to be opening before him, as for other young men of similar background, training and talents. But then the wholly unexpected happened. This was a period when the Jews of Francia were enjoying a considerable degree of favour at the hands of their rulers and rising to positions of eminence in imperial service. A Jew named Isaac, for instance, had been employed by Charlemagne as his envoy to the court of the Abbasid caliph Haroun ar-Rashid in Baghdad. Bodo met these prominent court Jews and was by them persuaded of the truth of the Judaic faith. An open avowal of conversion by such a person as Bodo would have been out of the question, so a subterfuge strategy had to be devised. In the year 838 Bodo sought the permission of the emperor to undertake a pilgrimage to Rome. It was willingly granted, and in the following year Bodo set off. In the course of the journey Bodo made his conversion to Judaism public and then diverted from his itinerary and crossed the Pyrenees into Spain, where he was beyond the reach of Frankish power. There he settled at Saragossa, had himself circumcized, adopted the name Eleazar and married a Jewish girl. He also compelled his nephew, who had been travelling with him, to adopt Judaism too. The defection of Bodo gave rise to the utmost dismay in Frankish ruling circles. As a contemporary annalist noted, 'It was only with difficulty that the Emperor could be persuaded to believe this news at all, which clearly showed to everyone what a very distressing episode this was for the Emperor and Empress and indeed for all those redeemed through the grace of the Christian faith.'[4]

The new convert immediately entered into controversy with the Christian intellectuals of Spain, notably a certain Paul Alvar of Córdoba (the son, incidentally, of Jewish converts to Christianity). The letters that passed between Bodo and Paul were preserved in a single ninth-century manuscript, printed in the sixteenth century and subsequently lost. At some date a pious Christian hand mutilated the manuscript to erase Bodo's anti-Christian arguments but they can be reconstructed with plausibility from Paul Alvar's quotations and allusions.[5] The tone of the polemic changed as the correspondence progressed. In Paul's earlier letters the recipient was 'Dear Eleazar' but in a later one Bodo had become 'the enemy of God, prophaner of the holy law, violator of churches, thief of God's treasures'. In part perhaps this was because Bodo showed himself such a gifted controversialist. At the heart of his argument lay an attempt to rebut the claim of the Christian church to be the New Israel, heir to the promises made by God to the Israelites of the Old Testament. This had always been one of the most sensitive issues in Judaeo-Christian polemic, for it was here that the claims of Christianity were most vulnerable. Bodo's arguments were not original but it is clear that they stung. They involved the exegesis of certain key biblical texts, notably Genesis xlix.10, 'The sceptre shall not depart from Judah, nor a lawgiver from between his feet, until Shiloh come: and unto him shall the gathering of the people be.'[6] Bodo quoted lavishly from the prophet Ezekiel to predict the future triumph of the Jews. Like others before and since his day he incautiously scrutinized the prophecies of Daniel to forecast the date of the Messiah's coming and decided that it was imminent. The Messiah would come in the year 867. Well, replied Paul Alvar, if either of us is still alive in twenty-seven years' time, we shall see. In addition to these arguments based on biblical exegesis, Bodo twisted the doctrines of the Incarnation and the Trinity into grounds for the accusations that Christians reverenced an ordinary mortal man as divine and that they worshipped three gods, not one. These also, particularly the latter, were criticisms which touched perennially sensitive nerves.

Bodo did not confine himself to literary exchanges. According to reports which reached the court of Louis's son Charles the Bald, king of western Francia, a few years later, Bodo had sought to persuade the Muslim ruler of Spain, the Amir Abd-ar-Rahman II, to put pressure upon the Christians under his rule to abandon their faith. The annalist Prudentius had heard that Spanish Christians were to be forced to adopt 'the insanity of the Jews or the madness of the Saracens'.[7] Such a course was beyond the capabilities, and probably the wishes, of the amir. However, Bodo's threats were sufficiently alarming for the Christians of Spain to petition Charles and his bishops to take measures to have him silenced – though it is not clear what, if anything, Charles could have done.

At this point the evidence peters out and the trail goes cold. We know nothing further of Bodo and can only hope that he did not live to experience disappointment in 867. What we *can* do is to provide him with a setting. The essential element in its background was the existence of numerous Jewish communities in Mediterranean Europe and its hinterland. These communities were long established: for example, St Paul's expressed intention of going to Spain to preach the gospel is held to indicate that Jewish communities existed there by the middle years of the first century. The population of this extra-Palestinian Jewry was reinforced by the diaspora, or dispersion, which followed in the wake of the Roman destruction of Jerusalem in A.D. 70. Our mental picture of late antique and early medieval society must therefore include a scattered but in the aggregate numerous Jewish population in Asia Minor, Egypt, north Africa, Spain, southern Gaul, Italy and Greece. This population was not exclusively urban by any means. There is plentiful evidence for Jews who were, for example, farmers. Nor was it, so far as we can tell, segregated. Jews seem to have lived interspersed among their Christian neighbours. The ghetto was a later development, feature of an age from the eleventh century onwards which experienced a rising tide of Christian hostility to Jews.

Such hostility was not unknown in the late antique and early medi-eval period. To take an example at random, we hear in a letter of Pope Gregory I from the year 599 about the desecration of a synagogue at Caraglio in northern Italy: the pope intervened to insist that proper restitution be made. But hostility seems, by and large, to have been sporadic and unsystematic. 'By and large', because of one significant exception to this rule which we shall come to in a moment. It is important to be clear about its most important characteristic: this was a *religious* enmity. It was not, in these epochs, either social or racial or economic. It is properly designated, therefore, anti-Judaic feeling: the term 'anti-Semitic' carries a burden of misleading overtones. The religious problem was at heart a simple one. In Christian eyes the Jews, even though they were or had once been the chosen people of God, had failed to heed the message of the Old Testament, had failed to recognize the Messiah and had failed to grasp that the New Israel had been re-embodied under God's new covenant in the Christian church. (Interestingly, the accusation that the Jews had been responsible for the death of Jesus under Roman authority, though not unknown, was not one which received much emphasis in this early period. It would be given more prominence in a later age which would dwell more tenderly upon the humanity of the Son of God.) This threefold failure made Judaism culpable. It was infuriating to Christian thinkers that the Jews stubbornly refused to admit to failure. It was still more infuriating that they fought back with reasoned attacks upon the Christian claims, attacks which had the potential to be persuasive – as in Bodo's case.

This was the nub of the problem, that Jews might make – indeed that Jews were steadily making – converts among Christians. The Christian clergy who furnish our sources do not, of course, tell us what the attractions of Judaism for the Christian laity were; though they drop some oblique hints, as will appear presently. But they do make clear that conversions were occurring. Now Roman law, as codified under the Emperor Theodosius II in the 430s and inherited by the barbarian monarchies of the west, guaranteed the free practice of their faith to the Jews but forbade Jewish proselytizing among the Christian population. Confessional traffic should be one way only. Every encouragement was to be given to Jews to adopt Christianity. This 'encouragement' could take harsh forms. Instances of forcible baptism of Jews were not unknown, though disavowed by leading churchmen such as Augustine and Gregory the Great. The latter sent a sharp rebuke in 591 to the bishops of Arles and Marseilles for permitting the compulsory baptism of Jews in Provence: it was contrary to the laws both of God and of man. It was reported, though on poor authority, that the Frankish king Dagobert I ordered all the Jews in Gaul to be baptized. A more reliable authority, Isidore of Seville no less, testified that the Visigothic king Sisebut gave orders for the forcible baptism of all the Jews in his realm. This decree was never fully carried out, but even its partial implementation created all sorts of problems for the authorities in Spain in the shape of crypto-Jews and lapsed 'returnees' from Christianity to Judaism.

It is Visigothic Spain which forms the exception mentioned above. In the course of the seventh century, church and state in Spain cooperated in systematic and relentless attacks upon Judaism. This is not the place to examine these in detail, but a light sketch is necessary. After the opening salvoes fired by Sisebut in about 620 we find King Recceswinth between 649 and 654 forbidding the celebration of the Passover, the observance of dietary laws and the performance of Jewish marriage ceremonies. He also prohibited Jews from initiating legal actions against Christians and from giving evidence against them in court. King Ervig (680–87) went further down the same road. Henceforward Jews were not to be allowed to observe their sabbath. On the other hand they were to be compelled to abstain from work on Christian Sundays and other holy days. These and other rulings were to be enforced by draconian monetary and corporal punishments. It was evidently the desire of the legislators to root out Judaic observances altogether from the Visigothic kingdom. Finally, in 694, King Egica gave orders for the entire Jewish population of Spain to be enslaved and their property to be forfeit to the crown. We can hardly doubt that the Jews of Spain looked upon the Arab conquerors of the Visigothic kingdom in the early eighth century as liberators.

The frantic and savage anti-Judaic persecutions undertaken by Visigothic kings and bishops in the seventh century have never been satisfactorily explained. As far as we know – and it's not far – the Jewish population of Spain was not in any exceptional way numerous or wealthy or influential. Yet the surviving texts of royal and ecclesiastical legislation against the Jews repeatedly expressed apprehension. Judaism was perceived as presenting some sort of threat to Christianity. It would be unwise to dismiss this perception as mere paranoia. It fits with the apprehensions about the leaching away of Christian vitality through conversions – whatever the law might say – to Judaism. A watchful eye was kept for anything that might smack of a Judaizing tendency. For example, we find Pope Gregory writing to the citizens of Rome in 602 prohibiting the observance of a Saturday sabbath after the example of 'the perfidy of the Jews'.[8] In Rome of all places! the enemy was within the very gates. As we might expect, eyes were particularly watchful and sanctions particularly drastic in Spain. King Chindaswinth (642–53) decreed the death penalty for Christians who adopted Jewish rites. A hint that these were not groundless fears may be picked up in the anti-Judaic polemic of the period. In 686 Archbishop Julian of Toledo, the leader of the Spanish church and one of the most notable scholars of that intellectually brilliant Spanish seventh century, wrote a work designed to counter Jewish claims that Jesus had not been the Messiah. It has been acutely observed by its most recent editor that 'the aim of the work is to convince the *Christian* reader [my italics] of the falsity of the Jewish claims'.[9] If Christians needed to be headed off from Judaism, it was surely because numbers of them were indeed drifting in that direction. Given the legal penalties in Spain for doing so, the fact seems almost incredible: but it is what the evidence suggests. These apprehensions continued in the era after the Islamic conquest of Spain, when churchmen no longer had the legal sanctions of a persecuting state at their beck and call. In about 730 the archdeacon of Toledo, Evantius, wrote a letter rebuking the Christians of Saragossa who feared 'with the Jews' that they would be ritually polluted by eating certain types of meat. In 764 Bishop Felix of Córdoba rebuked Christians who wanted to share fast-days with the Jews: they must 'leave off Judaizing', he warned them.[10]

These fears were not confined to popes and Spanish clergy. Agobard, archbishop of Lyons from 816 to 840, wrote several pamphlets which leave one in no doubt concerning his anxieties about Jewish proselytizing among Christians. He was worried about the presence of influential Jews at the imperial court. Bodo's conversion would show how right he was. He was worried about Jewish proselytizing in southern Gaul, especially in the regions of Narbonne and his own Lyons. It was not just an urban problem. As he pointed out in a letter to Archbishop Nebridius of Narbonne, peasants were being seduced into Judaism as well as townspeople. He was worried about the vulnerability of Christians who were exposed to Judaic practices in the course of everyday life: Christian servants in Jewish households, Christian friends and neighbours who attended Jewish dinner-parties or weddings. Agobard's successor at Lyons, Amolus, shared these apprehensions. In his *Liber contra Judeos* dedicated to King Charles the Bald he let slip the revealing fact that Christians in Lyons were attending synagogues instead of churches because the Jewish rabbis 'preach better than our priests'.[11] Both Agobard and Amolus were dismayed by the *Toledoth Yeshu*, a sort of parody of the gospels which was destined to have a singularly long life as a piece of anti-Christian mockery. In this curious text Jesus is demoted to being a gifted Jewish schoolmaster, no more and no less. 'Hosanna to the son of David' becomes a children's singsong which his pupils chant to him in class. One of his pupils is so stupid that Jesus nicknames him 'Rock'. Eventually unmasked as a magician, the schoolmaster is hanged. His pupils conceal the corpse in an aqueduct. Floods occur during the night, bearing the body away into oblivion. The loyal pupils claim that their master has risen from the dead. And so on: lively knockabout stuff, but obviously distasteful and worrying to high-minded churchmen.

Amolus also tells us of Jews who took jobs as tax-collectors in remote country districts. There they would make converts to Judaism by offering remissions to 'poor and ignorant' Christians who could not afford to pay their taxes. It is a revealing glimpse of the grimness of peasant life in the ninth-century Lyonnais. Amolus had learned about this practice from Jews 'who come over from their error to Christianity'. So there was evidently traffic in both directions. Agobard had sponsored missions to the Jews in Lyons. His too-zealous methods had provoked the Jewish community there to appeal to the Emperor Louis. And Louis had upheld their complaint, much to Agobard's angry embarrassment. The writings of Agobard and Amolus leave one with a sense of a certain fluidity of religious allegiance, of a degree of interpenetration between Judaism and Christianity in southern Gaul in the ninth century. They were worried that ordinary Christians – that vast majority who were *illiterati*, 'unlearned' – were failing to distinguish clearly between Christianity and Judaism. This may come as a surprise to readers who think that the two faiths have always been as different as chalk and cheese. Their anxiety offers us tantalizing hints about the laity's perceptions of religious faith and observance.

When the Jews of Lyons complained to the emperor about Archbishop Agobard we may presume that they addressed themselves in the first instance to the Jews who were attached to the imperial court, the sort of people who had converted Bodo. We get occasional glimpses of them. One has already been mentioned, the Jew Isaac employed by Charlemagne as an ambassador; the Emperor Charles the Bald had a Jewish physician named Zedekiah. These were very exalted people, close to the centre of power, well placed to act as lobbyists on behalf of local petitioners like the Jews of Lyons. These were patterns which were repeated elsewhere. In Muslim Spain, for example – or al-Andalus, as the Arabs called it – we encounter in the middle years of the tenth century the remarkable figure of Hasday ibn Shaprut. He was physician to the caliph of Córdoba, Abd-ar-Rahman III, and a prominent figure at court. He treated the Christian king Sancho the Fat of León for obesity. He was a scholar and a patron of poets. His network of contacts was very extensive. The Jewish doctor to the ruler of Egypt dedicated a medical treatise to him. He was a benefactor of the rabbinic academies of Iraq, which at that date were the most important centres of Talmudic scholarship and piety in the Judaic world. It is probable though not certain that he corresponded with the ruler of the Khazars of the southern Russian steppe who had adopted Judaism in the ninth century. It was widespread contact-networks such as this which had scared the Visigothic kings in the seventh century and rendered Bodo's defection so shaming in the ninth. That Christian discomfiture in the Frankish empire might be the subject of hilarity among the *gaon* of the academies in Baghdad was an unsettling thought.

The conversion of the Khazars, and of some among the Berber tribes of north Africa, to Judaism showed that Jews, like Christians, could make mass-conversions among barbarians. But the Khazars mattered to the Jews of the diaspora for a very much more important reason: they could point to the ruler of the Khazars as a Jewish king. This enabled them to uphold the promise of Genesis xlix.10: there still *was* a sceptre in Judah; therefore the Messiah had not yet come. It was a useful debating point in polemic with Christians, whose argument was that Jewish kingship had come to an end in the lifetime of Jesus the Messiah. There were other candidates for this Jewish royalty as the years passed. One at least was illusory, the claim that a prince of the house of David had been established in Narbonne by Charlemagne! This yarn did not appear before the twelfth century, and most – though not quite all[12] – historians are agreed that it was a fantasy. Yet truth has a way of being even stranger than fiction. It was reported of Raynard II, a French feudal baron who was count of Sens between 1012 and 1055, that 'so much did he admire the wicked customs of the Jews that he ordered his whole entourage to place before his name the title King of the Jews.'[13] Ludicrous, we might be tempted to think, but we should be wrong. Churchmen of the day took it seriously. It was, seemingly, Count Raynard's bizarre claim that impelled Bishop Fulbert of Chartres, the leading intellectual light of his day in northern France, to compose a treatise *Adversus Judeos* in which he rehearsed all the old arguments to counter Judaic interpretations of Genesis xlix.10.

The age of Fulbert of Chartres, who died in 1028, looks similar to that of Agobard in respect of the relations between Christians and Jews. In many ways the two epochs were similar, though as we shall see later there were signs of a shift in attitudes in the eleventh century which heralded an era of harsher prejudices. Historians of assumptions and mentalities, especially of medieval assumptions and mentalities, must not expect suddenness in the changes they try to chart. The old and well-tried can overlap and co-exist with the new and as yet uncertain. Thus it is that the tenth and eleventh centuries continued to display phenomena with which the period of Bodo and Agobard has made us familiar. There was further two-way traffic across the confessional divide. We encounter a certain Habaz, for example, 'once a Jew but later a Christian and a monk', in a monastery in northern Spain in the year 905.[14] Theodelinus, a notable abbot of Maillezais in the Vendée in the early eleventh century, was a convert from Judaism. So was Paul, a con-man who claimed to be able to turn copper into gold who attached himself to the retinue of Archbishop Adalbert of Bremen in about 1050. In about 1010 a certain Vecelinus, a clerk in the employ of the royal family of Germany – and therefore a figure, like Bodo, of some weight – renounced Christianity for Judaism. By far the most distinguished convert in the same direction was a high-ranking prince of the church, Andrew, archbishop of Bari in southern Italy, who declared himself a Jew in the course of a visit to Constantinople in about 1066 and subsequently fled to Egypt. We know this from a fragmentary text which survived in Cairo, apparently an autobiographical composition by Andrew himself. Christian sources maintained an absolute silence on the subject of his defection; surely the silence of consternation.

Archbishop Andrew's was clearly a *cause célèbre*, and one that we should dearly like to know more about. The shifts of confessional allegiance by lesser persons, whether respectable Leonese monks or shady alchemists in north Germany, seem to have been not uncommon. They may have been even more common, almost routine indeed, among that overwhelming proportion of the population of whose thoughts and hopes and fears we know nothing at all. It is characteristic of this age that there survives a fair amount of evidence for the harmonious co-operation of Christian and Jew. We can see this in the field of scholarship. Paul Alvar had had to concede to Bodo that Christians were ignorant of Hebrew – though this did not stop his asserting that the Jews had doctored their holy books to remove all testimony of Christ. Christian scholars who needed to elucidate Hebrew writings had to seek out Jews who could help them. Rabanus Maurus of Fulda did this when preparing his biblical commentaries, and Agobard learned some Hebrew from the Jews of Lyons. When a Byzantine embassy brought a sumptuous manuscript of the work of the first-century pharmacologist Dioscorides to the court of Córdoba in 949 the text was studied by an interdenominational committee of scholars consisting of a Greek monk, a Sicilian with a knowledge of

Greek, a group of native Spanish-Islamic scholars and our acquaintance the Jew Hasday ibn Shaprut. The renowned French scholar Gerbert of Aurillac – later Pope Sylvester II (999–1003) and the revered teacher of Fulbert of Chartres – seems to have had contact with Jewish mathematicians while he studied in Catalonia in the 960s. A century later the monk Sigebert of Gembloux, teaching at Metz, sought the assistance of the local Jewish scholars in elucidating the biblical text. The Englishman Stephen Harding, first abbot of Cîteaux, did likewise in seeking to establish a more accurate text of the Old Testament in the late eleventh century.

Another area of co-operation was that which may broadly be described as business.[15] We have evidence that a tenth-century archbishop of Narbonne employed two Jews, business partners, to manage the financial affairs of his see; their responsibilities including lending his money out at interest. If this is not quite what we might have expected, perhaps it is simply that our expectations require adjustment. Another intriguing case, from the eleventh century, is that of a Jew who sought papal assistance, no less, in bringing pressure to bear upon a bishop to get him to coerce Christian debtors into repaying their Jewish creditors. We hear of a Jewish merchant in eleventh-century France who dealt in luxury textiles and used a Christian church as a warehouse in which to keep his stock. Perhaps among his clients was the Christian noblewoman, possibly from the Rhineland, who commissioned a Jewish merchant to buy her a dress 'from overseas' valued at the very high price of thirty *solidi* (many hundreds of pounds in today's values): the likelihood is that the dress was made of silk from the Byzantine empire or some part of the Islamic world. We hear of a nobleman from the same area who commissioned a Jewish merchant to acquire a fox-pelt for making into a hat. We are not told what sort of fox, but may presume that it was no ordinary one. Possibly it was the white fox, whose fur was greatly prized. If so, it would have had to be imported from a long way away, northern Scandinavia or Russia.

That Rhineland aristocrats in the eleventh century could request Jewish businessmen to buy clothing in the Byzantine or Islamic worlds and furs which came ultimately from trappers in western Siberia suggests extensive Jewish trading networks. That they were indeed as far-flung as the intellectual contacts of a Hasday ibn Shaprut is shown by the business archive of Nahray ibn Nissim. Nahray was a Tunisian Jew settled in Egypt whose adult life fell in the second half of the eleventh century. A many-sided man, he was a trader, banker, scholar and devout communal leader. His business correspondence shows that from Egypt he traded in – among much else – tin from Spain, coral from the western Mediterranean, antimony from Morocco, textiles from Armenia, hazelnuts from Syria, spikenard from Nepal and rhubarb from western China or Tibet. In other words, his commercial operations embraced the entire Old World. His slightly younger near contemporary Isaac Nisaburi, that is Isaac of Nishapur, was a Persian-Jewish merchant resident in Alexandria. He traded, among other things, in Indian brazilwood, Spanish silk and Moroccan ambergis.

Their widespread network of contacts made the Jews, in Christian eyes, at once attractive and slightly sinister: attractive as the purveyors of exotic goods and exotic learning, sinister in the sense of being mysterious and unamenable to control. Rumours of distant kings and messianic expectations made Christian authorities uncomfortable. Discomfort was indeed the keynote in Christian relations with Judaism during the early Middle Ages. Twin but divergent shoots from the same stock, closely intertwined but unable ever to embrace, Christians and Jews seemed destined to experience that very worst form of enmity on which early medieval poetic sensibilities dwelt with darkest brooding, dissension within the kin.

The conversions from Judaism to Christianity, or vice-versa, which have been discussed were those of individuals. In this they differed from most, though not all, of the conversions to Christianity examined in earlier chapters. The phenomenon of conversion for Bodo was different from what it had been for, let us say, the warriors of Clovis or Edwin. Bodo, Vecelinus and Andrew of Bari were educated, thoughtful individuals who became convinced of the claims of the Judaic faith. Of course, there were 'group-conversions' to Judaism, among the Khazars or the Berbers, just as there were to Christianity. Equally obvious, there were occasions of accepting Judaism which had nothing to do with calm reflection; among the tax-burdened peasantry of the Lyonnais, or for an isolated Christian servant-girl in a Jewish household, or for Bodo's luckless nephew. The same could be said of conversions in the other direction. There was nothing calm or reflective about the passage to Christianity of King Sisebut's Jewish subjects. However, by and large there is fairly abundant evidence for voluntary and individual crossing of the religious divide between church and synagogue. Part of the reason for this must surely lie in the generally – if not

invariably – urban setting of such switches of allegiance.* It is a socio-
logical truism that the urban (or even quasi-urban) environment acts
as a solvent upon all sorts of loyalties and bondings which remain firm
in a rural setting – of family, neighbourhood, dress, speech, diet,
routines, habits of mind, and religious allegiance. Which is only to
make the probably obvious point that in the ninth or tenth centuries
it was easier to become a Jew in Lyons or Narbonne or Naples or
Toledo than it was in Pictland or Ulster.

The social environment of a town may have played what some would
term a 'facilitating' or 'enabling' role in conversion from Christianity
to Judaism. More important, one may suspect, were religious precon-
ceptions and expectations. These are bound to be difficult to recover
– difficult enough from the nineteenth century, let alone the ninth –
but one significant clue is afforded in the writings of Agobard and
Amolus. Agobard's astonishing admission that people found it difficult
to distinguish clearly between Judaism and Christianity prompts all
sorts of speculation about the manner in which the Christian faith was
presented to the laity. The average Christian layman or laywoman, we
should remember, was illiterate or of very restricted literacy. Even for
those who could read, access to books was so rare as to be almost
non-existent. Religious instruction, if any, came from a priesthood of
whose teaching capacities the Carolingian reformers had a uniformly
low opinion. Despite the obvious differences, there was much that
must have looked familiar about Judaic observances: a weekly holy
day, worship comprising liturgy, prayers, hymns and sermons, sacred
scriptures to a degree shared with the Christians, comparable exhortations and prohibitions. Above all, there was a common and a single
God. For early medieval churchmen in western Christendom the real
enemy was paganism, and paganism's defining characteristic was polytheism: a plurality of gods. Thus the principal emphasis of clerical
teaching was upon the singleness of the divine. Now of course it is
true that the doctrines of the Trinity and the Incarnation were taught,
fundamental as they are to the Christian faith. What sense otherwise
for Bodo to criticize them or for the author of the *Toledoth Yeshu* to
mock them? Nevertheless, one may suspect that during this period the

---

* In this context we may permit ourselves to consider a royal court (Bodo, Vecelinus)
a quasi-urban environment; though some readers might suspect here one of the slippery
deviations of which early medievalists have been known to be accused.

prime stress was on God's oneness. So when a Christian was invited by a Jewish friend to the local synagogue – there were at least twelve to choose from in eleventh-century Toledo – to hear one of those sermons which Amolus had to admit were so good, he would encounter a monotheism that was familiar.

A noted scholar of Old English literature, John Clark Hall, once observed that there was nothing in the epic *Beowulf* which might offend a pious Jew. The remark was made in the context of discussion about the presence or absence of Christian elements in that Old English epic. Scholars are unanimous today that *Beowulf* is permeated by Christianity; yet it was a Christianity, as Clark Hall's judgement showed, of a somewhat limited kind. The poem was composed for a primary audience of early medieval Germanic Christian warrior-aristocrats; people not unlike Bodo's kinsfolk in Alemannia, perhaps. Such Christians might have found it easier than we should expect to slip across the frontier that divided Christianity from Judaism.

Paul Alvar of Córdoba, Bodo's Christian opponent in the early 840s, was engaged a few years later in a different sort of religious controversy, one in which the enemy was not Judaism but Islam. During the 850s a number of Christians in Córdoba publicly denounced Islam and suffered the full penalty which Islamic law exacts for such insults, namely death. Paul knew several of those involved in this so-called 'martyr movement'. In particular he was a friend of the priest Eulogius, a leading member of the Christian community of Córdoba, historian of many of the martyrs in his work *Memoriale Sanctorum* (*In Memory of the Saints*), who was himself executed by the Muslim authorities in 859. Paul composed a *Vita* of Eulogius to commemorate his friend. He also wrote a work entitled *Indiculus Luminosus* (*The Shining Catalogue*), which was partially devoted to anti-Islamic polemic, partially to a defence of the martyrs against Christian critics who asserted that they had not been genuine martyrs on the grounds that they had voluntarily sought their own deaths.

These were troubled waters. As with Bodo, so with the Córdoba martyrs we must attempt to furnish a context. The immediate setting lies in Spain, but beyond it there looms the transformation of the Mediterranean world wrought by the rise of Islam in the seventh century. By the time of his death in 632 Muhammad the Prophet had established a community or people (*umma*) of believers in western

Arabia united in their submission (*islam*) to the will of the one and only God. Muhammad had been called to proclaim this unflinching monotheism in a series of visions and messages which he began to experience in middle life from about the year 610. The written record of these revelations would later constitute the text of Islam's holy book, the Koran. The teaching of the Koran laid five fundamental requirements upon those called *muslims* ('those who have submitted') which are known as the five 'pillars of Islam'. These were and are the affirmation of God and of His Messenger Muhammad; daily prayer at five stipulated times; fasting during the daylight hours in the holy month of Ramadan; almsgiving on a stipulated scale; and pilgrimage to Mecca at least once in a lifetime. Rituals were devised to accompany the performance of these duties, and a nucleus of commands and prohibitions as a guide for the devout to the way they should live their lives. Authority within the *umma* was indivisible: there was no priesthood in Islam, no distinction between 'church' and 'state'. Every Muslim was required to propagate the faith by means of *jihad*. The word docs not mean 'holy war', though it is often so translated. It means 'effort' or 'struggle' (in the way of Islam) against unbelievers. Such effort might take violent form but need not do so. Unbelievers were identified as polytheists and idolaters. Jews and Christians, fellow monotheists though not vouchsafed the final fullness of God's revelation through Muhammad, were specifically exempted from the attentions of *jihad*-doers. 'Peoples of the Book', they and their religious observances were to be respected.

Arabian society in Muhammad's day was, as it had always been, what anthropologists call 'segmentary'. Warfare between different tribes was the norm, its prizes livestock, women, slaves, merchandise and honour. There was no supra-tribal authority, though certain places at certain times might enjoy the precarious and temporary authority of sanctuary. Muhammad's birthplace Mecca was one such, a holy place for all the Arabs since time immemorial, the goal of pilgrimage, a place therefore of peace, of some modest trade, and of a settled semi-urban way of life in an Arab society which was still largely nomadic and pastoral. The creation of Muhammad's *umma* provided a principle of unity – *islam* – which was bigger than the tribe. Furthermore, it compelled the Arabs to turn their attentions elsewhere. Once all the inhabitants of Arabia had adopted Islam they could no longer raid one another because Muslim was not permitted to fight against Muslim. After

Muhammad's death, perhaps even before it, Arab armies began to strike into the settled lands bordering the eastern Mediterranean.

What ensued is well known and well documented but remains inexplicable: 'one of the most profoundly unintelligible series of events in history', in the words of a distinguished British historian, Fergus Millar. Within the next twenty years Islamic dominion had been imposed upon the provinces of the eastern Roman empire from Egypt to Syria and upon the entire Persian empire which then comprised approximately today's Iraq and Iran. The momentum of Islamic expansion appeared unstoppable. By 720 Islamic rule extended from the Pyrenees to the Punjab, from the Atlantic coast of Morocco to the mountains of the Hindu Kush and the shores of the Aral Sea. Raids were being launched into Gaul and against Sicily. Arab merchants were nosing their way down the east coast of Africa and across the Caspian to the great northern highway of the Volga.

The emergence, over against Christendom, of a 'second world' of Islamic faith and culture is a good deal easier for the modern historian to grasp and to delineate than it was for those who lived through the process in the seventh, eighth and ninth centuries. For a start, Christian observers were unaware that a new religion had appeared on the scene. To comment that they were 'unaware' is to risk caricaturing them as myopic dimwits. It would be more accurate to state that the idea of a 'new religion' was, strictly and literally speaking, unthinkable for the Christian intellectual of those times. You can only entertain the notion of a 'new religion' if you are accustomed to religious pluralism. We are so accustomed, but the people of the early Middle Ages were not. For them there was one faith, and that the Christian faith. Peoples who were not yet Christian posed no *intellectual* challenge. The Jews had been offered the faith but had rejected it. They would suffer for their rejection in the hereafter. Numerous pagans existed, but as the in-gathering of the nations proceeded along the lines foretold in the Bible they would all be duly shepherded into the Christian fold. Finally there were the deviants from Christianity, the heretics. But these too were destined to pass away just as, for example, the German barbarians had abandoned Arianism and become good Catholics. Islam was most plausibly interpreted as a Christian heresy. Manifestly it shared much with Christianity – monotheism, holy places like Jerusalem, veneration for patriarchs and prophets such as Abraham or Elijah, reverence for the Virgin Mary. And yet Islam had perverted Christianity by offering a parody of holy scripture, by denying Incarnation and Resurrection and Trinity, by exalting its own pseudo-prophet, by making war on Christians and seizing their holiest places. Pondering the matter, Christian scholars decided that they could identify the antecedents of Islam in the Bible. The Arabs were descended from Ishmael, the son of Abraham by his concubine Hagar, Ishmael the wild man, 'his hand against every man and every man's hand against him', who would 'live at odds with all his kinsmen' (Genesis xvi.12). (It is for this reason that Muslims were often referred to in medieval Christian sources as 'Hagarenes' or 'Ishmaelites'.) In short, Christian churchmen were able neatly to docket and explain Islam to their satisfaction. Further enquiries were unnecessary.

In accordance with Koranic precept Christians and Jews were tolerated provided they submitted peacefully to the imposition of Islamic dominion. We possess the occasional example of a capitulation treaty. In south-eastern Spain, for instance, a certain Theodemir formally submitted to the Islamic conquerors by a treaty dated 5 April 713. He was evidently a powerful local magnate, the lord of Alicante and of six other named towns near by. Theodemir and his people were guaranteed their safety and the free exercise of their religion in return for loyalty and the annual payment of tribute in money and in kind. Some religious groups found a welcome respite under Islamic rule from persecutions that they had experienced under a previous Christian dispensation. Such were the Jews of Spain, such too the Monophysite heretics of Egypt, better known as the Copts. Toleration was accompanied by some discriminatory measures. Christians and Jews had to pay a poll tax to their new masters. Christians were not allowed to build new churches or to indulge in religious practices which were obtrusive such as ringing bells or singing loud chants. They were strictly forbidden to show disrespect for Islam or to attempt to convert Muslims to Christianity. Sexual relations between a Christian man and a Muslim woman were forbidden. Christians were not allowed to possess various items of military equipment. They were to identify themselves as Christians by wearing a distinctive type of belt called a *zunnar*.

All in all, it looks a fairly comprehensive if not particularly burdensome package of discriminatory controls. However, there is reason to suppose that they were rarely if ever enforced in all their rigour during the early centuries of Islam. For a start, it was probably beyond the power of Islamic authorities in former Christian provinces to enforce

305

these rules strictly. It is easily forgotten that in such provinces the new Islamic masters were a small minority for some considerable time after the initial conquest. Take Spain by way of example: the so-called 'Islamic' conquest of the Visigothic kingdom between 711 and 718 was in actual fact a conquest by Berber armies led by a small Arab elite. The Arabs were fully Islamicized. But the pagan Berbers, who had only recently been conquered by the Arabs after a long and dogged resistance, were at best but lightly touched by Islam. The Spain of Theodemir was divided between populations of indigenous Christian Hispano-Romans, of semi-Islamic Berbers and of Islamic Arabs in proportions of perhaps something like 90%, 9% and 1% respectively.

The new ruling elites needed the administrative skills of their Christian subjects in order to keep the show on the road. In the period of the early Islamic conquests, roughly from Muhammad's day down to the middle of the eighth century, the Arabs had everything to learn about the culture of governing a settled society from the peoples they ruled. In this respect they were not unlike the Germanic kings who dismembered the western provinces of the Roman empire in the fifth century. When Boniface's kinsman Willibald, the later bishop of Eichstätt, was travelling in the east to visit the Holy Places in the 720s he and his companions were arrested on suspicion of being spies and imprisoned at Emesa (the modern Homs) in Syria. They were not ill-treated – they were befriended by a Christian merchant who sent food into the jail for them, and whose son was even allowed to take them out for a bath twice a week – but there seemed no prospect of their release. But then a fortunate encounter took place. They were visited in prison by a Spaniard who made careful enquiries about their story. This man had a brother who held high office at the court of the Umayyad caliph at Damascus as, in the words of the nun who took down Willibald's story many years later in Germany, 'chamberlain to the king of the Saracens'.[16] The brother used his exalted connections at the caliphal court to bring about the prisoners' release. We have no idea who these Spanish brothers were nor of the train of events which had brought them from Spain to Syria. What is remarkable is that within a very few years of the conquest of their country one of them had risen to influential rank in the directing circles of the Islamic *umma*. It was not unknown for Christian churchmen, too, to be so employed. The patriarchs of Alexandria were sent on diplomatic missions by their Islamic masters, were sometimes consulted for political advice and on at least one occasion – scarcely credible though it may seem – were solicited for their prayers. Such relationships as these could not easily co-exist with a rigorous enforcement of Islamic law. Instead, what we seem to witness in the early period after the irruption of Islam into the Christian Mediterranean world is a degree of co-existence of the two faiths; uneasy no doubt, but co-existence none the less.

Such discrimination as there was could be escaped by Christians who embraced Islam. But there was a built-in fiscal disincentive for the Muslim authorities to encourage conversion. Christians who adopted Islam ceased to pay the poll tax. The more conversions, the less money the authorities could raise in tax. Contrary to the popular western image, early medieval Islam was not on the whole a proselytizing faith. Nor, as already indicated, were the laws discriminating against Christians consistently enforced. We have evidence to this effect in the writings of Eulogius and Paul Alvar of Córdoba. For example, the monastery of Tabanos, which we shall see again, was founded in about 840 despite the ban on the building of new Christian churches; and it was a mere seven miles from the amir's palace in Córdoba, the centre of Muslim authority in the Iberian peninsula. It is further notable that Eulogius mentions this quite casually, in passing. Evidently the establishment of a new Christian monastic community in the middle years of the ninth century was no matter for remark.

Nevertheless, the fact is that throughout the formerly Christian lands which came under Islamic rule there did occur gradual but in the long term extremely numerous conversions from Christianity to Islam. Analysis of the patterns of name-giving in the families whose geneal-ogies were recorded in Islamic biographical dictionaries has made it possible to work out the rough tempo of conversion in the early Islamic world.[17] The graph or curve of conversion, consistently replicated on the basis of Persian, Syrian, Egyptian or Spanish genealogical materials, suggests that conversion to Islam from non-Islamic faiths was slow at first, then quickened, and finally flattened out, the whole process being spread over some three centuries. In the case of Spain only some 8% (of the final total Muslim population) had adopted Islam by about 800. This rose to about 12.5% by *c.* 850, thereafter doubled to 25% by *c.* 900, doubled again to 50% by *c.* 950, attained 75% in the early eleventh century and stood at 90% by about 1100. Certain cautions are needful. It is not claimed that these figures are accurate in detail;

they offer a rough approximation. It is important to stress that they are percentages (as stated above) 'of the final total Muslim population', not of the population of the Iberian peninsula as a whole. There always existed Christian communities or families or villages which never adopted Islam at all. We know very little about such enclaves, though it is to be hoped that with the aid of archaeology we might soon know more. On the analogy with comparable societies at other times and places we might guess that these Christian pockets could have been quite sizeable, especially in regions which were not easily penetrated by alien cultural influences, which lacked cultural porosity, such as remote rural or mountainous regions. Furthermore, the genealogical materials relate to families of note like those commemorated in al-Khushani's *History of the Judges of Córdoba*, composed in about 960. The affiliations revealed were those of the urban and the educated. Doubtless, too, we should make allowance for regional variations. The impulse to change religious allegiance might have been felt earlier and more strongly in the metropolis of Córdoba than in small provincial towns such as Lisbon or Segovia or Saragossa. There are parallels to be mulled over with the spread of early Christianity within the Roman empire.

What then were these impulses? How did conversion from Christianity to Islam take place in al-Andalus? These are questions to which it is difficult to find convincing answers. One way of approaching them is through the literature generated by the martyr movement of the 850s. The focus of Eulogius' *Memoriale Sanctorum* was, naturally, upon the *passiones*, the 'passions' or sufferings of the martyrs themselves. He was following literary models familiar to all Christian intellectuals, the accounts of the deaths of early Christian martyrs at the hands of Roman persecutors. However, in the course of introducing the martyrs to his readers he provided a certain amount of information about their background. The very casualness with which he furnished this information – as in the case of the monastery of Tabanos – is a guarantee of its reliability. These were matters ancillary to his main concern, mere backdrop to the tremendous drama of martyrdom.

What is really striking is the fluidity of religious affiliations revealed in these scene-setting narratives. Consider the case of Aurelius, executed at Córdoba in July 852, and his connections.[18] His father was a Muslim, his mother a Christian. Orphaned in infancy he was brought up a Christian by his *paternal* aunt: his Muslim father had a

308

Christian sister. Later on he was sent to other relatives, on which side of the family we do not know, to learn what Eulogius called *Arabica litteratura*, which is most plausibly understood as 'penmanship', letters in the most literal sense, rather than 'literature'; in other words, the calligraphic skills that he would need in later life, not impossibly for a career in Córdoba's expanding bureaucracy. These relations were Muslims, so Aurelius had to keep his Christian faith secret. When he grew up he was betrothed to a girl named Sabigotho. Her parents were Muslims: but her father had died while she was a baby and her widowed mother remarried, her second husband being a secret Christian who converted his new wife to his faith. So Sabigotho was baptized and brought up a Christian within the family, though to the outside world she, her mother and her stepfather presented themselves as Muslims. So when the secret Christian Aurelius was presented with his bride-to-be, a good Muslim girl chosen for him by his Muslim relatives, he discovered to his delight that she was a Christian too.

Aurelius had a relative named Felix. This man had been born to Christian parents, had adopted Islam, had subsequently decided that this had been a mistake and had switched back to Christianity: an intriguing spiritual odyssey. Naturally he had to conceal what in Muslim eyes was apostasy, so his Christian faith remained clandestine. He married a girl named Liliosa, who like Sabigotho was the daughter of secret Christians.

Aurelius and Sabigotho decided that they must make their Christian faith public. They knew well that this would leave them open to a charge of apostasy from Islam with all the terrible consequences that would follow. Together they embarked upon a course of self-denial and good works in preparation for what might lie ahead. Visiting and comforting captives was among these good works, and it was while prison-visiting that Sabigotho made a new friend, Flora, who was imprisoned at Córdoba.

Flora's story was particularly harrowing. She was another child of a mixed marriage, her father a Muslim and her mother a Christian. Her father died when she was very young and her mother brought her up a Christian. However, this had to be kept secret from her elder brother, who was an extremely zealous Muslim. Flora would later recall how difficult it had been to fast secretly in Lent. Eventually she ran away from home with her sister and the two young women took refuge in a nunnery. However, her brother tracked Flora down – we don't know what happened to the sister – and handed her over to the authorities as an apostate. She was imprisoned, which was when Sabigotho met her. Refusing to renounce Christianity, Flora was executed in November 851. Shortly after her death she appeared to Sabigotho in a vision, promising her that she too would win a martyr's crown. Sabigotho would know that the time for this was at hand, Flora told her, when a foreign monk should come to Spain to share her fate.

Aurelius and Sabigotho sold all their property and retired to the monastery of Tabanos. Felix and Liliosa did likewise. There they were joined by a visitor from abroad, a Palestinian monk named George who was an inmate of the famous monastery of St Saba, founded in the fifth century (and still there in the twentieth) between Jerusalem and the Dead Sea. Everything was happening as Flora had foretold. From Tabanos the five emerged publicly to denounce Islam and suffer the supreme penalty. They were executed in July 852.

The degree of intermingling between Christian and Muslim in the circles of Aurelius and his connections is something of which we should never have guessed had not the *Memoriale Sanctorum* of Eulogius come down to us. We should also bear in mind that we hear about these people only because they came to grief and suffered martyrdom. How large an allowance – and it is another of those unanswerable questions – should we make for families which did not come to grief? To put this in another way, supposing that Flora's brother had been a more pliant character, would we ever have heard of Flora? Quite probably not. If we had never heard of Flora we should never have been offered that tender and painful glimpse into the domestic arrangements of a ninth-century Córdoban household. It was difficult to fast secretly in Lent. Not impossible; just difficult. Evidently the strain upon Flora, and presumably not just during Lent, became so great that she could bear it no longer and fled. Flora took her religious duties as a Christian very seriously indeed. But many Christians did not. We have the explicit testimony of Eulogius and Paul Alvar to this effect. A large part of the psychological background to the martyr movement was anxiety about the Arabizing or Islamicizing tendencies evident among the Christian population of Córdoba. As far as we can tell, the diagnosis was correct. This was the period when the graph of the conversion-rate was beginning to curve steeply upwards. There are other indications, which we do not have the space to examine here, that Spain was becoming more Islamic in its culture in the middle years of the ninth century.[19] Córdoba's great mosque had just been enlarged by the Amir Abd-ar-Rahman II, to hold a swelling number of believers and to be an architectural assertion of Islamic faith. Eulogius and Paul were right to be worried as they contemplated their fellow Christians, especially the Christian youth, dressing like Arabs, chatting in Arabic, enjoying Arabic poetry, visiting Arabic baths. We must never forget the attractions of the street-life of a metropolis. A ninth-century cleric with the resoundingly Visigothic name of Leovigild composed a pamphlet about clerical costume, the *Liber de Habitu Clericorum*, because he was worried that the clergy were becoming neglectful about wearing proper clerical garb, with all the weight of its symbolism; a minor but telling indication of the way the wind was blowing. The more rigorous Christians felt themselves threatened. They were called to maintain purity and standards. We can recognize some perennially recurrent features of the culture of captive churches – anxiety, frustration, a sense of being at once betrayed by a world and chosen by God, a yearning to testify. These feelings were forced in the hothouse atmosphere of certain Christian communities, notably Tabanos, the monastery with which so many of the martyrs were connected. They were irrigated by exotic visitors like George of St Saba, who could tell of the sufferings of Christians elsewhere in the Islamic world and of their heroic steadfastness under persecution. Small wonder that an explosion should have occurred.

The explosion of the Córdoban martyr movement in the 850s was not welcome in other Christian quarters. Bishop Reccafred of Seville immediately condemned it on the grounds that voluntary martyrs were not true martyrs. Eulogius and Paul, as we have seen, composed the *Memoriale Sanctorum* and the *Indiculus Luminosus* precisely to answer such critics. In the eyes of such purists Reccafred and his like were traitors, Arabizers, collaborators. We do not possess Reccafred's answer to this accusation, but he might well have claimed – like the patriarchs of Alexandria – that prudent accommodation with the authorities protected his flock from molestation. These are cruel and all too familiar moral dilemmas.

Prudentius, surveying the worrying goings-on in his native Spain from the perspective of Troyes, had thought that Bodo the defector to Judaism wished to force the Christians of Spain into either Judaism or Islam. It is suggestive that Prudentius could lump together these two alternatives to Christianity: Anxieties about Arabizing must put us in mind of anxieties about Judaizing. Did Spanish Christians adequately distinguish between Christianity and Islam, or did they get muddled, just as Agobard's flock at Lyons got muddled between Christianity and Judaism? The monotheism of Islam could have been seen as seductive as the monotheism of Judaism. Faint evidence survives for what seems to have been lively theological discussion on the topic of the Trinity in Spain of the late eighth and early ninth century. Some of the participants drifted into heresy. One must not press the evidence too hard, especially when there is so little of it anyway, but it is striking that Trinitarian debate with ragged heterodox edges should have resurfaced after long lying dormant precisely in a part of Christendom which had fallen under the domination of the adherents of a rigidly unitarian monotheism. Was this completely coincidental?

A glimmer of an answer to this question comes to us from the other end of the Mediterranean.[20] Sometime about the middle of the ninth century, roughly contemporaneous with the Córdoban martyrs, an anonymous inmate of a Christian monastery in Palestine composed, in the Arabic language, a work of Christian apologetics which has been labelled the *Summa Theologiae Arabica*. One of the author's concerns was to castigate Christians whom he regarded as dissemblers or hypocrites. These were people who devised professions of Christian faith which were acceptable to Muslims, but only because they were, in the writer's judgement, evasive or ambiguous.

> By 'There is no god but God' they [Muslims] mean a god other than the Father, Son and Holy Spirit. According to what they say, 'God neither generates nor is generated' [*Koran* 112.3]. Nor according to what they say is the Holy Spirit anything other than a creature among creatures. So, their saying 'There is no god but God' is the same as what we say in words, but it is different in meaning . . . When we, the assembly of Christians, say 'There is no god but God', we mean a living God, comprising a living spirit which both enlivens and brings death; a mind which gives a determination to everything that it wills; and a word by which the being of everything comes about.

Now, the words 'There is no god but God' form, of course, the opening phrase of the Islamic *shahadah* or 'affirmation' of faith, the first and most fundamental of the Five Pillars. How remarkable to find this formula being employed by these 'dissembling' – or should we say 'convergent'? – Christians of ninth-century Palestine. The author of the *Summa* was in no doubt about the reasons for it. The formulation was acceptable to the Muslim masters of the dissemblers and, by implication, of worldly profit thereby to themselves. But purists like the author regarded them as traitors who implicitly denied the central Christian doctrines of the Trinity and the Incarnation. They were 'hypocrites among us, marked with our mark, standing in our congregation, contradicting our faith, forfeiters of themselves, who are Christians in name only. They disbelieve in their Lord and their God, Jesus Christ, the son of Mary; due to the calumny of strangers they disdain to describe for them any of their Lord's vicissitudes in the flesh.' This writer was not alone in his anxieties. The Syrian Christian theologian Theodore Abu Qurrah, writing in the early ninth century, attacked Christians who 'neglected the veneration of the holy icons' out of deference to Muslim sensibilities about idolatrous attempts to represent the holy. Further examples of similar anxiety could be quoted. These worries of the Palestinian and Syrian Christians bore resemblances to those of the Córdoban purists like Eulogius and Paul Alvar. And let us not forget George of St Saba – and other monastic travellers like him? – who linked the eastern and the western extremities of the Mediterranean. These were *shared* concerns.

Theodore and the anonymous author of the *Summa* wrote in Arabic. In Syria and Palestine it had displaced Greek as the language of theological discourse. It was to do the same in al-Andalus. Arabic became the language of daily life and therefore of worship for the 'Mozarabic' or 'Arabized' Christians of Spain who lived under Muslim rule. Arabic translations of the gospels and of a collection of ecclesiastical law have come down to us from tenth- and eleventh-century Spain. Other cultural elements were likely to wash in with language. The marking of time, for example: a Christian tombstone from near Carthage still bears an inscription in Latin of a sort, but uses Islamic alongside Christian chronology, being dated 'in the year of the infidels 397', that is A.D. 1007. One gets a sense of Christian communities quietly slipping into Islamic cultural garments. This is surely the answer to questions about the impulses which brought about conversion to Islam. We possess no evidence for what might be called 'conviction conversions', the sort of forces that impelled Bodo or Andrew of Bari into Judaism. Instead we must reckon with social pressures of great power but of near-invisibility in terms of the 'hard' evidence they have left of themselves for the historian. Marriage; neighbourhood; the peer pressure of youth; the need for a patron; business advantage; employment: these are the kind of pressures of which we must take account. They may not be noble, but they are certainly human. We may recall that back in the fourth century, when the Mediterranean world was still Roman, ecclesiastics had worried over the stampede into the Christian church of new believers whose motives for conversion were suspected of being shallow. Should we call them believers, or conformists? They were joining an 'establishment' which was perceived by them as 'here to stay'. So it was with the conversion to Islam in the former Christian provinces ranged from Syria to Spain.

The works of Eulogius and Paul Alvar come to us out of a historiographical void. The light that they shed is welcome, even though their polemical edge and their literary debts make them tricky to handle. But the light falls almost exclusively upon Córdoba.* And it is a light that fails us after the 850s. Thereafter we have no further detailed information about the Mozarabic Christian communities of al-Andalus and must be content with the few scraps of evidence that have come down to us. There were occasional further instances of 'martyrdom' – as, for example, that of Pelayo in 925, a young boy who had been sent to Córdoba as a hostage against the release of his uncle Bishop Hermogius of Tuy, who had been taken prisoner in a frontier battle. There is more plentiful evidence for pliant accommodation. In 953 an ambassador from the kingdom of Germany paid a visit to Córdoba where he met John, the bishop of the Christian community there. Bishop John outlined for his visitor's benefit the Mozarabic strategy of survival:

> Consider under what conditions we live. We have been driven to this by our sins, to be subjected to the rule of the pagans. We are forbidden by the apostle's words to resist the civil power. Only one cause for solace is left to us, that in the depths of such a great calamity they do not forbid us to observe our own customs ... For the time being, therefore, we keep the following counsel: that provided no harm is done to our religion, we obey them in all else, and do their commands in all that does not affect our faith.[21]

---

* One has to write 'almost exclusively' because one of the martyr narratives concerns the sisters Nunilo and Alodia, again children of a mixed marriage, from the northern town of Huesca in the foothills of the Pyrenees.

Communities that kept their heads down and gave no trouble would not be molested. A tombstone inscription reveals to us one Amaswinth who had lived for forty-two years a monk in a religious house in the mountains above Málaga before his death in 982. Occasional Christians rose to high office in service to the Muslim establishment in Spain. One such was Recemund, a civil servant who was sent on diplomatic missions to the Byzantine empire and to Germany. He became bishop of Elvira (later Granada). He was also a figure of some eminence in the intellectual life of al-Andalus, author of a work known as the *Calendar of Córdoba*, an important source of information about the agriculture and horticulture of tenth-century Spain. Altogether Recemund of Elvira puts one in mind of his colleague in governmental service, Hasday ibn Shaprut.

Neither the quiet monastic life of Amaswinth nor the busy official career of Recemund should blind us to a general trend towards diminution among the Christian communities of al-Andalus during the ninth, tenth and eleventh centuries. They were depleted by conversion to Islam, at its most intense between about 850 and 1050. They were also depleted by emigration to the Christian monarchies of northern Spain or beyond. The monastery of Samos, originally founded, as we saw in Chapter 5, in the middle years of the seventh century, was re-established in about 840 under the direction of an abbot who was an immigrant from the Islamic south. We hear of monks there in 857 who were recent arrivals from Córdoba, their departure suggestively falling in the decade of the martyrs. The given name of the annalist Prudentius was the characteristically Aragonese one of Galindo. (Prudentius, his name 'in religion', was the name of a fourth-century Christian Latin poet, also a native of Spain.) It would seem that his parents had migrated from the Pyrenean region to Francia in the early years of the ninth century. These patterns were repeated elsewhere. There was a steady stream of emigrants from Muslim Syria and north Africa into Christian Asia Minor and Italy respectively.

The Christian communities that were left behind became smaller, more isolated, more demoralized, more marginalized. While they were never completely cut off from their co-religionists elsewhere they were deprived of the nourishment of regular cultural contact with the heartlands of Christendom – heartlands which had moved away from the Mediterranean to the Frankish kingdom, and had therefore become less accessible. Deprived of 'intellectual oxygen', it has been well said,

315

they suffered 'slow asphyxiation'.[22] Of course, this is to generalize rather wildly. The Coptic Christian churches of Egypt flourish to this day. The example of Ethiopia suggests that isolation need not always mean loss of confidence and vitality. But further to the west the experience was bleaker. There, the Christian presence became a shadow of its former self. Pope Leo IX, writing to Bishop Thomas of Carthage in 1053, lamented the fact that there were only five bishops left in the whole of north Africa. There had been over 600 in Augustine's day! These remnant communities slowly faded away as the years passed. Some were an unconscionable time dying. At Gafsa, deep in today's Tunisia, research has revealed a little society of Berber Christians which – almost incredibly – survived into the fifteenth century.

Christianity in Muslim Spain might have gone the same way as it did in the Maghrib. Instead it was rescued, by the process known to Spanish historians as the *Reconquista*, the 'Reconquest'. This is a shorthand term for the expansion of the petty Christian principalities of northern Spain into the centre and south of the Iberian peninsula at the expense of the Arabo-Berber Muslim authorities of al-Andalus. The tempo of reconquest was at its most intense between about 1050 and 1250. By the middle of the thirteenth century the entire landmass of the Iberian peninsula had come under Christian control with the exception of the small enclave of Granada and its territory, which maintained a precarious existence as an independent Muslim amirate until 1492.

The Christian reconquest of Spain was roughly contemporaneous with the crusades directed against Islam in the eastern Mediterranean with the aim of regaining and holding the Holy Places for Christendom. Every schoolchild knows – or at least used to know – that the crusades were initiated by the preaching of Pope Urban II at the council of Clermont in 1095. The First Crusade achieved an initial fluke success, mainly because middle-eastern Islam was weak and divided, with the capture of Antioch (1098) and Jerusalem (1099). In its wake Christian principalities were established at Antioch, Edessa, Tripoli and Jerusalem; the so-called crusader states whose governing classes were drawn from the military aristocracies of western Europe, mainly France. Successive crusades in the twelfth and thirteenth centuries attempted to extend Christian territorial dominion in Syria and Palestine, ultimately to no avail. There were many and complex reasons for this, but the overarching one was a revival in the stamina of middle-eastern Islam. Although this revival has forever been associated with the name of Saladin, who reconquered Jerusalem in 1187, it is more accurate to say – and it is not to belittle his great achievements – that it started before his day and continued to gain momentum after it. Although much Christian ingenuity was devoted to the thirteenth-century crusades, and colossal amounts of Christian blood and treasure squandered in them, the last fragment of Christian territorial lordship on the Syrian mainland disappeared with the loss of Acre in 1291. Plans continued to be made for crusades to recover the Holy Land during the fourteenth and fifteenth centuries, and some expeditions were mounted, but no lasting success was registered.

What French historians of the *annaliste* school dismissively call the *histoire événementielle* of the crusades is – well, to be candid – pretty boring. But what might be called their moral history is of an intense interest and impinges upon our topic of mission and conversion. How did the notion gain acceptability that warfare directed against 'infidels' was not just in some sense sacred but also spiritually meritorious for the participant? Who were identified as infidels and what adjustments took place in Christian attitudes to them before and during the crusading epoch? Was mission perceived as an adjunct to crusading or as an alternative to it? What strategies for missions to infidels were devised during the age of the crusades? These and related questions have very properly attracted attention, stimulated research and generated some distinguished historical writing. This is not the place to pursue them further.[23] But the reader needs to be aware of them as we return to our rival monotheisms.

European Jewry was the first domestic victim of the crusading movement. During the preaching and preparation for the First Crusade in the course of 1096 Jewish communities in several towns, mainly in the Rhineland, were plundered, ill-treated and sometimes massacred. Here is an account of what happened at Worms:

> On the twenty-third of Iyar [18 May 1096] they attacked the community of Worms. The community divided into two groups; some remained in their homes and others fled to the local bishop seeking refuge. Those who remained in their homes were set upon by the steppe-wolves [cf. Jeremiah v.6] who pillaged men, women and infants, children and old people. They pulled down the stairways and destroyed the houses, looting and plundering;

317

and they took the Torah scroll, trampled it in the mud, and tore
and burned it . . . Seven days later, on the new moon of Sivan,
those Jews who were still in the court of the bishop were subjected
to great anguish. The enemy dealt them the same cruelty as the
first group and put them to the sword . . . The enemy stripped
them naked, dragged them along, and then cast them off, sparing
only a small number whom they forcibly baptised in their profane
waters. The number of those slain during the two days was
approximately eight hundred.[24]

The pogroms of 1096 came to constitute one of the turning-points
in the historical consciousness of Ashkenazi Jewry. Nothing would be
quite the same again. However, it has long been recognized that the
ghastly events of 1096 did not spring from nothing. The way had
been prepared by a gradual hardening of attitudes in the relations
between Christians and Jews in the course of the eleventh century.

In the year 1003 the ruler of Egypt and Palestine, al-Hakim, began
a persecution of the Christians in his dominions. It intensified over
the ensuing years and culminated in 1009 with the destruction of the
church of the Holy Sepulchre at Jerusalem. This wounded Christian
sensibilities at a particularly tender point. What is striking about Christian reactions to the outrage is that two nearly contemporary chroniclers attributed it to a Jewish plot. (They evidently did not know that
al-Hakim persecuted the Jews as well as the Christians.) One of these
was Rodulfus Glaber (or Ralph the Bald), whose comments on the
Judaizing Count Raynard of Sens have already been quoted. Writing
at Auxerre about thirty years after the event, Rodulfus tells this extraordinary story.

> In the same ninth year after the millennium the church at Jerusalem, which contained the Sepulchre of Our Lord and Saviour,
> was destroyed at the command of the Prince of Cairo. This is
> known to have begun in the way I am about to describe. Because
> of the fame of this monument, great multitudes of the faithful
> from all over the world were drawn to Jerusalem. Therefore the
> devil, driven by envy, sought to pour out the venom of his malice
> upon the practitioners of the true faith by using his accustomed
> instruments, the Jews. There were a great many of that race in
> Orléans, the royal city of Gaul, and they are notorious for being
> even more arrogant, envious and insolent than the rest of their
> brethren. They conceived a dastardly plot: they bribed one

318

Robert, a fugitive serf from the house of Moutiers-Sainte-Marie [a monastery in which the chronicler had resided for a time], who was no more than a vagabond masquerading as a pilgrim. With infinite precaution they sent him to the prince of Cairo with letters written in the Hebrew alphabet; the parchment strips were hidden inside the iron of his staff lest he should be robbed. The fellow set off and delivered these letters, which were full of evil and lies: they alleged that if he did not quickly destroy the venerable church of the Christians, then they would soon occupy his whole realm, depriving him of all his power. When the prince heard this he was transported with rage, and he sent some of his servants to Jerusalem to destroy the church.[25]

There was a sequel in western Europe.

Once they knew this all the Christians throughout the whole world decided unanimously to drive the Jews from their lands and cities. They became the objects of universal hatred; they were driven from the cities, some were put to the sword, others were drowned in rivers, and many found other deaths; some even took their own lives in diverse ways. So it was that after this very proper vengeance had been taken, very few of them were to be found in the Roman world. Then the bishops proclaimed that no Christian could have any kind of dealing with them. They exempted from this section those who wished to convert to the grace of baptism and renounce all Jewish customs and ways.

The same 'scapegoating' of the Jews is found in the independent account of the same events composed by Adhémar of Chabannes, a monk of Limoges who died in 1033. Adhémar's chronicle is our main source of information about the affairs of south-western France in the late tenth and early eleventh centuries. A few pages after his report on the destruction of the church of the Holy Sepulchre he has the following tale to tell, set at Toulouse in about the year 1020.

At this time Hugh, the chaplain of Viscount Aimeric of Rochecouart, was at Toulouse in attendance upon his lord for the celebration of Easter. It fell to him to deliver the blow to a Jew, as is always the custom there each Easter. He dashed the brain and the eyes out of that perfidious head onto the ground: the man died instantly. He was carried from St Stephen's cathedral and given burial at the Jewish synagogue.[26]

It is worth trying to unwrap this extremely nasty episode a little bit. Adhémar claimed that it was a 'custom': but this is its first reliably attested appearance in the historical record; it was probably a custom of fairly recent institution. The word translated 'blow' is the Latin word *colaphus*, transliterated from the Greek κολαφος. It was a rare word but it would have been familiar to all who heard the gospel readings in holy week because it is the word used in the Vulgate for the blows inflicted on Jesus by the Jews following the accusations of the high priest Caiaphas (Matthew xxvi.67). So, at the central festival of the Christian year, Easter, and at the most sacred place in the city of Toulouse, the cathedral, a representative of the Jewish community was publicly assaulted and humiliated by a cleric for the 'perfidy' of his people in a re-enactment in reverse of an episode in the passion of the Christian Saviour. (I do not think we may assume that the ritual was intended to inflict death on the victim. Adhémar tells the story – at least I think he does – because on this occasion matters went rather far; he does not say too far. Hugh was evidently a very muscular Christian indeed. Those who chose him for the job must have known that a blow from him would be likely to inflict more than just a bloody nose.) This was a publicly 'staged' ritual which was meant to convey something to the onlookers: what? Jewish responsibility for the death of Jesus; the fittingness, perhaps even the duty of Christian revenge; the ostracization of the Jews from Christian society; the permissibility of violence against them as enemies of God and man.

Symptoms of harsher Christian attitudes to Jews in the eleventh century, of which these are two, are not hard to find. Their causes are much more elusive. Hardening attitudes have been plausibly connected with the movement towards a more intense lay piety which was a marked feature of the eleventh and twelfth centuries. This was an age of enhanced religiosity, a wonderful vitality and experiment and creativity in the service of God; an age comparable in spiritual intensity to the sixteenth, seventeenth or nineteenth centuries.[27] The manifestations of this upsurge of piety may be seen, diversely, in the building of parish churches and cathedrals, the founding and endowment of monasteries, a renewed veneration for relics, a surge in the popularity of pilgrimage, changes in penitential practice, the wish to devise a Christian role for the armed knight, the attempts to recreate a religious life on the 'apostolic' model, the quest for a more positive role for women in the Christian life, the further elaboration of the liturgy, a new emphasis on preaching, the beginnings of religious drama, the transformation of Christian sculpture and painting – and much else besides. These were the positive features of the culture of the age. Its most disfiguring negative feature was a growth of intolerance. It is an observable if regrettable fact that groups identified as outsiders, as alien elements, as 'the Other' tend to become victims in ages of intensifying religiosity. This was the ill-fortune of the Jews from the eleventh century onwards. We move into an age of ever sharper Christian hostility towards the Jewish communities of western Europe. It was characterized by the ghetto, discriminatory laws, slanderous allegations, outbreaks of violence, financial victimization by governments, mass expulsions. Christian conversions to Judaism became rare and much more risky. In England a deacon who adopted Judaism was burned at the stake in 1222. He was not unique. The relatively free and easy traffic between the rival monotheisms that had marked an earlier age had gone.

In the next generation after the lifetime of Rodulfus Glaber and Adhémar of Chabannes, Pope Alexander II (1061–73) sent a letter to the bishops of Spain urging them to protect the Jews in their dioceses 'lest they be killed by those who were setting out to fight against the Saracens in Spain'.[28] It is our first surviving indication that violence against the Jews was to be anticipated from warriors who were going to campaign against Muslims and an uncanny apprehension of the dreadful events of 1096. The First Crusade may itself be considered a feature of the heightened religiosity of the age. It also exemplified a new cohesion and self-awareness in Christendom, moods which played their part in stoking up hostilities. A robustly self-conscious western Christendom found it easier to identify and focus its enmity upon those perceived as its foes, be they Jews, or Muslims, or even the unfamiliar Christians whom the crusaders encountered as they moved eastwards.

The age of the crusades saw a Christian recovery at the expense of Islam in the Mediterranean world. It took place on both land and sea. By sea the near-monopoly of long-haul trade by Islamic and Jewish merchants which had been characteristic of the tenth and eleventh centuries was broken. The future lay not with men like Nahray ibn Nissim but with the business communities of Venice, Pisa, Genoa, Marseilles and Barcelona. By land the Christian recovery took the form of territorial gain. In the crusading zone properly so-called, at the eastern end of the Mediterranean, gain was temporary: the crusading states on the mainland came and went within two centuries (though some of the islands remained in Christian hands for very much longer than that). Islam was re-installed there, and a shrunken Byzantine empire entered upon its last long agony, which would end with the fall of Constantinople to the Ottomans in 1453. Elsewhere in the Mediterranean world Christian gains endured and proved permanent. Sicily, conquered by the forces of north African Islam in the ninth century, was reconquered by Norman knights in the second half of the eleventh century. The landmass of the Iberian peninsula, as we have seen, came gradually under Christian control, leaving only Granada to be conquered in 1492. But reconstituted Christian power was no longer unitary as in the days of the Visigothic kings. Instead, political authority had fragmented into four independent monarchies: Castile, Portugal, Navarre and the federation comprising Aragón, Catalonia and Valencia, known to contemporaries as the 'Crown of Aragón'.

Territorial gain meant the incorporation of large numbers of people who were largely though not exclusively Muslim in faith under Christian rule. What stance did the Christian authorities in state and church adopt towards their new Muslim subjects? A number of written *ad hoc* agreements between conquerors and conquered has survived. Their general tendency was to guarantee to the Muslims freedom of worship and varying measures of communal autonomy in return for loyal submission and the payment of tax at widely varying rates. There were resemblances between this regime and that customarily granted by Islamic authorities to the 'peoples of the book' and exemplified in the submission on terms of Theodemir of Alicante in 713. The difference lay in this, that Muslim toleration of the protected peoples was an obligation laid down in the Koran, however grudgingly it might from time to time have been observed. By contrast, the status of Muslims under Christian rule depended not on any religio-legal sanctions but on tradition modified by any number of variables which might include self-interest, fanaticism, greed or whim. Consider, for instance, what happened at Toledo after its conquest by Alfonso VI of Castile in 1085. The king guaranteed the Muslims of Toledo the continued use of their principal mosque for Islamic worship. But in the following year his hawkish and over-zealous new archbishop of Toledo took possession of the mosque and turned it into his cathedral, 'a tabernacle of celestial virtue for all Christian people'.[29] Many mosques were turned into churches during the age of the crusades, the best-known example being the *mezquita* of Córdoba.

Self-interest dictated that the existing Muslim populations should not be displaced. Large tracts of land that came under Christian governance were thinly settled. The new authorities wanted to keep the inhabitants and to encourage immigrant settlers. There were of course wide variations from place to place. There was little immigration of Christian settlers to the countryside of the crusader states. By contrast, heavy immigration from mainland Italy in the twelfth and thirteenth centuries helped to swamp the Muslim population of Sicily. In Aragon an Islamic peasantry was sparse; in next-door Valencia it was exceptionally dense, outnumbering four- or even fivefold the Christian population. Forcible movements of people did take place in certain circumstances. Following a Muslim revolt in Sicily, made especially dangerous by the links between the rebels and their co-religionists in north Africa, the Emperor Frederick II in 1233 transferred some 20,000 Muslims from Sicily to mainland Italy, where they were settled at Lucera, near Foggia in Apulia. Ferdinand III of Castile insisted that every Muslim inhabitant should leave Seville after he captured it in 1248 so that it should thenceforward be an entirely Christian city.

In the eyes of churchmen the danger was that Muslims living under Christian rule might contaminate Christian citizens and lead them into error. They were a prey to the same sort of fears that Agobard and Amolus had experienced in ninth-century Lyons about the threat of the Jews to the spiritual well-being of their congregations. It was for this reason that steps were taken to keep Christian and Muslim apart. This might mean the enforced segregation of Muslims into ghettos, as at Murcia in south-eastern Spain, where Alfonso X of Castile ordered the construction of a wall between Christian and Muslim quarters in 1266. Such drastic measures were exceptional. More typically it meant a multitude of regulations affecting possible encounters in daily life. Spanish municipal law, whose regulations have survived in abundance, provides many examples. Christians and Muslims were to use the town baths on different days of the week. Christian parents must not employ Muslim nannies for their children. Sexual relations between Christian and Muslim – especially between Christian women and Muslim men – were harshly punished. Muslim proselytizing among Christians was strictly forbidden. Apostasy from Christianity to Islam incurred the death penalty.

Although it is demonstrable that some of the enactments relating to everyday social relations were more honoured in the breach than in the observance, it is likely that those dealing with religious allegiances were more effective. The cases of Christian apostasy to Islam of which we know tended to feature not 'born' Christians but 'new' Christian converts from Islam. The most celebrated example was Philip of Mahdia, born a Muslim in Tunisia, who became a Christian and rose to high governmental office in the service of King Roger II of Sicily, only to lapse back to Islam. He was burned to death at Palermo in 1154. Part of the trouble was that it was difficult to trust defectors from Islam in the context of intermittent military hostilities between Christian and Muslim. Baldwin I, the first Latin king of Jerusalem, stood godfather to a convert from Islam who took his name and prospered in the royal service. But in 1110 he was discovered plotting with the Muslims of Sidon to murder the king, so he was hanged. Not all such defectors were unreliable. Abu Sa'id, formerly the governor of Valencia, became a Christian in 1229, taking the name of Vincent, and remained thereafter a model of loyalty to his king, James I of Aragon, as well as an ostentatiously devout Christian who financed the refoundation of the bishopric of Segorbe.

Converts like Baldwin, Philip and Vincent were very prominent people. What were the options for conquered Muslims of lesser rank? One was emigration to independent Islamic countries. The exodus of Muslims from Spain and Sicily to Africa in the twelfth and thirteenth centuries matches the exodus of Christians at an earlier date from Africa to Italy or from Spain to Francia. Respected Islamic sages taught that it was a duty for the devout to escape living under Christian rule. But emigration was expensive. It was a feasible option for the well-to-do, but not for the poor. This was one of the reasons why the Muslims who remained under Christian rule tended to be people of lowly status who got a living in fairly modest walks of life. Muslims were encouraged to adopt Christianity, and we may be fairly certain that many did drift into the arms of the church at the same sort of rate and for the same sort of reasons that had nudged their ancestors from Christianity towards Islam back in the ninth and tenth centuries. One of the most widespread forms of encouragement was the offer of liberty to Muslim slaves who adopted Christianity. But this ran against the interests of the slave-owners, who stubbornly resisted such conversions. Pope Innocent III had to write a severe letter to the cathedral clergy of Barcelona in 1206 to reprimand them for colluding with the slave-owners in denying baptism to potential converts from Islam. The first version of Valencia's municipal law after the conquest of the city in 1238 offered freedom to slaves as a reward for conversion but the slave-owners made such a fuss that the clause was revoked. At that very time Pope Gregory IX was issuing guidelines which were intended at once to soothe the conscience of churchmen and to satisfy the rapacity of slave-owners: slaves should be permitted wherever possible to become Christians but this need not entail their liberation.

The surviving evidence suggests that there was not a great deal of will actively to set about converting the Muslim population – or the Jewish population – to Christianity. So long as the Muslims were docile and paid their taxes and maintained a low profile they could be left alone. Of missionary activity properly so-called there was practically none in the pre-crusading era, exception made for the eccentric Venetian hermit Anastasius, who tried to preach to the Muslims of Spain in the 1070s with conspicuous lack of success. In the course of the twelfth century voices critical of crusading began to be raised in advocacy of peaceful approaches towards the Muslims. It was in the thirteenth century, when the military approach was visibly failing, that the idea of a mission to Islam took hold of some of Christendom's leading spirits. Notable among these men were the famous preacher James of Vitry, who became archbishop of Acre in 1216; St Francis of Assisi, who preached before the sultan of Egypt in 1219; Domingo of Osma, founder of the Dominican order (d. 1221); Pope Innocent IV (1243–54); and King Louis IX of France (1226–70). The two new religious orders of friars, the Franciscan and the Dominican, were especially active in undertaking or promoting this new evangelical offensive.[30] Franciscans undertook missions to Morocco in 1219 and 1227 which ended in their martyrdom. It was a Spanish Dominican, Ramón de Peñafort, who established the first training college in which prospective missionaries could learn Arabic, at Murcia. Others followed at Valencia and Játiva. The most formidable Dominican intellect of the century, Thomas Aquinas, composed his *Summa contra Gentiles* at Ramón's prompting as a kind of theological textbook for missionaries. Another Dominican, Ramón Martí, wrote his *Pugio Fideo* ('The Dagger of Faith') for use in disputation with Muslims and compiled an Arabic–Latin dictionary, the first of its kind, for the use of missionaries in the field.

The thirteenth century was an age of expanding horizons and of high hopes. The thinking about missions and the experiments in evangelism to which those hopes and horizons gave rise continued buoyant for two more centuries. Thus it was that when new and inconceivably vast scope for missionary endeavour opened before the wondering eyes of Europeans in the sixteenth century in India, the Americas, China and Japan, Christian churchmen were anything but unprepared. They had been there before; they knew all about it. But they had not succeeded in their confrontation with the opponents who have been the subject of this chapter. Christian missionary efforts had not dented Islam at all. The rival monotheisms of Judaism and Islam were still in place. The colonial church of the crusader states had ebbed away, leaving a scatter of fine buildings and some grandiloquent titles of sees *in partibus infidelium* to swell the treasury of papal patronage. The missions to Africa had yielded martyrs and travellers' tales but no other fruit. In the central Mediterranean Sicily, re-Christianized by about 1300, was the showpiece of Catholic success; but it was a success that had been achieved rather by emigration and deportation than by conversion. In Spain, a bigger land with a bigger non-Christian population and feebler executive powers, the problems were more intractable. So intractable did they prove that in the end, two centuries later, the Christian authorities adopted a violent solution which was in itself an admission of failure, with the expulsion of the Jews in 1492 and the forced baptism of the Spanish Muslims from 1499 onwards.

CHAPTER TEN

A Certain Greek Named Methodius

It is manifest that the situation is the mission field, where agents animated, in some measure at least, by denominational zeal, subject to the influence of personal idiosyncrasies, and responsible only to far-distant authorities, are working side by side, may lend itself to friction unless principles of comity, written or unwritten, are acknowledged and observed.

World Missionary Conference 1910, Report of Commission VIII, 'Co-operation and the Promotion of Unity'

ANOTHER CASUALTY of the crusades was any hope of ever again harmoniously stitching together the eastern and the western halves of Christendom. The two main branches of the church – western, or Latin, or Catholic, and eastern, or Greek, or Orthodox – drifted apart slowly and imperceptibly over many centuries. Signs of strain were detectable in the lifetime of Constantine; sundering was not irreversible until the crusaders had sacked Constantine's city in 1204, 900 years later.* As well as long it was also complicated, messy and acrimonious.

It is easy, but an oversimplification, to point to the underlying differences of language, tradition and religious sensibilities and to proclaim that the split was inevitable. But there was much that was random and unpredictable about this parting of the ways. The irruption of Islam into the Mediterranean and of the Slavs into the Balkans and Greece both contributed to render communication between east and west more difficult. Neither could have been predicted, let alone controlled. Dates, incidents, encounters, misunderstandings, acquired only later and with hindsight a significance which they could not possibly have

---

* The armies of the Fourth Crusade had been intended to attack Muslim Egypt. Owing to a series of misfortunes and muddles – cock-up rather than conspiracy, though the question is endlessly debatable – the crusaders were diverted from their objective and stormed the Christian and imperial city of Constantinople instead.

had at the time. The Emperor Constans II visited Rome in the year 663. No one at the time could possibly have guessed that never again would an emperor from Constantinople set foot in Rome (at least until the very different circumstances of the fourteenth century). In 710 there occurred a papal visit to Constantinople. Who could have foreseen that the next such visit would not take place until 1979? When Pope Zacharias died in 752, no one could have predicted that there would not be another pope of Greek origin for nearly 700 years. Divergent practices between east and west existed from an early date. For instance, among the Greeks those who failed to receive holy communion on three successive Sundays were excommunicated, but this was not the case among the Latins. The Greeks used leavened bread in the celebration of the eucharist, the Latins unleavened – a difference, this, which was to cause intemperate squabbling in the eleventh century. How much divergence may there be, and over what range of issues, before a healthy diversity in unity – a favourite theme with Pope Gregory I – turns into a festering schism? Doctrinal quarrels, now for the most part forgotten like the Three Chapters dispute in the sixth century or the Monothelite controversy in the seventh, engaged energies from time to time. Only later, and only from a certain perspective, did they seem to fall into a pattern or progression, steps along a path that led inexorably to schism.

Differences over doctrine or practice became more frequent and more heated as time went by, their scars less easily healed. Intermittently between 726 and 843 the emperors in Constantinople enforced a policy of iconoclasm upon the church they governed. All religious images, in painting, sculpture, metalwork, wood, plaster, glass, whatever medium, were to be destroyed. It was an attempt to cleanse the church from any taint of idolatry by doing away with the images which focused the veneration, possibly the too unrestrained veneration, of the devout. The iconoclast tendency was denounced in the strongest terms by the authorities in the western church. This in itself was remarkable: never before had Rome so openly rebuked Constantinople. It was particularly unfortunate that the iconoclastic controversy took place at the same time as a significant change of bearings for the popes. They had always needed a powerful secular protector and had traditionally found one in the emperor. In a favourite image, the emperor was the earthly sword to complement the spiritual weaponry of the bishop of Rome. The distant and beleaguered emperors in

Constantinople could no longer fulfil this role, fighting as they were for their survival against an Islamic enemy to their east. But the need for protection was felt most keenly by the eighth-century popes, as Lombard kings of Italy cast predatory eyes upon Rome and its territory. So the popes looked north and west, to the kings of the Franks. We need not linger over the details. Suffice it to say that the alliance between the papacy and the Carolingian dynasty formed at that dynasty's inception in 751 led directly to the coronation of Charlemagne as Roman emperor at the hands of Pope Leo III in St Peter's on Christmas Day in the year 800. Charlemagne was already viewed with gravest suspicion at Constantinople because of his opposition to iconoclasm. But this was nothing less than usurpation.

Frayed tempers are calmed with time, relationships patched up. So it was between Rome, or Aachen, and Constantinople on this occasion. Frankish rulers were tactful, the emperors in Constantinople busied in other directions. But not long after the final ending of Byzantium's iconoclastic phase, which did not occur until 843, there was a further rupture. It started with an unseemly dispute over the patriarchate of Constantinople. In 858 the emperor deposed the Patriarch Ignatius and replaced him with Photius, whose name we shall be meeting again in this chapter. Ignatius refused to resign and an unholy row broke out. The papacy was drawn into it. At a council held at Rome in 863 Pope Nicholas I declared that Ignatius was the rightful patriarch and that Photius must be deposed. This assertion of papal authority gave great offence at Constantinople, and relations between the two churches were strained almost to breaking-point over the next few years. A climax was reached in 867 when Photius accused the Latins of doctrinal error and declared the pope deposed and excommunicate. The doctrinal innovation identified by Photius was the insertion of the notorious *Filioque* clause into the creed: that is to say, the addition of the word *filioque*, 'and from the Son', into that section of the creed which concerns the Procession of the Holy Ghost.* Later in the same year a new emperor, Basil I, effected a shaky reconciliation with Rome, restored Ignatius and sacrificed Photius. But relations continued strained for several years thereafter.

---

* In the Greek creeds the Holy Ghost 'proceeds from the Father'; in the Latin creeds 'from the Father and from the Son'. This is still today the major bone of doctrinal contention between Catholic and Orthodox churches.

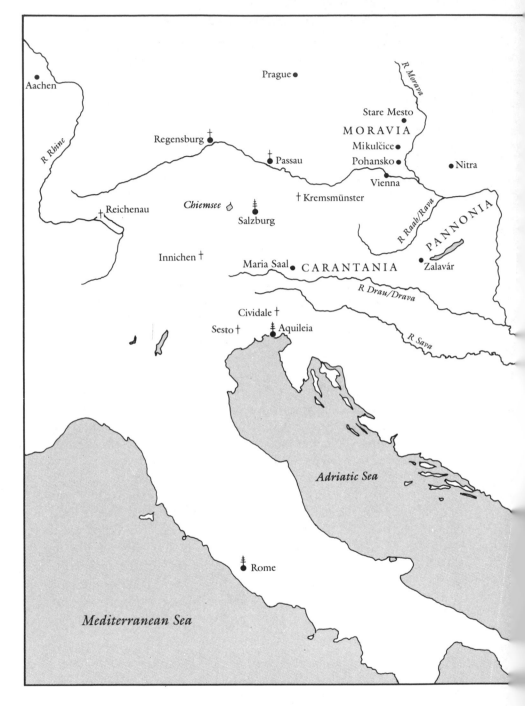

8. *The world of Cyril and Methodius in the ninth century.*

● Kiev

● Madara

● Pliska

R Danube

B U L G A R I A

Black Sea

† Preslav

Adrianople ♠

Constantinople ♠

MACEDONIA

† Olympus

† Ohrid

Thessalonica †

♠ Archbishopric

♠ Bishopric

† Monastery

Aegean Sea

irmium]

At precisely the same time, in the 860s, there occurred a flurry of missionary activity directed at the Slav peoples of central and eastern Europe. The surviving evidence generated by this activity presents us with some familiar themes, though heard from new directions, in the history of early medieval missions. It also sounds some that are rather less familiar. Notable among these is that of rivalry in the mission field between the great powers of the day, the Byzantine and the Frankish empires. This rivalry was conducted against a background composed from a particularly troubled episode, the Ignatian–Photian schism, in that long-drawn-out drifting apart which was eventually to sunder western Christendom from eastern. The Slavonic peoples of central Europe, initially the Moravians and the Bulgarians, were confronted, and not for the last time, with a question which has been fundamental to their sense of identity. Which way does central Europe face, eastwards or westwards?

The prehistory of the Slavs is extremely obscure. Their ancestors have been located by archaeologists in the cultures of the Dnieper system to the north of Kiev. From these origins migration took them in three directions: westward into Poland and Bohemia; southward across the Danube into the Balkans and Greece; and north-eastward into Russia. This slow drift of peoples seems to have been at its gradual busiest between about 550 and 700. It brought the western and southern Slavs into a frequently painful proximity with Christian Europe and therefore into the dim glow shed by the meagre sources which survive from those literate communities. From the seventh century onwards something approaching an outline narrative history of the western and southern Slavs becomes possible.

Impartial and rational enquiry has not on the whole been characteristic of the historiography of the Slavs composed in the nineteenth and twentieth centuries. Two tendencies in particular have served to restrict free investigation: nationalism and communism. The quest for the will-o'-the-wisp of a true ethnicity has spawned bogus scholarship, mendacious rhetoric, persecution, battle and inhuman crime. It is unhappily not yet dead, and not merely in the wilder corners of the Balkan states. To assert the Slav ethnicity of the inhabitants of modern Greece at an Athenian dinner-table remains imprudent. The Marxian underpinning of the communist regimes of eastern Europe required that historical activity should be directed towards establishing certain social features of the past, pre-ordained stages of material development leading to pre-ordained ends. This shackled eastern European historians during the second half of the twentieth century to a dreary search for 'the origins of the state'. It inhibited the emergence of techniques of historical enquiry which have proved fruitful elsewhere.

To the eye of the historian unhindered by such preoccupations the development of Slav societies in the early medieval period recalls that of the Germanic peoples who came into contact with the Roman world in late antiquity. Like the Germans, the Slavs were settled, village-dwelling peoples whose principal economic activity lay in an agriculture of mixed stock-herding and arable cultivation. Though they did not yet mint their own coin, they traded actively among themselves and with their neighbours. Like the Germans they were polytheists who worshipped a variety of gods diversely responsible for weather, fertility and the fortunes of war. The Slavs who pressed upon the Danube frontier of the Byzantine empire in the sixth century were perhaps a little poorer in material culture, less socially differentiated and less politically organized than the Goths of Dacia who had pressed upon that same frontier some two centuries earlier. Such assessments must be cautious, based as they necessarily are on imprecise rumours committed to writing by incurious Constantinopolitan men-of-letters and on perilous inferences drawn by archaeologists from potsherds and post-holes, beads and buckles. Whatever may have been the social development of the Slavs in the age of Justinian, it is certainly true that they showed themselves – again in this like the Germans – adaptable to a new environment, ready to appreciate the more advanced culture of their Christian neighbours. It was an appreciation which those neighbours were eager to encourage.

Byzantine diplomacy has been described as an 'intricate science and fine art, in which military pressure, political intelligence, economic cajolery and religious propaganda were fused into a powerful weapon of defensive imperialism'.[1] This formidable machinery was directed to manipulation of the Slavs from hostile foes into useful satellites and eventually grateful members of the imperial family of nations. The principality of Samo in Bohemia in the second quarter of the seventh century, briefly alluded to in Chapter 7, may have owed more to Byzantine gold than to the economic and social pressures issuing in 'pre-state formation'. Certainly, and surely not by chance, its existence was a thorn in the side – or the rear – of the Avars who had threatened

Constantinople itself in 626. If it had been principally the Virgin Mary who had saved the City of New Rome on that occasion, as contemporaries believed, Samo's Wends had played a modest part too. Frankish diplomacy was less sophisticated than Byzantine. Such as it was, however, it was directed to essentially the same ends, the prevention by whatever means of the emergence of too strong and hostile a neighbour beyond the eastern frontier zone. For both Franks and Byzantine Greeks the association of missionary activity with diplomacy was close. In the eastern empire the intimate interdependence of church and state, which dated back to the days of Constantine and Eusebius, rendered the association a near-identity. Diplomacy without mission was inconceivable. In the west the association was looser but still close, particularly in the context of the frontier. As we saw in Chapter 5, the desire of St Amandus to preach Christianity to the Slavs may plausibly be linked with King Dagobert I's political initiatives in the middle Danube area in the 630s. Already therefore by the middle years of the seventh century both Greeks and Franks were fishing in the turbid waters of Slavonic central Europe. It would remain to be seen whether their interests would prove complementary or divergent.

By the year 800 Slav cultures and the Slavonic language extended from the Baltic to the Peloponnese and from the Elbe to the Dnieper. Cultures in the plural, because there was diversity; language in the singular, because Slavonic was slower to experience internal divergence than the Romance, Germanic or Celtic branches of the Indo-European linguistic tree. This was to be of some significance for the progress of Christianity in two Slav principalities particularly, Moravia and Bulgaria. Moravia takes its name from the river Morava which runs in its lower course along the boundary between today's Czech Republic and Slovakia to its confluence with the Danube east of Vienna.[2] A naturally fertile region, the valley of the Morava was also a nodal point in a central European network of communications. The Danube with its affluents has always been a highway between east and west, while the plains of north-eastern Europe are linked by a southerly route threading through the passes known as the Moravian Gate to the plain of Pannonia (Hungary) and on to the Adriatic coast. Slaves, fur and amber had been traded from north to south along this route since time out of mind. Here in Moravia, in all probability, had lain the heart of Samo's ephemeral principality. After his time almost nothing at all is heard of Moravia in the written sources for over a century.

The archaeological record, however, does not fall silent. It shows that Moravia continued to be an important trading entrepôt mediating between north-west and south-east. New arrivals on this mercantile scene were the Arabs, or at any rate those who used their silver coin, hoards of which were deposited in Moravia from the second half of the eighth century onwards. It was along this central European trade route that there might have travelled the silk, ivory, pepper and incense which ended up in English monasteries. A hint of a grimmer commerce, but then as now a highly profitable one, is furnished by Charlemagne's prohibition in 805 on the trade in arms to the Slavs. Moravia became very rich through trade. Because its profits were not equally shared but went to the native traders and the chieftains who protected them, differentials of wealth, status and power in Moravian society were accentuated. These differentials are plainly visible in the Moravian cemeteries that have been excavated. In the ninth-century cemetery of Staré Mesto, for example, 53.4% of the graves were unfurnished with grave-goods, 40% were poorly or moderately furnished, 6% contained jewellery and/or elaborately decorated pottery, while only 1.6% contained the primary weapon of the warrior class, a sword. This cemetery was excavated in the 1950s, and cemetery archaeology has made such enormous strides since then as to be almost a different discipline; certainly a much more refined and exact one. The figures quoted above have to be treated with circumspection, any conclusions based upon them offered with caution. But even the most cautious interpreters agree that the archaeological evidence from ninth-century Moravia – not just from cemeteries by any means – indicates a growth simultaneously in material wealth and in social differentiation. The expansion of trade in range, volume and value led to an enhancement of the power of chieftains and princes. They alone could guarantee the peace which commerce required, command the power to keep roads and bridges in repair, ensure the supply of marketable goods such as slaves. Princes, merchants and customers alike favoured the concentration of trade at fixed points. Such places, naturally enough, were princely centres, crystallizations of human settlement round the residence of a powerful lord and his retainers who could protect and regulate commercial activity. Such market settlements, perhaps impermanent at first, gradually became permanent as crafts, or 'service industries', as they would be called today, struck root to serve the needs of the prince, his warrior entourage and the floating population of merchants – smiths, wheelwrights, grooms, potters, millers, bakers, tanners, weavers and so forth. In short, they became towns. The type case, in Moravia, has been excavated at Mikulčice, where a small agricultural settlement of the sixth century developed over the course of the seventh and eighth into a substantial town. By about 800 there were at Mikulčice a fortified acropolis, dwelling houses, workshops and plentiful evidence for industry and trade. To these were added only a little later several Christian churches.

This is to summarize the materialist explanation of the origins of the political formation rather grandly known as the 'Great Moravian Empire' of the ninth century. As an explanation it is almost convincing, but it omits other, contingent factors. One of these was military and political, namely the destruction of the Avar kingdom by Charlemagne in 795. The Moravian principality had probably been a tribute-paying dependency of the Avars, at any rate from time to time in the course of the eighth century. The removal of the hand of the Avars from the scene left a vacuum in the Danubian lands of central Europe. Who was to succeed to their power? Not just Charlemagne, but others as well, among them the rulers of Moravia. The first such prince of Moravia since Samo's day of whom we have more than the very faintest knowledge was named Mojmir and he ruled from sometime in the 820s until his death in 846. This long reign was in itself significant: it was longer than was usual in the kaleidoscopically unstable power politics of the Slav chieftains. Mojmir increased his power at the expense of his neighbours. In about 833 he expelled a certain Pribina, prince of the neighbouring Slav principality of Nitra, and annexed his territory: we shall hear more of Pribina shortly. One last thing we know about Mojmir is that he was baptized a Christian in or about the year 822, the officiant being a bishop from the Frankish empire, Reginhere (or Reginhar) of Passau. A few years later, in 831, east Frankish sources recorded a mass baptism of Moravians by the same Bishop Reginhere. The similarities with Paulinus at Yeavering two centuries earlier are striking.

Bulgaria presents contrasts with Moravia. It grew up not beyond the frontier zone of a Germanic kingdom but inside what had been for centuries the Roman imperial provinces to the south of the river Danube. Its rulers were much more imposing figures than the princes of Moravia, and their southern frontier lay within striking distance of the imperial capital at Constantinople.

Slav raiding parties had been crossing the Danube to push into the Balkans and Thrace throughout the second quarter of the sixth century while Justinian was looking the other way in pursuit of his heady dream of restoring Roman imperial power in Africa, Spain and Italy. Its vulnerability thus proved, the Danube frontier collapsed around the middle years of the century, just as the Rhine frontier had crumbled before the advancing Germans in the early fifth. The Slavs surged or drifted across the river and down through the Balkan provinces of the empire into Macedonia and Greece. By the 580s their raids were reaching as far south as the Peloponnese. By about 600 it was plain that imperial authority had lapsed throughout this inland area and had retreated to coastal strongholds such as Thessalonica, Monemvasia and Dyrrachium (Durazzo, Durrës). Even these were not wholly secure. Thessalonica was besieged by the Slavs in 612 and for the next two centuries remained a frontier town, with Slav settlements just outside its walls and Slavonic spoken in its streets and markets. It was the empire's tragedy that the military imperatives during most of the seventh century called from the east and the south: the Persian wars of the Emperor Heraclius followed by the hard-fought surrenders to Islam in Syria, Egypt and north Africa. No resources could be spared for the Balkans and Greece, which were in effect abandoned to the depredations and settlements of the Slavs.

The Bulgars were not Slavs. They belonged to a Turkic ethnic group and when we first hear of them early in the seventh century they were settled beyond the Black Sea to the east of the Sea of Azov, between the lower waters of the river Don and the mountains of the Caucasus. Later in the century they were displaced from this homeland by the arrival of the Khazars from central Asia and began to move westwards. Under their ruler, or khan, Asparuch they crossed the lower Danube and established themselves in what had been the Roman province of Moesia Inferior. The empire was compelled to acknowledge this barefaced land-taking in a humiliating peace treaty agreed with Asparuch in 681, unprecedented recognition of an independent barbarian kingdom on Roman territory. From this base the Bulgarian khans of the following century and a half increased their power over the north Balkan area by little and little and by fits and starts. They employed both diplomacy and war. In 716, when Constantinople was threatened by the Arabs, the Bulgars were able to extract territorial and commercial concessions in exchange for their aid. A century later, in 811, the great Khan Krum defeated and killed the Emperor Niceophorus I. It was the first time that an emperor had lost his life in battle since the death of Valens at the hands of the Goths in 378. Two years later Krum defeated Nicephorus' successor Michael I, sacked the city of Adrianople and burnt the suburbs of Constantinople. Only Krum's early death in 814 spared the empire further humiliations. Under his successors Omurtag (814–31) and Malamir (831–52) a fragile peace with the empire prevailed. The expansion of the Bulgar kingdom continued, however, south-westerly into Slav Macedonia and north-westerly into what had been the kingdom of the Avars. By the middle of the ninth century Bulgaria's zone of influence was bounded by the Black Sea, the Carpathian mountains, the valley of the Danube between modern Budapest and Belgrade, and Macedonia to the coastline of Albania on the Adriatic. Its heartland, however, conveniently for a modern understanding, lay in the regions which comprise the present-day state of Bulgaria.

Bulgaria's population in the ninth century was a mixed one. An elite of Bulgar warrior-aristocrats, or boyars, overlay a subject populace in which Slav and pre-Slav inhabitants were intermingled. Whatever the ethnic composition of the Bulgarian khanate, doubtless already as thoroughly scrambled as that of any other part of Europe, the Slavonic language was gaining in it at the expense of native Greek or incoming Bulgar. There has been much debate concerning the degree of survival of Romano-Byzantine culture under the impact of Slav settlement and Bulgar rule.[3] A persuasive case has been made for the continuity of some urban life in Bulgaria and thereby of some elements of Romano-Byzantine – or let us say simply Greek – civilization. Greek inscriptions on stone were being executed for Bulgarian patrons during the first half of the ninth century. The official documents of the khans were being drawn up in Greek. And if the colossal stone palace at Pliska is correctly attributed to the reign of Khan Omurtag, which seems likely though unproven, then he could call upon the services of Greek architects and craftsmen. It is most unlikely that *all* these monumental masons, scribes and architects would have been prisoners of war carried off from, say, what was left of Adrianople in 813 (though some may have been). It is reasonable to propose, therefore, some survival of Greek cultural activities under Bulgarian

17. St Cuthbert's pectoral cross, Anglo-Celtic work of the late seventh century. That even so austere and ascetic a churchman as Cuthbert could wear jewellery of an aristocratic magnificence conveys something of the tone of the early Anglo-Saxon church.

18. *Right* A stone from Papil (Shetland), carved probably about the year 800, apparently commemorating four abbots or bishops. The creature below them is probably the sculptor's attempt at the lion of St. Mark. The bird-legged and beaked human figures beneath were probably a later addition: they remain inexplicable.

19 and 20. A brooch found in a grave of the seventh century at Wittislingen (Bayern), Germany, not far from the Danube to the north of Augsburg. On the back it bears an inscription in Latin asking for God's blessing on its owner.

21. The Ardagh chalice, Irish, about 800, one of the most sumptuous pieces of ecclesiastical metalwork to survive from early medieval Europe.

22. The chalice presented by Duke Tassilo of Bavaria to his monastic foundation of Kremsmünster, near Linz, Austria, between 777 and 788.

23. *Opposite top left* A library catalogue written in English script at Würzburg in about 800. The fifth item in the left-hand column, reading *Historia Anglor-* (short for *Anglorum*) 'History of the English,' denotes Bede's *Ecclesiastical History.*

24 and 25. *Opposite* The resplendent covers of two gospel books. The earlier, *top right*, was made for Queen Theodelinda (cf. plate 9), whose name may be read in the narrow transverse bar at upper right, about the year 600. The second, *bottom left*, known from its provenance as the Lindau Gospels, was made in Germany under English stylistic influence early in the ninth century. The cover commissioned by Wilfrid for the Ripon Gospels (see Chapter 6) might have looked something like this.

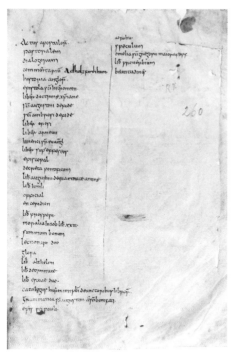

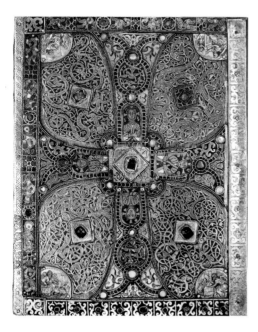

26. The Enger reliquary. This little casket for housing relics of the saints was allegedly given by Charlemagne to the Saxon leader Widukind on the occasion of his baptism in 785. It is more likely that it was made to Widukind's commission some twenty years later for presentation to the monastery which he founded at Enger in Saxony in the year 807.

27. The front panel of the enigmatic Franks casket, carved from whalebone in England about the year 700. The scenes depicted here are discussed in Chapter 8.

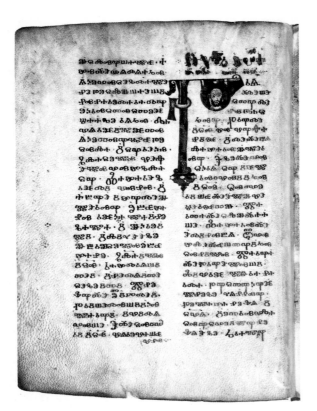

28. An example of Glagolitic script, the manner of rendering the Slavonic tongue in written form devised by Cyril and Methodius for their converts in Moravia.

29. The horseman of Madara,
c. 820. This rock-face relief
near Pliska in northern
Bulgaria marked a place sacred
to the Bulgarian's high god
Tengri.

30. The greater of the memorial
stones at Jelling in Denmark.
The runic inscription on this
and the other faces proclaims
that the stone was raised by
King Harald 'who made the
Danes Christian'. It dates from
shortly after 960.

31 and 32. The cross at Middleton, near Pickering in North Yorkshire, appears to commemorate a Viking warrior who had accepted Christianity. It dates from the first half of the tenth century.

33. The runestone at Frösö (Jämtland), Sweden, records that 'Ostman Gudfastsson had Jämtland made Christian'. It probably dates from the second quarter of the eleventh century.

34. This pillar, recovered from the River Zbrucz in southern Poland, is thought to be an idol of the Slav god Svantovit whose cult is discussed in Chapter 12.

35. *Right* Sainte-Foi, patron saint of the abbey of Conques (Aveyron), in the Rouergue district of south-central France, the object of a wide-spread local cult. This astonishing statue-reliquary covered in gold and gems probably dates from the tenth century.

36. *Below* The sundial at Kirkdale, North Yorkshire, with its accompanying inscription recording the rebuilding of the church dedicated to Pope Gregory, the apostle of the English, by Orm, the son of Gamel, in the middle years of the eleventh century.

rule, just as there was of Gallo-Roman culture in Frankish Gaul in the age of Clovis.

If Greek, therefore Christian too? Surely. We can posit the existence of pockets of Christianity in the surviving towns of Bulgaria. These could have been reinforced by the familiar process of seepage which we have seen at work in other contexts, whether in times of war by the movement of prisoners or in times of peace through the agency of merchants and diplomats. The khans were certainly suspicious enough of Christian prisoners of war to persecute them for their faith. The most distinguished victim was Manuel, archbishop of Adrianople, martyred in 813. The perceived danger, apparently, was that these exiled Christians would make converts among the Bulgars. It sounds a little reminiscent of the anti-Christian persecutions conducted by the Goths in Dacia in the fourth century. Perhaps the perception was correct. It was said that Khan Omurtag's own son Enravotas became a Christian, for which he was put to death by his brother Khan Malamir. The reality may have been a squabble over the succession, but the very fact that such an accusation could be made, or even just rumoured, is significant. Christianity was not for the Bulgar elite – except when its members left Bulgaria. We have a case from the year 815 of a boyar who departed Bulgaria, for reasons unknown but quite possibly as a political exile, and migrated to Constantinople where he was converted, receiving the Christian name Theodore and the high rank of *patricius*, 'patrician'. The leading spiritual counsellor of the day, the monk Theodore of Studios, in a letter congratulated his tame barbarian namesake upon his conversion to Christianity. The letter makes it plain that Theodore the boyar was not an isolated case. One of the stone inscriptions, dated 837, famously contrasted 'Bulgar' and 'Christian'. What might be called 'official' Bulgar paganism was very much alive. The celebrated rock-face relief known as the Horseman of Madara – at what was probably a cult-site not far from Pliska – is accompanied by an inscription (in Greek!) which refers both to Khan Omurtag and to the Bulgars' high god Tengri.

So matters stood in the middle years of the ninth century. There were to be far-reaching cultural changes for both Moravians and Bulgarians under their respective rulers Rastislav, who came to power in Moravia in 846, and Boris, who succeeded to the khanate of the Bulgars in 852. In the year 862 both rulers approached one of the great powers of the day and asked for Christian teachers to be sent to his kingdom. What may seem initially surprising is the choice of power to whom each turned. Rastislav addressed his request to the Emperor Michael III in Constantinople. Boris directed his to the ruler of the east Frankish kingdom, King Louis, known as 'the German', the grandson of Charlemagne. Initial surprise may ebb, however, if we look a little more closely at the background.

The seventh and eighth centuries were the unhappiest that the Byzantine empire had yet known in its long history. The reconstituted Mediterranean empire of Justinian was steadily eroded as the Lombards tightened their grip upon Italy and the distant Spanish province was lost in the 620s after campaigns by the learned King Sisebut. The Avars had overrun the Danubian provinces and besieged Constantinople in 626. The irruption of Islam in the middle east – sudden, unexpected, a bolt from the blue of which even Byzantine diplomacy had fatally failed to give warning – had hacked off in an almost unbelievably short space of time some of the empire's oldest and holiest provinces. Jerusalem fell to the Arabs in 636 and Palestine and Syria were quickly overrun. Alexandria and Egypt followed in the early 640s. Cyprus was lost in 649. Africa took a little longer, Carthage finally succumbing in 698. Twice the Arabs threatened Constantinople itself, in the sieges of 674–7 and 717–18. Meanwhile, as we have seen, the infiltration of the Balkans and Greece by the Slavs had effectively rolled imperial authority back into a few coastal cities. These reverses had seriously disrupted the empire's economy – particularly grievous being the loss of Egypt, Constantinople's bread-basket – at a time when the economy of the Mediterranean world as a whole was experiencing a prolonged recession in urban and commercial life. The appearance of bubonic plague in the Mediterranean from the second quarter of the sixth century, endemic thereafter for 200 years, further contributed to economic disruption and human dislocation. Turned in upon itself, humbled, bewildered, despairing, the empire then proceeded to tear itself apart in the long-drawn-out iconoclastic controversy, which convulsed the empire for over a century from its inception in 726.

But the empire was nothing if not resilient and it had come through this grim period. The Arab peril had begun to recede after the displacement of the Umayyad caliphate of Damascus by the Abbasid caliphate of Baghdad in the middle of the eighth century. The Avars were conquered by Charlemagne. The tempo of economic life began very

340

gradually to quicken once more. The incidence of plague slackened. Anatolia replaced Egypt as the agrarian hub of the empire. New administrative structures were devised for a slimmed-down empire. Little by little imperial authority was reaffirmed in Greece and the Balkans, its progress marked by the extension of the new administrative units known as *themes*. In our surviving documentation the theme of the Peloponnese is first recorded in about 800; that of Macedonia by 802; that of Cephalonia and the Ionian Islands by 809; that of Dyrrachium by about 825; that of Thessalonica by 836. From these coastal bases the re-Hellenization and re-Christianization of the Slav interior could be undertaken. Above all, the iconoclastic controversy was finally settled in 843 with the formal condemnation of iconoclasm and the 'Restoration of the Images' – still a major feast-day in the eastern churches – in a resounding affirmation of Christian orthodoxy and imperial authority. A new mood of self-confidence and self-assertion stole imperceptibly over the governing classes in church and state. One symptom or symbol of this mood was the re-foundation of the university of Constantinople by the Emperor Theophilus in the 830s. It was to prove a nursery of scholars, churchmen, administrators and diplomats in the course of the immediately following generations. The empire embarked upon its golden age, which was to last until the disasters of the eleventh century.

Another indication of the new mood was a revived sense of the imperative of mission. The key to understanding the Byzantine empire is the notion that the emperor was the divinely appointed instrument of God for the achievement of His purposes on earth through the diffusion of the orthodox – not quite yet but very nearly the Orthodox – Christian faith. It will be readily appreciated that this notion had its origins in what in an earlier chapter I called 'the Eusebian accommodation' in the age of Constantine. This process of diffusion was not quite the same thing as 'imperialism' in the crude sense in which the Saxons experienced it at the hands of Charlemagne; though the campaigning sceptres of Byzantine emperors could be sharp enough if the need arose. Rather, the east Roman notion was one of a community or family of peoples, loosely held together by a shared faith and culture in subordination to God's representative on earth, the father of the family, the emperor. It is no coincidence that the recovery of Byzantine fortunes in the ninth century was accompanied by a concern for Christian evangelism. It was a part of that intricate science and fine art of

Byzantine diplomacy. Thus, for example, the re-Hellenization of Greece and the Balkans meant both the Christianization of the Slavs who had settled there and, inseparable from it, their submission to imperial authority. Here is the bookish tenth-century emperor, Constantine Porphyrogenitus:

> The nations of those parts, the Croats and Serbs and Zachlumites, Terbuniotes and Kanalites and Diocletians and the Pagani, shook off the reins of the empire of the Romans and became self-governing and independent, subject to none . . . But in the time of Basil, the Christ-loving emperor [867–86], they sent diplomatic agents, begging and praying him that those of them who were unbaptised might receive baptism and that they might be, as they had originally been, subject to the empire of the Romans; and that glorious emperor, of blessed memory, gave ear to them and sent out an imperial agent and priests with him and baptised all of them that were unbaptised of the aforesaid nations, and after baptising them he then appointed for them princes whom they themselves approved and chose, from the family which they themselves loved and favoured.[4]

The conversion of Serbia did not go quite like that, but the passage shows us how governing circles in Constantinople looked out upon their world, and makes it a little easier to understand Constantinople's positive reaction to Rastislav's request for Christian teachers in 862. We are also better placed to understand the reluctance of Khan Boris to seek his teachers from the same quarter. The empire was the traditional foe of the Bulgarians. To accept Christianity from Constantinople would be to acknowledge the suzerainty of its emperor. Krum had made Bulgaria great, with Tengri's help, by defeating emperors, not by submitting to them. Boris, therefore, determined to look elsewhere.

Here for the moment we must leave the Byzantine empire and turn to the German background, best approached by way of the history of the church in Bavaria. After the withering away of Roman imperial rule in the provinces of Raetia and Noricum at the end of the fifth century a principality of Bavaria emerged there in impenetrably obscure circumstances in the course of the sixth century. By the year 600 Bavaria was on the way to achieving some stability under a dynasty of rulers of Frankish origin known as the Agilolfing family. Their relations with Merovingian Frankish royal power fluctuated in much the same way as did those of other principalities up and down the eastern frontier zone, such as the Frisians. Merovingian lordship over Bavaria seems to have been at its most effective during the first half of the seventh century; thereafter it declined in intensity, to such an extent that during the eighth century the Agilolfing dukes of Bavaria were to all intents and purposes independent sovereign rulers. Charlemagne put an end to this state of affairs when he deposed the last Agilolfing, Tassilo III, in 788 and incorporated Bavaria into his empire.

The geographical position of Bavaria meant that her relations with Italian powers to the south were as significant as those with the Franks to the west. Agilolfing lordship reached deep into the Alps and intermittently beyond them, a force to be reckoned with by Lombard kings at Pavia, Byzantine officials at Ravenna and popes at Rome. The Bavarian princess Theodelinda married, around the year 600, two successive Lombard kings and was the mother and regent for another, King Adaloald (the recipient of the letter from King Sisebut of Spain to which reference was made in Chapter 4). The last of the Agilolfings, Tassilo III, also married a Lombard princess.

As in the Rhineland in the sixth century, pockets of Christianity seem to have survived here and there in Bavaria, particularly at what had been Roman forts or towns. Such, for example, were Castra Batava (Passau) and Iuvavum (Salzburg) – though Salzburg was later to trace the foundation of her cathedral church to St Rupert, a political exile from the Rhineland who migrated to Bavaria in about 690. The Agilolfing dynasty seems to have been Christian from early on, by the early part of the sixth century, well before the time of Theodelinda. She busied herself with encouraging the spread of the faith in her native province, in testimony to which archaeologists have noted Italian influences in the early Christian archaeology of seventh century Bavaria. The Agilolfings welcomed clergy from outside, just as did, let us say, the Anglo-Saxons. Rupert was one such, so was Emmeram at Regensburg and Corbinian at Freising. So too was Boniface, when he re-organized the Bavarian bishoprics in 739–40. Yet another was the Irishman Virgil, who came to the continent as a *peregrinus* in 743 and gravitated to Bavaria, where he became bishop of Salzburg in 747. There may well have been Italian clerics active in Bavaria also, possibly emanating from the church of Aquileia in the extreme north-east of Italy.

A Christianized or re-Christianized Bavaria, situated on Latin Christendom's eastern frontier, naturally became a jumping-off point for missionary work among its pagan Slavonic neighbours. These were the Moravians to the north of the Danube and the Carantanians to its south, the latter squeezed between Bavarians and Avars in what is now eastern Austria and western Hungary.* We should bear in mind, too, that no neat dividing-line separated Bavarian from Slav; there were Slav settlements intermingled amongst the Bavarian and pre-Bavarian populations of the region. When Tassilo III, just after a visit to Rome, founded the monastery of Innichen in 769 it was 'because of the unbelief of the Slav peoples, to lead them into the way of truth'. A missionary role for this community was envisaged as clearly as for the monks of Echternach or Münster or Corvey. Innichen lies in the Austrian Tyrol on the upper waters of the river Drau (Drava). Its mission field lay down-river, among the Carantanians and beyond them the Croats. Kremsmünster – 'the monastery on the Krems', a little to the south of Linz – was another of Tassilo's foundations. Its surviving foundation charter, from the year 777, makes plain that this house too had missionary responsibilities among the Slavs. Virgil's successor at Salzburg, Alcuin's friend Arn, though a native of Bavaria had spent some time as a young man at the monastery of Saint-Amand in Flanders. It is likely that evangelistic concern was fostered in the young Arn by training in the community founded by the great Amandus. As bishop, and from 798 archbishop of Salzburg, Arn would put much effort into the evangelization of the Avars along the lines agreed in 796, and of the Carantanian Slavs. It was Arn too who, building upon foundations laid by the scholarly Virgil, encouraged the growth of a splendid library at Salzburg. This example was followed in others among the religious communities of Bavaria. Here as in other contexts we can see the close association of scholarship with mission.

The missionary activities of the churchmen of Salzburg among the Slavs of Carantania are described in some detail in a work known as the *Conversio Bagoariorum et Carantanorum* (*The Conversion of the Bavarians and Carantanians*).[5] This is a short pamphlet which was composed at Salzburg in 870 in somewhat turbulent circumstances

---

* I use the term 'Carantanians' to translate the Latin *Carantani* of our principal source. 'Carinthians' would be misleading because the territory they occupied was distinct from the modern Carinthia, the Austrian province of Kärnten.

which we shall come to later on. Briefly, the *Conversio* was a defence of Salzburg's ecclesiastical claims over its Slav neighbours against interlopers from the Byzantine empire. The clergy of Salzburg claimed the Carantanians for themselves because Salzburg alone and unaided had undertaken the task of evangelizing them. It would be an understatement to say that the *Conversio* is polemical and partisan. However, the story that it has to tell was firmly based upon records preserved at Salzburg and it seems to be credible not only in its main lines but in much of its detail too. As often, we need to be alert to the kind of things which its anonymous author chose not to tell us. The *Conversio* offers us one of the most lively accounts of the operations of an early medieval mission station that has come down to us, which makes it worth quoting at some length. Here is what it has to tell us of the growth of Christianity among the Carantanians during the episcopate of Bishop Virgil of Salzburg. I have inserted dates and modern place-names, where ascertainable, in brackets. The passage translated here opens during the sway in the 740s of the Carantanian chieftain called Boruth or Boruta.

> Not long afterwards the Avars began to press heavily upon the Carantanians with fierce attacks. Their leader at that time, by name Boruth, sent to the Bavarians telling them of the imminent attack of an Avar army and asked them to come to his aid. They came in haste, defeated the Avars, strengthened the Carantanians and subjected them and all their territory to the overlordship of the kings [i.e. of the Agilolfing dukes of Bavaria who were sometimes styled king]. They carried hostages with them back to Bavaria. Among these hostages was the son of Boruth, by name Cacatius [or Gorazd] whom his father asked to be brought up in a Christian manner and to be made a Christian; and this was done [*c.* 743]. He asked the same for Cheitmar [or Hotımır] his brother's son. When Boruth died [*c.* 750] the Bavarians . . . sent Cacatius, now a Christian, back to the Slavs at their request. The Slavs made him their duke. But he died in the third year after this [*c.* 752]. Once more, at the request of the Carantanians and with the agreement of King Pippin, Cheitmar, now a Christian, was sent back to them. Lupus the priest, ordained from the church of Salzburg to the island called Awa on the lake of Cheming [the Chiemsee] gave to Cheitmar his nephew, by name Maioranus, who had already been ordained priest. And because he was Cheitmar's godfather, Lupus the priest instructed him to submit himself

with a devout will to the church of Salzburg for ecclesiastical guidance. The Carantanians received Cheitmar and made him their duke. He was accompanied by Maioranus, who had been ordained by the holy Virgil in the church of Salzburg. Maioranus instructed Cheitmar to bow his head to that same church in God's service. And Cheitmar did this, and promised that he would be obedient to that see. This vow he kept, and every year he performed his service there, and he always received Christian teaching and ministry from Salzburg for as long as he lived.

After some time had passed the aforesaid Cheitmar, duke of the Carantanians, asked Bishop Virgil to visit his people and to strengthen them resolutely in the faith. At the time [*c.* 757] the bishop was unable to do this himself, but in his place he sent a bishop called Modestus to instruct that people, and with Modestus the priests Watto, Reginbert, Gozharius and Latinus, and Eckhard the deacon together with other clergy. Bishop Virgil gave Modestus permission to consecrate churches and to ordain clergy in accordance with canon law, and told him to undertake nothing which was contrary to the decrees of the holy Fathers. Going among the Carantanians they dedicated there the church of St Mary [Maria Saal, north of Klagenfurt] and another at the town of *Liburnia* [Lurnfeld, near Spittal] and another at *Undrimas* [Pölshals] and more in several other places. Bishop Modestus stayed there until the end of his life [*c.* 763].

On the bishop's death Cheitmar again asked Bishop Virgil to come to him, if it were possible. But Virgil declined, because the disturbances which we call *carmula* had broken out [*c.* 763; we do not know what the *carmula* was]. However, after taking advice, he sent the priest Latinus there. But not long afterwards, on the outbreak of further disturbances, Latinus came back. When the *carmula* had been suppressed Bishop Virgil sent out the priest Madalhoh and after him the priest Warmann.

When Cheitmar died [769] and disorder broke out there was no priest there for some years, until Duke Waltunc sent once again to Bishop Virgil and asked him to send priests there. The bishop then [772] sent them Haimo the priest and Reginbald the priest, and Maioranus the deacon and other clergy. Not long afterwards he sent there the same Haimo, and Dupliterus and Maioranus the priests, and other clergy with them. Later he sent them Gozharius the priest, Maioranus and Erchanbert; after them, the priests Reginbald and Reginhere; and then the priests Maioranus and Augustine; and later, Reginbald and Gundarius.

And all this was done in the time of Bishop Virgil [who died in 784].

Salzburg thus got its initial foothold among the Carantanians by means of the princely hostages, the son and nephew of Boruth. There are hints of an ecclesiastical dynasty in Lupus the priest – godfather of the returning Christian prince Cheitmar – and his nephew Maioranus. The team of clergy sent with Bishop Modestus consolidated Salzburg's ecclesiastical empire. When times were dangerous clergy would travel to and fro as circumstances permitted, some of them like Maioranus evidently making a speciality of the Carantanian 'run'. And there are further hints of family operations in the trio Reginbert, Reginbald and Reginhere, whose shared name-element suggests a blood relationship.

The *Conversio* also offers us the following tale, or perhaps we should say fable. It concerns a certain Ingo, incorrectly described in the text as a secular leader in Carantania. In reality he was probably another representative of the Salzburg clerical community active in the mission field during the last fifteen years of the eighth century. The tale sheds some light on the missionary tactics which the clergy of Salzburg liked to remember and celebrate at the time that this pamphlet was composed.

> Ingo used to invite serfs who were believers to his table, and those who were their lords, if unbelievers, he forced to sit outside like dogs, putting down bread and meat and glasses of wine that was cloudy in front of them, that thus they should take their food; but he ordered that the serfs should be served from golden plates. When the great men who had been excluded asked him, 'Why are you treating us like this?' he replied, 'You are not worthy, with your unwashed bodies, to have dealings with those who have been reborn in the holy fount [of baptism]. Out of my house and eat your food like dogs!' As a result of this they positively rushed to be instructed in the holy faith and be baptised. And so the Christian faith quickly grew.

The *Conversio* goes on to emphasize the continuing missionary responsibility of the church of Salzburg under Archbishop Arn (784–821) and the extension of this responsibility to embrace Pannonia as well as Carantania after Charlemagne's defeat of the Avars.* It relates

* Pannonia at this period may be understood as that area of today's western Hungary bounded by the rivers Raab (Rába), Drau (Drava) and Danube.

how Theodoric was consecrated a missionary bishop for Carantania-Pannonia by Arn in 799, and how Theodoric's successors Otto and Osbald were consecrated by Arn's successors Adalram (821–36) and Liupram (836–59).

The *Conversio* also dwells in some detail on the relations between the church of Salzburg and the Slav prince Pribina. The latter, as we have already seen, ruled a Slav principality next to Moravia based in the valley of the river Nitra (Neutra). Pribina had married a Bavarian and therefore Christian wife. The possible significance of this marriage is worth pondering in the light of such earlier mixed marriages as those of Ethelbert and Bertha or Edwin and Ethelburga. The *Conversio* records that Archbishop Adalram consecrated a church 'beyond the Danube in the place called Nitra'. This church, consecrated probably in about 827, may have been built for the use of Pribina's Christian wife and her entourage. A few years afterwards, in about 833, Pribina was expelled from Nitra by Mojmir of Moravia. The exile sought refuge at the court of King Louis the German, 'at whose command', the *Conversio* tells us, he was baptized a Christian. The ceremony took place in a church on an estate belonging – and surely not a surprise – to the church of Salzburg. Louis subsequently established Pribina at Moosburg (Zalavár) at the western end of Lake Balaton. Archaeologists have excavated the remains of a formidable stronghold there and, beneath the stone foundations of an eleventh-century church, the remains of its wooden ninth-century precursor. This neatly confirms the evidence of the *Conversio* that in 850 Archbishop Liupram consecrated a church built by Pribina 'at his fortress in the woods and marshes beside the river Zala', a description which corresponds to that low-lying country. The priest to whom the church was entrusted by the archbishop, one Dominic, had previously served in the chancery of Louis the German. There was thus no doubting who was in charge of ecclesiastical life at Zalavár. Dominic came as Salzburg's man. He was also a man whose previous administrative experience would have enabled him to school Pribina in the habits and techniques of Christian rulership. On the same journey Archbishop Liupram consecrated two more churches. One had been built by a priest named Sandrat, probably a native of the diocese of Salzburg, on land near Zalavár in the possession of Pribina's son Kocel (Kotsel, Chozil). The other had been built by Ermperht the priest, probably a member of a Bavarian family in the retinue of Pribina. At Pribina's request Liupram sent masons, carpenters, smiths and painters from Salzburg, who built two further churches at Zalavár. Before his death in 859 Archbishop Liupram had consecrated fourteen other churches at named places in Pannonia, at least one of which was dedicated to Salzburg's own St Rupert. All the successors of Dominic as priest to the princely court at Zalavár were drawn from the Salzburg community. Throughout his life Pribina never wavered in his devotion to the see of Salzburg, boasted the *Conversio*. After his death, probably in 860 or 861, his son Kocel inherited his power and his loyalties. In 864 Archbishop Adalwin of Salzburg spent Christmas at Kocel's court at Zalavár and subsequently consecrated six new churches, providing each with its own priest, presumably from Salzburg. In the course of the next three years he consecrated five more. Salzburg's grip on the Christian life of Pannonia must have seemed unshakeably secure.

Owing to the survival of the *Conversio* we are enabled to see with unusual clarity how Salzburg's 'ecclesiastical colonialism' worked. It cannot be doubted that had there survived a comparable narrative from the Bavarian bishopric of Passau it would have told a similar tale about the Christian life of Moravia. As things are, we have to make do with mere fragments of information: Mojmir's baptism in about 822, the mass baptism of his followers in 831. The archaeological record helps us a little. In addition to the princely residence, the houses and the workshops excavated at Mikulčice there were also discovered the foundations of several churches which dated from the first half of the ninth century, presumably commissioned by Mojmir and Rastislav. On the analogy of Zalavár we are probably on safe ground in assuming that these princely churches would have been staffed by incoming German clergy obligingly supplied by the bishops of Passau. At Pohansko, at the confluence of the river Dyje with the Morava, not far from today's Břeclav, there has been excavated a settlement, with a church, on a more modest scale than the princely centre at Mikulčice. If correctly interpreted as the dwelling of a nobleman we have here a hint of the adhesion of the Moravian aristocracy to the new faith.

King Louis the German and his Bavarian bishops would have regarded the Moravians, Carantanians and Pannonians as lying within the range of their influence, being in some sense subject to their authority. The Christianization of these peoples was a concomitant of their subjection. But we must be cautious about accepting the German view of matters uncritically. The Slav principalities were as awkward for a ninth-century German ruler to manipulate as, shall we say, the Frisians – or indeed the Bavarians – had been for Frankish kings of the eighth. Quite possibly, given their wealth, the Slavs were a good deal more difficult to manipulate. The pressure of German claims and German overlordship was one that varied in weight and intensity as to time and place. Rastislav owed his coming to power in Moravia in 846 to Louis's assistance: but within a few years he was harbouring German exiles and by the 860s he was playing an active part in the squabbling between the sons of the now elderly Louis over their prospective shares in the inheritance. If the political scene on the southeastern frontiers of Germany was more complicated than our sources permit us to take the full measure of, so too was the ecclesiastical one. Rulers like Rastislav and Pribina were perfectly capable of 'shopping around' in the ecclesiastical market-place. There is some reason to suppose that both men independently made approaches to the pope in about 860, presumably in an attempt to outflank the German bishops, though seemingly nothing came of these moves. The archaeological evidence reveals influences from another Italian quarter. Several of the early Moravian churches display architectural features which have their closest parallels in the north-east of Italy. If we ask how they came to be there, the most plausible answer is, through the agency of the church of Aquileia. The patriarchate of Aquileia, at the head of the Adriatic, long preceding Venice as a mercantile and Christian city, cherished long-standing if shadowy claims to the spiritual headship of the middle Danube region to her north. The monasteries in the hinterland of Aquileia – Cividale, Sesto and others – were as well-placed as Innichen or Kremsmünster to undertake missionary work among the Slavs. Already in 811 Charlemagne had been called upon to give a ruling in some contention between Aquileia and Salzburg over competing claims in the Carantanian region. One could not ask for clearer evidence that the narrative of the *Conversio* was being, well, economical with the truth in its portrayal of Salzburg's selfless and solitary efforts to bring God's word to the Carantanians.

There is therefore much that we do not and shall never know about the fluctuating pattern of relationships in the Danube basin during the middle years of the ninth century. If we knew a little more about them we might be able to recover the immediate background to the startling events of the 860s. We should also give much for a precise chronology of those events. But it is no good moaning about what we don't have. Let us instead try to make sense of what we do.

In 862 Khan Boris of Bulgaria had a meeting with King Louis the German on the Danube near Vienna. He sought an alliance with the German king as an escape-route from the prospect of Constantinople's stifling embrace, in return for which he undertook to accept Christianity from the German church. As an immediate riposte to this Rastislav of Moravia, feeling the pincers of Germans and Bulgarians closing upon him, sent an embassy to the Byzantine emperor Michael III requesting Christian teachers for his people. The Byzantine response was speedy and positive. Two brothers, Cyril and Methodius, were sent to Rastislav's court in the year 863.

Cyril and Methodius were very remarkable men. Their careers were recorded in *vitae* composed shortly after their deaths, which occurred respectively in 869 and 885. The *Life of Cyril*, possibly composed by his brother, must have been in existence by 882. The *Life of Methodius*, probably composed by his disciple Clement of Ohrid (Ochrida), seems to have been written in or shortly after 886.[6] Though these *Lives* were composed in accordance with hagiographical convention it is generally agreed that most of what they have to tell us is reliable. The brothers were natives of Thessalonica, the sons of a wealthy nobleman who occupied a high position in government service. Methodius was the elder of the two by several years, born in about 815. He studied law as a young man, entered the civil service and quickly rose to become what his biographer obscurely calls 'governor of a Slav province'. It is presumed that this indicates prominent administrative rank in one of the recently established themes of the northern Greek or Adriatic coastline. Methodius seemed to be on course for a distinguished career among the empire's governing elite. But in middle life he threw all this over and became a monk in one of the several monasteries on Mount Olympus.[*] This would have been in about 850.

His younger brother Cyril, meanwhile, was making a name for himself in the intellectual circles of the capital. Born in about 825, Cyril was a child prodigy, a precocious learner who quickly exhausted the scholastic resources of Thessalonica. A timely exercise of patronage

---

[*] Olympus in Bithynia, overlooking the Sea of Marmara, not the home of the gods in northern Greece.

enabled him to continue his studies in Constantinople. At the recently restored university he was fortunate to sit at the feet of Leo, known as 'the Mathematician' – though his expertise ranged much more widely – the foremost teacher of his day. Another of his masters was Photius, perhaps the most encyclopaedic intellect ever to flourish in Byzantium, later to become the distinguished and controversial patriarch of Constantinople. When Photius left the university to take up a leading post in the imperial chancery Cyril was promoted to the chair of philosophy which he had vacated. At the time he can hardly have been more than about twenty-four. Because of the intimate association in Constantinople between scholarship and government, the empire's leading professor of philosophy was in no sense withdrawn from the world. He was a public figure, potentially available for public service. The branch of service in which he was chosen to represent the empire was foreign diplomacy. This was partly because of his intellectual stature: envoys were often called upon to engage in scholarly debate with their opposite numbers. We may suspect that Cyril was chosen for this role also because of his extraordinary talent for languages. The first such embassy on which he served took him to the court of the Abbasid caliph al-Mutawakkil in Mesopotamia. Another took him to the ruler of the Khazars, beyond the Black Sea.

By this time the brothers had come together again. Cyril had spent some time with Methodius in his Olympian monastery in the mid-850s, and both brothers served on the Khazar embassy of 860–61. The Khazars had long occupied a critically important place in the web of Byzantine diplomacy. They had blocked the advance of Islamic armies through the Caucasus and on to the south Russian steppe, an advance which would have given access to and quite probably possession of Christian Europe. Now the Khazars were to be schooled for a new role, against new enemies. In June 860 a fleet of 200 ships had sailed into the Bosphorus. From them had disembarked an army of Scandinavian Vikings from what we now call Russia, who proceeded to plunder the suburbs on Constantinople. The attackers had achieved complete surprise and in the short space that their raid lasted they did considerable damage and inspired great terror. We can re-live something of that terror in two homilies delivered by Photius, now patriarch, one during the emergency and one immediately after the Vikings' departure. As during the Avar siege of 626 the Virgin Mary had not failed her beloved city. 'At the time when, denuded of all help and deprived of human alliance, we were spiritually led on by holding fast to our hopes in the Mother of the Word, our God.'[7] Constantinople's most precious relic, the Virgin's robe, had been solemnly processed about the walls; and the enemy had withdrawn. But human stratagem as well as divine aid had to be resorted to in an attempt to guard against this new enemy. Hence the embassy to the Khazars. They were to be persuaded to attack the Russians.

The biographers of Cyril and Methodius make no allusion to these political manoeuvrings. For them the Khazar embassy had a primarily religious goal: to urge the Khazars to become Christians. In the context of Byzantine diplomacy this made sound sense. Ideally, the Khazars were to be encouraged to turn themselves into good Christians and loyal sons of the imperial family of nations. In the event, Cyril and Methodius were too late. The Khazars had for long – and most intriguingly – been hesitating between Judaism, Christianity and Islam. By the middle years of the ninth century the influence of the Jewish rabbis in Khazar ruling circles was approaching dominance. During the third quarter of the century the Khazar people became officially Judaic in observance: 'the Thirteenth Tribe'.

What is interesting to us is that it should have been Cyril and Methodius who were chosen by the government in Constantinople to undertake an enterprise that had at least in part a missionary character. One can only assume that their inclinations in this respect were already known. One possible clue to the roots of their vocation could lie in the spiritual preoccupations of the monastic community to which Methodius belonged and to which Cyril had for a time been attached. In the first half of the ninth century monks from Mount Olympus were beginning to be active in the evangelization of the Alans, a semi-nomadic tribe who inhabited the fringes of the Caucasus, neighbours of the Khazars. Was the idea of mission one that was cultivated in the Olympian monasteries, rather as it was at, say, Luxeuil in the seventh century in Francia? We have one more hint that it might have been, which concerns the origins of the language known as Old Church Slavonic.

'You two are from Thessalonica, and all Thessalonians speak the Slav tongue well.' The words were allegedly spoken by the Emperor Michael III when he gave an audience to the brothers before despatching them to Moravia. The most enduring achievement of the brothers over the next few years was the creation of a Christian literature in the vernacular for their Moravian converts. This was written in an alphabet devised by Cyril, the so-called Glagolitic script.* According to his biographer the letters were revealed to Cyril by God, suddenly, in a flash of understanding. We may prefer to think that they were elaborated slowly, after much cogitation and experimental utterance of sounds and scribbling of characters. In other words, the devising of the alphabet could have taken a longish time, and since both men were clearly familiar with it by 863, it was not the work of one man alone but had evolved from discussions between the brothers (and possibly others as well). If the Glagolitic script did indeed develop in some such fashion, then clearly the encouragement of monastic superiors and colleagues in Mount Olympus may be assumed. This would reinforce our suspicion that communication with barbarians for missionary purposes was engaging the attention of the Olympian monks in the middle years of the ninth century.

Rastislav of Moravia is said to have asked for 'a teacher to instruct us in the true faith *in our own language*' (my italics). Because of the storm of controversy that blew up we have to treat this assertion cautiously. However, whether or not Rastislav requested vernacular teaching, this is what he got at the brothers' hands. Upon arrival in Moravia Cyril and Methodius instantly set about providing the Moravians with a Christian literature in Old Church Slavonic and in training a native Slav clergy. Their actions were controversial on three grounds. First, they were moving into a territory which the German clergy had been evangelizing for some time and regarded as their own. Second, they probably moved more swiftly in recruiting a native priesthood than the Germans had been accustomed to. Third, they translated the daily liturgy of the church into the vernacular. Now the Germans had no objection to vernaculars as such. As we saw in Chapter 8 there was at this very time a lively development of Old High German for the purposes of Christian instruction. The error, in German eyes, of which Cyril and Methodius were guilty was to translate *the liturgy of the sacraments* into the vernacular. Preaching, praying and professing the faith might be done in a convert's own native tongue; but baptism and the eucharist must be administered in Latin – and correct Latin too, as we may recall St Boniface insisting.

---

* This was not the same as Cyrillic script, which was devised about a generation later and, confusingly, not by Cyril.

The German clergy claimed that there were only three permissible liturgical languages, namely Hebrew, Greek and Latin. Cyril opposed this. It did not promote the calm exchange of views that he mocked his antagonists as 'Pilatians', because Pontius Pilate had composed the trilingual superscription attached to the cross above the crucified body of Jesus. Cyril had other objections, too, to the methods of the German clergy. These are alluded to only in one puzzling sentence in his *Life*. Its meaning is not clear in detail but its general drift is to the effect that Cyril accused the German missionaries of being too ready to compromise with pre-Christian beliefs and customs – among them, we might care to note, 'illegitimate unions' or consanguineous marriages. It is clear therefore that the differences at stake were not just about ecclesiastical power-politics but involved hard and important questions concerning missionary tactics. After some forty months, that is to say in the autumn of 866, Cyril and Methodius left Moravia and entered Pannonia. They took with them their body of trainee clergy so that they might be ordained to the priesthood by a bishop, presumably within the east Roman empire. It is possible that the timing of their departure was not unconnected with the appointment of Bishop Hermanrich to the see of Passau. This man was later to show himself fanatically anti-Greek; it was his bishopric that had lost the most by the brothers' work in Moravia. Cyril and Methodius were made welcome in Pannonia by Prince Kocel and remained there for about a year, teaching in Old Church Slavonic and training a native clergy, just as they had done in Moravia. We know, from the *Conversio*, how this initiative was regarded at Salzburg.

It was at this point that a new player took a hand. At some point in 867 Pope Nicholas I summoned Cyril and Methodius to Rome. Quite why he did so we do not know. The most natural explanation among the various possibilities is that the pope – one who had a particularly exalted conception of his office and its authority – was apprehensive of an unseemly dispute between rancorous German clergy and innovative Greek missionaries, particularly at a juncture when relations between Rome and Constantinople were fragile. The brothers travelled to Venice, where they debated the trilingual question with a distinguished body of clergy, some of whom at least must have been attached to the patriarchate of Aquileia. That church, as we have already seen, may have had some interest in the evangelization of the Slavs. After this encounter the party travelled on to Rome, arriving there in the autumn of 867. Pope Nicholas had just died; his successor Hadrian II received them.

Cyril and Methodius brought with them a pearl of great price, the relics of St Clement which they had acquired in the Crimea in the course of their embassy to the Khazars. Clement, an early successor to St Peter as bishop of Rome, had allegedly been exiled to the Crimea and martyred there by being flung into the sea with an anchor tied round his neck. It was almost certainly an apocryphal tale, but the arrival of the holy 'relics' of an early Roman martyr in 867 was greeted with jubilation and the remains were solemnly deposited by Hadrian II in the martyr-pope's own church of San Clemente, further to swell the spiritual garrison, the noble army of martyrs who defended the City. In the course of the discussions and enquiries which followed, Pope Hadrian was evidently impressed with the brothers and their work. He approved the Slavonic liturgy and had it celebrated in St Peter's. He ordained to the priesthood the native clergy trained in Moravia and Pannonia. Most important of all he prepared to appoint a bishop, who would be independent of the German bishops, for the new Slav churches of central Europe. It is likely that he wished to appoint Cyril to this office. However, Cyril fell ill towards the end of the year 868 and died in February 869. On his deathbed he charged his brother to carry on the work that they had together begun.

The immediate result of Boris's acceptance of Christianity from the Germans in 862 was a sharp military riposte from Constantinople. Boris had wavered from his orientation and had to be taught a lesson. As soon as the campaigning season of 863 opened, an imperial army was sent into Bulgaria and an imperial fleet cruised up the Danube. Boris capitulated, renounced his German alliance and agreed to accept Christianity from Constantinople. After instruction he was baptized by a Greek bishop sent from the capital, probably towards the end of 865. Following Byzantine custom he became the Emperor Michael's godson and took his name (though we shall continue to refer to him as Boris). He also received, from the Patriarch Photius, a long letter setting out the main points of Christian doctrine and sketching a portrait of the ideal Christian ruler for the convert khan to model himself upon. Mingling flattery with instruction Photius compared Boris with Constantine: a familiar theme. The patriarch's letter was cast in elaborate circumlocutions but between its stately lines could be read the message that conversion entailed subordination to the emperor in Constantinople.

The first domestic result of the acceptance of Christianity by Boris from Constantinople was a rebellion against him by the pagan boyars of Bulgaria. The little that we know about it indicates that the revolt was an extremely serious one which nearly cost Boris his throne and his life. He suppressed it with great savagery. It is probably correct to interpret this rising not as a 'pagan reaction' *tout court* but rather as an expression of revulsion against the idea of accepting Christianity with all sorts of menacing strings attached from Bulgaria's traditional enemy. Boris cannot have been unaware that in neighbouring Moravia the missionaries were employing the vernacular and training a prospective priesthood for what might turn out to be a largely self-governing Moravian church. It was evident from Photius's letter that there was no prospect of these things coming to pass in Bulgaria. For Boris the future looked unappealing: he had subordinated himself to the emperor in Constantinople, which his own magnates would not stand for. So as soon as he had put the rebellion down, in 866, Boris changed tactics. He decided to play again the 'western card' as he had done in 862, and once more appealed to King Louis the German. But in 866 there was this difference, that he also approached the pope.

The Germans eagerly grasped this opportunity of extending their influence, now threatened by Cyril and Methodius in Moravia, into Bulgaria. A German mission under Bishop Hermanrich of Passau was despatched to the khan's court: it was a significant choice of leader. Pope Nicholas I also responded positively. In November 866 a papal mission was despatched under an Italian bishop, Formosus of Porto (later himself to become pope between 891 and 896). He took with him a long letter from Pope Nicholas responding to queries put to him by Boris, and from one of the pope's answers it can be inferred that Boris had requested a patriarch for the nascent Bulgarian church, in other words a leader who might render it independent of Constantinople. Pope Nicholas stalled. He could take no action until his legates had reported on their mission. If the number of believers multiplied in Bulgaria, then bishoprics might be founded there. In the fullness of time it might be that one of the bishops could be chosen, not as patriarch, but as archbishop.

The ecclesiastical politics of the late 860s were complicated by all sorts of rivalries and suspicions. It is clear that Rome was apprehensive of Bavarian churchmen's propensity for empire-building. One of the first acts of the Roman delegation upon arriving in Bulgaria in the spring of 867 was to snub the Germans by sending Bishop Hermanrich back to Passau. Formosus of Porto established himself in place of the Germans at the court of Boris and his Latin missionaries set to work among his subjects. Boris and Formosus evidently got on well together. This seems to have raised other suspicions at Rome. Later in 867 Boris asked Pope Nicholas whether he might allow Formosus to become archbishop of Bulgaria. The pope blocked this on a technicality, the prohibition in canon law on the transfer of a bishop from one see to another. (And it *was* a technicality: no objections were raised when Formosus was transferred from the see of Porto to that of Rome in 891.) Nicholas's successor Hadrian II was equally unresponsive. When Boris suggested an alternative candidate for the proposed Bulgarian archbishopric this too was turned down. This last exchange seems to have taken place in the late summer of 869. By this time it must have appeared to Boris that he was not going to get what he wanted from Rome. His every effort for the last three years had been in vain.

Meanwhile the Greeks had not been idle. There were ferocious denunciations of the Latin mission of Formosus to Bulgaria, and beneath the tumult and the shouting the machinery of Byzantine diplomacy moved stealthily into action. It was put to the khan that Constantinople's position could be more accommodating than had appeared in Photius's letter of 865. By these means Boris was lured back into the Byzantine fold. In the winter of 869–70 the eighth ecumenical council met at Constantinople. In a move which one cannot help but suspect had been carefully rehearsed, delegates from Khan Boris appeared just before the council ended. They requested an authoritative and binding ruling on the issue, to which church, Rome or Constantinople, should Bulgaria look for leadership? The council was re-convened for an extraordinary session on 4 March 870. The question was debated acrimoniously. But the outcome could never have been in doubt. Attendance from the Greek east vastly outnumbered the clerical representatives of the Latin west. The decision was in Constantinople's favour. In the immediate wake of this ruling Boris courteously but firmly expelled the Latin clergy from Bulgaria and accepted an archbishop, bishops and numerous other clergy from Constantinople. These included many monks, 'called upon from the mountains and from the caves in the earth and sent there by the emperor'.[8]

The Byzantine establishment was going to take no chances this time; and its missionaries were going to tread more warily. As for Boris, he had skilfully saved face. The decision had been made by a council of the whole church, not imposed on him by emperor and patriarch. Presumably his boyars found this reassuring. As an earnest of his good intentions he sent his son Symeon to be brought up in Constantinople. No one was so tactless as to refer to the boy as a hostage.

After the death of Cyril in Rome in February 869 Pope Hadrian II prevailed upon his brother to accept the proposed Moravian bishopric. Accordingly Methodius was consecrated a bishop – with the titular rank of archbishop of Sirmium – with responsibilities for the Christian Slavs of both Moravia and Pannonia. He was also given the office of papal legate. In practice, then, he became a bishop without a fixed see – like Amandus or Boniface – firmly attached by his legatine office to the Roman church. He returned to his central European mission field in the spring of 870. His arrival there provoked howls of rage from the Bavarian bishops. At Salzburg, where it must have seemed that things had gone horribly wrong, the *Conversio* was hastily composed to rehearse and buttress that see's claims. Christianity in Carantania and Pannonia had been introduced from Salzburg, led from Salzburg, staffed from Salzburg – until the coming of 'a certain Greek named Methodius', until there arose 'the new teaching of the philosopher Methodius'. 'New' and 'philosopher' were not, for the anonymous author, terms of approbation. It was unfortunate for Methodius that he found German influence in the ascendant in Moravia, where Rastislav's nephew Svatopluk had just ousted his uncle with German aid. Methodius was arrested and taken to Regensburg, where he was subjected to the travesty of a trial on the charge of usurping episcopal rights and found guilty. His old enemy Bishop Hermanrich of Passau was with difficulty restrained from thrashing him with a horsewhip. Methodius was imprisoned in a Swabian monastery, probably Ellwangen, which was a proprietary house of the bishop of Passau. These events took place towards the end of 870.

Methodius remained a prisoner for two and a half years. At the end of this time he was released at the insistence of the new pope, John VIII, in about May 873. He returned to Moravia to continue his evangelizing work among the Slavs. These were difficult years, and the days of the Methodian mission in Moravia were numbered. On Kocel's death in 874 Pannonia was incorporated into the German kingdom and the archbishopric of Salzburg re-asserted its grip on the church there. Svatopluk of Moravia remained on reasonably good terms with the German opponents of Methodius, which enabled German clergy to enter Moravia again; the German priest Wiching established himself at Nitra, which under Svatopluk had displaced Mikulčice as the most favoured princely residence. At Svatopluk's request, and probably in the face of opposition from Methodius, Wiching was consecrated a bishop by John VIII in 880. The German clergy continued to resist the liturgical use of Old Church Slavonic and even went so far as to accuse Methodius of heresy. Though Methodius's orthodoxy was upheld by Rome he came to feel that John VIII was less warm in his support than he might have been. Bishop Wiching of Nitra remained an implacable enemy until and beyond the death of Methodius in April 885. As soon as Methodius had been removed from the scene Wiching prevailed upon Svatopluk to expel the Methodian clergy from Moravia and restore its church to German control and Latin liturgy. Accordingly the disciples of Methodius were unceremoniously ejected in the winter of 885–6.

From these ashes of the Moravian mission there arose a phoenix in Bulgaria. Two of Methodius' closest Slav disciples, Clement and Naum (or Nahum), managed to make their way to Bulgaria, where they presented themselves to Khan Boris. The encounter was to have momentous consequences for Bulgarian Christianity. In the ensuing fifteen years since the expulsion of the Latin clergy in 870, the popes had made repeated attempts to retrieve the position in Bulgaria, but to no avail. Boris's decision to face eastwards towards Constantinople remained firm. He worked actively to promote Christianity among his people. He established bishoprics – no less than seven, as later tradition would claim. He founded monasteries, notably the monastery of St Panteleimon near Preslav. He encouraged the adoption of Christianity by his boyars and their dependants. Boris 'thirsted after' such men as Clement and Naum.[9] Their arrival presented him with an opportunity for adopting two of the Cyrillo-Methodian initiatives in Bulgaria, the training of a native priesthood and the use of a vernacular liturgy. Both courses were acceptable to the highest authorities in Rome and Constantinople. (It is just conceivable that Methodius had urged their adoption in Bulgaria with the authorities while on a visit to Constantinople towards the end of his life in 881–2.) Both would render the church in Boris's dominions less foreign, more familiar to their Slavo-Bulgar population. Old Church Slavonic liturgies spoken or sung by home-grown priests might have an integrative effect upon Bulgarian society. I doubt whether this thought ever occurred to Boris, though some twentieth-century historians have shown little hesitation in attributing it to him. But he might well have been familiar with the royal psalmist's assurance that God's blessing and the earth's fruitfulness would be forthcoming when '*all* the people praise Thee'.

Be that as it may, Boris placed the weight of royal patronage behind the Moravian missionary initiatives imported into Bulgaria by Clement and Naum. Clement was despatched to Macedonia and spent the remainder of his life there teaching, preaching and writing. The zone of his activities was the region between Lake Ohrid and the Adriatic, roughly co-terminous with the southern half of modern Albania. It was said of him, doubtless with some exaggeration, that he 'unveiled the more profound scriptures' to no less than 3,500 pupils, many of whom presumably went on to become priests. We have a glimpse of his methods for teaching children to write the Old Church Slavonic alphabet, and it was later recalled that he had the ability simultaneously to teach his class and to copy out manuscripts: a useful talent. It is of great interest to learn that his teaching extended beyond strictly religious instruction. 'Since in the whole land of the Bulgarians the trees grew wild and there was a lack of cultivated fruits, he brought from the land of the Greeks all manner of cultivated [fruit] trees, and made fruitful the wild trees by grafting.' In the same manner had Wilfrid taught the inhabitants of Sussex to fish with nets. Clement founded a monastery on the shores of Lake Ohrid which became a notable centre of learning. Consecrated a bishop in 893, he laboured there until his death at a great age in 916.

His companion Naum stayed initially at the royal court – later he joined Clement at Ohrid – where he busied himself with the further Christianization of Khan Boris and his entourage. All went well until 889. In that year Boris abdicated because of ill-health and retired into the monastery which he had founded at Preslav. He handed over power to his eldest son Vladimir. His other son Symeon had returned from Constantinople by this time, having received there a first-rate education. On his return he had been installed in a monastery. These indications that Symeon was being groomed for an ecclesiastical career prompt one to wonder whether Boris contemplated some concentration of authority within the family. Was Vladimir to be the Bulgarians' khan while Symeon became their bishop or archbishop? If so, something resembling the situation in eighth-century Northumbria could have obtained, where King Eadbert wielded secular power while his brother Archbishop Egbert of York exercised spiritual. If this were Boris's intention, the scheme failed disastrously. Vladimir threw over the Byzantine alliance and attempted a rapprochement with the German King Arnulf, the grandson of Louis the German. This would in any case have made the position of the Greek clergy in Bulgaria vulnerable. But there was more to Vladimir's reaction against his father than just a change of political orientation. Vladimir sought to restore what a contemporary chronicler called 'the rites of paganism', and he seems to have received support from the more conservative of the boyars who had survived Boris's purge of 866.[10]

There has been much discussion of this curious episode. Some historians have claimed to detect a repetitive pattern in the process of early medieval royal conversions, one feature of which was the tendency for one among a ruler's sons not to follow his father into professing Christianity from motives of what might be called reasons of state. If numbers of the ruling elite declined to follow the king to the font there would thus remain an unbaptized son who could become a leader acceptable to them upon his father's removal from the scene. An Anglo-Saxon parallel is furnished by the son of King Ethelbert of Kent, Eadbald, who did not become a Christian during his father's lifetime and upon the latter's death in 616 restored pagan worship at the royal court.[11] However, it is difficult to accept that a ruler so devoutly Christian as Boris could have been capable of so cynical a manoeuvre in the interests of dynastic continuity, in the knowledge that it could lead – almost certainly would lead – to the destruction of all that he had striven for over the previous twenty-five years. As usual, we do not know enough about the circumstances to put forward any interpretation of these goings-on with confidence. Had Vladimir been an open pagan before 889, or a crypto-pagan who had outwardly conformed to Christianity? Had he been on bad terms with his father? Was he, a Christian, forced to make concessions to the boyars who feared that Boris had gone too far too fast and loathed everything Greek? The only honest answer to these questions is that we do not know. All that we do know is the sequel. Boris emerged from his monastery in 893, deposed his son and installed Symeon as khan in his place. Vladimir was blinded to unfit him for any future exercise of authority and became in effect a non-person in Bulgarian historical consciousness, his name omitted from lists of Bulgarian rulers which pass straight from Boris to Symeon. His work then done, Boris returned to his monastery, where he spent the remainder of his very long life. His obituary was written by his nephew Theodore, another inmate of Preslav: 'During the same year 907 on May 2, Saturday evening, there died God's servant . . . who lived in the pure and orthodox creed of our Lord Jesus Christ. This was the great, honest, pious master of ours, the Bulgarian khan by the name of Boris, whose Christian name was Michael. This same Boris converted the Bulgarian people to the Christian faith.'[12]

Symeon ruled the Bulgarians with conspicuous success until his death in 927. One of his first acts was to move the principal royal residence from Pliska to Preslav. Perhaps Pliska was tainted by its proximity to the cult-site of Madara and its associations with pagan rulers like Krum and Omurtag. Preslav was emphatically Christian, with its royal monastery harbouring Boris, its several other monasteries, its twelve-apsed 'golden church' commissioned by Symeon, its ceramic workshops which produced accomplished tableware decorated with Christian icons, its scriptoria for multiplying Christian texts and its scholarly ex-monk ruler. In the year of his accession Symeon summoned a council of all his magnates and churchmen to Preslav. It was in all likelihood at this council that a new alphabet was adopted for the writing of texts in Old Church Slavonic. This was the alphabet which we now call Cyrillic. Its letter-forms were close to those of the Greek alphabet, and it thus rendered easier the assimilation of Greek literary culture which Symeon with his Constantinopolitan education was eager to encourage. In this manner the Bulgarians kept their own distinctive script, but it was one which was significantly close to Greek. The same could be said of their culture as a whole, as it developed under the patronage of Boris and Symeon.

'You too are numbered among those great people who praise God in their own language.' So the Emperor Michael III in his letter addressed to Rastislav of Moravia, delivered by Cyril and Methodius at the beginning of their mission in 863. The greatest achievement of the brothers and their successors was the creation of a Christian literature in Old Church Slavonic for the Slavs and Bulgars. Before Cyril's death in 869 he and his brother, probably assisted by Clement, had translated for the use of the Moravians and Pannonians not just the liturgy of the ecclesiastical year but also the psalter and the four gospels. In addition to these Christian texts they had also translated a code of secular law known as the *Ecloga*. This had been promulgated by the Emperor Leo III in 726 for the purpose of making Justinian's legal codifications more accessible and thereby more useful in provincial courts of law throughout the empire. In translating this code the brothers also adapted its content to Moravian conditions. As with Clovis and Ethelbert the 'reception' of Roman law was an accompaniment to conversion. (We might care to note that in his long letter to Boris in 866 Pope Nicholas I promised that he would send him, in answer to his request, a code of secular law (*mundanas leges*): we do not know what this code might have been.) Between 869 and 885 Methodius translated, according to his *Life*, the entire Bible, the *Nomokanon* or collection of canon law, and a work vaguely described as 'books of the Fathers', which was perhaps a collection of sermons or of biblical commentary. After 886, in Bulgaria, Clement of Ohrid composed hymns, sermons and – probably – the *Life* of his master Methodius. He was therefore the first person to write *original* compositions, as opposed to translations, in Old Church Slavonic. Naum's encouragement of scholarship at the monasteries associated with the royal court was reinforced by the patronage of the learned Symeon. The so-called 'Preslav school' produced further translations and compositions in the late ninth and early tenth centuries. Symeon himself is said to have translated some of the sermons of St John Chrysostom. It was the duty of a Christian ruler to busy himself with the religious education of his people. His slightly older contemporary King Alfred of Wessex would have agreed.

The cultural response of the Bulgarians to their acceptance of Christianity had the speed and vitality of that of the Irish or the Franks or the Anglo-Saxons to theirs. Only forty years separated the baptism of Boris from the consecration of Symeon's golden church at Preslav. During that period a cultural revolution was set in motion. In the words of Clement of Ohrid, 'the rain of divine understanding came down upon my people'.[13] This image of peaceful irrigation masks the fact that the journey of the Bulgarians from paganism to Christianity had been a turbulent one. Those early and unsure days when Boris took the plunge and provoked the fury of his boyars are brought most vividly before us in a document of cardinal importance for our understanding of barbarian conversion. This is the letter of Pope Nicholas I sent to Boris in the autumn of 866. This extraordinary document, briefly referred to already, merits a close examination.

Its full title is the *Responsa Nicolai Papae ad Consulta Bulgarorum* (*The Replies of Pope Nicholas to the Questions of the Bulgars*), hereafter abbreviated to *Consulta*.[14] The envoys of Khan Boris who had visited Rome in 866 had put a number of queries to the pope, as Augustine of Canterbury and Boniface had done before them. It is important, as a first step, to get a sense of scale. Augustine, on behalf of his English converts, had put nine questions to Pope Gregory I. Boniface, from Germany, had on one occasion put twelve questions to Gregory II, on another occasion nine to Gregory III. The *Consulta* to which Pope Nicholas responded numbered no less than 106. The document constitutes by far the most extensive surviving body of advice offered by any early medieval pope in a missionary context, and this is what gives it its unique value.

At a first reading the *Consulta* appear a miscellaneous lot. The matter ranges from the treatment of the rebel boyars (Boris had been too savage in slaughtering all their children) to the permissibility of sexual intercourse during Lent (no); from the future organization of the church in Bulgaria (wait and see) to the procedure for dealing with Islamic books (burn them). Miscellaneous in content, the *Consulta* are also desultory in arrangement. The pope skips in three successive replies from a discussion of the use of judicial torture via the question of whether a widow might be compelled to enter monastic life to the prohibition of prayer for pagan ancestors. Superficially rambling and shapeless, the *Consulta* nevertheless reveal to a more attentive scrutiny what the new Bulgarian converts were worried about and how the pope proposed to calm their anxieties. Their information helps to answer some of the questions set out in the informal agenda in Chapter 1.

The *Consulta* are above all else concerned with behaviour, not with doctrine. In this they contrast with, or complement, the long letter of doctrinal exposition sent by the Patriarch Photius to Boris in 865. For example, there are eight answers to questions relating to the proper observance of Lent, and ten on the subject of Christian marriage. This all appears fairly straightforward, the commendation of seemly conduct to the newly converted. Look, the pope seems to be saying, this is how we do things and how you must try to do them too now that you are Christians. But looming behind these questions of behaviour was the vastly more weighty matter of ritual. Correctly performed rituals would propitiate this new and all-powerful God whom Boris had accepted, a conciliation which would yield a harmonious universe and a contented people. But if rituals were incorrectly performed, who could tell what might happen?

Boris had asked the pope, for example, whether the proper observance of Lent required abstinence from *ioca*. Nicholas replied a shade tartly that *ioca* were to be abstained from not just during Lent but at all other times of the year too. What was at stake here? The primary meaning of *ioca* was 'jests': our word 'joke' is derived from it. But I do not think that Pope Nicholas was trying to rein in the Bulgars' sense of humour. A clue is furnished by the context. Although the formal arrangement of the *Consulta* is haphazard there is a tendency for certain blocks of replies to be devoted to a single issue. Thus, Chapters 44 to 48 inclusive are all concerned with Lent, and it is in this block that the chapter about *ioca* (47) is situated. Now the chapter immediately preceding it is concerned with the permissibility or otherwise of waging war in Lent. The juxtaposition suggests that for the Bulgarians war and *ioca* somehow went together. This suspicion is confirmed by another response. The Bulgars have told him, writes the pope, that they have been accustomed, when advancing into battle, to observe particular days and hours, and to employ spells, *ioca*, chants and certain auguries: may they continue to do so now that they are Christians? A secondary meaning of *ioca* is 'play' in the sense of 'sports, activities, pastimes, performances'. The *ioca* that accompanied the spells, the chants, the seeking of auguries as the Bulgars advanced into battle, at the right hour of the right day, were surely some sort of war dances. It is evident from the *Consulta* that the rituals and ceremonies associated with warfare had a religious significance. Horses seem to have mattered in this context, as perhaps they had for Childeric. A standard made of a horse's tail was carried by the Bulgarian army into battle. The mind is bound to turn to the Horseman of Madara at the shrine of the high-god Tengri. Anxieties about the proper times for battle are apparent. The Bulgars asked the pope whether there was a certain day on which battle should not be hazarded: the underlying assumption here would seem to have been that some days are luckier than others. Another question starts with the admission that the Bulgars were reluctant to offer 'complete and suitable prayer' while on campaign. This has the air of an oblique way of saying that they could not at once abandon all their well-tried rituals of spells and chants and dances.

War loomed large for Khan Boris and his boyars, but similar kinds of anxiety about correct ritual behaviour can be detected in the *Consulta*, where they deal with day-to-day conduct in times of peace. Must women cover their heads in church? Is it really necessary, as the Greeks insist, to wear a belt when receiving the eucharist? May men wear their turbans in church? Is it true, as the Greeks claim, that no one should take a bath on a Wednesday or a Friday? May a Christian eat meat slaughtered by a pagan? Or by a eunuch? Is it necessary to abandon the ritual in accordance with which the khan is accustomed to eat at a table all by himself? Is it permissible to mark a table with the sign of the cross? Is hunting allowed in Lent? Can we continue to swear oaths on a sword? What is the correct posture for the hands at prayer? How should suicides be buried?

These were not trivial questions. They went right to the intimate heart of everyday life. What was Christianity going to mean for the way the Bulgars dressed, or washed, or ate, the way they made love or war, the way they did business or diverted themselves, the way they prayed, the way they disposed of their dead? How many of life's familiar landmarks had to change? How bewildering was it going to be? And how potentially offensive to their ancestral gods? Pope Nicholas treated the enquiries with all the seriousness they deserved. His answers were firm but also charitable. They were pervaded by the spirit – indeed they sometimes borrowed the very words – of one among his predecessors whom Nicholas hugely revered, Pope Gregory I. Just as Gregory had commended a policy of accommodation to the English mission in 601, so Nicholas sought so far as possible not to change Bulgar practice but to infuse it with a Christian tincture. This is notably the case with regard to war. The Bulgars were urged to carry the sign of the cross into battle in place of their horsehair standards. They should prepare for a campaign not with augury-seeking and chants and dances, but with prayers, masses, confession, almsgiving and other acts of mercy. This is not to say that Nicholas was pliable. He issued routine condemnations of the use of ligatures and phylacteries and curing stones for medicinal purposes. He took a notably harder line than his predecessors on questions about consanguinity and marriage.

But the general tone was accommodating. The Bulgars like the Anglo-Saxons were encouraged to rise by steps. Baptismal rebirth did not need to involve immediate and complete renunciation of everything that the old Adam – and Eve – had cherished. I think we may take it that Boris and his boyars – well, most of them; barring those who supported Vladimir in 889 – were reassured.

This brings to a close the first act in the conversion of the Bulgarians to Christianity. The years between 863 and 893 had certainly been unsettled. They ended with the Bulgars facing firmly eastward, towards Constantinople, but with their own alphabet and their own priests and their own Christian literature in the vernacular. A generation later, in 927, they would at last get what Boris had asked for in vain, their own patriarch. Bulgaria would remain thereafter in the commonwealth of eastern Christendom.

Moravian Christianity, its beginnings equally stormy, had found itself facing westward after 886. But the victory of the German clergy under Bishop Wiching was short-lived. In the last decade of the ninth century a new enemy appeared from the east in the form of the Magyars, semi-nomadic plunderers whose horsemanship gave them the same mobility which their ships gave to the Vikings of Scandinavia. They exploited speed, surprise and skill as mounted archers to launch raids upon the settled people to their west, and Moravia was the first to suffer. After bruising attacks in the early years of the tenth century the principality of Rastislav and Svatopluk was overwhelmed in the years 906–7. Organized Christianity was obliterated. The first chapter in the Christianization of central Europe came to an abrupt end.

CHAPTER ELEVEN

Scandinavians Abroad and at Home

Knowledge may have its purposes,
but guessing is always
more fun than knowing.

When Norsemen heard thunder,
did they seriously believe
Thor was hammering?
W. H. AUDEN, 'Archaeology',
in *Thank You, Fog*, 1974

THE EARLIEST Scandinavian encounters with Christianity occurred
when the natives of those northern homelands met it in the course of
their travels abroad. These travels did not begin in the age of the
Vikings, roughly defined as the ninth and tenth centuries, nor were
they exclusively concerned with pillage and plunder. Nevertheless, it
is broadly speaking true that the encounter between the Scandinavians
and the peoples of Christendom became closer and more intense in
the ninth century than it had been before, and that for many people
and institutions within Christendom that encounter was painful and
disruptive. It is conventional, if artificial, to divide Viking activity into
a phase of raiding followed by a phase of settlement. Religious communities suffered the most severely from the raids, and because they
were literate they recorded their discomfiture in writing and we can
read about it. The ecclesiastical slant of these sources composed by
the victims has had the effect of magnifying the violence of the Vikings
and of presenting an image of them as relentlessly hostile to Christianity. The violence was there, certainly, though we should do well to
recall that if the Saxons had been literate we should have heard something of the ferocity of the Christian Franks. Violence was not a Viking
monopoly. And about the hostility to Christianity we have to be a
good deal more circumspect before giving judgement.

The Vikings attacked religious communities principally because they were repositories of treasure – not just their own plate, vestments, books and so forth, but also the treasure of local lay society. It was another feature of the integration of early medieval monasteries into their social world that they played a role as places of safe deposit, bankers, for their friends and neighbours among the local aristocracy. Viking leaders needed treasure to reward followers, to prosecute ambitions at home, to buy ships and slaves, to finance trade, to purchase land or wives. Pillaging a monastery was therefore not unlike robbing a bank. It was not necessarily an act of hostility to Christianity as such, though it might have felt like that to the inmates. Canny predators do not annihilate their prey, because they want to come back for second and third helpings. So it was with the Vikings and the religious houses of Christendom. The predators wanted to cut and come again. Some communities, such as Iona, were repeatedly attacked. Many found it prudent to remove themselves from exposed coastal or riverine sites to safe havens inland. The monks of St Filibert's foundation at Noirmoutier at the mouth of the Loire, mentioned in Chapter 5, decamped by successive stages in the course of the ninth century further and further inland until they ended up at Tournus in Burgundy – where, by a tragic irony, they soon found themselves at the mercy of other, horseborne, predators in the shape of the dreaded Magyars. The monks of Filibert's other foundation, Jumièges, removed themselves to a new site near Cambrai. The community of St Cuthbert abandoned Lindisfarne and after much wandering and sojourning at different places in northern England finally came to rest at Durham towards the end of the tenth century. Columba's monks at Iona removed themselves to Ireland and established themselves at Kells. Monastic life, then, experienced severe disruption. So too did the episcopal hierarchy of the church. It is common to find interruptions to the succession of bishops in those areas subject to Viking attack and settlement. In Normandy the see of Avranches was vacant from 862 until 990. In Britain the see of Whithorn in Galloway, allegedly founded by St Ninian (see Chapter 3), disappears from view in the ninth century and was not revived until 1128. In north-western Spain the episcopal city of Tuy was sacked in 1015; no new bishop was appointed until 1070. These disruptions and discontinuities played havoc with the organization of the Christian church. However, it is important to bear in mind that this is not the same as obliterating

Christian belief. Furthermore, it is notable – and again surely not by chance – that the poorer religious communities seem to have been spared the Vikings' attentions. The ability of such inconspicuous establishments to survive, to continue to be a focus for local religious devotion, to maintain a degree of pastoral care, may have implications for our enquiries. Wherever the Vikings settled in mainland western Europe and the British Isles they lived intermixed with populations who were Christian, with whom they necessarily had relations.

The Vikings evidently had access to good intelligence. Their raids were for the most part not casual, opportunistic arm-chancings but operations that had been carefully planned in the light of sound information. It was not by coincidence that York was their target in 867 when two rival contenders for the throne of Northumbria had divided the kingdom in civil strife; nor that when they occupied Santiago de Compostela in 968 it was at a time when the kingdom of León was in turmoil during the minority of the infant king Ramiro III. The great *chevauchées* across northern Francia between 856 and 862, or across eastern England between 865 and 876, were systematic, not random. The Vikings knew what they wanted and where to find it.

Good intelligence presupposes communication. It has long been known that the Vikings came to trade as well as to raid. The point has been mightily reinforced by the archaeological investigation of their trading stations at Birka, Hedeby, Kaupang, Novgorod, Dublin, York, Lincoln, Fécamp, Rouen – to name but a few. Even pillage could bring negotiation in its train, the pillagers be rapidly transmuted into bargainers. Consider this famous inscription added to a luxury eighth-century English gospel book:

> I ealdorman Alfred and Werburh my wife obtained these books from the heathen army with our pure money, that was with pure gold, and this we did for the love of God and for the benefit of our souls and because we do not wish these holy books to remain longer in heathen possession. And now they wish to give them to Christ Church [Canterbury] to the praise and glory and honour of God, and in gratitude for his Passion, and for the use of the religious community which daily raises praise to God in Christ Church; on condition that they shall be read every month for the sake of Alfred and Werburh and Ealhthryth, for the eternal remedy of their souls, as long as God has foreseen that the Christian faith shall continue at that place.[1]

Alfred redeemed a very sumptuous and sacred book; the Vikings got their gold. The two parties had to talk to each other.

Alliances were frequently formed with the Vikings to exploit their military skills. In 850 one of the many petty Irish kings, Cináed of Ciannachta in Ulster, allied with a party of Vikings in the course of his hostilities with the king of Meath. In 864 Pippin II of Aquitaine, nephew of the West Frankish king Charles the Bald, allied with the Vikings in his rebellion against his uncle. In 900 Ethelwold, nephew of King Alfred of Wessex, allied with the Vikings against his cousin King Edward. In such a fashion, as allies or mercenaries, Viking bands became an additional element in an already unruly Christendom.

So there was a context of communication between the Vikings and those they visited; and there may be grounds for supposing that the attitude of the Vikings to Christianity has been misunderstood. This latter possibility has given rise to much debate among historians. Given the nature and sparsity of the materials bearing upon the problem, the matter is likely to remain controversial. How consistently, how aggressively heathen really were those whom the clerical chroniclers of western Europe labelled as 'pagans' or 'heathen men'? To answer this question we should need to know vastly more than we do about the pre-Christian religion of the Scandinavian peoples. But our knowledge of it is insecurely based. It is the same problem that we came up against when considering the conversion to Christianity of the Germanic invaders of the Roman empire: we know so little about what they were being converted *from*. Strictly contemporary sources such as Rimbert's *Vita Anskarii* (see Chapter 7) are laconic in the extreme. Rimbert tells us that many gods were worshipped in Sweden and that cult-sites existed. Well, we might have guessed this for ourselves. We possess a large body of material bearing upon the myth and cosmology of the Viking age, but this was for the most part not committed to writing until a much later date and in a changed cultural environment, the Iceland of the thirteenth and fourteenth centuries. Old Norse scholarship has detected 'early' deposits in this literary spoil heap – for example, the mysterious verses about the god Odin in the didactic poem *Hávamál*. But there is disagreement about how early is 'early', and arising from this about the extent to which these Odin passages might already have been touched by Christian influences. Even supposing that the antiquarian scholars of thirteenth-century Iceland faithfully recorded the thought-world of the Viking age – a large assumption –

they still leave us in the dark, as they themselves were surely in the dark, about belief, ritual, organization, the whole functioning of pre-Christian religious life and the degree of loyalty it commanded, in ninth-century Scandinavia.

We have some evidence for the interpenetration of paganism and Christianity. Consider what was recorded of one of the early Norse settlers of Iceland, Helgi the Lean: 'Helgi was called Christian, and yet was very mixed in his beliefs: he was baptised and professed faith in Christ, but he vowed to Thor for sea journeys and difficult undertakings.'[2] Helgi's voyage to Iceland might have required the protection of Thor; but he gave the name Kristnes, 'Christ's headland', to the settlement which he founded near the north coast. This story was not committed to writing until about 1130 and we are not called upon to accept it as the literal truth. Yet the spectacle of a mixture of religious belief which it presents to us gains colour from other evidence closer to Helgi's own day. The Saxon chronicler Widukind of Corvey, writing in about 968, observed that 'the Danes formerly became Christians, but nevertheless they continue to venerate idols according to heathen custom'.[3] This sounds like what was later to be said of Helgi, with the difference that the words were written by a near-contemporary in a Saxon monastery associated with missionary work in Denmark which had once housed St Anskar.

Archaeological expression of the beliefs attributed to Helgi lies to hand. It is assumed that Helgi had picked up his Christianity in the course of a sojourn in the Western Isles of Scotland preceding his voyage to Iceland. In 1882 there was discovered on the island of Colonsay the grave of a Viking warrior. The man had been buried, accompanied by his horse, beneath his boat. With him there had been deposited sword, axe, shield, spear, arrows, knife, harness, whetstone, silver pin, scales for weighing bullion, and two English coins which enabled the burial to be dated to the third quarter of the ninth century. It was roughly contemporary therefore with the earliest phases of the settlement of Iceland, which according to tradition started in the year 874. But this was not quite all. At each end of the rectangular enclosure of stones which framed the warrior's body had been set a small stone slab incised with a cross. Whatever might have been the dead man's beliefs, his kinsfolk or retainers who gave him this thoroughly traditional burial 'had encountered and to some extent adopted Christian ideas'.[4] In Denmark and in Sweden little soapstone moulds have been

373

found for the simultaneous casting of *both* the cross of Christ *and* the hammer of Thor. Of course, we cannot know the thoughts of those who made, distributed, bought, gave, wore or cherished these ornaments. But it must at least give us pause when we find that both could be worn at once, for example by the ninth-century woman buried near the thriving port of Hedeby in Schleswig or by the villagers of Pollista in central Sweden. During this period Christian churchmen developed the ritual known as *prima signatio* or 'prime-signing', that is the signing with the cross as a pre-baptismal stage of Christian initiation, which became a widespread practice in Scandinavia. Like baptism itself – and we might recall Notker's quips about Danish baptisms at the Frankish court – prime-signing was potentially ambiguous. Donor and recipient might often have viewed the ritual in different lights. Perhaps it was this very ambiguity which made it useful in the mission field.

This readiness to make room for a Christian deity alongside the traditional gods – reminiscent of the way favoured by King Redwald of the East Angles in Bede's story – does not suggest that the paganism of the Vikings was aggressive or intolerant. We should bear in mind too that though ninth-century Christendom was weak and vulnerable there was also much about its style and trappings that was impressive, even awesome. The encounter at Ingelheim in 826 was carefully staged to impress Harald Klak with the might of Frankish power. Just because we know so much about it thanks to the survival of Ermold the Black's poem, we must not fall into the trap of taking the occasion as unique. Suppose for a moment that some Anglo-Saxon Ermold had memorialized the visit of the Danish leader Guthrum to the court of King Alfred for baptism in 878. There were several such encounters of this sort in the course of the ninth and tenth centuries. And if Christian trappings were impressive, surely, too, the God who gave them? This was an argument that Bishop Daniel of Winchester had commended to Boniface back in the early eighth century.

The exportability of Scandinavian paganism must not be too readily assumed. Only in Iceland, it would seem, were the traditional religious observances of the homeland successfully transplanted. They co-existed, however, with the Christianity or quasi-Christianity or proto-Christianity of immigrants like Helgi the Lean, or of travellers from Iceland who encountered Christians in the course of voyages across the sea and embraced some of their teachings. In other regions where Scandinavian emigrants settled they were assimilated to the prevailing religious culture with varying degrees of speed and completeness.

We may start with the Western and Northern Isles of Scotland, that archipelago which stretches from Gigha to Unst. We last touched upon it to draw attention to its Christianization at the hands of activists fanning out from communities of Hibernian filiation such as Iona and Applecross. By the time that Viking raiders began to cruise these waters from the late eighth century onwards the people of the isles were in a formal sense Christian. Christianity seems to have survived the disruptive raids of the ninth century. So much is suggested, in the absence of contemporary written sources, by the bits and pieces of other evidence. The distribution of place-names with the Old Norse element *papa*, meaning '(Christian) priest', as for example in Papa Westray, Orkney, has been held to indicate the survival of Christian communities. Continuity of Christian site, as at the Brough of Birsay on mainland Orkney, where a church of the Norse period was built on the site of an earlier Christian settlement, might point in the same direction: though we need to enter the caveat that apparent continuity of site does not rule out interruptions in use. The slippery evidence of church dedications and the ambiguous evidence of certain memorial gravestones have been read as comparable indicators.

It is not much to go on. Iona provides us with a little more. As already mentioned, it was repeatedly attacked by Viking raiders. In one such attack in the year 825 a monk named Blathmac was killed for refusing to divulge the whereabouts of the hidden monastic treasure. His death was lamented shortly afterwards in Latin verses by Walafrid Strabo, monk and later abbot of Reichenau: a remarkable testimony to the cultural integration of Latin Christendom. For present purposes the interest of the story lies in showing that a Christian community continued to live at Iona even after the main body of Columba's monks had migrated to the safety of Kells. Further testimony to the continuing spiritual magnetism of Iona was the choice of the island-monastery as their royal mausoleum by the Scottish kings who finally displaced the kings of the Picts in the middle years of the ninth century. From Kenneth mac Alpin, who died in 858, for the next two and a half centuries nearly every Scottish ruler was buried at Iona. This devotion to the saint of Iona was communicated to some of the newcomers. Perhaps we can sense the hand of Columba's

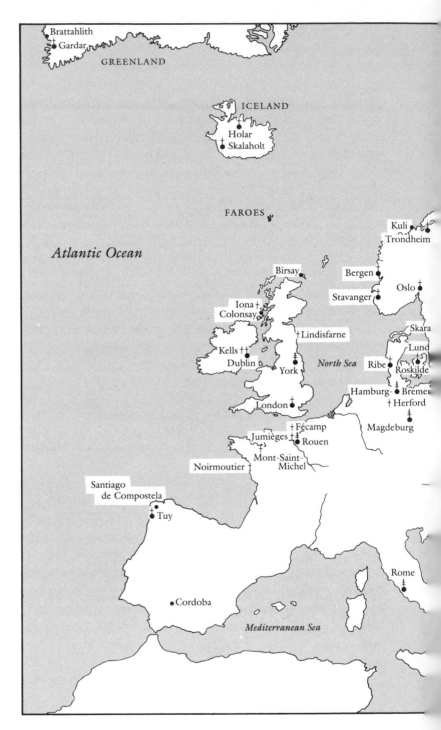

9. *Christianity in the Viking world, c. 1000.*

Archbishopric

Bishopric

† Monastery

Uppsala
rka

Baltic Sea

‡ Novgorod

Kiev

R Dnieper

R Volga

Caspian Sea

R Danube

Black Sea

‡ Constantinople

Baghdad

community behind Helgi the Lean's adoption of Christianity, or discreetly manifest in the burial rites of the warrior of Colonsay almost within sight of Iona. If we can trust the evidence of the Icelandic *Landnámabók*, the 'Book of Settlements' compiled in about 1130, Iona's influence may certainly be detected in the religious affiliations of Orlygr Hrappsson, nephew of the celebrated Viking Ketil Flatnose. Orlygr was fostered by a Hebridean bishop, otherwise unknown, named Patrick. When Orlygr wished to emigrate to Iceland in about 880 or so, Bishop Patrick told him to build a church there in honour of St Columba and provided him with timber, a bell, a missal and consecrated earth to lay beneath the corner pillars of the building. Orlygr did as he was bid, and founded a church dedicated to St Columba at his farmstead near Reykjavik.

In the light of this evidence, if light it may be called, it is possible to make out the beginnings of a process by which the Norse newcomers were assimilated to Christianity. By the 960s at the latest there was a bishopric of the Isles based at Iona. There may have been other incumbents of whom we know nothing between the shadowy Bishop Patrick of *c.* 880 and the better-attested Bishop Fothad of *c.* 960. When the Scandinavian ruler of Dublin, Olaf Cuaran, abdicated in 980 he retired to Iona to end his days there as a penitent. A grave-slab at Iona of about the same or slightly later date bears a runic inscription recording that 'Kali Olvirsson laid this stone over his brother Fugl'. These indications of Christian allegiance among the Scotto-Scandinavian elite of the Western Isles can be matched in the Northern. A Norse earldom of Orkney had emerged in impenetrably obscure circumstances by about the year 900. In the course of the tenth century we can trace marriages between members of the dynasty and women drawn from neighbouring princely or aristocratic families, brides who would certainly have been Christian. Earl Thorfinn Skullsplitter, for example, who died *c.* 963, married into the native aristocracy of Caithness. His son Earl Hlodver married Eithne or Edna, daughter of the king of Ossory. Their son Sigurd the Stout married a daughter of Malcolm II, king of Scots.

There exists a quasi-legendary story about the conversion of Earl Sigurd to Christianity. The hero of this tale was Olaf Tryggvason, king of Norway, who was said to have sailed to Orkney in 995 and compelled Sigurd at swordpoint to accept the new faith. It's in the highest degree implausible. The claim arose in the context of much later attempts to confect an image of Olaf Tryggvason as the heroic Christian warrior-king who single-handedly imposed Christianity upon Norway, the Northern Isles, the Faeroes and Iceland. The historical reality of Olaf Tryggvason, as we shall see, was not like this. The earls of Orkney must have been nominally Christian before the king of Norway appeared on the scene. By the next generation their Christianity was more than nominal. Sigurd's son Earl Thorfinn the Mighty, who died in 1065, had been fostered at the court of the king of Scots, his grandfather. He built a handsome church at Birsay, whose remains may still be seen. His son was given, for the first time in the dynasty's history, a Christian name, Paul. Thorfinn made a pilgrimage to Rome, travelling by way of Denmark. It was very probably on this journey that he had a meeting with Archbishop Adalbert of Bremen, who consecrated a certain Thorolf to serve as bishop of the Orkneys. One of Thorfinn's grandsons would achieve sanctity through martyrdom. Another would lead a pilgrimage to Jerusalem. The earls of Orkney had joined the club of Christian rulers.

The religious history of the Scandinavian settlers in Ireland presents us with variations on this theme of assimilation. The earlier history of Christian culture in Ireland had, of course, been vastly more distinguished – spiritually, intellectually and artistically – than that of its colonies in the Scottish islands. We must not make the mistake of supposing that Ireland had become some sort of cultural backwater after her clergy's great achievements in diffusing godliness and good learning in Francia and Britain in the seventh century. Irish scholars and pilgrims continued to traverse the European continent during the eighth and ninth centuries. How else but through their agency could Walafrid Strabo have learned so quickly of the killing of Blathmac of Iona? In its homeland the Irish church, though tainted in the eyes of austere critics by too intimate an association with secular society, continued to maintain the traditions and observances handed down by the early fathers whom it so much revered.

The Scandinavian, mainly Norse, settlements that occurred in Ireland after the initial phase of pillaging were different in character from those in the Western and Northern Isles. In Ireland the settlements were principally urban and mercantile. The new arrivals established themselves at bases on the sheltered east coast where they could overwinter and refit, bases which gradually assumed the character of permanent commercial settlements which attracted population and generated the necessary support-system of craft and industry. Dublin, where the Vikings first over-wintered in 841–2, was the most imposing of these early towns. Others were Wexford, Waterford and Limerick. Collectively the Irish Norse are often known as the *Ostmen*, the 'Easterners', from the location of their towns (though Limerick does not fit). They established themselves, thus, literally on the fringes of Irish society and they faced, so to say, outwards: to their fellow-members of the Scandinavian diaspora in the Isles or England or Normandy, and to more distant, risky but profitable enterprises like the slave-markets of Islamic Spain.

Owing to the excavations of the last thirty years, notably in Dublin, we now know a lot about the material conditions in which the Hiberno-Norse lived out their lives. We know what their houses and workshops were like, their cups and bowls and tools and combs and footwear. But we know practically nothing about their thoughts and beliefs. It will probably remain for ever obscure whether the immigrants were gradually assimilated into Irish Christian culture, or whether the Irish kept the Norse at arm's length and deliberately neglected their evangelization.[5] It is true that there is no evidence for any planned mission to the Hiberno-Norse. Yet this need cause us no surprise. For it is a rather remarkable feature of the Christianization of the Scandinavians who settled in western Europe at this period that it seems just to have happened without the agency of the organized missions which had characterized the previous Carolingian age. The absence of mission does not in itself do much for the 'separationist' case. On the other hand the 'assimilationists' can point to evidence for all sorts of interactions between settler and native. Trade, war, diplomacy, intermarriage, all wove the Norse into the texture of Irish society. It would be surprising if – at the very least in some instances – no modification of religious allegiance occurred as part of the process. The first Hiberno-Norse ruler of whose Christianity we have clear evidence was King Olaf Cuaran of Dublin. Olaf had ruled the Danish kingdom of York between 941 and 944, during which period he had been baptized at the court of King Edmund of Wessex. Driven from York in 944, Olaf returned to Dublin, where his father and grandfather had ruled over the Norse of Dublin before him. He presided over them for the remainder of a long life and abdicated in 980 to end his days, as we have already seen, in the monastic community of Iona. It is true that the little that we know of Olaf's Christianity points us away from Ireland, to England and the Isles. But he may not have had much choice about when or where he was baptized, and as for the place of his retirement and death, well, Iona was a very holy site and it was where kings were buried.

An assimilationist case can be made but should not be pressed too hard. The religious flavour of the Dublin Norse in the tenth century remains completely hidden. Light begins to creep above our horizon from about the year 1000. Olaf's son Sihtric 'of the Silken Beard' established a mint at Dublin in about 995. The coin that he struck there, in imitation of the royal coin of Anglo-Saxon England, bore Christian symbolism. Sihtric made a pilgrimage to Rome in 1028 and it was perhaps on that occasion that discussions were held about setting up a bishopric in Dublin. Sihtric founded Christ Church cathedral in Dublin – it shared a dedication with Earl Thorfinn's at Birsay – and at some point during his lifetime a bishop named Dunan was appointed to the new see of Dublin. Dunan's name suggests an Irish origin, but there is some reason – admittedly, very tenuous – for supposing that he had been consecrated in England, at Canterbury. Be this as it may, it is certain that Canterbury harboured, or came to harbour, ambitions over the see of Dublin, just as Bremen did over the church in Orkney. Dunan's successor Patrick, a monk of Worcester, was consecrated at Canterbury by its first Norman archbishop, Lanfranc, in 1074 and made on that occasion a written profession of obedience to him and his successors. When Patrick went back to Ireland he carried with him a letter from Lanfranc to King Guthric of Dublin in which the king was adjured to change the marriage-customs of his Hiberno-Norse subjects. This was a characteristic concern of high-minded churchmen in their dealings with the recently converted – consider Boniface or Pope Nicholas I – though what on earth King Guthric was meant to do about it remains unclear. Lanfranc commended Guthric's religious observances: 'many good reports of you . . . matters worthy of much commendation . . . cherished son of holy church . . .'[6] Polite epistolary commonplaces, perhaps; but the writer was in no doubt about Guthric's essential Christianity. Like the earls of Orkney the Ostmen of Ireland had joined the club. At about this time – somewhere between 1062 and 1098 – a new shrine was made to house a famous and holy relic, the *Cathac* of Columba, an early manuscript of the Psalter which was believed to have belonged to the founder of Iona.

The shrine for this quintessentially Irish relic was made at Kells. Its decoration shows Scandinavian stylistic influences and the artist who made it bore the Norse name Sihtric.

The quest for adventure, booty and trade also led the Scandinavians to look eastwards. Already by the time of Anskar's mission to the Sueones round Birka people of the same stock were drifting eastwards across the Baltic and up the Gulf of Finland, thence to turn inland to the south. Much later on the *Russian Primary Chronicle*, composed at Kiev early in the twelfth century, would present an idealized origin-legend about the doings of these ninth-century founding fathers. Its readers would be encouraged to look back to the heroic Viking Ruric, who settled his men at Novgorod; to earls Askold and Dir, who captured Kiev from the Khazars; and to Oleg, who made Kiev his capital, declaring that it would thenceforward be 'the mother of all the Russian cities' and furnishing thereby a pretext for rivers of tears to flow from patriotic Russian eyes through centuries to come. We do not need to believe these legends. Recent archaeological investigation and a more attentive scrutiny of the written sources combine to suggest that the rise of Kiev as an urban and political centre of any importance occurred in the tenth century rather than the ninth. The earliest significant concentration of Viking settlers in Russia seems to have been further to the east, on the Volga rather than the Dnieper. Archaeologists have found large quantities of Islamic silver coin, dating from the second half of the eighth century onwards, in the Volga basin. These hoards suggest that the Vikings had been growing rich on the profits of trade – in furs and slaves and amber – with the Islamic caliphate, its capital city recently (762) moved from the shores of the Mediterranean at Damascus to a new site at Mesopotamian Baghdad.

Apart from some rather insubstantial evidence for a couple of raids upon the Crimea and across the Black Sea to the coastline of Asia Minor in the 820s and 830s – recalling the Ukrainian Goths of the third century and the pastoral cares of Gregory Thaumaturgus – the earliest reliable notice of Russo-Byzantine relations comes from the year 839. As it happens, it occurs in a western rather than an eastern source, and one that we have already consulted for its information about scandalous goings-on at the other extremity of Christendom. In the very same entry which tells of the defection of the Deacon Bodo to Judaism the *Annals of Saint-Bertin* record the arrival in the Frankish empire of an embassy from Constantinople which was accompanied by men described as 'Rus'. They had been conducting a diplomatic mission to the imperial court and on their behalf the Emperor Theophilus sought permission for their return home by way of Frankish territory. The Frankish authorities, learning that they were Swedes, were apprehensive. We know nothing at all about the background to these manoeuvres but it is a reasonable guess, in the light of what we know about Byzantine diplomacy, that the government in Constantinople was trying to neutralize or defuse some perceived danger which was offered by these Rus.

That the danger was real enough was proved in 860 when the Rus attacked Constantinople. We have already encountered a part of the imperial response in Chapter 10, the sending of a mission which included Cyril and Methodius to the Khazars. Direct relations seem also to have been opened or resumed with the Rus of the Volga, for at some point between 862 and 866 an embassy from them, presumably a return embassy, visited Constantinople. What is germane to our enquiries is that the Rus ambassadors, who would of course have been prominent people, were baptized. In 867 the Patriarch Photius could proclaim, more than a shade optimistically, that the Rus were under the spiritual authority of a Christian bishop and had become the 'subjects and friends' of the emperor. A few years later, in about 874, a bishop was sent to the Rus by the Patriarch Ignatius.

This may not have added up to very much. The triumphalism of Photius may be as deceptive as that of Ermold the Black, the baptisms of the 860s perhaps as ephemeral in their effects upon the Rus as that of Harald Klak had been upon the Danes. The Greeks and the Franks read meanings into the sacrament of baptism which those who received it quite possibly did not. It is not impossible that the negotiations of 874 had been *primarily* concerned with securing Christian ministry for the Christian merchants – Greek, Armenian, Georgian – who visited Russia to trade there, not with converting the Rus people: there might be parallels with Anskar's visits to Birka. There is unsurprising evidence of the continuance of pre-Christian habits into the tenth century. The Arab traveller Ibn Fadlan could describe in 922 the offerings made by the Rus to their gods for successful trading, and the Emperor Constantine Porphyrogenitus included in his manual of imperial diplomacy an account of the sacrifices offered by Rus merchants as thank-offerings for safe passage of the Dnieper rapids.

Kiev's rise to prominence might have owed more to Byzantine diplomacy than the patriotic version of the *Russian Primary Chronicle* allows us to see – or indeed than its compilers were aware. The Rus based at Kiev on the Dnieper, hitherto a fairly insignificant bunch of itinerant traders, could be turned into a client state which might act as a buffer against other enemies and provide mercenary troops for the imperial armies, in return for privileged access to Byzantine markets and a share in Greek Christian culture. We can clearly see this relationship taking on substance in the middle years of the tenth century. Following hostilities between the Rus and the empire in 941 a treaty was made with Prince Igor of Kiev in 945. Its text demonstrates that by then there was a Christian community, with its own church, in Kiev: it might have been primarily composed of visiting Christian merchants, though that need not rule out the possibility that some native Kievans were also attracted to Christianity. After Igor's death his widow Olga governed the Kievan principality as regent for their young son Svyatoslav (in whom one may note the transition from a Norse to a Slav name). In 957 Olga paid a state visit to Constantinople – nearly half of her large entourage were merchants – where she was baptized by the patriarch. She took the Christian name Helena, which was the name of her godmother the empress as well, of course, as the name of the mother of the Emperor Constantine I, Helena the alleged discoverer of the True Cross. On her return to Kiev she built a church there in honour of the Holy Wisdom, its dedication echoing that of the most famous church in Constantinople, Justinian's Hagia Sophia. Byzantine expectations of Olga seem fairly clear. But like Boris of Bulgaria a century earlier Olga also flirted with the west. In 959 she sent an embassy to the court of Otto I of Germany, the most powerful ruler in western Christendom and one whose vigorous *Ostpolitik* was much concerned with the spread of Christianity among the Slavs. Otto despatched a mission under Adalbert, a monk of Trier who later became the first archbishop of the missionary see of Magdeburg. Adalbert could make no headway in Kiev in the years 961–2 and returned to Germany: we shall hear of him again.

It is possible that Adalbert's lack of success among the Russian elite owed something to the displacement of Olga as regent in Kiev by her son. If Svyatoslav was expected to play Constantine to her Helena he proved a disappointment to Byzantine hopes. The period of his rule at Kiev between 962 and 972 has been characterized as one of 'pagan reaction'. The phrase is no more helpful in this context than in some others. Svyatoslav had had to struggle against the rival claims of a kinsman, and had successfully done so with help from the north, a part of Russia where Christianity had as yet made no impact; so he was beholden to a pagan ally. It was later alleged that Svyatoslav had rejected the option of conversion to Christianity with the words, 'My retainers will laugh at me.' Apocryphal, no doubt, but the remark may hint at some of the realities of his fragile power, as well as reminding us of a recurrent anxiety among potential royal barbarian converts. Clovis would have understood Svyatoslav's reluctance; so would Boris.

It was his son Vladimir who took the plunge, becoming thereby Vladimir *Ravnoapóstolny*, 'ranking with the apostles'. As commonly, we possess a literary conversion legend elaborated at a later date, in this instance in the *Russian Primary Chronicle* of the early twelfth century, which has served to obscure the truth. The kernel of that truth, however, is not in doubt. Christianity came to Kiev from Constantinople, and, like the Bulgarians, the Russians were firmly locked into a Byzantine embrace. Vladimir was baptized at Kiev, probably in 988. He married Anna, the emperor's sister, a marriage alliance of unprecedented honour for a barbarian. Mission clergy were sent to Russia from the empire. Mass baptisms followed that of Prince Vladimir. Greek craftsmen were imported to build a new dynastic church at Kiev, the famous 'Tithe Church' consecrated in 996. Bulgarian clergy introduced the Old Church Slavonic liturgy. Vladimir established additional bishoprics in his principality, certainly at Novgorod and Belgorod, possibly elsewhere. He was said to have founded a school at Kiev where a native clergy might be educated. The first man of Russian birth to attain the episcopate was Bishop Luke of Novgorod, consecrated in about 1036. Customary law was written down in the vernacular, the *Russkaja Pravda* or 'Russian Law Code', and new law regulating the position of the church was promulgated by Vladimir.

His son Jaroslav 'the Wise', or 'the Crafty' (d. 1054), rebuilt the church of the Holy Wisdom on the grandest scale. It still stands, an extraordinary and moving monument, in its design, in its interior embellishment with mosaic and fresco, even – perhaps especially – in the graffiti which adorn its walls, a proclamation of what it meant to join the Byzantine family of Christian nations. He founded the monastery of St George at Kiev, and his Swedish wife Ingigard (Irene, Irina) founded the monastery of St Irene. Other monastic foundations

385

occurred. The children of Jaroslav and Ingigard contracted marriages which indicated clearly that the rulers of Kiev were acknowledged members of the royal commonwealth of Christendom. One daughter married King Andrew of Hungary; another, King Harald Hardrada of Norway. A third, named Anna after her grandmother the *porphyrogenita*, made the most imposing match of the lot, to King Henry I of France. Their son was christened Philip and it was thus that this Greek name entered the French royal family.

The Rus had settled in a random and uncontrolled way among non-Christian peoples but within reach of a Christian superpower. The Ostmen had settled in a similarly uncontrolled way among the Christian Irish, who were politically fragmented into a multitude of tiny kingdoms. In England and in Gaul the Vikings settled among Christians and in both areas they were, if not controlled, at any rate to a degree contained, by close political neighbours who were not indeed great powers but were none the less formidable kings, the house of Wessex in England and the West Frankish branch of the Carolingians in Gaul (or as we may now begin to say, France). In both the English and the French instances assimilation to the existing Christian culture seems to have been rapid. We have to say 'seems to have been' because the sources are, once again, thin.

In the early years of the tenth century – the traditional date is 911, though it has no good warrant – a band of Vikings was settled in the valley of the lower Seine round about the city of Rouen by agreement with the West Frankish or French king Charles, whom history has somewhat unkindly remembered as Charles 'the Simple'. The leader of these Vikings was a man named Rollo in our Frankish written sources, which may perhaps have been a rendering of Hrolf or Rolf. The first certain reference to the settlement occurs in a diploma issued by the king in the year 918 in which the claim was made on his behalf that in establishing the newcomers he had acted 'for the safety of the kingdom' (*pro tutela regni*), ambiguous words which may exaggerate the degree of royal initiative.[7] The settlement of Rollo and his men was an *ad hoc* response to a menacing situation by a hard-pressed ruler. Perhaps few on either side expected this Viking principality to last long. Across the Channel the Danish kingdom of East Anglia had lasted less than forty years (878–917) before being conquered by the king of Wessex, and a settlement of Vikings at the mouth of the

Loire in eastern Brittany would endure for a bare sixteen (921–37). However, Rollo's principality not only endured but prospered. By skilfully exploiting the gradual debilitation of the French monarchy in the tenth century, and the internecine hostilities of the territorial principalities into which it fragmented, Rollo's descendants expanded their lands into a duchy of Normandy which stretched from Mont-Saint-Michel in the west very nearly to Amiens and the valley of the Somme in the east. By the middle years of the eleventh century Normandy was one of the most formidable principalities in France. Rollo's great-great-great-grandson, Duke William II, conquered England in 1066.

As part of the treaty arrangements Rollo agreed to become a Christian. So, at any rate, we are informed by the usually reliable contemporary chronicler Flodoard of Rheims, and there is no reason to disbelieve him. What sort of a Christian Rollo turned out to be is hard to judge. The Aquitanian chronicler Adhémar of Chabannes later told a weird story about his last days: 'He was made a Christian by the Frankish bishops and as death approached he lost his senses. He had a hundred Christian captives beheaded in his presence in honour of the idols whom he worshipped, and then he distributed a hundred pounds of gold among the Christian churches in honour of the true God in whose name he had received baptism.'[8] All we need conclude from this is that a century later and in a distant part of France Rollo was remembered as a man who found it prudent to hedge his bets. Just so was Helgi the Lean remembered. More reliable reports than Adhémar's tell that Rollo welcomed back the monks of St Audoen to Rouen in 918 – they had fled to escape Viking predators in 876 – and provided them with endowments. We also know that he was buried beneath Rouen cathedral. We are told that he took a Christian wife. This is not much to go on, but it is congruent with what went on elsewhere. It suggests a barbarian convert well-disposed to his new faith.

Christian observance had been significantly disrupted by Viking depredation. There were interruptions to the succession of bishops, in Normandy as elsewhere. We have already cited the example of Avranches. Indeed, out of the seven episcopal sees of Normandy only at that of Rouen can an unbroken succession of prelates be traced, and that with difficulty, throughout the ninth and tenth centuries. There were monastic displacements: the monks of St Audoen, the monks of St Filibert at Jumièges, both houses vulnerably situated on the banks of the easily navigable river Seine. The pastoral ministry of the church to the laity, such as it was, may have been made more difficult in the areas of densest Scandinavian settlement which were, on the evidence of place-names, the Pays de Caux inland from Fécamp, the region of Bayeux, and the Cotentin peninsula in western Normandy. There was evangelizing work to be done, and the initiative in doing it was taken by the archbishop of Rouen. We can establish this from two letters, one from Pope John X to Archbishop Harvey of Rheims, and the other from the latter to Archbishop Guy (Wido) of Rouen, which can be dated to the period between 914 and 922.[9] The internal evidence of the texts makes it clear that the correspondence originated in a request, now lost, from Guy to Harvey seeking advice on the evangelization of the Scandinavian settlers, which Harvey then referred to the pope. It is possible that King Charles was also involved. It is interesting, in view of the story told by Notker, that one of the problems on which Guy sought guidance was that of successive baptisms undergone by a single individual. Harvey's letter to Guy consists of a fairly long series of extracts from earlier authorities concerning conversion-related matters. One of these extracts concerned the baptism of Clovis at the hands of St Remigius of Rheims. I think we may take it from this that the churchmen of Rheims were conscious and proud of a long evangelizing tradition – in which let us not forget Archbishop Ebo and his mission to the Danes in 823 – and felt responsibility for bringing the faith to the new arrivals in Normandy.

Rollo's descendants busied themselves with the work of Christian restoration. His son William Longsword welcomed St Filibert's community back from Cambrai to Jumièges. Under his son Richard I, whom Adhémar considered a 'most Christian' prince, further religious communities were re-established at Mont-Saint-Michel and Fécamp and the full complement of Norman bishoprics restored. The plum among them was kept in the family: Robert, archbishop of Rouen from 989 to 1037, was the son of Richard I. Robert's elder brother Richard II was famed far and wide for his ostentatious piety. A contemporary chronicler, the monk Rodulfus Glaber, recorded that he sent 100 pounds of gold to the church of the Holy Sepulchre in Jerusalem, and told how 'each year monks came to Rouen even from the famous Mount Sinai in the east and took back with them many presents of gold and silver for their communities.'[10] The fact seems scarcely credible; but it is confirmed from other sources. The dukes set an example which proved infectious among the Norman aristocracy of the eleventh century.

> The barons of Normandy were inspired by the piety of their princes to do likewise, and encouraged each other to undertake similar enterprises for the salvation of their souls. They vied with each other in the good work and competed in giving alms as generously as befitted their rank. Each magnate would have thought himself beneath contempt if he had not supported clerks or monks on his estates for the service of God.[11]

These religious communities had significant pastoral responsibilities and the evangelization of the Normans owed more to them than is readily apparent in the historical record. For example, the seventh-century monastery of Fécamp, once St Leger's prison, on its vulnerable coastal site, had fallen victim to the Vikings. It was restored by Richard I, who installed a community of clergy there, perhaps about the year 980 or so. His son and successor Richard II, wishing to reinstate there the fullness of monastic life according to a strict rule, called in the foremost monastic 'consultant' of the day, the Italian William of Volpiano, who was at that time the abbot of a famous monastery at Dijon in Burgundy. When William came to Normandy in 1001 he found at Fécamp, according to his biographer, that same Rodulfus Glaber who was quoted above, 'an inconsequential little congregation of clerics living in a carnal manner unfettered by the burden of the Rule'.[12] The writer, a Benedictine monk and an eager admirer of Abbot William, had only contempt for the clergy who had preceded the monks at Fécamp. We have to look to another source to find out what these clergy had been doing. A diploma recording a grant to the abbey by Richard I in 990 reveals that already by that date the community at Fécamp possessed at least twelve churches in the vicinity.[13] In other words, the clerics about whom Rodulfus Glaber was so dismissive exercised pastoral care which extended over a substantial area of the Norman countryside in a region where Scandinavian settlement had been heavy. To put it in a nutshell, the clergy of Fécamp were agents of evangelization – though we shouldn't have known this if we had only Glaber's account to go on. This role, initiated by the (unreformed) clerics, was inherited by the (reformed) monks and continued with the acquisition of more rural churches and the establishment by William of Volpiano of a school for the training of priests.

The Fécamp pattern can be replicated elsewhere. Take the monastery of St Evroul in the diocese of Sées in southern Normandy. We know a great deal about it and the local society in which it belonged because it was the home for many years of the monk Orderic Vitalis, whose *Ecclesiastical History* is one of the most lively and observant works of social history ever written and an incomparable guide to the doings of the Norman baronage in the eleventh century. The monastery had been founded by Evroul (Ebrulfus) in about 660, probably on the Columbanian model. In a document of the year 900 its inmates were referred to as *canonici*, 'canons', rather than *monachi*, 'monks'. The word 'canons' would at that time have roughly speaking been equivalent to the *clerici*, 'clerics', whom Richard I had settled at Fécamp. In the middle years of the eleventh century a local baron, William fitz Giroie, decided to re-found it as a monastery on strict Benedictine lines: a good example of the way in which the aristocracy of Normandy followed the example of their dukes. At that time, Orderic informs us, there were just 'two elderly clerics' living there. Orderic also names six churches which William's father Giroie had built on his estates. Two of them were within reach of St Evroul. Were these parish churches served by the two elderly clerics? It looks likely. Elsewhere Orderic tells us a little more about one of these priests. His name was Restold and he was a native of the Beauvaisis who had migrated to Normandy with his wife and son after being admonished to do so in a vision. How many men like Restold were there in tenth- and eleventh-century Normandy? We can only guess. These low-profile cider-priests with their wives and families were outrageously devalued by the snooty 'reformers' of the eleventh and twelfth centuries with their monastic bias and their uncomfortably novel standards. But they had done the job of keeping the show on the road and easing a post-Viking society into new cultural garments. The Christianization of Normandy owed much to them; and their spiritual – and sometimes biological – descendants staffed the rural parishes of Normandy for many centuries to come.

In England, Scandinavian settlement occurred in the second half of the ninth century in a swathe of territory to the east and north of Watling Street, the Roman road linking London and Chester. The nearest parallel to the 'contained' settlement of Rollo in the valley of the lower Seine is to be found in the treaty between King Alfred of

Wessex and the Danish leader Guthrum in the year 878 after Guthrum's defeat in battle. This is how Alfred's friend and biographer Bishop Asser described it:

> When [the hostages] had been handed over, the Vikings swore in addition that they would leave his kingdom immediately, and Guthrum, their king, promised to accept Christianity and to receive baptism at King Alfred's hand; all of which he and his men fulfilled as they had promised. For three weeks later Guthrum with thirty of the best men from his army came to King Alfred at a place called Aller, near Athelney. King Alfred raised him from the holy font of baptism, receiving him as his adoptive son; the unbinding of the chrisom on the eighth day took place at a royal estate near Wedmore. Guthrum remained with the king for twelve nights after he had been baptised, and the king freely bestowed many excellent treasures on him and all his men.[14]

The 'unbinding of the chrisom' was the ritual in which a fillet worn round the head to keep in place the chrism-oil used in baptism was removed after a week had passed since the ceremony. In the wake of this Guthrum and his army retired to East Anglia, which they had overrun nine years earlier (when King Edmund of East Anglia had been killed by them). Scandinavian settlement further north, in the eastern Midlands, Yorkshire and Cumbria, seems to have been less controlled; but that does not necessarily mean altogether disorganized. However, whereas the duchy of Normandy survived and expanded as in effect an independent principality, though formally subject to the nominal lordship of the king of France, the Scandinavian settlements in England were conquered by Alfred's successors. In 954 the last Scandinavian ruler, Eric Bloodaxe, king of York, was killed and the kings of Wessex thereafter ruled a single kingdom of England.

The writings generated directly or indirectly by Alfred's court circle – and very remarkable they were – presented like their Frankish counterparts, though not entirely consistently, an image of the Scandinavians as 'heathen men', committed pagans. The historical reality was probably somewhat different. In England as in Normandy there survives strikingly little firm evidence of a living and resolute pagan faith. In contrast, there is a fair amount of evidence, albeit patchy, for the assimilation of the newcomers to Christian habits. In East Anglia King Guthrum struck coins in his baptismal name of Athelstan, and they were marked with a cross. Coins were also struck to commemorate the 'martyred' King Edmund. Viking rulers in Northumbria also issued coinage of a Christian character. King Guthfrith of York seems to have been on good terms with the community of St Cuthbert, which he encouraged to return from precautionary exile and settled at Chester-le-Street in about 883. At his death in 895 Guthfrith was buried beneath York Minster. There are parallels here with the return to Normandy of the communities of St Audoen and St Filibert, and with Rollo's burial-place at Rouen. We cannot know what sort of a Christian Guthfrith really was. But he was canny enough to grasp that it was worth joining the company of St Peter (of York) and St Cuthbert. He was not alone in this. Under the title *Eiric rex Danorum* the name of Eric Bloodaxe features in the *Liber Vitae*, the 'Book of Life' of the community of St Cuthbert, that is to say the lists of those persons for whom special commemorative prayers were offered.

The example set by the rulers of the Scandinavian settlers was followed by their leading men, in England as in Normandy and elsewhere. There survives in England, mainly northern England, an abundance of stone sculpture from the Anglo-Scandinavian period of the tenth and eleventh centuries. Difficult to date and often to interpret, this corpus nevertheless permits some inferences to be drawn from it. It was clearly executed for patrons who were wealthy, in other words for persons of rank. It was decorated in a manner that displayed markedly Scandinavian stylistic influence, for patrons therefore of Scandinavian artistic taste. It shows a fascinating mixture of Christian and pre-Christian motifs. We can read in these mute stones a tale of the acculturation of the Viking settlers to their new environment. Take, for example, the memorial to a warrior at Middleton, near Pickering in North Yorkshire, probably erected in the first half of the tenth century (illustrated in plates 31 and 32). There he is, a warrior with his weaponry, accompanied or menaced by a big dragon on the reverse which may – but does not have to – set us thinking of the traditional mythology of the northern world. But he was also a Christian; or at any rate those who commissioned his memorial thought it appropriate that it should take the form of a cross. The Middleton cross is a simple piece – as simple as, though less puzzling than the Niederdollendorf stone referred to in Chapter 5.[15] For something much more elaborate and accomplished we might look at the Gosforth cross in Cumbria. This monument stands in a churchyard near the Cumbrian coast a few miles south of St Bees Head. It is a noble piece, carved from the local red standstone, standing over three and a half metres high. Its surfaces are densely sculpted by an artist of great vigour and subtlety whose distinctive hand can be recognized in other sculptural fragments at the same site. There is indeed such a concentration of sculpture at Gosforth as to suggest that some locally important Christian community existed there when the 'Gosforth Master' was working, generally agreed to have been the first half of the tenth century (and therefore roughly contemporary with the Middleton cross). The artist has juxtaposed Christian with non-Christian scenes in his decoration. There is a Crucifixion, but there are also scenes which represent the story of Ragnarök, the destruction of the gods in Scandinavian mythology. This marriage of Christian and pre-Christian iconography is something that we have met before in our brief consideration of the Franks Casket in Chapter 8. It directs attention to a familiar phase in the conversion process.[16]

Both the speed and the opportunities of integration into English Christian society are exemplified in the career of Oda, archbishop of Canterbury from 941 to 958. We are told on fairly good authority that Oda's Danish and presumably pagan father had come to England with the Viking invaders in the 860s. Oda was brought up a Christian, which presumably indicates that his father had adopted Christianity upon settling in England, perhaps on the occasion of marrying a Christian woman. The young Oda was attached to the household of Athelhelm, successively bishop of Wells (909–23) and Canterbury (923–6). Aided by this distinguished patron, Oda's rise in the governing circles of the English church was swift. He had become bishop of Ramsbury (i.e. Wiltshire) by about 925 and was promoted by the king to Canterbury in 941. It is astonishing that a second-generation Viking immigrant should have been able to rise to the highest ecclesiastical position in the kingdom. Undoubtedly Oda was a very able man; equally certain that he had powerful friends in church and state. But when all allowances are made we are left with a sense of immigrants who were eager to integrate themselves with the prevailing culture and of a 'host' society which was willing to make room for them.

The command structure of the church in England had been disrupted by the invasions, its endowments plundered. There are tell-tale gaps in the episcopal lists for the bishoprics of northern and eastern England. The see of Lindsey (i.e. Lincolnshire), for instance, was vacant for some eighty years, from *c.* 875 to *c.* 953. Already in the 890s Pope Formosus, whose concern for missions we have already seen evidence of in a Bulgarian context, was urging the English bishops to fill vacancies so that pastoral care should not be lacking. One cannot wholly suppress the unworthy thought that the removal from the scene of potential rivals might not have been unwelcome in certain quarters. In terms of territory and power the see of York – like that of Rouen – did rather nicely out of the Viking invasions and settlements. When the pattern of ecclesiastical government was restored it was sometimes on different lines from what had gone before, lines which re-drew boundaries in such a fashion as to enhance episcopal power. The two bishoprics of East Anglia had lapsed from *c.* 870, the bishops of London acting as caretakers during a long interruption. When restoration occurred in 955, presumably on the initiative of Archbishop Oda, only one of the two sees was restored. What had been the sees of Lindsey and Leicester back in the ninth century were amalgamated to constitute the enormous diocese of Dorchester (on Thames) in the 950s, whose seat was moved to Lincoln in 1072. Leicester's last pre-Viking bishop disappears from view in about 870; the see was not revived for over 1,000 years (1927).

Monastic life was also re-established, with the re-foundation of communities which had existed before the invasions began, such as Ely, Peterborough and Barking. New religious houses also were founded, such as Ramsey. In England as in Normandy we have to reckon with communities of clergy at which reformers looked askance but which very probably made a significant if unobtrusive contribution to the Christianization of Anglo-Scandinavian England. The will of Bishop Theodred of London (*c.* 951), a document which sheds some welcome light on the church life of East Anglia owing to the caretaker role alluded to above, reveals the existence at Hoxne (Suffolk) of 'God's community at St Ethelbert's church' of which we should not otherwise have known.[17] Excavations there have revealed the foundations of some of the community's not insubstantial buildings. The same document mentions other communities, at Mendham and at Bury St Edmunds, the latter being transformed into a Benedictine monastery in the 1020s. These three establishments are likely to have played a role in the pastoral life of tenth-century Suffolk. In Yorkshire the monastery founded by St Wilfrid at Ripon had been revived (if indeed it had ever died) as a community of priests under the supervision of the archbishop of York by 948 at the latest. Ripon was well placed to supervise church life in the northern reaches of the plain of York where, to judge by the place-names, the Scandinavian presence was particularly dense: like Fécamp and the Pays de Caux. Comparable re-emergences of former monastic sites as the hubs of local pastoral ministry may be found elsewhere in the north, at Repton in Derbyshire, for example, or at Beverley in the East Riding of Yorkshire. There were also new foundations of such colleges of canons, as they are sometimes called. Stow in Lincolnshire is a good example, apparently founded early in the eleventh century, well documented from the 1050s, when it found generous patrons in Earl Leofric of Mercia and his wife Godgifu (the 'Lady Godiva' of legend). Much of its very handsome church still stands. The first post-Conquest bishop of Lincoln tried to reform Stow into a Benedictine monastery by introducing monks from Eynsham in Oxfordshire. It sounds a little like what happened at Troarn in Normandy:

> To Gilbert abbot of Conches and his monks Roger de Montgomery entrusted the reform of the abbey of Troarn, driving out the twelve canons whom his father Roger had established there. After expelling these clerks, who were wholly given over to gluttony, carnal lusts and worldly profit, he replaced them with monks vowed to the discipline of the Rule. From that time monks under the authority of abbot Gilbert began to establish strict religious life there . . . and their successors, faithful to the charge committed to them, have carried on the tradition of sound observance . . . and still do so today.[18]

The difference was that at Stow the reform did not stick. The next bishop was no friend to Benedictinism and sent the monks back to Eynsham. Stow was sucked instead into the cathedral establishment: it became and remains a prebend of the cathedral church of Lincoln.

Very occasionally we can demonstrate continuity of pastoral function right across the caesura which is what the Viking invasions and settlement so often seem to represent. The case of Horningsea in Cambridgeshire may be quoted. Before the Scandinavian irruption

> . . . there was at Horningsea a minster of royal dignity with no small congregation of clergy. At the time when the [Danish] army was ravaging about that region, Cenwald the priest exercised sacerdotal office there. Then those Danes who had come together from paganism to the grace of baptism endowed that aforesaid minster with five 'hides' of land in Horningsea and two in Eye. When Cenwald died, Herolf the priest succeeded him there . . .[19]

395

We know this story simply because the endowments in question later became the subject of a lawsuit, the record of which was copied down and has survived. It must prompt one to wonder how many Cenwalds there might have been up and down the eastern side of England quietly getting on with their pastoral job during troubled times, of whom we shall never know anything at all.

We can learn something of their duties and of the expectations which authority held of them in a document known as the *Northumbrian Priests' Law*, a code of conduct probably drafted by Archbishop Wulf-stan of York (1002–23). Wulfstan was a realist who did not ask the impossible of his clergy. They must shave regularly, must not bring their weapons to church, must try to keep out of fights and must not perform in taverns as 'ale minstrels'. It was expected that they would be married but separations and second unions were forbidden. Restold of St Evroul and his wife would have felt quite at home. They were to be on the lookout for heathen practices: divination, sacrifices, witch-craft, idol-worship, the veneration of holy trees or stones or wells, 'or any such nonsense', as the archbishop robustly put it. Wulfstan was well aware that he led a flock whose Christian observances needed improvement.

Anglo-Scandinavian Christianity may not have been deep, but it was eager and it was pious. One indication of this may be seen in the foundation by the laity of churches in both town and countryside.* At Lincoln a man with the probably Old Norse name Eirtig founded the church of St Mary-le-Wigford and had the fact recorded in an Old English inscription incised on a re-used Romano-British gravestone: 'Eirtag had me made and endowed with possessions to the glory of Christ and St Mary.' Three men with Old Norse names founded the church of St Mary, Castlegate, in York at some point in the eleventh century and similarly recorded this act of piety in an inscription. At Norwich there were in existence at least forty-nine churches and chapels by the year 1086: it is likely that most of these had been founded by the citizens in the course of the preceding century and a half. In the middle years of the eleventh century it seems to have been fashionable among Yorkshire landowners to embellish the churches they built on their estates with inscribed sundials. 'Ulf ordered this

---

* For reasons which will appear in a later chapter it is not quite appropriate to call them 'parish' churches just yet, though this is what they became.

church to be built for himself and for Gunwara's soul' reads the inscription on one at Aldborough on the east coast of Yorkshire. Ulf was an important landowner in Yorkshire in the late Anglo-Saxon period. The best-preserved and the most ambitious of them survives at Kirkdale: 'Orm the son of Gamel acquired St Gregory's minster when it was completely ruined and collapsed and he had it built anew from the ground to Christ and to St Gregory in the time of King Edward and Earl Tostig. This is the day's sun-marker at every hour. And Hawarth made me, and Brand [was] the priest.'[20] Tostig was earl of Northumbria under King Edward the Confessor between 1055 and 1065; Orm was a prominent Yorkshire magnate. Both Ulf and Orm remind us of Giroie and his church-building enterprises in eleventh-century Normandy. As we shall soon see, hundreds of other landowners in eleventh-century Europe were engaged in similar activities.

In the same year in which Tostig became earl of Northumbria, 1055, a visitor from Iceland turned up at the court of Archbishop Adalbert of Bremen. His name was Isleifr (or Islef) Gizurrsson, and he asked to be consecrated as a bishop for the Icelanders. The see of Hamburg-Bremen had claims to the direction of Christian life throughout all the northern islands. Archbishop Adalbert, moreover, was never a man to let slip any chance of enlarging the sphere of his authority. We have already seen him consecrating a bishop for the Orkneymen. Accordingly, Islef was consecrated and sent back to Iceland as its first bishop.

The settlement of Iceland from Norway occurred in the period between about 870 and 930. It is commonly cited as the unique instance from early medieval Europe of the export of a native pre-Christian religious tradition from one environment to another. The statement needs some qualification. Leaving to one side the vexed question of whether there were Irish monks on Iceland before the arrival of the Norse, we can be certain of two things. First, some of the early settlers had already encountered Christianity in the Western Isles and adopted some of its teachings and observances. Such, for instance, were Helgi the Lean and Orlygr Hrappsson. Second, the early settlers were not exclusively Norse but also comprised natives of the Scottish islands and of Ireland who were Christians. Tenth-century Iceland, therefore, was not a purely pagan society but contained Christian elements within it. These elements were reinforced by contacts between the settlers and the Christianizing societies of mainland western Europe. The Viking world was one in which it was easy to move about. Merchants, mercenaries, fishermen, poets moved to and fro between Iceland and the continent in the course of the tenth century. It is not impossible that among visitors to Iceland there were clerics. A German bishop named Frederick, of whom nothing whatsoever is known, was rumoured to have visited Iceland at some point during the century.

We seem to be on firmer ground with another bishop, presumed German on the strength of his name, Thangbrand, who is said to have paid a visit to Iceland in 995. Our source for this is the *Islendingabók* ('Book of the Icelanders') of Ari Thorgilsson, composed in about 1125. Ari is normally judged a sober and trustworthy historian. What is more, his own foster-father had been baptized by Bishop Thangbrand. So the historicity of Thangbrand's visit looks at first sight reliable enough. Our difficulty is that Thangbrand has become attached to a conversion narrative of whom the hero was Olaf Tryggvason, king of Norway. In its main lines the story runs as follows. Thangbrand was sent to Iceland by King Olaf in 995 to convert the Icelanders. His mission being unsuccessful the king threatened to kill or maim some Icelandic hostages whom he held in Norway unless the Icelanders adopted Christianity. Two leading Icelanders, both converts to Christianity, Gizurr the White and Hjalti Skeggjason, went to Norway and freed the hostages by promising Olaf that they would try to bring about the conversion of their fellow Icelanders. On their return home the issue was debated at the Icelandic assembly, the Althing. Christian and pagan factions had formed and open conflict seemed to be on the point of breaking out. The arbitration of the president of the assembly, the 'lawspeaker' Thorgeirr Thorkelsson was sought. Thorgeirr withdrew for a day and a night, possibly undergoing some sort of divination ritual, and then pronounced in favour of Christianity. Accordingly, after this public debate and agreed arbitration, the people of Iceland became Christian. The year traditionally assigned to this decision is 1000. It all sounds too good to be true.

Well of course it *is* too good to be true. This conversion narrative is found in Ari's work and in subsequent works dependent on him composed in the course of the thirteenth century. It is likely that already before Ari's day certain elements in the tale had been tampered with in such a way as to bend the historical truth. Ari was simply reporting the received opinion of his time. Conversion narratives have

398

always to be treated with circumspection, and upon scrutiny almost invariably betray legendary elements. The role attributed to Olaf Tryggvason in the conversion of Iceland is probably as distorted as that attributed to him in the conversion of Earl Sigurd the Stout of Orkney. Indeed, the beginnings of conversion in Iceland may have resembled the early stages of conversion in Orkney as sketched above: a sort-of-Christian presence, even if only on Sundays, gathering adherents bit by bit. It is unlikely that Olaf Tryggvason ever exercised the influence over Iceland attributed to him in the narrative. On the other hand, the commercial and cultural ties of the Icelanders with Norway were close. If they were going to approach anyone about Christianity it would have been the Norwegians. Could this have been the reality behind the legend – an approach from the Icelanders expressing interest in Christianity? This, after all, is what Rastislav of Moravia and Boris of Bulgaria had done; and it might be what Ethelbert of Kent had done, as we saw in Chapter 4. So we can keep the embassy to Norway, but we may wish to scale down the part allotted to the king. We might also wish to juggle with the chronology of Thangbrand's mission. The sending of a German cleric from Norway to Iceland is in itself credible, because we know that there were German clergy active in Norway at the time. But surely Thangbrand must have been sent *after* the embassy, in answer to its request. This would fit better with the personal history of Ari Thorgilsson, who was born in 1067. Ari would not have had a near-septuagenarian foster-father if Thangbrand's mission had occurred a little later than the conversion narrative would have it.

Whatever the truth about the early stages of Icelandic Christianity its eleventh-century growth took place in a north German cultural setting. Gizurr the White sent his son to be educated at the Saxon monastery of Herford. This was Islef, later to become Iceland's first bishop. On his return to Iceland he established his episcopal seat at one of his family's properties, Skálaholt, where he founded a cathedral and a school for educating boys for the priesthood. His son and successor Gizurr was also educated at Herford, also consecrated a bishop in Germany. A second Icelandic diocese was founded at Hólar in 1106. The school founded there by its first bishop boasted a woman named Ingunn who taught Latin grammar and wove or embroidered scenes from lives of the saints, thus 'declaring God's glory not only with the words of her mouth but also with the work of her hands'.[21] Perhaps her work looked like the medieval figured textiles which are still to be seen in Norway's museums. The section of 'Old Christian Laws' included in the Icelandic legal compilation known as *Grágás* was committed to writing at about the same time that Ari put together his *Islendingabók* in the 1120s. Bede's work was known to Ari and to some extent furnished a model for him. When Bishop Thorlákr of Skálaholt lay on his deathbed in 1133 he asked to be read to from Pope Gregory the Great's *Regula Pastoralis*. The scene is familiar: literacy; Latin; written law; theology; history. Mediterranean religious culture had reached Iceland.

It is true that twelfth-century Icelandic Christian culture had some peculiar features. Clerical marriage was openly accepted. Bishop Gizurr Islefsson had a daughter who married Bishop Ketil of Hólar; after his death in 1145 she became a nun. It was assumed that lay patrons who built churches would pass them on to their heirs like any other property. Common enough in mainland Europe at an earlier date, this was now frowned upon and fast disappearing as lay owners surrendered power over their churches to their bishops. A separate ecclesiastical jurisdiction had not emerged in Iceland, with its apparatus of canon law, church courts, appeals procedures and bureaucracy. The poverty of the Icelandic environment was such as to inhibit the development of institutions which were taken for granted elsewhere. Monasteries were few and very small; no Icelandic monastery ever had more than five inmates at one time. Cathedral chapters did not develop – which was perhaps not altogether unwelcome to the bishops.

An even more peculiar outpost of European Christendom was to be found still further to the west in Greenland. Banished from Iceland in 982, Eric the Red found his way to those inhospitable shores and somehow supported himself for the three years of his exile. On his return to Iceland he sought to recruit settlers for the land which, in one of the most inspired pieces of mendacity in the whole history of advertising, he temptingly called 'Greenland'. Two settlements were established in the course of the next few years. We are told that there was a Christian among the earliest settlers. Again like Iceland, we possess a much later conversion narrative. According to this Eric's son Leif sailed to Norway in the year 999, where he was converted to Christianity by – no prizes for guessing – King Olaf Tryggvason. He returned to Greenland with a priest supplied by Olaf. His father was suspicious of the new faith but his mother Thjodhild accepted it and built a church near the family home at Brattahlith. She refused to share her bed with Eric until he too had accepted Christianity.

We need not accept this story as literal truth. However, in the usual morass of legend and tradition there are some certainties. Somebody did build a church at Brattahlith in the eleventh century. It was discovered and excavated in 1961–2, and proved to be a tiny rectangular byre-like structure measuring only about six by three metres externally, with a stone east wall, the remainder presumably of timber and turf, standing in a small circular graveyard defined by a ditch. It is entirely credible that the Greenlanders should have accepted Christianity in the wake of Iceland, though not necessarily in the person of Leif Ericcson, let alone from Olaf Tryggvason. The best evidence for this reception is to be found in the work of the chronicler Adam of Bremen, writing in the 1070s. Adam did not know much about Greenland, and he had his own axe to grind about the claims of the see of Bremen (to which we shall return a little later). However, there are signs that he had access to eye-witness information about Greenland. He knew that its people lived, like the Icelanders, 'in underground caves, glad to have roof and food and bed in common with their cattle'. This is probably a reference to the cladding of turf, several metres thick, with which all structures in Greenland had to be protected from wind and cold. Farms, byres, churches, all would have looked from the outside like gigantic mole-hills. Adam reported rather vaguely that the Christian faith 'has winged its way to them of late', and his account of Bishop Islef's consecration in 1055 could be read as implying that Greenland as well as Iceland was intended to fall within the scope of his pastoral supervision.[22]

Greenland did eventually get a bishop of its own. In 1125 Einar Sokkason went to Norway and asked King Sigurd Jorsalfari – 'the Jerusalem-farer', named after a pilgrimage he had undertaken in the years 1108–10 – for a bishop. A priest named Arnold was appointed and consecrated by the archbishop of Lund. Einar in gratitude presented the king with a polar bear – alive – which he had brought with him in his boat from Greenland. In the following year Bishop Arnold established himself at Gardar, where he built himself a cathedral and dwelling-house with appurtenant buildings: all these have been excavated.

The medieval settlements in Greenland produced no native historians. We are dependent for our knowledge of them entirely upon occasional references in European chroniclers such as Adam of Bremen and upon the remains of their material culture recovered by archaeologists. We know just enough to sense a certain vitality in the Christian culture of the settlements during the twelfth and thirteenth centuries. The cathedral at Gardar was rebuilt on a larger scale by Bishop Jon Smyrill, John the Hawk, whose episcopate fell between 1189 and 1209. It had glass windows and three fireplaces. The bones of a man who may have been Jon Smyrill have been excavated in the north transept. They were identifiable as the remains of a bishop by his gold episcopal ring and the crozier which had been placed across his body. This crozier had a finely carved head of walrus ivory, probably Icelandic work of the late twelfth century. It has been speculated that it could have been carved by the celebrated Icelandic artist Margret *hin haga*, Margaret the Dexterous, who worked to commissions from Bishop Pall of Skálaholt, whom Bishop Jon Smyrill is known to have visited in 1202–3.

Another episcopal concern is registered by the substantial tithe barn which stood near the cathedral, a massive blockhouse of a building, the sandstone lintel of one of its two doorways weighing about three tons. The laity whose arduous labours filled the bishop's ample garner worshipped in at least sixteen churches known from Norwegian documentary sources, most of which have been identified and several excavated, simple little buildings like that at Brattahlith. The markers found in their graveyards allow us to eavesdrop on the piety of the men and women who struggled to make a living in that harsh land: 'May the Almighty God bless and keep Gudleif'; 'Mary and Michael have me, Brigit'; 'Thorleif made this cross in praise and honour of God the Almighty'. And of those whose loved ones were wasted on the chill northern waters: 'This woman, whose name was Gudveig, was committed to the deep in the Greenland sea'.

This is not the place to pursue the fragmentary history of Christianity in the Greenland settlements or their pitiable end in the fifteenth century. They fell victim to a deadly combination of climatic deterioration, Eskimo hostility, European neglect and – very probably – physical and mental degeneration. The coming of Christianity to Greenland is but a footnote to the narrative of European conversion. But a heroic one and a confident one; testimony to the extraordinary buoyancy and optimism which distinguished the eleventh, twelfth and thirteenth centuries.

It will be obvious from the foregoing that the sources for the conversion of the Scandinavians abroad, in Ireland, Scotland, England, Normandy, Russia, Iceland and Greenland, are extremely sparse. They are a little more plentiful with regard to the Scandinavian homelands, but they present special problems of their own. There never was some Scandinavian Bede to compose an *Ecclesiastical History of the Northern Peoples* and thus to impose a welcome but perhaps deceptive order upon a muddled welter of tradition. There was very little in the way of early hagiography, which is such a boon to the historian of conversion in Francia. There was much late and legendary elaboration of the doings of two kings of Norway, Olaf Tryggvason and Olaf Haraldsson: we have already encountered some of the resultant difficulties. Our principal source for what follows in the rest of this chapter is a narrative which is in some respects akin to, though much ampler than, the *Conversio Bagoariorum et Carantanorum* (see Chapter 10). Its author was Adam of Bremen, and his work the *Gesta Hammaburgensis Ecclesiae Pontificum* (*Deeds of the Bishops of the Church of Hamburg*). Adam was a native of Swabia who migrated to the north of Germany in about 1065 and joined the cathedral establishment of the see of Bremen which had been united to that of Hamburg, as we saw in Chapter 7, since the year 864. He composed the bulk of his history between 1072 and 1076. Adam was learned, lively and observant. His work would be worth reading, if for no other reason, for its subtle portrait of the tremendous but flawed figure of Archbishop Adalbert (1043–72). Adam was passionately loyal to his adopted church. His principal motive in writing was to expound, justify and defend the claims of the see of Hamburg-Bremen to the evangelization of the northern peoples and the subsequent oversight of their religious life. Adam did for Hamburg-Bremen what the anonymous author of the *Conversio* did for Salzburg; but he did it on a larger scale, after more extensive research and with greater elegance. His history was what German scholars call a *Tendenzschrift*, a writing with a purpose.

We saw in Chapter 7 that attempts to convert the Danes were being made in the second quarter of the ninth century during the reign of Charlemagne's son the Emperor Louis the Pious. From that period we have the embassy of Ebo of Rheims, the baptism of Harald Klak and the beginnings of Anskar's mission. But after Anskar's death in 865 the Danish mission faltered. Rimbert's carefully crafted memorial to his master in the *Vita Anskarii* was a celebration of a glorious past by an unhappy present, composed at a time when Christian Europe was enduring the worst intensity of the Viking raids. This is not to say that Christianity disappeared from Denmark. Adam was probably right to judge, or guess, that something of the Christianity implanted by Anskar survived; and his hunch has received some archaeological confirmation. The Danes were aware of Christianity in the late ninth and early tenth centuries because they had Christian neighbours in Saxony, or because they raided and traded and fought as mercenaries in Christian lands across the sea, or because they had kinsfolk who settled in the British Isles or in France. There must have been many who had been prime-signed like Egil Skallagrimsson and 'had full contact with both Christians and heathens but kept whatever faith they were inclined to'.[23]

The stabilization of the East Frankish or German kingdom under a new dynasty from Saxony began during the reign of Henry I, or Henry the Fowler (918–36). He showed the Saxons how to defeat the Magyars, he restored morale and the influx of tribute by campaigns against the Slav tribes of his eastern frontier, and his prestige found expression in far-flung diplomacy, the summoning of church councils and showy royal progresses in Germany. By the 930s German kingship once again loomed large over the Danes as it had not done for nearly a century. It was to loom larger still during the reign of Henry's son Otto I, or Otto the Great (936–73). Restored confidence stimulated renewed concern for mission, much as it had done in ninth-century Constantinople. Archbishop Unni of Hamburg-Bremen undertook a missionary journey in Anskar's footsteps, dying in the course of it at Birka in Sweden in 936. Adam had heard that he appointed priests for the Christian communities in Denmark. In 948 Archbishop Adaldag even went so far as to create three Danish bishoprics, though there is no evidence that the German bishops he appointed to them ever so much as set foot in the Danish kingdom. Gorm, often called Gorm the Old, the king of the Danes, seems to have tolerated Christianity among his subjects but was not to be won over himself.

Gorm the Old died in 958. Harald, the son of Gorm, was the earliest convert to Christianity among the kings of Denmark (if, that is, we except Harald Klak whose reign was very short). Adam, predictably, attributed his conversion to the missionary activities of the church of Hamburg-Bremen. Fortunately, we possess two other sources, composed very shortly after the event, which shed a different light on the circumstances. The more important of the two is the chronicle of Widukind of Corvey, whose reference to an earlier conversion of the Danes – presumably in allusion to the work of Anskar – was quoted near the beginning of this chapter. Widukind was writing in the years 967–8. He tells an odd story of how the Christian faith was put to the test at the Danish court on King Harald's orders. In the manner of a judicial ordeal a hot iron was carried by a Christian priest named Poppo whose hand suffered no injury thereby. Persuaded by this miracle of the power of the Christian God, King Harald was converted and ordered all his subjects to follow his example. Widukind added the information that Poppo 'is now a bishop'. The only Poppo who fits is the Poppo who became bishop of Würzburg in 961. So Harald's acceptance of the new faith must shortly have preceded that date. A further inference is permissible. Because tenth-century German rulers kept a tight hold over their church and used episcopal appointments as a way of rewarding those who served them well, we may plausibly surmise that Poppo's mission had been sponsored by Otto I and that the bishopric of Würzburg was a reward for its successful outcome. Significantly, Adam of Bremen was confused about Poppo. One can see why: Poppo had not come from the church of Hamburg-Bremen. Rather, he was the representative of the looming presence of German kingship. If Bede had been reporting the encounter he might have put it that King Harald of the Danes received Christianity through the fraternal advice of Otto I.

Vivid and extremely solid testimony to Harald's public acceptance of Christianity is to be seen at Jelling in Jutland. The present church there, built in about 1100, is flanked by two enormous man-made mounds. Excavation has revealed that one of them contained a grave datable to the middle years of the tenth century by objects found within it. No human remains were found, but the grave-goods allow the inference that the grave had been that of a man, possibly also of a woman, of the highest status. Not long after its construction the mound and the grave within it had been opened up, presumably for the purpose of abstracting something from it. Beneath the church were discovered the remains of three successive earlier churches. The earliest church, of timber, had contained within it a prominently sited grave which, by analogy, could only have been the resting-place of a very important person (or persons). The human bones found within the grave were in some disorder, presumably because they had been moved there from some earlier resting-place. Finds of gold thread from textiles confirmed that these were the remains of a person (or persons) of rank and wealth, and the deposit could be dated to the middle years of the tenth century. Outside the church, and exactly halfway between the mounds, stand two stones. The smaller of the two bears a runic inscription which records that it was erected by King Gorm in memory of his wife Thyre. The larger is a monster hunk of granite standing about two metres high (see plate 30). Its irregular shape offers three surfaces for ornament. One of these is carved with a horned, prancing beast intertwined with a serpent. Another carries a representation of the Crucifixion. The third bears most of a runic inscription which also overflows on to the other two surfaces: 'King Harald ordered this monument to be made in memory of his father Gorm and his mother Thyre. That Harald won for himself all Denmark and Norway, and made the Danes Christian.'[24] It is clear enough what happened at Jelling. In the wake of his conversion in about 960 Harald built a church there in which he re-interred his parents in a Christian manner. His forebears were brought under the protection of this new and all-powerful God in a sort of posthumous Christianization. It was a neat solution to the problem which had worried Radbod of Frisia.

Harald's territorial claims need a little explanation. 'Denmark' meant the 'march' (*mark*) or frontier region of the Danes and indicated the eastern islands of modern Denmark together with the south-western parts of what we today call Sweden, the coastal strip between, roughly speaking, the modern cities of Göteborg and Malmö. 'Norway' indicated the coasts on either side of Oslo Fjord. A great part of Harald's considerable power rested on his lordship over territories which lay on *both* side of the seas which embrace the country of the Danes, the Skagerrak and the Kattegat. This gave him access to the high-quality iron ore of Telemark, and enabled him to exercise some degree of control over the lucrative maritime trade which passed between the Baltic and the North Sea. If Otto I had thought that Harald's acceptance of Christianity at German hands would make him a pliant satellite, his son and grandson were to find that this hope was wide of the mark. Harald was a very imposing king. The main witness to this is a series of colossal public works – the monuments at Jelling, the enormous forts constructed in Jutland, Fyn and Sjaelland, the massive causeway at Ravning Enge. Harald's pretensions may also be seen in the coinage he issued (with, for the first time, manifest Christian symbolism), the legislative activity attributed to him by Adam of Bremen, and perhaps in the organization of a royal fleet. When he died in 987 and was buried in the church which he had founded as the royal mausoleum at Roskilde, he left to his son Sweyn (Sven) a monarchy of formidable military potential. Sweyn, often known as Sweyn Forkbeard, was not slow in activating this potential. The kingdom of England was easy of access, wealthy, and at the time vulnerable during the troubled reign of Ethelred II, 'the Unready'. Sweyn turned his fleets in that direction and after some twenty years of hammering finally succeeded in conquering England in the years 1013–14 before dying suddenly in the moment of his triumph early in 1014. His son Canute (Knut) sought to reunite his father's conquests. He reconquered England in 1015–16, seized Denmark after his brother's death in 1019, and re-established Danish lordship over Norway by 1028. Canute presided over this far-flung but precarious Anglo-Scandinavian empire until his death in 1035. Thereafter its component fragments drifted apart.

The poet Thorleif Jarlsskald attributed the success of Sweyn Forkbeard in conquering England to the *gipta* or good fortune bestowed on him by God. *Gipta* was an important quality of the pre-Christian dispensation in the Scandinavian cultures. Etymologically related to the various words for *giving* in the early Germanic languages, it meant the luck or success 'bestowed' by the gods. It was readily transferable into a Christian context. Another skald or poet of the time could refer to the *gipta Hvítakrists*, the 'White Christ's good luck', or grace, bestowed in baptism (with allusion to the white garments of the recipients). Sweyn and Canute had *gipta* in abundance. We know little of Sweyn's religious loyalties. Adam of Bremen's story that he reverted to paganism is maliciously inaccurate, and indeed contradicted by some of his other reports about Sweyn. (Adam disapproved of Sweyn because he had been unsympathetic to the claims of the church of Hamburg-Bremen.) Sweyn was certainly a Christian of a sort. We know rather more about his son. As king of England Canute of course came into contact with the bench of English bishops, and especially with its most-commanding figure, Archbishop Wulfstan of York. Wulfstan took it upon himself to school Canute in the ways of Christian kingship. He played Remigius or Paulinus to Canute's Clovis or Edwin.

Canute was taught that gratitude to God for his good fortune as well as remorse for the blood he had shed was best expressed in lavish benefactions to the church and acts of ostentatious piety. We can read this in Canute's foundation of a minster church on the site of the battle of Ashingdon, or in the stagy translation of the body of the murdered Archbishop Alphege (Aelfheah) from London to Canterbury in 1023. Above all perhaps we can read it in Canute's pilgrimage to Rome and attendance there at the imperial coronation of Conrad II in 1027: the Viking conqueror has been refashioned into the pious king who was welcomed as an equal by the highest in Christendom. Archbishop Wulfstan drafted godly laws in Canute's name. The king's moneyers struck coin which bore the sign of the cross. He sought to buy regard with the giving of presents. A letter from the great Bishop Fulbert of Chartres survives which acknowledges a gift from Canute, in somewhat tactless terms ('We had heard that you were a pagan, but now . . .').[25] Was Chartres the only continental church to be the recipient of his patronage? We cannot tell, but it is unlikely that Canute neglected others in his eager strategies to be accepted.

Canute, in short, paraded himself after Wulfstan's grooming as the model Christian king. He set an example to other northern princes. It cannot be coincidence that so many among them undertook pilgrimages to Rome or even the Holy Places so soon in the wake of Canute's Roman journey of 1027 – Sihtric Silkbeard of Dublin, Duke Robert of Normandy, Earl Thorfinn of Orkney, Macbeth, king of Scots, Earl Tostig of Northumbria. Another fruit of his Christian schooling may be seen in the church life of Denmark. Canute could learn from the example of the reasonably well-conducted Anglo-Saxon church about the proper ordering of the churches in his homeland. Before Canute's day such organization as there was in the Danish church had been fluid. This had not escaped the notice of Adam of Bremen:

> Archbishop Adaldag consecrated for Denmark several bishops whose names we have found indeed, but on which see each was specifically enthroned we could not easily ascertain. I think the reason is that, with Christianity in a rude state, none of the bishops was as yet assigned to a fixed see, but that as each of them pushed out into the further regions in the effort to establish Christianity, he would strive to preach the Word of God alike to his own and to the others' people. This even now seems to be the practice beyond Denmark, throughout Norway and Sweden.[26]

The likelihood is that these early Danish bishops had been attached to the itinerant royal court. Canute set in motion the creation of an orderly structure of ecclesiastical government, though it was not completed until well after his death: seven Danish dioceses with agreed boundaries and fixed seats at cathedral towns, of which one, Lund, became an archbishopric in 1104. Canute also challenged the claims of Hamburg-Bremen to control the Danish church through bishops of German origin. Adam noted ruefully that Canute introduced 'many bishops' from England into Denmark and named three of them, of whom one – Gerbrand of Roskilde – can be confirmed from a contemporary and independent English source. Others, shadowy but plausible, can be added, such as the disreputable Henry, formerly Canute's treasurer, who went on to hold the office of bishop in Orkney – before Thorolf? another challenge to Hamburg-Bremen? – and ended up as bishop of Lund, where he drank himself to death. It is notable too that bishops of native Danish origin began to occur more frequently as the eleventh century advanced. Such, for instance, was Odinkar of Ribe: 'He was a noble of the royal Danish stock, rich in land, so much so that they say the bishopric of Ribe was founded from his patrimony. This Odinkar was taken to England by King Canute and there instructed in letters. After that he spent time in Gaul in search of learning, and acquired the reputation of being a wise man and a philosopher.'[27] One senses an emerging Danish *Adelskirche*, and there is more than a hint – in the rank, the wealth, the travels in search of wisdom – of such men as Benedict Biscop or Wilfrid.

These eleventh-century Danish bishops may have been, some of them, a roughish lot. Egilbert of Odense was an ex-pirate, Avoco of Roskilde was another drunk who met the same fate as the bibulous Henry of Lund, Christian of Aarhus was one of the leaders of a raid on England in 1069–70. One can readily imagine the reactions to them of smooth prelates like Fulbert of Chartres Yet it was the lead given by these bishops that enabled the Danish church to become firmly rooted in its native soil; literally so, with the foundation of rural churches by landowners for their people. Adam of Bremen tells us that there were 300 churches in Skåne by the time he was writing in the 1070s, 150 in Sjaelland and 100 in Fyn. The numbers are, of course, suspiciously round; but archaeological research has borne out his assertion of numerous church foundations from this period. The first Benedictine monasteries were founded in the 1080s. King Sweyn

Estrithson (Sven Estridsen: 1047–74) corresponded with popes Alexander II and Gregory VII. Sweyn's son, Canute IV (1080–86), was murdered at Odense when he was on the point of setting off to invade England; quickly identified as a martyr, he furnished the Danes with their own royal saint.

The political scenery in the lands to Denmark's north which we now call Norway and Sweden was, like the physical scenery, more rugged and less tamed. There was no unitary monarchy in these countries like the one which Harald Gormsson had managed to create in Denmark. Instead, there were regional divisions and local chieftaincies; overarching them from time to time, some fragile and temporary personal supremacy won by a beefy warrior tribute-taker might briefly form, only to crumble quickly away. There were in addition destabilizing pressures from the neighbouring Danes, for much of the period from the mid-tenth to the mid-eleventh century, it will be recalled, intermittently a threatening presence on the northern side of the Sound or Kattegat. When we speak in what follows of a 'king of Norway' or a 'king of Sweden' it is important to remember that this is a form of shorthand: at any one time before about 1050 there could have been several men who called themselves 'king' in Norway and Sweden.

A member of a Norwegian princely dynasty named Haakon was brought up at the English royal court as the foster-son of King Athelstan (925–39), the grandson of King Alfred of Wessex. Later Norse tradition would remember him as Haakon *Athalsteins fóstri*. The background to this seems to have been an Anglo-Norwegian alliance between Athelstan and Haakon's father King Harald Fairhair, formed in circumstances of which we know nothing. This was not without its effects upon Norwegian Christianity. Haakon's sojourn at the English court might be compared with that of Symeon, the son of Boris of Bulgaria, at the imperial court in Constantinople. It is inconceivable that the young Norwegian prince was not brought up a Christian at his foster-father's notably pious court. Furthermore, when he returned to Norway to become king – or to become *a* king – in about 946, it is impossible to imagine that he would have been unaccompanied by clergy, even if only by a domestic chaplain. The brother whom Haakon subsequently drove into exile was none other than Eric Bloodaxe, who became ruler of the Scandinavian kingdom of York. Eric too was a Christian, or became one after his arrival in England (947?), remembered, as we have already seen, in the prayers of the monks of St Cuthbert. Later tradition, for what it is worth, identified the reigns of Haakon (946–61) and of his nephew and successor Harald (961–72) as a period when Christianity made progress in Norway with royal encouragement. An eleventh-century English text from Glastonbury lists one *Sigefridus Norwegensis episcopus*, Sigefrid bishop of Norway, whose consecration may be tentatively dated to the 960s.

A few meagre scraps of information, but they do indicate that Christianizing impulses were reaching Norway from England as well as from Harald Gormsson's Denmark, and that they were doing so well before the appearance of Olaf Tryggvason towards the end of the century. We have already seen that later Icelandic tradition moulded Olaf Tryggvason into a missionary king who imposed Christianity upon his own people and others at swordpoint. Many of these later legendary accretions are sheer fantasy: the story that Olaf was prime-signed in Greece, for example, or that he was baptized by a hermit in the Scilly Isles. The strictly contemporary evidence of the *Anglo-Saxon Chronicle* tells us that he was confirmed – which shows that he had already been baptized – in England in 994. In the following year Olaf returned to Norway, with English money, in pursuit of his claims to be king. As in the case of his predecessor Haakon it is surely likely that he took clergy with him. Indeed, Adam of Bremen asserts that Olaf was accompanied by an English bishop; a significant admission from the upholder of the claims of Hamburg-Bremen. In the course of his short and violent reign (995–9) Olaf struggled to impose his authority upon the chieftains of northern Norway, particularly the jarls of Lade in the district of Trøndelag. In so far as this also involved imposing, or re-imposing, Christianity one can understand how it could furnish the seedbed for the luxuriant growth of myth in the course of the next three centuries.

Olaf Tryggvason was later regarded, in some quarters, as a saint. It is important to distinguish him from another sainted King Olaf, his distant kinsman Olaf Haraldsson, better known in England as St Olave. This second Olaf pursued an early career of 'desultory violence and robbery round the coasts of the Baltic and the North Sea'[28] which even took him as far afield as Spain. In the early years of the eleventh century he can be traced in England, fighting for King Ethelred against the Danes. It was probably at this time that he accepted Christianity. In 1015 he returned to Norway, managed to wrest lordship from the hands of the Danes and ruled as king for thirteen years. He was remembered as a vigorous encourager of Christianity. An enigmatic runic inscription from the island of Kuli, west of Trondheim, records that the stone on which it was incised was set up when 'twelve winters had Christendom been in Norway'. A case has been made – based on dendrochronological dating of the timbers of the bridge which is also mentioned in the inscription – for dating this event to the year 1022. Quite what happened in 1022 we shall never know. Perhaps it was the acceptance of Christianity by a local lord on the order of King Olaf. At the very least, it tells us that for the people who commissioned the Kuli stone the arrival of Christianity was a datable event from which the subsequent years could be numbered. King Olaf Haraldsson was said to have imported bishops and priests from England to help in the good work. One of these, Rodulf or Rudolf, can be identified in English sources: in later life he returned to England, where he became abbot of Abingdon and died in 1052. King Olaf was driven out of Norway by Canute in 1028 and took refuge in Russia. In 1030 he attempted to reclaim his throne but was killed at the battle of Stiklestad near Trondheim. Although the occasion of his death was entirely a matter of secular politics and his killers as much Christians as he was, Olaf Haraldsson was very quickly hailed as a martyr. His body was exhumed in 1031 and found to be incorrupt. It was translated to Trondheim, where miracles began to occur at the tomb. The cult may have been encouraged by Olaf's English clerics, and certainly spread with remarkable speed to and within England. Earl Siward of Northumbria founded a church in honour of St Olaf at York before 1055, his name featured among the martyrs in an Exeter liturgical book copied in about 1060 and there were four churches dedicated to him in London before the end of the century. His cult can also be traced among the Scandinavian Ostmen of Ireland and in Orkney, Shetland and the Isle of Man. In Norway the cult helped to focus loyalty upon Olaf's dynasty and associated it firmly with Christianity: both were important factors in the consolidation of kingship and church in Norway over the next century or so. By the end of the eleventh century Norway had territorial bishoprics at Oslo, Bergen and Trondheim, to which were soon added Hamar and Stavanger.

Kings in Sweden began to grope their way towards Christianity from the late tenth century onwards. Eric the Victorious, who died in about

995, was said by Adam of Bremen to have adopted Christianity but later to have lapsed back into paganism. If we can trust this report, it is not impossible that Eric's flirtation with Christianity was connected with his marriage to a daughter of Duke Mieszko of Poland. The ducal family of Poland had recently become enthusiastic Christians, as we shall see in the following chapter, and the Polish bride must have brought a Christian presence to Eric's court for the duration of the marriage. Eric's son by this union, Olof (*c.* 995–*c.* 1022), was striking apparently Christian coinage at Sigtuna, a little to the north of modern Stockholm, soon after his accession. Later legend would attribute his conversion to an English bishop. Adam credited Olof with the foundation of a bishopric at Skara, just to the south of Lake Vänern in western Sweden, and praised the missionary energies of its first bishop, Thorgaut, who had been despatched from Hamburg-Bremen. Bishop Thorgaut's existence is confirmed by the strictly contemporary and meticulous chronicler Thietmar of Merseburg. Olof's son and successor, Anund (*c.* 1022–*c.* 1039), was the first member of the dynasty to bear a Christian name, James. Adam could refer to him as the 'most Christian' king of the Swedes and claim that while he reigned Christianity was 'widely diffused' in Sweden. His half-brother and successor Emund earned no such golden opinions, but that was because he was no friend of Hamburg-Bremen. He expelled a bishop named Adalward who had been sent from there and replaced him with another bishop named Osmund. Adam did his best to discredit Osmund, alleging that his consecration had been irregular. But further information about Osmund comes from a surprising source, the house-history of the English monastery of Ely. After his episcopate in Sweden, at which the Ely author levied no criticisms, Osmund retired to England, of which he was probably a native, and ended his days as a monk of Ely. The conflict between Adalward and Osmund has the look of a case of rivalry in the mission field which became focused at a princely court. We have met such rivalries before, for example in ninth-century Moravia.

The evangelization of Sweden was undoubtedly a more complicated business than our surviving sources permit us to see. Bremen's claims were well-trumpeted by Adam, but even in his partisan pages we can detect influences from England – not just in the person of Bishop Osmund but of others too, such as the otherwise unknown English missionary named Wulfred who was martyred after smashing an image

413

of Thor with a battle-axe. Poland was another quarter from which influence played. In addition to King Eric's marriage we have the intriguing fact that Bishop Osmund had been consecrated by the archbishop of Gniezno. The sister of King Anund-James, Ingigard, married Jaroslav of Kiev, so we must make room, perhaps, for some Christian influences from Russia. And if from Kiev, quite possibly from Constantinople too? The Christianization of the northern peoples could never be a matter for unconcern to the sharp-eyed diplomats of New Rome. We must remember, too, the Swedish merchants and mercenaries who took the route to Mickelgard: 'Thorsten had this memorial made to Sweyn his father and Tori his brother. They fared out to Greece.' Very occasionally runic inscriptions tell us directly, if enigmatically, things about the progress of Christianity of which we should otherwise be entirely ignorant – a salutary reminder of how little we know. The northernmost runestone known in Sweden, at Frösö in Jämtland, carved probably in the second quarter of the eleventh century, reads 'Östman, Gudfast's son, had this stone raised and this bridge made, and he had Jämtland made Christian.' A local initiative by a local chieftain, we may suppose, but we know nothing of its context or results.[29]

Adam of Bremen has left us a famous but perhaps not wholly reliable account of a pagan cult centre at Uppsala. He probably owed his information to another bishop named Adalward, usually called 'the Younger' to distinguish him from the bishop of Skara who had crossed swords with Osmund. This second Adalward had been established as a bishop at Sigtuna by King Stenkil, probably in about 1060. He was driven out 'because the barbarous folk did not wish him to preside over them' and returned to Bremen to end his days there. Adam would have known him well. Adalward was an active evangelist who would travel about the country smashing idols and winning many converts. It wasn't quite the virgin territory that our informants imply. The many surviving runestones in the region with Christian inscriptions or decoration show that there were already large numbers of Christian families in the Sigtuna-Uppsala district: it was an area of mixed religious allegiances, not unlike Boniface's Thuringia. In company with another bishop, Egino – also from the Hamburg-Bremen stable – Adalward planned to put a torch to the pagan temple at Uppsala. Rumour of the plan got out.

Observing that the people murmured about this design of the confessors of God, the most pious King Stenkil shrewdly kept them from such an undertaking, declaring that they would at once be punished with death and he be driven from the kingdom for bringing malefactors into the country, and that everyone who now believed would quickly relapse into paganism, as they could see had lately been the case in Slavia.[30]

This is an interesting vignette. Stenkil's family connections seem to have been with the Swedish south-west. Adalward, therefore, as the nominee of a 'foreign' overlord, was going to have a hard row to hoe up in the north at Sigtuna. But the king was not going to sanction direct action in the Martinian tradition against pagan cult at Uppsala. His caution may have been justified. So much is suggested by the experience of King Inge I in the 1080s. He did try to end pagan cult at Uppsala. For this he was promptly expelled and replaced by his brother-in-law Sweyn, who agreed to countenance it and is therefore remembered as Sweyn 'the Sacrificer'. But Inge gathered an army, defeated and killed Sweyn and imposed Christianity. It was the end of the open celebration of pagan rituals at Uppsala. Tidings of it reached even as far as Rome, whence Gregory VII sent Inge a congratulatory letter. But observe the sequel. In the longer term Uppsala emerged superior to Sigtuna under the new Christian dispensation, a pagan holy place sanctified in a fashion that Pope Gregory I might have approved. The bishopric of Sigtuna migrated to Uppsala, which was raised to the rank of an archbishopric by Pope Alexander III in 1164. And when the Swedes too finally got their own royal saint, Eric 'the Martyr', killed – possibly in a drunken brawl – in 1160, it was at Uppsala that his cult took shape.

An elaborate cycle of narratives concerned with the coming of Christianity to Norway and to Iceland grew up in the Old Norse tongue and was committed to writing in thirteenth-century Iceland. But it may be employed by the modern historian only with the utmost caution; and prudent historians tend not to use it at all. There has not come down to us – and as far as we can tell there never did exist – a contemporary mission literature bearing upon the tenth- and eleventh-century conversion of the Scandinavians at home or abroad comparable with the missionary literature of the period which extends from the lifetime of Bede to that of Rimbert. It is a puzzling literary hiatus.

Take England by way of example: Bede's homeland; where Bede was widely read in the tenth and eleventh centuries, to judge by the surviving manuscripts of his work; where one of the restorers in the 1070s of Bede's own monastery, Turgot, had himself been a missionary in Norway. The Anglo-Saxon clergy had watched the eighth-century missions to continental Germania with interest, supported them generously and commemorated them in writing with pride. It is quite extraordinary that their successors never composed a single coherent literary work in celebration of the conversion of the heathen who had settled in England nor of the labours of English evangelists in Scandinavia. Why? A part of the answer might be, as suggested in the discussion of the Ostmen of Ireland earlier in this chapter, that *among Scandinavian settlers abroad* conversion was something that 'just happened' in the process of assimilation into a host culture; that the heathenness of those whom contemporary chroniclers called the 'heathen men' has almost certainly been exaggerated. But that still leaves us with the Scandinavian homelands. Apart from royal push and shove there is precious little evidence for missionary activity in the positive sense that we associate with Patrick or Amandus or Willibrord. Adam of Bremen might proclaim that 'the mission to the heathen is the first duty of the church of Hamburg': but the spectacle with which he presents us is of intermittently empire-building archbishops who grasped opportunities to send out clergy in an entirely pragmatic way. In other words, one could make a case for supposing that the conversion of the Scandinavian homelands to Christianity was also something that 'just happened'. It would not be a very strong case. However, we may be confident that the conversion of Scandinavia was gradual, piecemeal, muddled and undisciplined. Would the conversion of England or Germany look similar if we lacked the artful shaping of the Bedan or Bonifacian literary memorials? For the historian it is an unsettling question.

CHAPTER TWELVE

The Eastern Marches
from Wenceslas to Nyklot

Whatever happens we have got
The Maxim Gun, and they have not.
HILAIRE BELLOC, *The Modern Traveller*, 1898

IN THE EARLY TENTH CENTURY a new ruling dynasty emerged in the East Frankish or German kingdom out of the collapse of the Carolingian order which had provided a degree of cohesion in the course of the ninth. It is sometimes known to historians as the Saxon dynasty: its first member to rule as king of Germany, Henry I or Henry the Fowler (918–36) had previously been duke of Saxony. The duchy of Saxony was where the family had its greatest concentration of landed estates, of strongholds, of proprietary churches, of retainers; in short, of wealth and of loyalty; a place of safety in a dangerous world. This tenth-century shift of the dynastic centre of gravity in Germany to the north-east was to have far-reaching consequences. The dynasty is also known to historians as the Ottonian, taking its name from its most illustrious member, Otto I or 'the Great' (936–73). Otto was the foremost ruler of his day in western Christendom, a man whose forceful personality was felt far beyond the confines of his beloved Saxony. He defeated the barbarians on his eastern frontiers and pushed German lordship deep into the lands of the Slavs. He exercised suzerainty over the kingdom of Burgundy to his west, and could put pressure upon the rulers of the West Frankish or French kingdom. In 951 he took over what contemporaries called the *regnum Italiae* or kingdom of Italy, that is, roughly speaking, the northern half of the Italian peninsula, and in 962 he had himself crowned emperor at Rome by the pope, just as Charlemagne had done in the year 800. By this means he inaugurated that connection between Germany, Italy and the

417

imperial title which was to be such a key feature of European politics for the next three centuries.

In addition to imperial pretensions, the Ottonian ruling house also inherited the missionary responsibilities of their Carolingian predecessors. This was natural enough. There were the heathen, up and down their eastern frontier, Wends, Poles, Bohemians, Magyars, to say nothing further of the Danes to their north. The 'Everest' explanation for missionary activity – because the unbelievers were just there – is not to be despised. Like the Franks in that earlier epoch, the Germans of the tenth century were pushing eastwards. This *Drang nach Osten* was accompanied by the imposition of Christianity upon the peoples they conquered. In this fashion the Saxons formerly subjugated by Charlemagne became Christian *conquistadores* in their turn as they spilled into the region which their chroniclers called Nordalbingia, 'North-of-the-Elbe land'. The Slavs whom they encountered there were divided among a number of shifting tribal groupings – Wagrians, Abotrites, Polabians, Rugians and others – but it will be convenient in what follows to refer to these most north-westerly of the great Slav family of peoples, as contemporary German writers often did, as the Wends. They seemed at first to offer easy pickings to the heavily armed Saxon knighthood, in plunder and tribute and slaves and souls won forcibly for Christ by militant churchmen. But this mood of confident expansion received a sharp check in 983 when a Wendish uprising put a halt to the German advance. It would not be resumed for many years to come.

Further to the south the Ottonians encountered peoples who were more settled, more prosperous, more differentiated and more organized than the Wends. Poles and Bohemians, not unlike the Moravians in the ninth century, were coming under the rule of princely dynasties whose members looked westward to the political and religious culture – and to the markets – of the Germans with eyes that were at once respectful and wary. Missionary churchmen would have to proceed in a different manner from the crude methods favoured in Nordalbingia. Alliances, inducements, patience, tactful steering would be needed here. Further south again, and we come to eastern neighbours of the Germans who were of an entirely different ethnic and linguistic stock from the western Slavs. We saw at the end of Chapter 10 how the Magyars had swept away the newly Christian Moravian principality in the early years of the tenth century. Their raids painfully endured, withstood and contained over the next two generations, they were finally and decisively defeated by Otto I at the battle of the river Lech, near Augsburg, in 955. In the wake of their defeat the Magyars settled down on the plain of Pannonia (or Hungary) and became an eligible target for missionary attentions. To complicate matters, these Christian cultural influences would seep into Magyar society from two directions, for Greek as well as German clergy busied themselves with the evangelization of the new arrivals.

The eastern marches of Germany, then, from the Baltic almost to the Adriatic, presented in the tenth century a varied and a complex scene to the gaze of missionary churchmen. Diverse though the field was, with variables across time as well as region, the German clergy could rely on the consistent and full-hearted commitment of the very determined rulers of the tenth-century Ottonian *Reich*. The Ottonians were encouraged by their clerical advisers to think of themselves as following in the footsteps of Charlemagne. It was in Charlemagne's palatine chapel at Aachen that Otto I was crowned and anointed king in 936. At the ceremony he was reminded of a king's missionary responsibilities by Archbishop Hildebert of Mainz. In the following year Otto established a monastery right on his eastern frontier, at Magdeburg. Dedicated to the soldier-saint Maurice, whose relics were moved there from Burgundy in 960, lavishly endowed, a spiritual fortress which was the apple of the king's eye, Magdeburg became the seat of an archbishopric in 968. Its missionary duties were clearly spelled out in an imperial diploma, the document in which the emperor formally announced the foundation of the new see. Magdeburg was to be the metropolitan see for 'all the peoples of the Slavs beyond the Elbe and the Saale, lately converted and still to be converted'. Magdeburg was to be to the western Slavs what Hamburg was, or wanted to be, to all the peoples of the north. The first archbishop of Magdeburg was Adalbert of Trier, who had already had experience of missionary work on his journey to Kiev in the years 961–2. Suffragan bishops were founded at Meissen, Merseburg and Zeitz, and 'the venerable man Boso who has laboured so greatly to convert the Slavic people to God' was to have the choice of Merseburg or Zeitz. He was not the only missionary to be rewarded with a bishopric: we might recall Poppo, who had converted King Harald Gormsson of the Danes in about 960, and who was given St Kilian's see of Würzburg. Nor were Magdeburg and its suffragans the only sees to be established with

Abo
Uppsala
Tallinn
Dorpat
Novgorod
Osel
Pskov
Riga
Uxküll
R Dvina
Polotsk
Baltic Sea
Vilnius
Roskilde
Lund
Königsburg
Rügen
R Niemen
Gdansk
Marienburg
Segeburg
Kołobrzeg
Lübeck
Wollin
Marienwerder
Schwerin
Grobe
Chelmno
Hamburg
Stettin
Corvey
Havelburg
Dobrzyn
Poznán
Gniezno
R Vistula
Kiev
Magdeburg
Merseburg
R Elbe
R Oder
Prague
Krakow
Bamburg
Regensburg

	Catholic
‡ Archbishopric	
† Bishopric	

Passau
R Danube

	Orthodox
▲ Archbishopric	
▲ Bishopric	

Lechfeld
Salzburg
Esztergom
† Monastery
R Tisza
Czanád
Aquileia

10. *Eastern Europe and the Baltic, twelfth to fourteenth centuries.*

evangelizing purposes in mind. When the Emperor Henry II, the great-nephew of Otto I, founded the bishopric of Bamburg in 1007 it was partly in order that 'the paganism of the Slavs might be destroyed'.[1]

The missionary zeal of the imperial dynasty and of that very formidable body of men the Ottonian bench of bishops was not sustained only by ghostly patrons like St Maurice. It was also fed by a lively sense of history, of a missionary past which was a spur to emulation in the present. Archbishop Hildebert was not merely the occupant of St Boniface's see of Mainz; he had also been a monk of Boniface's monastery of Fulda. Otto I's first queen, the English princess Edith, was a compatriot of Boniface. Magdeburg had formed part of her dower lands, so we may assume her active role in encouraging her husband's new foundation. The Magdeburg community looked to Fulda, quite possibly more than to any other centre of learning, for the books which were an essential adjunct to evangelization. These books carried the memory of Boniface as missionary and martyr to the church of Magdeburg. When in 968 Pope John XIII sanctioned the creation of the new archbishopric the text of the papal bull announcing his decision referred to Boniface's apostolic role. Perhaps it was no coincidence that the missionary-martyr Adalbert (d. 997) – of whom more presently – had been trained at Magdeburg. Not for the first time we observe the association of mission and martyrdom.

The venerable man Boso chose Merseburg. We learn most of what little we know of him from the historian Thietmar, his successor as bishop of Merseburg between 1009 and 1018 and the author of a deservedly famous chronicle which is the liveliest memoir of its times. Thietmar was proud of the first bishop of Merseburg. By his preaching and baptizing Boso claimed 'an innumerable multitude in the east for Christ'. Boso knew the Slavonic tongue, and so did Thietmar, who records an anecdote about Boso's translation of the *Kyrie eleison* into Slavonic.[2] This was all very well, but the other side of the coin was that Christian and Saxon domination bore down very heavily upon the Wends. The bishoprics set up in 968 had to be supported with landed endowments – and by the compulsory payment of tithe. The German authorities made the same mistake which the Franks had made two centuries earlier and which Alcuin had pointed out to Charlemagne. The reckoning came in 983.

The Roncesvalles of the Ottonians occurred in 982 when Otto the Great's son Otto II was defeated by the Arabs at Cap Colonne near the 'toe' of Italy in Calabria, hundreds of miles away from his Saxon homeland. Just as the Frankish defeat at Roncesvalles in 778 had precipitated a Saxon rising, so did Cap Colonne a Wendish one. Thietmar's father Count Siegfried had been forewarned of it in a dream but the warning came too late. The north-eastern frontier collapsed. The fortress-bishoprics of Brandenburg and Havelburg were destroyed. The nunneries at Kalbe and Hillersleben were sacked. The Wends 'pursued our people like fleeing deer', as Thietmar, who was eight years old at the time, later recalled. It was humiliating. The Wends got as far west as Hamburg, which they burned and plundered. The archbishop of Magdeburg managed to get an army together and checked the raiders but there was no hope of restoring the frontier. The Germans were pushed right back to where they had been fifty years before, and their religion with them. Their settlements were abandoned to the encroaching scrub. Nearly two centuries later the priest Helmold of Bosau could describe the surviving traces of these settlements in the countryside of Holstein:

> There remain to this day numerous indications of that old occupation, especially in the forest which extends in a wide sweep from the city of Lütjenburg into Schleswig. In its vast and scarcely penetrable solitude traces of the furrows which had separated the ploughlands of former times may be described among the stoutest trees of the woods. Wall structures indicate the plans of towns and also of cities. In many streams ancient embankments, once thrown up to collect the tributary waters for the mills, show that all that woodland had once been inhabited by the Saxons.[3]

If Christianity came and went in tenth-century Nordalbingia, it came and stayed further to the south. Among the Bohemians Christianity had been a hovering presence for some time. In 845 some Bohemian chieftains had turned up at the court of King Louis the German at Regensburg, 'seeking the Christian religion', as the Fulda annalist put it, and the king 'ordered them to be baptised'. They may have been seeking more tangible things as well. It sounds somewhat like Harald Klak and his Danes at Ingelheim twenty years earlier. The Christianity planted in Moravia by the Cyrillo-Methodian mission of the 860s seeped westwards into Bohemia partly through the familiar conduit of lordship – Svatopluk of the Moravians being intermittently overlord of the Bohemians – and partly through the flight of clergy after the death of Methodius and the persecutions initiated by the German bishop Wiching (see Chapter 10). A little later, when Magyar raids began to pound their country, Bohemian leaders looked to the Germans for protection. Two of them came and submitted to the German king, again at Regensburg, in 895. The Fulda annalist does not tell of baptisms on this occasion, presumably because the leaders concerned were already in some sense Christian. One of them, Spytignev, was later said to have built the little rotunda-church of St Peter at Budeč, which still stands, though much restored. He or his brother Vratislav is alleged to have built a first wooden church at Prague.

What stands out from these hazy traditions is that Bohemian Christianity at the turn of the ninth–tenth centuries was being nurtured from southern Germany, Bavaria. Several of the early churches of Bohemia were dedicated to the saints particularly associated with Regensburg, such as Emmeram or George. It was at this time that a struggle for the kingship of Germany was being waged between the ducal dynasties of Saxony and Bavaria, and it was not to be until well into the reign of Otto I that Saxon-Ottonian hegemony went uncontested. Inevitably, this struggle spilled over into the German client-principality of Bohemia. In the second quarter of the tenth century the Saxon house challenged Bavarian influence in Bohemia. It was an influence worth having because Bohemia was rich from trade, just as Moravia had been in the ninth century. Prague, especially, prospered in the tenth century as the most important central European entrepôt for east–west trade. It was recorded of one Bohemian prince that he would reward his German priests most generously with gold and silver, furs, slaves and textiles. This open-handed prince was named Wenceslas.

Every English-speaking reader has heard of 'Good King Wenceslas', thanks to the enduring popularity of the Christmas carol composed in the nineteenth century by that great hymn-writer John Mason Neale. As not infrequently, it is the melancholy duty of the historian to be iconoclastic. Wenceslas (or Václav) was not a king, and we do not know enough about him to attempt a confident assessment of his moral worth. The principal thing which we know about him is the fact of his murder at the instigation of his brother Boleslas (Boleslav) in the year 929 at the age of about nineteen. Of the little else that we know of him for certain, two things are relevant here. One is that he built a church in Prague dedicated to St Vitus, a saint whose cult was anchored in Saxony, and specifically at the monastery of Corvey, with its strong missionary traditions and its demonstrable access in the tenth century to oriental textiles – they influenced its manuscript art – which could have come via Bohemia and the markets of Prague. The second is that he received relics of St Vitus for his new church from no less a person than Henry the Fowler, duke of Saxony and king of Germany, the father of Otto I; a gift which might in Saxon eyes have symbolized a relationship between lord and vassal. This is little enough to go on, but it permits the cautious inference that under Prince Wenceslas the Christian orientation of the Bohemians was being steered or at least nudged from Bavaria in the direction of Saxony.

Some historians have sought to connect this with the young man's cruel end, casting Wenceslas as the leader of a Saxon faction against Boleslas the leader of a Bohemian one. But the evidence does not allow this. Still less does it permit the ludicrous indulgence of seeing in Boleslas a patriotic Slav nationalist who thought his brother too pro-German. Such an interpretation, not without its adherents in some quarters even today, is part of the destructive legacy of modern nationalism whose myths historians have to cut away like bindweed lest they smother the truth. All other considerations apart, this myth disregards the fact that for the remainder of a long life Boleslas showed himself as 'pro-German' as his brother had been. We are still left wondering what the truth about the murder of Wenceslas was. He was not the victim of a 'pagan reaction', another favourite myth. Boleslas was as good a Christian as his brother, and indeed the fatal encounter took place as a result of Boleslas's invitation to his brother to attend the consecration of a church which he had built and to the feasting that would follow the ceremony. The hagiographical document known from its opening words as *Crescente fide* (While the faith was growing . . .), composed perhaps about 980, presented Wenceslas as particularly devout, a prince 'ruined by priests and like a monk' in the eyes of his opponents.[4] Some have inferred from this that Wenceslas was altogether too keen a Christian and met the fate of King Sigebert of Essex, who was murdered by his kinsmen in the mid-seventh century 'because he had devoutly observed the gospel precepts'. The trouble is that *of course* the anonymous author laid stress on Wenceslas's Christian virtue: that is what hagiography means; but we are no nearer an understanding of what Wenceslas was actually like. The truth about his murder was probably rather humdrum, a family feud that got out of

hand. Fratricide was not uncommon among the princely and aristocratic elite of tenth- and eleventh-century Europe.

Whatever the truth of the matter, Wenceslas was quickly hailed as
a martyr. The contrite Boleslas translated his brother's body to Prague,
probably in 932, where it was enshrined: a focus of devotion both to
faith and to dynasty. Christianity continued to make steady progress
in tenth-century Bohemia. Before the death of Boleslas (*c.* 967) a
bishopric of Prague had been founded, though the first incumbent
did not take up office until a few years later. The new bishopric was
placed among the suffragans of the archbishopric of Mainz – Prague
did not become an archbishopric in its own right until 1344 – and its
first bishop was a native of Saxony and a monk of Corvey. In respect
of its direction, then, the young Bohemian church was a 'colonial'
offshoot of the *Reichskirche* of the Ottonian emperors. But not in
every other respect, most notably the use of the vernacular. Old Church
Slavonic, introduced for liturgical purposes from Moravia, was retained
even after the tightening of German influence. Prayers, hymns, cat-
echisms and the earliest life of Wenceslas survive in Old Church
Slavonic.

With one exception all the first five bishops of Prague, down to
1030, were Germans. That exception was a Slav nobleman called
Vojtěch, who is better remembered by the German name which he
took, Adalbert. But since his remarkable career touched Poland too,
before we look at it in detail we must first say something of early
Christianity in Poland.

Spirited attempts have been made to derive the place-name Brandenburg from Brendan, and so to attribute the early implantation of Christianity among the Poles to the ministrations of that widely travelled
but elusive Irish cleric. While it is conceded that these attempts reflect
credit upon their authors' robust patriotism, it is generally agreed that
the celebrity of the Irish in the history of the expansion of Christianity
is sufficiently established upon the basis of less doubtful evidence. As
far as we can tell, Christianity entered Poland from Bohemia. It appears
to have done so, as so often elsewhere, as the result of a dynastic
marriage. In about 964 the Polish ruler Mieszko married Dobrava,
the daughter of Boleslas I of Bohemia. It was a name of happy omen,
commented Thietmar of Merseburg, airing his knowledge of Slavonic,
because Dobrava meant 'good'. She brought Christian priests and

books with her to Poland, and soon the heathen husband was brought to God by his Christian wife. Thietmar, in stressing Dobrava's role, showed a restraint rare among early medieval authors precisely in *not* quoting the traditional Pauline tag; of which we may make what we will. Mieszko was baptized in 966, though we do not know where, nor who were his sponsors. He established a new residence for himself at Gniezno (Gnesen), which had a chapel dedicated to St George. In this choice of saintly patron we might detect the influence of Dobrava, whose sister Maria was abbess of the nunnery of St George in Prague. By 968 Mieszko had his own bishop, Jordan, who established a mission station at Poznań (Posen), which in the course of time became the seat of a bishopric. Bishop Jordan's affiliations are unfortunately unknown. The likelihood is that he was German by origin or training. Mieszko of Poland, like his father-in-law Boleslas, was to some degree the client or vassal or subordinate of Otto I. Widukind of Corvey could describe him as 'the emperor's friend', and Thietmar as Otto's 'faithful man': Mieszko paid the German emperor tribute and sent troops to serve on his campaigns. It is inconceivable that Otto I and his clerical advisers could have been indifferent to the progress of Christianity among the Poles. A faint clue to one source of German influence might be afforded us in the appearance of Mieszko's name in a necrology from Fulda (with which we might compare the commemoration of Eric Bloodaxe by the monks of St Cuthbert). Boniface was a patron worth having and his monks at Fulda, as we have already seen, had a keen sense of mission. Mieszko's second wife was a German girl of very high family, the daughter of Dietrich, margrave of the north-eastern frontier. The alliance was so important to both parties that she had to be hauled out of the nunnery of Kalbe to exchange a heavenly for an earthly bridegroom. Thietmar was shocked at this, though he admitted that she subsequently performed many Christian good works.

A German contribution to early Polish Christianity is undeniable. It was strengthened after 983 when German rulers needed a friendly Polish principality to balance the hostility of the Wends and the potential hostility of the Danes. This was the background to the celebrated visit of the Emperor Otto III to Gniezno in the year 1000. The journey, its symbolism and significance, has long held the attention of scholars, who have read it as a charged expression of the *Reichspolitik* of Otto III. In doing so they have attributed to that rather confused

426

young man grandiose and misty ideas which he quite possibly never entertained. The fundamental purpose of the journey was devotional. Otto III went to Gniezno as a pilgrim. The shrine which he went there to venerate was Adalbert's.

Vojtěch was born in 956 into a Bohemian aristocratic family who were rivals of the ruling dynasty of Wenceslas and Boleslas I. His parents were devout believers, and in this a neat illustration of the Christianization of the tenth-century Bohemian elite. They sent him to Magdeburg, where he studied in the 970s under the direction of its first archbishop, Adalbert, whose name he adopted and whose missionary ideals he presumably absorbed. He also had some contact with the imperial court. In 983 he was appointed to the bishopric of Prague with the support of the Emperor Otto II but against the wishes of Duke Boleslas II of Bohemia: in addition to the family rivalries mentioned above, this was a time when German–Bohemian relations were undergoing some strain. Dealings between Adalabert and Boleslas, at best guarded, were soured by Adalbert's attempts to implant a more emphatic observance among the newly Christian Bohemians. He singled out for attack the polygamous marriage customs of the laity, clerical marriage and the sale of Christians into slavery. There are familiar themes sounded here, echoing previous controversies in the mission fields of early medieval Europe. After five years Adalbert's position became untenable. In 988 he left Prague and went to Italy, where he threw himself on the mercy of the Empress Theophano, widow of Otto II and regent for the infant Otto III. After toying with the idea of a pilgrimage to Jerusalem, a stay at Montecassino and an encounter with the renowned hermit and spiritual counsellor Nilus, Adalbert settled at the Roman monastery of San Alessio (St Alexis), where he spent the years 989 to 991. But the situation was far from satisfactory. Although his early biographers – two of them writing before 1004 – played this down, Adalbert was a bishop who had abandoned his flock. It was a matter of scandal that he should be pottering about Italy as a hanger-on at the imperial court and a sampler of fashionable forms of the religious life. In 992 his ecclesiastical superior, the archbishop of Mainz, ordered him to return to his duties; and the summons was conveyed by a high-level delegation from Bohemia, led by the brother of Boleslas II. Adalbert gave in and returned to Prague.

His second spell as bishop of Prague was no happier than his first.

After further quarrels with Boleslas Adalbert again departed into exile and went back to Rome in 994. It is an indication of the seriousness of the dynastic rivalries back in Bohemia that in 995 four of Adalbert's five brothers were slain by Boleslas II. In Rome Adalbert attached himself to the circle of talented intellectuals who had gathered at the court of the teenage Otto III. The archbishop of Mainz continued to thunder for Adalbert to return to Prague. Reading between the lines of his biographers one can sense that Adalbert was something of an embarrassment. He was a runaway bishop with a talent for stirring up trouble who was given to eccentric behaviour. On more than one occasion he rose in the night to clean the shoes of the entire imperial court: praiseworthy humility, of course, this nocturnal spit-and-polishing, but distinctly odd and demeaning behaviour in a bishop. The Ottonian age looked to its bishops for *gravitas*, majesty and command.

However, in 996 a role was found for Adalbert as an evangelist. Mieszko had commended his country to the pope shortly before his death in 992.* At a time of rivalry between Poles and Bohemians over territorial claims in Silesia, Adalbert, as an enemy of the Bohemian ruling house, would be *persona grata* among the Poles. As a native Slav speaker he was well-equipped to reinforce the young Polish church. Missionary endeavour was acceptable for a bishop in exile: Wilfrid in Frisia was a precedent. Adalbert would come as Rome's man, to reinforce the links forged by Mieszko. He would also come as Otto III's man, with his Magdeburg training, and his participation in those heady Roman seminars where Otto's imperial *renovatio* was adumbrated and plans were sketched for a Christian empire which would enfold all the peoples of eastern Europe in its embrace. So, after a round of pilgrimages which took him to the shrine of St Martin of Tours among other places – and we note the continuing connection between pilgrimage and mission – Adalbert set off for Poland in the winter of 996–7. He passed through Gniezno in the spring and went on to the very fringes of Polish settlement in the region of Gdansk. Impulsive as ever, Adalbert pushed on across the river Vistula accompanied only by his kinsman Radim, Christian-named Gaudentius, and a Polish disciple Bogusza/Benedict, in an attempt to bring Christianity to an entirely unfamiliar people, the Prussians, whose language he did

---

* There are formidable documentary and interpretative problems about this so-called 'Donation of Poland', which I here pass over.

not speak and among whom he would be beyond the protective arm of Polish weaponry. Something went terribly wrong. As usual the precise course of events remains uncertain. But the outcome is all too clear: on 23 April 997 Adalbert was killed.

Gaudentius and Benedict, who were spared, brought Adalbert's body back to Gniezno and buried it there. His life had been something of a shambles, but his death made him almost overnight a martyr. Otto III was intimately associated with the growth of his cult. He built a church in honour of the martyr at Aachen in that same year of 997. The first *Life* of Adalbert was composed in 999 by John of Canaparo, a Roman nobleman who was a monk of San Alessio, on the basis of information supplied by Gaudentius. In the same year the saint was formally canonized – a fairly novel procedure – by Pope Sylvester II, Otto's former tutor and a member of that imperial 'think-tank' to which Adalbert had once belonged. When Gaudentius was consecrated archbishop of Gniezno in 999 he was referred to as 'the archbishop of St Adalbert the Martyr'.

A second *Vita Adalberti* was composed in about 1004. The author of this life was a young German aristocrat, a distant connection of Thietmar of Merseburg, named Bruno of Querfurt, who had become a monk at San Alessio after serving in the household of Otto III. He was instrumental in sending two Italians to Poland, where they founded a religious community and settled down with three Polish companions to learn the Slavonic tongue in order to equip themselves for missionary work. Bruno planned to join them there but was detained in Germany by the need to attend upon the new emperor, Henry II. (Henry had succeeded Otto III on the latter's early death in 1002.) While he was in Germany, all five members of the community were butchered by robbers. In 1004 Bruno was consecrated *archiepiscopus gentium*, 'archbishop of the pagan peoples', another in that line of missionary bishops with no fixed see. During the next five years Bruno's missionary influence can be traced between the Ukraine and Sweden. A man of great talents and prodigious energies, he might have accomplished much. But he followed in the footsteps of his hero Adalbert and went to work among the Prussians. At their hands he too met his death, in 1009.

Bruno of Querfurt tells us that Adalbert had also preached the gospel to the Hungarians; and since Bruno himself had dealings with them his information commands respect. This activity fits into a context of Bavarian missionary work among the Magyars after their settlement in Pannonia. However, German churchmen had here been preceded by Greek. The Magyars had raided to the south as well as to the west during the first half of the tenth century. They frequently preyed upon Macedonia and Thrace, twice appeared before the walls of Constantinople and once struck as far south as Attica in Greece. Byzantine diplomacy lumbered into action as it had when faced by the Rus in the ninth century. As early as the 920s a cleric named Gabriel was sent on a mission to the Magyars, though how he fared we do not know. About twenty years later an imposing delegation from the Magyars arrived in Constantinople. One of its leaders, a chief named Bultsu, was baptized. The Emperor Constantine Porphyrogenitus was godfather, the new convert was loaded with rich presents and given – a rare and signal honour – the imperial title of *patricius*, 'patrician'. The occasion was splendidly illustrated in the manuscript, now in Madrid, of our main informant, the chronicler Scylitzes, with a picture of the emperor hovering by the font from which his new spiritual son was about to emerge. However, if the establishment in Constantinople thought that they had thereby welcomed the Magyars into the Byzantine family of Christian nations, they were to be disappointed. As soon as he returned to his own people Bultsu apostasized and went back to making war upon his Christian neighbours. He was among the leaders of the raid into Germany which was defeated by Otto I at the river Lech in 955 and had the misfortune to be captured there. As an apostate he could expect no mercy. Otto had Bultsu hanged at Regensburg. But on other occasions the Byzantines were luckier. A few years after Bultsu's baptism another Magyar chief named Gyula was given the same treatment. When he returned to his people he brought with him a monk named Hierotheus who had been consecrated a bishop for the Magyars by the patriarch of Constantinople. We are told that Gyula thereafter lived at peace with the eastern empire and that Hierotheus made many converts.

Greek influence among the Magyars, which was to continue strong for two centuries to come, was concentrated in the eastern half of the lands they settled, roughly speaking to the east of the river Tisza (Thiess). Missions from Germany were active further to the west, in Pannonia proper and the valley of the Danube. The missions overlapped and bickered, as in ninth-century Moravia. The leading German activists were clergy from the churches of Bavaria. Wolfgang of Regensburg had been a monk at Reichenau as a young man and the missionary traditions of that house (see Chapter 7) may have influenced him. Another influence upon him was Udalric, the veteran bishop of Augsburg, who 'discovered' him at Reichenau and ordained him priest to fit him for missionary work. Udalric's memories went back to the darkest days of Hungarian raiding about the year 900 and he had become bishop of Augsburg as early as 923. He had accompanied Otto I's army to the battlefield of the Lechfeld in 955, and in the wake of that triumph he had busied himself with the evangelization of the Hungarians during the remainder of his fifty-year-long episcopate. It was under Udalric's influence that Wolfgang undertook the work of missionary preaching in Pannonia. Promoted to the bishopric of Regensburg in 973, Wolfgang continued active in the evangelization of the Magyars until his death in 994.

Wolfgang owed his promotion to episcopal rank, after the death of his patron Udalric in extreme old age, to a new patron, his slightly older contemporary Pilgrim, bishop of Passau from 971 to 991. Pilgrim was an ambitious man who concocted pseudo-historical traditions about the early renown of his see and sponsored – or at any rate acquiesced in – the forgery of papal privileges purporting to grant to Passau, rather than to Salzburg, the rights of a metropolitan archbishop over the Hungarians. In a (genuine) letter to Pope Benedict VII requesting papal confirmation of these spurious claims Pilgrim excused himself from coming to Rome in person to present his case on the grounds that he was too busy converting the Hungarians 'along the lines that I have learned from the deeds of the English' – another testimony to the pervasive effect of Bede's exemplary account of how a mission should be conducted. The same letter reveals that Pilgrim's apprehensions about rivalries in the mission field were not confined to his neighbour at Salzburg. It contains an elaborate statement of credal orthodoxy which laid special stress on his adherence to the *Filioque* clause (see Chapter 10, p. 329), which was the most contentious point of doctrinal difference between Greek and Latin churches. Pilgrim was in effect giving the pope a guarantee that 'the neophyte people of the Hungarians' (as he called them) would not be contaminated by theological error if their Christianization were left in the hands of the churchmen of Passau.[5]

The abandonment by the Magyars of a nomadic way of life and

their permanent settlement in the Pannonian plain was followed by the expansion of east–west trade through the region and the gradual consolidation of power in the hands of a single princely dynasty, the Arpads. It is a familiar pattern. This does not mean that conversion to Christianity would follow as the night the day; but we may, by now, be unsurprised to learn that it did so follow. The earliest ruler of the settled Magyars to adopt Christianity was Geza, probably round about 980. The adoption took the form – again, not unfamiliar – of simply adding the Christian deity to his pantheon of traditional gods. When his bishop taxed him with this Geza is said to have replied 'that he was a rich man and well able to afford sacrifices to all his gods'; so at least Thietmar of Merseburg had heard.[6] Thietmar had also heard tales about Geza's wife, that she was a hard drinker, rode like a knight and had killed a man with her bare hands. Bruno of Querfurt reported that Adalbert's missionary dealings were more with her than with her husband, because 'she held the whole kingdom in her hands'. Thietmar knew her by a Slav name, not a Magyar one. He rendered it Beleknegini and tells us that in Slavonic this means 'beautiful lady' (more accurately, actually, 'white lady'). Had Geza married into a Christian Slav family – like Mieszko of Poland – and was this one means by which Christianity got a toehold at the Magyar court? If so, then the coming of Christianity to Hungary was evidently a rather more complicated matter than the Passau version would have had it; or, for the matter of that, the Constantinopolitan version.

These matters are very uncertain. We are on firmer ground in the next generation. Geza's son Waik married into the Ottonian dynasty: his bride was Gisela, the sister of Duke Henry of Bavaria, who would become the Emperor Henry II in 1002 upon the death of his young kinsman Otto III. The marriage took place before the death of Geza in 997 and it is inconceivable that it could have occurred if Waik had not been converted to Christianity. He took the name Stephen as his Christian name. In 1001 the emperor and the pope jointly gave him the title of king and a royal crown in token of it. Stephen commended himself and his people to the patronage of St Peter, and Pope Sylvester licensed the foundation of a Hungarian archbishopric with its subordinate bishoprics. In the course of time the archbishopric became settled at Esztergom (Gran). The earliest Hungarian monastery was established at about the same time as the archbishopric.

King Stephen – later to be canonized – ruled Hungary until his death in 1038. Reliable sources for Hungarian history in the eleventh century are meagre, but one can sense that in the course of his reign the Christianization of his people made progress. Like other newly converted rulers Stephen issued Christian legislation, the so-called *Decretum sancti Stephani* (Edict of St Stephen), which required church attendance, sabbath observance and Lenten fasting. His laws included also a plan, to what degree implemented we cannot tell, for covering the Hungarian countryside with a grid of churches. Every ten settlements (*villae*) were jointly to build a church and endow it with land and livestock; the king would provide vestments and furnishings, the bishop a priest and liturgical books. Intermarriage with the aristocracy of southern Germany bonded the Magyar elite into a network of Christian families. Hungarian prelates turn up from time to time in our patchy evidence as attenders at German church councils or other ecclesiastical gatherings, such as the consecration of the new cathedral at Bamburg in 1012. King Stephen attracted visitors from abroad. The English royal family, fleeing from Canute, found a refuge in Hungary. A Venetian pilgrim stopped off and became a renowned hermit in Hungary, where he ended his days as bishop of Czanád. Many pilgrims to Jerusalem from western Christendom took the land route across eastern Europe, where a string of *xenodochia* – resting places or hospitals – grew up to serve their needs. Contemporaries were impressed. All that Bruno of Querfurt could find to say of his hero Adalbert was that he had cast 'the shadow of Christianity' over the Hungarians. But a generation later Rodulfus Glaber, composing this section of his *Histories* before the death of King Stephen, could be more positive: 'The people of the Hungarians, who previously were accustomed cruelly to prey upon their neighbours, now freely give of their own for the sake of Christ. They who formerly pillaged the Christians . . . now welcome them like brothers and children.'[7]

Christianity was firmly established in the new principalities of eastern Europe by the early years of the eleventh century. Of course, there were to be growing pains. The accord between Poland and Germany broke down during the reign of the Emperor Henry II and debilitating warfare ensued. Dynastic instability troubled the kingdom of Hungary after Stephen's death. There was only slow progress in setting up the suffragan bishops of both Gniezno and Esztergom. All this and more might be said: but there could be no going back.

After the millennium there was a certain loss of German initiative, even though German cultural influence remained strong among Bohemians, Poles and Hungarians. Although the approach to the eastern barbarians had softened from the strong-arm crudities of Otto I's day to the eirenic subtleties of the *fin-de-siècle* Roman court of Otto III, the stress on imperial and German leadership had remained consistent. This changed after the millennium. A different and a bleaker mood can be sensed in Thietmar of Merseburg's *Chronicon*, 'that great and sombre memorial', as its most acute modern critic has called it.[8] Thietmar looked back to the good old days of his boyhood and beyond, before the collapse of the north-eastern frontier in 983. He had his doubts about Otto III's Polish policy, and could reveal himself in such an outburst as this: 'How unequal the comparison of our forebears with our contemporaries! When the mighty Count Hodo was alive, Mieszko [of Poland] would never have dared while wearing his fur coat to enter a house where he knew him to be, nor to remain seated when the count got to his feet.' Thietmar dwelt approvingly on Bishop Ramward of Minden's action in 997 when he carried his processional cross into battle with the Slavs as a standard, a *vexillum* like the 'royal standards' celebrated in Venantius' great hymn (see Chapter 5), which Thietmar would have known. That was the way to treat them: hit them hard with Christianity! And yet this from a bishop of a frontier see who harboured a strong sense of zeal for the salvation of the souls of his flock, not least the Slavs among them. There is no easy route to the understanding of Thietmar and his world.

In the context of this particular enquiry it is really rather remarkable that Thietmar had so little to say about missions to the heathen; the more so in that the history of his family, of which he was intensely proud, had been closely bound up with the implanting of Christianity in the eastern marches of Saxony. True, he told of the martyrdom of Adalbert, but he did not linger on it. It is difficult to think of much in the way of common ground between those fellow-bishops Thietmar and Adalbert, and altogether impossible to imagine Thietmar cleaning the shoes of Otto III's courtiers. Thietmar had rather more to say about Bruno: but then, Bruno was a kinsman of his; Bruno was family. Did Thietmar's reticence on the subject of missions spring from a sense of disquiet? Towards the end of his life he looked out from Merseburg upon a world of new Christian societies beyond Germany's eastern frontier. Bohemians, Poles, Hungarians, all had been converted. But in his own back yard, at his very doorstep indeed, were the Wendish tribes of Nordalbingia who had rejected the Christianity imposed on them by Thietmar's revered forebears. The Wends were a standing reproach to any conscientious bishop, and especially to a man with Thietmar's capacity for unease and his strong sense of the proper ordering of human relations. No wonder that the tone of his chronicle was sombre.

The Wends were to remain a reproach for many years. This is not to say that Christianity made no progress among them at all. Other considerations apart, the archbishops of Hamburg-Bremen as well as those of Magdeburg had every reason for encouraging their evangelization. The sack of Hamburg in 983 had been a reminder of the vulnerability of the north-eastern marches of Germany, and the missionary claims of the see of Willehad and Anskar could not remain mute, especially in a changed world where newly Christian Danes and Poles were chafing under German ecclesiastical tutelage. Those claims speak to us in the pages of Hamburg-Bremen's eleventh-century historian Adam, to whose reports on the conversion of Danes and Swedes we have already had recourse. With Adam's help we can follow the chequered history of another client principality.

In the course of the eleventh century a Christian ruling family emerged among the peoples known as the Wagrians and the Abotrites. These were the most westerly of the Wendish Slavs, who inhabited the regions of Oldenburg and Mecklenburg, flanking what is now Lübeck. The earliest member of the family of whom a fair amount can be known was a certain Gottschalk. His father, described by Adam of Bremen as 'a bad Christian', had none the less placed his son to be educated in the Saxon monastery of Lüneburg, the premier family house of the ducal dynasty of Saxony. There is no suggestion that Gottschalk had been intended for a permanent monastic life. He had simply been sent to the best available institution for educating him and, doubtless in the eyes of the Lüneburg monks, for instilling in him a respect for the Saxon establishment. Perhaps it was in the course of his education at Lüneburg that Gottschalk acquired his German name. But matters did not work out smoothly. His father was killed by a Saxon in his service – itself an interesting hint at the complexities of a fluid frontier society – and Gottschalk left Lüneburg in order to avenge him. In the course of making war upon the Saxons he was captured by Duke Bernhard of Saxony. The two men must have known one another well, for Bernhard would have been a frequent visitor to the family monastery and mausoleum at Lüneburg. It was a small world. Bernhard released Gottschalk, apparently on condition that he should go into exile. Gottschalk accordingly attached himself to the great Canute, at that time (*c.* 1029) king of Denmark, England and Norway, to whom it is possible that he was distantly kin through his mother. Gottschalk remained in the service of Canute and his two sons, which takes us to 1042, when the last of them died. After this he returned to his native land and established himself in power there.

Adam of Bremen, writing within a decade of Gottschalk's death, was his enthusiastic admirer, not least because Gottschalk 'loved the church of Hamburg like a mother' and was a regular visitor there. He married a daughter of King Sweyn Estrithson of Denmark (1047–74), the grandson of Canute. Energetic, valorous and prudent, he subdued many of the Slavs to him as tribute-payers and was an active propagator of Christianity among them as far as the river Peene at the frontiers of Pomerania. Churches were built, German priests imported and religious communities established. The bishopric of Oldenburg, which had led a precarious existence from its foundation in about 970 and at best a shadowy one since the disasters of 983, was re-established. Another bishopric was founded at Mecklenburg by the expansionist Archbishop of Hamburg-Bremen, and entrusted rather surprisingly to an Irishman named John. Adam offers a glimpse of Gottschalk himself preaching in church to his subjects 'because he wished to make clear in the Slavonic speech what was abstrusely preached by the bishops or priests'.

A new client principality seemed to be in the making, in loose subordination to Saxony and with a colonial Christian church. But then another check was administered, as severe as that of 983. In 1066 an uprising of his Slav subjects took place, directed against Gottschalk and the Christian establishment associated with him. Gottschalk was slain by the insurgents. Bishop John of Mecklenburg was tortured and beheaded. Monks at Ratzeburg were stoned to death. Gottschalk's Danish wife was summarily expelled. It was a setback of the utmost seriousness which caused concern in distant places: we saw in the previous chapter how uneasy it made King Stenkil of Sweden. The bishoprics of Mecklenburg and Oldenburg would lie vacant for nearly a century, from 1066 until 1149. In trying to explain the catastrophe Adam of Bremen took refuge in a cloud of biblical quotation and looked to the inscrutable judgement of God. (The ability to make sense of reversal has always been a crucial part of the church's missionary success.) He also reported the opinion of his friend King Sweyn of Denmark, Gottschalk's father-in-law: 'I have also heard the most veracious king of the Danes say, when in conversation he commented on these matters, that the Slavic peoples without doubt could easily have been converted to Christianity long ago but for the avarice of the Saxons. "They are," he said, "more intent on the payment of tribute than on the conversion of the heathen." '[9] Modern historians have pointed to good Wendish military intelligence. German kingship was critically weakened during the minority of the Emperor Henry IV, and in the mid-1060s there was strife between the ducal house of Saxony and the abrasive Archbishop Adalbert. The Wends, like the Vikings, were masters of timing.

Two features of this story strike the historian of conversion. One is the detachment of Prince Gottschalk from his subjects and the other is the strength of militant pagan resistance among the Wends. Gottschalk had been moulded in an alien environment – a Saxon monastery, the Anglo-Danish royal court – and when he returned to his native land it was as a warlord who imposed himself upon the Wends by force. It would be wide of the mark to adopt a romantic interpretation casting Gottschalk as the beloved exile who came back to the warm embrace of his own people. He used Anglo-German techniques of lordship and he attempted to impose what the Wends looked upon as a German religion. It is by no means clear that, for the Wends, being ruled by Prince Gottschalk was any better than being ruled by the dukes of Saxony. The revolt of the year 1066 was not surprising.

Because Christianity was so closely bound up with alien lordship the Wendish uprisings of 983 and 1066 – and lesser ones in between, which for simplicity's sake I have omitted were anti-Christian. The Wends had developed a pagan faith of their own which was both militant and organized. This presents us with the spectacle of something new in the history of early medieval conversion. Even the Saxons, bitterly though they had resisted the Christian Frankish onslaught in the eighth century, had not created a coherent religious alternative. But this is just what the Wendish Slavs did.

Thietmar of Merseburg is our earliest witness. He inserted an account of Wendish paganism into the sixth book of his *Chronicon*. Although it is in parts difficult to interpret, and although it can be shown that he erred in some respects, it is as always worth paying careful attention to what the bishop of Merseburg has to tell us. Thietmar described a temple which stood near the Tollensee – a lake in the modern district of Neubrandenburg, to the west of Szczecin (Stettin). This temple stood within a gated triangular enclosure deep in a forest. It was elaborately constructed of wood, and it was decorated on the outside with the carved images of gods and goddesses. Inside the temple there were more images of gods, who were decked out in helmets and coats of chain mail: the defensive armour which was one of the hallmarks of the superior military technology of the Wends' German enemies. Battle standards were kept in the temple except when they were taken out on campaign. The temple was tended by a priesthood whose duties were to conduct sacrifices and to foretell the future by interpreting auguries. Thietmar described, in a particularly difficult passage, how auguries were sought in the manner in which a led horse would pace between spears fixed upright in the ground. He tells us that the supreme god was called *Zuarasici* and the place of his worship *Riedegost*. But he or his informant probably slipped up here, confusing deity and place. Adam of Bremen, our next witness, correctly names the god, not his place of worship, *Redigast*, and the place as *Rethra*. Adam also tells us that when Bishop John of Mecklenburg was killed in 1066 his severed head was offered on a spear's point to Redigast. An anonymous writer at Magdeburg about a generation later also refers to the sacrificing of Christians and the offering of their heads to idols. In another passage Adam stated that the image of the god Redigast was of gold and that the temple was hung with the extremely rare and sought-after Byzantine silk textile known as *purpura*, 'purple'. (In certain respects Redigast's temple did not differ from some of the greater Christian churches. They too had their golden images, of which the most famous surviving example is the tenth-century statue of Ste Foi at Conques in the Auvergne. They too might be hung with *purpura*, if they could afford it, as was Wilfrid's monastery church at Ripon. They too might shelter some of war's accoutrements, and be adorned with elaborate wooden carving.) If Adam's information was correct, the temple at Rethra evidently disposed of considerable wealth. The point is confirmed by the information contained in the early accounts of the missionary activities of Bishop Otto of Bamburg in Pomerania in the 1120s. His biographers described colossal quantities of gold in the temple of a god named Triglaus at

Szczecin. This wealth came in part from voluntary offerings to the gods. However, at Szczecin it also came from a sort of tax, not impossibly modelled upon the Christian tithe. The earliest biographer of Otto of Bamburg, writing in the early 1140s, recorded that it was customary for the worshippers of Triglaus to offer him a tenth of the spoils of war. Helmold of Bosau, too, referred to a kind of temple tax. He noted that 'statutory taxes' were sent every year 'from all the provinces of the Slavs' to the shrine of the great god Svantovit, to whom also a Christian chosen by lot was sacrificed once a year. Yet another historian, the Danish chronicler Saxo Grammaticus who wrote towards the end of the twelfth century, has left a fascinating account of the cult of Svantovit on the Baltic island of Rügen.

> There was a level space in the middle of the town [Arkona, on Rügen] in which there was to be seen a very finely-constructed temple of wood, venerated not merely for its splendid adornments, but for the holy image set up inside it. The outside of the building shone with laborious painting, consisting of the shapes of various things crudely and primitively depicted. There was only one way in. This shrine consisted of a double set of enclosures, the outer one of walls covered with a red roof, the inner resting on four pillars and resplendent with hangings, in place of walls. There stood in the temple a huge image bigger than any man, astonishing for its four heads and four necks, two facing the front and two the back. And one gazed to the right, and one to the left, both before and behind. He was made to be clean-shaven and crop-headed, so you would think the ingenious craftsman had imitated the Rugian style of hair-dressing. In his right hand he bore a horn decorated with various sorts of metal, which the priest skilled in his worship used to fill every year with drink, in order to foresee the next year's crops from the state of the liquor. On the left side, the arm was represented as bent inward with a bow. A tunic was carved, reaching down to the shanks, which were made of different kinds of wood, jointed to the knee so inconspicuously that the place of the join could only be discovered on minuter inspection. The feet appeared level with the ground, their base lying under it. Nearby, a bridle and saddle and many emblems of the divinity were to be seen. The wonder of this was increased by a gigantic sword, of which the scabbard and hilt were not only painted with exquisite skill, but enhanced with silver.

439

Perhaps the idol looked a little like the one found in the river Zbrucz in Poland which is illustrated in plate 34. Saxo went on to describe the various rituals and observances which were involved in the cult of Svantovit.

> It was worshipped in this way: once a year, after harvest, a general gathering of the whole island in front of the idol's temple would sacrifice animals and hold a solemn religious feast. On the day before he was due to officiate, the priest used very carefully to sweep the sanctuary (which he alone could enter) with a broom, taking care not to breathe inside the building; for as often as he needed to breathe in or out he ran to the door, lest the presence of the god should be tainted with the breath of a man. The next day, the people kept watch outside the doors, and he took down the cup from the image, and inspected it closely: if any amount of the liquor he had put in had gone away, he thought this meant a dearth in the following year. If he saw no lessening of its usual fullness, he would prophesy a good season. Depending on this augury, he warned them to use this year's harvest either sparingly or liberally. Then he poured out the old wine at the feet of the image as an offering, and filled the empty cup with fresh; and playing the part of a cupbearer, he worshipped the statue and petitioned him in a ritual incantation for increase of wealth and victory for himself, his country and its people . . . They spent the rest of the day feasting greedily, using the sacrificial meat for their merriment and gluttony . . . A coin was paid annually by every man and woman as a contribution to the worship of this image. Also it was assigned a third of the spoils of war, as if these had been got and won by its help. This god also had three hundred horses appointed to it, and as many warriors to ride them, all of whose gains, whether obtained by force or theft, were consigned to the priest's keeping; and out of these spoils he wrought different sorts of emblem and various ornaments for the temple, which he locked in chests containing piles of time-eaten purple [i.e. *purpura*] as well as a mass of money. Here was to be seen a huge quantity of public and private gifts, contributed with the anxious prayers of those who sought advantage from it.

And there is much more besides, too much to quote here.[10] Now it must at once be emphasized that the foregoing is culled from the works of authors widely separate in time, between *c.* 1000 and *c.* 1200, though less so in space. Paganism was neither static nor unitary; none the less, there is a consistency about these reports which is arresting. Wendish paganism, or paganisms, in the eleventh and twelfth centuries was, or was becoming, organized, funded and warlike. Displacing it would not be easy. This was the more so because the society which sustained it and which was sustained by it was so successful. Triglaus and Svantovit had made their worshippers rich, as pagan gods were expected to do. The southern shores of the Baltic were experiencing during this period the same sort of commercial and urban expansion which Denmark and Sweden had enjoyed in the age of St Anskar. Adam of Bremen called Wolin (Wollin), at the mouth of the Oder, 'a noble city, a very widely renowned trading place and' – in a surge of recklessness – 'truly the largest of all the cities of Europe'! An exaggeration, of course: but archaeological investigation has confirmed that vigorous urban growth was taking place at Wolin. And not only there. So too at Mecklenburg and Dobin, at Rostock and Demmin, at Karenz on Rügen, at Usedom and Szczecin, and further east at Kołobrzeg (Kolberg) and Gdansk. This burst of urban prosperity fostered local gratitude to the gods who were doing so well by their worshippers. The inhabitants of the town of Gützkow paid 300 talents, evidently a very large sum of money, for the construction of a new temple in about 1120. They were proud of it in the same way that Christian townspeople were proud of their new churches. When Otto of Bamburg wanted to destroy it in the course of his Pomeranian mission they begged him not to. Could they not, they asked, turn it into a church? Pope Gregory I would have approved.

But another Pope Gregory may be held indirectly responsible for a further obstacle to successful missionizing among the Wends. This was Hildebrand, pope as Gregory VII from 1073 to 1085, who has given his name to the Hildebrandine or Gregorian reform of the western church. The Gregorian reform was an extraordinarily complicated process, but it is sufficient to say here that in essence it was an attempt to liberate the institutional church from the grip of the secular world so that it should be better placed – this, at any rate, was the hope – to mould a more thoroughly Christian society. Many existing customs came under the chilly appraisal of the reformers and were found wanting. Gregory VII directed his attack upon the practice of lay investiture; that is, the custom by which the German emperors invested newly appointed bishops with the pastoral insignia, ring and staff, of their office. It was in this ritual and its symbolism that there was concen-

441

trated the habit of secular direction of the church. From the opening of the investiture dispute in 1075 until its final resolution in 1122 the German emperors Henry IV (1056–1106) and Henry V (1106–25) were at loggerheads with successive popes. There was much more to the dispute than a squabble over episcopal appointments. There were territorial conflicts in Italy which repeatedly occasioned absence from Germany for the emperor and his armies. The papal challenge to imperial power over the church furthermore called into question important features of the system of government which had grown up in tenth- and eleventh-century Germany. Existing stresses in the structure of power in Germany, exacerbated during the troubled years of Henry IV's minority, meshed with the struggle between empire and papacy. In the course of a prolonged crisis the governing classes of Germany experienced something akin to paralysis of will and initiative.

Looking back from the vantage point of the 1160s, Helmold of Bosau commented thus on the period of strife: 'Constantly weighed down by domestic concerns, there can be no doubt that the imperial Henrys [IV and V] held back the conversion of the Wends not a little.' He was absolutely correct. There is a striking absence of evidence for any evangelizing activity after Gottschalk's murder in 1066. Gottschalk was supplanted by the pagan Prince Cruto, and his son Henry – imperially named – fled into exile in Denmark. After a long absence Henry returned and fought his way back to power among the Wends in 1093 with Saxon and Danish help. He presided over them, a puppet ruler under German overlordship, until his death in 1127. But his long reign witnessed little progress of Christianity among his subjects. 'There was in all Slavia not a church or a priest except only in the stronghold which is now called Old Lübeck because Henry very often sojourned there with his family.'[11] Christianity was effectively confined to the ruling family. Thus at the opening of the twelfth century the frontier between Christian and pagan on the north-eastern marches of Germany had not significantly altered since the days of Charlemagne, three centuries earlier. Already a source of embarrassment, the situation was in danger of becoming a scandal.

Wendish paganism was finally overthrown in the course of the twelfth century. Partly this was owing to what might cumbrously be called the geo-politics of the Baltic mission. In plain language, Wendish paganism became steadily more isolated. Christianity slowly became more robust in the monarchies of Denmark and Sweden. Missionary zeal revived in Germany after the end of the investiture dispute. Perhaps more important still, the Wends were isolated by the Polish conquest and Christianization of Pomerania, the territories to the east of the lower Oder between Szczecin and Gdansk. The Poles had long harboured designs upon the tribes of this region and their rich trading ports. As early as the year 1000 a bishopric had been founded as a missionary base, a suffragan see of the new archbishopric at Gniezno, at Kołobrzeg on the Pomeranian coast, but it lapsed after only a few years. During the eleventh century a Christian presence in Pomerania was probably confined to the Scandinavian merchants who frequented those coasts in search of slaves and salt and amber. Polish ambitions were revived towards the end of the century and Boleslas III of Poland had completed the military subjugation of the Pomeranians by about 1120.

Their subsequent conversion and Christianization followed a familiar pattern.[12] The leading warlord of Pomerania, Vratislav (Warcislaw), had been baptized a Christian in his youth while held prisoner for a time in Germany. Shrewdly throwing in his lot with his conquerors, he at once promoted the faith among his leading men and ensured his own continuing tenure of power until his death in about 1134. (And not just his own: his descendants governed Pomerania for five centuries to come.) According to Helmold, Vratislav established a bishopric on the island of Usedom, at the gateway to western Pomerania hard by the mouth of the river Oder. He also protected and encouraged the mission that was sent into Pomerania in the wake of the Polish conquest. This was led by a distinguished German bishop, Otto of Bamburg. As a young man Otto had served in the household of the princess Judith, a sister of the Emperor Henry IV who had married Duke Ladislas of Poland in about 1088. Accompanying the bride to her new home, Otto made influential contacts in Poland and became fluent in the Slavonic tongue spoken by Poles and Pomeranians alike. His earliest biographer, a monk of Prüfening (a house founded by Otto) who had perhaps accompanied the bishop on his missionary journeys, was impressed by his linguistic skills. 'He learned the language of that people so well that if you were to hear him speaking that barbarian tongue you would never have guessed that he was a German.'[13] Returning to Germany and a distinguished career first as a civil servant and subsequently from 1102 as bishop of Bamburg, Otto did not forget either his Polish friends or the language. Neither did the ducal family forget him. His experience and skills made him a natural choice to lead a mission to Polish Pomerania. Otto's first missionary journey took place in the years 1124–5. Before setting off he sought papal permission to undertake it. It was a tactful way both of underlining the restoration of harmony between emperor and pope in 1122 and of acknowledging increasingly insistent claims from Rome to be the directing force in Christian missionary endeavour.

Otto found Pomerania no easy field to till. He toured its booming towns but his preaching fell on deaf ears. At Szczecin, for instance, he spent nine weeks but his preaching was greeted with hails of stones. His hand was wounded and his pastoral staff was damaged. The sequel is instructive. Otto reported back to Duke Boleslas of Poland, who threatened the people of Szczecin with reprisals unless they accepted Christianity; which, not surprisingly, they decided, after debate, to do. Fortified by the threat of fire and sword, Otto baptized many converts in Pomerania: 22,165, to be precise, according to his biographer. The writer also tells us of other methods employed by the bishop of Bamburg to hasten conversion. 'He refreshed poor converts and those of modest means with copious measures of food and drink, and also gave them clothes in no small quantity. However to the sons of the noble and powerful he gave rings and sword-belts, sandals, cloth of gold and other precious gifts.' It is not quite fair to say that Otto bribed the Pomeranians into Christianity. But he certainly knew how to get on in a society to which reciprocal gift-exchange was of the utmost importance – like many of his missionary precursors, such as Patrick and Wilfrid. Temples and idols were destroyed. Churches were built. The triple silver-plated head of the image of the god Triglaus was sent off to the pope as a token of victory over paganism. Otto's instructions to his converts have survived; they enjoined sabbath observance, infant baptism with godparents, canonical marriages, confession, burial in Christian cemeteries according to Christian rites: familiar themes. Pomeranian society was to be reshaped by the Poles as surely as Saxon society had been reshaped by the Franks in the eighth and ninth centuries.

But Otto's triumphalism was premature. As soon as he had turned his back on Pomerania to return to Bamburg there was large-scale apostasy among the new Christians, and he had to return for a second tour of duty in 1127–8. His biographer assures us, as he was in duty bound to do, that it was more successful – even more successful –

than the first. Yet he closed his account with a revealing admission. Otto had wanted to appoint a bishop for the Pomeranians. He had even gone so far as to send an episcopal ring to Rome for papal blessing. But no bishop seems to have been appointed during Otto's lifetime. 'What with one thing and another (*vario rerum eventu*), he never managed to carry out what he had intended.' The first reference to a bishop in Pomerania east of the Oder occurs in a papal letter of 1140, the year after Otto's death. The name of this bishop was Adalbert and he had been a disciple of Otto's, based at Wolin since 1125. We must not be deceived by his German name. Adalbert was a Pole from the household of the duke, presumably named after the martyr who rested at Gniezno. Whatever the conversion of Pomerania might have meant to the Pomeranians, to the Poles it meant the acquisition of an ecclesiastical colony.

The isolation of the Wends by means of the conversion of the Pomeranians did not make them any friendlier towards Christianity. Indeed, it may have made them more defiantly and defensively pagan. This was certainly the stance adopted by their prince, Nyklot, who had emerged as a successor to Henry, son of Gottschalk, as overlord of the Wends by about the year 1130. Yet the conquest and conversion of the Pomeranians did serve to highlight in other quarters the enduring non-Christianity of the Wends and the desirability of bringing this state of affairs to an end. Helmold of Bosau, our liveliest contemporary source, was uncomfortably aware that the progress of the Christian faith among the Wends had been painfully slow. He was clear in his mind that their conversion was an urgent and a sacred task. Given to quotation from the Old Testament, he presented the Saxons as a chosen people like the Israelites, who should wage holy war to eliminate the idolatry of the Wends and to save their souls. Helmold chafed at delay; he wanted the secular authorities to get on with the job. He deplored the tardiness of the imperial Henrys, as we have seen, and later he would be maddened by the vainglorious diversions of Duke Henry the Lion of Saxony. Helmold could present the wars as just, for among the westernmost Wends the Saxons were simply repossessing lands which had once been theirs. His reports on signs of earlier occupation buried in the woodlands of Holstein, quoted earlier in this chapter, were not innocent recollections of youthful country rambles: they had a point. Retrieval of lost property, as lawyers had agreed for centuries, was just cause for a just war. Like Thietmar, Helmold was not against the Wends as such. He simply wanted them converted. What he was against was any obstacle that stood in the way of this, be it imperial political embarrassment or frivolous ducal ambition or the rapacity of Saxon knighthood.

Looking back from the time when he was composing his *Chronica Slavorum* in the 1160s, Helmold judged that a turning-point had come with the death of the Emperor Henry V and the accession of his successor Lothar in 1125. The damaging quarrels with the papacy were over. The new emperor had a Saxon frontiersman's priorities. Count Adolf of Holstein, appointed in 1130, was a man after Helmold's heart, brave but also devout, 'a warrior of the Lord rooting out the superstitions of idolatry', as he put it in the obituary notice he composed after the count's death in battle in 1164.[14] Above all, there was a resumption of missionary initiatives on the north-eastern frontier. Helmold associated this with his revered master Vicelinus or Vizelin. Vizelin was a native of Hamelin (Hameln) who, after study abroad at the cathedral school of Laon in northern France, returned to Saxony in about 1125 and there experienced a missionary vocation. Commissioned by his own archbishop of Hamburg-Bremen to preach Christianity among the Slavs, Vizelin established a missionary base at Faldera in 1127 from whence he could make evangelistic forays into the land of the Wends. He attracted a community round him at Faldera, which came to be referred to as 'the new monastery', now Neumünster in Schleswig-Holstein. With the assistance of the Emperor Lothar and Count Adolf of Holstein, further mission communities were founded at Segeburg and Lübeck. Despite a period of upheaval following the death of Lothar in 1138, and despite the indifference or hostility of the Wendish prince Nyklot, Vizelin's mission prospered. More recruits arrived, among them Helmold, churches were built, priests were trained at Neumünster. At the same time Count Adolf was encouraging immigrants to come from western Germany and the Low Countries to settle in the countryside of Holstein and Wagria and to populate the town of Lübeck, which he had moved to a new site in 1143. In 1149 the archbishop of Hamburg-Bremen revived the sees of Oldenburg and Mecklenburg, vacant since 1066, and appointed Vizelin bishop of Oldenburg. He did not enjoy the honour for long but suffered a stroke in the summer of 1152 and after a long illness died towards the end of 1154. His successor Gerold moved the seat of the bishopric from Oldenburg to Lübeck in 1160.

These changes and initiatives in the north-east of Germany must be set in the context of the military subjugation of the Wends in a series of campaigns spread through the second and third quarters of the twelfth century. This makes the operation sound organized, which it wasn't. Progression was neither steady nor linear; the process was characterized by the muddle which is so perennial a feature of human affairs. Four episodes will give some flavour of it. In 1134 King Eric II of Denmark led an expedition against the people of the island of Rügen. They successfully besieged the fortress of Arkona, which was also the cult-centre of the god Svantovit. When the Arkonians surrendered they were forced to undergo baptism, but did so, according to Saxo Grammaticus, with insincerity: 'they went to the pool rather to quench their thirst, than from zeal to enter the faith, and refreshed their war-weary bodies by pretending to undergo the holy rites.' They were provided with a priest to minister to them, but as soon as Eric had set sail for Denmark 'the priest and the doctrine were expelled together', and the people reverted to the worship of Svantovit.[15]

Thirteen years later the so-called 'Wendish Crusade' took place. There had been a sharp worsening of Saxon–Wend relations in the early 1140s when Count Adolf of Holstein had seized some of Prince Nyklot's territory and settled immigrants upon it with Vizelin of Neumünster to minister to their religious needs. When Pope Eugenius III proclaimed a crusade to recover the city of Edessa in Syria, lost to the forces of Islam in 1144, the Saxons sought and were granted the same spiritual privileges in their own wars against the pagan Wends as were enjoyed by the crusaders in the east. The Danes decided to join in too. Accordingly, in the late summer of 1147, Nyklot was attacked by Danish fleets and Saxon armies. The land forces were notionally under the command of a bishop, Anselm of Havelburg, appointed by the pope as his legate to lead the campaign. They were accompanied by at least six other bishops, including the archbishops of Mainz and Hamburg-Bremen. Despite the novel ecclesiastical character of the expedition, what actually happened was reassuringly traditional. Nyklot and the Wends were chased up and made a sulky peace with the Saxons. Tribute and plunder were exacted, Christian captives were freed, a heathen temple was burnt down and some Wends were dunked in the waters of baptism in token of surrender at Dobin. Helmold judged that the baptisms were false, like those at Arkona in 1134. The whole campaign, he thought, was marked by infirmity of purpose, and though it had been imposing in conception it in fact achieved little. Others thought so too. 'It didn't work,' commented the abbot of Corvey, another churchman who had accompanied the armies. The first official crusade in northern Europe was not a great success in terms of the conversions it had been intended to bring about.

Nyklot survived until 1160, when he was killed in a minor skirmish, allegedly trying to prove to his sons that he was braver than they: not seldom a foolish prank for elderly fathers. If Helmold was correct in hinting at conflict between the generations, the sequel to this third episode is perhaps not surprising. Nyklot's son Pribislav proved notably less hostile to Christianity than his father. The Cistercian monk Bern, appointed to the bishopric of Mecklenburg by Henry the Lion of Saxony in 1160, showed himself skilled in exploiting this. Pribislav became a Christian under Bern's shepherding and within a few years had negotiated a deal with Henry the Lion by which he should govern a principality of Mecklenburg under Saxon overlordship, somewhat along the lines of that made a generation earlier between the lords of Pomerania and the rulers of Poland. (Pribislav's family lasted even longer in Mecklenburg than did Vratislav's in Pomerania, until 1918.)

King Valdemar I of Denmark finally conquered Rügen in 1168, assisted in this by contingents from Mecklenburg and Pomerania and episcopal participants in Bern of Mecklenburg and Absalom of Ros-kilde. Arkona was conquered again. The idol of Svantovit was over-thrown, chopped up and disposed of as fuel for cooking the victors' dinner. His temple was demolished: Saxo Grammaticus reported that 'a demon was seen to leave the inner shrine in the form of a dark animal and suddenly vanish from the sight of the bystanders'. The powers of darkness had been comprehensively and visibly worsted. Svantovit's temple treasure and estates enriched King Valdemar and the bishopric of Roskilde. The people of Rügen accepted Christianity once more, but two features differentiated 1168 from 1134. In the first place, there was more robust consolidation: Valdemar provided the means for building churches – twelve churches had been built on the island by the time that Helmold was writing in or before 1172 – and resident priests had been appointed. (Twelve churches on Rügen, an island of approximately 370 square miles in extent, is about one church per thirty square miles, which means that no inhabitant of Rügen would have had to walk more than five or six miles to attend church. This is about the same density of parish churches as in Touraine in the time of Gregory of Tours (see Chapter 2). In some respects, therefore, there had been accomplished in four years on Rügen what it had taken two centuries to achieve in Touraine.) Bishop Absalom took no chances about asserting the church of Roskilde's rights over this very lucrative new addition to the diocese. Second, Prince Jaromir of Rügen became an enthusiastic Christian and was permitted – like Pribislav at Mecklenburg – to maintain himself in power under Danish lordship conditional upon payment of tribute and good behaviour. Jaromir knew on which side his bread was buttered. 'Acting in the capacity of an apostle,' enthused Helmold, 'partly by assiduous preaching, partly by threats, he converted the folk from their natural wildness to the religion of a new life.' We may be sure he did.[16]

In 1163 a clerk drafted a charter recording a donation from Duke Henry the Lion of Saxony – the greatest German nobleman of his day after his kinsman the Emperor Frederick Barbarossa, son-in-law of the king of England, virtually an independent ruler of his duchy of Saxony – to the cathedral church of Lübeck. In the preamble to the record he put the following words into Henry's mouth: 'As heavenly grace has granted success to our campaign, we have been able to triumph over the Slav hordes in such a way that we have led the obedience of the humble to eternal life by baptism, and the defiance of the proud to eternal death by spilling their blood.' A recent author has pointed out that this is an isolated sentiment, occurring only once in the six-score surviving documents given in Henry's name, and that therefore it 'should not be taken too seriously'.[17] But somebody drafted it, and important people thought it a fitting thing that the sentence should stand. It casts a vivid light on the spirit of the age.

The triumphalism of Henry the Lion, or at any rate of his secretarial staff, may be offset by one last and very human vignette supplied by Helmold. In the early days of 1156 Helmold accompanied Bishop Gerold to keep the feast of the Epiphany – a season particularly associated with mission because of the 'showing forth' of Christ to the gentiles – at Oldenburg. 'The city was entirely deserted, having neither defences nor any inhabitant, only a tiny chapel which Vizelin of holy memory had built there. In the bitterest cold, amid banks of snow, we went through the mass there. Apart from Pribislav and a few others, not a single Slav attended the service.' It is a revealing glimpse of the task which faced the missionaries. Three days later, journeying towards Lübeck, Helmold assisted the bishop to cut down and burn a grove of trees sacred to the god Prove, 'not, however, without fear, lest perchance we should be overwhelmed by a tumult of the local people'.[18] It was dangerous work. In the following chapter he let slip that an idol was still being worshipped at Plön. But Plön was just across the lake from his own church of Bosau, almost within sight of where he wrote!

The Wends might have been bullied into a formal acceptance of Christianity in the middle years of the twelfth century; but their hearts and minds had yet to be won. Christianization in these lands of the northern Slavs meant 'Germanization': a colonial church, a church of the German ascendancy, was imposed upon them. Cherished patterns of cultural identity were broken up: immemorial ways of doing things, of exploiting a land, of dealing with authority, of placating the forces which governed a hostile world. Little that was positive was proffered in exchange. No native Wendish clergy was encouraged; no Christian literature in Old Pomeranian developed. The converts were cowed and resentful. Some missionaries, such as Helmold, were aware of this and uneasy. But his was not an environment which set much store by the patient winning of souls.

CHAPTER THIRTEEN

Mission into Church

Regarding the ultimate object of a mission to be the
settlement of a native Church, under native pastors, upon
a self-supporting system, it should be borne in mind
that the progress of a mission mainly depends upon the
training up and the location of native pastors, and that,
as it has been happily expressed, 'the euthanasia of a
mission' takes place when a missionary, surrounded by
well-trained native congregations, under native pastors,
is able to resign all pastoral work into their hands, and
gradually to relax his superintendence over the pastors
themselves, till it insensibly ceases; and so the mission
passes into a settled Christian community.

HENRY, VENN, of the Church Missionary Society, 1860

WHEN THE ENGLISH EVANGELIST Willehad established a Christian community at Bremen in about 780 it was a mission-station in a hostile
environment, a vulnerable outpost among the Saxon tribes as yet
incompletely subjugated by Frankish arms. Three centuries later, the
archbishopric of the twinned sees of Bremen and Hamburg had
become an institution of an almost unrecognizably different character:
rich in lands, buildings and treasures; proud of its traditions chronicled
by Adam in his *Gesta*; claimant to patriarchal rights over churches
scattered from Sweden to Greenland; a power within the German
monarchy. A mission had turned into a church.

Christian ecclesiastical organization grew and spread upon the trellis
furnished by the urban framework of the civil administration within
the Roman empire. Fixity and territoriality were its principal features.
Bishops were the central figures in the government of the church.
Typically, therefore, within the Roman world, a bishop would be based
in a town and his diocese would be co-terminous with the town's rural
hinterland. The city which was the capital of the civil province would

451

be the seat of a senior bishop, who might come in the course of time to be designated a metropolitan bishop or an archbishop. The structure of church government which thus evolved has proved remarkably durable and resistant to change. Indeed, in parts of the former empire such as southern France or mainland Italy, the Roman bones can still be discerned beneath the churchly tissue of today. Shifts in the pattern in response to changing realities have occurred from time to time, but they have tended to occur sluggishly and reluctantly. Aquileia, at the head of the Adriatic, was the metropolitan see of north-eastern Italy from an early date: even if the church of Aquileia had not been founded, as was its clergy's boast, by St Mark, it had achieved a position of commanding eminence by the fourth century. The years passed, and the city decayed. By the tenth century at latest Venice had succeeded Aquileia as the most vibrant urban settlement of the region. But the archbishops of Aquileia hung on in their shrunken community, surrounded by the crumbling reminders of a glorious imperial past. It was not until the middle of the fifteenth century that reality was bowed to and the seat of the archbishopric translated to Venice. Or consider another example of institutional conservatism, drawn from the north-western quarter of the Iberian peninsula. The archbishopric occupied by St Martin in the sixth century and St Fructuosus in the seventh was situated at what had been the Roman provincial capital, Bracara Augusta, the modern Braga. Its subordinate or 'suffragan' bishops were scattered across the Roman province of Gallaecia (Galicia) between the Atlantic and the Bay of Biscay. Violently disrupted by the Islamic conquest of Spain in the eighth century, this structure of ecclesiastical government was lovingly put together again as the region was repossessed bit by bit for Christendom by the kings of León in the course of the ninth and tenth. The keystone was put in place when the archbishopric of Braga was definitively restored – there had been an earlier false start – in about 1070. In the following century an independent monarchy of Portugal broke away from the kingdom of León, taking Braga with it but not the towns of Galicia. The bishops of the Galician sees were thereafter politically the subjects of the kings of León but ecclesiastically the suffragans of the archbishop of Braga, who was the premier churchman in the kingdom of Portugal. Relations between Portugal and León tended to be at best uneasy, at worst actively hostile. The non-coincidence of political and ecclesiastical jurisdictions was a source, over the years, of considerable tension and difficulty. Yet such was the force of conservatism that no sorting-out was attempted before the end of the fourteenth century.

Naturally, ecclesiastical authority recognized that in the course of missionary operations a certain fluidity of arrangements would have to be tolerated. We know of those major missionary bishops who for much of their operational careers were not tied to a fixed see: for example, Amandus, Willibrord, Boniface, Methodius, Anskar, Bruno of Querfurt. But such fluidity was distasteful to the upholders of Roman administrative traditions within the church. The restoration or the creation of a grid of territorial bishoprics with fixed urban seats remained the ideal. Pope Gregory I wanted the nascent English church to be governed by two metropolitan bishops at London and York, each of them presiding over twelve subordinate bishops. In this plan, announced to Augustine in 601, he was probably trying to restore an earlier Romano-British ecclesiastical organization (about which it is likely that he knew more than we do). But Pope Gregory evidently knew little about the realities of power in early Anglo-Saxon England. When Augustine reached England in 597 he found himself in the kingdom of King Ethelbert of Kent. Augustine's mission was dependent upon Ethelbert's goodwill. Indeed, as we saw in Chapter 4, it is possible that it had been called into being in the first place by a request originating with Ethelbert's Frankish and Christian queen. Augustine and his companions had to work with and through the Kentish royal court. Now, London lay beyond the direct reach of Ethelbert's power; it formed part of the kingdom of the East Saxons, or Essex. Rather, the former Roman city of Canterbury was, in Bede's words, 'the metropolis of Ethelbert's empire'. Accordingly, Augustine fixed his episcopal seat at Canterbury, where it has remained to this day. The conformation of secular power structures could, in this fashion, wrench the organization of a new church out of the Roman mould designed for it.*

England was a region where the possibility of reviving an earlier Roman pattern existed. It is notable that over much of Anglo-Saxon England – not all of it – the bishops' seats did come to be fixed in

---

* Bulgaria may present a not dissimilar spectacle, though we possess no surviving papal blueprint for the government of its church such as we have from the pen of Gregory I for the English. The 'Canterbury' of Bulgaria, so to say, was Preslav, seat of the khan's authority, seat therefore of the Bulgarians' premier bishop. Its 'London' could have been such a former Roman city as Philippopolis (Plovdiv), which lay beyond the immediate grasp of Khan Boris.

what had been Roman towns – for example, Winchester, Leicester, Worcester. Problems would arise when missionaries came to plant Christianity in regions where no existing or dormant Roman civil network survived. Sooner or later the question would have to be faced of the exportability or otherwise of the Roman model of ecclesiastical administration. It was in Ireland, an island untouched by Roman governance, that the question was first posed insistently. Palladius came from a Romanized cultural environment and may be presumed to have designed to establish a Roman pattern of territorial dioceses governed from fixed centres. But Patrick's six years of exile in the forest of Foclut beside the western ocean must have taught him that such a pattern could not be imposed upon Ireland. Instead of the grid of a former imperial administration, the controls upon an emergent Irish church would be furnished by the endlessly shifting influences of unstable princely *tuatha*, of clans and clients and patrons and retainers, of an unstable world in which the kaleidoscope of power could be set spinning by a poor harvest or a cattle-raid that went wrong. We know too little of Patrick's conduct of his mission in Ireland to guess with any confidence how he solved the problem. However, it is a reasonable assumption that he and his successors as bishops among the Irish attached themselves to royal courts which were for most of the time itinerant. A *tuath* or kingdom might thus get its own bishop, but a *tuath* was not quite the same thing as a territory. A bishop might find himself spending time at a favoured royal residence or staging-post in the course of journeying, such as Cashel, but that was not the same as having his own fixed episcopal seat. The results may have looked rather odd to critics in Patrick's day and later, but these arrangements worked well in Ireland and elsewhere outside the Roman or formerly Roman world. The association of episcopate with royal or princely power in such a manner as to depart from accepted organizational practice is a good example of that adaptability which is such a critical ingredient of successful evangelism. There was nothing peculiar to Ireland in this association. We can see it again and again in successive missions. In seventh-century Northumbria the royal stronghold at Bamburgh stood cheek by jowl with the episcopal establishment at Lindisfarne, giving rise to the harmonious co-operation between King Oswald and Bishop Aidan so memorably recorded by Bede. We can see the same association in ninth-century Pannonia: Pribina, the Salzburg clergy and the settlement at Moosburg (Zalavár), which was at once princely and ecclesiastical, and might have become the seat of a bishopric had not the Magyars wiped out the Pannonian church. So too in tenth- and eleventh-century Scandinavia, where missionary bishops attached to royal courts tended to settle at royal places such as Roskilde. Many such instances could be cited from medieval or – consider Moshoeshoe of Lesotho – post-medieval contexts.

This manner of solving the problem of ecclesiastical organization in non-Roman or 'barbarian' regions reinforced the tendency for the emergent church to bear the character of – to use that useful German term again – an *Adelskirche* or 'church of the nobility'. Bishops attached to itinerant royal courts dealt primarily with kings, princes, high-born warriors, and the women who wove aristocratic dynasties together in marriage. The persons they influenced were the grand and the rich, those who could afford to lay out their ample wealth in founding religious communities which they could people with their kinsfolk and dependants. Naturally, the church of which they were the patrons had an aristocratic character. (Of course, we must not make the mistake of implying that Mediterranean bishops were immune to considerations of status or that they lacked kinsfolk. Neither must we suppose that 'Roman' organization could not co-exist with aristocratic direction: consider Frankish Gaul.)

The goal of achieving fixity and territoriality of diocesan arrangements was never lost sight of. And it was eventually achieved, at any rate formally so, on even the most unpromising of terrains. Provinces of Magdeburg, of Gniezno, of Esztergom little by little emerged after setbacks and false starts, parcelled out into territorial bishoprics. In 1152 a papal legate, Cardinal Nicholas Breakspear – the only Englishman ever to become pope, as Adrian IV (1154–9) – visited Norway and overhauled its church structure. He elevated the bishopric of Nidaros or Trondheim to metropolitan status and confirmed its suffragans as Olso, Bergen, Hamar and Stavanger on the Norwegian mainland, together with the bishoprics in the Norwegian sphere of influence overseas in Orkney, the Sudreys (the Western Isles from Lewis to Man), Skálaholt and Hólar in Iceland, and Gardar in Greenland. In the same year another cardinal, John Paparo, was busy on the same lines in Ireland. The church council over which he presided there completed a programme which reforming churchmen had been striving to achieve over the previous forty years, the dividing up of Ireland into orderly territorial dioceses. After John Paparo's visit the church in Ireland was organized into four archbishoprics of Armagh – which held the primary – Dublin, Cashel and Tuam, presiding respectively over eleven, five, twelve and six suffragan bishops. With minor modifications this pattern was to hold sway until the Reformation.

It must not be supposed either that the pattern of church government was achieved without contention or that it displayed regularity and uniformity. Archbishops quarrelled with one another over their respective rights and suffragans. Bishops squabbled over diocesan boundaries. Kings sought ecclesiastical autonomy for the churches under their patronage which would reflect political autonomy. Acrimony and litigation could persist for centuries. Distant echoes of it can still be heard today. The official title of the archbishop of York is 'Primate of England'; that of the archbishop of Canterbury is 'Primate of *All* England'. The difference springs from five centuries of strife between the seventh and the twelfth, and this conflict in a sense sprang from Pope Gregory I's letter of 601 in which he had proposed an alternating primacy between the two sees; in this displaying an uncharacteristic degree of optimism about the clerical capacity for harmonious co-operation. Ecclesiastical politics are rarely compounded of sweetness and light.

On the other hand the lack of regularity and uniformity in the diocesan pattern of western Christendom is a matter of concern to us. There was variation in the density of bishoprics on the ground as between one region and another, disparity therefore in their territorial extent. In the year 600 there were 250 bishoprics in Italy – and that figure conceals further regional variations, for 197 of them were in the centre and the south, only fifty-three in the north. Comparable densities were to be encountered round the eastern – not the western – shores of the Mediterranean, in Greece or Asia Minor or Egypt or Africa. By contrast, in England on the eve of the Viking invasions there were only sixteen bishoprics; in the area that was to become Normandy there were only seven; and in the vast ecclesiastical province of Mainz, which stretched from the Elbe to the Alps, there were only twelve. These disparities had significant consequences. The bishop was and is the central figure in the day-to-day life of the Christian church. As pastor, teacher and judge the role of the bishop in his diocese was of critical importance. Only he could ordain priests and consecrate churches. Only he exercised jurisdiction in matters spiritual and had responsibility for supervising monastic life. (The Greek term from which our word 'bishop' derives means literally 'overseer'.) And if the exclusive right to instruct, baptize and administer penance to the laity was gradually slipping from the bishop's grasp (see Chapter 8), he possessed in the developing rite of confirmation a means for continuing to oversee the spiritual life of the laity under his charge. It was an accepted maxim of canon law that the number of bishops should increase as the body of believers swelled. But even in the youngest and theoretically most malleable of churches this was difficult to bring about. It was, for example, one of the issues at stake in the conflict between Archbishop Theodore of Canterbury and Bishop Wilfrid of York in the second half of the seventh century. At its greatest extent Wilfrid's diocese of York stretched from the Firth of Forth to the river Trent. Theodore, a Greek habituated to the micro-dioceses of the eastern Mediterranean, wanted to split it up into smaller and more manageable units. Wilfrid resisted, and unseemly quarrels ensued which proved sharply divisive in the early English church. Historians have been quick, perhaps too quick, to condemn Wilfrid for his resistance to Theodore; York's case against this assertion, or extension, of Canterbury's authority was a strong one. Be that as it may, thoughtful observers such as Bede were convinced – whatever the rights of the matter – that big diocesan units needed to be subdivided so that bishops could the more intensely conduct that pastoral ministry which alone could save souls. As Bede complained to Archbishop Egbert of York in 734, there were 'numerous estates and villages of our people' where no bishop 'is seen for many years at a stretch'. It was a matter of grave concern.

Big bishoprics were generally rich bishoprics. Although humility and self-denial were fitting episcopal virtues routinely lauded in many a hagiographical text, missionary churchmen were well aware – perhaps an unpalatable truth – that episcopal wealth, might and display would win converts. Christians are rich and powerful, pagans poor and feeble. It was one of the arguments which Bishop Daniel of Winchester commended to Boniface in his famous letter on missionary strategy. Boniface knew that showy books impressed the heathen, for he said as much when requesting a Kentish abbess to send him the epistles of St Peter copied out in letters of gold. The same theme was being sounded four centuries later in an account, in one of the early biographies of Otto of Bamberg, of divergent methods in the evangelization of the Pomeranians. He had been preceded by a missionary named Bernard – apparently a native of Spain; how he got to the Pomeranian mission field is anyone's guess – a man of humble disposition who travelled about barefoot and unkempt to preach the word. He had had no success at all because the Pomeranians had despised him. 'How can we believe that you are a messenger of the most high god, since he is glorious and filled with all riches and you are contemptible and so poor that you cannot afford shoes?' His advice to Otto was couched in a manner that Daniel of Winchester would surely have understood and approved:

> That foolish people, ignorant of the truth, saw my poverty and the wretchedness of my clothes and thought that I had come there not through love of Christ but because of my own needs. So they disdained to hear the word of salvation from me and sent me away. If you, dear father, wish to make any gains in the brute hearts of these barbarians, you must go there with a noble retinue of companions and servants and a plentiful supply of food and clothing. Those who, with unbridled neck, despised the yoke of humility will bow their necks in reverence for the glory of riches.[1]

Bishoprics had to be adequately endowed if they were to function properly. When a Mercian bishopric was set up for Chad in 669 it was fixed at Lichfield not because this had been a Roman town – it had not – but because it was the focal point of an enormous royal estate which King Wulfhere of Mercia was prepared to donate to the church. (It was also close to one of the principal residences of the Mercian kings at Tamworth.) Generally speaking, the greater churches of Christendom's missionary territories were generously endowed: a Trier or a Canterbury, a Salzburg or a Magdeburg. Certainly their incumbents could command greater resources than their counterparts in the modest little bishoprics of Italy or southern Gaul, a Siponto or a Todi or a Savona, a Vence or Vaison or Antibes. These resources lay not simply in the landed endowments of the bishopric, steadily growing by means of the gifts and legacies of the devout or the guilty. What is notable is the speed with which the overseers of the young churches acquired the right to levy taxes on their flocks. Though bishops were negligent about their pastoral duties, as Bede complained, 'there is not a single man', he continued, 'who is exempt from paying tributes (*tributa*) to the bishop.' It is likely that Bede's 'tribute' was the same as the due referred to as *ciricsceat* or 'church-scot' in the lawcode promulgated by Bede's contemporary King Ine of Wessex. It was apparently a tax levied on households; probably not therefore the same as tithe, of which more below. Penalties for not paying it were heavy. We do not know at what rate it was levied, but a significant pointer to its incidence is furnished in a clause of the *Penitential* attributed to Archbishop Theodore: 'Church tribute must not be levied in such a manner as to cause suffering to the poor.' This ruling would not have been required if the tax had not been burdensome. It is also of great interest to learn that bishops in England rapidly became entitled to a share in the spoils of war; a third of the booty, according to Theodore's *Penitential.* Add to all this that the property of the church was protected by formidable legal sanctions, and that at least in some of the Anglo-Saxon kingdoms and for some of the time the church was exempt from royal levies of taxation, and one can sense the potential for very considerable concentrations of wealth.

The illustrations above have been drawn from seventh- and eighth-century England. There is reason to suppose that analogous arrangements were to be encountered elsewhere. Irish churchmen exacted tax. The archbishopric of Salzburg profited from Charlemagne's conquest of the Avars in Pannonia. *Tributa* were rendered to the see of Magdeburg by the Slavs who lived to the east of the Elbe. The seizure of temple treasures by Liudger in eighth-century Frisia was to plunder Satan, and the booty was shared – two-thirds to Charlemagne, one-third to the church – in the proportions which Theodore had stipulated in England. There are later parallels to this – for instance, in the enrichment of the bishopric of Roskilde with the god Svantovit's estates and treasures on the island of Rügen.

Riches were necessary for furnishing and maintaining the infrastructure of a bishopric. We tend to think of episcopal accoutrements in terms of the few treasures that have survived, such as Cuthbert's pectoral cross and portable altar or the book at Fulda with which Boniface vainly tried to defend himself. We must not forget the less exotic but absolutely essential underpinning of an episcopal establishment. The large retinues, like those about which Alcuin had complained, had to be clothed, fed, mounted and armed. How revealing that when Otto of Bamburg entered his chosen mission field in 1128 with thirty wagons in his train the Pomeranians took this for an enemy army. Retainers were not menials; so we must make allowance for servants, grooms, cooks, laundrymaids. Already a lot of people, and somehow they must eat and drink and sleep. We may think of the carts as groaning under the weight of canvas and rope, poles and pegs, sheep-skins and cooking-pots and emergency fuel and candles, flour and bacon and beer. Axles break, tack frays, weapons rust. So there must be craftsmen who can exercise various skills as wheelwrights, saddlers, armourers and smiths; and they will need tools and anvils and horse-shoes and nails and grease and leather and packthread. And this is but to consider the absolutely basic equipment of an itinerant episcopal household. If in turn we consider the more exotic activities of a cathedral establishment we can appreciate the need for resources on an ample scale. For example, the production of books was inseparable from the work of Christian evangelization. It was a long and complex series of operations from the slaughter of a calf and the messy and smelly business of turning its skin into vellum that could be written upon, to the final outcome in such masterpieces as the Codex Amiat-inus or the Book of Kells. Neither should we forget the associated crafts (ink-making, mixing of pigments, bookbinding), nor the labori-ous training with quill and brush, nor the false starts, nor the sudden shower which ruined a day's work hung out to dry on the scriptorium's washing-line. Amiatinus and Kells were of course luxury productions, among the very finest books which human skill has ever produced. But even everyday texts designed for use rather than ostentation or devotion – such as, say, the Weissenburg catechism alluded to in Chap-ter 8 – would have required precious resources of materials, training and skills in their making.

Resources on a vast scale were needed for episcopal building works, which meant primarily but by no means exclusively the cathedral church of the diocese. Not a single cathedral church from the mission-ary territories survives in its entirety to the present day. The churches that do survive, whether or not built on episcopal initiative, whether whole or (more usually) fragmentary, are of modest size. Because the architects of the succeeding Romanesque age mastered the art of constructing enormous churches – Speyer or Cluny or Durham – we tend to look a little patronizingly upon their early medieval prede-cessors. But we should not underestimate the challenge of constructing a cathedral church at any time. Surviving fragments; literary descrip-tions; archaeological investigation; disciplined imagination: by a com-bination of means we can in some measure recover the work of masons and carpenters and glaziers and bellfounders, we can hear the singing and breathe the incense, see the play of candlelight upon the dull gold of votive crown or the shimmering surface of silk or mosaic, reach out and touch with lips or fingertips the resting-place of saint or relic. All this was a part of the work of evangelization. It did not come cheap.

Endowments were needed, finally, for supporting people – people who ranged from the community itself to those whom our sources refer to, in an undifferentiated manner, as 'the poor'. Charitable work had held a high priority for churchmen ever since the earliest days of organized Christianity, and modern research has emphatically endorsed Edward Gibbon's judgement that this 'very materially conduced to the progress of Christianity' in the Roman world.[2] It was customary to set aside a fourth part, in some parts of the church a third part, of ecclesiastical revenues for the relief of the poor. It was a wide category, including all those who fell through the supportive networks of kinsfolk, neighbours or patrons – widows and orphans, refugees and travellers, the underemployed and the unlucky, the incapacitated and the captive. There were also the genuinely destitute, of whom we get a startling glimpse in a ninth-century Latin poem about a Northumbrian monastery, 'shut out at the gates, laying their cold limbs in the rubbish to warm them'.[3] We should think of communities such as Inishmurray (plate 7) as surrounded not just by the 'general mess of a life-support smallholding': they were ringed by a human detritus too.

In the mission field the episcopal community was not the static cathedral chapter that it later became – its concerns narrowing to the annual liturgical round, the upkeep of buildings, the distribution of preferment and the pursuit of litigation. Whether travelling with a largely itinerant missionary bishop such as Amandus or Boniface; whether setting out from a base on round-trip missionary journeys as vividly described in the *Conversio Bagoariorum* discussed in Chapter 10; or whether being planted out, as by Wilfrid or Fructuosus or Pirmin, to found new monastic mission-stations: the episcopal household or cathedral community – for it was only later that they came to be differentiated – played a central role in evangelization.

In any Christian missionary enterprise the formation of an indigenous priesthood to take over the running of a new church from alien founders is a significant and often a delicate step. Early medieval

Europe was mercifully free of some of the complications which have bedevilled this step in other missionary settings, such as the apparatus of modern colonialism or differences of skin pigment. It is generally observable that converts will be steadier when they are guided by teachers who speak their language and share their culture. There are as usual several variables. Patrick was of British rather than Irish birth, but he had presumably become a fluent Irish speaker in the course of his exile. Gifted linguists must have included Ulfila, Cyril and Methodius; and many other characters whom we have encountered must have been more than adequate in the necessary foreign tongues. The cultural gap or divide between mission and recipients presents other variables. That between England and Frisia in the age of Willibrord, or between Saxony and Sweden in the age of Anskar, was not the same as that between, let us say, the Constantinople of Photius or Constantine Porphyrogenitus and the Moravia of Rastislav or the Kiev of Olga.

We have only snippets of information to guide us. Straws in the wind, perhaps, but sufficiently blown in the same direction as to suggest a fairly rapid recruitment of a native clergy in recently converted societies. Patrick tells us that he ordained priests in Ireland, presumably of Irish birth. In Adomnán's *Life of Columba* we catch a glimpse of a priest of Pictish origin named Eogenán: he possessed a hymnal written out by the hand of Columba himself which had the magical property of being impervious to water. In England the first bishop of Anglo-Saxon stock was Ithamar, who succeeded Paulinus of Rochester (formerly of York) in 644. Further native bishops were consecrated during the next few years, which suggests that ordination of English converts into the priesthood had been progressing steadily from at latest the 630s. We have witnessed seventh-century bishops in Francia such as Amandus and Eligius ransoming captives who seem to have included young Englishmen and, as Amandus' biographer pointed out, 'some of them later became bishops, priests or distinguished abbots'. The thirty Danish boys whom Willibrord brought back from his abortive mission to Denmark may have been intended as future mission-priests (though Alcuin, Willibrord's biographer, did not state this in so many words). Liudger's great-uncles were brought up in Willibrord's household, and as we saw in Chapter 7 they were proudly remembered in the family as 'the first of all the Frisian people to take up clerical office'. Sturm, the first abbot of Fulda, was a native of Bavaria who had been placed as a child by his parents in Boniface's household to be fostered by him. Priests of Danish birth are mentioned in Rimbert's *Life of Anskar:* one of them had been fostered in the household of Archbishop Ebo of Rheims. Cyril and Methodius trained clergy among their Slavonic converts, and on his deathbed in 885 Methodius designated one of them as his successor. Two of these clergy, Clement and Naum, played an important part in the Christianization of Bulgaria in the early tenth century. Oda, who became archbishop of Canterbury in 941, was the son of a Danish immigrant-convert. The see of Prague, founded shortly before 967, received its first native bishop, the ill-starred Vojtěch/ Adalbert, in 983. Roughly fifty years after the acceptance of Christianity by King Harald Gormsson the first bishop of demonstrable Danish birth, Odinkar of Ribe, was appointed. The earliest native Russian bishop was Luke of Novgorod, again promoted some half-century after the baptism of Vladimir of Kiev. It is the same time-lag, a couple of generations, that we can witness between the arrival of Augustine in Kent in 597 and the consecration of Ithamar in or shortly after 644. We can see it again in Iceland: Islef Gizurrsson, the first native bishop, was consecrated in 1055, about fifty years after the formal acceptance of Christianity.

The pattern is a fairly steady one. There seems to have been a willingness to launch a native clergy in the new churches as quickly as was consistent with the acquisition of the necessary training. (An exception to this rule was the Baltic area in the twelfth and thirteenth centuries, as we shall see in the following chapter.) Naturally, there was an element of risk in this strategy. Would education, even rudimentary education, stick? We might recall Boniface's shock at the priest who could not recite the Latin baptismal formula correctly. Could a native clergy be trusted to remain thoroughly indoctrinated with Christianity in the home cultural environment? Perhaps these anxieties were only, or were principally, felt by rigorists such as Boniface. Realists, such as Wulfstan of York in the *Northumbrian Priests' Law* (see Chapter 11) were prudently minimal in their expectations. In a word, they were accommodating: and accommodation, as we saw in Chapter 8, was a potent means of advancing Christianization.

A native clergy can address the people in their native tongue. Adalbert of Prague was a highly educated man who had hobnobbed in Rome with the leading intellectuals of the day, presumably in Latin; but he could talk to the Poles in their own language. Islef Gizurrsson had been sent to Germany for a good Latin education at the monastery of Herford; but he could preach to his countrymen in Old Norse. It needs to be emphasized that during the early Middle Ages, and throughout those parts of Christendom where the primary language was not one of the branches of Romance, ways and means were sooner or later devised for conveying Christian teaching and conducting at least some parts of Christian worship in the Celtic, Germanic and Slavonic vernaculars. This can be regarded as another example of the techniques of accommodation, another potent means of advancing Christianization. It is easier to find an identity in a faith which welcomes the language of the convert – within certain limits – than in one which spurns it. Here again, as we shall see, the Baltic area proved the exception, in an age which was less inclined to be accommodating.

It will also matter that in other respects too the clergy should not be too sharply differentiated from the laity. The married, tavern-haunting, weapon-bearing priests of eleventh-century Normandy or Northumbria – and doubtless of most other parts of Christendom too – may have scandalized the stricter sort of churchman. But in their manner of life, their behaviour, their dress, there was little to distinguish them from their flock. One may suspect that in certain ways this facilitated an effective ministry. Not all agreed. A prime aim of the Gregorian reformers of the eleventh century was to set the priesthood apart from the secular world as a separate, disciplined and above all celibate caste. These measures were intended to improve standards of ministry. Did they in practice render improvement even more difficult of attainment? Did the digging of a gulf between clergy and laity make the former less accessible to the latter? These are nice questions, and their investigation is not easy. One thing is clear, however, and that is that some of the effects of the reformers' work may be seen in the mission field of the twelfth and thirteenth centuries.

Eleventh-century Normandy and Northumbria supported a dense network of local churches and local priests. So did the other parts of western Christendom which had experienced several centuries of Christianization. (Obviously, matters were different in the newly missionized areas such as Hungary or Sweden.) In leaping from episcopal households in a missionary context to the well-meant attempts of Gregorian reformers to smarten up the parochial clergy we have cut all sorts of corners. How did pastoral ministry function below the rank of bishop?

How did a network of churches come into existence in countryside and town?

It seems that units of pastoral responsibility progressively fragmented until this process was halted by the freezing effects of the linked growth of clerical bureaucracy and canon law, and of the vested interests bound up with property and tithing rights. The evidence relating to this evolution is – it need hardly be said – thin in quantity and patchy in distribution. In consequence it is hard to interpret in a manner which will command widespread assent. One particular complication lies in the terminology employed in our surviving documentation and the shifting meaning of certain words over time or place. For example, the Latin word *parochia* came to mean 'parish' but for long had signified 'diocese'. The term *monasterium*, as we have already seen, need not indicate what we might understand as a 'monastery'. Other terms present comparable difficulties: *cella, domus, locus, plebs, sedes*, even the word *ecclesia* is not without its problems. In addition to sliding nuances of meaning, generalization is rendered awkward by the sheer variety of arrangements that came into being. Structures of pastoral care differed from place to place depending on local circumstances of environment, piety or power. Some very able scholarly work has in recent years shed light on the evolution of a network for the conduct of spiritual ministry. Yet the dawning light reveals ever more variety, rendering it still harder for the historian to attempt any general characterization.[4]

We may begin with the churches founded in the early days of a mission in the wake of the establishment of the bishop's own cathedral church. Such churches have been called by various names, none of them entirely satisfactory. I shall here refer to them as 'principal churches', which is colourless and cumbersome but has the virtues of neutrality. These principal churches might be founded by a missionary bishop and his immediate successors, like those founded in Touraine by successive bishops of Tours from Martin onwards (see Chapter 2). They might be established by a monastic founder, as Columbanus' Luxeuil, Annegray and Bobbio, or Boniface's Amöneburg, Fritzlar, Ohrdruf, Tauberbischofshcim and Fulda (see Chapters 5 and 7). They might be founded by a royal or princely patron – as, for instance, Duke Boleslas II of Bohemia, who was reported to have founded twenty such churches, or King Stephen of Hungary, whose plan for a grid of churches was touched on in Chapter 12. Episcopal, monastic and

465

princely initiatives should probably be thought of as complementary, not competing. But we should give due weight to the fact that because only a bishop could consecrate churches and ordain priests, in the last resort episcopal control of the network was in canon law (if not always in fact) decisive. The principal churches tended to be planted at significant centres of settlement or authority, frequently at or near sites associated – for instance, as a favoured residence – with the local ruling elite. It is notable that the Czech and Polish words for 'church', *kostel* and *kościół*, derive via German *Kastel* from Latin *castellum*, 'castle, defended lordly site'. Principal churches might be staffed by a small community of clergy, in which case they were often referred to in our sources, confusingly for us, as *monasteria*, which passed into the Old English vernacular as *mynster*, which has left its mark on the English countryside in such names as Beaminster, Leominster or Southminster. Churches of this type, typically, exercised a pastoral ministry over a fairly wide area and a scatter of settlements, in which ministry the crucial element was the right to baptize. This was delegated to the principal church by the bishop and carefully controlled by him. The means of control lay to hand in the annual distribution of chrism, the oil used in addition to water in the sacrament of baptism, which remained a jealously guarded episcopal monopoly. These churches were supported, in addition to landed endowments, by the right to exact tithe.

In Italy, where such churches were and still are known as *pievi* (from the Latin *plebs*), episcopal supervision remained tight. One may suggest that this was because of the small size of the typical Italian diocese. Let us take an example from Lucca, where an abundant early medieval documentation has survived in the diocesan archives. In the year 763 a certain priest named Ratpert was appointed by Bishop Peredeus of Lucca to the *pieve* of San Genesio at Vallari. A document which survives to this day in its original form was drawn up by Osprando the deacon to record the terms of Ratpert's life tenure of San Genesio. He was to be resident, to perform all the liturgical offices, to keep the altar lights burning day and night, to be obedient to the bishop, and to preserve and if possible to increase the endowments of the church in his charge.[5] Because of this close episcopal supervision, the further fragmentation of the pastoral unit of the *pieve*, of the principal church, tended in Italy not to occur. Lesser churches were indeed founded, offspring of the principal churches, especially by landowners for the tenantry on their estates. These lesser churches tended to be referred to as *oratoria*, 'oratories' or 'chapels'. However, they were subordinate in status to the principal church, and in particular they possessed neither baptismal nor tithing rights. The diocese of Luni, between Pisa and Genoa, is not unrepresentative. Its modest territory, an approximate rectangle of some sixty by forty kilometres, held thirty-five *pievi*, enumerated in a papal bull of 1148: on average, therefore, each *pieve* had a territory of about sixty-eight square kilometres (roughly twenty-five square miles). The earliest evidence for a rural oratory or chapel, archaeological not documentary, appears to come from the seventh century – which is strikingly contemporaneous with the mission of Columbanus and the founding of Bobbio. This rural pattern was replicated in the episcopal cities of Italy. The bishop's cathedral was the urban *pieve* and the subsidiary city churches which were founded did not normally enjoy rights of baptism, burial and tithe. The strict episcopal control of the sacrament of baptism in the cities of Italy finds glorious architectural expression in the baptisteries which stand – significantly – right next door to a number of Italian cathedrals to this day.

This Italian pattern of pastoral ministry was not repeated elsewhere in western Christendom except to some degree in south-eastern Gaul, that other land of very small bishoprics. Where dioceses were larger, episcopal control was necessarily more intermittent. Moreover, the laity's desire to have a church dispensing the sacraments of salvation near at hand, within easy reach, was strong. Accordingly the multiplication of churches below the level of principal churches was accompanied by a devolution of rights that were closely controlled in Italy, in particular that critical right to administer baptism. This devolution of episcopal monopolies was what created the network of what we now call parish churches across most of Europe outside Italy. It did not go any further. Oratories or chapels might be created within a parish territory but they did not acquire (save in a few exceptional cases) the parish rights of baptism, burial and tithe. In sum, on the Italian model we find a three-tier structure of cathedral church, principal churches or *pievi*, and chapels; on the non-Italian, a four-tier structure of cathedral church, principal churches, parish churches and chapels.

Use of the word 'devolution' may convey overtones of some orderly process, of proposals discussed, decisions made, recommendations implemented. It should not. The creation of an ecclesiastical parish may sometimes have been a self-conscious and orderly act – we shall see an example of this presently – but we may suspect that in the majority of instances the evolution of the parish as a unit of pastoral ministry was something that just happened unobtrusively – and almost invisibly to the eyes of the historian – as the Christian population grew or the principal church ceased to function because ransacked by Vikings or appropriated by a king as a convenient source of patronage. The evolution of the parish as a defined territory within which such ministry was exercised is a different matter. The critical factor in territorial definition was the compulsory payment of tithe. Now tithe had long been regarded as an obligation on the conscience of the devout, but it did not become a legally enforceable burden until, in the Frankish kingdom, the reign of Charlemagne's father Pippin the Short (751– 68). In England comparable legislation was issued two centuries later. The compulsory payment of tithe by the laity had two significant effects. In the first place, obviously enough, it provided the churches with a handsome source of income. Second, it necessitated clarification on the issues of who pays from which land to which church. If the farm at A pays tithe to the church of X and the neighbouring farm at B pays tithe to the church at Y, then a parish boundary comes into existence along the line of the hill, valley, stream, marsh, wood, road or dyke which separates the farmland of A from that of B. We must not assume that Carolingian or Anglo-Saxon royal legislation was implemented overnight. But the pressure to implement was there, and we can see the pressure being exerted, for example, in some of the voluminous writings of Archbishop Hincmar of Rheims in the third quarter of the ninth century.[6] Generally speaking, the ninth and tenth centuries seem to have been the main age of parish formation in France and Germany, the eleventh and twelfth in Britain. The distribution of surviving baptismal fonts is a rough and ready indicator. The commissioners who conducted the Domesday survey of England south of the Tees in the year 1086 assumed that a village settlement would be a parish with a church and a resident priest who exercised baptismal rights and was supported by the payment of tithe. This model of parochial organization was exported in its main lines to the missionary frontiers of Christendom in Spain or among the Slavs and Magyars.

It is not often that we can witness the foundation of a parish. But in the Archivo de la Corona de Aragón in Barcelona there survives this account of just such an occurrence. In the year 922 a church was consecrated in the name of St John the Baptist at the village of Mundarn in the district of Berga, high in the Pyrenees to the north of Barcelona. It had been built on the order of a lady named Emma, who was abbess of the nunnery of San Juan de las Abadesas. Emma was a very great person, the daughter of Count Wifred the Hairy of Barcelona (d. 898), who had been the uncrowned king of the Spanish March (though nominally subject to the king of West Francia). Wifred had founded the nunnery in about 892 and had installed his daughter as its first abbess: a familiar arrangement in every sense. Emma presided over San Juan de las Abadesas for fifty years. Evidently an active and decisive woman, she devoted her considerable energies, among other things, to the organization of pastoral ministry on the monastic estates. It needs to be borne in mind that the southern slopes of the Pyrenees were densely populated in the early medieval period, more so than they are now. Also, that whatever rural pastoral organization had existed in the Romano-Visigothic period (if any) had been disrupted during the period of Islamic rule which had come to an end only during Emma's father's lifetime and to some degree owing to his efforts. This was a region, therefore, which needed the masterful organizing hand of such as she. So she commissioned the building of the church at Mundarn and then invited the local bishop, Rodulfo (or Ralph) of Urgel – who was her brother – to come and dedicate it.

The Catalans of that age had a widespread respect for the written word. Emma and her brother were careful to have the arrangements recorded in writing. She provided the new church with vestments and books: a chasuble, stole, maniple and alb; a missal, lectionary, psalter, antiphonal and a selection of 'uplifting homilies from the holy Fathers of the Catholic church' (*sermones ad exortandum sanctorum catholicorum patrum*). In addition to this generous gift of liturgical equipment she also gave a house on the south side of the church as a residence for the parish priest together with various plots of land for his support. Bishop Rodulfo consecrated the church and laid down the boundaries of its parish: '. . . on the south side the Sierra de *Taxo*, then to Leutard's estate, then running along the Cardona road beside the property of Count Miro [another brother] called *Miralias*, thence to the land of the monastery of St Saturninus, and so to the boundary of the parish of Caserras and then along the boundary of the parish of Espuñola . . .' It is of some interest to find the new parish defined in relation to the boundaries of two existing parishes. Within these boundaries, went on the bishop, all the inhabitants must pay tithes and first-fruits to their new parish church. The ministry of chrism must be performed at the fixed times and in accordance with canonical usage. The new parish must also pay an annual due to the parent monastery.[7]

It is rare to possess a detailed record of the deliberate establishment of a parish. The elements are all there: devolution of episcopal rights coupled with maintenance of episcopal control through the ministry of chrism – a two-way ministry, bishop administering chrism-oil to priest, and priest to the newly baptized; a church building; provision of endowment in house, glebe, vestments and books; delimitation of boundaries; stipulation about payment of tithe and other renders; safeguarding of the rights of the patron – and one can be certain that such a patron as Abbess Emma would be vigilant in her supervision of whomsoever she chose as priest. The Mundarn charter is precious not only because of its rarity but also because we can detect in it what might almost be termed an element of routine. The few comparable documents bearing upon Emma's pastoral activities contain the same kind of information arranged in a similar way and employing similar verbal formulae. One gets a sense, in studying these rare survivals, that setting up a new parish in Catalonia in the early tenth century was something that people knew how to do. It was not some unfamiliar new departure.

Not all founders of rural churches were as high-minded or as generous as Abbess Emma. Consider, for instance, this ruling from a church council held at Braga in the year 572: 'If anyone builds a church not out of devotion to the faith but to satisfy cupidity – in such wise that he shares the offerings of the laity with the clergy on the grounds that he founded the church on his own land – no bishop should sanction such an abominable proceeding, nor presume to consecrate a church founded not out of love for the saints but as a species of investment.'[8] The implication is that landowners were doing this, and that some bishops were conniving in it. The ruling gains in interest when we consider who was responsible for it. The answer is, Bishop Martin of Braga, whom we encountered briefly in Chapter 2. He it was who presided over the council in 572, guided its deliberations and probably drafted its decrees. Martin, it may be recalled, was concerned with rural evangelization, the author of the tract *De Correctione Rusticorum* which was designed to assist in that work. Martin was also very probably responsible for drawing up another document, known to historians as the *Parochiale Suevorum*, which was a list of churches in his own diocese of Braga and in the dioceses of his suffragan sees, the bishoprics of Gallaecia. This list, it will not occasion surprise to learn, bristles with all sorts of problems, but three observations may be made about it with some confidence.[9] First, its very existence is testimony to a conscientious bishop's concern for the network of rural churches which assisted the evangelization of a remote corner of Christendom. Second, the churches listed were probably those in which the bishop had a direct supervisory interest. That is, they were what were earlier termed the principal churches of the dioceses of the north-western quarter of the Iberian peninsula. Thirdly, while the list does not constitute a complete census of all churches or chapels then in existence, whether built by bishops or landowners or village communities, we may be reasonably certain that not a great many other churches, apart from those listed, would then have been in existence.

How rare it is for the historian of early medieval religion to be able to employ statistical evidence. But in Braga, very unusually, it is possible. Braga was a huge diocese, which extended over almost the whole of the northern part of the modern state of Portugal as far south as the river Douro. In Martin's day there were thirty principal churches, including the cathedral church, in its entire enormous extent. Five centuries later one of Martin's successors commissioned a survey for administrative purposes of the parish churches not of the whole diocese but of a small segment of it, about a tenth of its whole territory, the region lying between the rivers Lima and Ave. This survey seems to have aimed at a complete listing of all existing parish churches. In the area surveyed there were 573 such churches. Now, this flourish of a statistical demonstration has to be qualified because of that giveaway phrase above about 'not a great many other churches'. We simply do not know how many churches, in addition to the principal churches, there might have been between the rivers Lima and Ave in Martin's time. If we were to make an estimate – a generous one – and guess that there were, say, perhaps as many as seventy churches of whatever type in the area, we should still be left with the astonishing statistic that some 500 churches were built there between *c.* 570 and *c.* 1070. But the figure is even more astonishing than a church a year. For about a century and a half (*c.* 720–870) the region was under Muslim rule

471

and Islamic law forbade the building of new Christian churches. And for a good half-century thereafter (*c.* 870–920) the region remained a vulnerable frontier zone or no man's land in which conditions were unpropitious for church-building. It must be emphasized that these are not hard and fast figures. None the less, it is difficult to avoid the conclusion that something like 500 churches were built in the course of something like 300 years.

These figures gain in credibility because they can be matched elsewhere. We move 800 miles from Braga north-east to the English county of Kent. When Augustine arrived at the court of King Ethelbert in 597 there must have been few if any functioning churches outside the town of Canterbury. (Some cautions were noted in Chapter 4 in relation to the place-name Eccles: see p. 109.) About five centuries later a survey somewhat akin to the Braga one was undertaken. It listed 407 parish churches in Kent. Here too we must make allowance for periods inimical to church-building; notably, in the case of Kent, the age of the Viking wars between *c.* 830 and *c.* 900. Yet here in south-east England, as in northern Portugal, the rate of foundation was prodigious. It may have been equally so in other areas of western Christendom. Adam of Bremen's report that 300 churches had been built in Skåne within the first century or so after the acceptance of Christianity was alluded to in Chapter 11, where a prudent caution was counselled about accepting the figure uncritically. In the light of the figures from Braga and from Kent, perhaps we can relax our scepticism a little. Naturally, there were wide regional variations in the rate of church foundation. In the diocese of Hamburg there were only four principal churches (*baptismales ecclesias*) – and, we may guess, precious few others – when its union with the see of Bremen was mooted in the middle of the ninth century. The Saxon diocese of Paderborn had only twenty-nine parish churches by the year 1000 after some two centuries of existence. The provision of a parochial network was a long-drawn-out business. In up-country Norway and Sweden it went on well into the thirteenth century.

Who built these village churches which became – outside Italy – parish churches? Here is one lay patron who tells us about his church-building activities in his own words: 'Know, my lord, that King Edgar [of Scotland, 1097–1107] your brother gave me Ednam [near Kelso, Roxburghshire] when it was uninhabited, which with his assistance and my capital [*pecunia*] I have settled, and have built there from its foundations a church which your brother the king caused to be dedicated in honour of St Cuthbert and endowed with one carucate of land.'[10] The quotation is from a letter to Earl David, later King David I of Scotland (1124–53), sent by his vassal Thor Longus and referring to events that had taken place during Edgar's reign. All sorts and conditions of people founded these rural churches – bishops, abbots and abbesses, lords and ladies of the manor, the village community clubbing together. The vast majority, however, seem to have been the lords of estates like Thor Longus, or Giroie in Normandy or Orm in Yorkshire whom we met in Chapter 11. There can be little doubt that most of these churches were at first very modest structures, and over much of western Europe more likely to have been of wood rather than of stone. (Obviously, natural resources and local building traditions varied from region to region. Round the Mediterranean good timber for building was in shorter supply than it was in, say, Germany. We might guess that Abbess Emma's church at Mundarn was built of stone from the outset, like so many churches of this date that still stand in Catalonia.) The examples of Hordain and Staubing, mentioned in Chapter 8, are representative. One of the early biographers of Dunstan, who was archbishop of Canterbury between 960 and 988, told a pleasing tale of how he went to consecrate a new church of wood at Mayfield in Sussex. When he got there he discovered that the building had been incorrectly oriented, so he put his shoulder to it and pushed it round until the alignment was correct. If we are to believe the story – and it may have lost nothing in the telling – Mayfield church cannot have been bigger than a modest garage. Not all wooden churches need have been small, however, and we may be sure that some, perhaps most, were richly decorated. Carpentry was a highly developed, highly regarded skill across the Slavonic, Germanic and Celtic lands. Remarkable decorated wooden churches survive in Scandinavia to this day, such as Urnes in Norway.

Replacement of wooden by stone churches was a feature of the period from the tenth century onwards. In a well-known passage the eleventh-century chronicler Rodulfus Glaber dwelt on this process of reconstruction: 'it was as though the whole world were everywhere clothing itself in a white mantle of churches.'[11] We occasionally get a glimpse of the process. Bishop Ethelric of Durham (1041–56) demolished a wooden church at Chester-le-Street to replace it with one of stone. When his workmen were digging the foundations for the new church they found a hoard of gold and silver coin, presumably Roman. The bishop appropriated the find and gave it to the East Anglian monastery of Peterborough, where he had formerly been a monk. He left no good reputation behind him at Durham when he resigned the bishopric to retire to Peterborough, though our Durham informant conceded that he used the money to good effect down there, laying it out in the building of churches near by. It is a nice conceit that we might owe the magnificent late Anglo-Saxon tower at Barnack, six miles from Peterborough, to the prudence of a Roman military pay-master and the rapacity of an eleventh-century bishop. Two centuries later, in the diocese of St Andrews, Bishop David de Bernham conse-crated 140 new churches in the course of his episcopate between 1240 and 1253, ninety of them between October 1241 and October 1243, or nearly one every week. It is probable that these would have been for the most part rebuildings.

The great majority of these churches were what historians call 'pro-prietary' churches, that is to say that they remained in some sense the property of the founder and his heirs or successors – like the proprietary monasteries of an earlier age of which something was said in an earlier chapter. Because most founders were secular persons like Orm Gamels-son or Thor Longus, rather than ecclesiastical institutions such as the nunnery of San Juan de las Abadesas, this meant that possession of the church remained in the family. The founder and his heirs would nominate the priest, who might well himself be a member of the family. To give but one example among many, when in 994 a Galician donor gave a church 'which came down to me from my ancestors' to the cathedral of Santiago de Compostela he stipulated that 'if there should be a man of my family' in the future who should wish to enter the priesthood, 'let him have the church under your lordship'. The family was not going to let go.[12] If churches could be inherited in this manner, so too they could be partitioned, sold, given, lent, or leased like other property in the active land-markets of tenth- or eleventh-century Europe. A prime example is furnished by the account in Domesday Book of the recent fortunes of the church of St Mary in Huntingdon:

> The jurors of Huntingdon say that the church of St Mary of the borough and the land which is annexed to it belonged to the church of Thorney [abbey], but the abbot gave it in pledge to the burgesses. Moreover, King Edward [the Confessor, 1042– 66] gave it to Vitalis and Bernard, his priests, and they sold it to

Hugh, the king's chamberlain. Moreover, Hugh sold it to two priests of Huntingdon, and in respect of this they have the seal of King Edward [i.e. legal proof of title]. Eustace has it now without livery, without writ, and without seisin.[13]

The church had passed through the hands of six owners, seven if we count the acquisitive Eustace, the new Norman sheriff, in the space of about a generation. It had been the subject of 'what can only be described as speculation in real estate'.[14] This was perhaps an extreme case, but countless examples could be offered of the traffic in proprietary churches. They were worth trafficking in because they were valued sources of revenue. Building a church was, among other things – quite possibly for some founders more than other things – a form of investment for the lord of an estate, because in addition to nominating a priest the proprietor would take a cut of the church's income. In other words, Martin of Braga's apprehensions had been all too justified. Domesday Book, once more, is a most revealing source in its candid inclusion of churches among the appurtenances of a landed estate alongside mills or stud farms or fisheries or ironworks and its listing of the annual revenue they yielded to their lords. The architectural arrangements of some surviving churches reflect the proprietary church system in the provision of a western gallery at first-floor level where the lord's family could sit comfortably removed from their smelly tenantry below, who could have thus been left in no doubt about who was in charge. Parish boundaries too reflect the proprietary origin of rural churches. The provision of churches by lords for their dependants meant that when parish boundaries hardened they tended to do so along the lines of the estate. It is in many cases demonstrable that parish boundaries are identical with the estate boundaries as described in documents of the ninth, tenth or eleventh centuries; and it may be suspected in many instances where no demonstration is possible.

In the year 849 Pope Leo IV wrote to the clergy and people of Brittany in response to their request for guidance on various matters of church government and discipline.[15] His letter makes it clear that the Bretons had evolved a pattern of Christian ministry which differed from that which was prevalent among their Frankish neighbours. It is a reminder that there were marked regional variations in the arrangements made for pastoral ministry. The point has already been made but it can bear repetition. Even within the relatively narrow confines of the British Isles there was regional diversity in the organization of pastoral care. Diversity occurred in part because central direction of the western church had never existed, in part because local episcopal initiatives tended to be intermittent – and this despite the good intentions, to which one must give full credit, of the prelates assembled in council in seventh-century Spain or eighth-century England or ninth-century Francia or tenth-century Germany. Pastoral ministry had just untidily grown, and had been shaped in the process of growth by local variables of landscape, climate, economy and settlement pattern. So it was various. It was also unstable. This was largely because it was linked to local networks of landownership and settlement, and these networks were themselves shifting and unstable, though steadily gaining in fixity and permanence throughout the period from the ninth century to the twelfth. Neither must we forget that devout acts, like the founding and endowing of a church or the choosing of a pastorally conscientious priest to serve in it, were themselves unpredictable, the outcome perhaps of the presence of a pious lady of the manor, or of a chance encounter with a hermit, or of compunction in the wake of the miraculous cure of a sick child. Piety is not necessarily a quality passed on from generation to generation. This was a point not lost on contemporary observers. The English monk William of Malmesbury thought that there had been a sad falling off from the pious standards of yester year among the Anglo-Saxon aristocracy on the eve of the Norman conquest. 'They didn't go to church in the mornings in a Christian fashion; but in their bedchambers, lying in the arms of their wives, they did but taste with their ears the solemnities of the morning mass rushed through by a priest in a hurry.'[16]

William was a churchman of high standards: he wrote in a moralizing literary tradition and he lived in an age when over much of western Europe the proprietary church system was coming under attack. The Gregorian reformers' objective of prising apart the church and the world ensured that it must be one of their principal targets. And they achieved a considerable degree of success. The passage of proprietary churches from lay into ecclesiastical hands was one of the most far-reaching changes which came over the western church in the course of the eleventh and twelfth centuries. Owners were encouraged to surrender their churches into the trusteeship of bishops, and their proprietary rights were watered down into a right of patronage. That is to say, patrons could continue to nominate priests, though bishops could in theory override a lay nomination on the grounds of unsuitability. That is to give but the barest indication of how the new system of lay patronage worked. A thicket of legal literature quickly sprang up about it. The workings of ecclesiastical patronage at parish level were by no means alone in this. The Gregorian reform movement spawned an unprecedented amount of lawmaking and codifying from the second half of the eleventh century onwards. The major landmarks were, first, the collection known as the *Decretum* edited by the Bolognese canonist Gratian in about 1140, an unofficial corpus but widely used because of its comprehensiveness and clarity of arrangement, which held the field as the standard textbook of canon law for about a century. It was superseded only in the 1230s by a collection officially sponsored by Pope Gregory IX, compiled by the Spanish Dominican Ramón de Peñafort (whose missionary concerns were briefly noted towards the end of Chapter 9). Concomitant with this mushroom growth of the law of the church were its predictable adjuncts: multiplication of church courts, proliferation of ecclesiastical lawyers, development of educational institutions to train this new clerical bureaucracy. A new force had arrived in the western church. As is often the case the new legal establishment rapidly became a powerhouse of inertia and resistance to change, its workings cumbersome and tortuous, its concerns bound up with the preservation of vested interests, its procedures arcane and impenetrable, its fees outrageous, its capacity for procrastination almost limitless.

The effect of the growth of canon law upon the parochial organization of the western church was to freeze it in its tracks. From the twelfth century onwards it became exceedingly difficult to create a new parish; so difficult as to be to all intents and purposes impossible. The discredited proprietary church system, for all its faults, had had the virtue of flexibility. Whatever the motives of the proprietor, he had been able to respond to changing circumstances. If new land were colonized and brought under the plough and a new village thereby created, he could run up a church for the new settlement on his own initiative. After the twelfth century this was no longer possible. Reformers, lawyers and bureaucrats – then as always a sinister alliance – had erected obstacles formidable enough to thwart lay and local initiatives.

The consequences of this change were felt more directly in the towns than in the countryside. Between about 900 and 1300 the towns of western Europe experienced a phase of demographic growth and economic expansion which was without precedent and would not be matched again until Europe's second urban boom in the eighteenth and nineteenth centuries. (It's another sweeping generalization; of course there was all manner of regional diversity.) This medieval phase of urban expansion posed problems for Christian ministry as serious as did that later surge of growth in the age of the industrial revolution. As in the countryside, needs could be met at first, in the pre-reform period, by local lay initiatives. To take one example already mentioned in Chapter 11, the church of St Mary Castlegate in York: the inscription on the surviving dedication stone records that it was founded by three men, presumed laity; the stone once bore a date, now illegible; the foundation is probably to be dated to the first half of the eleventh century. Excavations at York have established that the area near the church had become by that date one of intense occupation, pulsing with industrial and commercial life. St Mary Castlegate, planted in the midst of this thriving scene, was surely intended to meet perceived religious and social needs.[17]

In examining the multiplication of urban churches we find something of the same contrast between Mediterranean and transalpine Europe that we encountered when looking at rural ministry. By and large, episcopal control over urban church life remained more firm in the south than it did in the north. We have already pointed out that there was in Italy a tendency for the episcopal city to remain a single ecclesiastical parish. This did not mean that no urban churches were founded apart from the bishop's cathedral. Far from it. When the Magyars attacked Pavia in 924 it was said that they sacked forty-four churches. Yet the town of Pavia remained a single parish, or *pieve*, under the control of its bishop. The situation was different in northern Europe. Incredible though it may seem, there were over 100 churches in London by the middle of the twelfth century, most of which became fully fledged parish churches by the usual tests of baptism, burial and tithe, even though they passed out of the hands of the laity who had been (for the most part) their founders. London might have been an extreme case, but there were many northern cities with a dense concentration of parish churches. Norwich, for instance, had at least forty-nine by the year 1086. Even so relatively new a

Christian town as Novgorod had thirty-two churches by about 1100.

The clericalization and bureaucratization of the church in the age of the Gregorian reform put an end to the free-and-easy provision for urban pastoral ministry of earlier days. The result was that the institutional church could no longer quickly and effectively respond to changing pastoral needs. The beginnings of a reaction to this state of affairs may be discerned in the twelfth century. Evangelical movements, or tendencies, or sects, began to develop among the laity. The Waldensians were evangelical preachers founded in about 1174 by a merchant of Lyons, Valdes, from whom they took their name. The Humiliati of Milan, Cremona and other north Italian cities were groups who attempted, from about 1180 onwards, to lead an apostolic life in which simplicity and manual labour, almsgiving and preaching, were conjoined. Both of these sects spread widely in Germany and southern France. (The Waldensians still exist in small numbers in Piedmont.) Francis of Assisi sought after his conversion in about 1205 to combine a life of absolute poverty and mendicancy with evangelical preaching. The religious order which he founded spread with astonishing speed throughout western Christendom. The groups of women known as Beguines, who came together to lead an apostolic life, were active from about 1200 in the towns of the Low Countries and the Rhineland. All of these movements, and others, were distinctively, if not exclusively, urban. All were implicitly, and sometimes outspokenly, critical of the existing arrangements for pastoral ministry in the established church. All were regarded with suspicion, even the early Franciscans, by the ecclesiastical authorities; and some experienced persecution as heretics. These movements are not our concern here, because their mission was not to the heathen but was primarily an internal mission to a European family of believers which was already firmly if nominally Christian. They witness here to the tensions and dissatisfactions within the western church in the wake of the Gregorian reforms. 'If it ain't broke, don't fix it' is a maxim which ecclesiastical – and perhaps all other – reformers would do well to keep at the forefront of their minds.

The evolution of a parochial network was one of the most significant, as it was one of the most enduring, achievements of the emergent civilization of medieval Europe. We have undoubtedly more to learn about it from the patient fieldwork of archaeologists and topographical historians. What has been offered above is no more than a light sketch, but I hope enough to render plausible any claims made for the role of this network in the process of Christianization. To begin with the sacrament of initiation: it is obvious that it is easier to have a child baptized when a church where the ceremony can be performed is readily accessible. Evidently, from the figures quoted above, it was a good deal easier to seek baptism in the diocese of Braga in the eleventh century than it had been in the sixth. In the diocese of Luni most parents would have had a *pieve* to which they could carry their baby within about an hour's walk of their homes. These illustrations are not unrepresentative, though they must be balanced by the recollection that there were parts of Christendom where the necessary travel must have been much more arduous, even dangerous. At life's end the dead were interred in a Christian cemetery attached to the local parish church. If persons died while absent from home, efforts were made where feasible to bring the corpse back for burial in the home parish. By the tenth century at latest guilds and confraternities existed whose members were pledged to perform this service. Some of their statutes have survived. The guild brothers of Abbotsbury in Dorset, for example, whose statutes date from the middle years of the eleventh century, were sworn to bring back a member's body, fittingly escorted, from as much as sixty miles away. That was not the end of the matter: they were required also to pray earnestly for the dead man's soul.

At cradle and at grave, then, the parish was a stimulus to and focus for local pieties. And in between? We have to tread with caution here because we have so little evidence about how parochial life was lived before the thirteenth century. What little we do have is for the most part normative or prescriptive; statements about how episcopal authority – Hincmar of Rheims, Udalric of Augsburg, Wulfstan of York – thought that parish priests and their people should conduct themselves. We know how parishes were meant to work, but practically nothing of how they actually did. Compulsory payment of tithe at the very least gave parishioners a grumpy material interest in what went on. He who paid the piper may have had more opportunity for calling the tune than we shall ever know. There is plenty of evidence for voluntary expenditure on pious causes, conspicuous still the building or rebuilding of village churches, that 'white mantle' of freshly dressed stone or whitewashed rendering which so impressed Rodulfus Glaber in the eleventh century. Multiplication of churches made church attendance easier, just as it made baptism more accessible. We have not the remotest idea how regular or otherwise the laity may have been in their attendance, though we have a fair amount of reliable – non-prescriptive – evidence that festivals and special occasions such as dedications or the enshrining of a saint's relics could attract large crowds. (It may be, however, that we should connect these occasions rather with cathedrals, monasteries and principal churches than with the humbler parish churches.)

We know what churches were meant to possess in the way of liturgical equipment and we can show that some, such as Abbess Emma's Mundarn, did indeed possess a complete tally. As against this, we can show that some did not; and we might care to bear in mind the implications of Bishop Udalric of Augsburg's ruling that priests must not pawn church vessels and vestments to merchants or innkeepers. In any case, possession of churchly equipment does not tell us anything certain about its use. Was Abbess Emma's volume of 'uplifting homilies' in regular use for the instruction of those villagers of Mundarn who bothered to go to church? Or did it gather dust and cobwebs in a corner of the church (perhaps to be hurriedly buffed and placed prominently on a lectern when the abbess paid one of her visits)? Was it even traded in for wine at the village tavern? These are among the many questions which we cannot answer. The likelihood is that there was very little in the way of instruction for the laity by means of preaching before the thirteenth century. Such instruction as there was could have come by way of commentary upon the Lord's Prayer and the Creed, which the parish clergy were meant to teach to their parishioners. As time went by, it could additionally have come by means of images. The presentation of scenes from scripture as religious drama – for example, the Easter play – dates from the tenth and eleventh centuries. In the following chapter we shall encounter a particularly *mouvementé* episode of religious theatre at Riga in the early thirteenth. Stone sculpture, on font or doorway or capital, representing sacrament or judgement or biblical scene, began to be widespread after about 1100. Local parish churches shared in a modest way in the skills that were developed in the regional workshops which enjoyed artistic patronage. Thus, for example, the sculptural styles pioneered at Cluny and maintained at Autun and Vézelay are traceable in several humbler Burgundian churches. Wall-paintings probably decorated many more parish churches than we might now guess. The general effect may be gauged from the magnificent collection of frescoes from Catalan churches to be seen in the Museu d'Art de Catalunya in Barcelona (if you're lucky enough to find it open).

Slowly, painfully slowly, the European laity became more deeply imbued with Christian values. It is difficult to isolate a distinctively parochial contribution to the process, but two lines of approach seem promising. One concerns names. Open at random any collection of medieval documents and compare the names of witnesses to deeds from the mid-tenth century with those of their counterparts in the mid-twelfth. At the earlier date names of local ethnicity predominate – Frankish names in Francia, Lombard names in Italy, Celtic names in Brittany and Wales, and so forth. By the later date, as like as not, local names will have given way to the Christian names of apostles and evangelists, saints and martyrs. It is not an invariable rule but it is fairly reliable. The choice of name for a child is formally sealed at the baptismal font. One may legitimately infer the influence – not the exclusive influence, of course – of the parish priest. The second concerns pilgrimages. By about the year 1000 the Latin word *peregrinatio* had shed its earlier meaning of lifelong 'exile for Christ' and had come to mean what we normally understand by 'pilgrimage' today, a round-trip journey to a holy place and then home again. Pilgrimage in this sense was being presented by churchmen as one of the more desirable religious exercises for the Christian laity. In the course of the eleventh century there appeared for the first time the phenomenon of mass pilgrimage: large parties of pilgrims organized by local church leaders in such a manner as to render the devout exercise possible for those who would not otherwise have been able to afford it. In 1064, for instance, a party of several thousand pilgrims led by four bishops went from Germany to the Holy Land. We know nothing of individual motivations, but it is surely likely that ordinary people of this sort would have been compliant to the local pressures of neighbourhood. One may again infer the influence of the parish priest. But we know so little about the parish clergy of that epoch. Unsung heroes, perhaps? They 'have no memorial and are perished as though they had never been'.

CHAPTER FOURTEEN

The Sword Our Pope: the Baltic and Beyond

The face of Europe coarsened and the war cast its heroic
and chivalrous disguise and became a sweaty tug-of-war
between teams of indistinguishable louts.
EVELYN WAUGH, *Scott-King's Modern Europe*, 1947

FROM THE TWELFTH CENTURY ONWARDS the tone of western Christian
approaches to the remaining heathen changed subtly but decisively. It
is as though some invisible frontier had been crossed. There was steady
demographic growth, the slow but remorseless pressure of people upon
resources. There was the gradual development of an ideology of crusading during the course of the twelfth century, the notion that certain kinds
of warfare against the enemies of Christendom were not merely justified
but holy, awarding positive spiritual merit to participants. There was an
increasing concern in the western church with education. And there was
the foundation of new religious orders specifically devoted to missionary
work. Each of these requires a closer examination.

Demography is a notoriously difficult field of study for the historian
of the Middle Ages. No unbroken statistical series have survived. In
their place, sorry (but challenging) substitutes, the historian is presented with random and isolated nuggets of documentary or archaeological evidence whose interpretation presents formidable problems.
There is, however, general agreement that between about 800 and
about 1300 the population of Europe grew at a slow but steady pace
until, on the eve of the demographic check administered by the great
pandemic of the Black Death of 1347–9, it stood at a high point
which would probably not be reached again until the seventeenth
century. On Europe's frontiers the effects of this growth in population
were most visible in a thickening of both rural and urban settlement

and the opening up of new lands for cultivation in the much less densely populated areas of the 'new Christendom' which had been added on to the 'old Christendom', the nucleus of Charlemagne's day. The phenomenon can be observed in regions as far apart and as different one from another as Portugal, Ireland, Sweden and Hungary. On the eastern frontiers of Germany the language and ethnicity of the Magyar, Slav and Baltic peoples was penetrated by those of enormous numbers of farmers and miners, merchants and craftsmen, attracted by varying material inducements (low rents, tax concessions, etc.) from regions of overpopulation further to the west. The settlers thus laboriously 'milked' came mainly, but not exclusively, from other parts of Germany. This mingling of peoples was to have far-reaching consequences, some of them still with us in the late-twentieth century.

Settlement was an expensive business requiring capital investment on which the return would be slow. Necessarily therefore it tended to be organized by the greater persons or corporations of secular or ecclesiastical life. Such, for instance, were the two leading frontier lords of north-eastern Germany in the middle years of the twelfth century, Count Adolf of Holstein (whom we met briefly in Chapter 12) and Albert 'the Bear', margrave of Brandenburg. Here is what Helmold of Bosau had to say about the latter's settlement operations in his *Chronica Slavorum*:

> At that time Albert, the margrave whose by-name is 'the Bear', held eastern Slavia . . . In the end, as the Slavs gradually decreased in number, he sent to Utrecht and to places lying on the Rhine, to those, moreover, who live by the ocean and suffer the violence of the sea – to wit Hollanders, Zeelanders and Flemings – and he brought large numbers of them and had them live in the strongholds and villages of the Slavs. The bishopric of Brandenburg, and likewise that of Havelburg, was greatly strengthened by the coming of the foreigners, because the churches multiplied and the income from tithes grew enormously . . . Because God gave plentiful aid and victory to our leader and the other princes, the Slavs have been everywhere crushed and driven out. A people strong and without number have come from the bounds of the ocean and taken possession of the territories of the Slavs. They have built cities and churches and have grown in riches beyond all estimation.

In this association of Christianity and material prosperity one can catch faint echoes of Daniel of Winchester; and perhaps closer ones of the sort of sermons that Helmold preached to the villagers of Bosau.

Monks were colonizers of new land as well as the laity. Especially notable in this respect were the Cistercians or White Monks, the most celebrated of the new religious orders which had emerged as alternatives to traditional Benedictine observance in the early years of the twelfth century. Marked in their early days by a regime of simplicity and austerity, the Cistercians sought to plant their houses in marginal lands far from human habitation. Not surprisingly, therefore, we find them on the ever-moving frontiers of Christendom. Consider, for example, this line of descent from Morimond, a daughter-house of Cîteaux founded in 1115, from which in turn sprang many of the Cistercian communities of Germany and eastern Europe. Altenkamp, in the Rhineland, was a daughter-house of Morimond founded in 1123. From Altenkamp descended Amelungsborn in Saxony, of which Bishop Bern of Mecklenburg-Schwerin (1158–91), an important figure in the immediate post-missionary phase of that region, had been a monk. From Amelungsborn was colonized Doberan in Mecklenburg, founded with Bishop Bern's encouragement by Pribislav, the son of Nyklot, in 1171. From Doberan descended Dargun in Mecklenburg and Buków in Pomerania. Now, it is not correct to characterize the Cistercians as a 'missionary order'. From the outset they set their face against preaching and pastoral work in favour of a life of seclusion. However, they were part of a church which was expanding at the expense of heathendom. They could mould churchmen who went on to be active in the mission field, such as Bern of Schwerin, Conrad of Lübeck, Eskil of Lund, and others whom we shall meet presently. And we may guess that by their very existence and their reputation for holiness of life they exerted the same sort of indirect influence upon the process of Christianization as had those earlier 'frontier' monks, the seventh-century disciples of Columbanus at Luxeuil or Bobbio or Weltenburg.

We have already had occasion, in Chapter 9, to take note of the circumstances of what historians – though not contemporaries, who did not know that it was the beginning of a series – call the First Crusade. It has long been recognized that the origins of the idea of crusade need to be sought far back in the recesses of the eleventh and the tenth centuries, and indeed beyond. Historians have been rather slower to grasp that the notion of crusade was by no means fully fledged or clear-cut by the time that Pope Urban II preached at Clermont in 1095, nor by the time the crusading armies captured Jerusalem in 1099, nor, indeed, by 1146 when Pope Eugenius III initiated what we call the Second Crusade. The 'crusade-idea' was fed by rivulets which sprang from diverse and sometimes unlikely starting-points, which trickled slowly and uncertainly in their early courses: it did not flow in a single strong current, some would argue, until the better part of a century had passed since Urban's pontificate.[1] So we must beware of assuming that a crusading ideology could be transferred to the Christian frontier in the Baltic region in the immediate wake of the fall of Jerusalem. This is one reason – not the only one – for being sceptical about an early dating for the puzzling document known as the *Magdeburger Aufruf* or 'Magdeburg Appeal'. This is a letter from an anonymous writer apparently attached to the church of Magdeburg, addressed to the clergy of Saxony, the Rhineland and Flanders, appealing for military aid in a proposed expedition against the Wends.[2]

The writer judged the war against the Wends to be just because 'the most cruel gentiles have risen against us and prevailed'. In other words, to campaign against them was but to repossess lands which had once been Christian. (We have encountered this argument already in the pages of Helmold of Bosau.) He went on to tell atrocity stories about the torture of Christians at the hands of the pagans and about the sacrifice of Christians to the Wendish god Pripegala. Then he turned to the example of the crusaders who had liberated Jerusalem in 1099. Just so must Christian armies liberate 'our Jerusalem, once free, but now enslaved by the cruelty of the gentiles'. The author infused much biblical quotation and allusion into his text, some of it from such surprising quarters, given his subject-matter, as the *Song of Songs*. It seems reasonably certain that he was acquainted with one of the early written accounts – there were several – of what Pope Urban had said at his speech at Clermont in 1095. The letter also has analogies with another class of document, the so-called *excitatoria*, broadsheets which were intended to stimulate enthusiasm for the crusade. Like them, the Magdeburg letter appealed to covetous instincts:

> These gentiles are most wicked, but their land is the best, rich in meat, honey, corn and birds; and if it were well-cultivated none could be compared to it for the wealth of its produce. So say those who know it. And so, most renowned Saxons, Franks, Lorrainers, and Flemings, this is an occasion for you to save your

souls and, if you wish it, to acquire the best land on which to live.

Both the date and the content of this document have been much discussed. A favourite date is *c.* 1108, though I should be inclined to place it rather later, say 1120–25. The question of whether it can be called a crusading document has also been examined. There is general consensus that on a strict definition of crusading it may not be so described; a point whose force is blunted by the reflection that strict definitions of crusading had not been formulated in the early twelfth century. These questions of date and definition need not concern us here. What is significant is that in the first quarter of the twelfth century a writer in northern Germany could present the Wendish wars as being comparable to the expedition which had resulted in the reconquest of Jerusalem.

As the twelfth century advanced the frontier wars of the German north-east gradually took on the emerging character of crusades. The participants in the Wendish crusade of 1147, briefly touched on in Chapter 12, received the same spiritual privileges as the warriors of the Second Crusade to Syria and Palestine in the years 1147–8. This was made formally explicit by Pope Eugenius III, a former Cistercian monk, in a letter of April 1147.[3] In the same letter the pope forbade prospective campaigners from accepting money from the conquered as the price for allowing them to remain pagan. This is a most interesting prohibition, revealing not only that conversion was among the aims of the expedition but also that people *had* been known to accept money in lieu of baptism. Mission and crusade had come together. This was revealed still more clearly in a celebrated letter from St Bernard, abbot of Clairvaux (where Pope Eugenius had been a monk) and the most potent spiritual force in the Europe of his day. Bernard had preached the Second Crusade to a huge and rapturous audience at Vézelay in Burgundy – Vézelay, where an unknown sculptor of genius had recently completed in the western portal of the abbey church of St Mary Magdalen one of the most powerful artistic renderings ever executed of the church's duty of universal mission. Bernard's letter of a few months later on the subject of the crusade against the Wends stated that the crusaders were setting out 'to convert those nations' (*ad convertendas nationes illas*) and indicated that he shared some of the pope's misgivings: 'We expressly forbid that for any reason whatsoever they should make a truce with those peoples, whether for money or for tribute, until such time as, with God's help, either their religion [*ritus*] or their nation be destroyed.'⁴ This theme of the union of crusade and mission was repeated by subsequent popes. Pope Alexander III encouraged the Scandinavian kings to fight against 'the Estonians and other pagans of those parts', promising the same remission of sins as that enjoyed by crusaders and looking forward to the conversion of the subjugated. Innocent III wrote in the same fashion to King Valdemar II of Denmark in 1209: 'gird yourself manfully to root out the error of paganism and spread the bounds of the Christian faith.'⁵

The medieval papacy attained the zenith of its power in the pontificate of Innocent III between 1198 and 1216. In terms of the institutional machinery of papal government Innocent was the beneficiary of the initiatives taken during the reforming era of the previous century and a half. He had access to the means of implementing his decisions which would have been the envy of Gregory VII. In a word, where Gregory had presided, Innocent governed. We need not dwell here on the process of change that had brought this state of affairs about, nor on the means by which papal government worked, save to note two significant features. First, written communication between the papal curia and the churches on Christendom's periphery became routine where formerly it had been rare. Second, the activity of papal legates – that is, churchmen appointed to act as the pope's representatives in a given region – became more pronounced. Correspondence between the curia and the rulers of Scandinavia, of which a couple of instances were cited in the last paragraph, is an example of the first. As for the second, the re-organization of the Irish church by Cardinal John Paparo or of the Norwegian church by Cardinal Nicholas Breakspear (see Chapter 13), may stand as examples. But the single most important effect of the changes was that the popes could play a more assertive and direct role in the mission field than they had ever done before.

The reform of the church had generated, and was itself assisted by, an educational revolution. From the second half of the eleventh century onwards the monasteries lost their long pre-eminence as centres of learning to the schools attached to the cathedral churches of Europe. Some of these cathedral schools, first and most famously Paris, developed into self-regulating universities. The monastic syllabus of studies had been conservative and backward-looking. The learning of the schools was dynamic and progressive; it quickly led to new departures of immense significance in Europe's cultural history, particularly in the disciplines of theology and law. From the middle of the twelfth century a training in the schools became a necessary qualification for a career in the higher ranks of the church. This too had implications for the mission field. After the twelfth century the management and direction of evangelistic endeavour fell more and more into the hands of heavyweight intellectuals, who believed with the usual arrogance of intellectuals that they had all the answers. For such persons it was no longer enough to dunk the convert in the waters of baptism and leave the rest to God's grace and human habit. The convert must be taught as well, and taught along lines acceptable to Roman bureaucrats and Parisian professors. This would involve defining in new and stricter ways the nature and extent of the cultural baggage which the convert might be allowed to carry across the threshold of conversion. That is why, to put it bluntly, we do not have a rich vernacular literature in Old Prussian or Old Finnish to stand alongside the glories of Old English or Old High German literature.

During the twelfth century a number of the new religious orders found themselves associated more or less closely with the missions on Christendom's frontiers. Besides the Cistercians, there were also the Augustinians and the Premonstratensians. These were orders of canons, not monks, the main difference being that canons were not excluded from the secular world as monks (in theory) were, but were permitted to undertake pastoral work among the nearby laity. The Augustinians took their name from the great Augustine of Hippo because they believed – erroneously – that the Rule of life they followed had originally been devised by him. In actual fact the Augustinians emerged as an order of canons gradually and obscurely in eleventh-century Italy and France, among groups of devout persons who were trying to re-create what they thought was a more 'apostolic' manner of life. Their hallmark was diversity. Their Rule allowed all sorts of variations in their routine of community life, and differing spiritual and pastoral priorities from house to house. It was this diversity which made them adaptable to the demands of evangelizing the newly and nominally converted. In north-eastern Germany their association with missionary work was close. Vizelin's mission communities at Neumünster and Segeburg were houses of Augustinian canons. Several cathedral chapters adopted the Augustinian Rule – for example, Lübeck when the bishopric of Oldenburg was moved there in 1160. Segeburg had close links with the early Livonian mission. Meinhard, the first bishop in Livonia, had been a canon of Segeburg; so too had some early members of the cathedral chapter of Riga. The priest Henry, who wrote the history of the Livonian mission, had been educated there.

The Premonstratensians were an offshoot of the Augustinians. The order was founded by an eccentric German aristocrat named Norbert whose early life had been spent in the glittering surroundings of the imperial court. Converted to the religious life after a fall from his horse in about 1114, Norbert adopted a regime of ferocious asceticism (it killed his first three disciples) and developed a manner of life in which the task of preaching occupied a high place. His first house was founded at Prémontré – hence the order's name – in the northern French diocese of Laon under the patronage of a sympathetic local bishop. (At that date, before the rise of the Parisian masters, the schools of Laon were the most renowned in western Christendom.) Norbert returned to Germany in 1126 when he was appointed to the archbishopric of Magdeburg. He immediately set about establishing communities in and beyond eastern Saxony, which had grown into quite a network by the time of his death in 1134. Because of the special conditions of north-eastern Germany these were from the first associated with the missionary initiatives of the mid-twelfth century (among which we must not forget those of Otto of Bamburg, whom we encountered briefly in Chapter 12). For example, the Premonstratensian house at Grobe, on the island of Usedom, founded from Magdeburg in 1155, was situated near one of those developing Baltic towns where pagan cult had been strong in the recent past. The Saxon bishop and papal legate who led the Wendish crusade of 1147, Anselm of Havelburg, was a Premonstratensian who had been a friend and admirer of Norbert as well as one of his suffragan bishops, and who had persuaded his cathedral chapter at Havelburg to adopt the Premonstratensian Rule.

These monastic and canonical initiatives of the twelfth century were reinforced early in the thirteenth by the orders of friars, of which the two earliest and most celebrated were the Friars Minor or Franciscans, founded by St Francis of Assisi in 1209, and the Friars Preachers or Dominicans, founded by St Dominic in 1216. These two orders had quite different priorities. Dominic founded his order of friars for the express purpose of countering heresy in general, and the Albigensian or Cathar heresy in particular. The Dominicans were therefore men of advanced intellectual training whose primary duty was preaching and teaching. It rapidly became apparent that such men were ideally qualified for missionary work in the changed circumstances of the thirteenth century. Francis, as we saw in Chapter 13, had sought to live a life of apostolic poverty. His disciples were to live by begging or by the labour of their hands and to preach by example. Higher education had at first no place at all among Franciscan priorities. But the Franciscans were soon drawn into the schools, and within a generation of their founder's death in 1226 were beginning to find themselves, like the Dominicans, undertaking missionary functions. Although neither of the new orders of friars was a missionary order pure and simple, it so turned out that many who were active as missionaries in the thirteenth and fourteenth centuries were Franciscans or Dominicans.

Papal direction, supported by bureaucratic and academic resources; greater reliance upon coercive force, justified by the ideology of crusading; the committed expertise of missionary or quasi-missionary religious orders: this was indeed a changed and changing world. The new act in the drama of missionary history which opens from about 1200 was long to endure. The techniques and experiments of the thirteenth and fourteenth centuries furnished models and precedents and warnings (not much heeded) for the missionaries of the fifteenth and sixteenth centuries. The spiritual conquest of Prussia and Livonia points ahead to that of Mexico and Peru. This is but one of many indications that there was not much that was 'medieval' about thirteenth-century Europe.

When thirteenth-century writers referred to 'Livonia' they meant, approximately, the territories which extended from the lower valley of the river Dvina (Daugava, Duna) to the Gulf of Finland; something like the modern republics of Latvia and Estonia. There had been frequent and fertile interactions between Livonia and her neighbours in the centuries prior to the thirteenth. Danish and Swedish merchants, adventurers, pirates, exiles and mercenaries had made their ways to those shores. Coin hoards witness to a sporadic German merchant presence in the twelfth century. Russian chieftains from Novgorod or Pskov would raid Livonia for slaves from time to time, sometimes claim lordship and tribute. There may even have been some mild Russian interest in evangelism from such centres as Polotsk, where a bishopric is attested from about 1100. Rumours circulated that clergy from Sweden visited Livonia's coasts in the twelfth century, though they cannot be substantiated. In the latter part of the twelfth century Livonia presented an inhospitable environment and an unstable compound of endlessly warring chieftains. These were deterrents to potential visitors. But the rewards of trade, particularly the opportunity to acquire the luxury furs that commanded such a high price in the west, were too tempting to be disregarded. Christianity could ride into Livonia on the merchants' ships. Not for the first nor for the last time commerce and Christianity – in David Livingstone's famous linkage – could flourish hand in hand.

So it was in a German merchantman that an Augustinian canon named Meinhard, an inmate of Vizelin's foundation of Segeburg in Holstein, arrived at the mouth of the Dvina in the Gulf of Riga in about 1180 to set up a mission station. He built a church up-river at Üxküll (Ikskile), and he cunningly displayed the superiority of German technology by importing masons who built a fort of stone wherein the local people would be safe from Lithuanian slave-raiders. He made a few converts, but there were many backsliders among them. On a return visit to Germany Meinhard was consecrated a bishop by Archbishop Hartwig of Bremen; an indication that the cathedral community at Bremen had not abandoned its claims to an ecclesiastical empire in the far north. He also sought and received, in 1193, the approval of Pope Celestine III for his mission.

Meinhard died in 1196. His successor, chosen by Archbishop Hartwig, was Berthold, abbot of the Cistercian house of Loccum in Westphalia. Arriving in Livonia in 1197 he quickly found his position untenable and returned to Germany to report that stronger methods were needed. Accordingly a crusade was preached by Pope Celestine, a crusading army was recruited in Saxony and under Berthold's leadership made its way to Livonia in 1198. A battle was fought in which the Livonians were defeated, but only at a particularly heavy price: Bishop Berthold's horse bolted into the ranks of the enemy, by whom he was set upon, killed and shredded into little bits. The Livonian mission had gained a martyr but lost a leader. The Saxon crusaders trailed home. The remaining clergy, perilously exposed at their base at Üxküll, hung on for a while but when in 1199 the Livonians decided that all Christian priests should be killed they went back to Germany. The Livonian mission had to all intents and purposes collapsed.

We owe this narrative to the chronicler Henry of Livonia. He was a Saxon, educated perhaps at the Augustinian house of Segeburg. He went to Livonia as a young man in about 1205 and apparently stayed there for the rest of what seems to have been a long life – he is last traceable in 1259 – working as a mission-priest. He composed his chronicle between 1225 and 1229. It is a detailed year-by-year narrative account of the mission, sober, factual and – whenever we can check its assertions against independent evidence – accurate.[6] Like all works in the slippery genre of missionary literature, his chronicle has to be handled with caution. Nevertheless, Henry is among our best witnesses to the changing world of thirteenth-century missions. In the early years of the Livonian enterprise we can already see some of these changes: papacy, Augustinians, crusaders. We can see them too in Henry's long account of the unfortunate Bishop Berthold's successor. This was Albert of Buxtehude, Henry's revered master and the hero of his narrative, who presided as bishop over the Christian presence in Livonia from 1199 to 1229.

Albert was one of those larger-than-life characters whose powerful personality can still be felt thumping through the measured Latin of Henry's *Chronicle*. He was a man of forceful and decisive measures. Appointed by his uncle Archbishop Hartwig in 1199, Albert led a crusading army from Lübeck in 1200 and re-established a missionary base at the mouth of the river Dvina. Grasping that Üxküll was too dangerously far inland, he moved the seat of the Livonian bishopric downriver to a new settlement which he founded for it in 1201. This was the origin of the city of Riga. The site had been carefully chosen for its commercial potential: a good harbour for German and Scandinavian merchant shipping. Albert reinforced natural advantages with a papal mandate, getting an order from Innocent III to the effect that merchants must in future use Riga in preference to any other Livonian port. Every year Albert went back to Germany in person to conduct recruiting tours. These yielded several kinsmen: at least four among his brothers went out and did nicely for themselves, one becoming provost (or dean) of Riga and another the first bishop of Dorpat in Estonia. They yielded in addition not just clergy and soldiers, but also the citizenry of Riga – businessmen, shopkeepers, craftsmen, clerks, publicans, and their families. Riga became and long remained a German colonial outpost in a hostile land. Henry of Livonia well brings out its vulnerability in the early days, of which he had had experience. Riga was threatened not just by hostile Livonians, its wooden dwellings and warehouses perilously naked to fire-arrows, but also – and with inescapable regularity – by the privations of cold and hunger. When in 1210 some Frisian shippers arrived with large numbers of sheep, Henry found it worthy of mention in his chronicle: milk, meat and wool! There must have been moments when it looked as though Riga would not survive. But Bishop Albert had boundless confidence: he also had faith. From the outset Riga was an emphatically Christian city, or better, a Christian citadel, an embattled fortress boldly reared in Satan's territory. Protected by water, and very soon by a wall, the earliest nucleus of the city sheltered the cathedral, the bishop's palace, a garrison of Christian knights and a church dedicated to St Peter. The Petrine dedication indicated Roman loyalties and the expectation of help, both terrestrial and supernatural, from the papacy. The cathedral was dedicated to the Blessed Virgin Mary. Albert capitalized upon the surge of Marian devotion which had swept twelfth-century Christendom, and in his more expansive moments would assert the special patronage of the Virgin for the Livonian mission. Here he is lecturing Pope Innocent III at the fourth Lateran council in 1215.

> Holy Father, [he said] as you have not ceased to cherish the Holy Land of Jerusalem, the country of the Son, with your Holiness' care, so also you ought not to abandon Livonia, the land of the Mother, which has hitherto been among the pagans and far from the cares of your consolation and is now again desolate. For the Son loves His Mother and, as He would not care to lose His own land, so, too, He would not care to endanger His Mother's land.

Riga quickly became a commercial and civic success. But it was a tense and jumpy sort of place. This comes over in one of Henry's anecdotes. Bishop Albert had staged what Henry called 'a very elaborate play of the prophets' in the town, 'so that the pagans might learn the rudiments of the Christian faith by an ocular demonstration'. It was characteristic of his showmanship and his inventiveness; characteristic too of his age's obsession with new paths in education. Large numbers of both converts and pagans were accordingly brought within the city walls – the native Livonians normally lived outside in a sort of Baltic *apartheid* – so that they could be made to watch the play.

An interpreter was on hand to explain what was happening. Perhaps he did not do his job very well; perhaps the acting was too realistic. For whatever reason, while Gideon's army was fighting the Philistines the audience took to flight, 'fearing', wrote Henry, 'lest they be killed'. Fortunately the panic was calmed and the play continued. It is a revealing moment. Violence marked the relations between natives and incomers at all times. Henry calmly reports the routine burning of crops and houses, the slaughter and the maiming, the torture of prisoners, the enslavement of women and children, the rending apart of Bishop Berthold's corpse. It was traditional: the Livonians and their neighbours had been carrying on like this since time out of mind. The coming of the Christians introduced novel features to the scene, such as a superior military technology. It did not long remain a Christian monopoly but was quickly diffused and shared, not invariably with the results intended. 'The Russians made a little machine [a *ballista*] like that of the Germans, but not knowing the art of throwing rocks they hurled them backwards and wounded many of their own men.'

A mixture of tradition and innovation characterized the Livonian mission under Bishop Albert's leadership. The network of his kinsfolk is reminiscent of the missionaries of an earlier age like Wilfrid and Liudger. The tactic of trying to work through a 'tame' native chieftain, by name Caupo, recalls the use made of Gottschalk or Pribislav among the Wends. Caupo was sent off to Rome in 1203 to be paraded in front of the pope and to be impressed by the might and majesty of Christendom. The experience made him 'most faithful' but it did not endear him to his Livonian followers. 'Because of the persecution of the Livonians he fled to the city [of Riga] and lived there with the Christians for almost a whole year.' Albert recruited workers in the mission field by the same methods that earlier leaders such as Eligius or Amandus had employed. The priest re-named John had been ransomed from captivity as a boy, sent off to Segeburg to be educated, brought back to Livonia and installed in a fort between Riga and Üxküll to evangelize the country people round about: he was martyred in 1206. Whether these traditional missionary techniques would be found acceptable in the changing religious climate of the thirteenth century remained to be seen.

Innovation can be seen in Albert's frequent requests for papal guidance. They bore fruit in a barrage of instruction and exhortation, and in the visits of papal legates such as Bishop William of Modena in 1226–7, who sought to impose order and structure upon the young Livonian church. Innovation can also be seen in Albert's emphasis on education, on the re-fashioning of converts in a more sharply defined Christian mould. It can be seen most clearly of all in the implanting in the Baltic of religious orders dedicated to missionary warfare. Here we must digress a little.

In southern France in the early eleventh century, bishops and abbots had formed the habit of coming together in council in the face of increasing levels of disorder and social dislocation in the wake of the collapse of the Carolingian empire to proclaim what was called the Peace or the Truce of God. These were prohibitions of violence shown towards certain peoples or in certain places (the Peace), or at certain times and seasons (the Truce), and they were enforced by spiritual sanctions such as excommunication. But fallen human nature was found to require more sharply immediate curbing, so the ecclesiastical authorities acquired the habit of permitting – sometimes even commissioning – groups of knights, as we might say vigilantes, to enforce observance of the peace. In this fashion the novel idea that knights might band together to employ force in a worthy cause under ecclesiastical leadership took root in western Christendom. From then onwards we can trace confraternities, 'brotherhoods', of knights who would come together for some specific purpose, military or quasi-military, with the approval of the church. Such confraternities tended to be ephemeral. There was no need for them to outlive the accomplishment of the purpose for which they had been founded. For example, the confraternity of Belchite was established in 1122 in order to defend the Aragonese town of that name, on the exposed frontier between Christian and Muslim in eastern Spain, from Islamic counter-attack. We know that the brotherhood was still in existence in 1136, but thereafter we hear no more of it. Presumably it faded away when the frontier had become more secure and its services were no longer required. However, a few of these bodies became permanent institutions. The most prominent such was the order of the Temple.

This confraternity originated in the second decade of the twelfth century as a group of knights who bound themselves together by taking the monastic vows of poverty, chastity and obedience for the purpose of escorting pilgrims on the dangerous roads between the Palestinian coastline and Jerusalem. (They owed their name to the fact that they were allotted a residence in the city which was thought to stand on the site of King Solomon's temple.) Quite soon, however, the military skills of the Templars were being employed by the rulers of the crusader kingdom of Jerusalem – always chronically short of reliable troops – as a Christian knighthood in the ceaseless struggle with the forces of middle-eastern Islam. In the years 1127–8 the first master of the order, a knight from Champagne named Hugh of Payens, visited western Europe to raise funds and recruits. At a church council held at Troyes, in his homeland, presided over by a papal legate, formal ecclesiastical approval was extended to the Templars. Still more important, Bernard of Clairvaux (who may have been a remote kinsman of Hugh) wrote a pamphlet which was influential in publicizing them. It was called *De Laude Novae Militiae* (*In Praise of the New Knighthood*). In a short compass, and with all the eloquence of which he was a master, Bernard outlined the salient features of what must have seemed a contradiction in terms to some contemporaries, a way of life by which a man could achieve salvation by doing battle with the enemies of God. With papal approval and Cistercian advocacy the Templars were irresistible. Their twelfth-century success, not just as warriors but also as the hapless recipients of generous donations which forced them to become international bankers as well, was a spur to emulation.

The Templars were copied wherever Christian and Muslim faced one another. In Spain and Portugal the military orders of Calatrava, Santiago and Alcántara, as well as some smaller ones such as Aviz and Mountjoy, were founded in the third quarter of the twelfth century. In the crusading states of Outremer an order was founded by German participants in the Third Crusade in about 1190. It came to be known as the Teutonic Order of St Mary's Hospital in Jerusalem. Its recruitment was mainly German and its primary purpose was the defence of the Christian presence in the Holy Land.

This, then, was the background to Bishop Albert's initiative in founding, in about 1202, a military religious order specifically devoted to the forwarding of the church's mission. The order was formally entitled the Fratres Militiae Christi de Livonia, the 'Brothers of the Knighthood of Christ of Livonia', though commonly known as the *Schwertbrüder* or Sword Brothers. In founding the order, Bishop Albert killed three birds with one stone. In the first place they were a permanent and a professional presence. They were not amateurs who went home to Germany at the end of the campaigning season, like the crusaders in 1198, thereby undoing all its hard-won achievements. The Sword Brothers were always there to act as garrison or field-force for the defence of episcopal lordship in Livonia. Secondly, they were from the first closely associated with mission. Their job was to subdue the heathen so that they could then be baptized and taught by priests like Henry. Thus the offensive warfare waged by the Brothers would contribute to a durable Christian society. This was a new departure for a military order. The earlier ones had been concerned with the traditionally just task of repossessing lands which had once been in Christian hands. Papal approval was forthcoming from Pope Innocent III and his successor Honorius III for the dual task of subjugating the heathen and defending the missions. Clearly, in practice, there was a very fine line indeed between these tasks on the one hand and imposing Christianity at the point of the sword on the other. Thus, imperceptibly, the link between institutionalized aggression and spreading the Christian faith became closer. Finally, Albert made sure that the Brothers were not autonomous. The Templars had been answerable only to the pope, and this had made them a state within a state in Outremer, with disastrous political and military consequences for the crusader kingdom of Jerusalem. The Sword Brothers were subordinate to the bishop of Riga, at least in theory. As matters turned out the relationship would prove exceedingly tempestuous.

A second order was soon founded in the north-east in imitation of the Sword Brothers. This was the order of the Fratres Militiae Christi de Livonia contra Prutenos, the 'Brothers of the Knighthood of Christ of Livonia against the Prussians', commonly known as the Knights of Dobrin. This order was founded by the Cistercian bishop Christian of Prussia in about 1207 and it was given the fort of Dobrin (Dobrzyn) on the Vistula to serve as its military base. It had the same characteristics as the order of the Sword Brothers.

The two Livonian orders did not enjoy independence for long. The Knights of Dobrin were always a small band, and their vulnerability to a take-over was increased when their patron Bishop Christian was taken prisoner by the Prussians and spent several years in captivity. The Sword Brothers quarrelled with successive bishops – soon archbishops – of Riga, for example over the division of the spoils of war. They were said to be, as we might say, over-zealous in their treatment of native Livonians. Ugly rumours made their way back to Rome, but the Brothers resolutely refused to allow themselves to be inspected.

And then finally, in 1236, the Sword Brothers were decisively defeated in an incautious campaign against the Lithuanians, a disaster which effectively annihilated the order.

The beneficiaries were the Knights of the Teutonic Order. Their role in the crusader states gradually dwindled as those states themselves dwindled in the course of the thirteenth century. (I drastically simplify a complicated story.) From the 1220s the Teutonic Order's activities were diversifying on to Latin Christendom's eastern frontier, first in Hungary and then in the Baltic. They were on hand to swallow up the Knights of Dobrin and to pick up the pieces after the wreck of the Sword Brothers, thus acquiring geographically distinct responsibilities in Prussia and Livonia. Although in theory they remained committed to fighting Muslims in Palestine and Syria, this objective became unrealistic after the fall of Acre in 1291, the loss of the last Christian outpost on the Syrian mainland. The headquarters of the Teutonic Knights was transferred initially to Venice, where they waited for a generation for the next crusade. But it never came. In 1309 the order finally came to rest at Marienburg (Malbork) in Prussia, in formal recognition of what had long been the case, that its primary military role lay in the subjugation of the heathen peoples of the north-east.

But in the early thirteenth century the Sword Brothers had been a significant new force in the extension of Christian dominion in the Baltic. Henry of Livonia brought his narrative to an end with the conquest of the island of Ösel (Saaremaa) at the mouth of the Gulf of Riga in 1227 and the mass baptism of its inhabitants. It was one of the last of Bishop Albert's triumphs. *Sic Riga nationes rigat.* 'Thus does Riga water the nations.' It was a pun of which Henry never tired. Heavy-footed though his wordplay might be, Henry remains an attractive figure, in his devotion to duty, in his generous loyalties, in his surprising talents – he once saved lives by charming some hostile Estonians by his playing of the harp. Above all he was at heart a man of peace, like the chronicler Helmold of Bosau whom we met in Chapter 12. Henry was well aware that coercion might be necessary, but it should be limited. It was a means, not an end. The end was saving souls, and that could be accomplished only by baptizing, teaching, preaching, church-building, getting on with the converts in their own language (at which Henry was skilled). When he finished writing everything seemed to be going well. He ended his chronicle on a note of optimism.

For another generation or so Henry's optimism might have seemed justified. Christendom's frontiers steadily expanded in the north-east, despite setbacks like the destruction of the Sword Brothers in 1236. In Prussia the Teutonic Knights gradually subjugated the area between the Vistula and the Niemen. Bishoprics were established at Chelmno (Kulm) in 1232, at Marienwerder in 1243 and at Königsberg (Kaliningrad) in 1255 – the latter named in honour of King Ottokar of Bohemia, who had gone crusading as a guest of the Knights in 1254.[7] In uneasy partnership with the archbishops of Riga they did likewise in the northern, Livonian zone of their operations. In Estonia a crusade led by the Danish King Valdemar II and Archbishop Andrew of Lund in 1219 led to the foundation of a town, like Riga, at Tallinn (Reval, Kalyban) and the setting up of a bishopric there. German settlers and Dominican friars consolidated the Christian presence. An episcopal see was founded at Dorpat – one of Albert of Riga's brothers its first bishop, another its first dean. Still further to the north, across the gulf, lay Finland. Swedes had been raiding and trading there for many years, and stories – almost certainly apocryphal – would circulate of a 'first Finnish crusade' led by King Eric IX and Bishop Henry of Uppsala in the middle years of the twelfth century. Be that as it may, there seem to have been some modest Christian communities among the people of south-west Finland, known as the Suomi, by about 1200. In 1209 Pope Innocent III sanctioned the creation of a bishopric, whose seat came in time to be fixed at Turku (Åbo). Thomas, its incumbent from about 1220 to 1245, was an Englishman, a patron of the Dominican friars and an active missionary to the inland regions.

But Henry of Livonia's optimism would prove misplaced, as perhaps even he came to realize as his long life wound to its close. A chilly wind began to blow on every frontier of Christendom as the thirteenth century unfolded, which may have had its effects upon changing attitudes in the mission field. New and aggressive Muslim powers emerged in north Africa, the Merinids in Morocco and the Mameluks in Egypt. The plight of what was left of the crusader states of Outremer steadily worsened until the last guttering remnant of Christian dominion was snuffed out in 1291. A terrifying menace emerged from central Asia in the form of the Mongols, whose raids were probing as far west as Silesia and Hungary in the 1240s. Swedes, Danes and Teutonic Knights came face to hostile face with the adherents of the Greco-Russian Orthodox churches as they pushed eastwards into Finland,

Estonia and Livonia. By this time the crusades – and especially the Fourth Crusade, which had sacked Constantinople in 1204 – had sharpened the animosity between the rival Christendoms of Greek east and Latin west. Inland to the south of Riga a new and powerful heathen principality of Lithuania was beginning to flex its muscles. We shall return to it shortly. Finally, on the Baltic doorstep, it was becoming ever plainer that subjugated Prussians and Livs and Estonians, Tavastians and Karelians and Vods, did not want the Christianity that was being thrust upon them by the orders of friars and knights.

It was in certain ways like eighth-century Saxony all over again. The pagan peoples of the eastern Baltic perceived in Christianity a threat to all that they held most dear. They resisted it stubbornly. The Christian aggressors, largely but not exclusively the Teutonic Knights, exasperated, met resistance with violence. To take one example, the people of Ösel, whose subjugation and baptism Henry of Livonia had celebrated, apostasized and rebelled in 1260 in the wake of a serious defeat for the Teutonic Order at the battle of Durbe.

> The Öselians were glad that the Brothers had lost the battle on the Dvina and welcomed the news. Soon they took counsel with one another and decided to live free and oppose the knights of God, for it was a cause of heartfelt sorrow to them that pure Christianity had taken root in their land. All the Öselians, young and old, broke away and left not a single Christian alive in all their territories. Later many of them were destroyed for doing this.

This information, and the detailed description of the harsh reprisals which followed, comes from the *Livländische Reimchronik* or *Livonian Rhymed Chronicle*, a history of the Livonian crusades in verse composed in about 1290 by an anonymous author who was probably a member of the Teutonic Order.[8] It is an unsettling document. The Rhymer shared emphatically in the new order of assumptions which came to the fore in the thirteenth century. For him, Christian service in Livonia was about unremitting war against pagans. A Christian army could 'yearn for battle like a hungry falcon'. God had sent the Knights to Livonia 'so that we should expand our dominion'. It was good therefore to slaughter pagans: 'Many were killed before the land was conquered, but to break a stubborn stone one has to strike hard . . . They took [a camp on Ösel] by storm and slew both young and old;

501

very few who had been inside survived.' For the Knights, the most glorious of deaths was in battle with the enemies of God. It was martyrdom, as the rhymer could say of the 150 Brothers 'martyred' at the battle of Durbe, or of the fifty-two who 'spilt their blood for God' on the winter's ice in 1270 while attempting to subdue – yet again – the stubborn Öselians. The Knights themselves put the nub of the matter like this in 1309. 'The sword is our pope.'[9]

The residence of the bishop of Ösel at Kuressaare (Arensburg) was built as a great stone blockhouse with a watchtower at one corner and few windows.[10] Its stones speak as eloquently as does the Rhymer's verse of the spirit of the Baltic crusades. And just as the Rhymer never so much as mentions a pastoral ministry to those of the subjugated pagans who were left alive, so the residences of Christian authority such as Arensburg or, on a vaster scale, the Order's headquarters at Marienburg, are striking for what they are not. They were not there to offer to the defeated a faith which might come with the passage of time to be inclusive – as another anonymous poet, the author of the *Heliand*, had sought to present it to the Saxons back in the ninth century. These buildings were designed as tools of colonial dominance. And that, roughly speaking, is the theme of the Christianization of the lands which came to constitute the so-called *Ordenstaat* or 'Order-state', the effectively independent political entity ruled by the Teutonic Knights on the shores of the Baltic during the fourteenth and fifteenth centuries.

By the middle years of the thirteenth century Christianity had reached as far north as it effectively could. At the top of the Gulf of Bothnia, inside the Arctic Circle, visitors from the south encountered the nomad Lapps. Suppliers of furs and feathers to a chain of trafficking which led ultimately to the wardrobes and mattresses of the European super-rich, the Lapps became attached to the demand economy of the settled world. But the religion of that settled world has never found a permanent haven among nomads, whether in Lapland or along the eastern and southern desert fringes of the Mediterranean. From time to time the churches of Norway would claim jurisdiction over the Lapps; so too the Orthodox churches of northern Russia. But there is no indication that these claims meant anything. The Lapps probably knew a little about Christianity, may have borrowed elements from it, as they previously had from Nordic heathenism, into their own pagan religious culture: but that was about the limit of it. Christianity did not strike roots among the medieval Lapps.

The Lapps were a mysterious people of whom settled Europeans knew little that was accurate. Except by those who traded with them, they could be ignored. The same could not be said of the Lithuanians. In the course of the thirteenth century the warlords of the Niemen (Nemunas, Neman) river system had built up a strong if unstable principality by means of the intelligent exploitation of circumstances which bear some resemblance to those exploited with equal skill by barbarian warlords of an earlier day, such as the Slav princes Pribina and Rastislav in the ninth century. Lithuania was well placed to link the commerce of the Baltic to that of the Black Sea and thus to grow rich on the profits from tolls and protection money. The primary agrarian products which were the staples of the Lithuanian economy – grain, hides, flax, honey, cheese – could be shipped downriver for sale to the cold and hungry burghers of Riga. The spoils of incessant warfare with neighbours to east and west yielded a human booty which could be sold into slavery or, if worth it, ransomed. A system for the exaction of military service made it possible for Lithuania's leaders to put effective armies regularly into the field. Their soldiers had mastered the art of operating in a challenging terrain in such a manner as to be frequently baffling and often fatal to their enemies. Skilled leadership, military expertise and the effective exploitation of wealth combined to bring about an expansion in the scope of Lithuanian hegemony in the course of the thirteenth and fourteenth centuries. From a nucleus around Vilnius in about 1200 the territory of what came to be known as the grand duchy of Lithuania was roughly co-terminous with the modern republic by about 1250. A century later it encompassed in addition what we now know as Belarus, parts of eastern Poland and some of the northern Ukraine (including Kiev).

Lithuanian rulers of the time would have seen the favour of their gods made manifest in their wealth and military might. Lithuanian paganism worked – like the Wendish paganism of the eleventh and twelfth centuries – and would prove hard to displace. As usual, we can discover not a great deal about it. We hear of a god called Perkunas, of the sky and of war, who may have been worshipped as a high god, supreme in Lithuania's pantheon. There were many other gods and goddesses, of cows and bees and flax, of dawn and winter and lakes and death, and swarms of lesser spirits and goblins. There were priests and priestesses, sacred places in woods or at rocks and streams, sacrifices both animal and occasionally human, auguries to be read in the behaviour of horses, snakes and pigs. The extent to which all this devout apparatus was organized into what has been called 'a sort of counter-church' remains debatable.[11] Some Christian writers of the fourteenth century thought that it had. One of them even claimed, implausibly, that the Lithuanians had a sort of rival pope of their own. It is not impossible that the pre-Christian traditional religion of the Lithuanians could have been as organized as the worship of Triglaus or Svantovit may once have been among their near neighbours the northern Slavs.

Naturally, there were contacts with Christianity. Raiding brought Christian captives into Lithuania just as it had done into Gothic Dacia long ago in the age of Gregory Thaumaturgus and Ulfila. The territorial expansion of Lithuania brought Christians both Latin (Poles) and Orthodox (Russians) under the rule of the grand dukes, just as Frankish expansion in Gaul had brought many Christians under the rule of Merovingian kings such as Childeric and Clovis. These Christian subjects of the grand dukes were very numerous; they could have outnumbered the ethnic, pagan Lithuanians in the proportion of something like seven or eight to one by the second half of the fourteenth century. A writer of the mid-thirteenth thought that the Lithuanian aristocracy would be easy to convert because so many of its members had been brought up by Christian wet-nurses and nannies![12] Foreign merchants brought their faith with them, just as they had done in earlier centuries to the ports of the north German and Danish coastlines. It was not by chance that a Catholic church built for them in Vilnius in the early fourteenth century was dedicated to St Nicholas, the patron saint of merchants. The lure of western, specifically German expertise was strong. In 1323 the Grand Duke Gediminas sent an open letter to Lübeck, Bremen, Magdeburg and other cities appealing for immigrants with skills as smiths, carpenters, masons, tanners, millers and so forth. The settlers were encouraged to bring their faith with them; indeed, copies of the letter were sent to the Franciscan and Dominican convents of Germany. A complicated web of diplomacy bound the Lithuanian ruling dynasty into the princely houses of Christendom. At least five daughters of Gediminas were despatched in marriage to Christian husbands. One expatriate Lithuanian prince, Daumantas, became ruler of the Russian statelet of Pskov, adopted the Orthodox faith and after his death in 1299 was revered as the patron saint of Pskov under the title of St Timofey.

Nevertheless, Lithuania remained officially pagan. As Gediminas put the matter to papal envoys in 1324, 'Christians worship their god after their own fashion – the Russians according to their rite, the Poles according to their rite – and we worship god according to our rite: we all have one god.'[13] This remarkable statement may be interpreted as evidence of a certain tendency towards monotheism in the religious development of the Lithuanian elite, which parallels a similar tendency among other peoples of pre-Christian Europe (though doubtless some allowance must be made for the gloss which the envoys put upon what they had heard in their report to their master the pope). If there were such a tendency it did not necessarily make that elite more sympathetic to Christianity. The grand dukes found that it was prudent to move very cautiously in any contemplation of an official change of religious allegiance. They had to respect the susceptibilities of their leading men just as Clovis or Edwin had had to do, or risk a bloody confrontation of the sort which had nearly cost Khan Boris of the Bulgars his life. Christian priests who sought publicly to make converts among pagan Lithuanians did so at the risk of their lives. Two Franciscans from Bohemia who did just this were executed in about 1340. Right to the very end the full panoply of pagan ritual was maintained for state occasions. The Grand Duke Kestutis, who died in 1382, was cremated at Vilnius splendidly adorned and armed, and with him his horses, hounds and hawks. It was a magnificent send-off, thoroughly traditional in character. None of those who witnessed it could have guessed that the obsequies of Kestutis would prove to be the last pagan state funeral in European history.

The prospect of an official acceptance of Christianity proved to be the strongest diplomatic card held by Lithuania's rulers. They played it again and again, with great skill, throughout the thirteenth and the fourteenth centuries. Grand Duke Mindaugas (*c.* 1219–63) accepted Roman Christianity from Pope Innocent IV in 1251 in order to detach the Teutonic Order from a hostile coalition formed against him by the Russians of Galicia-Volynia to his south. The proper motions were gone through. The pope granted him the status of a king and sent him a royal crown, just as his predecessor had bestowed title and crown upon King Stephen of Hungary two and a half centuries earlier. Mindaugas built a cathedral at Vilnius which was excavated in the

1980s. It was of brick and stone, not of wood, which was the traditional building material in Lithuania, and it was in the new 'gothic' architectural style. But contemporaries were unconvinced of his sincerity. Mindaugas, like Redwald of East Anglia long before, seems merely to have tackled on another god to the existing pantheon. His baptism 'was only for appearances – secretly he made sacrifices to the gods', as a Russian chronicler commented. When political pressures had eased, in 1261, Mindaugas renounced Catholicism. The cathedral at Vilnius was demolished and a pagan temple built in its place.

Grand Duke Gediminas (1315–41) flirted with Greco-Russian Orthodox Christianity early in his reign. He sponsored a short-lived metropolitanate in Lithuania for his numerous Orthodox subjects which was theoretically obedient to the patriarch of Constantinople. There was an Orthodox church in Vilnius for visiting Russian merchants. But he also toyed with Catholicism, putting out feelers to Pope John XXII in 1322 and hinting that he might accept Roman Christianity. (His correspondence with the pope was handled by two Franciscan secretaries.) A fascinating glimpse of the dispassionate calculations of this complex world of diplomacy and *Realpolitik* is furnished by a report of the papal envoys on this occasion. They wrote that Gediminas's decision not to accept Christianity had been taken *on the advice of a Dominican friar*. This man, Nicholas, seems to have been the grand duke's adviser on his religious policies and we should very much like to know more of him than we do, what his background was and how he had come to occupy this position in the counsels of Gediminas. Brother Nicholas, it seems, had urged that if Roman Christianity were to be adopted it should only be at the hands of a more powerful protector than the pope's current man-on-the-spot, the archbishop of Riga.

It was indeed a tangled web. From whom you accepted Christianity, and what might come with it in the way of political advantage, mattered to the rulers of the Lithuanians in the fourteenth century just as much as these factors had mattered to earlier rulers of Franks, Anglo-Saxons, Danes, Moravians, Bulgarians, Magyars or Wends. Similar manoeuvring continued during the reign of Gediminas's successor Algirdas (1345–77). Approaches were made to the pope on three occasions and to the patriarch on two. The controlling factor throughout was the Teutonic Order. The *Ordenstaat* commanded the most remorseless war-machine in north-eastern Europe and was slowly but surely making territorial gains. In 1346, for example, just after the succession of Algirdas to the grand duchy, the Order had bought out Danish claims over Estonia, thus strengthening its position on the shores of the Gulf of Finland. Lithuania was unavoidably the principal target of the Knights' aggression. This was partly because it was the only pagan state left in Europe. It was partly because the westernmost spur of Lithuanian territory in the lower valley of the river Niemen cut the Order's Prussian lands off from its Livonian and Estonian ones. Rulers like Gediminas or Algirdas needed only to glance at the fate of the Prussians or the Livonians to see what was involved in Christianization at the hands of men animated by the ideals of the Rhymer. So they fought back like tigers; but it was a losing battle.

For over a century the grand dukes of Lithuania hesitated between east and west, Orthodoxy and Catholicism, Constantinople and Rome.* During the same period the pressure of the Teutonic Order became steadily more intense. A sharp crisis, of dissension within the Lithuanian ruling dynasty, finally precipitated matters. The successor of Kestutis, Jogaila, decided in 1385 to opt for Roman Catholicism, but a Catholicism that came to him not from the Order but from Poland. In the year 1384 the throne of Poland was inherited by the ten-year-old princess Jadwiga. Poland was worth a mass. The Lithuanian diplomats moved swiftly. In the summer of 1385 a plan was agreed for the dynastic merger of Poland and Lithuania. Jadwiga and Jogaila were to marry, their two countries were to be joined and the pagan Lithuanians were to accept Catholic Christianity. It all went ahead as planned. On 15 February 1385 Jogaila was baptized at Cracow under the name of Władysław (Ladislas). Three days later he was married to Jadwiga. On 4 March he was crowned king of Poland. His leading men were baptized and in their turn undertook to bring about the baptism of their dependants. Medieval Latin Christendom was at last formally complete.

---

* Strictly speaking, for most of the period, Avignon rather than Rome: the papacy was based at Avignon from 1309 to 1378.

CHAPTER FIFTEEN

Slouching Towards Bethlehem

The great thing is indeed that the muddled state too is one of the very sharpest of the realities, that it also has colour and form and character, has often in fact a broad and rich comicality, many of the signs and values of the appreciable.

HENRY JAMES, Preface (1909) to *What Maisie Knew*

THE ACCEPTANCE OF Christianity in Lithuania put the last piece of a jigsaw puzzle into place. It has been a long haul from Gregory Thaumaturgus to Jogaila Algirdaitis, from the age of Origen to that of Chaucer. The events of 1386 did mark the culmination of a process. Something was over. Something had been accomplished.

Accomplished in a formal sense, at any rate. But Christianization was as slow in Lithuania as it was elsewhere. In the earliest surviving text in the Lithuanian tongue, a catechism composed by the Protestant pastor Martin Mazvydas published in 1547, the author thought it appropriate repeatedly to condemn the cult of the god Perkunas. In a letter written shortly afterwards to his patron Duke Albert of Brandenburg, the friend of Martin Luther, Mazvydas lamented the irreligion of his flock. They did not go to church, did not abstain from work on Sundays, did not know the Lord's Prayer, did not receive the sacraments. The sentiments might have been expressed by Caesarius of Arles or Gregory of Tours, by Bede or by Hincmar. 'If I may be frank, they know the true Christian religion as much as infants in their cradles do.'[1] The pre-Christian practice of cremation was not abandoned in parts of Lithuania until about Mazvydas's day. The dead were being interred in non-Christian burial grounds, sometimes accompanied by a bull or a horse, until far into the seventeenth century, the age of Pascal and of Milton, of Leibnitz and Newton and Locke.

The lamentations of Mazvydas were being echoed by his contemporaries in Germany, where Christianity had of course been established for half a millennium longer than it had in Lithuania. Investigation of the parochial visitation records of the sixteenth and seventeenth centuries has yielded to a modern enquirer evidence of 'an adult population on whose everyday lives and thoughts the formal religion appears to have made scarcely an impact' and of 'pastoral incompetence so egregious as to be scarcely believable'.[2] A visitation in Saxony in 1584 found that the parishioners were 'completely ignorant . . . they drink brandy all day long on Sundays and are unmoved by warnings and punishments'. Another in 1617 reported that the laity were 'like the dumb beasts of the field, without an inkling of the word of God'. Diviners and soothsayers had been outlawed in Saxony by Charlemagne; but they were still doing a lively trade in the sixteenth century. Typically, in one parish in 1579, the visitors found 'an old woman with a crystal, and people run to her whenever something troubles them'.

When Mazvydas referred to 'the true Christian religion' he meant the religion of Protestants. True religion meant going to church every Sunday to hear scripture and catechism expounded. His letter to Duke Albert reveals that in Lithuania in the middle years of the sixteenth century the cult of the saints was a lively matter, that people would travel – sometimes quite far – to join in the festivities of saints' days, would light candles for saints in their own homes. But for Mazvydas this veneration of the saints was 'abominable idolatry . . . a papist custom'. These judgements bring us face to face once more with a difficulty we have encountered on several occasions in the course of this book. The laity had been encouraged by their priests to revere the saints with festivities and with candles. Then in the sixteenth century their priests started to tell them that this was idolatrous. Fashions in piety had changed. Requirements had become stricter. The line between the encouraged and the unacceptable had been redrawn in a different place. It is that most perplexing question on the agenda outlined in Chapter 1: what makes a Christian?

We must resist the temptation of supposing that with reference to the sixteenth and seventeenth centuries the question could be answered simply on sectarian lines. Naturally enough, any one branch of the luxuriant tree which was Christendom – Catholic, Lutheran, Calvinist, whatever – would have claimed exclusive access to the correct answer, and until recently the answers given have been robustly defended by protective traditions of sectarian historical writing. But it is striking to the historian of that period today that pastoral anxieties were shared, were interdenominational, and so too – at any rate up to a point – were pastoral remedies. 'The common man cannot even say the Lord's Prayer or the Ave Maria with the right words, and does not know the Apostles' Creed, to say nothing of the Ten Commandments.' The reference to the Ave betrays the Catholic origin of this cry of dismay. Remove that, and the sentiment could have been uttered by Martin Mazvydas or any of the Lutheran inspectors of Saxon parishes. In fact the words occur in a letter from the archbishop of Salzburg in Catholic Bavaria to the elector Maximilian I in the year 1608.

Building upon the widespread evidence of lax observance, of shared concerns and overlapping remedies, the French historian Jean Delumeau has boldly suggested a re-interpretation of the Christian history of the early modern period.

> On the eve of the Reformation, the average westerner was but superficially christianized. In this context the two Reformations, Luther's and Rome's, were two processes, which apparently competed but in actual fact converged, by which the masses were christianized and religion spiritualized . . . If the seventeenth century was the golden age of Christianization, especially in France, it was because the missionaries tried to reach the rural world, whereas the preachers of the fourteenth and fifteenth centuries had contacted above all the urban public.[3]

Delumeau had earlier made a special study of Brittany. He discovered that the most bizarre religious observances were being practised there in the seventeenth century. Breton villagers made offerings of bread and butter at springs, or of grain round the boundaries of fields. (Martin of Braga had been complaining of such things in his *De Correctione Rusticorum* in sixth-century Galicia.) They put stones out as seats near the domestic hearth on the eve of St John the Baptist's day so that returning ancestors could sit in warmth when paying a family visit. The wives of fishermen would collect dust from churches and then throw it into the air while muttering charms to secure favourable winds for their seafaring menfolk. Faced by such practices the high-minded clergy of seventeenth-century France saw themselves as missionaries on their home territory. St Vincent de Paul held that his mission was to 'the poor people of the fields' as well as, more famously, to prisoners in the galleys. The Lazarist order which he founded was designed to undertake a rural mission. Julien Maunoir spent his pastoral career in Brittany administering correction to the rustics there. His biographer Fr. Boschet entitled his memoir of Maunoir, published in 1697, *Le parfait missionaire*. In it he wrote revealingly that the Breton mission brought about 'something akin to what the pagans experienced when the first apostles preached to them'. Things were as bad as that. Some thought they were a great deal worse. It was, to an extent, despair of the condition of the church in Spain which led the 'Twelve Apostles of Mexico' to set sail in 1519. The church in the Old World was beyond redemption. They would build the just city, the City of God, in the New.

In other words, their predecessors had got it all wrong, made a mess of things, let standards slide. Reforming do-gooders are almost invariably priggish. In a sense they have to be, for their credibility depends upon the alleged mistakes of others. This is not to deny that on occasion reformers may have every justification for righteous indignation at the lack of zeal of their forerunners. After all, standards *do* slide. Targets of excellence have to be proclaimed. From a certain point of view Christian history is all about the intermittent reiteration of standards of observance. The archbishop of Salzburg in 1608 was echoing – whether he was aware of it or not – the concerns expressed in the correspondence that passed between his predecessor Archbishop Arn and his counsellor Alcuin of York eight centuries beforehand; there are continuities of pastoral concern because there are discontinuities of behaviour (or continuities of Original Sin). Irish monasticism had taught Christendom new forms of evangelism and spirituality in the early Middle Ages, but by the end of the Middle Ages it had sunk into such torpor and corruption as might have caused astonishment even to an abuse-hardened parochial inspector from sixteenth-century Saxony. Abbess Emma of San Juan de las Abadesas had conscientiously established rural churches in tenth-century Catalonia. Five centuries later the same region was notorious as one where standards of pastoral ministry were among the most slovenly and degraded to be encountered anywhere in western Christendom. If Vincent de Paul and Maunoir saw rural France as missionary territory in the seventeenth century, so did their successors in the nineteenth.

Backslidings and refurbishments are easy enough for the historian to cope with. The trouble is that the shrill denunciations of reforming rhetoric can easily conceal – are sometimes intended to conceal – changing assumptions, expectations and definitions from view. Standards of observance have not been unvarying. It may be that historians of the Delumeau tendency have been gulled by that rhetoric. Other historians of early modern Christianity have taken a different view. Here are the carefully chosen words of John Bossy, in his thoughtful introduction to the English translation of Delumeau's book. 'I think it is possible to believe that the rural church of medieval Europe did, in its own mode, transmit a respectable view of Christianity to the average rustic.' It is a judgement that must command respect. It is moreover one that can to a degree be tested and measured in the light of the surviving evidence. Consider the case of England. Recent investigation by such historians as Eamon Duffy has revealed the exuberant vitality of traditional lay piety in the later Middle Ages.[4] These widespread pieties of later medieval Europe (not just England) sprang from earlier foundations which rested deep down, which went back to the pastoral impulses generated by the fourth Lateran council of 1215, and beyond to the age of church-building at which we looked in Chapter 13. Contemplating this evidence of active, vibrant, pullulating religiosity, the judgement of yet another distinguished scholar that later medieval England was 'in the fullest sense a Christian country' is irresistibly persuasive.[5] But the reformers of the sixteenth and seventeenth centuries would not have agreed. They found these pieties wanting. They judged them superstitious, idolatrous, blind, popish. Godliness was defined by the reformers in new ways.

For the historian of medieval missions and the conversion of the new barbarian arrivals in the late- or post-Roman worlds and their eastern and northern neighbours considerations such as these can be discouraging. It was pointed out in Chapter 1, and on more than one occasion in subsequent chapters, that because we are so ignorant about the content and workings of pre-Christian traditional paganisms we can know very little indeed about what people were being converted *from*. Because of the ceaseless process of redefinition of expectations and requirements – as well, of course, as the paucity of evidence – it is almost equally difficult to make out what they were being converted *to*. Small wonder that for the historian a muddled state does indeed all too frequently seem one of the very sharpest of the realities.

The 'received notions' about conversion held by most western historians largely derive – possibly more than they are aware – from the very influential study by William James (brother of Henry) published in 1902 under the title *The Varieties of Religious Experience*. James was a high-minded New Englander, son of a theologian, a man of intense intellectual cultivation who held chairs at Harvard, successively of psychology and of philosophy, for twenty years. His studies of religious experience focused upon 'cases' who were literate and articulate, drawn predominantly from the British and North American cultures of the period between about 1600 and 1900, and to a great degree from what might be broadly termed the Protestant and evangelical tradition: educated persons who could recount the odyssey of an individual soul. Conversion, for James, was something intense and individual and spiritual. This was a perception of the experience that was widely shared in the Anglo-American world of the nineteenth century. These assumptions lie behind what is the most famous single study of the subject which has reference to the early centuries of the Christian era, Arthur Darby Nock's *Conversion. The Old and the New in Religion from Alexander the Great to Augustine of Hippo*, published in 1933, in which the author paid tribute to William James in his opening chapter. Nock's book is still a marvellously fresh and invigorating read, the essential starting-point for any study of religious change in antiquity. Here is his definition of conversion.

> By conversion we mean the reorientation of the soul of an individual, his deliberate turning from indifference or from an earlier form of piety to another, a turning which implies a consciousness that a great change is involved, that the old was wrong and the new is right . . . Judaism and Christianity demanded renunciation and a new start. They demanded not merely the acceptance of a rite, but the adhesion of the will to a theology, in a word faith, a new life in a new people.[6]

Nock's was a 'high and dry' understanding of the process of conversion. Historians, especially academic historians, approve of the educated and the articulate. During the period embraced by this book there lived only two persons whose spiritual odysseys may be charted in some detail. The first is St Augustine of Hippo (d. 430), who both in his *Confessions*, briefly alluded to in Chapter 1, and in his voluminous other writings, has left us an unsurpassed account of the progress of a soul towards and within Christianity. The second is St Anselm of Aosta, monk and abbot of Bec in Normandy and finally a reluctant archbishop of Canterbury (d. 1109). Anselm's spiritual portrait was painted not only in his own letters and meditations and treatises but also in the remarkable biography by his friend and disciple the English monk Eadmer. Both Augustine and Anselm were highly intelligent, widely cultivated men who wrote of their beliefs and emotions and spiritual struggles with fluency and directness. They were in this wholly uncharacteristic of their respective ages or of any age that came between them. The overwhelming majority of persons who accepted Christianity during the period of our study were neither literate nor articulate. When they received the faith they did so, for the most part, millions and millions of them, because they were told to or because they were born into it. The struggles they experienced in the course of their usually short lives were not spiritual but the harshest of material ones – just how to keep on going in a world that was chronically short of food, warmth and health. How much did Augustine's Christian faith have in common with that of the up-country Numidian farmers who cultivated the hinterland of his native town of Thagaste? Not a great deal, we might guess. And it is surely implausible, we may suppose, to imagine that Anselm's spiritual quest was in any manner shared by the goatherds of his childhood Alpine valleys, or by the apple-growers of the Roumois, or by the flinty farmers of east Kent.

In describing their own spiritual growth, in articulating interiority, Augustine and Anselm were wholly exceptional. This is, of course, not to claim that they were unique in their experience of an intense individual religious faith. We may think of Patrick's extraordinary account of his vocation to become a missionary; we may speculate about what the unwritten *Apologia pro Vita Sua* of Bodo might have told us about the spiritual currents which carried him from Christianity into Judaism. But the spectacle of early medieval conversion to Christianity – or indeed to Islam, or indeed in some circumstances (consider the Khazars) to Judaism – is generally not one of individuals acting upon conviction. Nock's 'reorientation of the soul' does not seem the most appropriate way to describe the passage into Christianity of the subjects of Clovis or Ethelbert or Widukind or Boris or Olaf Tryggvason. Harald Bluetooth claimed that he had 'made the Danes Christian', not that he had reoriented their souls.

So what had he done? What *did* conversion mean to these people? As a way into this baffling question we might care to latch on to some of the words used by contemporaries to describe the process. It is immediately striking that 'conversion' was rarely so used. True, we do occasionally find the Latin word *conversio* employed to indicate what we understand by 'conversion', as by the anonymous author of the *Conversio Bagoariorum et Carantanorum Libellus*, composed at Salzburg in 870. But generally speaking the word *conversio* tended to be used to indicate not the shift from paganism to Christianity but the transition within a Christian dispensation from a less to a more intense form of the Christian life. It was the term most frequently employed for an individual's decision to adopt a 'regular' life, that is a life lived according to a rule, as by a monk or a nun. The words used to describe a ruler's or his people's adoption of Christianity tended to be verbs such as 'accepting' or 'submitting to'. 'At that time the West Saxons accepted the faith of Christ.' 'The fierce necks of the Saxons bowed to the light yoke of Christ.' Pribina received Christianity 'at the command of' King Louis the German. On the evidence of verbal usage alone conversion was presented as a fairly passive operation and it could involve the exercise of authority. What you accepted or submitted to might be described as a *fides*, which we usually translate 'faith' but which was often used with a rather wider meaning along the lines of 'body of Christian observance' or even with the social sense of 'Christian community'. It might also be described as a *ritus*, more than a 'rite' in the narrow sense, rather a 'set of cultic or propitiatory rituals', or as a *lex*, literally 'law', but by extension 'customs, tradition, right behaviour, proper way of doing things'. The body of words, of which this is but a sample, the semantic field, seems not to be about individuals but about collectivities and solidarities; not about theology but about conduct and disposition. *Pace* Nock, there was nothing 'mere' for early medieval men and women about the acceptance of a rite. The Northumbrians who grumbled about the abandonment of the *veteres culturas* knew this, and so did Bede, as ever didactic, who recorded the story. So did the Bulgars: worries about the correct performance of ritual lay at the heart of all those questions which they put to the pope in 866.

Acceptance of new ways of doing things implies at least some degree of dissatisfaction with the old – remembering always that such stirrings are possibly far from a readiness to jettison the old altogether. Anthropological study of modern societies which experience the transition from traditional polytheism to a world monotheism such as Christianity or Islam has highlighted the solvent effect of social change and dislocation upon age-old religious loyalties.[7] One such solvent is compounded of proximity to, interaction with and movement into a culture which is perceived as enjoying a more advanced civilization (in terms of wealth, technology, order, authority and so forth). In the course of this book we have seen repeated examples of the process at work. The Germanic outsiders who lived along and within the porous frontier zone of the Roman empire in the fourth and fifth centuries, for example, never ceased to admire its power and its wealth even when they felt cowed and humiliated by it, even when they entered it to share it out among themselves. This is readily intelligible. The post-Constantinian empire was an immensely imposing structure whose like has not been seen again in fifteen subsequent centuries of Europe's history. If worldly prosperity was a sign of divine favour – and there is every reason to suppose that the 'empirical religiosity' of the Germans led them to suppose that it was – then the High God of the Christians was worth cultivating. Entry to the empire, the process by which outsiders became insiders, meant adopting the empire's God. It was part of the business of changing your identity and self-perception from barbarian to a kind of Roman. So they all did it, though some more quickly than others. The Visigoths, as far as we can see, accepted Christianity very soon after their entry to the empire as refugees in 376. By contrast, those offshore islanders the Anglo-Saxons were in this context as in some later ones notably slow; but they joined in the end, and with a zeal not always matched in subsequent couplings to Europe. Comparable juxtapositions in later centuries precipitated similar religious changes, due allowance being made for the variables of circumstance. Settlement within the eastern Roman empire brought the southern Slavs and the Bulgars, eventually, into the Christian fold. Proximity to and relationship with the Frankish kingdom and its successor the Ottonian *Reich* brought Christianity to Frisians, Carantanians, Bohemians, Magyars, Poles. The Vikings respected western European civilization even as they looted it and settled within its boundaries, and the shrewdest of them, Canute, became (or was presented as) the most ostentatiously Christian ruler of his day. It is a moot point whether any European paganism has ever survived the movement of its adherents into a different environment. The only possible example from the period surveyed in this book is the case of Iceland. But it is not a convincing one, partly because there seems to have been a modest Christian presence from the first among the settlers, partly because they were not joining a culture perceived as dominant but settling on an uninhabited volcanic rock in the middle of the Atlantic.

The imposition of alien rule and with it the imposition of Christianity as an instrument of cultural dominance was a variant form of interaction. The conquest of Saxony by Charlemagne in the eighth century is a good example. It involved the violent and calculated dislocation of Saxon society so that it could be remade in a Frankish and Christian image. The savagery was a little mitigated by the efforts made to heal cultural wounds in the course of the following century, and the character of Saxon Christian culture in the tenth century suggests that these efforts had not been in vain. Further to the east, along the southern and eastern shores of the Baltic, dislocation was equally violent and calculated in the course of the twelfth and thirteenth centuries: the difference was that there no efforts were made to heal its wounds at all.

Economic development was an enormously powerful engine of cultural change. The extension of trading networks, the growing volume and value of commodities traded, the access to unfamiliar and exotic goods, the growth of a merchant class, the circulation of coin, the unequal sharing of the wealth generated, the indirect profits made by princely authority, the development of markets and towns, the need they generated for crafts and services, the migrations they called into being, the adaptation of custom and law to embrace new problems and situations: these characteristics of medieval economic development combined to react with tremendous disruptive force upon earlier, simpler patterns of relationship and behaviour and cultic observance. Commerce was an agent of critical importance in the diffusion of Christianity. It is difficult to measure or to pinpoint this in any scientifically accurate manner, but one may be confident that the coming of Christianity to, let us say, the Frisians, Moravians, Danes, Bohemians, Russians and Wends had more than a little to do with the economic precocity of these various peoples at diverse times between the seventh and the twelfth centuries.

The advance of political authority was another solvent of traditional ways. It tended to be closely related to economic change because so often princes found that they could enhance their power by acting as facilitators of commerce – protectors of merchants, guarantors of the peace of the market, providers of roads and bridges and town walls, strikers of coin, takers of tolls and so forth. Of course, the growth of authority was not exclusively related to economic development. It might depend on contingent forces operative at dynastic level. Dynastic marriages, for example, could open princely eyes to all manner of desirable ways of doing things in the country from which his bride had come. Vladimir of Kiev got more than a wife in the Emperor Basil II's sister Anna; he also got access to the most commanding source of imperial expertise in the Christian world. The growth of princely authority could change a traditional society and its religious observances by means of command or patronage or sanctions. There are plentiful indications, in the situations we have surveyed, that the adoption of Christianity and the consolidation of secular power were often inextricably bound up together.

These considerations may suggest an answer to a question that was posed but left unanswered in Chapter 9: why were the Slavs resistant to Christianity in the seventh century, and the Danes in the eighth, while both were readier to accept it in respectively the ninth and the tenth centuries? Perhaps because at the earlier dates the solvents of tradition had not begun their work of breaking down and dissolving the barriers to change. Later they had.

Christendom – late antique, early medieval, high medieval – knew that it was attractive to outsiders by reason of its wealth and power. These widespread perceptions furnished the activists in the diffusion of Christianity with their trump cards. They also possessed an unshakeable self-confidence founded upon those heady and tremendous assurances about God's purposes which they read in the Bible. Riches and order confirmed and strengthened their confidence. They could play these cards again and again, and almost always with success because manifestly the Christians were almost always the winners and the pagans the losers. Become a Christian and get rich: this was at the heart of the arguments commended to Boniface by Bishop Daniel of Winchester in his letter on missionary tactics. And let us remember too Bede's commendation of the 'prudent words' addressed by the Northumbrian high priest Coifi to King Edwin: 'None of your followers has devoted himself more earnestly than I have to the worship of our gods, but nevertheless there are many who receive greater benefits and greater honours from you than I do and are more successful in all their undertakings. If the gods had any power they would have helped me more readily, seeing that I have always served them with greater zeal.' Crude stuff, no doubt about it – though one can hear stuff as crude from street-corner evangelists today – but it was persuasive. It was persuasive because it reflected what the 'empirical religiosity' of early medieval Europeans, pagan and Christian alike, expected their cult to do for them.[8] Heathens possess 'only the frozen lands of the north'. How right Bishop Daniel was: by 1400 the only heathens left in Europe were the Lapps.

These perceptions by outsiders were justified. Christian spokesmen were not indulging in deceitful boasts or sleight of hand. It is still inadequately appreciated that Christian Europe in the early Middle Ages was both wealthy and well managed. The view that the early medieval economy was in some sense 'primitive' or 'under developed', long ago abandoned by medievalists, is still widespread. It deserves the strongest possible emphasis that such a judgement is without foundation. Medieval Christendom was densely settled – the population was almost certainly much higher than the usual estimates that have been made – and efficiently exploited. Furthermore, it commanded, partly by inheritance from a Roman or pre-Roman past, partly by means of fertile improvisation, orderly structures and techniques of power (family, community, hierarchies, kingship, literacy, law, taxation and so forth) which were demonstrably effective, and which were above all flexible and adaptable to novel social circumstances.

Not the least remarkable of such ordered structures was the institution of the Christian church. What Gibbon called the 'union and discipline of the Christian republic' has long been acknowledged as one of the prime explanations of the growth of Christianity in the Roman world. Some of the facets of this structure which have relevance for the study of conversion have been touched on, and there is no profit in repetition. The important point to grasp is that the varied paganisms which expanding Christianity encountered were lacking in union and discipline. Christians were organized, pagans were not (though as we have seen there might have been some movement in that direction among the northern Slavs and the Lithuanians). This made all the difference.

The institution of monasticism in a fashion exemplifies it. Only wealthy and ordered societies could afford the foundation and endowment of monasteries on the scale that we witness in early medieval Europe. If the pace and scale of foundation slackened towards the end of our period, that was partly because by then Christendom was reaching into genuinely marginal regions (Norway, Iceland, Finland) which could not afford the indulgence, partly because new religious orders were coming to the fore in the mission field to replace monasticism; there were always more friars than monks on the shores of the Baltic. Monastic communities had the resources, the discipline and the adaptability to enable them to contribute weightily to the dual processes of conversion and Christianization. We have seen repeated examples of this in the course of this book.

The willingness to commit wealth to the church was, for the aristocratic elite who possessed nearly all of it, as much a way of establishing a new Christian identity as was, for their rulers, the founding of bishoprics, the issue of written codes of law or the wearing of pope-given crowns. We can see this in the noble patrons of Columbanian monasticism in Gaul, in the deployment of the 'abundant patrimony' of Fructuosus, in the colossal expenditure by Benedict Biscop on the books which made Bede's work possible, in the endowment of the see of Ribe by that Danish *grand seigneur* Bishop Odinkar, and in countless other examples.

Old cultural habits sloughed off, new cultural garments assumed: was it a merging or a distinction, a bridge or a void? As usual there is no single nor simple answer. But generally speaking, missionary churchmen were rather more willing to countenance a strategy of adaptation, along the lines commended by Pope Gregory I, before about 1200 than they were after that date. The strategies were diverse and variable but they were in general disciplined and well thought through. They were emphatically not the kind of sentimental mishmash that some have supposed them. For example, the notion widely entertained today, especially by dewy-eyed ecologists, that the spirit of the so-called Celtic church was a pollen-strewn blend of love and nature and Irish mythology is one of the silliest misconceptions which the mushy credulity of our age has devised.

The liberty permitted to the convert of carrying a certain amount of traditional cultural equipment, as it were a duty-free cultural allowance, over the threshold of Christianity facilitated that transition for the individual. It also transmitted messages of reassurance to others. The shock of the new could be softened, in this manner, for (let us say) the followers of a convert king. Immemorial sensibilities did not need to be harshly bruised. Pressures could be quietly acknowledged but did not need to be publicly yielded to. Face could be saved. From whom a barbarian ruler accepted Christianity, on what terms, with what strings attached, mattered in ways which could be literally those of life or death, as we have seen. The too-precipitate acceptance of Christianity from Constantinople by Khan Boris in the wake of military defeat led to the boyars' revolt and nearly cost Boris his life. The long-drawn-out dalliance between the grand dukes of Lithuania and the Christian churches are unusually well documented. But one can sense comparable hesitations and calculations in earlier and more obscure contexts. Ethelbert of Kent could not accept the faith from the Britons of whom he was the overlord, nor from the Franks because it might look like an acknowledgement of *their* overlordship; so he turned to the pope instead. Some historians have found this a persuasive way of interpreting Ethelbert's conversion.

Calculation and hesitation, diplomatic nicety, considerations of *Realpolitik*, greed, self-promotion, the hard-nosed search for political advantage: the historian of conversion must take account of all these more or less ignoble foibles. An impious age such as that in which we live is apt to be embarrassed or bewildered by the concerns of more pious epochs. So it is convenient – it is sometimes even verifiable – to explain the acceptance of Christianity, or explain it away, by pointing to Clovis's wish to enlist the support of the Gallo-Roman episcopate, or to the desire of the Rus merchants for favourable trading terms in Constantinople, or to Gediminas's need for German technical expertise. It is as well to remind ourselves, as King Edwin's mysterious nocturnal visitor placed before him in Bede's tale, that what was at issue was not the here and now but the eternal things: a God who could give salvation.

The conversion of Europe to Christianity certainly had its epic moments, duly highlighted by the hagiographers. There the scenes are unforgettable passages of assertion, of confrontation, of triumph: Martin's destruction of the temple at Levroux; the debate at Edwin's court; Boniface felling the sacred oak of Geismar; the murder of Wenceslas; Gizurr's speech to the Icelanders at Thingvellir; the destruction of the idol of Svantovit on Rügen. There were many other moments which were far from epic; all the more accessible and human for it. Dozy Friardus in a harvest field with a wasps' nest near the Loire; the exorcism of a poltergeist from a country house in the Rioja by Emilian; infanticide at Tauberbischofsheim and its sequel; Flora fleeing from her brother in the streets of Córdoba; a Viking funeral on the island of Colonsay; Einar sailing from Greenland to Norway with a live polar bear; Helmold of Bosau saying Epiphany mass in a deserted church amid snowdrifts; Henry of Livonia playing his harp to the Estonians. All these, and countless other vignettes, have something to convey to us of the flavour of Christian life while the peoples of Europe were experiencing conversion. Identifying the pious Christian act or the devout Christian person in the distant past is a matter for temperament and judgement as much as – probably more than – it is a matter for historical enquiry. We must not shirk enquiry, of course. But it so soon becomes mired and snagged by worries about the status of the evidence (authorial sources, methods, intentions, *topoi*, etc.) and by vain attempts to find a means of distinguishing between the genuine – or even the 'genuine' – and the conventional or the assumed. At a certain point one just has to take the plunge, without any concomitant incitement to others to take it too. Temperament and judgement lead me to hazard that it was an act of piety in Ulfila to translate the Bible into Gothic; in an unknown Saxon monk to compose the *Heliand*; in King Harald Gormsson to re-inter his parents in a Christian manner; or in Orm the son of Gamel to rebuild the ruined minster of St Gregory at Kirkdale.

Looking out of the window beyond the desk at which this book has been written, into the varied greens of the Yorkshire countryside in June, the only living creatures that meet my eye are five young Frisian bullocks chomping away at the lush grass of one of my fields. The further boundary of that field is formed by a stream called the Ellerker Beck. The Ellerker is a modest stream – you can jump across it except when it is in spate – but in that part of its course it has a significant additional function. As well as of a field it marks the boundary of a parish. The parish is cigar-shaped, long and thin. Here at its southern tip it reaches right down into the marshy clays of Ryedale, a bare thirty-five metres or so above sea-level. Its northern end stretches up into the heather and bracken of the North York Moors, beyond the reach of tillage, above the tree-line. Essentially it is the parish of a single valley, the valley of a stream larger than the Ellerker named the Hodge Beck, which runs roughly north–south until its confluence a couple of miles from here with the river Dove, which in turn runs into the Rye a few miles further to the south. The valley of the Hodge Beck is usually known as Kirkdale because in it, isolated from any present-day settlement, there stands the church rebuilt by Orm the son of Gamel in the middle years of the eleventh century.

The bounds of the parish of Kirkdale are probably identical with Orm's estate (or one of Orm's estates we should say, for he was a rich man). In certain fundamental respects its agrarian routines today cannot have changed much since the time of Orm: farming is like that. The Frisian bullocks in my field are not mine but belong to a local farmer who rents the grazing from me. He farms right up at the top end of the parish, at the margins of cultivation, where the soil is thin and the untamed vegetation of the moors sneaks back over the dry-stone walls. The bullocks are born in a foldyard at his farm in winter, but as soon as winter is over (which was not until May this year) they must be brought down to fatten on the pasture of the southern meadows. So it must have been in Orm's day nine centuries ago; so it probably was nineteen centuries ago when the valley perhaps belonged to the estate of the Roman villa whose foundations may be seen in the neighbouring dale to the west. Livestock of all sorts, not just bullocks, was and is regularly shifted about in a micro-system of seasonal transhumance. Until recently, that meant herding the stock along the main artery of the parish, the valley bottom, and that in turn meant going past St Gregory's minster. The church rebuilt by Orm, with its dedication to the apostle of the English, may originally have been founded by the monks of Lastingham, three centuries or more before his time. The oldest object now within the church is a sculpted stone slab which takes the history of a place of Christian worship on the site reliably back to the eighth century. The original founders chose a spot where the floor of the valley is very narrow, barely more than about a hundred metres wide. Anyone driving livestock up or down the valley would have to pass close to the church. The spot would have been frequented also by travellers on an east–west axis along what is still the principal thoroughfare running along the foot of the moors. Until a recent re-routing of the road in the interest of motor traffic this thoroughfare crossed the Hodge Beck a couple of hundred metres south of the church. Isolated it may be, but still a nodal point in a system of local communications; where hills meet plain. Brand, the priest appointed by Orm, would have been accessible to all and sundry.

About a mile above St Gregory's minster the Hodge Beck, as though reluctant to meet and contend with the unyielding clay of the plain, plunges underground – except when in spate during the autumn and winter months. It is a most extraordinary sight. At one moment the beck is burbling merrily along; the next moment it is draining away among the strewn limestone boulders of its bed. The spates of winter tumble and shift these boulders, opening to human view parts of the stream's underbed normally invisible. Thus it is that sometimes, in spring, you will find the mouth of a cavernous fissure down which you can peer ten, fifteen, twenty feet, down which indeed you could even climb were not its walls so perilously unstable. And down these fissures the water trickles away out of sight. It is like peering into another world. At a lesser distance below the church the waters of the Hodge Beck re-emerge as mysteriously as they had earlier disappeared. Not in some triumphal, fountainous gushing forth, but oozingly, almost imperceptibly, as you walk from a dry stream-bed to a damp one, from a damp one to a puddled one, from a puddled one to a flowing one. I have sometimes wondered whether this strange behaviour of an otherwise prosaic watercourse had made the valley in some way numinous, sacred, long before the coming of Christianity; whether it was for that very reason that a Christian church was founded there in the first place.

14 June 1996

FURTHER READING

CHAPTER 1

Peter Brown, *The World of Late Antiquity, from Marcus Aurelius to Muhammad* (London, 1971) is a sparkling introduction to the period which stretches from the second to the seventh century. He has recently extended and updated it in *The Rise of Western Christendom. Triumph and Diversity A.D. 200–1000* (Oxford, 1996) without, unfortunately, the splendid illustrations of its predecessor. R. A. Markus, *Christianity in the Roman World* (London, 1974), is an excellent place to embark on study of the rise of a new faith. It may be supplemented by two books of very different, but complementary, scope and character: Ramsay MacMullen, *Christianizing the Roman Empire* (New Haven/London, 1984), and Robin Lane Fox, *Pagans and Christians* (London, 1986). On Augustine I have found especially stimulating R. A. Markus, *Saeculum. History and Society in the Theology of Saint Augustine* (Cambridge, 2nd edn., 1989). The same author's masterly study *The End of Ancient Christianity* (Cambridge, 1990) contains an opening chapter which is particularly thought-provoking for the matter of the present book. On the sources for Edwin and Paulinus see the note on further reading for Chapter 4 below.

CHAPTER 2

For Gregory of Pontus see Stephen Mitchell, *Anatolia: Land, Men and Gods in Asia Minor*, vol. II, *The Rise of the Church* (Oxford, 1993). For Martin of Tours and his successors see Clare Stancliffe, *Saint Martin and His Hagiographer. History and Miracle in Sulpicius Severus* (Oxford, 1983), and her earlier paper 'From Town to Countryside: the Christianisation of the Touraine 370–600' in D. Baker (ed.), *Studies in Church History*, vol. 16 (1979). John Matthews' brilliant study of *Western Aristocracies and Imperial Court 364–425* (Oxford, 1975) contains more that is germane to our topic than might be suspected from the title. Peter Brown's *The Cult of the Saints* (London, 1981) was a work of seminal importance; and there is much that is of relevance to our enquiries in his volume of collected essays, *Society and the Holy in Late Antiquity* (London, 1982). His researches have been developed by Raymond Van Dam, *Saints and Their Miracles in Late Antique Gaul* (Princeton, 1993). There is very little work in English on the Christianization of the countryside in Spain, though aspects of it are treated in the fine article by J. N. Hillgarth, 'Popular religion in Visigothic Spain', in Edward James (ed.), *Visigothic Spain. New Approaches* (Oxford, 1980). On St Samson and his setting see Charles Thomas, *And Shall These Mute Stones Speak? Post-Roman Inscriptions in Western Britain* (Cardiff, 1994), ch. 14. A good introduction to Pope Gregory I is to be found in Jeffrey Richards, *Consul of God. The Life and Times of Gregory the Great* (London, 1980).

CHAPTER 3

The standard work on the Goths is Herwig Wolfram, *History of the Goths* (London, 1990), and the most detailed investigation of their relations with the empire is to be found in P. J. Heather, *Goths and Romans 332–489* (Oxford, 1991). Peter Heather and John Matthews, *The Goths in the Fourth Century* (Liverpool, 1991), is a volume in the series 'Translated Texts for Historians' published by the Liverpool University Press; an invaluable work which is a great deal more than just translations. There is a colossal bibliography on Patrick, too many of its items by the pious, the hostile or the deranged. The sanest and the most intelligent recent treatment known to me is to be found in Charles Thomas, *Christianity in Roman Britain to A.D. 500* (London, 1981), chs. 12–14. This may be supplemented by a collection of specialist papers edited by David N. Dumville, *Saint Patrick A.D. 493–1993* (Woodbridge, 1993), among which that by T. M. Charles-Edwards, 'Palladius, Prosper and Leo the Great: mission and primatial authority', is particularly illuminating. For the Irish social context Harold Mytum, *The Origins of Early Christian Ireland* (London, 1992), can be recommended and the subsequent development of Christianity in Ireland can be followed with the aid of Kathleen Hughes, *The Church in Early Irish Society* (London, 1966). The best introduction to Columbanus is by way of his own works, which have been edited and translated by G. S. M. Walker, *Sancti Columbani Opera* (Dublin, 1957): and see also the further reading for Chapter 5 below.

CHAPTER 4

The *Decem Libri Historiarum* of Gregory of Tours have been best edited by Bruno Krusch and Wilhelm Levison in the *MGH SRM*, vol. I. There are English translations, both under the (incorrect) title *History of the Franks*, by O. M. Dalton (Oxford, 1927), and by Lewis Thorpe (Harmondsworth, 1974). On Clovis see J. M. Wallace-Hadrill, *The Long-Haired Kings* (London, 1962), ch. 7; Ian Wood, *The Merovingian*

Kingdoms 450–751 (London, 1994), ch. 3; and Ian Wood, 'Gregory of Tours and Clovis', *Revue Belge de Philologie et d'Histoire* 63 (1985). The Latin text of Bede's *Historia Ecclesiastica Gentis Anglorum* has been edited with a facing English translation by B. Colgrave and R. A. B. Mynors (Oxford, 1969). Of the numerous translations of Bede the most easily accessible and accurate is that by Roger Collins and Judith McClure (World's Classics: Oxford, 1994). J. M. Wallace-Hadrill, *Bede's 'Ecclesiastical History of the English People': A Historical Commentary* (Oxford, 1988), the posthumously published work of a commanding scholar, supplements but was not intended to replace the magnificent commentary by Charles Plummer which accompanied his edition of *Baedae Opera Historica* (Oxford, 1896). On Ethelbert and Edwin see Henry Mayr-Harting, *The Coming of Christianity to Anglo-Saxon England* (London, 3rd edn., 1991), and Ian Wood, 'The mission of Augustine of Canterbury to the English', *Speculum* 69 (1994).

CHAPTER 5

J. M. Wallace-Hadrill, *The Frankish Church* (Oxford, 1983) – a marvellous book – is the best starting-point (ch. 4) for an exploration of the impact of Columbanus on Gaul. It may now be supplemented with Ian Wood, *The Merovingian Kingdoms 450–751* (London, 1994), ch. 11. There is a clutch of specialist papers in H. B. Clarke and M. Brennan, *Columbanus and Merovingian Monasticism*, in the series *British Archaeological Reports, International Series*, vol. 113 (1981). Paul Fouracre and Richard A. Geberding have now provided us in *Late Merovingian France. History and Hagiography 640–720* (Manchester, 1996) with a very useful collection of translated documents-and-commentary which contains materials relating to, among others, Bathild, Audoen, Leger and Gertrude of Nivelles: it comes in the series 'Manchester Medieval Sources'. Patrick J. Geary, *Aristocracy in Provence. The Rhône Basin at the Dawn of the Carolingian Age* (Stuttgart, 1985) is a translation and commentary upon the will of Abbo, founder of Novalesa. On Christianity in Spain the English reader should start with Roger Collins, *Early Medieval Spain. Unity in Diversity 400–1000* (London, 2nd edn., 1995), ch. 3. The same author's *The Basques* (Oxford, 1986) is the best account of that mysterious people and furnishes a context for the unsuccessful missionary activities among them of St Amandus.

CHAPTER 6

Henry Mayr-Harting, *The Coming of Christianity to Anglo-Saxon England* (London, 3rd edn., 1991) is the best introduction to its subject. On Ireland, Michael Richter, *Medieval Ireland: The Enduring Tradition* (London, 1988), and Dáibhí Ó Cróinín, *Early Medieval Ireland 400–1200* (London, 1995), are commended; and on Scotland, Alfred P. Smyth, *Warlords and Holy Men. Scotland A.D. 80–1000* (London, 1984). Patrick Wormald's paper on 'Bede, *Beowulf* and the conversion of the Anglo-Saxon aristocracy' in Robert T. Farrell (ed.), *Bede and Anglo-Saxon England*, in *British Archaeological Reports* 46 (1978) is a very stimulating and wide-ranging piece of work. So too are the essays of James Campbell, easily accessible in collected form in his *Essays in Anglo-Saxon History* (London, 1986), among which the first six have relevance in one way or another to the theme of this chapter.

CHAPTER 7

The classic work in English remains Wilhelm Levison, *England and the Continent in the Eighth Century* (Oxford, 1946). J. M. Wallace-Hadrill, *The Frankish Church* (Oxford, 1983), ch. 6, is a splendid survey which may be supplemented with Ian Wood, *The Merovingian Kingdoms 450–751* (London, 1994), ch. 18. The editor's own contribution to T. Reuter (ed.), *The Greatest Englishman. Essays on St Boniface and the Church at Crediton* (Exeter, 1980) is valuable. On Charlemagne the best book in English is Donald Bullough, *The Age of Charlemagne* (London, 2nd edn., 1973). On the Carolingian renaissance and the ideas that underpinned it see Rosamond McKitterick, *The Frankish Church and the Carolingian Reforms 789–895* (London, 1977) and the collection of essays edited by the same writer entitled *Carolingian Culture: Emulation and Innovation* (Cambridge, 1994). For Anskar, see the superb essay by Ian Wood, 'Christians and Pagans in ninth-century Scandinavia' in Birgit and Peter Sawyer and Ian Wood (eds.), *The Christianization of Scandinavia* (Alingsås, 1987). Inevitably, there is a vast literature on the subjects embraced by this chapter in languages other than English, especially in German. At the time of writing the most compendious guide to this literature in an English publication is to be found in the chapter-by-chapter bibliographies in Rosamond McKitterick (ed.), *The New Cambridge Medieval History*, vol. II (Cambridge, 1995).

CHAPTER 8

The character and length of Chapter 8 turned out such as to deserve a fuller array of reference in the endnotes than was appropriate for the other chapters of this book. Accordingly, the further reading for that chapter is to be found in those notes. It might be fitting to mention here, because it had not been published when I composed Chapter 8, the excellent chapter (no. 24) by Julia M. H. Smith, 'Religion and Lay Society' in Rosamond McKitterick (ed.), *The New Cambridge Medieval History*, vol. II (Cambridge, 1995) with its accompanying bibliography at pp. 1002–6. For the same reason I draw attention to Michael Richter, 'Models of Conversion in the Early Middle Ages' in Doris Edel (ed.), *Cultural Identity and Cultural Integration. Ireland and Europe in the Early Middle Ages* (Dublin, 1995).

CHAPTER 9

Bernhard Blumenkranz, *Juifs et Chrétiens dans le monde occidental 430–1096* (Paris, 1960) is the fundamental work, which may be supplemented by his collected essays, *Juifs et Chrétiens: patristique et moyen âge* (London, 1977). For one series of episodes see Robert Chazan, *European Jewry and the First Crusade* (Berkeley, 1987). For Islam, with special reference to Spain, see Thomas F. Glick, *Islamic and Christian Spain in the Early Middle Ages* (Princeton, 1979), and more recently his *From Muslim Fortress to Christian Castle. Social and Cultural Change in Medieval Spain* (Manchester, 1995), briefly at the end of Chapter 3. The martyrs of Córdoba have attracted much attention: see Kenneth B. Wolf, *Christian Martyrs in Muslim Spain* (Cambridge, 1988), and Jessica A. Coope, *The Martyrs of Córdoba. Community and Family Conflict in an Age of Mass Conversion* (Lincoln, Na./London, 1995). For the later period, there is a useful collection of essays edited by James M. Powell on *Muslims under Latin Rule 1100–1300* (Princeton, 1990).

CHAPTER 10

There is a fine introduction by Dimitri Obolensky, *The Byzantine Commonwealth. Eastern Europe 500–1453* (London, 1971), chs. 1–5. For a closer focus on the process of conversion there is ample narrative treatment in A. P. Vlasto, *The Entry of the Slavs into Christendom* (Cambridge, 1970). Z. Vána, *The World of the Ancient Slavs* (London, 1983) may be recommended for its maps and illustrations. These works may now be supplemented by Jonathan Shepard, 'Slavs and Bulgars', being

Chapter 9 of Rosamond McKitterick (ed.), *The New Cambridge Medieval History*, vol. II (Cambridge, 1995), which is accompanied by a formidable bibliography slightly longer than the text of the chapter itself for those who might want to explore the topic further; also by Mark Whittow, *The Making of Orthodox Byzantium 600–1025* (London, 1996), ch. 8. For the kingdom of Germany see Timothy Reuter, *Germany in the Early Middle Ages 800–1056* (London, 1991), and specifically on Bavaria there is W. Menghin, *Frühgeschichte Bayerns* (Stuttgart, 1990). Henry Mayr-Harting, *Two Conversions to Christianity: The Bulgarians and the Anglo-Saxons* (Stenton Lecture 1993: Reading, 1994) is a stimulating exercise in comparative history to which this chapter owes much.

CHAPTER 11

General treatments of the Vikings are legion and of very variable quality. The best introduction known to me is Peter Sawyer's *Kings and Vikings. Scandinavia and Europe A.D. 700–1100* (London, 1982), and the best account of their homeland is Birgit and Peter Sawyer, *Medieval Scandinavia: From Conversion to Reformation 800–1500* (Minneapolis/London, 1993).

The geographical scope of this chapter is so wide that my suggestions for further reading are more than usually summary in order to prevent the list becoming forbiddingly long. For **Scotland**, see Barbara Crawford, *Scandinavian Scotland* (Leicester, 1987), and for **Ireland** for the period down to about 950 Alfred Smyth, *Scandinavian York and Dublin* (2 vols., Dublin, 1975, 1979), and for the subsequent period John Watt, *The Church in Medieval Ireland* (Dublin, 1972).

On **Russia**, to the books by Obolensky and Vlasto listed among the items of further reading for Chapter 10 may be added Mark Whittow, *The Making of Orthodox Byzantium 600–1025* (London, 1996), ch. 8, and the more formidable work of Simon Franklin and Jonathan Shepard, *The Emergence of Rus 750–1200* (London, 1996).

For **Normandy**, David Bates provides an indispensable guide in *Normandy before 1066* (London, 1982), and for **England** Pauline Stafford does likewise in *Unification and Conquest. A Political and Social History of England in the Tenth and Eleventh Centuries* (London, 1989).

Iceland may best be approached through Dag Strömbäck (trans. Peter Foote), *The Conversion of Iceland* (London, 1975), and Jesse L. Byock, *Medieval Iceland. Society, Sagas and Power* (Enfield, 1993). On **Greenland** see Finn Gad (trans. Ernst Dupont), *The History of Greenland*, vol. I (London, 1970), and Knud Krogh, *Viking Greenland* (Copenhagen, 1967).

On the **Scandinavian homelands** the essays in Birgit and Peter Sawyer and Ian Wood (eds.), *The Christianization of Scandinavia* (Alingsås, 1987) form a stimulating introduction and may be followed up with two papers by Lesley Abrams, 'Eleventh-century Missions and the Early Stages of Ecclesiastical Organisation in Scandinavia', *Anglo-Norman Studies* 17 (1995), and 'The Anglo-Saxons and the Christianization of Scandinavia', *Anglo-Saxon England* 24 (1995). Canute's piety is well evoked by M. K. Lawson, *Cnut. The Danes in England in the Early Eleventh Century* (London, 1993). Peter Sawyer sorts out the very complicated history of eleventh-century Swedish kingship in *The Making of Sweden* (Alingsås, 1989), and there is a good introduction to the rune-stones in Sven Jansson's *Runes in Sweden* (Stockholm, 1987). Phillip Pulsiano (ed.), *Medieval Scandinavia: An Encyclopedia* (New York/London, 1993) is a useful reference work, in which Peter Foote's article 'Conversion' is a masterpiece of thoughtful compression.

CHAPTER 12

The best starting-points for Germany are Timothy Reuter, *Germany in the Early Middle Ages 800–1056* (London, 1991) and Alfred Haverkamp, *Medieval Germany 1056–1273* (Oxford, 1988). The works by Obolensky and Vlasto listed among the items of further reading for Chapter 10 are useful for the Slavs and Magyars. Geoffrey Barraclough (ed.), *Eastern and Western Europe in the Middle Ages* (London, 1970), with contributions by distinguished German, Czech and Polish scholars, is a good introduction to the complex interactions indicated by its title. Henry Mayr-Harting, *Ottonian Book Illumination: An Historical Study* (2 vols., London, 1991) is a fascinating work of much wider scope than the title might suggest. Bernard Hamilton, 'The monastery of San Alessio and the religious and intellectual renaissance of tenth-century Rome', most easily accessible in his collected essays, *Monastic Reform, Catharism and the Crusades (900–1300)* (London, 1979), casts light on the role of that house in fostering missionary impulses. Very little of the voluminous work in German has been made available in English translation: a welcome exception is Friedrich Lotter, 'The Crusading Idea and the Conquest of the Region East of the Elbe' in Robert Bartlett and Angus MacKay (eds.), *Medieval Frontier Societies* (Oxford, 1989). There is a first-rate article on the conversion of the Pomeranians by Robert Bartlett, 'The conversion of a pagan society in the middle ages' in the journal *History* 70 (1985).

CHAPTER 13

General overviews are provided by Bernard Hamilton, *Religion in the Medieval West* (London, 1986), and Colin Morris, *The Papal Monarchy. The Western Church from 1050 to 1250* (Oxford, 1989): the latter work is wider in scope than the first half of its title might suggest; a magnificent survey of its vast subject. Specifically on parishes, Richard Morris, *Churches in the Landscape* (London, 1989), chs. 1–6, is a good introduction to the English and Welsh evidence, while M. Aubrun, *La Paroisse en France des Origines au XVe Siècle* (Paris, 1986) performs the same function for the French scene. Regional studies are constantly enlarging our understanding of the evolution of local ecclesiastical arrangements. Among fairly recent examples might be cited: John Blair (ed.), *Minsters and Parish Churches: The Local Church in Transition 950–1200* (Oxford, 1988) for England; Elisabeth Magnou-Nortier, *La Société laïque et l'église dans la province ecclésiastique de Narbonne de la fin du VIIIe siècle à la fin du XIe siècle* (Toulouse, 1974) for southern France; E. von Guttenberg and A. Wendehorst, *Das Bistum Bamberg*, vol. 2, *Die Pfarrorganisation* in the series *Germania Sacra: II Abt., Die Bistümer der Kirchenprovinz Mainz* (Berlin, 1966), with good maps, for central Germany. James A. Brundage, *Medieval Canon Law* (London, 1995) is a succinct introduction to its subject. R. W. Southern, *Scholastic Humanism and the Unification of Europe* (Oxford, 1995), part 2 ('Turning Doctrine into Law'), is a penetrating analysis of a twelfth-century turning-point.

CHAPTER 14

For the general context of the expansion of west European Christendom Robert Bartlett, *The Making of Europe: Conquest, Colonization and Cultural Change 950–1350* (London, 1993) is now the liveliest introduction, though a little weak on the religious perspective. Easily the best book on the topics embraced by this chapter is Eric Christiansen's *The Northern Crusades. The Baltic and the Catholic Frontier 1100–1525* (London, 2nd edn., 1997): a masterly and very readable study. By contrast, William L. Urban, *The Baltic Crusade* (De Kalb, Ill., 1975), though careful, is pedestrian. On the military orders a good starting-point is Alan Forey, *The Military Orders from the Twelfth to the Early Fourteenth Century* (London, 1992). The best way into Lithuania is via the series of very able and clear articles by Michał Giedroyć under the general title of 'The Arrival of Christianity in Lithuania', published in *Oxford Slavonic Papers* 18 (1985), 20 (1987) and 22 (1989). They may be supplemented by the dense but rewarding study of S. C. Rowell, *Lithuania Ascending: A Pagan Empire within East-central Europe 1295–1345* (Cambridge, 1994). Two specialist collections indicate the directions of present research: *Gli Inizi del Cristianesimo in Livonia-Lettonia* and *La Cristianizzazione della Lituania* in the series *Pontificio Comitato di Scienze Storiche, Atti e Documenti* (2 vols., Vatican City, 1989). For the enormous literature on all these matters see the bibliography in Rowell's book (above) and the annual reviews in such journals as the *Zeitschrift für Ostforschung*.

NOTES

ABBREVIATIONS USED IN THE NOTES

DLH   Gregory of Tours, *Decem Libri Historiarum*

EHD   *English Historical Documents*, vol. I, edited by Dorothy Whitelock

ET   English Translation

HE   Bede, *Historia Ecclesiastica Gentis Anglorum*

J   P. Jaffé, *Regesta Pontificum Romanorum* (in the 2nd edition of 1885)

MGH   *Monumenta Germaniae Historica*

MGH SS   *Scriptores*

MGH SRG   *Scriptores rerum Germanicarum in usum scholarum*

MGH SRM   *Scriptores rerum Merowingicarum*

PL   *Patrologiae cursus completus, series Latina*, edited by J.-P. Migne

CHAPTER 1

1. Ramsay MacMullen, *Roman Social Relations* (New Haven/London, 1974), p. 45.

2. Eusebius, *Oration in Praise of the Emperor Constantine*, i.6, in the translation of Ernest C. Richardson in the series *Nicene and Post-Nicene Fathers* (Oxford/New York, 1890), p. 583.

3. Origen, *Contra Celsum*, ii.30, in the translation by Henry Chadwick quoted in R. A. Markus, *Saeculum. History and Society in the Theology of Saint Augustine* (Cambridge, 1970), p. 48.

4. F. E. Cranz, in R. A. Markus (ed.), *Augustine. A Collection of Critical Essays* (New York, 1972), pp. 411–12.

5. For these quotations see Prudentius, *Contra Symmachum*, ii.815–17; Optatus, *De Schismate Donatistarum contra Parmenianum*, iii.3; Orosius, *Historia adversus paganos*, v.2 (respectively

PL, lx.235; xi.1000; xxxi.921).

6. E. A. Thompson, *The Visigoths in the Time of Ulfila* (Oxford, 1966), p. xvii.

7. Augustine, *Confessions*, viii.6 (*PL*, xxxii), in the translation of R. S. Pine-Coffin (Harmondsworth, 1961), pp. 167–8.

8. B. J. Kidd (trans.), *Documents Illustrative of the History of the Church*, vol. I (London, 1933), no. 29, pp. 55–7.

9. Augustine, *De Civitate Dei*, xix.17 (*PL*, xli.645–6), in the translation of H. Bettenson (Harmondsworth, 1972), p. 878.

10. Augustine, *Letters*, no. 199, chs. 46–8 (*PL*, xxxiii.922–3): in the translation by Sister Wilfrid Parsons (Fathers of the Church: New York, 1955), vol. IV, pp. 393–6. For some of the other biblical passages on the in-gathering of the nations see Psalms xxii.27; l.1; Isaiah lxvi.18–19; Revelation vii.9.

11. A. Hamman, in A. di Berardino (ed.), *Encyclopedia of the Early*

535

Church (English trans., Cambridge, 1992), p. 717. On the stirrings of a missionary consciousness in the circles frequented by Prosper, see T. M. Charles-Edwards, 'Palladius, Prosper and Leo the Great: mission and primatial authority', in D. N. Dumville (ed.), *Saint Patrick A.D. 493–1993* (Woodbridge, 1993), pp. 1–12.

12. Prosper of Aquitaine, *De Vocatione Omnium Gentium*, ii.16 (*PL*, li.704).

CHAPTER 2

1. This is the summing-up of a recent authority, Stephen Mitchell, *Anatolia. Land, Men and Gods in Asia Minor*, vol. II, *The Rise of the Church* (Oxford, 1993), p. 63: 'There is no reason to quarrel with the judgement that Christianity made more headway in Asia Minor . . . than anywhere else in the Roman world in the third century A.D., but its progress was irregular and the map of Christian progress resembles an irregular patchwork quilt not a simple monochrome blanket.'

2. R. Van Dam, 'Hagiography and history: the life of Gregory Thaumaturgus', *Classical Antiquity* I (1982), pp. 272–308 (at p. 274).

3. Quoted by Ramsay MacMullen, *Christianizing the Roman Empire* (New Haven/London, 1984), p. 65.

4. J. N. Hillgarth (trans.), *Christianity and Paganism 350–750. The Conversion of Western Europe* (Philadelphia, 1986), pp. 55–6.

5. These works by Sulpicius Severus have been translated by F. R. Hoare, *The Western Fathers* (London, 1954): quotations in the text have been taken from this source.

6. Gregory of Tours, *Glory of the Confessors*, translated by R. Van

Dam (Liverpool, 1988), ch. 2. p. 19 (slightly abbreviated).

7. Also translated by F. R. Hoare in the volume referred to above, note 5.

8. Caesarius of Arles, *Sermons*, trans. M. M. Mueller (Fathers of the Church: New York, 1956), vol. I, p. 263.

9. Hillgarth (trans.), *Christianity and Paganism* (above, note 4), pp. 59, 62.

10. Gregory of Tours, *The Miracles of the Bishop St Martin*, Book I, ch. 26: trans. R. Van Dam, *Saints and Their Miracles in Late Antique Gaul* (Princeton, 1993), pp. 219–20.

11. Gregory of Tours, *Life of the Fathers*, x.1: translated by E. James (Liverpool, 2nd edn., 1991), p. 72.

12. Braulio of Saragossa, *Life of St Emilian*: translated by C. W. Barlow (Fathers of the Church: New York, 1969), *Iberian Fathers*, vol. II, pp. 113–39.

13. *Vie des Pères du Jura*, trans. (into French) F. Martine, *Sources Chrétiennes*, vol. 142 (Paris, 1968).

14. The Latin text was edited by R. Fawtier in the *Bibliothèque de l'École des Hautes Études* 197 (1912): there is an English translation by T. Taylor, *The Life of St Samson of Dol* (London, 1925).

15. Gregory of Tours, *Libri Historiarum* x.29: translated by O. M. Dalton, *The History of the Franks by Gregory of Tours* (Oxford, 1927), II, p. 466.

16. J. M. Pardessus (ed.), *Diplomata, Chartae, Epistolae, Leges ad res Gallo-Francicas spectantia* (Paris, 1843–9), I, no. clxxx.

CHAPTER 3

1. Gregory's *Canonical Letter* has been translated in Peter Heather and John Matthews, *The Goths in the Fourth Century* (Liverpool, 1991),

pp. 5–11. All quotations relating to Gothic matters in the course of the immediately following pages are drawn from this admirable collection unless otherwise stated.

2. Gibbon, *Decline and Fall*, ch. 37 (1818 edition, vi.264).

3. P. J. Heather, *Goths and Romans 332–489* (Oxford, 1991), p. 105.

4. For this suggestion see Charles Thomas, *Whithorn's Christian Beginnings* (Friends of Whithorn Trust: Whithorn, 1992).

5. Patrick's works have been many times translated: my quotations from them are based, with minor adaptations, on the version of A. B. E. Hood, *Saint Patrick: His Writings and Muirchú's Life* (Chichester, 1978). The most recent editor of Patrick's works takes an altogether different view of his Latinity from that proposed here: see D. R. Howlett, *The Book of Letters of Saint Patrick the Bishop* (Dublin, 1994).

6. Edited and translated by M. J. Faris, *The Bishops' Synod* (Liverpool, 1976), pp. 1–8.

7. A monastery 'would have looked like any other sixth-century hamlet with huts, plots and the general mess of a life-support smallholding': Charles Thomas, *And Shall These Mute Stones Speak?* (Cardiff, 1994), p. 311.

8. Edited and translated by A. O. and M. O. Anderson, *Adomnán's Life of Columba* (Edinburgh, 1961). This translation has been revised and reprinted with excellent introduction and notes, by Richard Sharpe, *Adomnán of Iona, Life of St Columba* (Harmondsworth, 1995).

9. Jonas of Bobbio, *Vita Columbani*, edited by B. Krusch in *MGH SRM*, vol. 4, ch. 3: there is a partial translation of this work by Edward Peters, *Monks, Bishops and Pagans: Christian Culture in Gaul and Italy*

500–700 (Philadelphia, 1975) at pp. 75–113.

CHAPTER 4

1. Peter Heather and John Matthews, *The Goths in the Fourth Century* (Liverpool, 1991), p. 106.

2. P. J. Heather, 'The crossing of the Danube and the Gothic conversion', *Greek, Roman and Byzantine Studies* 27 (1986), pp. 289–318 (at p. 292).

3. Most easily accessible in the somewhat free translation by Lewis Thorpe for the Penguin Classics series: Gregory of Tours, *History of the Franks* (Harmondsworth, 1974).

4. The letters of Avitus and Remigius have been translated in J. N. Hillgarth, *Christianity and Paganism 350–750. The Conversion of Western Europe* (Philadelphia, 1986), pp. 76–8.

5. ibid., pp. 79–80.

6. Bede, *HE*, i.25.

7. Edited and translated by Bertram Colgrave, *The Earliest Life of Gregory the Great by an Anonymous Monk of Whitby* (Cambridge, 1985): the story of the encounter is in ch. 9.

8. J 1386: translated *EHD* 1, no. 161.

9. J 1751.

10. J 1432: translated *EHD* 1, no. 162.

11. J 1518: translated *EHD* I, no. 163.

12. J 1825, 1827.

13. This crucial sentence occurs in *HE*, ii.5.

14. J 2008, 2009.

15. Alcuin, *The Bishops, Kings and Saints of York*, edited and translated by Peter Godman (Oxford, 1982), line 218.

16. *MGH Epistolae* 1, pp. 671–5; also in J. Gil, *Miscellanea Wisigothica* (Seville, 1972), pp. 19–27. There are some grounds for supposing that Adaloald was already a Catholic, but perhaps King

Sisebut did not know this.

17. J 2019.

18. J. M. Wallace-Hadrill, *Bede's 'Ecclesiastical History of the English People': A Historical Commentary* (Oxford, 1988), p. 65.

19. Martin Carver (ed.), *The Age of Sutton Hoo* (Woodbridge, 1992), p. 366.

20. For what follows I rely on L. Thompson, *Survival in Two Worlds. Moshoeshoe of Lesotho 1786–1870* (Oxford, 1975), especially Chapter 3, 'The King and His Missionaries'.

CHAPTER 5

1. Gregory of Tours, *Life of the Fathers*, vi.2: translated by E. James (Liverpool, 2nd edn., 1991), pp. 34–5.

2. *The Irish Penitentials*, edited and translated by L. Bieler (Dublin, 1963), p. 97.

3. Guy Halsall, 'Social Change around A.D. 600: an Austrasian perspective', in Martin Carver (ed.), *The Age of Sutton Hoo* (Woodbridge, 1992), pp. 265–78 (at p. 273).

4. Jonas of Bobbio, *Vita Columbani*, edited by B. Krusch in *MGH SRM*, vol. 4, ch. 27.

5. *Vita Audoini*, edited by W. Levison in *MGH SRM*, vol. 5, ch. 4. Since this chapter was drafted this text has become available in an English translation in Paul Fouracre and Richard A. Geberding, *Late Merovingian France. History and Hagiography 640–720* (Manchester, 1996), a very useful volume which also contains a translation of the *Vita* of Queen Balthild.

6. *Vita Amandi*, edited by B. Krusch in *MGH SRM*, vol. 5; translated, together with the will of Amandus, in J. N. Hillgarth, *Christianity and Paganism 350–750* (Philadelphia, 1986), pp. 139–49. Both the

authorship and the date of composition of the *Vita Amandi* are controversial. It would be inappropriate to dwell on the difficulties here. Suffice it to say that the interpretation offered in my text is widely if not unanimously accepted.

7. *Diplomata, Chartae, Epistolae, Leges ad res Gallo-Francicas spectantia*, edited by J. M. Pardessus (Paris, 1843–9), II, no. ccccxxxviii.

8. The *Vita* of Fructuosus has been edited by M. C. Díaz y Díaz, *La Vida de San Fructuoso de Braga* (Braga, 1974).

CHAPTER 6

1. Bede, *HE*, iii.8. Bede's *Ecclesiastical History* is the principal source for this chapter. Quotations not otherwise identified may be assumed to be from this work.

2. A. O. Anderson, *Early Sources of Scottish History* (Edinburgh, 1922) I, p. 211.

3. Alan Thacker, 'Monks, preaching and pastoral care in early Anglo-Saxon England', in John Blair and Richard Sharpe (eds.), *Pastoral Care before the Parish* (Leicester, 1992), pp. 137–70 (at p. 137).

4. Felix, *Life of Saint Guthlac*, edited and translated by B. Colgrave (Cambridge, 1985), ch. 34.

5. Translated *EHD* 1, no. 170.

6. *Two Lives of Saint Cuthbert*, edited and translated by Bertram Colgrave (Cambridge, 1940), Anonymous, ii.5 (p. 84).

7. *Cartularium Saxonicum*, edited by W. de G. Birch (London, 1887), vol. II, no. 841 (49c).

8. *The Life of Bishop Wilfrid by Eddius Stephanus*, edited and translated by Bertram Colgrave (Cambridge, 1927), ch. 2 (p. 6). All quotations relating to Wilfrid which occur in the text over the next few

pages are taken from this source unless otherwise stated.

9. Aldhelm, *The Prose Works*, translated by Michael Lapidge and Michael Herren (Ipswich, 1979), Letter xii (p. 169).

10. For a fine piece of detective work in elucidating the nature of *purpura* see C. R. Dodwell, *Anglo-Saxon Art: A New Perspective* (Manchester, 1982), pp. 145–50; also Gervase Matthew, *Byzantine Aesthetics* (London, 1963), p. 90.

11. Alcuin, *The Bishops, Kings and Saints of York*, edited and translated by Peter Godman (Oxford, 1982), line 579.

12. *Vita Samsonis* (see Chapter 2, note 14, Ch. 16).

13. *Ep.* 114 (Dümmler), translated by Stephen Allott, *Alcuin of York, His Life and Letters* (York, 1974), no. 6 (p. 8).

14. James Campbell, 'Elements in the background to the life of St Cuthbert and his early cult', in G. Bonner, D. Rollason and C. Stancliffe (eds.), *Saint Cuthbert, His Cult and His Community to A.D. 1200* (Woodbridge, 1989), pp. 3–19 (at p. 12).

15. A. W. Haddan and W. Stubbs (eds.), *Councils and Ecclesiastical Documents relating to Great Britain and Ireland* (Oxford, 1871), vol. III, p. 177; translated by John T. McNeill and Helena M. Gamer, *Medieval Handbooks of Penance* (New York, 1938), p. 184.

16. *Urkundenbuch des Klosters Fulda*, edited by Edmund E. Stengel (Marburg, 1913, repr. 1956–8), nos. 23–7.

17. *Ep.* 20 (Dümmler), trans. Allot no. 26.

18. *Ep.* 128 (Dümmler), trans. *EHD* I, no. 203.

19. On the problems of translating this passage see G. R. Owen-Crocker, *Dress in Anglo-Saxon England* (Manchester, 1986), pp. 88–9.

20. Haddan and Stubbs (eds.), *Councils*, III, pp. 369, 450.

21. *Die Briefe des heiligen Bonifatius und Lullus*, edited by M. Tangl (Berlin, 1916, repr. 1955), no. 116: trans. *EHD* I, no. 185.

CHAPTER 7

1. *Die Briefe des heiligen Bonifatius und Lullus*, edited by M. Tangl (Berlin, 1916, repr. 1955), no. 109.

2. Alcuin, *Vita Willibrordi*, edited by W. Levison, *MGH SRM*, vol. 7, ch. 6: translated by C. H. Talbot, *The Anglo-Saxon Missionaries in Germany* (London, 1954), p. 9.

3. Tangl no. 107 (= J 2160); trans. Talbot, pp. 71–2.

4. D. Parsons, 'Sites and monuments of the Anglo-Saxon mission in central Germany', *Archaeological Journal* 140 (1983), pp. 280–321 (at p. 282).

5. Willibald, *Vita Bonifacii*, edited by W. Levison, *MGH SRG*, ch. 6; trans. Talbot, p. 46.

6. Letters referred to here are (in order) Tangl nos. 23, 33, 32, 30, 38, 35, 75, 76, 63; all except 32 and 38 are translated in Talbot; all are translated in E. Emerton, *The Letters of St Boniface* (New York, 1940).

7. Tangl no. 63; trans. Talbot, pp. 116–18.

8. Tangl nos. 21 (= J 2164), 46; the latter trans. Talbot, p. 96; both trans. Emerton.

9. Tangl nos. 46, 47: no. 46 trans. Talbot, p. 96; both trans. Emerton.

10. *The Fourth Book of the Chronicle of Fredegar*, edited by J. M. Wallace-Hadrill (London, 1960), *continuationes*, chs. 9, 27.

11. Tangl no. 93; trans. *EHD* I, no. 181.

12. *Vita Lebuini*, edited by A. Hofmeister, *MGH*, *SS*, XXX, ch. 6; trans. Talbot, pp. 231–2.

13. *Annales Regni Francorum s.a.* 776, in R. Rau (ed.), *Quellen zur karolingischen Reichsgeschichte* (Berlin, 1955, repr. Darmstadt, 1966), pp. 32–4.

14. *Capitularia Regum Francorum*, edited by A. Boretius, *MGH Leges, sectio II*, no. 26, pp. 68–70; translated in H. R. Loyn and J. Percival, *The Reign of Charlemagne* (London, 1975), no. 11, pp. 51–4. The capitulary cannot be dated except within the range 775–90, but about 785 seems plausible.

15. Tangl no. 121; trans. *EHD* I, no. 187.

16. Altfrid, *Vita Liudgeri*, edited by W. Diekamp (Münster, 1881): the parts relating to England (chs. 9–12) have been translated in *EHD* I, no. 160.

17. Alcuin, *The Bishops, Kings and Saints of York*, edited and translated by Peter Godman (Oxford, 1982), line 218.

18. Alcuin, *Epp.* 107, 110 (Dümmler): the letter to Arn translated (in part) in Stephen Allot, *Alcuin of York* (York, 1974), no. 59; that to Charlemagne translated in Loyn and Percival, no. 33.

19. Alcuin, *Ep.* 6 (Dümmler): trans. Allott, no. 55.

20. Ermold le Noir, *Poème sur Louis le Pieux*, edited and translated by E. Faral (Paris, 1932), line 2434.

21. I have used the spirited if free translation of Lewis Thorpe, *Two Lives of Charlemagne* (Harmondsworth, 1969), pp. 168–9.

22. Rimbert, *Vita Anskarii*, edited by G. Waitz, *MGH SRG* (1884), ch. 6. There is an English translation by C. H. Robinson, *Anskar, Apostle of the North* (London, 1921).

CHAPTER 8

1. Garth Fowden, *Empire to Commonwealth. Consequences of Monotheism in Late Antiquity* (Princeton, 1993), pp. 91, 125.

2. Bede, *HE*, v.9.

3. *Ep.* 48 (Tangl); trans. Talbot, p. 97.

4. Alcuin, *Vita Willibrordi*, chs. 10–11; trans. Talbot, p. 10.

5. R. Morris, *Churches in the Landscape* (London, 1989), p. 62.

6. Succinctly and neutrally by T. Reuter, *Germany in the early middle ages 800–1056* (London, 1991), pp. 65–9.

7. *Ep.* 59 (Tangl); trans. (in part) Talbot, pp. 107–16.

8. S. T. Driscoll, 'The relationship between history and archaeology', in S. T. Driscoll and M. R. Nieke (eds.), *Power and Politics in Early medieval Britain and Ireland* (Edinburgh, 1988), pp. 162–87.

9. Gregory of Tours, *DLH*, v.43.

10. The relevant extracts from the *Vita Barbati* are printed in E. Salin, *La Civilisation Mérovingienne*, vol. IV (Paris, 1959), pp. 477–80, 486. There is a condensed English translation in T. Hodgkin, *Italy and Her Invaders*, vol. VI (Oxford, 1895), pp. 293–8. I am grateful to Ian Wood for directing my attention to St Barbatus.

11. K. Hughes, *Early Christian Ireland: Introduction to the Sources* (London, 1972), p. 227.

12. *Ep.* 23 (Tangl); trans. *EHD* I, no. 167.

13. *Vita Columbani*, ch. 13.

14. A. O. and M. O. Anderson (eds.), *Adomnán's Life of Columba* (Edinburgh, 1961), ii.33 (pp. 399–405).

15. Bede, *HE*, iv.22.

16. J. Knight Bostock, *A Handbook on Old High German Literature*, 2nd edn. revised by K. C. King and

D. R. McClintock (Oxford, 1976), pp. 27–8.

17. Valerie I. J. Flint, *The Rise of Magic in Early Medieval Europe* (Oxford, 1991), p. 324. I record here my indebtedness to a very able, learned and thought-provoking book from which I have learned much.

18. Gregory of Tours, *DLH*, viii.15.

19. *HE*, iv.3, in the translation by Charles Thomas, *The Early Christian Archaeology of North Britain* (Oxford, 1971), p. 147.

20. Bede, *Vita Sancti Cuthberti*, ch. 23: edited and translated by B. Colgrave, pp. 232–5.

21. Anonymous, *Vita Sancti Cuthberti*, ii.8: edited and translated by B. Colgrave, pp. 92–3.

22. Bede, *HE*, i.30 (= J 1848).

23. Frederick S. Paxton, *Christianizing Death. The Creation of a Ritual Process in Early Medieval Europe* (Ithaca/London, 1990).

24. In what follows I have leant heavily upon (in order of publication): Bailey Young, 'Paganisme, christianisation et rites funéraires mérovingiens', *Archéologie Médiévale* 7 (1977), pp. 5–81; Edward James, 'Cemeteries and the problem of Frankish settlement in Gaul', in P. H. Sawyer (ed.), *Names, Words and Graves: Early Medieval Settlement* (Leeds, 1979), pp. 55–89; Donald Bullough, 'Burial, Community and Belief in the early medieval west', in Patrick Wormald (ed.), *Ideal and Reality in Frankish and Anglo-Saxon Society* (Oxford, 1983), pp. 177–201; Bailey Young, 'Exemple aristocratique et mode funéraire dans la Gaule mérovingienne', *Annales: Economies, Sociétés, Civilisations* 41 (1986), pp. 379–407. I am also grateful to Edward James for some helpful conversations on the subject.

25. Anonymous, *Vita Sancti Cuthberti*,

iv.13: ed. and trans. Colgrave, pp. 130–31.

26. There is an excellent aerial photograph of it in Wendy Davies, *Wales in the Early Middle Ages* (Leicester, 1982), p. 26, fig. 11.

27. There is a good introduction in R. McKitterick, *The Frankish Church and the Carolingian Reforms 789–895* (London, 1977), ch. 6, and an update in Cyril Edwards, 'German vernacular literature: a survey', in R. McKitterick (ed.), *Carolingian Culture: Emulation and Innovation* (Cambridge, 1994), pp. 141–70. For the *Heliand* I have rested heavily upon J. Knight Bostock, op. cit. (above, note 16). D. H. Green, *The Carolingian Lord* (Cambridge, 1965) is difficult but rewarding on the Germanic words used to render the concept of the Christian 'Lord'.

28. The translation is that of R. I. Page, *Runes* (London, 1987), p. 41.

29. Respectively, T. D. Kendrick, *Anglo-Saxon Art to A.D. 900* (London, 1938), p. 122, and Lawrence Stone, *Sculpture in Britain: the Middle Ages* (Harmondsworth, 1955), p. 14. In what follows in this paragraph I have taken my cue from Flint, *The Rise of Magic* (as in note 17 above), pp. 372–3.

30. For what follows see Boniface, Ep. 59 (Tangl): trans. Talbot, pp. 107–16.

31. They certainly existed in sixth-century Gaul: see Gregory of Tours, *DLH*, ix.6, for his encounters with two impostors in the 580s. They were also to be encountered in ninth-century Bulgaria: Pope Nicholas I warned the newly Christian Bulgars about the hazards of pseudo-priests in 866.

32. Gregory of Tours, *DLH*, viii.15.

33. J. N. Hillgarth, 'Popular religion in Visigothic Spain', in E. James (ed.),

Visigothic Spain. New Approaches (Oxford, 1980), pp. 3–60 (at p. 27; quotation at the end of this paragraph, p. 23).

34. See Rosamond McKitterick, *The Carolingians and the Written Word* (Cambridge, 1989), and the collection of essays edited by the same writer as *The Uses of Literacy in Early Medieval Europe* (Cambridge, 1990).

35. Readers who may be wondering about the Romance vernaculars may consult Roger Wright, *Late Latin and Early Romance in Spain and Carolingian France* (Liverpool, 1982).

36. See Peter Cramer, *Baptism and Change in the Early Middle Ages* (Cambridge, 1993).

37. Felix, *Life of Saint Guthlac*, edited and translated by B. Colgrave (Cambridge, 1985), ch. 10.

38. See Alexander Murray, 'Confession before 1215', *Transactions of the Royal Historical Society*, Sixth series, 3 (1993), pp. 51–81.

39. Bede, *HE*, i.27. Subsequent citations relating to consanguinity and marriage are taken from (not in order): Boniface, *Epp.* nos. 26, 33, 50, 51 (trans. Talbot, pp. 81, 89, 100–101, 105); *MGH*, *Concilia* II.1.20 (trans. Meyvaert, see below); Theodore, *Penitential* II.xii.25 in Haddan and Stubbs, *Councils* III, p. 201 (trans. McNeill and Gamer, p. 210). For a magisterial investigation of some of the textual problems connected with Gregory's letter to Augustine see Paul Meyvaert, 'Bede's text of the *Libellus Responsionum* of Gregory the Great to Augustine of Canterbury', in Peter Clemoes and Kathleen Hughes (eds.), *England before the Conquest. Studies in Primary Sources presented to Dorothy Whitelock* (Cambridge, 1971), pp. 15–33.

CHAPTER 9

1. *Two Lives of Saint Cuthbert*, edited and translated by B. Colgrave (Cambridge, 1940), Bede, ch. 3 (pp. 160–64).

2. Rudolf of Fulda, *Vita Sanctae Leobae*, edited by A. Holder-Egger in *MGH SS* XV.i, ch. 12: translated by C. H. Talbot, *The Anglo-Saxon Missionaries in Germany* (London, 1954), pp. 216–18.

3. Bede, *HE*, iii.30.

4. *The Annals of Saint-Bertin*, translated and annotated by Janet L. Nelson (Manchester, 1991), year 839 (p. 42). The author of these annals, Prudentius, a native of Spain who later became bishop of Troyes, was at this period a member of the imperial court who must have known Bodo well.

5. The best edition of these texts is to be found in J. Gil (ed.), *Corpus Scriptorum Muzarabicorum* (Madrid, 1973), vol. I, pp. 227–70, being nos. xiv–xx among Paul Alvar's correspondence.

6. Quoted from the Authorized Version: I leave to one side the formidable textual problems of this passage.

7. *Annals of Saint-Bertin* (as above, note 4), year 847 (p. 64).

8. J 1867.

9. *Sancti Juliani Toletanae Sedis Episcopi Opera*, edited by J. N. Hillgarth (Turnhout, 1976), introduction, p. lxvi.

10. *Corpus Scriptorum Muzarabicorum* (as above, note 5), I, pp. 2–5, 58: and see the illuminating discussion in Roger Collins, *The Arab Conquest of Spain 710–797* (Oxford, 1989), pp. 65–71.

11. *PL*, cxvi, col. 170.

12. It has been defended by A. J. Zuckerman, *A Jewish Principality in Feudal France 768–900* (New York/London, 1972), a work

which displays more ingenuity than real historical acumen.

13. Rodulfus Glaber, *Historiarum Libri Quinque*, edited and translated by John France (Oxford, 1989), III, vi.20 (pp. 127–8).

14. *Colección Documental del Archivo de la Catedral de León (775–1230)* (León, 1987), vol. I, no.19 (p. 31).

15. In what follows I draw upon the work of I. A. Agus, *Urban Civilisation in Pre-Crusade Europe* (Leiden, 1965), which under a misleading title brings together much fascinating material derived from rabbinical *responsa* literature.

16. Hugeburga of Heidenheim, *Hodoeporicon Sancti Willibaldi*, edited by O. Holder-Egger, *MGH SS* XV (i): translated in Talbot, *Anglo-Saxon Missionaries* (as above, note 2), pp. 162–3.

17. Richard W. Bulliet, *Conversion to Islam in the Medieval Period: An Essay in Quantitative History* (Cambridge, Mass., 1979) is the fundamental work. See also the same author's article 'Conversion stories in early Islam' in Michael Gervers and Ramzi Jibran Bikhazi (eds.), *Conversion and Continuity. Indigenous Christian Communities in Islamic Lands, Eighth to Eighteenth Centuries* (Toronto, 1990), pp. 123–3. Bulliet's other essay in the same collection, 'Process and Status in Conversion and Continuity' (pp. 1–12), is also warmly commended.

18. For what follows, see the *Memoriale Sanctorum*, ii.8, 10 in *Corpus Scriptorum Muzarabicorum* (as above, note 5), II, pp. 408–15, 416–30.

19. I have attempted a brief characterization of this process in my book *Moorish Spain* (London, 1992), ch. 3: attentive readers will notice that the author's interpretation of Bulliet's figures on conversion is incorrect.

20. For what follows I am indebted to Sidney H. Griffith, 'The first Christian *Summa Theologiae* in Arabic: Christian *Kalam* in ninth-century Palestine', in Gervers and Bikhazi (eds.), *Conversion and Continuity* (as above, note 17), pp. 15–31.

21. *Vita Iohannis abbatis Gorziensis* in *PL*, cxxxvii.239–310 (at col. 302), translated in Colin Smith, *Christians and Moors in Spain* (Warminster, 1988), vol. I, no. 15 (p. 65).

22. M. Talbi, 'Le christiansime maghrébien de la conquête musulmane à sa disparition', in Gervers and Bikhazi (eds.), *Conversion and Continuity* (as above, note 17), pp. 313–51 (at p. 329).

23. For those who wish to do so the best starting-point is still the classic study by Carl Erdmann, *Die Entstehung des Kreuzzugsgedankens* (Stuttgart, 1935), of which a long-overdue translation into English was provided by M. W. Baldwin and W. Goffart, *The Origins of the Idea of Crusade* (Princeton, 1977). Among recent works on the 'prehistory' of crusading Marcus Bull, *Knightly Piety and the Lay Response to the First Crusade* (Oxford, 1993) is particularly able and thought-provoking. Specifically on mission, Benjamin Z. Kedar, *Crusade and Mission. European Approaches toward the Muslims* (Princeton, 1984) is warmly recommended. And see also below, Chapter 14, for crusade and mission in the Baltic region.

24. *Chronicle of Solomon bar Simson*, translated by S. Eidelberg, *The Jews and the Crusaders. The Hebrew Chronicles of the First and Second Crusades* (Madison, 1977), p. 23.

25. *Historiarum Libri Quinque* (as above, note 13), III, vii.24.

26. Adhémar of Chabannes, *Chronicon*, edited by J. Chavanon (Paris, 1897), III, 52 (p. 175). For a succinct discussion of some of the problems of this passage see B. Blumenkranz, *Juifs et Chrétiens dans le monde occidental 430–1096* (Paris, 1960), pp. 318, 382–3.

27. The period has been magnificently surveyed by Colin Morris, *The Papal Monarchy. The Western Church from 1050 to 1250* (Oxford, 1989). The classic introduction remains R. W. Southern, *The Making of the Middle Ages* (London, 1953).

28. J 4528. Long suspect, this letter is now widely accepted as genuine, though its date, context and interpretation remain problematic.

29. *Privilegios reales de la Catedral de Toledo 1086–1492*, edited by J. A. García Lujan (Toledo, 1982), vol. II, no. 1 (pp. 15–20). For a recent discussion of this murky episode see Bernard F. Reilly, *The Kingdom of Leon-Castilla under King Alfonso VI 1065–1109* (Princeton, 1988), pp. 181–3.

30. For the friars and missions, see Colin Morris, *The Papal Monarchy* (above, note 27), chs. 18 and 19, with good bibliographies.

CHAPTER 10

1. Dimitri Obolensky, *The Byzantine Commonwealth. Eastern Europe, 500–1453* (London, 1971), p. 47.

2. Imre Boba, in his book *Moravia's History Reconsidered* (The Hague, 1971), argued that the Moravian principality should be located much further to the south in the vicinity of the Roman city of Sirmium (today's Srem Mitrovica, to the west of Belgrade). This view has not on the whole commended itself to other enquirers, though it continues to find defenders such as Charles R. Bowlus, *Franks, Moravians and Magyars. The Struggle for the Middle Danube 788–907* (Philadelphia/London, 1995).

3. See Henry Mayr-Harting, *Two Conversions to Christianity: The Bulgarians and the Anglo-Saxons* (Reading, 1994), pp. 5–6 and references there cited.

4. Constantine Porphyrogenitus, *De Administrando Imperio*, edited by G. Moravcsik and translated by R. J. H. Jenkins (Budapest, 1949), ch. 29, pp. 124–6.

5. The Latin text has been edited, with a translation into German and an elaborate commentary, by Herwig Wolfram, *Conversio Bagoariorum et Carantanorum. Das Weissbuch der Salzburger Kirche über die erfolgreiche Mission in Karantanien und Pannonien* (Vienna, 1979).

6. The *Lives* were composed in the language known as Old Church Slavonic. A translation into French may be found in F. Dvornik, *Les Légendes de Constantin et de Méthode, vues de Byzance* (Prague, 1933), pp. 349–93: subsequent quotations in the text are my own translations from this edition. There is said to be an English translation by Marvin Kantor, *Medieval Slavic Lives of Saints and Princes* (Ann Arbor, Michigan, 1983), but I have been unable to track down a copy of this work. For the sake of clarification it should be explained that the names Cyril and Methodius were the names taken by the brothers 'in religion'. The given name of Cyril was Constantine and that of Methodius was (probably) Michael. Although Methodius is always referred to as Methodius, Cyril is sometimes called Constantine (as, for example, in the title of Dvornik's book, above) and sometimes, cumbrously, as Constantine-Cyril. For simplicity's sake I shall refer to them throughout by the name that each

finally chose for himself, Cyril and Methodius.

7. *The Homilies of Photius, Patriarch of Constantinople*, translated by C. Mango (Cambridge, Mass., 1958), Homily IV, pp. 95–110 (at p. 102).

8. Quoted from the *Chronographia* of the Continuator of Theophanes by Vassil Gjuzelev, 'The Adoption of Christianity in Bulgaria', in his volume of essays *Medieval Bulgaria, Byzantine Empire, Black Sea, Venice, Genoa* (Villach, 1988), pp. 115–203 (at p. 158). I am grateful to Henry Mayr-Harting for kindly supplying me with a copy of this article.

9. Quoted from the *Vita* of Clement attributed to Theophylact of Ohrid, by Dimitri Obolensky in his essay 'Clement of Ohrid' in his *Six Byzantine Portraits* (Oxford, 1988), pp. 8–33 (at p. 21). Quotations relating to Clement in the following paragraph are drawn from the same source.

10. The phrase is quoted from the German chronicler Regino of Prüm by Henry Mayr-Harting, *Two Conversions to Christianity: The Bulgarians and the Anglo-Saxons* (Reading, 1994), p. 16.

11. For this argument see A. Angenendt, 'The conversion of the Anglo-Saxons considered against the background of the early medieval mission', in *Angli e Sassoni al di qua e al di là del mare*, being *Settimane di Studio del Centro Italiano di Studi sull'Alto Medioevo*, vol. 32 (Spoleto, 1986), pp. 747–81.

12. Quoted by Gjuzelev (see above, note 8), pp. 185–6.

13. Quoted by Obolensky (see above, note 9), p. 32.

14. J 2812. The best edition of the text is that by E. Perels in *MGH, Epistolae* VI, pp. 568–600, where it features as no. 99 among the letters of Pope Nicholas; there is an older edition in *PL*, cxix, cols. 978–1016. There is no published English translation that I am aware of. Failing that, the fullest discussion of it in English is to be found in the article of Richard E. Sullivan, 'Khan Boris and the Conversion of Bulgaria: a case study of the impact of Christianity on a barbarian society', *Studies in Medieval and Renaissance History* 3 (Lincoln, Nebraska, 1966), pp. 53–139.

CHAPTER 11

1. *EHD* I, no. 98.

2. *Landnámabók*, edited by J. Benediktsson (Reykjavik, 1968), p. 253.

3. Widukind of Corvey, *Rerum Gestarum Saxonicarum Libri Tres*, edited by G. Waitz, K. A. Kehr in *MGH SRG* (Hanover, 1904), iii.65 (p. 117).

4. Anna Ritchie, *Viking Scotland* (London, 1993), p. 83.

5. For a recent summary of the debate see Dáibhí Ó Cróinín, *Early Medieval Ireland 400–1200* (London, 1995), ch. 9 and references there cited.

6. *The Letters of Lanfranc, Archbishop of Canterbury*, edited by Helen Clover and Margaret Gibson (Oxford, 1979), no. 9, pp. 66–9.

7. *Recueil des Actes de Charles III le Simple, Roi de France*, edited by P. Lauer (Paris, 1949), vol. I, no. 92.

8. Adhémar of Chabannes, *Chronicon*, edited by J. Chavanon (Paris, 1897), III.20 (p. 139).

9. The letters have been studied in depth by Olivier Guillot, 'La conversion des normands peu après 911', *Cahiers de Civilisation Médiévale* 24 (1981), pp. 101–16, 181–219.

10. Rodulfus Glaber, *Historiarum Libri*

Quinque, edited and translated by
John France (Oxford, 1989), I.v.21
(pp. 36–7).

11. *The Ecclesiastical History of Orderic
Vitalis*, edited and translated by
Marjorie Chibnall, vol. II (Oxford,
1969), pp. 10–11.

12. Rodulfus Glaber, *Vita Domni
Willelmi Abbatis*, edited and
translated by John France (above,
note 10), ch. 7 (pp. 272–3).

13. The diploma is printed in *Recueil
des Actes des Ducs de Normandie
(911–1066)*, edited by Marie
Fauroux (Caen, 1961), no. 4
(pp. 72–4), and the places are
mapped by David Bates, *Normandy
before 1066* (London, 1982), map
10 (p. 273).

14. Asser, *Vita Alfredi*, ch. 56, in the
translation of Simon Keynes and
Michael Lapidge, in their *Alfred the
Great* (Harmondsworth, 1983),
p. 85. The authenticity of Asser's
work has been vigorously – some
might say intemperately –
impugned at inordinate length by
Alfred Smyth in his study *Alfred the
Great* (Oxford, 1994). I find
Professor Smyth's argument
ingenious but not persuasive.

15. There is a good and rightly cautious
discussion of the Middleton cross in
Richard N. Bailey, *Viking-age
Sculpture in Northern England*
(London, 1980), pp. 209–14.

16. The most recent discussion of the
Gosforth cross is to be found in
Richard N. Bailey and Rosemary
Cramp, *The British Academy Corpus
of Anglo-Saxon Stone Sculpture*,
vol. II, *Cumberland, Westmorland
and Lancashire North-of-the-Sands*
(Oxford, 1988), pp. 100–104 (for
the cross), 100–109 (for the
Gosforth stones as a group).

17. *EHD* I, no. 106.

18. *Orderic Vitalis* (as in note 11
above), II, pp. 20–23.

19. *Liber Eliensis*, edited by E. O. Blake
(Camden Society, vol. 92: London,

1962), II, ch. 32 (pp. 105–6).

20. For these inscriptions see Elisabeth
Okasha, *Hand-list of Anglo-Saxon
Non-Runic Inscriptions* (Cambridge,
1971), nos. 1, 64, 73, 146.

21. Quoted by Dag Strömbäck, *The
Conversion of Iceland*, translated by
Peter Foote (London, 1975), p. 92.

22. Adam of Bremen, *Gesta
Hammaburgensis Ecclesiae
Pontificum*, edited by
B. Schmeidler, in *MGH SRG*
(Hanover, 1917), iv.36. There is an
English translation by Francis J.
Tschan (New York, 1959) in which
these passages occur at pp. 217–18.

23. *Egil's Saga*, translated by Christine
Fell (London, 1975), ch. 50
(p. 74).

24. For a succinct discussion, with good
illustrations, see Else Roesdahl,
Viking Age Denmark (London,
1982), pp. 171–6.

25. *The Letters and Poems of Fulbert of
Chartres*, edited by Frederick
Behrends (Oxford, 1976), ep. 37
(pp. 66–9).

26. Adam of Bremen (above, note 22),
ii.26 (trans. Tschan, p. 71).

27. Adam of Bremen (above, note 22),
ii.36, conflated with scolium 26
(trans. Tschan, p. 79).

28. *Encomium Emmae Reginae*, edited
and translated by Alistair Campbell
(Camden Society, vol. 72: London,
1949), appendix III, p. 76.

29. For these two runestones see Sven
B. F. Jansson, *Runes in Sweden*,
translated by Peter Foote
(Stockholm, 1987), pp. 45–6, 119.

30. Adam of Bremen (above, note 22),
iv.30 (trans. Tschan, p. 210). The
reference to 'Slavia' is probably to
the risings against Christian and
German overlordship among the
Slavs of what is now Mecklenburg,
for which see Chapter 12 below.

CHAPTER 12

1. *MGH, Diplomata, Otto I*, no. 366 (pp. 502–3); *Henry II*, no. 143 (pp. 169–72).
2. Thietmar of Merseburg, *Chronicon*, edited by J. M. Lappenberg, F. Kurze, in *MGH SRG* (Hanover, 1889), ii.36, 37 (pp. 41–2). A Slavonic version of the *Kyrie* has come down to us, though not necessarily Bishop Boso's.
3. Helmold of Bosau, *Chronica Slavorum*, edited by G. H. Pertz, in *MGH SRG* (Hanover, 1868), i.12 (p. 30): translated in Francis J. Tschan, *The Chronicle of the Slavs by Helmold Priest of Bosau* (New York, 1935), p. 72.
4. This and other documents have been translated by Marvin Kantor, *The Origins of Christianity in Bohemia, Sources and Commentary* (Evanston, Illinois, 1990): a useful collection, though maddeningly arranged; quotation from *Crescente fide* at p. 147. For Sigebert, see Bede, *HE*, iii.22.
5. Pilgrim's letter is printed in P. Labbé and G. Cossart, *Sacrosancta Concilia*, vol. IX (Paris, 1671), cols. 716–18. The more important forged papal bulls are J 767 (attributed to Pope Symmachus, 498–514), 3614 (Leo VII, 937–9), 3644 (Agapetus II, 946–55) and 3771 (Benedict VI, 972–4).
6. Thietmar, *Chronicon* (see note 2 above), ix.4 (p. 241), though he got Geza's name wrong.
7. Rodulfus Glaber, *Historiarum Libri Quinque*, edited and translated by John France (Oxford, 1989), I.v.22 (pp. 38–9).
8. Karl Leyser, *The Ascent of Latin Europe* (Oxford, 1986), p. 19. (This inaugural lecture has been reprinted in Karl Leyser (ed. T. Reuter), *Communications and Power in Medieval Europe. The Carolingian and Ottonian Centuries* (London/Rio Grande, Ohio, 1994), pp. 215–32.)
9. Adam of Bremen (above, Chapter 11, note 22), iii.23 (trans. Tschan, p. 133): other references in this and the preceding paragraphs are to ii.66 and iii.19, 20 and 50.
10. For the foregoing see Thietmar vi.23, 24 (see note 2); Adam, ii.21 and iii.51 (see Chapter 11, note 22); Helmold, i.52 (see note 3). The anonymous document known as the *Magdeburger Aufruf* is translated in Louise and Jonathan Riley-Smith, *The Crusades. Idea and Reality 1095–1274* (London, 1981), no. 13, pp. 75–7. Saxo Grammaticus, *Danorum Regum Heroumque Historia*, xiv.39, for which see the translation and magnificent commentary by Eric Christiansen, *British Archaeological Reports, International Series*, vol. 84, 118(i) and 118(ii) (Oxford, 1980–81): for Rügen and the cult of Svantovit see pp. 494–8.
11. Helmold of Bosau (above, note 3), i.34, 40 (trans. Tschan, pp. 123, 137).
12. A rare English-language contribution is furnished by the excellent article of Robert Bartlett, 'The conversion of a pagan society in the middle ages', *History* 70 (1985), pp. 185–201.
13. *Monachi Prieflingensis Vita Ottonis*, edited by R. Köpke, in *MGH SS* XII (Hanover, 1856), i.2 (p. 884). Succeeding quotations relating to Otto are from this source.
14. Helmold of Bosau (above, note 3), ii.5 (trans. Tschan, p. 263).
15. Saxo Grammaticus (above, note 10), xiv.1 (trans. Christiansen, p. 352) and editorial commentary.
16. Saxo Grammaticus, xiv.39 (trans. Christiansen, pp. 493–511); Helmold, ii.12 (trans. Tschan, pp. 274–6).
17. *Die Urkunden Heinrichs des Löwen*,

Herzogs von Sachsen und Bayern, edited by K. Jordan (Leipzig-Weimar, 1941/49), no. 53 (pp. 86–7): translation quoted from Alfred Haverkamp, *Medieval Germany 1056–1273* (ET, Oxford, 1988), p. 194. There is a detailed discussion in Käthe Sonnleitner, 'Die Slawenpolitik Heinrichs des Löwen in Spiegel einer Urkundenarenga', *Archiv für Diplomatik* 26 (1980), pp. 259–80. The 'recent author' is Friedrich Lotter, 'The crusading idea and the conquest of the region east of the Elbe', in Robert Bartlett and Angus Mackay (eds.), *Medieval Frontier Societies* (Oxford, 1989), pp. 266–306 (at p. 298).

18. Helmold, i.82, 83 (trans. Tschan, pp. 217–19).

CHAPTER 13

1. Quoted by Robert Bartlett, 'The conversion of a pagan society in the middle ages', *History* 70 (1985), pp. 185–201 (at p. 198).

2. Gibbon, *Decline and Fall*, ch. 15 (1818 edition, ii.341). For a fine discussion of the significance of Christian almsgiving see Peter Brown, *Power and Persuasion in Late Antiquity: Towards a Christian Empire* (Madison, Wis., 1992), ch. 3, 'Poverty and Power'.

3. Ethelwulf, *De Abbatibus*, edited and translated by A. Campbell (Oxford, 1967), lines 480–81. For the 'life-support smallholding' see Chapter 3, note 7.

4. Recent scholarship can be appreciated in the valuable collection of essays edited by John Blair and Richard Sharpe, *Pastoral Care before the Parish* (Leicester, 1992), and in the debate on the so-called 'minster hypothesis' in the journal *Early Medieval Europe*, vol. 4 (1995) and 5 (1996), with contributions from John Blair, Eric

Cambridge, David Rollason and David Palliser.

5. *Codice Diplomatico Longobardo*, edited by L. Schiaparelli, vol. 2 (Rome, 1933), no. 173, pp. 133–5. For a clear exposition of Italian arrangements see Catherine E. Boyd, *Tithes and Parishes in Medieval Italy* (Ithaca, 1952).

6. There is a good discussion of these matters in J. Devisse, *Hincmar, Archevêque de Rheims 845–882* (Geneva, 1976), vol. 2, pp. 829–46.

7. *El archivo condal de Barcelona en los siglos IX y X*, edited by F. Udina Martorell (Barcelona, 1951), no. 73, pp. 208–9. Compare in the same collection nos. 10, 102, 103, 146.

8. *Concilios visigóticos e hispano-romanos*, edited by J. Vives (Madrid/Barcelona, 1963), p. 83 (= II Braga, ch. 6).

9. The text was edited with an illuminating discussion by Pierre David, *Études historiques sur la Galice et le Portugal du VIe au XIIe siècle* (Lisbon/Paris, 1947), pp. 1–82.

10. *Early Scottish Charters*, edited by A. C. Lawrie (Glasgow, 1905), no. xxxiii, pp. 25–6.

11. Rodulfus Glaber, *Historiarum Libri Quinque*, edited and translated by John France (Oxford, 1989), III.iv.13 (p. 116).

12. *Tumbos del Monasterio de Sobrado de los Monjes*, edited by Pilar Loscertales de García de Valdeavellano (Madrid, 1976), vol. 1, no. 48, p. 82.

13. I quote from the translation in D. C. Douglas and G. W. Greenaway (eds.), *English Historical Documents*, vol. 2 (London, 1953), p. 862.

14. Frank Barlow, *The English Church 1000–1066* (London, 1963), p. 193.

15. J 2599, and see the discussion in

Julia M. H. Smith, *Province and Empire, Brittany and the Carolingians* (Cambridge, 1992), pp. 177–85.

16. William of Malmesbury, *De Gestis Regum Anglorum*, edited by W. Stubbs (London, 1889), iii.245, p. 305.

17. On the church in the towns, a good starting-point is C. N. L. Brooke, 'The medieval town as an ecclesiastical centre', in M. W. Barley (ed.), *European Towns: Their Archaeology and Early History* (London, 1977), pp. 459–72; on the case of England see the fine study by James Campbell, 'The church in Anglo-Saxon towns', *Studies in Church History* 19 (1979), reprinted in his collected *Essays in Anglo-Saxon History* (London, 1986), pp. 139–54.

CHAPTER 14

1. For a recent and lively discussion see C. J. Tyerman, 'Were there any crusades in the twelfth century?', *English Historical Review* 110 (1995), pp. 553–77.

2. The best edition of this letter is to be found in the *Urkundenbuch des Erzstifts Magdeburg*, edited F. Israel and W. Möllenberg (Magdeburg, 1937), no. 193 (pp. 249–52): English translation, L. and J. Riley-Smith, *The Crusades. Idea and Reality, 1095–1274* (London, 1981), no. 13 (pp. 75–7). There is an interesting discussion of the text by Peter Knoch, 'Kreuzzug und Siedlung: Studien zum Aufruf der Magdeburger Kirche vom 1108', *Jahrbuch für die Geschichte Mittel- und Ostdeutschlands* 23 (1974), pp. 1–33.

3. J 9017.

4. Bernard, *Ep.* 457, in *PL*, clxxxii, cols. 651–2: translated in Bruno Scott-James, *The Letters of St Bernard of Clairvaux* (London,

1953), no. 394 (pp. 466–8).

5. J 12118 (1171–2); A. Potthast (ed.), *Regesta Pontificum Romanorum 1198–1304* (Berlin, 1874–5), no. 3809 (1209): the latter translated by the Riley-Smiths (as above, note 2), no. 14 (pp. 77–8).

6. Henry's chronicle was edited by W. Arndt in *MGH SS*, XXIII (Hanover, 1874): there is an English translation by James A. Brundage, *The Chronicle of Henry of Livonia* (Madison, Wis., 1961).

7. The 'knightly package tour' is well described by Christopher Tyerman (whose phrase it is, p. 267) in his fine study of *England and the Crusades 1095–1588* (London, 1988), ch. 10 and references therein, especially the articles by Jeremy Catto and Maurice Keen.

8. I quote from the prose translation by Jerry C. Smith and William L. Urban, *The Livonian Rhymed Chronicle* (Bloomington, Ind., 1977): quotation in text, lines 6105–16.

9. Quoted by S. C. Rowell, *Lithuania Ascending. A Pagan Empire within East-central Europe, 1295–1345* (Cambridge, 1994), p. 225, note 199.

10. There is a photograph in Eric Christiansen, *The Northern Crusades* (London, 1980), plate 3(b), and see also his remarks on architecture at pp. 211–12.

11. The phrase is Eric Christiansen's, *The Northern Crusades* (see previous note), p. 137.

12. See M. L. Colker, 'America rediscovered in the thirteenth century?', *Speculum* 54 (1979), pp. 712–26, for this remarkable text which came to light (no less remarkably) in Dublin some years ago.

13. Quoted by Michał Giedroyć, 'The Arrival of Christianity in Lithuania: early contacts (thirteenth century)',

Oxford Slavonic Papers 18 (1985), pp. 1–30 (at p. 13).

CHAPTER 15

1. Mazvydas's letter is translated in A. Musteikis, *The Reformation in Lithuania* (New York, 1988), appendix B, pp. 87–92.
2. Gerald Strauss, *Luther's House of Learning. Indoctrination of the Young in the German Reformation* (Baltimore/London, 1978), pp. 277, 282. Subsequent quotations from pp. 275, 280–81, 291 and 304.
3. Jean Delumeau, *Catholicism between Luther and Voltaire* (ET, London, 1977), pp. 161, 190. The book was first published in 1971. Despite the focus indicated by the title the author makes clear that he believes his thesis to be applicable in Protestant contexts too (e.g. George Fox, John Wesley and others in England).
4. See his brilliant book *The Stripping of the Altars. Traditional Religion in England 1400–1580* (New Haven/London, 1992).
5. Maurice Keen, *England in the Later Middle Ages* (Harmondsworth, 1990), p. 271.
6. A. D. Nock, *Conversion* (Oxford, 1933), pp. 7, 14.
7. I have in mind the debate initiated by Robin Horton's article 'African Conversion' in the journal *Africa* 44 (1971). This and subsequent contributions furnish much thought-provoking material which the medieval historian may care to use sparingly and judiciously.
8. So there might be a clue here to the problem of what they were converted *from*. In the wise words of Michael Wallace-Hadrill, 'a good source of information about Frankish paganism is Frankish Christianity' (*The Frankish Church*, Oxford, 1983, p. 33).

INDEX

This index is selective: not every one of the thousands of persons and places mentioned in this book is listed in it. As a rough and ready rule of thumb, not adhered to with strict consistency, only those who feature more than once in the text are to be found in the index. Regional or ethnic entries, of the type 'Frisia, Frisians' are intended to help the reader to plug the resultant gaps. Thus, for example, although King Stenkil of Sweden is mentioned more than once in the text (pp. 415, 436 if you must know) he does not feature in the index (an instance of non-adherence to the rule above); but he can be tracked down under 'Sweden, Swedes'. The category-entries, in lower case, are sometimes precisely focussed (e.g. 'drunkenness, clerical') but at others gather all sorts of matter in their fairly generous embrace (e.g. 'language', 'mortuary practice').

Persons of the same name are listed in chronological order; see for example the nine Gregorys. The following abbreviations are used: Archbp - Archbishop; Bp - Bishop; K - King; St - Saint.